REVOLUTIONARY JEWS FROM SPINOZA TO MARX

THE SAMUEL & ALTHEA STROUM
LECTURES IN JEWISH STUDIES

SAMUEL STROUM, BUSINESSMAN, community leader, and philanthropist, by a major gift to the Jewish Federation of Greater Seattle, established the Samuel and Althea Stroum Philanthropic Fund.

In recognition of Mr. and Mrs. Stroum's deep interest in Jewish history and culture, the Board of Directors of the Jewish Federation of Greater Seattle, in cooperation with the Jewish Studies Program at the University of Washington, established an annual lectureship at the University of Washington known as the Samuel and Althea Stroum Lectureship in Jewish Studies. This lectureship makes it possible to bring to the area outstanding scholars and interpreters of Jewish thought, thus promoting a deeper understanding of Jewish history, religion, and culture. Such understanding can lead to an enhanced appreciation of the Jewish contributions to the historical and cultural traditions that have shaped the American nation.

The terms of the gift also provide for the publication from time to time of the lectures or other appropriate materials resulting from or related to the lectures.

Revolutionary Jews from Spinoza to Marx

The Fight for a Secular World of Universal and Equal Rights

JONATHAN I. ISRAEL

A Samuel and Althea Stroum Book

UNIVERSITY OF WASHINGTON PRESS
Seattle

Revolutionary Jews from Spinoza to Marx is published with the assistance of a grant from the Samuel and Althea Stroum Endowed Book Fund.

Composed in Minion Pro, typeface designed by Robert Slimbach

25 24 23 22 21 5 4 3 2 1

Printed and bound in the United States of America

UNIVERSITY OF WASHINGTON PRESS
uwapress.uw.edu

LIBRARY OF CONGRESS CATALOGING-IN-PUBLICATION DATA
Names: Israel, Jonathan, 1946– author.
Title: Revolutionary Jews from Spinoza to Marx : the fight for a secular world of universal and equal rights / Jonathan I. Israel.
Description: Seattle : University of Washington Press, [2021] | Series: The Samuel & Althea Stroum Lectures in Jewish Studies | "A Samuel and Althea Stroum Book". | Includes bibliographical references and index.
Identifiers: LCCN 2020051726 (print) | LCCN 2020051727 (ebook) | ISBN 9780295748665 (hardcover) | ISBN 9780295748672 (ebook)
Subjects: LCSH: Socialism and Judaism—Europe—History. | Jewish socialists—Europe—Biography. | Communism and Judaism—Europe—History. | Judaism and politics—Europe—History. | Jews—Europe—Politics and government. | Enlightenment—Influence.
Classification: LCC HX550.J4 I77 2021 (print) | LCC HX550.J4 (ebook) | DDC 321.09/4092392404—dc23
LC record available at https://lccn.loc.gov/2020051726
LC ebook record available at https://lccn.loc.gov/2020051727

The paper used in this publication is acid free and meets the minimum requirements of American National Standard for Information Sciences—Permanence of Paper for Printed Library Materials, ANSI Z39.48–1984.∞

In memory of Robert Wistrich (1945–2015)

CONTENTS

ACKNOWLEDGMENTS

This book originates in two lectures given at the Stroum Center for Jewish Studies of the University of Washington, in Seattle, in May 2017, as part of an annual series that began in 1975. I would like to thank all the participating colleagues for their stimulating and helpful comments during the symposium on Spinoza and modern Jewish thought that took place there in connection with and between the Stroum Lectures, an event organized by Michael Rosenthal, whose remarks and suggestions were invaluable. My warm thanks also to Noam Pianko for his help in arranging the book's publication, to the staff of the University of Washington Press, especially Lorri Hagman, for all their hard work and care in preparing the book for the press, and to my wife, Annette, for her very extensive help in the final editing and revision of the text.

The book's title recalls Robert Wistrich's *Revolutionary Jews from Marx to Trotsky* (1976). Robert Wistrich (1945–2015) was my friend and longtime discussion partner with whom during the 1960s, in the senior classes of our northwest London secondary school, Kilburn Grammar, I frequently discussed the question of what made "Jewish revolutionaries." At Kilburn Grammar, we were both taught by an unusually gifted history teacher, Walter Isaacson (1909–1999). A German Jewish refugee from Nazism, Isaacson was an altogether exceptional and inspiring mentor who filled us, and many others, with a sense of the tremendous drama of modern history and the intellectual excitement that comes from connecting general history with the history of ideas and philosophy. Subsequently, Robert and I were both undergraduates at Queens' College Cambridge, and intensively resumed our dialogue, not least about "Jewish revolutionaries." To my immense regret, Robert Wistrich died unexpectedly in May 2015. I dedicate this book to his memory.

REVOLUTIONARY JEWS FROM SPINOZA TO MARX

Introduction

Jewish revolutionaries of all kinds, during the late nineteenth century and early twentieth, became a familiar feature of underground movements, subversive journalism, café opposition and philosophical theorizing about man and society. Karl Marx (1818–1883), a Jew by birth and early upbringing, living most of his life in exile, was arguably the greatest revolutionary of them all. Eventually, the conspicuous role of Jewish revolutionaries, notably in the Russian Revolution, with Leon Trotsky (1879–1940) foremost among them, came to be widely noted and commented on. Though triumphantly celebrated in some quarters, it was more often indignantly deplored and denounced.

Until the 1870s, there were in the Russian Empire including the bulk of divided, suppressed Poland, the regions where most Jews then lived, too few revolutionary Jews to make much impact on the contemporary imagination or echo through the general mass of the Jewish population. From the perspective of the Jewish people as a whole, one might easily suppose the comparatively small number of Jews plausibly counted as "revolutionaries" prior to 1870 had little connection with the burgeoning phenomenon that arose more dramatically in the 1870s. But this would be an error. During the 1860s and 1870s, the great majority of Jews in the Russian Empire still remained strikingly quiescent and submissive in the face of mounting oppression and the new pogroms. The main response of the Jewish majority to the large-scale pogroms of 1881–82 was to dream of, or actively plan, emigration to the United States or elsewhere, with great numbers soon leaving for America, Britain, South Africa, Brazil and Argentina. Meanwhile, Jewish revolutionaries of the 1870s, the first decade when they became numerous enough to form a substantial pan-European network, tended to be partly or wholly estranged Jews rebelling against their families, former college students often eager to flout the conventions and sexual mores of their time.[1]

Alienation from their background, partial or comprehensive, was a state of mind such rebels shared with a long line of earlier estranged Jews steeped in secular education dotting the pre-1850 landscape of early modern history providing the focus of this volume, rather than with the great bulk of the Jewish population of their own time. Among these revolutionaries of the 1870s were Yehudah Leib Levin (1844–1925), Aaron Shmuel Lieberman (1845–1880), Mark Natanson (1850–1919), the Bakuninist Pavel Axelrod (1850–1920) and Aaron Zundelevich (1852–1923) from Vilna, who helped set up the first secret revolutionary press in Petersburg. Student activists prominent in the early revolutionary cells of the 1870s and 1880s, in Russia, most had been exiled temporarily and often first absorbed Marxism or other socialist ideologies in Berlin, or another main city outside Russia. But whether fully or only partly estranged from Jews and Judaism, the revolutionary activism of both the pre- and post-1850 eras generally sprang, we shall see, from much the same resentments and anxieties that shaped the broader cultural evolution of the rest.

Some Jewish revolutionaries, including Marx and Trotsky, and numbers of others, disassociated themselves in every way from specifically Jewish issues, problems and concerns, including language and culture, wanting nothing more to do not just with their parents' and grandparents' religious commitments but with their former cultural and social background. Others, though, like Yehudah Leib Levin of Minsk, a socialist, Hebrew poet and eventually socialist-Zionist, Lieberman, a Hebrew and Yiddish editor from a shtetl, near Grodno, and Isaac Kaminer (1834–1901), another socialist and Hebrew poet, and later Nachman Syrkin (1868–1924), the founder of Zionist socialism, and the stirring, upright Russo-American feminist anarchist revolutionary Emma Goldman (1869–1940), the classic freethinking "rebel woman," originally from Kovno (Kaunas), in Lithuania, explored and deeply pondered the vast complexity of the Jewish predicament and crisis, Goldman during her long, deeply disillusioning stay, clashing with the Bolsheviks, in early Soviet revolutionary Russia (1920–21).

This is unsurprising. The traumatic Russian pogroms of 1881–82 focused a whole generation of Jewish revolutionary minds on the question of Jewish survival and the Jewish future. While some ignored or buried the question, or acknowledged the crisis's severity but insisted the answer to the Jews' particular plight was the general emancipation of society on a socialist basis, others combined striving for general emancipation with confronting the special predicament of the Jews. Figures like Lieberman, Kaminer, Levin,

Syrkin and Goldman loathed the oppression and tight censorship of the Czarist-aristocratic police state, the lay ignorance on which it rested and what they saw as the Orthodox clergy's buttressing that repression with the credulity and subservience they instilled in the minds of the Russian and Ukrainian peoples, and were passionately committed to general emancipation. But at the same time, they pondered and debated the specific problems of the separate Yiddish-speaking proletariat centered on what, in Czarist times, had been the "Pale of Settlement," the western fringe of the Russian Empire (including Poland, White Russia, much of the Ukraine and Lithuania) to which most of the Jewish population remained legally restricted.[2] Their very revolutionary commitments led to their becoming steeped in issues of Jewish identity, social development, education reform and group survival.

Pre-1848 "Jewish revolutionaries," such as David Nassy, Zalkind Hourwitz, Baer Joselewicz, Junius Frey, Abraham Furtado, Hartog de Hartog Lémon, Ludwig Börne, Heinrich Heine and Moses Hess, mostly fit this latter pattern rather than the classic Marxist anti-Jewish typology or mold but in a way that has never been properly studied as a category, typology and age-old historical process. This is relevant to some later revolutionary traditions when we consider that fighting for Jewish emancipation during the eighteenth and nineteenth centuries, in some quarters remained firmly tied to a far broader, more general concern with human emancipation from oppression. In any case, there is a need to identify, characterize and explain the modern Jewish revolutionary consciousness as it first emerged from the late seventeenth century onwards down to the young Marx, a development noticeably gaining momentum down to the mid-nineteenth century. A social, cultural and intellectual development slowly gestating since the seventeenth century, the phenomenon accelerated from the 1770s, gaining momentum, after 1800, and in Russia from the 1860s, especially from the growing attendance of European Jews at secularized secondary schools and universities.[3]

This book traces the historical development of a revolutionary consciousness rooted in the Jewish predicament and circumstances of Jewish society that exerted an enormous impact not only on Jewish life but, burgeoning also outwards, the entirety of the modern Western world. It is an argument partly about Jewish emancipation standing in broad agreement with that recently published by David Sorkin claiming Jewish emancipation as the most decisive, central development of modern Jewish history, and one commencing far earlier than the late eighteenth-century world of Moses Mendelssohn and the Berlin *Haskalah* [or Jewish Enlightenment], which historians have traditionally identified as its starting point.[4] Jewish emancipation was a struggle which in many respects never ended but continued incomplete, yielding all manner of problematic and difficult consequences down to our own time. This account agrees with Sorkin further in seeing many of the steps toward a less marginalized, discriminated against and restricted Jewish environment within general society as arising through gradual, cumulative tendencies which mostly, however, failed to attain complete resolution and release from the oppressive burdens of the past. The powerfully attractive model of "unconditional, full emancipation," as Sorkin calls it, if often a mirage, remained essentially a revolutionary agenda certainly down to 1917, a vision inseparable from the French Revolution and subsequent revolutions of the nineteenth and early twentieth centuries.[5]

Within this wider span there was a decisive early period, from the later seventeenth century until the mid-nineteenth, roughly 1670–1848, when preoccupation with Jewish emancipation was intense among both an upper crust of highly educated Jews and some elements among wider Western society and, though still mostly pre-socialist in character, this commitment could turn distinctly revolutionary. If, from the late nineteenth century onwards the Jewish people's quest for liberation and a life of freedom became essentially migratory, socialist or Zionist in character, what chiefly characterized the earlier pre-1848 phase, apart from the fact that its secular, non-mystical and non-Christianizing manifestations hardly yet affected the devout Jewish masses, was that these manifestations were invariably specifically Enlightenment commitments and concerns, not least with regard to the central rift between gradualism and arguing for an uncompromising revolutionary sweep, a rift one finds likewise within the Enlightenment as a whole.[6]

Intellectuals, then, of one sort or another are the main protagonists of this story. Not entirely shut out of the Western world's academic system down to the Napoleonic era, in the later phases, after 1800, these intellectuals were increasingly products of the university world. The 1848 revolutions in Austria began in Vienna among crowds attending Metternich's funeral. Conspicuous among the printed flyers agitators distributed was an ode by a noted Jewish poet, Ludwig August Frankl (1810–1894), a graduate of Vienna and Padua universities and fervent advocate of the rights and dignity of all the Habsburg Empire's peoples, entitled "Die Universität" [The University]:

dubbed by Wistrich "the Marseillaise of the Vienna rising," it extolled university students as humanity's prime freedom fighters—man's principal hope for a better future.[7]

The book's focus, then, is on an enlightened intellectual elite arising first at the fringes of mainstream Jewish and non-Jewish society but eventually invading the wider sphere of general learning, the sciences, academe and the student body, creating small networks sworn to redeem mankind, as they saw it, from universal misery, oppression and credulity. In their eyes, the alienated intellectual fringe to which they belonged, rather than the exploited proletariat (as yet barely identified as the future redeeming agent), was the spearhead of general emancipation. This applied even to Marx himself down to 1844, the year he became "Marxist"; for in the years prior to that he was not a socialist of any sort but a philosophical democratic radical. Hence, certainly down to the 1848 revolutions, the phenomenon examined here belonged to the world of what is nowadays labeled by historians the "Radical Enlightenment" rather than the Enlightenment generally, or early socialism. In fact, even after the Jewish quest for emancipation became basically socialist in character, from the 1870s, Jewish workers, artisans and peasants were still largely missing from the picture. Until the early 1880s, and the worst of the pogroms, the story remained consistently one of an intelligentsia with no following, only potential pull, and little else.

The purpose of this book, then, is to ask what exactly transformed a fringe of eighteenth- and early nineteenth-century Jewish society, including the young "pre-Marxist" Marx, into the world's most resolute, intellectually driven, and theory-preoccupied revolutionaries. Its central thesis is that in its origins modern Jewish revolutionary consciousness, like the modern revolutionary consciousness as a whole, was the direct offspring and fruit of the Enlightenment—the veritable seedbed of "modernity"—yet not of the whole undifferentiated Enlightenment but rather just one particular segment of it.

Certainly, the entire Enlightenment, commencing among intellectuals, scientists, jurists and writers in the late seventeenth century, with Newton, Leibniz, Bayle and Locke among its principal forerunners, including later the *Haskalah,* the specifically Jewish Enlightenment, was a secularizing, rationalizing intellectual movement aiming at the general amelioration of society, education and religion. From the outset, the entire Enlightenment constituted an international movement for the general betterment of mankind striving in particular to render society more tolerant and open-minded, more averse to superstition and credulity, more adjusted to up-to-date science, less tied to dogma, ecclesiastical authority and tradition. Before long, the general Enlightenment also bred a compelling political logic that concentrated on transforming early modern royal absolutism into a more socially responsible, benevolent style of government less rooted than earlier monarchy in tradition and precedent, less fixated on dynastic glory and on imposing religious uniformity in the manner of Philip II of Spain or Louis XIV of France. During the Enlightenment era, especially after Frederick the Great came to the throne in Prussia, in 1740, kingship in Europe, including in Catherine the Great's Russia, increasingly professed and in part genuinely aimed to be "enlightened," that is, show dedication to the general well-being and welfare of society as a whole. By the eighteenth century's last quarter, mainstream Enlightenment reformism had also begun having a far-reaching impact on eastern Europe and its Jews as well as the West.

All this exerted what the progressive-minded saw as a broadly positive impact on society. Efforts to rationalize and reform the convoluted legacy of the past, however, could only stretch so far while still conserving the basically monarchical and aristocratic frame, the social and institutional structure of early modern Europe. Restrained by royal courts, ecclesiastical authority and limited education, mainstream Enlightenment unavoidably stayed within clearly defined limits, defending the privileged status of nobility and churchmen throughout Europe, reaffirming the strongly hierarchical stratification of society prevalent everywhere, including the ghetto and *shtetl* where merchant elite and rabbinic oligarchies long presided over Jewish communities. Consequently, the social and intellectual impulses powering the Enlightenment also nurtured a profound and comprehensive social, political and intellectual internal rift within the Enlightenment, between enlighteners respecting the limits and those defying them, between restrained, intentionally partial versus bold, uncompromisingly revolutionary visions of change. The chief cause of the unavoidable rift that developed was that one side of the Enlightenment expressly deferred to the admonitions and requirements of faith, throne and noble status whereas the other side emphatically condemned these as illicit and needing to be demolished. Here was a split of overriding importance (rarely fully explained in the historiography) inherent in the prevailing conditions of life, fundamentally affecting every aspect of society and culture—and inevitably basic to all political and social thought.

The rebellious offshoot, the more sweeping radical tendency within the Enlightenment challenging the existing status quo, deliberately fomented theories and attitudes that were fundamentally anti-monarchical, anti-aristocratic and anti-ecclesiastical, ways of viewing the world combining rejection of religious authority with what developed into democratic republicanism. Until 1789, when it first came out into the open, this insurgent offshoot, the Radical Enlightenment, remained a veiled underground in intellectual as in political and social life, unseen by or inconspicuous to most.[8] Largely hidden from view, it was a dimension of the wider Enlightenment, the world of forbidden texts, or *clandestina*, that has increasingly attracted attention among historians in recent decades and without which one cannot make sense of the Enlightenment's fraught, fiercely contested, convoluted relationship to modernity, secularization, revolution and universal and equal rights.

Enlightenment, then, is the key to the story, and as far as the revolutionary consciousness Jewish and non-Jewish goes, especially the divergent radical tendency originating in the late seventeenth century as an irreligious, democratic republican and freethinking underground comprehensively rejecting monarchy, aristocracy and clergy. Always rejecting religious authority outright, it was a tendency that from the 1770s developed into an open, widely diffused, confidently undisguised challenge to the old order, an emphatically "universal and equal rights"-based democratic republican revolutionary challenge aimed at dismantling the prevailing social, religious and cultural system. It also rejected outright the deference to hierarchy, faith, precedent and long-standing stratified "rights" integral to the more moderate type of Enlightenment associated with Locke, Montesquieu, Voltaire and Hume.

Democratic republicanism embracing "universal and equal rights" consequently first entered the stage of the modern world as the preserve of very small networks confined originally mainly to northwestern Europe, but which after 1770 rapidly penetrated vast tracts of the world, first to North America, then South America, Czarist Russia and the rest of eastern Europe, generating a formidable democratic republican vanguard that first materialized as a serious political force in the "Paineite" democratic wing of the American Revolution (1775–83) and, from 1789, the French Revolution.

But the French Revolution's defeat, followed in 1813–15 by the downfall of Napoleon, ensured the ideology of "universal and equal rights" and democratic republicanism was then comprehensively pushed back and by no means only in Europe. From 1814, conservative reaction, mounting resistance to secularism, democracy and "universal and equal rights" among the devout and most of society allied to the old elites, lent fresh edge in North America by the "Great Awakening," the persistence of slavery until the 1860s in the southern states, and a tenacious oligarchic tendency in state and federal legislatures, and, in Europe, by such fervent Counter-Enlightenment writers as Chateaubriand, De Maistre and Bonald, dominated the scene. It was a general reaction that reaffirmed aristocratic and ecclesiastical dominance of society and, as part of this, restored and stiffened formalized discrimination against the Jewish minority. A parallel phenomenon was the intensifying reaction against the *Haskalah* in Jewish Eastern Europe, spearheaded by a rigid conservative orthodoxy and the separatist Jewish spiritual renewal of the Hasidic movement.

Reaffirming traditional values, political, social and religious, proved a powerful mechanism. Yet, such reaction, including the rampant Toryism dominant in England between 1789 and 1832, had the effect also of stiffening, entrenching and, beneath the surface, widening the culture of revolutionary opposition to post-1814 suppression of "universal and equal rights," of stimulating anti-aristocratism, anti-clericalism and rejection of what to a considerable extent were still popular deferential attitudes. Not least, it intensified Jewish resentment at the survival, and in many lands re-imposition, of legal and political restrictions on Jews and Judaism. The very force of reaction, by fueling the growing frustration and anger at the heart of the now vigorous opposition to the existing *status quo*, further mobilized the Radical Enlightenment tendency as chief motor of the revolutionary consciousness, Jewish and non-Jewish, down to the 1848 revolutions.

Prime examples of the Radical Enlightenment's escalating clash with majority attitudes arose from the prolonged thwarting of Jewish emancipation in lands such as Bavaria, Austria, Switzerland and Hungary. Bavaria is a classic instance of the uniqueness of the Jewish issue. During the Napoleonic period, the new Bavarian monarchy made up for its earlier lagging behind the rest of German enlightened reform by steaming ahead rapidly on every front, cutting back the sway of the Catholic Church in education, cultural affairs and reducing discrimination against non-Catholics more energetically than almost anywhere else outside France. Jewish rights, except with regard to access to general education, was the one great exception, the regime pulling back, in 1821, from even those advances previously made to lessen restrictions on Jews' right of residence, right to purchase property, subjection to special taxes, and much else. With regard to Jewish emancipation, the Bavarian monarchy bowed to popular and church pressure, especially following the violent upsurge of antisemitism accompanying the "Hep! Hep!" riots of 1819–22.[9]

Initially, the 1848 revolutions seemed to propel the cause of democratic values forward once again. On 4 June 1848, Bavarian Jews received the right to vote and stand for public office. On 3 August 1848, Jews were admitted to serve on Bavaria's newly introduced juries. In Hungary too, a country where the Jews had not yet begun to invade the universities and the medical and legal professions on the spectacular scale that marked Hungary out after 1860, the events of 1848 lent new impetus to all reforming tendencies, including the reform movement within Judaism itself, rapidly deepening the rift between Jewish orthodoxy and "Reform Judaism." There too, as in Austria and Switzerland, prospects for emancipation looked highly promising initially. A Hungarian Jewish revolutionary especially intoxicated by the gains of the 1848–49 revolutions, Ignać Einhorn (1825–1875), grandson of a rabbi of Vagújhely, in western Hungary, near the Slovakian border, possessing a solid training in Hebrew and Jewish studies, and working as a journalist in Budapest, emerged as perhaps the most notable Jewish activist equally committed to Jewish emancipation and Hungarian national renewal on a revolutionary basis, his *Zur Judenfrage in Ungarn* [On the Jewish Question in Hungary] having appeared in 1847, just prior to the eruption.[10]

The spectacular revolutionary wave convulsing many European capitals during 1848–49, including Paris, Rome, Venice, Berlin, Munich and Vienna as well as Budapest, all cities where Jews conspicuously participated in the insurgency against Europe's rulers, briefly intoxicated Jewish revolutionaries like Marx, Hess, Einhorn, and many others throughout the Austro-Hungarian Empire, Germany, Poland and Lithuania.[11] As the months passed, however, not a few, Einhorn among them, became dismayed and eventually profoundly shocked and disillusioned by what to them was the stunningly hypocritical failure of the revolutionary "liberals" to press the cause of Jewish emancipation in the face of surging prejudice and reaction steered by both the Protestant and Catholic clergy. Hungary's so-called "liberals," and the progressive Magyar nobility, Einhorn considered a particularly blatant instance of such base retreat. Appalled by the upsurge of popular antisemitic protest and then pogroms in Hungary, in 1848, which, in the end, succeeded in blocking enactment of Jewish rights by the revolutionary legislature in early 1849, Einhorn despaired of sufficiently enlightening Hungarian society in the foreseeable future to render Jewish equality a realistic goal in his time.

The story was the same in Bavaria. In the same spring of 1849, full civil emancipation for Jews initially passed the Bavarian legislature's Lower House by 91 votes to 40. Backed by the "liberal" Maximilian II (r. 1848–64), the newly enthroned popular "King Max," and his ministers, and the Lower House, the final triumph of Jewish emancipation in Bavaria looked assured. But the Church was not beaten yet: a renewed powerful push by conservative aristocrats, clergy and the religiously devout here too succeeded in stopping the process in its tracks. More than five hundred petitions, mostly organized by Catholic or Protestant clergy, bombarded the legislature demanding the reversal of Jewish emancipation, offering as justification the need for Bavarian society's "Christian character" to be safeguarded. Much of the public expressed joy and profound gratitude for their success. Revolutionary Jews, by contrast, felt utterly dismayed. Nevertheless, Einhorn, like many others, still hoped Jewish emancipation and integration alongside the majority would eventually prevail, if not soon in Hungary or Bavaria, then in Protestant Germany, Switzerland and France, where Enlightenment had accomplished more and traditional prejudices appeared to have been trimmed back further. If emancipation once triumphed in the most enlightened countries, supposedly, eventually it would triumph everywhere. But it was not until 1861 that Bavarian Jews finally gained freedom of movement and residence, and release from most other disabilities, nearing full emancipation. Final removal of all discriminatory measures and special taxes in Bavaria had to wait until 1881.[12] Hungary approached full Jewish emancipation only in 1868.

Admittedly, in early modern times social hierarchy based on elaborate stratification, presided over by royal absolutism and buttressed by theology, condemned most Europeans to one form of servility or another, ranging from outright serfdom to merely lacking political rights, servility predominating throughout Europe and to an extent still the Americas, and was hence still not ending for the great majority of people generally even by 1848. For centuries, the Western world's *ancien régime* had locked most of society into its system of legalized subjection—subordination increasingly regarded by some as systematic oppression. Armed with judicial codes, entrenched practices and, especially, religious justification, hierarchy's defenses remained formidable. Compared to the wealth, status and "rights" of the privileged upper strata, prior to 1848, the vast majority were vastly humbler and lowlier than they later became. At the same time, society's entrapment in hierarchy and theology generally received unstinting popular support in lands stretching from Russia and Hungary, to Britain and Spain. That was the Radical Enlightenment's great predicament.

If government either side of the Atlantic prior to the American Revolution (1775–83) rested mainly in the hands of monarchs, princes and aristocratic oligarchies, usable land, not just in Europe and Russia but also in much of the New World, was owned or leased out mostly by large aristocratic landowners and (in Catholic lands) ecclesiastical foundations. Long-distance and colonial trade remained heavily regulated by rulers with key components, notably chartered, government-approved monopolistic companies, like the English, Dutch, Danish and French East and West India and Africa companies, controlled by elite cliques of privileged, well-connected and wealthy investors. Moreover, many vestiges of the old pattern remained in place after the American Revolution and after the Spanish American revolutions of the 1820s; for even inside the United States, until the late 1860s, neither the privileged political status of big landowners nor special status for clergy bolstered by special church taxes and blasphemy laws, nor the subordinate position of substantial particular groups, most strikingly the black population, was yet ended, even in theory.

Through the guild system, early modern arts and crafts too were rigorously confined to narrowly defined qualified groups with higher education dominated by a restricted segment of professors and teachers exclusively belonging to whichever church was locally dominant. Since the Reformation, this nearly always meant one or other of four politically hegemonic and privileged ecclesiastical spheres—Catholic, Lutheran, Calvinist and Orthodox. Some kingdoms, notably Prussia and post-1688 Britain, even awkwardly embodied two publicly supported authorized state churches, the Lutheran and the Calvinist in the former, the Anglican and Scottish Presbyterian (Calvinist) in the latter within the same state, creating coexisting privileged domains for academics and clergy adhering to the presiding ecclesiastical spheres. The greatest political, naval and military power of the late eighteenth and early nineteenth centuries, Britain, was in many respects (prior to the 1832 Great Reform Act) typical of the *ancien régime* system of domination of society but looked exceptional due to the aristocracy rather than the royal court dominating and to the exceptional vigor of popular ardor for Loyalism, that is, for crown, church and defending the aristocracy's social hegemony.

Hegemony of aristocracy, privilege and confessional thinking, and the vast organized subordination of the great majority, was universal and widely supported. In these circumstances, given the continuing prevalence of illiteracy, *ancien régime* society's often stiflingly repressive features generated more endemic unfocused, non-intellectual grievance than argued, reasoned rejection. Anger and resentment were widespread among a wide range of social strata and groups. But resentment took a more highly literate, argued form only in very restricted circles. The situation guaranteed the prevalence of inarticulate, non-intellectual grievance, which also meant, once a match was put to the dry wood, that the Western Hemisphere's sustained general revolutionary upheaval (1775–1848) continued its menacing, dizzying career for many decades. Everywhere, the Western world seethed with unfocused dissatisfaction, a resource sometimes captured and steered, it is true, by the much smaller revolutionary-minded fringe; but this happened only sporadically, precariously and briefly, without any consistency. A wide spectrum of groups stood behind the broad dissatisfaction, resulting in frequent disturbances and insurrections, but with only a narrow, highly educated opposition fringe preparing the ground and pointing the way toward the overthrow of the old aristocratic-monarchical-ecclesiastical order. This is the reason, often overlooked, why Radical Enlightenment remained for so long the only available general motor toward far-reaching social and political renewal on the basis of democratic representative republicanism and "universal and equal rights."

Sustained revolutionary momentum capable of replacing the old institutional framework with a new social vision could grow only where a prepared seedbed of ideas justifying rejection of the existing social and political order and the religious authority sanctioning it existed. Consequently, where these intellectual tools were lacking, where there was no linking of general frustration and social grievance to a comprehensive philosophy restructuring the social, moral and political order according to basic new principles, even the most furious dissatisfaction could go no further than sporadic outbreaks of aimless protest and violence usually fairly quickly suppressed. As was repeatedly seen also before 1789, with the eighteenth century's earlier mostly short-lived Old World peasant risings and New World slave revolts, it made no difference how profound and widespread wretchedness, distress and misery were, where the necessary intellectual spearhead in the form of a highly educated ideological vanguard presenting a blueprint for a new order was lacking, popular resistance, no matter how deeply felt, brooding, conspiratorial and violent, invariably led nowhere.

A great many diverse groups, broad segments comprising the great majority (from 1775 outside the United States at least), were legally and institutionally under royal, aristocratic and ecclesiastical sway on both sides of the Atlantic, oppressed by a combination of social hierarchy, religion and popular ignorance. This needs emphasizing since, generally speaking, historians eager to extol "national history" have tended to play down the discrimination, exploitation and segregation still prevailing. Until 1789, lifelong, inescapable subordination was the fate of most, including practically all women whether within or outside of marriage (at the time essentially a religious institution), servants, serfs, slaves, artisans, small tenant-holders, seamen, soldiers, those born out of wedlock, homosexuals and nearly all religious minorities. Even so, due to their outsider status, lingering partial or actual ghettoization in many parts and age-old denial of Christian teaching, Europe's Jews found themselves trapped in an extra-degraded space of legalized discrimination and organized scorn upheld by laws and governments as well as religion, education and society, that had long been, and often still was, deeper and more oppressive than *ancien régime* subordination of other social strata apart from serfs and black slaves.

Jews were subject to restrictions imposed with varying degrees of rigor in every European land, specially devised marks of exclusion and humiliation along with a systematic intellectual exclusion that applied to few others. Even in England and Holland, regarded at the time as the two most tolerant European countries, Jews were heavily discriminated against down to the early nineteenth century, viewed with hostility by most of the population as well as by government, law and by military, ecclesiastical and academic institutions. The psychological response, we have seen, was mostly passive and sullen, but not always. There was some scope for action, as the Polish-Lithuanian Jewish radical Baer (Berek) Joselewicz (1764–1807) showed with Yiddish posters he put up, in early October 1794, in the Jewish quarters of Warsaw, a city inhabited by some 6,750 Jews, then amounting to just over 8 percent of the total of 81,000, with a substantial proportion earning their living as a middle segment, concentrated in a particular sector of the crafts, mainly tailors, hatters and furriers, wedged between the wealthy merchants and the poor, peddlers and the like.[13] In support of Tadeusz Kościuszko (1746–1817), Poland's greatest hero and a supporter of Jewish as well (in the New

World context) as black emancipation, a rebel leader who directly appealed to Poland's Jews in the great synagogue of Kazimierz (Cracow), Joselewicz in 1794 raised a Jewish fighting contingent to help the Poles resist Russian imperial annexation of the Polish heartland: "why should we, the most oppressed people in the world, not take up arms to free the Fatherland?" His contingent was quickly crushed by the Russians in the ensuing battle for Warsaw.

But this rare and quickly extinguished Jewish call to arms—"let us rise up like lions and leopards, and with God's help devour the puffed-up great [the Russian crown and nobility]"—could occur only because Joselewicz spoke and read Polish, German and French besides Yiddish and had personally witnessed the beginnings of the French Revolution, in Paris, in 1789.[14] One of the very few other "Polish" Jews who had anything like his secular breadth of vision, or closeness to the enlightened ideals of Kościuszko at the time, was Salomon Polonus (dates unknown) of Vilna, a physician trained in Amsterdam. On the defeat of the 1794 rising, Joselewicz fled to join the crowd of other revolutionary exiles huddling in Paris.

The restrictions confining Jewish life in most of Europe extended eastwards as far as Warsaw, Posen, Lublin and Cracow, Polish "crown cities" with specially designated "Jewish" suburbs such as Kazimierz in Cracow and Praga in Warsaw, with non-Jewish merchant elites dominating the city center and ensuring tough restrictions on Jewish life and settlement remained in place. But, farther east, in the vast, less urbanized parts of the Polish-Lithuanian "commonwealth," in the many small towns and villages of eastern Poland, Belarus, Lithuania and the Ukraine under the nobility's control, Jews heavily dominated retailing and commerce. Not infrequently Jews were the numerical majority in these small townships, presiding to the point that, locally, a kind of reverse pattern of hierarchy prevailed, if not in law and institutions then certainly psychologically, on the level of everyday conversation and humor. More literate, internationally connected and hence also better-informed than the rest of society below the level of aristocracy and clergy throughout fringe Europe east of Warsaw and Cracow, here at any rate Jews could reciprocally scorn their still more servile, credulous and exploited, if less discriminated against Christian neighbors, an important element in the psychology of the subsequent modern Jewish revolutionary consciousness. Here, Jews often evinced contempt for the apparent backwardness and illiteracy of the local peasantry and non-Jewish townsfolk.[15] This was evident not least in Joselewicz's home town in Lithuania, Kretinga, or the small town of

Mir (Mirz), southeast of Grodno, the town nearest the village where the most subversive eighteenth-century Jewish philosopher, Solomon Maimon (1753–1800), originated.

Still, disdaining the backwardness of others is rarely justified. The early modern Jewish world proved just as vulnerable to being swept off its feet by popular ignorance and superstition as any early modern religious bloc. Longing for redemption, for the chains to drop and prison walls to crumble, for persecution to cease, was so intense, especially in the aftermath of the "Chmielnicki massacres" of 1648, when many thousands of Jews were slain by insurgent peasants and Cossacks in the Ukraine and southeastern Poland, and all east European Jewry deeply traumatized, that when the "false Messiah" Sabbatai Zevi (c. 1626–1676) and his entourage proclaimed his message of salvation to the Jewish world in 1665–66, the resulting frenzy knew no bounds. Hebrew letters sent from Ottoman Lands announcing the "great news" swept the Near East, Mediterranean and Europe, fomenting the greatest convulsion to shake the Jewish world of the entire early modern era. But what most shocked Rabbi Jacob Sasportas (c. 1610–1698), the bitterest, most resolute critic of the false message in western Europe and staunchest foe of the frenzy, was not the mass emotion, unrestrained jubilation and dancing in the streets, or temporary throwing aside of Jewish observance, but the utter failure of the Jewish establishment, of the rabbis and scholars, to stand up to the credulous mass and stem the tide, the total failure to apply reason and argument as brakes to control the crisis.[16]

The Jewish impulse to self-emancipate was first identified as a key collective—part mystical, part secularizing—historical phenomenon central to modern Jewish history as a whole by the great historian Simon Dubnow (1860–1941), following the 1880–81 pogroms in Russia. Born near Mogilev, in what is today Belarus, Dubnow spent many years in Petersburg, Odessa and Vilna, mastered the sources in Yiddish, Hebrew, Russian and German, remaining always ambivalent about a Jewish return to the Holy Land but never about the need to escape appalling religious hatred, persecution and discrimination. He was the first to offer a general historical schema interpreting the phenomenon of self-emancipation from the time of Sabbatai Zevi, and of the greatest early modern Jewish philosopher, Benedict de Spinoza (1632–1677), onwards, clearly identifying the overall tendency as an impulse to escape, whether via emigration to the New World, by revolution, or Zionism, from the misery and oppression that permeated nearly the entirety the Old World's Jewish population.[17]

During the 1750s, the upsurge of mysticism and frenzy associated with another powerful messianic movement, the "Frankist" movement in Poland and the Ukraine, proved once again how profound was the inner pressure for release. But mid-eighteenth-century Frankism, recognized Dubnow, also confirmed that the deep, instinctive rebellion of many poorer, less educated Jews participating in these great movements since the 1660s was as much directed against the rigid discipline, austerity and control exercised by the learned Jewish elite and community organization as against external oppression. Integration with the Christian population and escape from stern sexual and other inhibitions were unmistakable features of the Frankist episode.[18] Soon afterwards, with the rise of the new orthodox mysticism known as Hasidism, associated with the Israel Baal Shem Tov, "the Besht" (c. 1700–1760), though the infringing of Jewish observance was (largely) absent, other features of the Jewish mass rebellion during the late eighteenth century and early in the nineteenth, prior to the onset of modern revolutionary consciousness, were abundantly evident.[19] Hasidism, which later became an essentially conservative tendency, originally represented a parallel revulsion against the learned elite especially in the Hasidic rejection of asceticism, push to re-enchant the world, and in its self-immersion in the world and its wonders, and its exalting the holiness of something like Rousseau's "simple souls" against the sophistication and social elitism of high learning. The Jewish tailor or other artisan often felt contempt for the Talmud student, remote from the economic harshness of daily life; the Talmud student often felt disdain for the artisan. A pure heart and the joy expressed in music and dancing were as attainable, or more so, by the scarcely literate as by the erudite; meanwhile, in their thirst for wonder cures and the mystical wisdom of particular village Hasidic rabbinic dynasties attuned to the Besht, the Hasidim surpassed anything to which the yeshiva students were prone.[20]

Eventually, Hasidism would become almost entirely a reactionary culture. Still, the element of rebellion against the world around them embodied in Hasidism remained strong through the late eighteenth century and beginning of the nineteenth. One strand of this popular revolution among east European Jewry, the Lurianic (Cabbalistic) doctrine of *Tzimtzum*, or "divine self-limitation in things," lived on in what has been termed "Hasidic pantheism," and was deliberately used as a bridge between east European Jewish proto-revolutionary longing and Spinozism by the rebellious philosopher Solomon Maimon (1753–1800) in his autobiography [*Lebensgeschichte*] of 1792. Around 1770, Maimon made a pilgrimage to the "court" of the most important Hasidic leader in the period immediately after the death of the Besht, namely Dov Ber, the "Maggid [Holy Man] of Mezrich" (c. 1710–1772). Maimon traveled from his native district, Mir, today in Belarus, southeast of present-day Lithuania, south into the Volhynia region of northwest Ukraine, to the west of modern Kiev, to the court of the Maggid. For the rest of his life, Maimon, while ridiculing the enthusiasm of the Maggid's devotees, and the exaggerated leadership cult surrounding Dov Ber—who rarely appeared among his followers but, when he did, was attired wholly in white satin—he also saw something of real value in Hasidism's core doctrines reconciling intellect with sensualism and merging oneself in the world. Refusing to agree that Spinozism is a form of "atheism," Maimon closely identified Spinoza's metaphysics with the Lurianic doctrine of *Tzimtzum*, explaining Spinoza's synthesis of God and the world as a similar form of "acosmism," a denial that anything is ultimately separate from God, that all particular things are limited extensions of God's infinite being as modes of His substance, so that in Spinoza's philosophy it is not God who does not exist separate from reality but rather the world separate from God.[21] Unsurprisingly, the pantheism of Lurianic *Tzimtzum* was also a key element in the messianism of Sabbatai Zevi; nor was Maimon the only commentator on eighteenth-century German philosophy to see a deep connection between Spinozism and the wellsprings of Jewish mysticism from Sabbatai Zevi to Dov Ber.

The final result of the abortive but frenzied spiritual uprisings of 1665–66, Frankism, and that emanating from Mezrich in the 1760s and 1770s, was not, of course, the redemption sighed for by the impoverished, oppressed Jewish masses of Poland-Lithuania and Czarist Russia, but disillusionment, disappointment and humiliation to add to their other woes. Unquestioning belief, prostration before wonders, in the end provided no release from marginalization and oppression. Repression and legal marginalization remained the unrelenting lot whether of those living openly as Jews in organized Jewish communities or those dwelling, as in the pre-1820 Spanish and Portuguese trans-Atlantic empires, where Judaism was officially forbidden altogether. In Iberian lands, many descendants of Jews remained inwardly loyal to their old religion, but had no choice but to dwell under precarious cover, adhering secretly under outward pretense of being "Christians."

In Spain, Portugal and throughout Ibero-America, these concealed crypto-Jews, or "New Christians" as they were known (in Portugal and Brazil, *cristãos novos*), found themselves ceaselessly denounced, along with the rest of Jewry, in the most vitriolic terms. "Judaism" they heard endlessly reviled in school, university and church as the worst of evils, that which is most opposed to Christianity, without being able to utter a word of dissent openly, remaining under permanent surveillance and constant threat of persecution by the Inquisition. Although normative Judaism had been forbidden in Spain since 1492, persecution notably intensified from the mid-sixteenth century, becoming an obsessive effort to extirpate all traces of Jewish tradition and culture, persecution that continued on a considerable scale until the 1720s and in Portugal the 1740s. Nevertheless, tenacious secret study of Judaism and loathing and repugnance for theology and churchmen, both monks and secular clergy, persisted widely among these so-called *conversos.*

Consequently, almost everywhere, Jewish society proved fertile ground for incipient revolutionary inclinations, despite rabbis and Jewish community elders, anxious to protect the limited formal toleration available outside the Iberian world—not least in the vast kingdom of Poland-Lithuania—striving to avoid unnecessary friction. Eager to maintain their own privileged status within their communities, Jewish community leadership habitually demanded submission and quiescence toward the prevailing status quo. In the Netherlands, the communities' official leadership, and most of the membership, remained more solidly loyal than virtually any other group of Dutch society to Orangism and what, from 1813, became the royal house. Yet, at times, and bitterly at odds with the mainstream, surged a contrary tendency tenaciously refusing to bow down. Rejection of the established order, and from 1789 zeal for the new revolutionary consciousness, consequently, also meant outright revolt against Jewish religious authority too. Fusing opposition to community leadership with resistance to the wider status quo became a natural, logical, even unavoidable response abundantly encountered among the estranged and restless fringe. While many social groups in early modern Europe shared to some degree the sense of grievance feeding the revolutionary ferment once it began, independent-minded Jews with both stronger grounds and often higher literacy levels than other disadvantaged groups, remained a distinctive category especially apt to be attracted to uncompromising revolutionary hostility to social rank, monarchical forms and religious authority.

While moderate *Haskalah*, like the moderate Enlightenment generally, was rather more acceptable to mainstream society than its radical counterpart, there were obvious social and intellectual reasons why many Jews were drawn in practice to radical in preference to moderate Enlightenment ideas.

Admittedly, for many decades it remained much harder to learn about radical ideas. Before 1775, Radical Enlightenment languished under wraps, hiding in the shadows of clandestinity. But the Western world's mainstream Enlightenment anchored in Locke, Voltaire, Montesquieu, Hume, Wolff, Kant and Adam Smith took scarcely any interest in the predicament of the Jews either as a religion or social group, indeed often, as with Voltaire and Frederick the Great, displayed unmistakable repugnance rather than sympathy. Voltaire's elegant world of courts and aristocracy looked down on the Jews as a repository of blind religious obedience and unthinking observance stuck in perversely narrow social roles, an ugly, irrelevant, annoying remnant from a distant past partly responsible supposedly for the theological dogmatism and "priestcraft" rife in contemporary society, for the "Pharisaic" intolerance and bigotry all enlighteners despised.[22]

Radical Enlightenment, by contrast, mostly (if not always) proclaimed Jewish traditionalism and obscurantism, and the Jews' widely scorned narrow occupation-structure focusing on money and trade, to be not inherent disfigurement manifesting an innate, allegedly unchanging malign and defective character as was generally supposed, or anything deemed the Jews' own fault, but the result rather of age-old oppression perpetrated by an unjust and overbearing system. This was first clearly affirmed in the *Reasons for Naturalizing the Jews in Great Britain and Ireland* (1714) by John Toland (1670–1722). Jewish society's reliance on money-lending Toland explained as resulting from intolerant restrictions and disabilities. He was to be followed here by a long list of radical enlighteners: Jewish concentration on petty trade, money-changing and finance, the constricted scope disfiguring Jewish economic life, and reinforcing anti-Jewish sentiment, stemmed not from innate characteristics, or inborn traits, but general oppression imposed by the real culprit—which in radical eyes was essentially an alliance of "kings and priests." Certainly, some Radical Enlightenment writers, like d'Holbach and the pre-1800 Fichte, at times lapsed into the familiar antisemitic tropes, attributing alleged inherent defects and supposed innate reprehensible traits; but in the context of their radical arguments overall this line of rhetoric where it occurs was illogical and self-contradictory.

Since Enlightenment thinkers like Toland, Diderot, d'Holbach and Condorcet had little confidence in the present intellectual level of ordinary people, appraised not as individuals but as a bloc, radical enlighteners always rejected "pure democracy" on the model of ancient Athens, scorning the purity of "simple souls" eulogized by Rousseau.[23] True democratic republicanism by their definition must always follow "reason" and advance society's "common good," which meant government by a representative legislature (as in Toland), or what Spinoza calls "great councils," enabling the most capable and intellectually most eminent to assume the lead in speaking publicly, framing laws and making decisions. Enlightenment radicals rejected direct government by the majority in favor of government in the interest of the majority by the most "rational," which, again contrary to Rousseau, meant spurning all notion of "natural equality" in favor of a politically constructed "equality of rights" introduced by human government subsequent to the "state of nature." Equal rights for radical enlighteners were a humanly devised construct aimed at evening up the natural vast diversity and inequality of men.

For radical enlighteners, then, there was no such thing as equal "natural rights" prior to the state, only "rights" subsequently devised to render society fairer and more amenable to vesting sovereignty in the "common good," as Spinoza terms it, or "general will" in the anti-Rousseauist sense used by Diderot, d'Holbach and Condorcet. Here is a point on which several central figures in this book, such as David Nassy and Junius Frey, laid particular stress. Wherever representation for all is demanded, without separate orders or privilege entering the picture, where Toland's "Commonweal or Good of all" is pursued "indifferently," as he put it, without any hereditary advantage or special consideration for any particularly favored group or authorized religious voice intervening, with frequent elections and meetings of the legislature, equality before the law, and full freedom of expression, all requisite criteria of the category "Radical Enlightenment" are met. This, as the great poet Heinrich Heine was keenly aware in the early nineteenth century,[24] was very much *his* tradition, an intellectual legacy rooted in a clandestine philosophical underground in which Toland had centrally figured.

For radical enlighteners, the cramped, disfigured character of early modern Jewish society, like all human ills, was entirely the fault of ignorance allied to a perverse value-system fueled by theology, intolerance and bigotry, by which they meant aristocracy and "Christian values" allied to royal despotism. Oppression of Jews, together with the antisemitic sentiment fueling it, resulted, in radical eyes, from the same systems of belief and assumptions operating to the disadvantage of society overall, but rooted in notions fervently trusted in, despite this harming their own interest, by the unknowing and credulous majority. While, like Spinoza and Toland, radicals by no means rejected what they conceived of as original unadulterated "Christianity," viewed purely as a moral doctrine, their aversion to post-Apostolic Christian "mysteries" and theology, their hostility to churches and churchmen, was inseparably tied to their repudiation of the existing monarchical-aristocratic form of society. This approach in turn spurred radical thinkers to take a closer, more urgent interest than moderate enlighteners or traditionalist theologians did in traditional Jewish critiques of Christian belief and dogma. Hence, the Radical Enlightenment stance rendered one very small fringe of society dramatically readier than all the rest to contemplate the dismantling of the repressive wall of disabilities and exclusions separating Jews and Judaism from the rest of society. Understandably, given how it assigned blame for the centuries-old stifling restrictions of the past, and its sympathy for the Jewish plight and Jewish arguments, Radical Enlightenment was peculiarly qualified and equipped, in a way no other tendency of the age could conceivably be, to attract powerfully aggrieved independent-minded Jews to its revolutionary thrust.

Jewish emancipation became a realistic proposition from the moment Europe's former predominantly theological view of the world began to crumble under the impact of Enlightenment ideas. While this did not occur on any scale before 1770, the first glimmerings of what was to come were perceptible earlier. Toland, an Anglo-Irish convert from Catholicism to Protestantism and then freethinking, was the first to propose lifting all restrictions and disabilities on the Jews and by means of a "General Naturalization" elevate them to full equality with Christians. Typically for radical thought, he laid the entire blame for the problem of Jewish marginality and separation squarely on the churches together with those backing ecclesiastical direction under what he thought of as the insidious alliance of priests and princes to cheat and exploit everyone else.[25] Few in Britain at the time agreed with him; but Toland was convinced the Jews' narrow occupation range, their focusing almost entirely on petty trade and money-lending "wholly proceeds from Accident and not from nature," the prime factor being irrational prejudice and the Jews' exclusion from public office, the professions and most handicrafts by laws, ecclesiastical decree and general discrimination.[26] The Jews' "most inveterate enemies were the priests, who devoutly offer'd up those human sacrifices" [the victims of the Crusaders and of medieval popular anti-Jewish outbreaks] "not only to share their goods with the rapacious prince, but also to acquire the reputation of zeal and sanctity among the credulous vulgar. Everything, in short, tho' ever so false or impossible, serv'd for a handle good enough to rifle, or expel or slaughter the Jews."[27]

Where earlier advocates of Jewish reentry to lands from which they had been expelled in the Middle Ages, like Rabbi Menasseh ben Israel (1604–1657), invoked Jewish commercial and financial usefulness, the mercantilist concerns of early modern governments,[28] Toland, a champion of anti-theological naturalism, universalism and egalitarianism, was the first to demand Jewish reintegration on the basis of universal common rights and values, claiming that in essentials Jews were the same as everyone else. Populace and clergy might disagree, and the vast majority did, but Toland's cutting analysis of the Jewish question could not be answered by emphasizing Jewish separateness, or peculiarities as a people, "by no means disprov'd from their present general occupation of exchange to which they are driven out of necessity" and not at all "from choice or inclination." Originally, in biblical times, Jews had been shepherds, farmers and builders; once accorded equality, with all disabilities lifted, they would again devote themselves to "building, farming and all sorts of improvement like other people."[29]

But Toland, historians and philosophers have come to recognize, was scarcely an original thinker. Rather, he followed Spinoza in all main lines of his thought, and especially in rejecting Locke's basic dualism, his separation of reality into two fundamentally distinct dimensions—physico-empirical reality subject to direct experience, on the one hand, and the sphere "above reason" [*supra rationem*], of religious authority, mysteries and theology, on the other. By replacing Lockean dualism with Spinozist monism, Toland effectively removed moderate Enlightenment's chief philosophical lynch-pin, erasing the floor supporting all theology and thereby negating the entire Lockean approach to divine providence, religious authority, divinely ordered natural justice and law. This turned the Bible and Jewish history into being simply parts of universal history without possessing any specially elevated, separate or sacred character. It was thus no accident that Toland as a Spinozist republican, and inveterate foe of "priestcraft" and denier of Lockean *supra rationem*, became the West's first writer openly and publicly to proclaim Jewish equality. All humanity Toland conceived as one without there ever having been any Revelation to one group or prophet, or "inclinations" or characteristics specific to any one people delivered by God or nature.[30]

But here too, Toland was echoing Spinoza. To those convinced of the need for Jewish separateness as a religious community under rabbinic direction, Spinoza replies that "no people is distinguished from another with regard to understanding and true virtue, and hence in these spheres God does not choose one nation above another."[31] Either Jews must form their own separate polity, he held, or integrate further into the societies around them. Yet, the Jewish experience in Iberian lands undoubtedly left a profound impression on Spinoza too: despite his basic stance, he appreciated more than most what it means to recognize Judaism as historically the first and most purely monotheistic of all religions.

Rather than a people apart, to be shunned, the Jews were as "obedient, peaceable, useful and advantageous as any [people]," indeed more so, suggested Toland, than many; besides, "both in their origine and progress, [they were] not otherwise to be regarded than under the common circumstances of human nature."[32] No entity apart, neither better nor worse than others, the Jews were not a people once chosen by God and then discarded, having never been specially "elected" in any theological sense in the first place. Their biblical history has no supernatural dimension. Assiduously blending anti-monarchism, anti-Scripturalism and anti-ecclesiasticism with anti-populism, Toland squarely assailed existing society, ideas and institutions. Relegating Jewish history to a fringe of universal history, at the same time he presents the Mosaic Law as a great republican landmark of enduring significance, one of a series of monumental proto-republican ancient legal codes, along with those of Solon, Lycurgus and Numa. Moses urgently required reconceptualization and reevaluation by scholars, contended Toland, being no divinely directed prophet but rather a "Pantheist or, in more recent language, a Spinozist."[33]

Only by rejecting the world of the "credulous vulgar," contended Toland, can one reach a just and true appraisal of things. However, with the clergy and ignorant multitude constantly on the lookout to block every emancipating proposal, and ordinary folk unknowingly colluding with priests, princes and aristocracy against their own interest, thereby preventing the emergence of a free, secular society, the common view of things is not just hopelessly misinformed, he maintained, but also exceedingly dangerous: "I am not ignorant how much the world is govern'd by prejudices, and how far some, who wou'd not be counted of the vulgar, are yet sway'd by vulgar errors."[34] As with Spinoza, Toland's "multitude" does not categorize the masses as a social category but rather embraces the whole of society at all levels, encompassing everyone unable to grasp the reality of things, including most kings, princes, aristocrats, churchmen and academics as well as most (but by no means all) ordinary folk. The fight was on to rescue the unjustly downtrodden from enforced marginality as part of the wider struggle to secularize and democratize modern society, a fight that would be long, bitter and inconclusive, against fundamentally false ideas sanctioned by government, nobility, churches, and universities but also by the common people, that could perhaps never be fully won.

Since it was the early Enlightenment that first created space for the modern revolutionary Jew, the roots of the phenomenon need to be looked for at an earlier point than the historiography has traditionally suggested, and certainly many decades prior to the French Revolution. The first revolutionary Jews, such as Nassy, Hourwitz, Maimon, Joselewicz, Furtado, Pereyra, Frey and Hartog Lémon, represent a wholly new dimension of Jewish life later including Börne, Heine and Hess, figures who became activists in radically non-religious revolutionary movements while at the same time aiming to rescue their own people by emancipating them as a people and culture, integrating them via equal rights into what radicals envisaged as the universal democratic society of the future. Dismantling traditional structures of authority and thought, held Enlightenment radicals, would rescue from theologically sanctioned oppression not just the Jews but all the downtrodden of society. Occasionally, some consideration was given to the idea that Jewish emancipation was simply not feasible without their acquiring their own independent geographical sphere; the late Diderot, for example, wondered whether a Caribbean island, Jamaica perhaps, might be a possibility. But the main concern was to integrate the Jews, once freed from *ancien régime* structures of authority, morality and thought, within general society while enabling them to retain elements of their separate identity as a religion and people.

During the eighteenth century, then, came into existence a distinctively "Jewish" Radical Enlightenment rejecting rabbinic authority and the sway of Torah and Talmud that needs careful differentiation from the better-known mainstream *Haskalah*. This latter, more moderate, traditionalist and, to most Jews, more acceptable reformist trend did not challenge Jewish religion or tradition as such, or reject separate community organization, peoplehood or religious authority, and therefore did not deny the God-given character of Scripture or the "election of the Jews" as a chosen people, in the manner of Spinoza and Toland.[35] Nor did it commit to overturning either the basic political and social format of *ancien régime* society. And yet, so marginalized was early modern Jewish status that it inevitably gave rise within itself to a covert revolutionary strand: for Jews, as one scholar expressed it, *Haskalah* was an escape route from "centuries-old preoccupation with religion allowing them to become Europeans" without specifying where any given individual's intellectual odyssey would eventually lead.[36]

Mainstream, or "moderate," *Haskalah* commenced with the endeavors of Moses Mendelssohn (1729–1786), in Berlin, in the 1750s and 1760s. Grounded in Jewish communities, schooling and tradition, it spread from Germany westwards to France and Holland and eastwards into Poland, Lithuania and the Ukraine. *Haskalah* aimed at gradually, gently reforming Judaism and the Hebrew language, modernizing the teaching of Judaism and education of Jewish youth, but within the orbit of continuing observance, Hebrew learning and rabbinic guidance while minimizing friction with conservative rabbis and community elders. Some key figures following in Mendelssohn's footsteps in eastern Europe, like the Galician rabbi Nachman Krochmal (1785–1840), nevertheless came under unremitting pressure from the Hasidic orthodox. More than a few such Jewish moderates were denounced by the strictly orthodox as heretics and crypto-Karaites. Moderates, fast gaining ground among the wealthy Jewish elite of Warsaw and other east European cities by the end of the eighteenth century, and radical enlighteners alike, retaliated by labeling the growing host of Hasidic and non-Hasidic orthodox and ultra-orthodox as unenlightened, "superstitious" and fanatical, provoking a contest that did not cease in the nineteenth century but blasts on loudly in Israel even today.[37]

Krochmal, having taught himself German by the age of twenty, and become steeped in Mendelssohn, Lessing, Maimon, Kant, Fichte, Schelling and later Hegel, emerged among the most prominent of the southern Polish Jewish enlighteners, both in Lemberg (Lvov), a noted center of Jewish *maskilim* (enlighteners) and Zolkiev. Studying German and the German classics, which he deemed vital, was precisely the main route out of the *shtetl*, for "enlightened" and emancipated eastern European Jews generally, for the Jewish elites throughout Poland, Hungary, Slovakia and Bukovina between the 1780s and 1848.[38] Among Krochmal's chief arguments for a modernized, rationalized Judaism attuned to Kant and other recent developments in philosophy was what he considered the morally negative effects of the narrowly traditionalist distortion of Judaism, which to his mind strict orthodoxy represented. Counter-Enlightenment orthodoxy threatened to alienate all the scientifically and intellectually aware from Judaism. Such religious traditionalism Krochmal dismissed as anti-scientific "superstition" driving the ignorant toward a pernicious distortion of the opposite kind to that perpetrated, equally reprehensibly, by radicals denying the spiritual realm altogether being caught in what he saw as the trap of Spinozism.[39]

The philosophical viability of a modernized Judaism, urged Krochmal, crucially depends on finding the middle way, rejecting rabbinic obscurantism and ignorance on one side while repelling Spinoza's assault on divine providence and teleology, on the other, and hence on rescuing the notion that God is distinct from nature, that nature is the creation of a knowing, purposeful, benign God. In his *The Guide of the Perplexed of the Time,* left unfinished at the time of his death, in 1840, Krochmal sought to apply Kant's categories to the burgeoning modern Jewish predicament with a view to blocking Spinoza and renewing the philosophical viability of a creator God delivering the moral order to mankind through Revelation.[40]

Set on compromise, moderate *Haskalah* took care to conserve the core structures of Jewish tradition and religious authority. But it also edged the Jewish people more toward broad social and political reform. It supported efforts to remove the special disabilities, fiscal burdens and restrictions imposed by society, law and government, the measures keeping Jews fenced into permanent marginality. Meanwhile, as regards freeing Jews from persecution, ghettoization, disabilities and restrictions, radical enlighteners ventured well beyond thinkers like Mendelssohn or Krochmal, and it was they who opened the way to the advent of the Jewish revolutionary consciousness. Given these concerns it is not surprising that not a few Jews opting for a more decisive rupture with the past broke entirely with their Jewish background and ties while others, in recent years dubbed the "radical Haskalah," likewise broke dramatically with the rabbis and observance, but at the same time showed a dogged resolve to uncover what they saw as a truer or deeper, more universal and more secular "Jewish reality" or truth that, for them, lay beneath the world of rabbinic Judaism and observance. The latter strove to bring out what they saw as a hitherto largely underground but fundamental aspect of Jewish tradition reaching back deep into the Middle Ages, and fundamental to Jewish thought.

Among this group the figure of "Baruch Spinoza," the greatest foe of all thinking conventional, respectable and traditional whether Jewish or Christian, was often assigned a pivotal role in the chain of underground "Jewish" tradition. Among devotees of this Jewish wing of the Radical

Enlightenment from the 1850s onwards, urging a more drastic and comprehensive emancipation for the Jews and for everyone, rather ironically, stepping well beyond the bounds fixed by his father, was Krochmal's own son, Abraham Krochmal (c. 1823–1895). Tellingly, Abraham Krochmal was the writer who, with a touch of humor, first coined the ringing modern secular democratic Jewish epithet "Rabbenu Baruch" [our Rabbi Baruch].[41]

ONE

The Subversive Background of a Revolutionary Thinker

Though the most notorious single rebel against rabbinic Judaism of the early modern era, Spinoza nevertheless viewed the Jews and Judaism as having played a primary role in world history in a number of fundamental respects.

"No one can deny," Spinoza reminded a former disciple, Albert Burgh (1650–1708), in 1676, "that all other [modern Western religious] sects have issued from [the Jews]." Burgh, who had converted from Protestantism to Catholicism, in Italy, had written from Florence urging Spinoza finally to "acknowledge" in the face of Christian teaching, "the folly of your philosophy and that your philosophy is madness." He should retrieve his soul "from eternal damnation" while there was yet time by repenting and submitting to the Church, to the eternal truth proclaimed by the Church which is manifest for all to see. Christianity's history, replied Spinoza, in early 1676, offers nothing proving it is the truth: rather, judged as a religion, Judaism's history is more remarkable as well as much the longer.

Burgh insisted on the martyrdom of those who suffered painful deaths for the sake of their faith as irrefutable evidence of Christianity's special divine status. But Jewish steadfastness, replied Spinoza, had endured longer than that of any other persecuted faith: the Jews "have remained steadfast over some thousands of years with no government to constrain them, solely through the efficacy of superstition," their faith enduring "unmoved and unshaken in spite of the bitter hatred of heathens and Christians." As for trusting in the Catholic Church's integrity, tradition and authority, this Spinoza deemed entirely deluded. There are indeed men of learning and character in every church but as the "vices of priests and popes" reveal for all to see likewise countless despicable types. In fact, no church exists "better arranged for deceiving the people and controlling men's minds" than the Catholic Church except only the Islamic which as regards deceiving humanity, he wrote, far surpasses it.[1]

Burgh exalted Christian martyrs as the foremost sign their faith was sent by God. But the Jews' "chief source of pride," replied Spinoza, is their "boasting far more martyrs than any other nation, a number daily increased by those who have suffered for the faith they profess with amazing steadfastness. I myself know, among others, of a certain Judah called 'the faithful' who, in the midst of the flames when already believed dead, started to sing the hymn which begins 'To thee, O God, I commit my soul,' and so singing, expired."[2] This remark is thought to refer to an episode, the burning alive of a Jewish prisoner in the *auto-da-fé* at Valladolid on 25 July 1644, who became legendary among western Europe's Sephardic congregations being earlier celebrated by Menasseh ben Israel, in his *Esperança de Israel* [Hope of Israel] (1649/50). Menasseh's *Esperança* was a book Spinoza kept beside him until the day he died, very likely because its Spanish version (also published in Latin), includes a dedication to the *parnasim* [elders] of the Amsterdam Portuguese Jewish synagogue of that year, 1649, the third in order listed being his own father, Michael d'Espinoza.[3]

This martyr, "Judah el Creyente" (1619–1644), whose real name was Don Lope de Vera y Alarcón, an "Old Christian" Catholic, from a noble family, relates Menasseh, having taught himself Hebrew and studied the Old Testament at Salamanca, became persuaded of the truth of Jewish teachings, renounced Catholicism and adopted the name "Judah." For this, he was imprisoned and subjected to unremitting pressure to coerce him back. Finding it deeply perplexing, inexplicable even, that "Judah" should remain so stubborn when not even of Jewish descent, the Inquisitors long kept him incarcerated; but rather than yield to their bludgeoning and dogma, and his parents' entreaties, he refused to abandon his conviction, dying at the stake aged just twenty-five.[4] Judah "deserves the praise of martyrdom," averred Menasseh. Being "very learned in the Hebrew and Latin tongues," he embraced Judaism on the basis of acquired learning; and considered it "insufficient" to believe only secretly: "he discovered himself to many others" and whilst locked up in darkness for five years "yet discovered the light to many," defying the "great number of doctors" summoned to retrieve him for Christ.[5] Such martyrs "obtained immortal glory more precious than this life."[6]

Spinoza disagreed, citing the episode only to show the truth of Christianity is in no way proved by what, to him, was its comparatively short and mediocre record of martyrdom. To his mind, Judaism's possessing many more "martyrs" than Christianity, thousands executed by the Inquisition in Spain and Portugal alone, was no cause for celebration and does not make Judaism any truer or more authentic than Christianity. For martyrdom, held Spinoza, is not remotely rational. Jewish separateness was justified, he thought, when Jews possessed their own polity, bound by Mosaic laws, as a people with its own land; but there could be no justification for separate communities, dwelling under separate laws and rules amidst peoples and within polities that were not their own. Iberian crypto-Judaism bred attitudes that amounted, Spinoza thought, to fanaticism and "superstition" little different in essence from the blind fanaticism of the Inquisition. The two were equally reprehensible to his mind rather than opposed phenomena, both barriers to human well-being steeped in credulity. Assuredly, no clearer confirmation of the tight connection of religious authority with coercive despotic rule could be found than the close entwining of theology with royal power manifested by the Inquisition. Numerous members of both Spinoza's mother's and father's families had been victims of the Portuguese Inquisition; and those whose family had been powerfully impacted by Inquisitors and their *autos-de-fé* tended to acquire earlier than other Jews, a politicized as well as vehement abhorrence of the early modern Iberian theater of power as an all-crushing combination of royal and aristocratic splendor decked out with theological sanction and fervor.

The Iberian and Ibero-American *auto-da-fé* was a religious ceremony, certainly, but also a staged spectacle put on to impress the unenlightened mind with pomp and grandeur, projecting each social class's separate submission to the joint hegemony of royalty and social hierarchy backed by theology's all-crushing supremacy over all human thought, belief and culture. Displaying its ability to pulverize dissent utterly, the Inquisition simultaneously paraded the unquestioning support of attendant massed ranks of gentry and royal officialdom all bowing before church, clergy and ecclesiastical coercion. No-one was exempted from acquiescing in this vast powerhouse of repression triumphantly uniting church, monarchy and society. In the eyes of Portugal's and Spain's obstinate crypto-Jews, though, this overweening repression was just pernicious superstition fanatically supported by the ignorant and semi-literate. Nothing better illustrated the shackling of everyday misguided notions of ordinary men and women to unbending authority, religious and secular, the stunning effectiveness of the spectacle and mighty chorus blending faith, power and ignorance, than the "Holy Office."

Outwardly, the Inquisition appeared daunting, but in reality amounted to nothing whatever without royal and aristocratic backing and reliance on unquestioning faith. Without the crown directing, the people's fervor and the nobility's support, the Inquisition, in truth, far from being fully empowered to blight the lives of thousands, was totally powerless. There could be no more vivid illustration of the Radical Enlightenment's central claim that the misery and wretchedness filling our entire world stems from entrenched ignorance rooted in ordinary belief exploited by the insidious alliance of clergy and state, a pact constituting the very essence of tyranny. Nothing more clearly exemplified the Radical Enlightenment's logic than the Inquisition. It was the very embodiment of theology wedded to despotic power holding sway over all of society, learning and culture. Defying the Inquisition, inevitably, was a psychological as much as intellectual or religious response.

An Inquisition story diffused by Menasseh and the poet Daniel Levi de Barrios, among others, circulating in Amsterdam when Spinoza neared adulthood but still remained within the Jewish fold, was that of Tomas Treviño de Sobremente (1592–1649), the sole example from New Spain (Mexico) of a crypto-Jew burned alive at the stake without being garroted first. The rest of the thirty or so crypto-Jews "martyred" by the Holy Office in early modern New Spain for reverting to Judaism after being "reconciled," were burnt as corpses, after ritual strangulation, a "mercy" accorded sentenced *relapsos* provided they first kissed the cross before their deaths before the vast throng chanting their hatred of heresy to signal final submission to the Church. Braving the "theater" of secular and ecclesiastical power combined during an *auto-da-fé* by rejecting, amidst the parading of the condemned, the "mercy" of escaping the agony of being thrust into the flames alive was not easy. The Mexico City Inquisition files show that Tomas's refusal to bow down stemmed from his highly irascible loathing of clergy and bigotry. Abjuring the cross at the last moment was as apt to be stubborn pride as anything.

Crypto-Jews in their thousands defied king and church, in secret, within and outside the Inquisition dungeons, in their homes and those of relatives.

Commemorating these "martyrs" tortured and executed in Iberian lands persisted, as Spinoza noted, in poetry, prayers, sermons, chronicles and letters throughout the western Sephardic world. But very few went to the stake refusing prior strangulation; and where this happened, as exemplified by Treviño de Sobremente, it might be less religious faith that so moved these few than personal rebellion. Being burned alive at the stake, in front of people, clergy and seated gentry, needed a particular temperament that might not be in any meaningful sense religiously devout. From Treviño de Sobremente's trial records, key details emerge about his bearing and attitudes.

Born near Valladolid, in northern Spain, he later confessed to having been taught fragments of Judaism in secret, as a boy, by his mother, and imbibing several Hebrew and Spanish-language prayers—he could recite the *Shema* in Hebrew. Emigrating to Mexico as a young man, he left his family behind, including his mother, who died at the stake, at Valladolid, in 1623. Tomas built up some capital, initially in southern Mexico, as a shopkeeper, at Oaxaca, later in Mexico City, but lost his fortune when, the Inquisitors, having confiscated his parents' property in Medina de Rioseco, in Castile, seized his own earnings in Oaxaca, after his first trial for "judaising" in 1624–25. At the end of his eventful life with his money and belongings confiscated for the third time, in Mexico City, he is recorded as remarking with sour humor: "I have been a source of profit to the Holy Office."

Between being ceremonially "reconciled" in 1625 and his execution in 1649, Tomas Treviño notoriously ignored the restrictions applying to "reconciled" heretics by riding horses and wearing costly clothing (for which he had an inordinate liking), bravado risking not just re-arrest and long incarceration but, should he be caught, given his relapse into crypto-Jewish observance, eventual certain execution. Risking re-arrest and being burnt at the stake, he continued observing practices nurtured by the crypto-Jewish group in New Spain, after 1625, among a furtive constantly nervous network, in deep secret. But, unlike the others, temperamentally, he could not help flaunting a proud, rebellious air such as most individuals in his position would have scrupulously avoided. On one occasion, in 1638, he got into a scrap with a Spanish officer abusing someone as a "New Christian." Furious, not caring about the scandal, Tomas grabbed the captain by the scruff of his neck swinging him in the air to publicly insult and humiliate him.[7]

Such near suicidal rebellion is of historical as well as psychological interest and occurred also in other instances. The New Christian scholar and skeptic Uriel da Costa (1583–1640), threw himself into an emotional state of defiance, on arriving in Hamburg, in 1614, and later in Amsterdam, as a Jewish heretic and virtual deist, displaying deeply felt aversion to the modern "Pharisees," with their stifling observance and rules,[8] openly antagonizing the Jewish community elders, as he had the Catholic clergy and Inquisition earlier. Repeatedly censured by the rabbis and elders of Venice, Hamburg and Amsterdam, he was publicly flogged and ritually humiliated for defying the Amsterdam Jewish community when Spinoza was a child, before finally committing suicide, shooting himself when Spinoza was aged eight.[9]

Spinoza's paternal grandfather, whose synagogue name in later life was Isaac de Espinoza, died a practicing Jew in Rotterdam, in 1627. But he was born around 1559, a "New Christian" in Lisbon, where he was called "Pedro Rodriguez Spinoza"; later, he lived in Vidigueira,[10] an inland southern Portuguese town near Évora, in the Alentejo region, the seigneurial rights over which once belonged to the great navigator Vasco da Gama, and now pertained to the latter's descendants. Center of a wine-producing area, this market town was where Pedro's wife's family resided.[11] This lady, Spinoza's paternal grandmother, Mor Alvares, likewise stemmed from a resisting crypto-Jewish family. Her own grandfather, Manoel Alvares, had been seized by the Inquisition in Vidigueira along with other relatives, in 1570.[12] Several of her uncles and cousins were burnt for judaising in the Évora *auto-da-fé* of 1574. Subsequent arrests, late in Philip II's reign, landed more family members, including Spinoza's maternal great-grandfather, Gabriel Alvares, secretary of an orphanage and a local tax-collector, in prison in 1597, together with two sons and other relatives who were tortured and stripped of their possessions. Part of the family, including Pedro Rodríguez Espinoza (alias Isaac d'Spinoza), fleeing Portugal, in 1597, joined Spinoza family members who had previously fled to Nantes, in western France.

Furthermore, where Iberian scholars of crypto-Jewish background and allegiance, like "Judah," took up arms against Christianity, they could do so more vigorously and confidently than orthodox Jews, being specially fitted for such a role by their "Christian" background and university training. If few could match Spinoza's witheringly sarcastic, deeply emotional loathing of the spiritual claims that rallied ordinary folk behind social and political pretensions underpinning *ancien régime* hierarchy and religious authority, many felt comparable aversion to churches, churchmen and post-Apostolic theology, and for royal support for ecclesiastical sway. A great many from all walks of life had been traumatized by the Inquisition or other forms of religious repression in sixteenth- and seventeenth-century Europe and the New World. But the scholars alone among the hated and condemned possessed the intellectual apparatus with which to punch back hard, vilifying theological cultures that had so murderously desolated their families and family circles in lands from which they themselves, or in Spinoza's case his parents and grandparents, had been mercilessly coerced for generations—and then by stealth managed to escape. Such men rebelled initially only privately, brooding secretly and in tiny clandestine groups at universities such as Salamanca, Osuna, Alcalá and Coimbra, but later diffused their heartfelt passionate rebellion far and wide using more effective methods.

CRYPTO-JUDAISM LINKED TO POLITICAL SUBVERSION

These figures loathed and rebelled against religious coercion. But equally they execrated the political tyranny that made it possible. Sweeping away the one was impossible without sweeping away the other. In this way, they forged the world's first genuine intellectually grounded revolutionary framework. The fate of Spinoza's own branch of the Jewish people, the western Sephardim, had for centuries been inextricably entwined with that of the Spanish monarchy and, in the case of his family, especially the realm of Portugal. King Ferdinand of Aragon (r. 1479–1516), a monarch Spinoza held in some regard, following his marriage to Isabella of Castile, in the year 1492, "compelled the Jews to accept the religion of his kingdom or go into exile [so that] a large number of Jews converted to the Catholic faith." These, relates Spinoza, "were granted the privileges of native Spaniards and were considered worthy of all positions of dignity." Consequently, "they immediately integrated with the Spanish, so that in a short time there were no remnants of them left and no memory of them."[13]

In Portugal and its colonies, by contrast, matters developed very differently. Instead of being integrated into Portuguese society, the great mass of those Spanish Jews who had migrated to Portugal to avoid forced baptism in 1492, and those already living in Portugal, "those whom the king of Portugal compelled to accept the religion of his country [in 1497]," remained a largely separate caste, shunned by most of Portuguese society. "Although they submitted to this faith," as Spinoza expresses it, "they continued to live apart from all men, doubtless because [the monarch] declared them unworthy of all higher positions."[14]

The Portuguese so-called *cristãos novos* [New Christians], legally defined as a separate caste formally excluded from all privileges and public offices being of Jewish origin, remained a distinct, scorned and, wherever slack in their outward "Christianity," persecuted minority. This fraught outcome sharply contrasted with the *converso* position elsewhere, trapping generation after generation in a way Spinoza judged disastrous as a context for individual life, despite their conserving vestiges of Jewish prayer and observance and keeping alive a sense of ancient Jewish identity. Full assimilation of Jews converting to Christianity in Spain, especially admittance into the social and political corpus of those among whom they lived, Spinoza deemed preferable both politically and as the best way to counter the otherwise unrelenting hatred and persecution Jewish separate existence incurs.[15] Assimilation, to him, was the only practical alternative to restoring Jewish political independence, if hatred and persecution of Jews, and their legal marginalization and lack of access to public affairs and officeholding, was to cease.

For these reasons, besides family background, Portugal and Spain represented in Spinoza's mind, and those of close relatives, a peculiarly relevant if decidedly fraught contrast. Social and political circumstances, especially legalized and institutionalized discrimination in Portugal, together with superstition, were the principal factors, urged Spinoza (here following the remarkable statesman and historian Antonio Pérez (1540–1611)—as he repeatedly does when discussing Iberian political history), explaining why Portuguese New Christians remained more committed to crypto-Jewish belief and practices than their Spanish counterparts and, hence, long remained a readily identifiable, legally separate grouping while also being more hated and persecuted than Spain's *conversos*.

Portugal and Spain contrasted in their respective trajectories as regards converted former Jews. Yet, from 1580, the destinies of Portugal and Spain came to be tightly linked politically and culturally following the union of crowns, that year, in the person of Philip II. After that, during the late sixteenth century, many Portuguese crypto-Jews re-emigrated back to Spain whence they had come nearly a century before, but this time, as in Portugal, long conspicuously stood out as a readily identifiable, scorned and marginalized minority, often, surviving Inquisition trial records show, nurturing their now typically "Portuguese" New Christian resentment of Iberian majority attitudes, a resentment both religious and political. Portugal's last king before the union of crowns, King Sebastian I (r. 1557–78), was a youthful idealist who dreamt of renewing the Crusades against the Islamic world, but on invading Morocco, in 1578, was at once crushed by the Muslims "with all his nobles," as Menasseh ben Israel described the battle of Alcazar-al-Quibir, and killed.[16] His eventual successor, Philip II of Spain (r. 1556–98), on becoming king of Portugal (r. 1580–98), personally resided in Lisbon in 1580–81. But doubts lingered about the identity of the remains Philip proclaimed to be those of his Portuguese predecessor and ordered royally entombed in December 1582, in the great Hieronimite monastery at Belém, near Lisbon.[17] This magnificent monastery, built under Manoel I (1469–1521), the monarch who founded Portugal's overseas empire and forcibly converted Portugal's Jews to Christianity, henceforth served as Lisbon's royal pantheon. Yet, doubts as to whether the Belém relics were really those of Portugal's lost "martyr" king persisted, turning into an obdurate underground mystique of emotional aversion to the union of Portugal with Spain, mystical longing for independence fervently embedded in the Portuguese popular consciousness.

Belief that Portugal's lost youthful "King Sebastian" was not in fact dead but would miraculously reappear one day at the head of his army to rescue his people from alien tyranny, and generally put the world to right, evolved into a political opposition undercurrent called *Sebastianismo*, a proto-revolutionary popular impulse, almost an ideology, that long persisted in the collective Portuguese psyche fueling resentment and grounding the alluring promise of eventual salvation. It was a way of collectively opposing the forced union and increasingly heavy hand of Philip II's absolutism, and hankering after Portugal's lost liberties, in a concealed manner, and, for both New Christians and other heterodox persons to subtly resist the now greatly reinforced and expanded sway of the Inquisition. Prior to Philip's arrival, Sebastian had been briefly succeeded on the throne by an interim regent, his great-uncle, Cardinal Dom Henrique (1578–79), a firm ally of Spain and the Inquisition, and foe of New Christians.[18] During this cardinal's brief reign, Philip had quietly prepared the ground for Portugal's absorption into his vast global monarchy; leaving nothing to chance, he prepared an army to powerfully press his claims as Sebastian's legitimate heir the moment Dom Henrique died.

However, there remained an obstacle in that many Portuguese dreaded his succession and preferred to acknowledge Philip's rival "Pretender" to the crown as the veritable heir to Portugal's throne. This was Dom Antonio, Prior of Crato (1531–1595), an illegitimate grandson of King Manoel and nephew of the cardinal.[19] To thrust aside this inconvenient rival, Philip assiduously courted the nobility, promising there was no risk to their privileges or social predominance. Meanwhile, a simultaneous clash of court factions was in progress in Madrid and now reached its climax with hard-liners eager to press Philip's claims everywhere in the most forceful fashion, led by the Duke of Alva, gaining ground, and Philip's formerly powerful chief secretary, urging a gentler approach, Antonio Pérez being dismissed.

In Madrid, planning the invasion of Portugal, in 1580, was consciously viewed as a step toward global mastery.[20] Absorbing Portugal, noted one adviser, "would be the principal, most effective, and decisive instrument and remedy for reducing the Netherlands to obedience and means for controlling England." Commanded by Alva, the same authoritarian figure who imposed fiercely intolerant Castilian absolutism in the Low Countries between 1567 and 1573, the army of invasion was made ready. Alva's ruthless and bloody drive to crush the Dutch rebels, records Spinoza, had brought numerous Calvinists, Lutherans and other religious dissidents "to all kinds of martyrdom."[21] But before Alva could invade Portugal, Dom Antonio was proclaimed "king" and enthroned in Lisbon, on 23 June 1580, amid fervor stoked by aversion to the prospect of Castilian dominance. Dom Antonio reigned for a month before the Spanish troops appeared and crushed his adherents, on Lisbon's outskirts, on 25 August 1580.

After this battle, Portugal and its empire were fully in Philip's grasp and the country's historic liberties and privileges were considerably curtailed. Another repressive consequence was the marked further strengthening of the Inquisition's powers. Despotism was the order of the day but despotism emphatically blending faith and crown together, not monarchical absolutism alone. The year 1580 was indeed decisive in expanding the Spanish world empire and conjoining religious intolerance to royal hegemony, the "revolution" in Portugal further tightening the alliance between royal and ecclesiastical sway. Yet, for many Portuguese, despite the high clergy and most nobles siding with Philip, Dom Antonio remained Portugal's rightful "king." The invasion could not entirely eradicate the menace to Philip this flamboyant, defiant princeling, not remotely a sincere churchman, represented. His mother, Violante Gomes, had been a New Christian and for years, against the wishes of his grandfather and uncle, he had fostered many connections with New Christians. The English envoy, Edward Wotton, sent by Elizabeth I to Lisbon in 1579, informed Francis Walsingham, head of the English secret service at the time, a statesman deeply concerned in Portuguese affairs, that

Dom Antonio also had numerous bastard children by New Christian women.[22] Later, during his prolonged exile in France and England, his relations with Portuguese *conversos* outside Portugal of necessity remained close since this exiled fringe, including the Spinoza family at Nantes, were the only Portuguese element at hand with any significant financial resources, shipping and legal clout, in a position to help keep his cause alive.

Menaced by the intensification of persecution of judaisers following Philip's invasion, neither Portuguese crypto-Jews in Portugal, nor those dispersed elsewhere, remained politically inert. Spinoza's own family, we know, figured among the more active judaisers at Nantes, as well as in Portugal. "At Nantes, the Portuguese community were divided in the late sixteenth century," as one authority expressed it, "between judaisers and Catholics." Among the former was Abraham d'Espinoza, Spinoza's great-uncle, brother of his grandfather, Isaac d'Espinoza, who later settled in Rotterdam. Abraham figured among the two or three leading merchants among the ten or so Portuguese New Christian families residing in Nantes around 1600 who, despite living, like all the Marranos dwelling in France's western ports at the time, outwardly as New Christians, remained an active judaiser. Still more significant, his active crypto-Judaism was widely known in crypto-Jewish circles internationally. For in 1615, the heads of the Amsterdam Portuguese Jewish marriage dowry society appointed "Abraham d'Espinoza" their organization's principal representative in Nantes, which means that he then headed the crypto-judaising faction among the Nantes Portuguese, and was reliably known to the Dutch Sephardic community to be among the most committed crypto-judaisers to be found in late sixteenth- and early seventeenth-century western France, a dissident with long-standing experience.[23]

Spinoza's father, Michael d'Espinoza, born in Vidigueira in the 1590s, left Portugal as a child with his father, in 1597.[24] Dwelling ostensibly as Portuguese "Christians" at Nantes, the d'Espinoza family was henceforth part of an international Marrano diaspora network among the most widely dispersed yet socially cohesive religious and cultural groupings of the early modern Atlantic world. The Nantes Portuguese merchant community remained extremely small throughout this period compared to those in Bordeaux and Bayonne, never rising above ten or a dozen families. Like the Rouen Portuguese community, moreover, the Nantes "Portuguese" remained sharply divided throughout, until the 1620s, between active judaisers and pro-Spanish Catholics. Later, the crypto-Jewish element withered away, due to the active judaisers transferring to Holland, leaving the remaining Nantes Portuguese definitively opting for a Catholic future.[25]

Philip II, long confronted by resistance and active subversion in the Low Countries, now faced the same in Portugal. Following Alva's victory and sacking of Lisbon, Dom Antonio, to Philip's exasperation, escaped to France. Though his reign in Portugal had lasted a mere few weeks, many Portuguese in and outside of Portugal during the 1580s and 1590s lent the exiled Prior of Crato their support.[26] Formally, all mainland Portugal and its African and New World colonies submitted to Philip, except the Azores. There the local governor held out for the Pretender, who, determined to continue the struggle, established his headquarters on the west coast of France, where he eventually mustered a sizeable force of fifty-eight vessels and some six thousand men, mostly French, often Huguenots, fitted out and supplied from Nantes with the help of the Portuguese (judaising) merchants there.[27] With this fleet he sailed to the Azores in the summer of 1582.[28] Dom Antonio, along with William of Orange (1533–1584), also known as William the Silent, who led the revolt against the Habsburgs beginning in 1568, in the Low Countries, was now one of the two international heroes most resolutely challenging Philip's world hegemony and whom the Spanish monarch most aspired to assassinate or imprison.[29] Acclaimed king in the Azores, Dom Antonio actually reigned in Terceira, from July to November 1582, as "king of Portugal," receiving munitions and supplies from Nantes. His fleet was defeated by a Spanish armada, from Cadiz, in late July 1582, off the island of São Miguel, and Terceira was conquered by Spanish troops, in 1583. The Azores' regional privileges and liberties were duly cropped. But Dom Antonio, chief focus of Portuguese revolutionary aspirations throughout the Atlantic world, eluded Philip's clutches yet again, escaping back to France with a few supporters.

The Portuguese Marrano diaspora's support for Dom Antonio's cause evolved into what, at the time, was a well-known movement of international subversion, combining crypto-Judaism with political subversion, obvious not least to Philip himself and frequently commented on by his diplomats. From Venice, for example, the Spanish ambassador reported during the late 1580s that Dom Antonio was endeavoring to add an alliance with the Ottoman Turks to his many pacts with Philip's enemies headed by the Dutch rebels, England's Queen Elizabeth and Henri IV of France. "Cada dia se descubren nuevos judíos que vienen de Portugal" [every day new Jews are discovered coming from Portugal], he wrote, adding, in July 1590, "y todos ellos son apassionadíssimos por don Antonio de Portugal que parezce que viene esta plaga de rebellion con la judería" [and all of them are extremely passionate for Don Antonio of Portugal so that it seems this plague of rebellion comes together with Judaism].[30] The same envoy, a few weeks later, again mentioned this mobilizing of Jews and New Christians and their conjoining of Jewish political and religious subversion, observing that both those Portuguese returning to Judaism in the Venetian ghetto, and those living in Venice outwardly as "Christians," ardently backed Dom Antonio's cause working as spies, suppliers, financial backers and assistants to his agents.[31]

Nantes and its vicinity remained pivotal to Dom Antonio's tenuous communications with Portugal and the Azores and retained a special importance for the Portuguese Atlantic anti-Habsburg revolution. In 1584, despite being continually menaced by agents and supporters of Philip and the Catholic League, Dom Antonio himself resided for a time at the castle of Sarzeau, four miles south of Vannes, near Nantes, and during 1585 for some months in Nantes itself, striving to revive his flagging cause in Portugal and the Azores and issuing letters of marque for fees (and a cut of the proceeds) and licensing French and English privateers to raid shipping belonging to Philip II's subjects. Receiving and sending out messengers, Dom Antonio spun a complex web of negotiations with Elizabeth, William the Silent, and likewise Prince Maurits, the new Dutch Stadholder after William was assassinated by an agent of Philip (with the sanction of his priestly confessor), in July 1584. Philip certainly aimed to murder Elizabeth and Dom Antonio too, likewise with ecclesiastical sanction, if he could.[32] Nearly trapped several times by pro-Spanish French Leaguers, in August 1585, Dom Antonio fled, via Huguenot La Rochelle, to England, where Elizabeth offered refuge. Already his ally at a distance, Antonio Pérez, another fugitive from Philip's vengeance, became personally acquainted with Dom Antonio in the summer of 1593, when the two leaders found each other simultaneously quartered for the interim in England, at Windsor.

Personifying Portuguese anti-Spanish insurgency, Dom Antonio died after later returning to France, in 1595, ending what adherents termed his fifteen-year "reign" (1580–95). He was succeeded as Pretender to the Portuguese throne (recognized and supported by the Dutch States-General and by Prince Maurits) by his illegitimate heir, Dom Emmanuel van Portugal (c. 1588–1636), who at a very early age married a daughter of William the Silent, Countess Emilia of Nassau (d. 1629), a lady who thereupon converted to Catholicism to perform her new subversive Iberian courtly role. This "royal" pair resided at the castle of Wychen, near Nijmegen, in Gelderland.[33]

Continuing disaffection in Portugal and among the Portuguese Atlantic diaspora undoubtedly had some material effect on the course of the great events shaking the Western world in the 1580s and 1590s. Elizabeth could count on a stream of intelligence, Walsingham's papers show, supplied from Lisbon by Dom Antonio's supporters, including detailed reports on the preparations for the great Spanish Armada against England.[34] After the Armada's defeat, in 1588, Walsingham, collaborating with Dom Antonio, persuaded Elizabeth to send a smaller counter-armada to strike at Spain, using some of the English veterans stationed in the Netherlands, an unsuccessful venture with which Maurits and the States of Holland, under Oldenbarnevelt's guidance, readily collaborated. Portugal was chosen as the target largely due to Dom Antonio's urging, especially the illusion he worked hard to implant in English and Dutch minds that the mere sight of an Anglo-Dutch fleet would suffice to bring the Portuguese out into open revolt against Philip's tyranny.[35]

That all three main rebellions against Philip II's global absolutist-ecclesiastical hegemony—the Dutch, Portuguese and that of Aragon (1591–92)—became deeply entwined in secretive ways was, of course, due to the political circumstances of the time. Their interaction also became an integral part of the propaganda of the Dutch Revolt, the legacy of Dom Antonio and his son Emmanuel, and part of a wider political mythology interweaving the worlds of Philip's and Alva's four principal adversaries—William of Orange, Elizabeth, Dom Antonio and Antonio Pérez. By the time international great power rivalry became a key concern of Spinoza's philosophy, in the 1660s and 1670s, Louis XIV of France had long since displaced the Spanish crown as chief threat to the Dutch Republic and chief absolutist challenge to the freedoms proclaimed by all republican theorists of democratic republican stamp, with Spinoza, after 1670, indisputably foremost among them. Nevertheless, in Spinoza's two major political texts, Philip rather than Louis always remains the chief embodiment of tyranny, intolerance, repression of basic liberties and the forging of royal pacts with churchmen representing the acme of despotism thereby connecting the destiny of Spinoza's own native land, Holland, with that of his father and all his immediate forebears, Portugal.

Spinoza's antipathy to monarchy, to all dominant churches, and his preference for republican forms of government were so pronounced as to be positively emotional and no doubt originated partly in an inherited ideological impulse. His mother and father belonged to families that for decades had opposed Philip's grasping religious and political tyranny. Nor was it an accident that the poetry of the *converso* João (Moshe) Pinto Delgado (1580–1653) featured among the small number of *converso* texts still surviving in Spinoza's personal library when he died, since the poet's family figured among the judaising Portuguese *conversos* living in Rouen in the early seventeenth century, leading a marginal existence strikingly parallel to that of the Spinozas in Nantes.[36] Pinto Delgado's Spanish poems, published at Rouen, in 1627, were dedicated to the Spanish crown's greatest seventeenth-century foe, Cardinal Richelieu. Later, Pinto Delgado transferred to Amsterdam during the years 1636–40, serving as one of the *parnasim* (governing council elder) of the Amsterdam *yeshiva* Talmud Tora, and its attached school at around the time Spinoza began his schooling. As I. S. Révah and Miiriam Bodian have pointed out, Pinto Delgado's poetry contains lines memorably echoing the *conversos*' fusing of political with religious subversion, one passage strikingly encapsulating the split between Spanish and Jewish allegiance, underlining the contrast, certainly deliberately, by reworking a famous phrase from a sonnet dedicated to Philip II by a renowned Spanish poet, proclaiming: "una Monarca, un Imperio y una Espada" [one monarch, one empire and one sword]; Pinto Delgado's rebellious countervailing lines answer that this was a false unity—there is only one "king" rightly venerated, "un Dios, un pueblo, una Ley" [one God, one people, one Law].[37]

Spinoza himself explained his family's and group's tenacious crypto-Judaism in terms of "superstition" baked hard by mistaken Portuguese royal policy and the multitude's ignorance and bigotry, this being just one of several arcane social phenomena which he knew intimately through not just family and upbringing but also his brief experience (1654–56) as a Sephardic merchant plying his trade in Amsterdam. As a youth reared in a mercantile household and destined for commerce, and still more after his father's death, in 1654, while heading the family firm in the years 1654–56, Spinoza participated directly in a far-flung mercantile network, personally managing what remained of his father's import-export trade with Portugal, France, Brazil, Morocco and the Canaries. Commerce and mercantile politics were topics about which he knew a good deal. He presumably also knew something of the political dimension of his grandparents' activities. Among the earliest surviving Amsterdam notarial deeds concerning the Nantes Portuguese Jews is a power of attorney assigned by a leading Amsterdam Portuguese merchant, Manoel Rodrigues Vega, to Spinoza's grandfather's brother, Manoel Rodrigues (alias Abraham) d'Espinoza of Nantes, the same who was the local representative of the Amsterdam dowry society, authorizing him to reclaim a cargo of textile goods seized *en route* to northern Portugal from a ship by Spanish troops based at the coastal town of Blauet, at the mouth of the river of that name, in Brittany.[38] These troops belonged to a force Philip sent to Brittany, in 1590, to support the French Catholic League fighting to prevent the Protestant contender, Henri IV (r. 1589–1610) securing the French throne, part of the Spanish drive to prevent a *de facto* toleration and general Catholic-Protestant compromise in France aimed at ending the civil war there.

These Spaniards, charged also with blocking Dom Antonio's efforts and stopping Henri IV extending his control over the Nantes region, stayed in Brittany, impinging directly on the lives of the Portuguese New Christian community until the close of the Spanish-French war, when they withdrew under the terms of the Peace of Verdun (1598). As the personage appointed to reclaim the seized cargo, Abraham d'Espinoza must have been not just a stubborn crypto-Jew loathing the Catholic League but also well-known among Dutch Sephardic merchants, the Nantes merchant community and the local town government, as somebody experienced in local legal procedures reliably known to oppose Spain's presence and the Catholic League's aims.

An interesting parallel arose half a century later, in July 1651, at a time of friction between England and Portugal, when Spinoza's father, Michael d'Espinoza (c. 1587–1654), appointed the Portuguese Marrano, Antonio Fernandes Carvajal, his agent, to represent him before the London High Court of the Admiralty. He was authorized to reclaim two of Michael's consignments of olive oil seized on the high seas in peacetime, before the First Anglo-Dutch War began, by English Parliamentary vessels from Dutch vessels returning from Portugal. These olive oil consignments of "Michael d'Espinoza" were declared to belong to him "alone as real property without anyone under the crown of Portugal, or any enemy of the Republic of England owning any part or portion of the olive oil."[39] Well-known to the Cromwellian authorities, Fernandes Carvajal was the leader of the London Marrano community, a veteran opponent of Spanish power as well as founder of London's first Sephardic synagogue.

After transferring to Holland in 1623, Spinoza's father for some years continued in partnership with his uncle Abraham d'Espinosa. During the 1630s and 1640s Michael enjoyed enough commercial and financial success to join the Amsterdam Sephardic community's general and educational boards of elders, becoming a leading figure in the Amsterdam Jewish community. When Abraham died, in 1638, the partnership was dissolved and whatever cash Michael had in hand, belonging to Abraham, was paid out to the latter's son and heir, Jacob d'Espinosa, who had spent years in the Ottoman Near East and, in a notarial deed of January 1639, is described as visiting Amsterdam but "living at Great Cairo in Palestine."[40] One main line of commerce Michael and Abraham jointly plied, a notarial deed of 1639 records (as does other evidence), was with Salé in Barbary, at the time among the chief corsair bases in Muslim North Africa, and a port with which Dutch Sephardic Jewish merchants developed a close relationship as suppliers of naval munitions and weapons destined for the Salé corsair fleet engaged in piratical operations against "Christian," and especially Spanish, shipping.[41] As a boy of six, still too young to grasp much about the complexities of Portugal, the Inquisition, Catholicism and the Prior of Crato, Spinoza heard more tales, one supposes, than most northern European Sephardic boys about life in Morocco, Egypt and other Muslim lands.

For one family to encounter Judaism, Christendom and Islam simultaneously and possess direct knowledge of Islamic as well as several Christian countries was unusual. The Sephardic Jewish diaspora straddled the Muslim as well as Catholic and Protestant worlds. But Dutch Sephardic families mostly bridged the Catholic and Protestant spheres without extending, like the Spinozas, to direct links, over many years, with Islamic lands too. Spinoza's confident comparisons between Islam and Christianity, and conviction, expressed in the 1675 letter to Burgh, for example, that Islam alone curbs individual liberty politically, culturally and socially more than Catholicism, owed more than a little in all probability to early impressions and his wandering Near Eastern uncle. Spinoza's proneness to lump Catholicism, Protestantism and Islam together as all oppressive in their social, legal, political, and cultural characteristics but in different degrees, was fundamental to his thought, much like his classifying churches as all essentially oppressive political and social mechanisms with none possessing any claim to be thought divinely sanctioned, justified or favored or have special moral validity.

THE "HIGHEST GOOD" IS AN INDIVIDUAL AND SOCIAL PROJECT

During the 1630s, prior to amalgamation of the three Amsterdam Sephardic synagogues into one united community, in 1639, Michael served as a *parnas*, or governing council elder of the Beth Ya'acov congregation, and in 1635–36, before Spinoza himself started school, was among the elders supervising Amsterdam Portuguese Jewish community education. In July 1637, Michael was appointed his congregation's delegate to the communal dowry society's governing board, among the principal tools of communication between Sephardim in Holland and crypto-Jews in western France, Portugal and Brazil. From 1642, Michael rose higher still in the Sephardic social hierarchy becoming an elder, or *parnas,* of the now united Amsterdam Portuguese (Talmud Torah) community. Michael never joined the ranks of the wealthy top tier of the Sephardi merchant elite, but by the 1640s was an affluent, respected figure prominent among the community's broader upper crust.[42] Trade, wealth and communal service, Spinoza must have heard repeated often enough, as a child, were what rescued his parents and their entire social group, stretching from Portugal to Brazil, and Holland to Morocco and the Near East, from dire straits, from tyranny, Inquisition, intolerance and poverty, securing standing and prestige in the world.

According to the autobiographical passages at the beginning of his *Treatise on the Improvement of the Understanding* (c. 1659), Spinoza, when young, struggled for years to combine devotion to study with business and family obligations. The reliability of these passages is sometimes questioned because they rhetorically echo well-known passages from antiquity. But while, to enliven his writing, Spinoza often utilized unacknowledged quotes from ancient Roman texts, he was too serious and to the point to permit fictions to intrude if remote or irrelevant to what he wished to say. Indubitably, we should take these autobiographical passages literally, especially as they pertinently fit the actual facts of his situation: "after experience had taught me that everything that usually occurs in everyday life is vain and futile, and I realized all things of which I was fearful have nothing intrinsically good or bad in them, except insofar as the mind is influenced by them, after a time I decided to enquire where there is anything which is the true good, discernible as such in itself and by which alone the mind is affected when everything else is stripped away."[43] He pursued the "highest good" while continuing with his routine family and soon also commercial activities, which proved, however, far easier in theory than to do in practice.

For years, Spinoza sought to stick to the course family and status marked out for him, combining affluence and communal eminence with philosophy. But so difficult did he find reconciling family, commercial and synagogue affairs with his quest for truth that he eventually concluded he must abandon his present life, if he was at all serious about persevering in his quest: "I say 'decided at length' because, initially, it seemed inadvisable to abandon something certain for something uncertain. I could see, of course, the advantages acquired through honor and wealth from which I would be excluding myself should I devote myself seriously to something different and new; and that if the highest happiness does lie in those things, I would then have to do without them. Equally, if it does not, and I devoted myself to them, then again I would fail to attain the highest happiness."[44] "So I used to ponder whether it might be possible to establish my new way of life, or at least certainty about it, without changing the outward order and form of my everyday existence. Often I attempted to do so but always in vain."[45]

Changing a life course focused on family, trade, synagogue and community, to single-minded pursuit of the "highest good" was the most critical, decisive step of Spinoza's life. It required agonizing soul-searching and happened only after prolonged self-questioning, hesitation and doubt. Those "things," enjoyment and social status, that for years prevented his abandoning his honored place amidst a privileged commercial elite in favor of his philosophical quest, were the same goals, he explains, that usually appeal to humans: "for generally what one encounters in life that men esteem the highest good, to judge by their activities, may be classified under three headings—riches, status and pleasure; and so distracted is the mind by these that in the end it cannot consider any other good."[46] But even long after deciding that blending commonplace preoccupations with the quest for truth does not work, escaping the harsh predicament of seeking to combine them proved exceedingly difficult.

Spinoza's later distinction between moneymaking for self-aggrandizement and to domineer in a communal context and earning the wherewithal to buy necessities, became crucial to his wider critique of ordinary thinking—the everyday notions and prejudices that undermine and vitiate "happiness," the true goal of human life. His critique of moneymaking heavily emphasized the difference between money as means to what we need and money as financial-commercial capital, the latter, however used, being an instrument of power, social control and pride rather than of exchange for basic needs, he cast in a negative light. Aged twenty-two when his father died, Spinoza's eventual break with the synagogue, with the past and family status, also confirmed his subsequent unconquerable austerity in financial matters which, understandably, fused with his day-to-day direct experience and recollections of his father's rejected firm to engender an anti-mercantile, anti-business mentality. In this respect, Heine and Marx would later pick up the thread where Spinoza left off.[47]

Trade, working in groups, collaboration, Spinoza recognizes repeatedly in his writings, are essential to raising the level of human existence. Without trading, exchanging the things they make, individuals can hardly provide for their needs on their own, states the appendix to *Ethics* IV: "Money has provided a convenient means of acquiring all these items. That is why thinking about money usually occupies the minds of the multitude more than anything else. For they can hardly conceive any species of joy without the accompanying idea of money as its cause." For those who "seek money," neither from "need nor for necessities," though, "but because they have acquired the arts of money-making and pride themselves on it very much," amassing wealth soon becomes a positive vice vitiating the individual's pursuit of happiness in many respects.[48]

After prolonged vacillation, Spinoza finally took the plunge, helped, I have argued elsewhere,[49] by a catastrophic drop in his father's firm's fortunes. Following his father's demise, in 1654, Spinoza continued for two and half years more (1654–56) as family head, running the firm together with his younger brother, Gabriel (Abraham d'Espinoza), while keeping up the position his father had attained within their religious community. Until 1655, there was no indication of collapse in his finances or unwillingness to pay his hitherto substantial synagogue dues. Since his father had been ailing for years and long been bedridden, Spinoza, as the oldest surviving son, had, presumably, ever since his elder brother Isaac d'Espinoza died, in 1649, been marked out for the presiding role in family business affairs. Unlike more fringe members of the Amsterdam community at the time, he remained a loyal, regular community member, paying his dues until late 1655, only lapsing from doing so, and from paying into communal charities, as has often been noted, rather abruptly, in late 1655.[50]

Some sudden, dramatic change obviously occurred in the mid-1650s to account for Spinoza's plunging into a scandalous crisis which irreparably disrupted his relations with family, community, rabbis and *parnasim*. And while his preexisting intellectual commitments doubtless played some part, something new clearly occurred to explain why the long, slow, outwardly placid inner process of alienation suddenly erupted, in late 1655, in real drama. As Jarig Jelles, among his first non-Jewish friends, someone who probably knew him already before the *herem* [ban], later attested, Spinoza had long been immersed in Bible study, and at a later stage also Cartesian philosophy, engaging in inward rebellion against rabbinic authority before his public break with the synagogue; and other biographical evidence confirms this.[51] The arrival of a fresh subversive intellectual influence in the shape of free-thinking Dr. Juan de Prado, who arrived in Amsterdam in 1655, and was a companion of Spinoza's for a time, may also have contributed, but was probably not as crucial as historians Gebhardt and Yovel later surmised. Some more basic change engineered the sudden dramatic switch from private inner to open public rebellion, given the latter entailed sweeping disruption to every aspect of his life, permanent forsaking of family, home, status and wealth, a break Spinoza admits to having previously found exceedingly difficult.

Despite his image in the later literature as an isolated recluse, the mature Spinoza obviously considered himself more realistic, worldlier and savvier politically than most philosophers, even than Machiavelli and Hobbes. That he thought himself more, not less, adept in everyday affairs than others is confirmed by several remarks, including his observation at one point that the true philosopher is not less but rather more worldly than the common merchant, which he substantiated by retelling the tale of the ancient philosopher Thales of Miletus (c. 625–547 BC). Thales, growing tired of friends chiding him for his poverty, demonstrated that his poverty was from choice, not necessity, and that he knew well enough how to amass what he deemed unworthy of his efforts. Having ascertained, from natural signs, that a bumper olive harvest was coming (Portuguese olive oil being among the principal commodities in which the Spinoza firm traded),[52] Thales hired all the olive presses in Greece before they were needed; then, with the olives being harvested and the equipment required, he rented out at a high price what he had hired cheaply, amassing huge wealth within a year "which he then dispensed with a generosity equal to the shrewdness with which he had acquired it."[53]

A key part of the disruption of 1655 in Spinoza's life was assuredly the financial collapse of the family firm. For a time, from the end of the Dutch-Spanish conflict (effectively 1647), Dutch commerce with the Iberian peninsula, Morocco and the Caribbean, and the Spinoza family firm with it, had blossomed spectacularly; but, in 1651, began a steep slump driven by the First Anglo-Dutch War (1652–54), which heavily disrupted Dutch overseas trade and shipping, with numerous ships and cargoes lost. The collapse started in the months preceding the war, from late 1650, when the English were already seizing Dutch cargoes on the high seas, which was the main reason for the Republic declaring war with England. The cargoes seized included several belonging to Spinoza's father. An ensuing disastrous fall in family fortunes, made worse by the general Dutch recession, was reflected in a spectacular drop in the family's *imposta* and *finta* assessment, the variable annual amount based on a register of assessed wealth compiled by community officials, that family heads contributed to synagogue and community to cover costs and rabbinic salaries, and support the poor.

By late 1655, all prospect of continuing wealth and status had vanished. However, this grave family setback could of itself not release Spinoza from the tangle of worldly complications impeding his intellectual quest. Rather,

TABLE 1.1. The *imposta* and *finta* payments of the head of the Spinoza family to the Amsterdam Portuguese Jewish community (1648–1658)

YEAR	FAMILY HEAD	*IMPOSTA* (GUILDERS)	*FINTA* (GUILDERS)
5405 (1644–45)	Michael de Spinoza	28	12.10
5408 (1647–48)	Michael d'Espinoza	14.5	12.5
5409 (1648–49)	Michael d'Espinoza	41	12.5
5410 (1649–50)	Michael d'Espinoza	75	12.5
5411 (1650–51)	Michael d'Espinoza	35	12.5
5412 (1651–52)	Michael d'Espinoza	68	12.5
5413 (1652–53)	Michael d'Espinoza	46	12.5
5414 (1653–54)	Baruch Spinoza	17.7	12.5
5415 (1654–55)	Baruch Spinoza	22	10
5416 (1655–56)	Baruch Spinoza	0	5
5417 (1656–57)	Abraham d'Espinosa	0	0
5418 (1657–58)	Abraham d'Espinosa	0	0
5419 (1658–59)	Abraham d'Espinosa	0	0
5420 (1659–60)	Abraham d'Espinosa	0	0

Sources: GA Amsterdam 334, inv. no. 173, pp. 17–268; inv. no. 174, pp. 8–41; see also Van der Tak, "Spinoza's Payments," 190–91; Revah, "Aux origines," 367; Israel, "Philosophy, Commerce," 139.

it hurled him into a morass, leaving him more instead of less encumbered than before. Loss of fortune removed the allurement of rank and wealth hitherto barring pure devotion to truth, but simultaneously deposited heaps of debt and legal dispute only fully revealed after sorting through his deceased father's affairs. The solitary bright spot was that to his mind failure and loss in worldly terms can readily be transformed into constructive austerity bringing welcome release from deadening subjection to debt and legal complications. Mounting legal and financial difficulties now removed all motive to hold back. The community would never have taken the initiative in expelling the honored son of one of its leading families or taken the initiative in any public confrontation. Had Spinoza kept to his earlier long-standing discretion, confining his anti-Scriptural thoughts to private discussion, he would have remained stuck with his failure and debts. Almost certainly it was Spinoza himself who now precipitated the open confrontation and defiance of rabbinic authority precipitating his expulsion and complete rupture with family, congregation and rabbinate.

An outspoken dissident openly challenging rabbinic and communal authority was impossible for rabbis and *parnasim* to ignore. Expulsion from the community under the *herem* of 1656 meant permanent abandonment of his family's former status within the community. But it freed Spinoza from the mass of complications of his father's overseas dealings and family and community obligations had landed him in. He never forsook, though, his inherited obsessive preoccupation, deeply characteristic of the Marrano diaspora, with how the few defying the beliefs of mainstream society can effectively challenge what the deluded "multitude" believes, and those who enforce coercive belief, by creating a clandestine underground of conviction and political scheming designed to subvert dominant structures of authority, faith and power, a hidden conspiracy of like-minded subversives fighting the existing order like his d'Espinoza forebears in Portugal, and comrades like De Prado, in Spain.

Striving for happiness, Spinoza believed, though an individual quest on one level, is ultimately inseparable from social and political milieu, hence also a collective quest. The strategy adopted must be simultaneously an individual *and* group effort. In Jewish circles, Spinoza's break with the synagogue was afterwards rightly remembered as not just exceptional, involving matters of principle on an individual basis, but involving also a wider rebellion against communal authority with far-reaching implications for community and organization. Daniel Levi de Barrios (c. 1625–1701), who later emerged as the virtually official chronicler and poet of the Amsterdam Sephardic Jewry in the 1680s, in his *Triumpho del Govierno Popular* (Amsterdam, 1683), records that "Benedito Spinosa, cast out of Amsterdam Judaism for his bad opinions, composed a book [against the rabbis] which looks like a vase of gold but is filled with the poisonous liquor that [claims] the Jews have no obligation to observe the Law of Moses ever since they no longer have a state of their own." This refers to Spinoza's lost *Apologia*, his Spanish-language text demolishing the claims of the rabbis, a text never published that Spinoza nevertheless circulated and read among friends.[54]

Yet, in the end, there is a sense in which the young Spinoza of 1656 did not after all wholly forsake pursuit of status and honor. While abandoning conventional wealth and communal status to seek the "highest good," he did not confine his attention to pure thought and reclusive investigation but, from the outset, as Toland and others afterwards remarked, strove to establish a hidden sect, a secretive oppositional underground eschewing old dogmas while seeking new goals aimed at renewing and transforming our world fundamentally. As with Marx nearly two centuries later, it was an ambition in which, in the end, both succeeded to an astounding extent, Marx via a revolutionary new social and economic theory pivoting on the justified anger of the proletariat and the principle of class warfare, Spinoza by undermining the world's religious leaders, shaking the mighty edifice of faith and credulity via a devastating mix of new Bible criticism with a republican, democratic, individually emancipating political philosophy based on the "common good," a system steeped in a philosophy of freedom, collective reason and "true religion," designed to replace priestcraft and redefine "true religion" as in essence just "justice and charity."

Spinoza's revolutionary career began in conscious, deliberate rebellion against rabbinic authority. Without such open revolt nothing remotely like the uniquely severe form of *herem* the community imposed on him would ever have been contemplated. Defying rabbis and congregation was the first step in building an activist philosophy amounting to a generalized assault on "superstition," miracles, theology and ecclesiastical authority, so abstracted from its specific historical context by nearly all modern professional philosophers and scholars that the reader unfamiliar with the dense fabric of his life and circle might easily imagine that, for him, assailing the repressive and irrational belief-structures dominating existing society was a purely abstract, generalized philosophical project arrived at through pure meditation on his own. Hence the need to ask what were the consequences and, as he saw it, practical benefits for society generally, including the Jews, that he envisaged following from his broad assault on prejudice and the monarchical-ecclesiastical sway of rabbis and *parnasim* as well as Philip II, the Inquisition and Calvinist bigotry?

REVOLUTIONARY GOALS

In confronting the ignorant and bigoted majority, Spinoza's projected future democratic republic offered an enriching, emancipating perspective but also a militant, even coercive aspect. However concealed and buried it may be, the true aim of society "and every state," argues the *Tractatus Theologico-Politicus* (or *TTP*) (1670), is not just to enable men to live securely (as in Hobbes), but freely and "satisfyingly" avoiding strife and providing scope for every individual to develop his or her potential to the utmost.[55] The "foundation and purpose" of Spinoza's democratic republic is "to avoid the follies of appetite and, as much as possible, constrain men within the limits of reason, so that they may dwell in peace and harmony." The moral order underpinning Spinoza's republic thus possessed a double role, constraining and encouraging: its institutions, while promoting everyone's individual liberty, happiness and emotional stability, must simultaneously ensure the bigoted element, no matter how numerous and ignorant, are "forced to be free" in the sense of being compelled by rational laws to respect the freedom of others, for otherwise no individual's liberty is secure. This two-way constraining and enriching constitutes Spinoza's "common good," the "algemeene accorderende interest" [general agreeing interest] first spelled out in a published text by his older associate and Latin teacher Franciscus Van den Enden, in his *Vrije Politieke Stellingen* (Free Political Propositions) (1665), that is the "general will" as Diderot, d'Holbach and Rousseau later renamed this concept in the 1750s.

This key concept of "general will," the most anti-Hobbesian strand of all the many anti-Hobbesian, anti-Lockean and anti-Rousseauist elements composing the radical democratic republican political thought tradition rooted in Spinozism, was a doctrine from which Rousseau later significantly departed, forging his own divergent version of "general will," his concept being based not on reason, as with Spinoza and Diderot, but on the common sentiment of the people. Spinoza's and his circle's "general interest" was what best supports individual pursuit of worldly happiness for all, a common good directed by popular sovereignty subjecting all law, theology, ecclesiastical authority, and Revelation to its supremacy; it is the collective power of the citizens where their individual interests are treated as equal and social elites and churches stripped of all means to dominate. It was a revolutionary recipe democratic in form and content sharply profiling an array of common pitfalls and opponents.

Rousseau borrowed his "general will" in the early 1750s initially from Diderot. But both derived the concept directly or indirectly, more distantly, from Spinoza and his circle, especially the idea that "whoever refuses to obey the general will shall be constrained to do so." Unlike Diderot and Rousseau, Spinoza, one might object, lacks a specific term for the "general will." Nevertheless, he carefully delineates the collective principle defining how the ignorant and superstitious, finding nothing in the "highest good" that philosophy delivers "they can touch or eat," must be constrained to conform to the "common good" through well-framed laws. In Spinoza's view the "common good" is (at the present) generally not understood, but, whether it is grasped or not, his "common good" always exists, is best understood by philosophers and remains of overriding importance for everyone in both its negative and positive aspects. When Spinoza explains the difference between "slavery" and political liberty in chapter 16 of the *TTP*, he contends that humans live in freedom only "in a state and government where the *salus* of the whole people, not that of the sovereign is the supreme law" [ubi salus totius populi, non imperantis, summa lex est].[56] "Salus" here means the common "well-being," "prosperity" and vigour, or better still, the "common good."[57]

Conceiving the individual's perfecting his intellect to be the path to "summum nostrum bonum" [our highest good] is pivotal in both Spinoza's *Ethics* and his political treatises. Because most individuals, including most elites, do not respect the highest good, preferring to pursue their own private interest instead, it is always best for the state to be governed by a group executive with powers of decision diffused as widely, into as many hands, as possible. Hence, democracy is inherently better than aristocracy while in aristocratic republics, like Spinoza's native Dutch Republic, the more the ruling oligarchy is broadened, power shared and decision-making made dependent on consultation and discussion, the more individual self-interest is curbed and the better the "common good" is served. Promoting non-Rousseauist "general will" defined by reason, as forged by Spinoza and inherited later by Diderot, d'Holbach, Condorcet, Volney and Destutt de Tracy, who all term it *volonté générale* but employ the term with a sharp, deliberately and consciously anti-Rousseauist twist, requires full freedom of thought, and freedom of expression and to publish, and also, raising the general intellectual level. Removing freedom of expression Spinoza declares totally destructive of the "Republicae salus," the well-being of the republic.[58] Conceding liberty of saying what one thinks to all not only may be accorded without damaging the "peace of the republic," affirms the last page of the *TTP*, but "such freedom is essential to it." Issuing decrees about doctrinal issues on the part of the sovereign state, on the other hand, is "completely useless." Subordinating religion, piety and religious leaders—whatever most people think—to the "peace and interests of the state," Spinoza, at the start of chapter 19, calls adjusting religion to the "peace and utility of the republic" [reipublicae paci et utilitati accommodari].[59]

In Spinoza's late text, the *Tractatus Politicus*, "small councils must be prevented from gaining power at the expense of great councils," as had unfortunately happened in the early modern republics of Venice and Geneva. Spreading power broadly is always indispensable for ensuring the "common good is attended to" [ut communi bono consulatur].[60] "Hence, wherever a few decide everything out of their inclination," as Spinoza expresses it in chapter 9 of the *Tractatus Politicus*, both "liberty [libertas] and the common good [communeque bonum] are lost."[61] It is totally wrong to argue, as one scholar has, that while "Spinoza prefers both democracy and aristocracy to monarchy, . . . it is not at all clear what his preference is between democracy and aristocracy."[62] Nothing could be more mistaken. For, on the contrary, in both the *TTP* and the *Tractatus Politicus*, Spinoza invariably expresses preference for democracy as against both monarchy *and* aristocracy, a stance inherent in his conception of the "common good."[63]

In the *TTP* the democratic republic stands superior to monarchies and aristocratic republics partly because there "all remain equal as they had been previously in the state of nature,"[64] partly because it affords more liberty to all than monarchy or aristocracy, but especially because it best promotes the "common good." "Spinoza's main motivation" for opting for democracy, it is sometimes argued, stems from a somewhat "naïve form of realpolitik" supposing "a large group of people with a vast variety of conflicting desires is unlikely to agree on extremely irrational policies."[65] But that is just one reason Spinoza offers as to why big councils are preferable to small ones, and why in political matters the democratizing principle is the right path to amelioration. The chief reason offered in the *Tractatus Politicus*, where arguing for democracy's superiority is less emphatic than in the *TTP* but still clear, is that private vested interest preying on the majority is more easily veiled in small than big councils while clashing individual wills, motives and desires in large councils lend collective reason more scope for resolving disagreement, shaping the outcome and promoting the "common good."

At odds though this may sound with the usual canon of Western political thought, Spinoza was more comprehensively committed to fighting monarchy, aristocracy, superstition and populism, and thus, according to radical enlighteners, considerably more useful than Hobbes, Locke, Rousseau or Kant, more effective in battling mankind's greatest curses, the three great curses that Spinoza's projected *revolutio* seeks to conquer—namely, tyranny, religious repression and popular thinking rooted in ignorance. By contrast, Rousseau, by rejecting representative democracy and dispensing with safeguards for dissenting minorities and freedom of expression, was less likely appeal to spokesmen of a small religious minority anxious to secure equal civic rights and freedom of expression. In fact, Rousseau's system presents evident and serious dangers, a lesson painfully confirmed by the horrors of Counter-Enlightenment *Robespierrisme* during the French Revolution.[66]

Spinoza was not the "source, origin, or originator" of the Radical Enlightenment's "modernity" as numerous scholars misconstrue the argument. Radical Enlightenment originated in the inevitable revulsion of some against the then prevailing forms of persecution and oppression. But the Dutch Golden Age *was* the Radical Enlightenment's original seedbed in the sense that it was in late seventeenth-century Holland rather than England that democratic republicanism was first explicitly and systematically pitted against aristocratic republicanism, bringing out the innate antagonism between the two tendencies, more conspicuously than one then found among republicans elsewhere, or at any point prior to the American Revolution. The first to emphatically assert the superiority of democratic republicanism over aristocratic republicanism and couple democratic republicanism with rejection of religious authority, explaining why religious authority needs eradicating along with monarchy and aristocracy to achieve political liberty, or at least doing so in print, were actually the Brothers De la Court, Franciscus Van den Enden and Adriaen Koerbagh, all of whom preceded Spinoza in this respect.[67] But Spinoza was the only great philosopher among them and most incisive and effective in converting their common stock of ideas into a ready-for-action, fully systematic philosophy.[68]

Spinoza accordingly possesses a special status in the struggle for emancipation of minorities and the downtrodden, and hence in the history of "modernity." If German, Polish and other central European Jews dominated the Jewish revolutionary tradition after 1800, in its earlier stages, until the 1780s, Jewish involvement with Radical Enlightenment remained largely the preserve of Sephardic Jews of Iberian heritage; and, among them, it was initially persons of crypto-Jewish background with exceptional academic training who proved likeliest to convert inherited group abhorrence of the prevailing status quo and Christian theology into theories directly challenging the existing order. This is reflected in the life histories of Uriel da Costa, Juan de Prado, Spinoza, Orobio and others, all these being exceptionally equipped intellectually to mount full-fronted challenges to the existing order and its legitimating agents, in a way most of the Jewish learned of the time (being restricted to Torah and rabbinic studies) and nearly all the rest, including most womenfolk, were then clearly unequipped to do. With their command of philosophy, Bible criticism, Western languages and Latin, and also political theory, these figures were uniquely furnished to stand and fight the greatest Leviathan of their time—religious orthodoxy dragging popular sentiment into alliance with political despotism, hence, the most prone to adopt revolutionary attitudes and thinking.

Spinoza opted for the rejectionist irreligious front of dissident former Marranos. For the rest of his life, he remained resolutely unrepentant under rabbinic ban while for over a century his principal books remained under the Dutch States-General's general prohibition. The unflinching defiance he turned against rabbis, he soon projected likewise against all churches and Islam, thus proceeding in reverse order to Uriel da Costa. Religious authority of whatever stripe he undermined by denying all miracles, revelation, divine providence and all other *supernaturalia*. The Scriptures to his mind were neither holy nor divinely revealed. But if his views on rabbinic authority, or "pharisaic arrogance" as he terms it, remained unreservedly negative, his perspective on the Jewish people and their traditions remained more complex, combining harsh criticism with several positive aspects.

The republic the Hebrews constructed under the Old Testament Judges, before opting for monarchy, he judged among the most exemplary states known to history, a view reaffirmed later by Toland; Jewish martyrology surpasses all other martyrology. But, equally, Jewish rejection of Spinoza, despite the rabbinic *herem*, never proved final or absolute. From the 1750s, his lingering presence became a problem for modern Jewry, as growing ambiguity increasingly shrouded perceptions of the Jews' foremost heretic. If radicals always had the best grounds for claiming him, in the 1750s, Moses Mendelssohn attempted to shift the broader Jewish perspective by presenting him as foundational to mainstream German philosophy, the true founder, rather than Leibniz, of the Leibnizian-Wolffian doctrine of the "pre-established harmony." In Mendelssohn, one first finds the seeds of a revived Jewish preoccupation with Spinoza among the central European secularizing Jewish mainstream. Later, the same phenomenon characterized also the enlightened vanguard in eastern Europe. Seeking to restore Spinoza's standing, redeeming and reabsorbing his philosophy in part into the fabric of modern Jewish identity, was a trend eventually reaching full fruition in Weimar Germany.[69] Driving this remarkable turnaround was the perceived usefulness as tools against discrimination and antisemitism of Spinoza's plea for freedom of thought and expression, democratic republican and universalist political theory, and fierce critique of priestcraft and popular prejudice.[70]

Spinoza in effect headed a group opening the door to an entirely new kind of Jewish anti-rabbinic revolutionary secularism destined to play a notable part in the history of the Enlightenment and the revolutionary era down to Karl Marx's close engagement with Spinoza's writings in the early 1840s, and modern Jewish history more generally down to 1933. To express the thread of continuity differently, one of those raised in the Pale of Settlement who witnessed the early 1880s pogroms, Nachman Syrkin (1868–1924), expelled as a boy from his Mogilev gymnasium for protesting at a teacher's antisemitic remarks, and later, with his younger ally, the Marxist Zionist Dov Ber Borochov (1881–1917), a founder of socialist Zionism, proclaimed as the true forebear and architect of Jewish socialism, Moses Hess (1812–1875), especially on account of his *Rome and Jerusalem* (1861), a book Syrkin translated and published in Yiddish.[71] But Hess himself venerated as his own greatest hero and moral inspiration, the figure he judged the world's foremost opponent of the repressive prevailing status quo, namely Spinoza.

Although, like many other revolutionary Jews down to the mid-nineteenth century, Spinoza did not believe Jews could survive as a secular entity without rites, ceremonies and observances to safeguard their separate identity,[72] his militant secularism and rejection of the supernatural, combined with his idea that the democratic republic best advances individual as well as collective freedom, including that of the Jews, helped establish a new kind of secular moral order, and thus, paradoxically perhaps, turned his philosophy into the foundation of an eminently recognizable novel type of secular Jewish identity. For this reason, Spinoza came to be elevated behind the scenes, underground, as a kind of reverse Old Testament prophet pointing the way to a universal revolutionary awareness, a trend that eventually culminated in the thought of Heine and Moses Hess.

TWO

Spinoza and the Origins of the Modern Revolutionary Consciousness (1650–1677)

A key dimension of Spinoza's lifelong project of fighting "superstition" and "ignorance" conceived as the universal platform of tyranny, religious and political, was his Portuguese *converso* background's proven serviceability as a resilient oppositional underground sworn to fight divine right monarchy. "Spinoza has often been read as a revolutionary thinker," remarks Michael A. Rosenthal, in an article about Spinoza's political thought.[1] This is certainly true; yet, for many or most experts today, Spinoza was decidedly "no democrat," as one commentator expressed this view, but rather a somewhat conservative thinker in no way a revolutionary.[2]

A major aim of this present book, in response, is to try to push back against what verges on becoming the prevailing view and show why the long-standing perception of Spinoza as a "revolutionary," democratic republican, and highly subversive force, needs reaffirming more strongly, not dismissing. Using the term "revolution" in relation to Spinoza is problematic, objects Rosenthal, because he and his contemporaries never used the term "revolution" [*revolutio*] in anything like its modern meaning. Certainly, the highly abstract style of Spinoza's philosophy and his preference for generalities rather than discussing particular contexts other than the Bible and ancient Hebrew commonwealth, encourages his portrayal as a remote, austere thinker little connected with the whirl of affairs around him. His potentially subversive democratic political theory, many view, consequently, as not just abstract but in some sense secondary, non-essential to his principal concerns, which modern philosophy teachers tend to see as confined to his metaphysics and ethics. Here professional philosophers are apt to mislead. For as Hermann Cohen recognized long ago, Spinoza's two political treatises, though works of philosophy and Bible criticism too, are in the first place fiery hands-on polemical interventions in his contemporary world.[3]

The three great and most intractable ills burdening and degrading mankind, according to Spinoza, namely tyranny, ignorance and religious authority, at first sight appear to be separate malaises only remotely connected. But, in his view, closer investigation leads to the realization that they are interdependent and mutually buttress each other. Hence, all three must be assailed together, held Spinoza, and, though impossible wholly to eradicate, must be emasculated by means of a single subversive strategy. In this respect, he was a profoundly revolutionary figure. Monarchy, the dominant system in Europe in his time, he deemed altogether undesirable, a defective system of government, and pernicious political ideology, the foe of human happiness chiefly responsible for the prevalence of war and all the misery it causes, given most wars in his time, like the Eighty Years' War in the Low Countries (1566–1648), sprang chiefly from unbridled royal ambition tied to religious doctrines useful for bolstering absolutist pretensions and power. Yet, while monarchy is reprehensible, and insidiously linked to religious authority and ordinary thinking, of humanity's three great adversaries, popular ignorance he judged the worst and most fundamental, since it is ignorance that feeds the credulity making monarchy and religious policing possible. Most avoidable human wretchedness in other words, Spinoza sees as directly stemming from popular "fanaticism," most people's inability to grasp the reality of things. Spinoza's three chief targets, moreover, all had a particular connection with Holland's struggle to free herself from Spain's world empire forged by the Habsburg Emperor Charles V (king of Spain, r. 1516–55) and culminating in global reach under Philip II (r. 1555–98).

Correctly understanding Spinoza as a pivotally important world-"revolutionary" requires first gaining a glimpse of the specific context in which Spinoza was immersed during the years 1665–77 when composing his political texts, the *Tractatus Theologico-Politicus*, or *TTP* (1670), and the *Tractatus Politicus* (1676–77), a tumultuous background essentially Dutch and beset with conflict. In 1667–70, the embattled Johan de Witt (1625–1672), leader of the republican-minded oligarchy governing the Dutch Republic in the years 1650–72, and his following, faced deepening difficulties aggravated by a worsening ideological deadlock in which the Republic was then trapped. While the United Provinces accorded religious minorities an unprecedented degree of toleration, and individuals an exceptional degree of personal liberty and freedom of expression, the ruling oligarchy's support among the public was much too narrow to ensure the Republic's stability and long-term survival. When Spinoza turned to writing his final text, the *Tractatus Politicus* (left unfinished at his death in 1677), the De Witt regime had recently been violently overthrown in the midst of Louis XIV's invasion, in 1672.

During 1672–73, French troops occupied half the now deeply fragmented Republic's territory, provoking a crisis such as the country had not witnessed since the darkest days of the struggle against Alva and Spain. The "True Freedom," as De Witt called his republican ideology, was toppled, disastrously in Spinoza's view, by a frantic, desperate popular upheaval fired by fervent Orangism, loyalty to the princely house, and a religious intolerance that in its fury raged against the old oligarchy and religious dissent. Amidst a tide of suspicion and talk of betrayal, this "theologico-political" fury, after transferring power to the young Prince of Orange, William III (1650–1702), the new Stadholder, literally tore De Witt and his brother to pieces in the street. De Witt supporters suspected William III himself of complicity in this to Spinoza's mind disastrous "*revolutio*." Certainly, William encouraged the wave of popular fury and initiated the ensuing purge of Holland's town governments of anti-Orangist republicans and republican political thinking, as likewise the post-1672 drive in the universities against the new philosophies of Descartes, Hobbes and Spinoza, all deemed pernicious by conservative Calvinist theologians (the young Stadholder's close allies). Confronting all this, Spinoza viewed the unreasoning popular rage and role of the Calvinist preachers with horror, and the stadholderate as a ruinous anomaly contradicting the basic principles of the state, a vestige of the past that should never have survived after the great Revolt against Philip II and the setting up of the post-1572 newly constituted Republic.[4]

In 1672, William and his supporters seized control with overt Reformed Church (Calvinist) backing, taking full advantage of the public Church's popular support, or what Spinoza called the multitude's gullibility and proneness to being misled, by means of a *revolutio* at The Hague, where Spinoza lived at the time. The change significantly diluted the United Provinces' republican character, and reduced freedom of expression for which the Republic was then still everywhere the measure. The new regime promoted church authority and displayed unmistakable courtly tendencies, swiftly transforming the command structure of the army, for example, by bringing in nobles, often Huguenots or other foreign foes of Louis XIV, to dominate the high command. There was also now greater scope than before for curbing fringe religious sects and suppressing religiously subversive texts, not least Spinoza's *TTP*, albeit Orangist city governments had already begun suppressing Spinoza's writings on a local basis before the Orangist coup, as for instance at Leiden, in 1670.[5]

No politically and philosophically committed writer then living in Holland, much less The Hague, the epicenter of the struggle for the soul of the Republic, could avoid being caught up to some measure in the furious political turmoil, or reacting to the menace to free expression and religious toleration and mounting reaction against the new philosophy. Even before the coup of 1672, it was quite impossible not to be acutely aware that the Republic was caught in a far-reaching political and intellectual crisis that profoundly threatened its essential character. For all its many achievements and excellent features, De Witt's Republic had throughout been spectacularly fraught, tense and precarious, ominously subject to rifts and faction-fighting among its rival power elites.

The Dutch Republic of Spinoza's time fell victim, then, to ferocious internal ideological conflict pitting two irreconcilable blocs—Orangists versus De Witt's "True Freedom"—against each other. This Dutch crisis, the more discerning recognized, stemmed chiefly from lack of a sufficiently broad support base to uphold the republican values of the "True Freedom." As Spinoza explains in his *Tractatus Politicus*, "those who in fact held the sovereignty [in Holland] were far too few to be able to govern the people and repel powerful opponents. Hence, the latter could plot against them with impunity and finally managed to topple them." The oligarchic Republic's dramatic overthrow, in 1672, resulted therefore "not from wasting time in useless deliberations [as opponents claimed] but the Republic's defective constitution and the fewness of its legislators."[6] Yet, despite major weaknesses—the limited number of those participating in the exercise of power and totally inadequate support base—a republic like that of the Dutch, contended Spinoza, is indisputably inherently superior both to monarchy and all republics ruled by smaller, more aristocratic oligarchies or a dominant city ruling a substantial territory such as, in his time, Venice, Genoa and the major Swiss cantons like Zurich and Bern.[7] Spinoza's ideal republic, the objective of his revolutionary thought for all human society, then, conserved the best of De Witt's

"True Freedom" strengthened by much wider representation and far broader support.

Orangists offered a more authoritarian, less republican, more theologically tinted regime, and unfortunately for anti-Orangists it was they who were unquestionably the stronger faction in terms of popular backing. This had been the case since the Republic's founding. Allied to the strict Calvinist Counter-Remonstrants, in the years 1617–19, Maurits of Nassau (Stadholder, 1585–1625) had already demonstrated the vulnerability of the Arminian, Grotian and republican legacies to his Orangist blend of princely house with religious backing by overthrowing and then executing Johan van Oldenbarnevelt (1547–1619), who had played a key role in the Dutch struggle against Spain. A second near fatal confrontation flared in 1650 when, at the point Spinoza was reaching maturity, Stadholder William II, again allied with the Calvinists, dragged the Republic to the verge of a ruinous civil war. Fortunately, for the republican-minded, the United Provinces' freedoms and stability survived on that occasion owing to the conveniently timed death of this overweening prince, later that year, from smallpox. The political crisis of 1672 confronting Spinoza was thus the third great menacing *revolutio* of the Dutch Golden Age.

But why exactly was support for De Witt's "True Freedom" too restricted for any kind of solidity or stability? How could that support be broadened?[8] Both sides were driven by ambition and quest for power. But where Orangists could rely on Calvinist doctrine, preachers and the common people's faith for political and ideological muscle, the republican faction, despite displaying stronger commitment to freedom of thought and conscience, freedom of the individual and the press, ruling out the hereditary principle from allocation of offices and power, and welcoming Cartesianism into the universities, was unable sufficiently to convince the public of the value of such principles. Hence the potential relevance of Spinoza's revolutionary strategy, his design to weaken religious authority while simultaneously advocating democratic in place of oligarchic republicanism. Because Spinoza rejects direct democracy (as all Radical Enlightenment thinkers invariably did) and equal access to the supreme council for all, the mistake is sometimes made that he rates aristocratic republicanism above democratic republicanism.[9] This misconception stems partly from Spinoza's unfamiliar terminology: he confines "democracy" to mean direct government by the entire people, something he viewed negatively due to the people's ignorance; what he advocated was government by "great councils," wide representation via non-hereditary representatives acting in the name of society as a whole, hence representative democracy.

During the 1650s, when Spinoza first embarked on his philosophical career, in the wake of William II's death from smallpox with no adult Stadholder available, the Republic's intrinsic political predicament had appeared less urgent than later. Early on, politics was not among Spinoza's chief concerns. During 1655–56, rebelling against rabbinic authority and forsaking all interest in commerce and Jewish community life while deeply immersed in Bible studies and Cartesianism, he was not yet a champion of democratic republicanism. If his own inner rebellion against rabbinic authority and his father's commitment to the synagogue commenced years earlier, prior to meeting the veteran freethinker of *converso* background, Juan de Prado (1612–1670), on the latter's arrival in Amsterdam, in 1655, his alliance with De Prado rendered that rebellion more public and at that early stage helped confirm it as his main project but did not yet hitch it to the republican bandwagon.

Still, the question of republics and republicanism was already a nagging issue in the background. For the First Anglo-Dutch War (1652–54) had a devastating impact on Dutch shipping and commerce, decimating the Spinoza family business, doubtless one factor behind the unconcealed aversion to Cromwell expressed in the *TTP*. Loss of his father's cargoes presumably lent extra edge to Spinoza's passionate aversion to war and later psychological explanation of England's aggression against the Dutch, which, in the *TTP*, he interprets as arising from deliberate deception via propaganda, directed by an imperious, autocratic statesman (Cromwell) needing to distract compatriots from the unedifying realities of his domestic policies and repression of opponents. Cromwell sought to disguise the fact that despite executing their king, Charles I, in January 1649, the English had entirely failed, in Spinoza's view, to rid themselves of autocracy and despotism. War with the Dutch perfectly distracted attention from perceiving Cromwell's tyranny for what it was. The English, concluded Spinoza, had simply no idea what a genuine republican revolution is and how to achieve it. A successful and true "*revolutio*" in the new sense Spinoza gives it, is characterized by its enhancing and elevating society's general well-being and, by definition, as he explains his terms, this must mean comprehensively replacing the ills of monarchy, aristocracy and religious authority with the democratic republic based on the representative principle.[10]

Among humanity's most urgent concerns, essential if men are to follow the path to general improvement, held Spinoza, is to learn how to avoid tyranny and war. If Philip's absolutism and the Inquisition were universal scourges that had uprooted his own family in Portugal, England's failure in the 1640s, due to inadequate ideas, helped no one apart from Puritan preachers and in its failure wrought extensive damage. By late 1655, Spinoza was wholly estranged from Jewish observance, rabbinic authority and commerce; but something of his Sephardic inheritance still helped shape his intellectual career and political development: for his entire upbringing, like Juan de Prado's, had immersed them in far-flung international clandestine subversion organized by the Portuguese Jewish and *converso* trans-Atlantic diaspora to which they belonged. This "diaspora within a diaspora" was a mercantile and family religious underground, certainly, but equally an Iberian trans-Atlantic network with long-standing political ramifications,[11] in effect concrete evidence that a highly motivated underground fraternity can work as an effective, enduring intellectual vanguard subverting dominant structures of authority and belief, by winning converts, as Prado and the young Spinoza did in the late 1650s, drawing in others, including young students, to their biting religious skepticism, virtual atheism and neo-Epicureanism.

Despite the finality of his departure from the synagogue, on 27 July 1656 (6 Av 5416), and denial of rabbinic authority still echoing later in numerous hostile references to "Pharisaic" presumption and ignorance in the *TTP*, one must not underestimate Spinoza's subsequent continuing involvement with the religious, political and cultural predicament of the Portuguese New Christians in Iberian lands, northern Europe and across the Atlantic (his younger brother migrated to the Caribbean)—his connection with fellow Jews both returning and not returning, to normative Judaism. The Iberian context remained relevant especially in the late 1650s, immediately following his departure from the synagogue. Two separate notarized submissions to the Madrid Inquisition, in 1659, provide detailed testimonies, lodged against Spinoza and Juan de Prado, registering their philosophical subversion of religion, submitted respectively by a Spanish American Augustinian friar and a Castilian army officer, earlier stranded for months in Holland, in an Amsterdam hostel frequented by Spanish- and Portuguese-speakers where both passers-through happened to encounter De Prado and Spinoza.

Their reports, based on conversations held more than two years after his ejection from the synagogue, reveal the Spinoza of 1658 to be already, years before publishing anything, "a good philosopher," having studied at Leiden, as the friar explained, able to dispute conventional notions of religion in Spanish, and criticize clergy and university professors apparently more ably than the older, more academically trained De Prado.[12] After leaving the Jewish community, Spinoza, evidently, stayed not only in De Prado's company but in that too of other Iberian Jews, including at least two conventionally observant members of the Sephardic congregation, a physician, Dr. Miguel Reynoso [alias Dr. Abraham Israel Reynoso], and Samuel Pacheco, a chocolate and tobacco dealer, persons hence contravening the communal ban imposed two years previously on conversing with the outcast.[13] Apart from Spinoza, the rest of the group had indeed spent most of their lives in the Iberian Peninsula, precariously concealed as crypto-Jews or, in De Prado's case, radical unbelievers, and now, in Spinoza's company, joined in the intellectual debate going on around him.

Reynoso's high academic and social status—he possessed a medical doctorate from Coimbra—quickly brought him onto the Amsterdam Sephardic community's governing board, or *Mahamad*, on which he served in 1654.[14] Before fleeing Spain around 1646, he had lived in Seville and known De Prado in Andalusia. Spinoza doubtless learnt much from these men, especially about clandestine crypto-Jewish life and Iberian academic philosophy—and the legacy he now so eagerly embraced resisting the universal monarchical-aristocratic-ecclesiastical system of Iberian oppression.[15] But there was also much they could not teach him. Drawn to such fringe Jews, partly by language, he already then showed an equal or greater fascination for outlying Christian sects like the Socinian Collegiants, mystical Millenarians, and Quakers he encountered in Amsterdam who similarly cherished freedom of discussion and to philosophize while roundly rejecting salaried clergy and the prejudices of "the multitude." One point Spinoza undoubtedly took to heart from all this was that intellectuals fleeing the Inquisition armed with university doctorates, like De Prado, Reynoso and Uriel da Costa earlier, with their Latin erudition and experience of clandestine research and debate, made particularly formidable adversaries of mainstream Christian theology, rabbinic authority and scholastic philosophy combined.

The role of universities in generating clandestine dissent and intellectual subversion in Spinoza's day was of considerable relevance to what was to come. For attendance at universities, not only at the outset but also later when German Jews became revolutionaries, especially in the aftermath of the

Napoleonic reforms, contributed decisively to the growing revolutionary ferment. This occurred both at Germany's newly founded universities like Berlin, Bonn and Munich, and older ones like Halle, Giessen, and Königsberg. The same phenomenon then recurred following the reforms of Czar Alexander II (r. 1855–81) enabling Jews, for the first time, to attend Russia's gymnasia, state-supported higher education colleges, and universities in significant numbers: entry into higher education institutions provided access to secretly circulating banned texts, political ideas and literature, laying the social, cultural and intellectual basis for a burgeoning Jewish social revolutionary consciousness.

It was not Czar Alexander II's intention, of course, to create a mass Jewish intelligentsia focused partly on Moscow and Petersburg and partly on the regional capitals of the Pale of Settlement, Vilna, Grodno, Odessa, Kovno, Mogilev, Vitebsk and Minsk. But due to overconcentration in towns, and their eagerness to learn Russian and to study, rapid proliferation of Jewish intellectuals of what horrified Czarist officials and churchmen considered the wrong sort, was the effect. By 1872, when the first signs of groups of Jewish students forming in Russia to study and discuss revolutionary ideas emerged, 2,362 Jewish students had attended the new "gymnasia." By 1881, the year of Alexander II's assassination by revolutionaries, 27 percent of all students studying in Vilna's gymnasia and no less than 35 percent in Odessa, were Jewish. These were astounding proportions in an empire where Jews constituted just one-third of 1 percent of the total population.[16] Government efforts followed to reverse this highly disturbing trend. To limit numbers of Jews being educated at state expense, a *numerus clausus* of 10 percent was imposed, in July 1887, on universities and gymnasia within the Pale of Settlement, and 5 percent on those outside the Pale. Increased hours were also assigned to compulsory instruction in the Russian Orthodox faith in response to ecclesiastical pressure. But "the harm" was done: the old placid Jewish acquiescence in the Czarist-aristocratic-Orthodox system of control and uncontested airing of Christian theology, proved irretrievable.[17]

The Spinoza of the 1650s formulated his ideas in speech and writing more readily and fluently in Spanish than any other language. "I do wish that I could write," he remarked, in January 1665, in a letter "in the language in which I was brought up. I would then perhaps better express my thoughts."[18] Spinoza's written and spoken Dutch remained always imperfect. His mother tongue, scholars often remark, was Portuguese; but the words "in which I was brought up" here probably denotes Spanish rather than Portuguese since Spanish was the language of instruction and the textbooks used in the community schools he attended as a boy. Spinoza's admission here ties in also with Salomon van Til's report echoed by Levi de Barrios, and later by Bayle,[19] that Spinoza originally wrote up his objections to the rabbis, his first book, the lost *Apologia* of 1656, "in Spanish." The listed titles in his personal library at the time of his death prove that Spinoza in later years continued reading Spanish (but not Portuguese) literature, especially Cervantes, Góngora and Quevedo. Spinoza, then, originally formulated the elements of his revolutionary political ideology, along with his critique of religion, in the Spanish language. He did so contemplating the Dutch Revolt (1566–1609) which produced the thriving Republic in which he lived, Portuguese opposition to union with Spain, and the Aragonese Revolt of 1591–92, the three revolts against Philip infusing and shaping not just Spinoza's complex relationship to Spain and Portugal—but his critique of the English Revolution of the 1640s and account of the three main political crises (1618–19, 1650 and 1672) of the Dutch Golden Age.

That "theologico-political" subversion was so deeply ingrained in Spinoza's consciousness, family traditions, the social group among which he grew up explains why his chief targets, the structures of authority he sought to undermine, were religious, political and intellectual all at the same time. As Philip II's Spain was the headquarters of absolutist monarchy, Inquisition persecution, intolerance and superstition, while Holland was the then world's chief repository of republicanism, liberty of expression and individual freedom, Iberia under Philip's sway became not just a key theme of his personal vendetta against "superstition," intolerance and obsolete scholasticism, but more broadly the counterpart, the sociopolitical antithesis, of the Dutch Republic. Later, during the 1660s, Spinoza would add, his correspondence with Henry Oldenburg, secretary of the Royal Society, shows, a further standing example of the pervasively pernicious consequences of monarchy for society—Charles II's England.

Not only are "the multitude" of whatever social category, from kings downwards, as distinct from discerning individuals belonging to the subversive underground, blind to the reality of things, and especially of how men are continually deceived politically and religiously, held Spinoza, but assuredly one must also doubt the competence of academics too, especially as regards constructive application of the results of study and philosophizing to society and politics. The best books about politics, he asserts in the preface to his

Tractatus Politicus, are not by theorists or philosophers but statesmen: "for they have experience for their mistress which teaches nothing inconsistent with practice."[20] The foremost statesman he had in mind, his texts reveal, was Antonio Pérez (1540–1611), chief secretary of Philip II from 1565 to 1579, the ally of Dom Antonio, who having been Philip's right-hand man eventually became his leading adversary.

Given Spinoza usually prefers generalities to particular political contexts, it is striking that he several times returns to the topic of Philip's reign, especially the Dutch Revolt and the 1591–92 Aragonese Revolt. In chapter 18 of the *TTP*, Spinoza repeats the fairly conventional claim that the States of Holland "did not, to our knowledge, ever have kings but only counts [Philip II's official titles included that of "Count of Holland"], to whom the right of government was never transferred." Willing to justify armed rebellion where it succeeds in improving conditions for general well-being and reducing ecclesiastical sway, Spinoza dilutes his usual admonition against popular resistance to rulers here by denying the Dutch Revolt was a "rebellion." For the States of Holland had "always reserved to themselves the authority to remind [Holland's medieval counts] of their duty, retaining the power to defend their authority and the citizens' liberty, and rescue both from them, should they become tyrants, and generally hold them in check, so that the counts could do nothing without the permission and approval of the States." From 1572, Spanish tyranny was indeed effectively checked in the northern Netherlands—by a massive revolt against royal authority lasting decades (1566–1609).

A vast tyranny such as that of Philip II was not invulnerable to the assaults of a thinker such as himself, concluded Spinoza. Philosophy can combat oppression by planting in men's minds the realization that the true cause of their being the wretched victims of kingly and aristocratic disdain for their well-being, of oppression, lies in their own ignorance and credulity. Here lay the seed of organized intellectual subversion eventually nurturing more republican, democratic and tolerant structures, hence the ground-plan of Spinoza's revolutionary undertaking embarked on from the 1650s onwards, his unheard-of staggeringly ambitious project, to use the sarcastic phrase of the French *érudit* Thévenot, in 1673, referring to what he saw as Spinoza's breathtaking presumption, his scheming to "reform the world."[21]

Like Uriel Da Costa and De Prado, after they settled in Holland, Spinoza looked on the Jewish religion, and messianic expectation for the future, with deep skepticism. But he shared with the other great Sephardic rebels, and the

Marrano diaspora at large, the same set of chosen political and intellectual adversaries, starting with the bitterly resented Inquisition to which his own toleration theory has aptly been termed "the antithesis."[22] For there was no fighting the Inquisition without looking well beyond it, given the Inquisition could zealously persecute and torture at will only due to men's beliefs and unstinting support from below and above. It was not Christian teaching that rendered oppressive churches and Inquisitors so terrifyingly formidable. Without unquestioning faith and monarchy, the Inquisition was nothing. Philip, meanwhile, proved notably more vigorous in bolstering the Inquisition and extending religious repression wherever he could than his predecessors, not least in Portugal. Philip aspired to world mastery, and "superstition" was his strongest weapon. He used it and every other resource at hand, including assassination, to further his absolutist reach, proclaiming his fiercely intolerant tyranny to the world as a war of "true faith" against heresy, a crusade Spinoza's entire family had suffered from and loathed to the depths of their beings.

Spinoza and his post-1656 comrades, De Prado and Dr. Reynoso, assailed too what to them was the blinkered scholasticism and Aristotelianism of Spain and Portugal's universities—Salamanca, Alcalá de Henares, Évora and Coimbra—essential props to the repressive faith they fought with which De Prado and Reynoso had long familiarity. For Iberian academic scholasticism never wavered in its long-standing pact with church and repressive theology linked to imperious persecuting monarchy. Against the old scholasticism, the young Spinoza first avidly embraced the new "scholasticism" of the mid-seventeenth-century Dutch universities, the burgeoning academic Cartesianism of the day. But it was not long before he was subverting the "new scholasticism" too. By 1660–61, when his first essay in metaphysics, the *Korte Verhandeling* (1660), was circulating in limited circles in manuscript, Spinoza, observed the visiting Danish physician and naturalist Olaus Borch (1626–1690), was already becoming known as a philosophical adept subverting academic Cartesianism's hegemony from within: "from being a Jew," noted Borch in September 1661, Spinoza "became a Christian, and is now practically an atheist; he lives in Rijnsburg and excels in Cartesian philosophy, indeed surpasses Descartes himself in many things with his clear and compelling concepts."[23]

In both the *TTP* and the *Tractatus Politicus,* Spinoza contends that it is altogether natural for monarchies to deceive their subjects, foment strife and war and oppress individual liberty and men's pursuit of happiness. The prime virtue of democratic republics, by contrast, lies in their safeguarding freedom of judgment and discussion; hence the democratic republic cannot survive without permitting free expression of differing views. Equally, republican values favor international and religious peace. Also, the individual liberty and toleration natural to the republic assists the progress of knowledge and science and thus society's efforts to counter ignorance, intolerance and "superstition." All this renders democratic republics intrinsically superior to all monarchy and every other form of state whether priestly rule or aristocratic republics like Venice and Genoa. Society must strive to rise from the degraded level of men's existence under kings, aristocrats, oligarchs and priests, the sway of faith and superstition, to salvage human happiness collectively and on an individual level together, attaining general improved well-being by adopting democratic republican forms.

However, the sophisticated revolutionary consciousness needed to prevent such efforts being swiftly crushed must be disseminated first, Spinoza perceived, via a long preliminary phase of gestation using clandestine networks diffusing forbidden ideas horizontally below the surface, unseen. Marrano experience proved there was no other effective way to attack overwhelmingly powerful tyranny which is political and religious simultaneously. For the "multitude," that is most people at all social levels, possessing little grasp of philosophy, politics, "true religion" or anything else shaping men's lives, is always unpromising revolutionary material, indeed so irrational and unpredictable it must be excluded, as far as possible, from the complex revolutionary scenario his project envisaged. Revolutionary in vital respects, Spinoza's *TTP* is nevertheless the very opposite of rabble-rousing or insurrection-friendly.[24]

"Superstition" and ignorance, holds Spinoza, can be fought only by providing more freedom of thought and eroding authoritarian regulation of education and the press. "Ignorance," he assured Oldenburg, with a skeptical eye on Charles II's post-Cromwellian England, that is "superstition" and belief in miracles, is indeed "the source of all evil." Halfway measures wrapped in theology such as the English attempted in the 1640s should be wholly avoided; only effective removal of autocracy and religious authority can conquer mankind's universal entrapment in ignorance: "but truly, whether kings will ever concede the bringing forward of a remedy for this evil [i.e., ignorance], I doubt very much [Verum an huic malo remedium adhibere reges unquam concedent, valde dubito]"[25] Spinoza was no optimist regarding the chances of elevating humanity by eradicating kings and autocrats together with aristocracy and religious authority, and to his mind there is no chance of a better world without eliminating autocracy, "small councils" and ecclesiastical supervision as well as kings. An activist of a kind, but pessimistic about "the multitude," the way forward, he believed, was for his brand of revolutionary subversion and activism to continue secretly at work nurturing more contexts like that of De Wittian Holland systematically encouraging fundamental erosion of monarchy, clergy and aristocracy while favoring the progress of the arts and sciences.

Putting philosophy to practical use subversively and by so doing helping raise the level of human happiness generally was his aim. Nowhere does the conventional myth of Spinoza, the reclusive, isolated thinker, more completely clash with the reality of his life and thought than in his extraordinary boast, at the beginning of his *Tractatus Politicus*, echoing Machiavelli, that virtually all previous writers on politics, presumably including Machiavelli and Hobbes (of whom Spinoza is much more subversive than most scholars have traditionally been willing to concede), "never conceived a political system which can be put to any use, but have produced either obvious fantasies, or schemes that could only be put into effect in Utopia, or the poets' Golden Age where, of course, there was no need for them whatever."[26] Spinoza aimed to elevate political theory onto a wholly more "realistic" level, yielding tangible improvements. His "realism" has always attracted a few: if Bolívar was among them, Henry Kissinger remarked, in an interview, of December 1972, that Spinoza and Kant were the two philosophers who had "influenced me most."[27]

Spinoza never sought to justify armed revolt as such; rather, he urges genuine revolution, fundamentally transforming the political, legal, religious and educational framework. His Dutch Revolt was assuredly no rebellion in the ordinary sense; rather, the States "rescued" the Dutch from monarchical despotism. The right of sovereignty had been "always vested in the Dutch States, and was the principle the last Count of Holland [i.e., Philip II] strove to usurp. Hence it is by no means true that the [Dutch] rebelled against him when they recovered their original power which they had by then almost lost."[28] Spinoza's account of the Dutch Revolt as coming just in time to prevent tyranny consolidating was a way of justifying the rebel republic as an invaluable improvement in political and social circumstances while denying the efficacy of mere violent, unstructured armed revolt against legitimate monarchy, of justifying anti-monarchical revolution while adhering simultaneously to an anti-insurrectionist stance. Spinoza here is distinguishing armed rebellion powered by common grievance and discontent, which he considers useless effort and waste of lives, from well-directed, politically organized emancipating initiatives arising from intellectual subversion of the kind he favored.

Spinoza's comments on Roman history further illustrate his distinctive preference for purposeful planned rejection of tyranny and oppression over unfocused violent resistance, an order of priorities, he thinks, the English had dismally failed to grasp. "Admittedly, the Roman people [under the Roman Republic] could much more easily get rid of a tyrant and change their form of government [than the English], the right to choose the king and his successor being in the hands of the people [. . .] indeed, of the six kings [the Romans] had in earlier times, they slaughtered three." But when finally they tired of kings altogether, "all they achieved thereby was to choose many tyrants [i.e., the Roman senate], instead of one, and these kept them wretched in ceaseless strife, caught in foreign and civil wars, until finally the form of state once again became monarchical [with Augustus and the establishment of the empire] except only, as in the English case, for the change of name."[29]

Thus, the Romans too, despite the advantage of their republican origins, ultimately failed to extricate themselves from the thicket of monarchical tyranny nearly everywhere ensnaring mankind. Casting off tyranny bolstered by religious authority is far from being a simple process. If both the Romans and the seventeenth-century English had dismally failed to escape monarchical and aristocratic tyranny and achieve the democratic republic, Spinoza's first and primal example of this supreme test in the field of politics, the Hebrew Republic of Old Testament times, had indeed come closer to the mark, at least fleetingly, by adopting the principle of "theocracy," which, in Spinoza, as earlier in Maimonides and before that in Philo, does not mean rule by clerics or priests but rather the sovereignty of "God." Having escaped bondage in the Egypt of the pharaohs, the Israelites created what in Spinoza's view was—here as usual directly opposed to Hobbes—an imagined sovereignty which, though based on "inadequate ideas," had the great advantage in practice of requiring all to share equally in an imagined non-human sovereignty creating real possibilities of stability and a successful democratic republic: "the Hebrews did not transfer their right to another person but rather all gave up their right equally, as in a democracy."[30] In the longer run, however, despite their special advantage here, the ancient Hebrews disappointed too, being no more able to jump the formidable hurdle than the Romans, or the English later, transferring effective sovereignty first to Moses as God's interpreter, then to Aaron and the Levites, and then Joshua. Finally, the Hebrews slid ruinously into monarchy, which, besides more wars and other pitfalls, exposed their body politic to clerical sway with more splits, sects and false prophets disrupting society even more than before.[31]

Nothing is more difficult than creating a stable collective sovereignty guaranteeing the basic freedoms to all, equally. Spinoza's account of the Aragonese Revolt in the *Tractatus Politicus* warmly praises the medieval Aragonese for establishing a form of monarchy with so many constitutional checks and legal restrictions boxing in the crown and court as to be the nearest thing Spinoza could conceive to an ideal—that is, totally emasculated—monarchy. So splendidly did this medieval kingdom function that the Aragonese "continued for an incredible length of time unharmed, the king's loyalty toward his subjects being as great as theirs toward him." This happy scene lapsed only when the "kingdom fell by inheritance to Ferdinand of Castile, who first had the surname of Catholic; for the liberty the Aragonese enjoyed began to displease the Castilians who therefore ceaselessly urged Ferdinand to abolish their rights." Basing himself on Pérez's account,[32] Spinoza lauds Ferdinand for being wise enough not to try to suppress Aragon's institutions. "Accordingly, the Aragonese retained their liberties after Ferdinand's time, though no longer by right, but the favor of their too powerful kings, until the reign of Philip who oppressed them with better luck, but no less cruelty, than he did the United Provinces."[33]

Pérez's political career and reflections offered a unique thread enabling Spinoza to weave together in his mind the Aragonese insurrection (1591–92) with the Dutch Revolt and, though more in the background, the Portuguese revolt. A copy of *Las obras y relaciones del Ant. Pérez secretario de estado, que fue del rey de España, Don Phelippe II deste nombre* [The Works and Historical Accounts of Antonio Pérez, Former Secretary of State of the King of Spain, Philip II] (Geneva, 1644), a text of more than a thousand pages, brimming with the hardheaded, steely realism and political psychology characteristic of this author, was one of only two political works in Spanish found surviving in Spinoza's small personal library at the time of his death in 1677 (listed as no. 96 in Offenberg's reconstruction).[34]

It was this work plainly that provided the basis for Spinoza's analysis of the Aragonese Revolt. Pérez's tendency to exaggerate Philip II's malign character and misdeeds, and inflate his own importance,[35] did nothing to lessen Spinoza's taste for his commentary. Rather, Spinoza fully shared Pérez's post-1590 conclusions about the unrelieved rottenness of royal courts and monarchs. Relishing Pérez's pithy exposition of his experience-based views about politics, Spinoza cites him with rare concurrence and approval. No-one who reads history can fail to know, he remarks, clearly alluding to Pérez (mentioned on the same page), that "the good faith of counsellors [of kings] has generally turned to their ruin; so that, for their own safety they find it necessary to be cunning and not faithful."[36] For both writers, a viable theory of politics must be based on reason, nature, experience and grasp of the unchanging mechanics of self-interest—on understanding that "ninguno fue tan amigo de su vecino," as Pérez expressed it, "que no lo sea de sí más" [that no one loves his neighbor so much that he does not love himself more].[37]

The prolonged Dutch and Portuguese uprisings confronted the Escorial with a general challenge: how should local laws, "liberties" and traditions of the vast empire's different realms be integrated under the crown? Two opposed factions evolved, we have seen, a hard-line Castilian, imperialist view, linked to ruthless religious intolerance, that of Alva, and a less repressive faction more conciliatory toward local particularist tendencies headed by Ruy Gomez, prince of Eboli, first, and, then, after his death in 1573, by Pérez. The Madrid court factions' rivalry was a struggle for power but also of principle. The Alva faction was the more Castilian in outlook; their opponents placed more emphasis on conserving elements of the Dutch, Flemish, Aragonese and Portuguese constitutions, seeking conciliation and a degree of autonomy rather than outright submission.[38] Pérez, having become Philip's secretary of state (1566–78), in succession to his father, Gonzalo Pérez, lost his initial modesty on growing accustomed to exceptional power close to the king. Over time, he took to advising Philip more and more forthrightly, until finally he overstepped the mark.[39]

Pérez's fall from grace, in 1578–79, coincided with a broad shift in Philip's general strategy from a more cautious, inward-looking stance to a grandiose Atlantic imperialism soon to have an immense impact on Portugal and the Portuguese New Christians.[40] Arrested in connection with the murder of a courtier, Juan de Escobedo, in which the king was complicit, Pérez was imprisoned in Madrid and kept under varying degrees of custody for eleven years (1579–90) until finally, helped by accomplices, he managed to escape to the Aragonese capital, Zaragoza. Himself Aragonese, Pérez sought refuge under that kingdom's famed *fueros*, or historic privileges. When Philip tried to seize him, in May 1591, circumventing the *fueros* by arresting him via the Inquisition, the one Aragonese institution not bound by elaborate checks, an angry local disturbance erupted over the Inquisition's exceptional powers, which had been resented by some in that realm for decades.[41] The Inquisition's important prisoner was forcibly set free by a rioting mob yelling, "viva la Libertad!"

A second Inquisition attempt to seize the conspirator, now Philip's foremost domestic opponent, in September 1591, triggered a full-scale uprising (albeit largely confined to Zaragoza), which freed him for the second time from the Inquisition dungeons. This armed rising enabled Pérez to escape to France, and then England, where he raised a wider banner of rebellion against monarchical tyranny linking his cause to that of Dom Antonio of Portugal and William of Orange's son, Prince Maurits, in the Netherlands. Philip's response was to gather a Castilian army to crush the insurrection. On entering Zaragoza, in November 1591, royal troops launched a rigorous crackdown with several dissident nobles being arrested and executed.[42] A defeated gathering of the Aragonese Cortes [parliament], held at Tarazona, in June 1592, was compelled to acquiesce in a wide-ranging curbing of Aragon's constitution and laws and the bolstering of royal powers and prerogative. The Aragonese Revolt was thus a perfect instance of what Spinoza considered the completely useless, counterproductive outcomes of popular insurrection against tyrants lacking a previously long-prepared clandestine intellectual ground-plan.

Outliving Dom Antonio by sixteen years, Pérez evolved down to his death, in Paris, in 1611, into the era's foremost international publicist propagating political theory attacking Philip's absolutism. His trenchant, bitter style—the favor of princes is "false, feeble, deadly, the shadow of death itself"—greatly appealed to Spinoza as the measure of autocrats generally. Spinoza found especially attractive Pérez's analysis of the mechanics of politics, his judgments and array of maxims summing up the reality of political life.[43] "Nam (ut Ant. Perezius optime notat)," Spinoza remarks at one point, "imperio absolute uti principi admodum periculosum, subditis admodum odiosum, et institutis tam divinis quam humanis adversum, ut innumera ostendunt exempla. [For as Ant. Pérez very well observes, an absolute dominion is to the prince very dangerous, to subjects very hateful, and to the institutes of God and man alike opposed, as innumerable instances show.][44] Pérez's actual wording is only slightly altered: "el uso del poder absolute es muy peligroso a los reyes, muy odioso a los vasallos, muy ofensivo a Dios y a la naturaleza, como lo muestran mil ejemplos" [exercising absolute power is very dangerous for kings, very hateful to their subjects, and very much opposed to God and nature].[45] The borrowing here, as has been noted, is unmistakable;[46] but it is also highly ironic that amidst one of the world's greatest texts of democratic republicanism, its author should, virtually word for word, cite the very personage who, behind the scenes, had served as most intimate adviser of the very monarch figuring in Spinoza's thought as the supreme symbol of royal arrogance, oppression and religious intolerance.

Opposing tyrants like Philip, Cromwell, Charles II and Louis XIV was central to Spinoza's political thought just as subversion was ingrained in his cultural background and personal experience. Some scholars maintain that, Spinoza's *Political Treatise*, in contrast to the *TTP*, is notable for its abstraction, for the negligible work performed by history and experience."[47] This view is again greatly mistaken. The very opposite is the case. While there is no evidence suggesting that when he crossed the "water line" entering French-occupied territory, in July 1673, Spinoza was really entrusted with high-level secret communications from The Hague, in the service of the Republic, or went to meet the commander of Louis XIV's invading French army, Condé, at the latter's request, as many supposed at the time, the trip should nevertheless be deemed characteristic of his engaged and subtle activism. Venturing forth into a danger zone, Spinoza crossed the "water line" dividing the French from the remaining Dutch defenses, carrying safe-conducts from both the French and Dutch sides, and stayed for a time at Utrecht, ignoring unpleasant rumors rife back at The Hague with hostile onlookers insinuating that he was engaging in some treasonable activity, conniving with the French.

At Utrecht, Spinoza held long discussions with Colonel Jean-Baptiste Stouppe, brother of the French military governor of French-occupied Utrecht, as well as Professor Graevius, a Cartesian expert well connected with the French court, and with republican-minded regents, sounding them out and evaluating the scene while explaining what he hoped could be achieved in the near future, by way of blunting the Dutch anti-Cartesian reaction, and gains of the Calvinist clergy once the French were finally forced to evacuate the Dutch eastern provinces as already seemed likely and as happened shortly afterwards. Stouppe's anti-Dutch propaganda pamphlet, *La religion des Hollandois,* written just before Spinoza's visit but published afterwards, a text which appeared in French but also in Dutch and German,[48] was the very first publication ever to report Spinozism's existence as a movement and force in society, describing it as an established philosophical creed which, Stouppe affirms, exhibited a notoriously clandestine character.

By the time of the invasion of 1672–73, explained Stouppe, Spinoza possessed a "grand nombre de sectateurs qui sont entièrement attachez à ses sentiments" [great number of *sectateurs* who are entirely attached to his views], persons who took pains not to reveal themselves openly because their leader's *Tractatus Theologico-Politicus* destroys "absolutely the foundations of all religions." As far as Stouppe was concerned, no-one could doubt the revolutionary implications of Spinoza's philosophy. The *Tractatus Theologico-Politicus* "a pour but principal de détruire toutes les religions, et particulièrement la judaïque et la Chrétienne, et introduire l'Athéisme, le libertinage, et la liberté de toutes les religions" [has for its principal goal to destroy all religions, and especially the Jewish and Christian faiths, and introduce instead atheism, libertinage and liberty of all religions].[49] Spinoza contends further, reports Stouppe, that religions were invented for public utility with the aim of persuading citizens to live honestly, behave virtuously, and obey their magistrates, goals Spinoza supports not because he thinks there is any hope of compensation after death but simply for the excellence of virtue itself and the advantages this brings to the virtuous in this life.[50] Here then, sketched by Stouppe, was a clandestine organization seeking a radically secular and tolerant society, with religious authority entirely stripped from government, law and institutions, partly derived from a subversive crypto-Jewish tradition that Spinoza had adapted as his own. A revolutionary project seeking to substitute democratic republics for monarchy and aristocracy, it replaced religious authority with free thought, freedom to publish and criticize, and a secularized moral order.

The ultimate antidote to persecution, superstition and ignorance in Spinoza's eyes is, of course, his own philosophy, or something like it. But absolute rulers, their power depending principally on "superstition," will inevitably oppose every attempt to demystify society, and overcome "superstition" and "ignorance" with all their power. "It may indeed be the highest secret of monarchical government," affirms Spinoza in the preface the *TTP,* "and utterly essential to it, to keep men deceived, and disguise the fear that controls them with the specious name of religion, so that they will fight for their servitude as if they were fighting for their own safety, and will not think it humiliating but supremely glorious, to spill their blood and give their lives for the glorification of a single man."[51] Yet, according to Spinoza, it is impossible to combat the sturdy edifice of tyranny, authority and belief rendering mankind generally wretched by means of mass insurrection or inciting the people to defect; to succeed thoroughgoing, genuine *revolutio* requires subtler methods, and a favorable institutional context such as the Aragonese and Dutch possessed (but the English did not) before their respective revolts.

"I know it as impossible to rid the common people of superstition," explains Spinoza, at the close of the *TTP*'s preface, "as to rid them of fear."[52] This is why he did not want the common people to read his work "and make a nuisance of themselves by interpreting it perversely, as they do with everything." If fundamental change is to come—that is, genuine revolutionary transformation based on sound thinking—it cannot be achieved by mass intervention but only by infiltrating hidden adherents and discerning sympathizers horizontally among the elites to tilt things in the right direction. It was highly educated, Latin-reading officeholders, freethinkers like De Prado and Reynoso, and university students, who must first be swayed. His intimate circle during the 1660s when he wrote his principal mature works were indeed mostly graduates—physicians, lawyers and independent gentleman scholars. Thus the political revolution Spinoza the revolutionary sought to instigate he envisaged as arising chiefly through veiled infiltration of ideas designed to undermine "superstition," an underground movement quietly disarming and overcoming by discrediting theology, vilifying popular credulity and eventually rupturing the vast theologico-political apparatus keeping humanity in misery and chains.

Defeating oppression imposed by tyrannical autocrats, whether royal heirs or Cromwell-type upstarts, Spinoza deems impossible without first inculcating a heightened awareness of what tyranny is, creating a climate where the better informed and more aware can take the lead. But how exactly does a clandestine subversive politico-philosophical movement, fed partly by a Jewish subversive tradition reaching back to the Middle Ages, and replenished by crypto-Jewish experience in Iberian lands, aiming to undermine all organized religion linked to tyranny, aspire to resolve the world's injustice and shortcomings? Spinoza was not just devising the downfall of tyrants but pondering how to propel constructive new principles effectively enough to actually ameliorate society and human life.

It soon became clear "what these fine principles were," commented Cornelis Bontekoe (1644–1685), a Cartesian physician living in The Hague in the late 1670s, renowned for the hegemony of tea among his medical remedies, a highly controversial figure who attended the auction of Spinoza's belongings after his death, hoping to acquire the dead philosopher's books. What Spinoza aspired to became plain to all, explained Bontekoe when he published his *Tractatus Theologico-Politicus* with which he strove to overthrow not only the "ware philosophie" [true philosophy] of Descartes but all religion and truth, and propagate his own pernicious philosophy in an underhand manner. "And from that time onwards he made it his task to sow his perverse seed in secret; for which reason he left Rijnsburg for Voorburg, and moved finally to The Hague, evidently thinking he would find more scope there for his diabolical *politica* and other atheistic ideas among the frivolous youth and other men of the world who are often much inclined towards such evil, as indeed he succeeded in doing and still today one finds his creatures in that place."[53]

Spinoza's writings rather than Spinoza himself created his network of disciples, or what Bayle called his "secte," at The Hague, Amsterdam, Rotterdam and other Dutch towns and set out his concrete political agenda. But he was by no means without persuasive power in conversation, nor alone in wanting to weaken religious authority to promote toleration and individual liberty, reduce persecution and, linked to this, end passive acceptance of divine right monarchy, nor in believing democratic republicanism, true citizenship and pursuit of happiness are furthered only where ecclesiastical direction, Christian, Jewish and Muslim, is effectively bridled. At the core of Spinoza's "realistic" conception stands his principle that the more the power of kings and autocrats is curbed by constitutional checks and committees and by discrediting the religious sanction tyrants need, and the more the clergy's power to invade politics is curtailed, the better for society. Viable opposition to structures of authority based on ignorance, faith and tyranny works only by making converts to "philosophy" and then infiltrating hidden sympathizers into the professions and positions of influence. The political revolution Spinoza aimed to further was thus a veiled process of intellectual subversion aimed at disarming kings, priests, fanatics *and* the ignorant surreptitiously, inconspicuously and peacefully.

Through combating religious "superstition," popular prejudice and tyranny conjoined, toleration can be established, freedom of expression extended, oppression checked, peace strengthened, science and the arts promoted, and useless wars and vainglorious self-sacrifice for completely worthless, meaningless causes cut back. Such gains are only achieved wherever the stultifying "glory" of kings and blind religious faith are sufficiently discredited to become objects of general contempt. Toleration, republics and democracy, proclaimed Spinoza's hidden creed, benefit men, whereas monarchs, ecclesiastics and ordinary belief, whether Christian, Jewish or Islamic, do not. Since royal tyranny and absolutism can only be undermined by weakening "superstition" and "ignorance," and the common people cannot be emancipated from "superstition" directly, the only practicable revolutionary strategy and politics available is to nurture republican, demystifying ideology clandestinely.

Like Bontekoe earlier, Bayle would later confirm that Spinoza did indeed succeed in insinuating his subversive influence everywhere, adding that his adherents included university students, preachers and professors. Spinoza was not infrequently viewed in the late seventeenth and early eighteenth centuries, as Bayle projected him, as the culminating manifestation of "godlessness" in the world. For Bayle, Spinoza was the thinker who imposed shape and order, summing up and reinforcing two thousand years of monism and rejection of *supernaturalia* in European thought and culture and who, consequently, had a unique and unrivaled status as an undermining influence, here dwarfing Machiavelli, Vanini and even Hobbes. And certainly he did exert an unparalleled impact on shaping the attitudes, terminology and orientation of the entire clandestine materialist tendency within the Western world down to the mid-nineteenth century. Still, Spinoza's objective was never to attack individual personal devotion (where genuine) as such, especially where manifested as "charity and justice," the true essence of "religion" in his eyes, but always rather to gain social, educational and political benefits by weakening authorities, doctrines and institutions nourishing "superstitious" belief-structures, ordinary thinking buttressing archaic laws, despotism, persecution, bigotry, ecclesiastical authority and monarchy.

A Dutch theological author, writing in Zeeland, in 1700, building on Bayle's depiction when reviewing the entire history of the world's "godlessness" running from the Greek thinkers via the Italian Renaissance to Vanini, concludes: "however, no-one brought godlessness to a higher point, putting it on the throne and erecting its banners everywhere than the devious Spinoza. France, England—the cadet-school of monstrous opinions, yes the Netherlands and also other lands produce a countless horde who adore him as something wondrous. The greatest minds have imbued his views and without fear openly avowed themselves to be atheists."[54] Another who adopted this perspective was the prominent Reformed theologian Herman Alexander Röell

(1653–1718), who knew the Dutch universities intimately, and was sufficiently worried by what he uncovered to exclaim—as reported by the eighteenth-century historian of philosophy Jacob Brucker—"utinam inauditum esset in Belgica nostra execrabile illud Spinosae nomen, quem tota armenta sequuntur ducem!" [Would that that execrable name of Spinoza were unheard of in our Netherlands, that one whom whole herds follow as their leader!].[55]

Another Bayle contemporary observing Spinoza's clandestine underground sect was Jacques Basnage (1653–1723), early modern Europe's foremost historian of the Jews. A Huguenot preacher from Rouen who moved to Holland after Louis XIV's Revocation of the Edict of Nantes ended religious toleration in France, in 1685, Basnage settled first in Rotterdam, where he became friendly with Bayle, and afterwards The Hague, serving in both as a Reformed pastor. Spinoza, he notes, in his celebrated history of the Jews, the *Histoire des Juifs*, published at Rotterdam in 1706, was the first leader of a sect who neither sought to impose his views on others nor whose followers sought to turn his views into dogmas of belief. Spinoza's was a fundamentally new kind of movement functioning by persuasion, using philosophical arguments alone, which, it turned out, somewhat paradoxically, was part of its power.[56]

Incorrect surmises about Spinoza's conjectured remoteness and marginality to the main developments of Western thought, reinforced by the tendency in Kant, Fichte and Hegel to veil the extent of their preoccupation with Spinoza, resulted in his being broadly left aside by historians and philosophers of modernity. Many basic errors occur in historians' accounts of modernity and this is only one. But this oversight encouraged a misconception reinforced, arguably, by other errors in historians' account of the rise of modern democratic republicanism—especially the glaring failure of the so-called "Cambridge school" of political thought to separate the English tradition of aristocratic republican thought from continental European traditions of democratic republican theory.[57] Failure to recognize Radical Enlightenment democratic republicanism as the prime ingredient of the early modern revolutionary consciousness before Marx is undoubtedly the chief reason for the systematically defective picture projected by the conventional canon of modern masters of political thought, misreading rendered worse by highly questionable interpretations of the French Revolution lending a wrong emphasis to Rousseau and the divergent version of "general will" presented by Rousseauism.

For a more historically accurate and balanced picture of the role of the revolutionary consciousness in modern Jewish history, and the rise of secular, democratic "modernity" more generally, the well-worn usual notions pivoting on English republicanism and Rousseau need some pretty brusque clipping back, and for Spinoza, as he deserves, to be allotted a more central role in the emergence of democratic, free speech modernity than Hobbes, Locke, Rousseau or Marx. Is this going to happen? Probably not, but that does not make it any the less requisite.

THREE

Orobio de Castro and the Enlightenment Myth of the Sephardic Universal Iconoclast

Long before 1789, it was obvious that only some kind of revolutionary upheaval could rescue the Jews of the world (and many others) from misery and oppression. In a way, the messianic surges and mystical ferment surrounding Sabbatai Zevi (1626–1676)—and, in eastern Europe at least, Jacob Frank (1726–1791)—were Jewish collective acknowledgments of just such a realization. Given the reality of such sentiments, it is hardly surprising that a secularized "messianic" Sephardic "revolutionary figment," the image of a Spinoza-like prophetic figure redeeming Jews and Christians alike, should have begun circulating during the early eighteenth century.

Both Judaism and Christianity, during the early Enlightenment decades of the late seventeenth and early eighteenth centuries, confronted entirely new challenges to religious authority. Rabbinic Judaism during the Middle Ages and the early modern era undeviatingly focused on conserving Jewish community integrity, observance and religious authority. Jewish orthodoxy made scant effort to proselytize or openly combat Christian (or Islamic) doctrine. Rather, Judaism became an enclosed, tradition-bound, purely defensive strategy, designed to conserve a vulnerable, fenced-in, exposed fringe anxious to minimize inter-communal tension and conflict. Medieval public disputations, intimidating events for Jews, only reinforced this ghetto-oriented passive avoidance strategy.

However, coercive forced Christianization in the Iberian world and the Inquisition changed this picture fundamentally. Repression of crypto-Judaism in the Iberian Peninsula was so brutal and relentlessly oppressive from the late fifteenth century onwards as to massively help provoke the new species of underground, university-trained, Latin-reading Jewish militancy, searching for surreptitious ways to hit back at the oppressor, forging a quite new, more combative Jewish mentality rigorously examining the Christian West's theology and intellectual culture specifically looking for weaknesses, every path by which to chisel away at tyranny of conscience. This new intellectual culture nurtured a conspiring, deliberately concerted clandestine group mentality, devoted to undermining religious authority and ecclesiastical hierarchy, and every political and legal institution it sanctioned, from within.

Juan de Prado, Spinoza's ally of the late 1650s, and other seventeenth-century Jewish "deists" followed in the footsteps of Uriel da Costa (1584–1640), who, having studied law at Coimbra in 1600–1601 and 1605–8, had dismayed the rabbis of western Europe. Fleeing Portugal, in 1614, Da Costa, having rejected Christianity, reacted too against the normative Judaism he encountered at Hamburg. From around 1616, he began formulating a detailed critique of the Jewish Oral Law and the "Pharisaic" priestly (rabbinic) tendency, and then incorporated this into a treatise denying the soul's immortality. A Jewish opponent at Hamburg championing the soul's immortality, Dr. Samuel da Silva (1570–1631), afterwards published parts of Da Costa's text without his knowledge, at Amsterdam, in 1623, to rebut him. Now under rabbinic ban at both Hamburg and Venice, Da Costa moved to Amsterdam still propagating his heresies. For his "arrogance," "wickedness" and "wrong opinions," at Amsterdam he was placed under a still more severe *herem* (ban).[1] He hit back with the full version of his *Examination of Pharisaic Traditions* (Amsterdam, 1624), which precedes (and also differs from) Spinoza in claiming that the body of Jewish tradition and observance called the "Oral Law is not a true tradition, nor did it originate in the [Mosaic written] Law."[2]

Appealing to the city government, the synagogue elders claimed Da Costa's militancy threatened Christianity no less than Judaism. The magistrates ordered his book suppressed and publicly burnt. According to the now silenced Da Costa, an emblem of revolt against both Christian and Jewish religious authority, individual moral choice and free will constitutes the true path to salvation. By fostering scorn for human life, oblivious to men's inevitably being guided more by needs and "the hardships of this world," immortality of the soul taught alike by "Pharisees," the papacy and Luther, sanctioned a pernicious repressive edifice of observance, priestly intercession and ecclesiastical mediation falsely professing to help rescue individuals from eternal punishment. A fatal doctrine, it wretchedly misleads the credulous, building a hypocritical, deceitful ecclesiastical voice obscuring the true moral order.[3]

After a tumultuous thirteen-year battle with the Amsterdam community rabbis and elders, Da Costa ended his life by suicide, in April 1640. A prime feature of Da Costa's and De Prado's revolt, soon followed up and built on by others, was the search for fresh criteria drawn from the burgeoning arsenal of hermeneutics and philosophical reason for testing the truth content of theological claims. They forged a militant secularized "philosophy" combating Church teaching and rabbinic rule together along with the edifice of officially approved scholastic philosophy. Meanwhile, without adopting the anti-rabbinic stance of a Da Costa or De Prado, other ex-*converso érudits* emerging from a similar background, likewise powerfully rounded on their Iberian scholastic university teachers. A particularly notable example was Isaac Orobio de Castro (1617–1687). After escaping and reverting to normative Judaism, Orobio cultivated a distinctively Iberian Jewish fiercely anti-passivist attitude to the Christian world.[4]

During the early seventeenth century, theologians already bitterly deplored the emergence of anti-theological "philosophy" as a *machine de guerre* for secretly assailing Christianity, rightly viewing this new phenomenon as potentially massively subversive. Crypto-Averroism over recent centuries, and neo-Epicureanism since the fifteenth century, had already earlier created a widespread philosophical underground, especially in Spain and Italy, opposing all religious authority, especially Christian teaching. But these currents had spread clandestinely, silently, without openly challenging the dominant status quo.[5] Late seventeenth-century theologians Catholic, Lutheran and Calvinist alike, felt renewed and much greater alarm at the upsurge of a more activist post-Epicurean and post-Averroist assault.

This was again fostered in secret but, when ready, sprang out challenging the dominant structures publicly, as Uriel da Costa had attempted to do.

Dubbed by the Dutch Calvinist theologian Melchior Leydekker (1642–1721) the "het rijk der philosophen" [empire of the philosophers], this more combative intellectual vanguard menaced European society's millennia-old Christian "kerkelijke Republijk" [church (oriented) republic], threatening to overthrow the whole system of authority and morality underpinning the institutional and legal edifice of Western trans-Atlantic society. For law, education, behavior, health care and politics were all embedded in ecclesiastical sanction and theology coexisting beside a silenced, marginalized, and quiescent Talmud-based, rabbinic Judaism.[6]

This post-1650 crisis was unprecedented. Practically all Dutchmen, Leydekker pointed out, including the Jews, had for millennia unreservedly believed in *supernaturalia*—wonders, Satan, demons, magic and witchcraft as well as divine revelation and providential signs. Until the mid-seventeenth century, society faced no risk whatever from unbelief, what to him was the vileness of secular philosophy, to its dominant, comprehensively confessionalized, church-based shepherding of men within enclosures fenced off by its uncompromisingly theological vision of the world. Theology reigned supreme. All Christendom stood secure in the unquestioned hegemony of faith, devotion and clergy. But recent years had revealed unmistakable symptoms of a fatal new malaise. Jews, moreover, noted Leydekker, during the 1692–93 public "Bekker controversy" over whether sorcery, magic, diabolical powers and witchcraft really exist, were especially prone to this malaise, to openly repudiating their own forefathers' acceptance of the miraculous, the wondrous and of *supernaturalia*. Frighteningly, even Menasseh ben Israel (1604–1657), eager for compromise and reconciliation between Judaism and Christianity, had admitted to Gisbertus Voetius (1589–1676), the hard-line Calvinist preacher known as the "Calvinist pope" of Utrecht, that he sincerely "did not know whether devils exist." If people do not believe in devils, magic, miracles and supernatural happenings, then religious leaders lose their authority and social power! Modern Jews, more than others, charged Leydekker, were becoming skeptics, deserting the supernatural in droves, becoming allies witting and unwitting of the godless *philosophen* dismantling the world's unquestioning trust in the wondrous: in Holland, "de hedendaagsche Joden zijn mede in haar geheel Sadduceen" [the modern-day Jews are *en bloc* all Sadducees], swarming toward a philosophical rationalism trampling faith, belief, and religious authority underfoot.[7]

ISAAC OROBIO DE CASTRO (1617–1687)

Here, the convoluted legacy of Orobio de Castro has special relevance. Trained in Spanish universities, a lifelong foe of Christian teaching who dared insist on the "falsity" and lack of proof of the miracles allegedly performed by "that man" more openly than anyone else,[8] and former clandestine ideological comrade of De Prado, in Spain, Balthasar (alias Isaac) Orobio chose to use philosophy as the ally of Jewish orthodoxy, in defense of rabbinic authority and as a weapon against De Prado's "deism" and Spinozism. But with this strategy, Orobio contributed to fresh tensions within Western Judaism, and between Judaism and Christianity, in a way that eventually caused the real Orobio's profile to become submerged under a post-1700 paradoxical legend, a fictional "Orobio de Castro" who, like his real persona, was indefatigably at war with Christianity and deism, but unlike his real persona, combated all religious institutions and authority. This fictional "Orobio," aided by the real Orobio's writings, was reworked and manipulated by later authors, in particular Veyssière de La Croze, the marquis d'Argens, and d'Holbach, into a prophetic revolutionary "Spinoza" figure who proved a potent tool of the Radical Enlightenment.

Orobio, more than any other Jewish figure in the years following Spinoza's death, strove to reconcile Judaism with philosophical reason by assailing Christianity's foundations and pretensions while also pointing to the deists' inconsistencies and castigating the waywardness of hesitant New Christians. The real Orobio had no thought of ending up as an underground icon of generalized clandestine revolt against all religious authority and faith-bound repressive moral codes, but such was his remarkable fate.

In Spain's universities, Orobio had become a Latin-reading subversive and uncompromising foe of every Christian claim. Secretly, he remained such as a practicing doctor, first in Seville as personal physician to Don Antonio de la Cerda, duke of Medinaceli, and then other Andalusian towns, including San Lúcar de Barrameda and Cadiz. Arrested for "judaising" by the Inquisition, in 1654, he spent two years in Inquisition dungeons before appearing in the Seville *auto-da-fé* of June 1656, just a month before Spinoza's expulsion from the synagogue in Amsterdam. Publicly "reconciled" to the Church, as the expression went, once released he spent several more years underground in Andalusia before fleeing, in early 1660, to Bayonne in southwestern France, where he had relatives and a sizeable Portuguese crypto-Jewish community had evolved. Though less oppressed than their co-religionists in Iberia, French

"New Christians" still lived a double life, outwardly conforming as "Christians" while not infrequently inwardly remaining crypto-Jews. Godfather at a Bayonne baptism, on 24 June 1660, Orobio testified to notaries under his "Christian" name "Balthasar Alvares de Orobio."[9] After moving to Toulouse to teach at the university there, he next transferred to Amsterdam, in late 1662, definitively reverting to normative Judaism.

Integrating into the Amsterdam Sephardic community, Orobio discovered, like Da Costa and De Prado before him, was no easy matter for intellectually alert crypto-Jews escaping from Iberia. Disoriented after reaching France and then Holland, in Amsterdam he turned for guidance especially to Rabbi Moseh Raphael d'Aguilar (c. 1625–c. 1679), now the leading figure among the Sephardic rabbis there, a skilled educationalist ardently committed to instilling a love of grammar and rhetoric into his students. Earlier, d'Aguilar had migrated with a party of Sephardic emigrants from Holland to Dutch (northeastern) Brazil, where the first organized Jewish community in the New World was founded in the early 1630s at Recife (Pernambuco). There d'Aguilar remained until the Dutch surrender of their Brazilian enclaves to the Portuguese, in 1654, when he returned to Amsterdam, resuming his career there. In June 1659, he was appointed to succeed the recently deceased Menasseh as rabbi and also teacher of Hebrew and Talmud to Jewish youth, at a salary of four hundred florins yearly.[10]

Earlier one of Spinoza's teachers, a pupil of Saul Levi Morteira, d'Aguilar offered rabbinic guidance that helped shape Orobio's entire subsequent outlook. Orobio especially consulted his mentor in Judaism regarding troubling questions long weighing on his mind during his protracted transition from crypto-Judaism in Spain and France to Jewish orthodoxy in Holland.[11] In particular, how should one interpret Isaiah chapter 53, which Christians traditionally construed as predicting Jesus the Messiah? Before composing his own later notorious treatise on the topic, he conferred closely with d'Aguilar.

If Orobio's Hebrew, Talmudic and rabbinic knowledge remained sparse, his expertise in medicine and philosophy reaching back to his youth was impressive enough: having studied at Osuna and Alcalá de Henares, he had taught for a time at the University of Seville (1641–43). Setting up again as a high-society physician, his varied academic career, mastery of Latin and competent French rapidly advanced his post-1662 career and social standing. When in the summer of 1679, Ernst August, Elector of Hanover (1629–1698), while touring the Dutch Republic with his wife, fell ill with fever, the ducal couple, parents of the future King George I of England, lodged, while he recuperated, in the luxurious Amsterdam home of the Sephardic patrician Jeronimo Nunes da Costa (alias Moseh Curiel) (1620–1697), Agent of the Crown of Portugal in the United Provinces.[12] Orobio was the physician Nunes da Costa summoned to tend the duke, confirming that by then he had achieved preeminence in the Western Sephardic medical and secular cultural world. Jeronimo owned reputedly the best town garden in Amsterdam and had become an eager patron of Sephardic literature, poetry and learning during the very years that the young Spinoza was struggling to turn his back on wealth and status; he liked impressing visiting noblemen and the Sephardic social upper crust with his family's elegant lifestyle and high level of refinement.[13] Deeming himself a cultural envoy for a new kind of Judaism, as well as diplomat of standing, Jeronimo sought to show he was neither segregated from the world nor deaf to general cultural developments, and made a point of encouraging writers, poets and intellectuals, Jewish and non-Jewish, in order to project an emancipated image of the Amsterdam Sephardic community.

Somewhat ironically in the circumstances, the Elector's wife, the elderly, not always discreet Duchess Sophia, happened to be the sister of the very same Karl Ludwig, Elector of the Palatinate (1617–1680), who, five years earlier, in February 1674, had invited Spinoza to accept a chair in philosophy at his University of Heidelberg. Spinoza's decision to decline had caused something of a stir. Having "given long consideration to the matter," he had explained that the Elector's promising he would enjoy the "most extensive freedom to philosophize" had left him still uncertain as to "within what limits freedom to philosophize [in the Palatinate] must be confined"; besides, "if I am to find time to instruct young students, I must give up my further progress in philosophy."[14] How the Elector himself felt about Spinoza turning him down remains unknown. But Sophia's letters to her brother show that, by 1679, she had imbibed an unusually keen and sympathetic interest in Spinoza and, only a few months prior to meeting Orobio, had perused the (clandestine and forbidden) French version, published in 1678, of Spinoza's *Tractatus Theologico-Politicus*, a text now notorious in Germany, France and Holland alike.

Writing to her brother, on 9 March 1679, Sophia made the extraordinary (and distinctly un-Calvinist) remark that Spinoza's book was assuredly something exceptional "and altogether according to reason." If Spinoza had unfortunately already died, as her inquiries indicated, then "je pense, que les amateurs de la foy sans raison l'ont empoisonné, car la plupart du genre human vit du mensonge" [I think the lovers of the faith have, without justification, poisoned him, given the greater part of humanity lives in accord with lies]. She for her part loved truth and found it astounding, considering how many books got written, that no one had praised in writing what Spinoza says about the vastly relevant subject of universal deception, rumor and delusion.[15] Whether she asked Orobio's opinion of Spinoza's philosophy, and about Jewish attitudes toward Spinoza, his death and influence, we can only guess. But certainly during the weeks spent under Orobio's care in Jeronimo's splendid mansion with its store of rarities, curiosa, exotic imports and fine books, Spinoza's challenge to our world of "lies" remained firmly planted in her mind.

Settling in Amsterdam permanently, Orobio became a bulwark of Jewish orthodoxy and ally of rabbis, but unlike the rabbis remained a zealous adversary of Catholic academe and all Christian teaching. But while there was no doubt where he stood, he made no pronouncement in public at all about Spinoza through the 1660s and 1670s. He explained his silence later by saying he had long believed Spinoza's philosophy to be no serious threat to the synagogue, not because its content was not menacing, it was, but because he judged Spinoza's texts too difficult for the unlettered and too fallacious for the erudite. By the mid-1680s, however, Orobio conceded he had misjudged: Spinoza had in fact penetrated widely, not least among the Jewish public. Not only were unlettered folk becoming contaminated by Spinoza's "pestilential dogmata," even exalting in them, but, surreptitiously, certain men of learning also embraced his "wretched doctrines."[16]

That the Marrano experience in the Iberian Peninsula and the trauma associated with it fueled not just implacable hostility to Christian teaching, which he shared, but also fierce revolt against Jewish observance, tradition and religious authority, was hardly a revelation to Orobio. In the Spanish academic world, one of his own closest crypto-Jewish allies, De Prado, had later become Spinoza's ally and comrade in subversion. As a young man frequenting Spanish universities in the 1630s, De Prado, like Orobio, Reynoso and other erudite "New Christians" prided himself on furtively gathering scraps and fragments of buried Jewish knowledge in academic libraries.[17] Orobio's originally close friendship with De Prado was interrupted for some years when the latter left Alcalá to complete his medical studies elsewhere. But still in Spain, the two had met again later, in 1643, when Spinoza was eleven. Now, though, to Orobio's amazement, his formerly crypto-Jewish ally had discarded Judaism for a secret philosophical "deism" maintaining men can obtain salvation via any law and any sect. To this view, he was apparently converted in Seville by Juan Pinheiro, another Alcalá-trained Marrano physician and clandestine dissident who, before dying, around 1662, "converted" also other Marrano graduates to deism.[18]

Orobio and De Prado, both outstanding New Christian *érudits,* endeavored to thrash out their differences in clandestine discussions at Lopera, a small town near Córdoba. All men enjoy equal spiritual status, held De Prado, irrespective of what religion they profess, Judaism, Christianity and Islam being, much as Spinoza contended later, all man-made social and political contrivances, none being divine revelation. Arriving in Holland seven years before Orobio, in mid-1655, De Prado had joined the Sephardic congregation and the city's *collegium medicum* as a practicing physician, but soon allied with the young Spinoza, each reinforcing the subversive inclinations of the other. Together they had launched a joint challenge to rabbinic authority, clashing openly in particular with Rabbi Saul Levi Morteira in discussions at the community's advanced Talmudic classes.[19] Still, in defying the community publicly, De Prado remained more hesitant than Spinoza and, for tactical reasons, more willing to placate and be reconciled. Recanting following his first ban, it was not until nearly two years after Spinoza's departure that "Daniel de Prado," as he was known in the synagogue, was likewise definitively expelled, in February 1658. Rabbis and *parnasim* [governing council elders] placed him under the major *herem*, like Spinoza earlier, for persevering "in his evil and false opinions contrary to our holy Law, and because his views were instrumental in disaffecting a number of young students."[20] When later in 1658, Daniel attempted, via his son, David de Prado, to get also this ban lifted, the rabbis remained adamant: inquiries into De Prado's teaching and opinions persuaded them he adhered to crypto-Averroist notions long circulating clandestinely in Spain, believing there is no divine providence, that the world was not created but exists eternally, that the Mosaic Law has no divine foundation, that rabbinic chronology is nonsense, and that the soul dies with the body.[21] Less openly defiant than Spinoza, De Prado was scarcely less seditious.

Until the mid-1680s, Orobio's surviving manuscripts show, his escalating dispute with his former friend De Prado, now dwelling in Antwerp, in his mind vastly overshadowed his rejection of Spinozism and the *theologi politici*, as he occasionally called Spinoza's adherents. Orobio's polemical manuscripts attacking De Prado, commencing with his *Tratado contra la impiedad de los deistas, que niegan la Sacra Escriptura* [Treatise against the Impiety of the

Deists, Who Deny the Sacred Scripture], date mainly from the years 1663–64. It was here that Orobio drew his distinction between two main types of former New Christians in their conflicting responses on first encountering freedom in lands where returning to Judaism was permitted. Most adopted a humble attitude, admitting their ignorance of Hebrew and Jewish law and deferring to "those who, having been raised in Judaism and being learned in the Law, are in a position to explain it"; such men, "because they do not suffer the horrible disease of pride," are easily healed "from the sickness of ignorance." Others, though, having distinguished themselves in secular learning in medicine and philosophy at Iberian universities, despite arriving just "as ignorant of the Law of God," often came "filled with vanity, pride and arrogance, deeming themselves very wise" and hence cannot be cured of their sickness of mind. "They think they will lose reputation as erudite men if they agree to learn from those educated in the sacred Law, and so feign great science by contradicting whatever they do not understand." Their pretensions to superior knowledge, though rebuffed by the rabbis, nevertheless impress some people "who, due to their youth or natural perversity, presume to be clever" and thus the revolt perpetrated by Uriel da Costa, De Prado and Spinoza had become a vast communal malaise—rebellion against religious authority. Orobio rejected both deism and philosophical atheism on the ground that man is naturally limited so that his reason, though essential, is insufficient to determine God's will without divine revelation.[22]

For the rest of his life Orobio adhered to Jewish orthodoxy. But in the world of letters during the eighteenth century his reputation and legacy came to be manipulated in a particular direction by the Enlightenment's furtive subterranean culture. Due to his renown, stress on reason and resolute anti-Christianity, much of his legacy evolved into something wholly detached from Jewish orthodoxy and hence from the real Orobio. Subversive underground writers, in effect, re-invented "Orobio" as an anti-rabbinic Jewish icon representing the primacy of philosophical reason, absorbing this image into the clandestine radical intellectual world alongside De Prado and Spinoza, a fictitious anti-religious philosopher among radicals. The real Orobio did not believe scholarship and science on their own could demonstrate to a non-believer that God exists and had created the world, and that faith is indispensable. But philosophy could, he believed, do some of the work of proving Orthodox Judaism rests on, and is allied to, "reason," and recalling religious "rebels" from their wayward path. In particular, all those anxious for the truth must ensure that whatever religion they are asked to accept actually conforms to reason as far as human reason extends, and that no one slips into believing, as Christians do, what manifestly conflicts with philosophical reason. When Calvinist theologians with whom he debated affirmed Original Sin, for example, through Adam's Fall, Orobio replied that man's rational soul cannot be perpetuated as our bodies are, descending from Adam. Soul is not transferred by body, hence, Calvinist doctrine violates "reason" as well as totally lacks any (valid) basis in Scripture, and therefore, like every specifically Christian doctrine, in his opinion, has no possible demonstrable validity.[23]

Orobio shared some points of agreement with other late seventeenth-century anti-Trinitarian and anti-Calvinist theologians, including his later debating partners, Philippus Van Limborch (1633–1712), Jean Le Clerc (1657–1736) and the great John Locke (1632–1704). These all maintained, like Orobio, that religion requires some extensive purging of impurities, cleaning up and being rendered rational as far "reason" stretches. Also, for them, what relies on faith alone must be clearly shown to be above or "beyond reason," *supra rationem*, and in no way in conflict with reason. This was the essence of Locke's philosophy, his celebrated doctrine (relentlessly assailed by Bayle and Toland) of *supra rationem*. Orobio readily fitted among the early Enlightenment milieu convinced religious questions are open in part to a philosophical approach. The problem was that unlike the Remonstrant leader, Van Limborch, and Locke, Orobio, having opposed Christian teaching all his life, now mobilized their own argument full-frontally against Van Limborch's, Le Clerc's and Locke's cherished doctrine. Anti-Lockean no less than anti-Trinitarian, Orobio in this way threatened all "rational" Christianity, what Locke, Le Clerc and Van Limborch termed *supra rationem*, including Original Sin, pronouncing their stance wholly in conflict with reason. His views were hence potentially more disturbing in the wider trans-Atlantic context than those of Locke and his allies,[24] and the real Orobio's legacy easily reworked into the fictional "Orobio" that became a tool of the Radical Enlightenment against all moderate, mainstream thinking reconciling reason and faith.

Six years after Spinoza's death, in 1683, a soon famous, much-publicized debate between Orobio and Van Limborch was staged in a house in Amsterdam. The original dialogue was afterwards expanded with further written exchanges between the participants, into an intricate discussion to which Le Clerc and Locke also contributed. All involved took the debate with great seriousness. Locke wrote to Van Limborch, in February 1685, requesting a second chance to study "those writings of your own and Don Balthasar which you lent me some time ago."[25] Van Limborch, Le Clerc and Locke regarded the encounter as a major event on which a great deal hinged. Especially novel was the concurrence of both sides in banishing all hint of the harsh acrimony and polemical ire characteristic of medieval Christian-Jewish disputations. In this respect the encounter represents a landmark on the path to modernity. The finalized text of what came to be recognized as a new type of Christian-Jewish dialogue eventually appeared, presumably with Orobio's agreement, at Gouda, in 1687, shortly before his death, under the title *De Veritate religionis christianae Amica Collatio con erudito judaeo* [On the Truth of the Christian Religion, an Amicable Debate with an Erudite Jew].

An "amicable debate" and step toward enlightened objectivity though it was, the publication still adhered to the well-worn path of "Christian teaching" presented as incontrovertible truth in the manner most readers would expect, with the Jew being allotted well under half the space of the Christian, and the Jewish arguments appropriately belittled by appearing in far smaller print underneath Van Limborch's pronouncements.[26] A Dutch version appeared under the title *Vriendelyke onderhandeling met een geleerde Jood over de waarheit van den christelycken godsdienst* [Friendly Discussion with a Learned Jew on the Truth of the Christian Religion] at Amsterdam, in 1723. Widely noted in several countries, a second Latin edition appeared at Basel, fifty-three years after the first, in 1740, but without additional comment simply reproducing the original preface.[27] What guaranteed the encounter's exceptional character and lasting importance was Orobio's skill in surmounting the bias and using his academic background, and the relatively free air of debate in Amsterdam, to present telling arguments resting particularly on issues of historical evidence.

Orobio relied for his critique entirely on the common European philosophical and scientific inheritance, deliberately bypassing Jewish tradition, apart from a few references to Maimonides, thereby offering the Christian world a wholly novel kind of non-Scriptural Jewish critique of Christianity and defense of Judaism.[28] Reviewing the debate in the *Bibliothèque Universelle et Historique*, Le Clerc conceded that Orobio's writings show "much more subtlety and reasoning power than one ordinarily finds in the writings of those of his religion," a backhanded but significant compliment.[29] The outcome was unprecedented also in that Van Limborch, Le Clerc and Locke all rejected traditional Christian theological approaches to Jewish objections. They concurred in Van Limborch's virtual Socinian strategy of insisting Christianity's essence is precisely its rationality. Accordingly, he purposely steered clear of the Trinity. As eager as Orobio to avoid wrangling over disputed Scriptural passages and Hebrew citations, Van Limborch paralleled Orobio by defending Christian doctrine using external sources and "reason" alone, without invoking Scripture, theology or church authority. Locke positively enthused over the result, declaring Van Limborch's revolutionary championing of Christianity through reason rather than biblical references immensely valuable. His friend, he did not doubt, had thoroughly "vanquished the Jew."[30] Locke later followed a similar path in his *Reasonableness of Christianity* (1695), which likewise seeks to demonstrate Christianity's truth while avoiding the questionable support of the Hebrew Bible, indeed minimizing the Old Testament's significance for Christianity. Locke judged Christianity superior to Judaism in a universal and absolute sense, demonstrated by reason, making it both necessary and certain the Jews would eventually convert.[31]

Van Limborch, Le Clerc and Locke, eschewing the original Hebrew sources, pursued a strategy of deliberately downplaying the Old Testament's relevance, questioning its clarity and reliability in ways that reflected Socinian influence and that of the renowned French Bible critic Richard Simon (1638–1712), as well as Spinoza.[32] Van Limborch saw no difficulty in keeping silent on whether the Old Testament does or does not announce, refer to or prefigure Christ. By saying nothing about this, he could navigate close to admitting the Old Testament says nothing about Christ while yet still securing his goal by asserting the overriding legitimacy and reasonableness of Christianity. Claiming the new revelation, the New Testament is ultimately what matters, that it stands in unique splendor as its own proof and justification, Van Limborch pronounced it unmistakably God's Word given the rationality of its spiritual guidance, perfection of its moral content and the Apostles' unimpeachable testimony regarding Christ's miracles and resurrection.

Van Limborch's and Locke's invoking the New Testament alone, Locke stressing especially the Pauline Epistles, without claiming any link with Hebrew texts, thrust Orobio into a potentially precarious position never yet confronted by rabbinic defenders of Judaism. Medieval and early modern predecessors defending Judaism invariably sought to avoid outright collision by wholly circumventing the New Testament. They concentrated on rebutting interpretations of key passages of Isaiah and the like in the Hebrew Bible that Christians supposed point to Christ's coming. Orobio, by contrast, was left with no choice—albeit, presumably also saw it as an open invitation—but to launch into a full-frontal offensive on the New Testament itself and renew his in the past oft-repeated denial that Christ was the Messiah, echoing what he had maintained many times before clandestinely, culminating in his unpublished manuscript *Prevenciones divinas* composed around 1669, but now reiterating these points explicitly in print, something never done previously and in the past deemed outrageous blasphemy and still strictly prohibited in most Western lands.[33]

Risking the severe reaction bound to be felt by readers, Orobio, as he had so often in clandestine debates in Spain, questioned the New Testament's validity, integrity and legitimacy, but did so now in print, refusing to admit any grounds for acknowledging the Gospel's alleged rationality or reliability as a source. Still guarded regarding the person of Christ himself, he spared no effort to throw doubt on the Apostles' testimony and Gospel text's integrity. Why are the Gospels written in Greek, a language of which neither Christ nor the Apostles had any knowledge? Toward the Apostles he was as unsparing as Spinoza, classifying them as ignorant, confused and unreliable dullards of low birth, without prestige or standing in the society of their time and devoid of trustworthiness. Van Limborch's maintaining the Gospels are their own justification Orobio rejected outright. As for Van Limborch's and Locke's contending Christianity's truth is manifest from the astounding speed with which so many lands and peoples adopted the new faith, Orobio countered—well before Bayle followed him here—by pointing out that "Mohammed propagated his sect in still shorter time, more spectacularly and over even more regions of the world. So great was the number of believers [in Islam] that the Arabs and Moors then conquered all of Spain," easily overrunning the Christians, hardly a ringing endorsement of providential support for the latter, a point later likewise made by the Huguenot radical subversive Jean-Frédéric Bernard.[34] Neither had Christianity's advent transformed our world's moral climate or elevated humanity's well-being in any noticeable way, whereas the Scriptures make it clear that the Messiah will be a "king" who will lead his people back to their Promised Land and introduce a world era of peace.[35] Rather, it was obvious the world remains just as steeped in error, superstition, ignorance, credulity, idolatry and wickedness as before. Here Orobio switched to an objection he had long raised in debating with Christians: is it not illogical to charge the Jews with "blindness" and obstinacy in denying Christ when "China, Tartary, Persia, Arabia, Turkey, the Americas, and Africa teem with nations roundly denying the Christian Messiah?"[36] Why would any reader guided by reason see grounds for trust in the Gospel's claims?

Van Limborch's affirming the Gospels offer the mind perfection and complete clarity on spiritual matters, his proofs of their reliability, their being what Locke too considered to be "infallible truth," greatly impressed Locke but struck Orobio as nonsense. The Reformation and post-Reformation Wars of Religion clearly demonstrate that it is impossible to find any clarity in Christian teaching. Rather, the Gospels present so many "difficulties, doubts and disputed interpretations, that the New Testament can be pronounced the single greatest cause in the world of hatred, persecution, theological strife and dispute," this point being a favorite theme also of his rabbinic mentor d'Aguilar and all his ex-*converso* circle. By rendering even the Hebrew Bible a bone of contention, Christianity surpasses all other faiths in engendering division, conflict arising especially from "so many different sects" and theologies all fighting for irreconcilable interpretations of Scripture.[37]

Erudite journals of the day did not question that Orobio lost the contest, underwriting Locke's and Le Clerc's evaluation of the debate as a "triumph" for Christianity. Van Limborch crushed the Jew's objections with "much force and erudition," agreed the sixteen-page review in the Rotterdam journal *Histoire des Ouvrages des Scavans*, in 1687.[38] But while Van Limborch, Le Clerc and Locke harbored no doubts and remained eager to publicize the disputation,[39] others, including Christian traditionalists, were less sure. Indeed, before long, the celebrated disputation began to exert a noticeably disturbing impact. The ten-page review appearing in the Leipzig *Acta Eruditorum* for 1688 confirmed the undeniable superiority of "Limborchius's" Christian claims over those of the unspecified "Judaeus," but was less confident that Van Limborch had pulled off a fully satisfactory victory from a Christian perspective.[40] If Socinians and near Socinians drew satisfaction, orthodox Calvinists, Lutherans, Anglicans and Catholics remained uneasy, one or two even becoming indignant.

A veteran Voetian (i.e., strict Calvinist) professor of theology, at Leiden, Herman Witsius (1636–1708), devoted a lengthy section of his *Meletemata Leidensia* (1703) to evaluating the discussion, entitled "Orobii et aliorumque obiectiones adversus Jesu et Apostolorum miracula refutatae," that revealed not just that the dispute was still vividly remembered at the start of the new century, but that the controversy had disconcertingly positioned Orobio's stance at the forefront of the Jewish response to Christian claims thereby lending new prominence to Jewish and deist denial of Gospel claims and Christ's miracles. In fact, the Orobio debate had become a source for the now increasingly widespread scoffing at the Apostles' once universally accepted unchallengeable integrity. Via his ill-judged published dialogue, complained Witsius, Van Limborch foolishly opened the door to Orobio's highly damaging critique. A lasting platform had been provided for tarring the "reputation" and "honor" of the Apostles. It was disgraceful that Orobio had been allowed to disparage the Apostles as untrustworthy witnesses, "men of the humble plebs of very low fortune!"[41] Arminians or Socinians might see no problem in accepting that "one can prove much more easily and clearly that the New Testament books are by the authors whose name they carry and have not undergone any considerable changes to the text" than justify traditional claims of a divinely ordained progression from the Old Testament to the New. But authentic Christians were appalled at seeing the Old Testament so marginalized and cast in doubt.[42]

Orobio, explained Basnage, a former pastor of Rouen (1676–85) now at The Hague, "suspected that it was the Greeks who had composed [the Gospels], since the Hebrew language was that of the Jews." Was it conceivable, he reports Orobio as querying, that God suddenly desired men's salvation to depend on unquestioning faith in the Christian Messiah when over many centuries he had repeatedly commanded in the Books of Moses and Prophets that men were to believe solely in Him, and adore only Him. Basnage, author of the best-known history of the Jews of the age, and Bayle's closest ally in his last years, devoted no fewer than sixteen pages to discussing Orobio's life and writings, conceding that his thrusts against Van Limborch were formidably incisive and of lasting significance.[43] Among preachers and theologians, it was possibly Bayle's friend Basnage who contributed most to preparing the ground for the remarkable eighteenth-century career of the fictive "Orobio."

Worst of all, for the theologians, furtive reports began circulating among the underground Radical Enlightenment fraternity that the truth of the matter was quite the reverse of what Van Limborch and his allies claimed. Behind the scenes, not a few onlookers concluded that it was actually Orobio who had got the better of Van Limborch, Le Clerc and Locke, rather than the other way around. This troubling rumor gained further currency through

Leibniz's curious remark in his *Theodicy* (1716), referring to Orobio, using Bayle's phrase, "as a very able Jewish physician" who refuted Van Limborch, "so I have heard say, in a work posthumously circulated, but unpublished."[44]

OROBIO AND THE RADICAL ENLIGHTENMENT (1687–1740)

Especially unsympathetic, then, to Van Limborch's and Locke's claims was the freethinking underground which by the 1680s had gained a foothold in Holland, England and France alike. Among the foremost figures of the early radical tendency engaged in writing and diffusing clandestine manuscripts was Henri, comte de Boulainvilliers (1658–1722), a leading propagator of underground *spinosisme* in France. Among Boulainvilliers's unpublished reading notes, bound in six volumes, conserved today at the Bibliothèque Nationale, in Paris, survives his "Extract from the Book of Van Limborch, *De Veritate religionis christianae* where the latter answers the arguments of the Jew Orobio." Boulainvilliers, weighing either side's arguments, concludes that Orobio's are the more cogent and convincing.[45] With his innovative strategy and reliance on philosophy rather than biblical text, Orobio in this way acquired a bigger reputation for subverting Christianity in Holland, France, England and Germany among clandestine radical freethinkers than any other contemporary Jewish thinker apart from Spinoza. It was this that drove the subsequent evolution of the eighteenth-century fictive "Orobio de Castro," a distorted image that acquired an underground momentum of its own. "Orobio" came to be remembered not just as rationalizing Christian apologetics' greatest foe, but due to the freethinkers' efforts, as a universal subversive propagating a generalized Spinozism.

Basnage unwittingly contributed to this development by drawing attention, for the first time, in the revised 1716 edition of his history of the Jews, to Orobio's unpublished Spanish manuscripts to which Leibniz was presumably referring. In his unpublished work Orobio advanced still bolder, more incisive objections to Christian teaching than in his toned-down published writings, objections, Basnage pointed out, scholars could no longer ignore, but had to answer. When Basnage first published his *Histoire,* in 1706, he had only just discovered Orobio's, Morteira's, Montalto's and d'Aguilar's anti-Christian manuscripts, a body of literature hidden from official eyes and the general public, conserved in Spanish and Portuguese manuscripts in Amsterdam, a hidden collection originally intended only to dissuade wavering Portuguese New Christians fleeing Spain and Portugal, or sheltering in

France, from embracing Christianity. Secreted away in the Portuguese synagogue, these documents, the historian Richard Popkin demonstrated, came to light via a major book auction, the sale of the 6,124 volumes of the Bibliotheca Sarraziana, in The Hague, in September 1715. Astoundingly, the collection included copies of no fewer than four unpublished anti-Christian tracts by "Doctor Yshak Orobio," including that on Isaiah, the *Exposición del Capitulo 53 Ysaias*, the auction catalogue ascribing these to "that most renowned and acute Jewish doctor, Orobio de Castro," texts "assiduously and expensively sought for by the erudite," so far in vain.[46] Basnage, like the erudite republic of letters more broadly, was taken aback by what emerged, though he was grateful for the fresh ammunition provided against "le spinosisme" (as he misconstrued Orobio's writings against his former friend De Prado as being). Much of Basnage's discussion of Orobio is in fact devoted to his polemics against the unmentioned "Daniel De Prado," material Basnage and others wrongly assumed was directed against Spinoza and Spinozism.[47]

Erudite freethinkers, commented Basnage, confirming a fact known in freethinking circles for years, had eagerly sought Orobio's manuscripts and willingly paid handsomely for copies, a point echoed afterwards in several German accounts of the anti-Scripturalism of the *Naturalistas*, as the freethinkers were called in Latin.[48] One notable freethinker who contrived to procure Orobio's manuscripts before Basnage was the English "deist" (in fact, atheist) Anthony Collins (1676–1729), former friend of Locke and celebrated bibliophile whose library, outstripping even the Sarraziana, was among the largest in Britain, by the 1720s boasting nearly seven thousand volumes.[49] A hardened foe of Christianity and all theology and, like Toland, rejecting Locke's "above reason," Collins was a radical enlightener perfectly aware that the most subversive reflections on such topics in his day derived from Spinoza, Spinozism and Dutch and Sephardic sources more generally. In *A Discourse of the Grounds and Reasons of the Christian Religion* (London, 1724), Collins refers several times to Orobio as a learned Jew who taught at Alcalá and Seville, was a "great master of School-Divinity after the mode of the Spanish universities," and conducted the "famous controversy with Limborch concerning the truth of the Christian religion," which Collins counted among the three "most important" Jewish anti-Christian texts of the age.[50]

A collaborator of Collins resident in London, the Huguenot refugee editor Pierre des Maizeaux (1673–1745), commenting on the hard-hitting texts of Orobio, Morteira and the Karaite, Isaac ben Abraham of Troki (c. 1533–c. 1594), the writer of another soon widely cited anti-Christian tract, likewise noted the extreme difficulty of obtaining copies. Remarking, after Collins's death, on the unobtainability of Morteira's text, he added that the "same may be said with respect to Orobio and Rabbi Isaac's [i.e., Isaac of Troki's] books"; however, "Mr Collins found means to get them when he was in Holland, but paid dear for them. It is more than probable that these," he wrote in an appended note, "are the very copies he purchased; and the only ones extant in the libraries of Christians in England."[51] During his life, Collins twice visited the Continent, mainly to frequent Dutch bookshops and freethinking groups, in 1710 and 1713, hence must have acquired Orobio's manuscripts by 1713 at the latest.[52] Orobio's manuscripts he placed among the most important of the usually unobtainable clandestine category, mentioning one, the *Prevenciones divinas*, by name. Powerful too, noted Collins, was Morteira's "Providentia divina," the "foremost book [the Jews] have against Christianity," a work, likewise unknown to the outside world as the Jews "forbid, under pain of excommunication, to lend it to any Christian, for fear of drawing a storm upon themselves for producing such strong objections against the Christian Religion," for which reason "no copies are to be procured of it, but by the greatest accidents."[53]

Surviving pre-1700 copies of these hitherto concealed tracts of Orobio, Morteira, Isaac of Troki, Montalto and d'Aguilar starting from the 1660s, are invariably in Spanish and derive exclusively from the libraries of wealthy Portuguese Jewish patricians of Amsterdam and The Hague, from the "cabinets" of figures like Jeronimo Nunes da Costa and his son, Alvaro, and the families Lopes Suasso, Belmonte, Teixeira, and de Pinto. These pre-1700 copies destined for Sephardic readers fetched high prices reflected in their fine script, sometimes adorned with pen-drawn illustrations and handsomely bound in gold-worked leather bindings. But only after 1713 did these texts penetrate the wider clandestine philosophical literature forming the backbone of the Radical Enlightenment. They continued to do so for the rest of the latter's fully clandestine phase lasting until the late 1740s.[54] Soon after Collins's second visit to Holland, a small stream of these manuscripts became available in French translation. The catalogue of Jewish manuscripts conserved in Amsterdam public collections today shows that production of these illicit translations continued until around 1740 and then abated.[55]

These illicit texts, or *clandestina*, very slowly seeped from wealthy Sephardic homes into other circles, an inevitable consequence given that even before 1700, the more eye-catching exemplars of these Spanish-language texts apparently were occasionally shown to amenable, freethinking visitors like

Leibniz's friend, the Duchess of Sophia of Hanover. A copy of Morteira's "Providencia de Dios con Ysrael" [God's Providence with Israel] bound in gold-worked leather, rendered in a "very skilled italic writing" by the renowned scribe Judah Machabeu, in 1664, today in the Amsterdam Bibliotheca Rosenthaliana, has each chapter beginning with "drawn ornamental borders and decorated initials." It later belonged to the opera-loving, wealthy and flamboyant Sephardic rentier Francisco de Liz, who in the early eighteenth century resided in style at The Hague.[56] Among embellished copies of Orobio's *Prevenciones divinas* surviving today in Amsterdam is one dating from 1713 prepared by a certain Michael Lopez Pinto, with "aquatints depicting scenes from the Old Testament."[57]

At least some translators of these texts into French undertook the task for ideological reasons rather than payment. Illustrative of deliberate Jewish rather than gentile deist subversion of Christianity was "D.D.L.P.," probably Daniel de la Penha (d. 1750), the younger son of the Rotterdam Sephardic merchant Joseph de la Penha (1658–1731). A copy of D.D.L.P.'s rendering of Isaac of Troki's main anti-Christian text, *Hisuk Emuna*, dated "in the year of the Creation 5490 at Rotterdam" (i.e., 1730), conserved today in Paris, has a preface yielding several clues regarding his motivation and attitude. He translated the text, he states, to promote a better future harmony and balance between the world's religions by weakening Christianity. Isaac of Troki's work he thought more suited for this than the texts of Doctor Orobio or Saul Levi Morteira, because the latter argue on purely philosophical grounds, whereas "au contraire," Isaac of Troki "se sert très peu de la philosophie" [uses philosophy very little].[58] Orobio's approach seemed to him problematic and lacking force, because it distracts attention from Scripture's real teaching. There will one day be just one Law and one monarchy, on earth uniting Jews and Christians, declares De La Penha, but this messianic utopia of the future will realize itself in purely religious and in part neo-Karaite terms.

Of importance too, then, was a specifically Jewish messianic strand of clandestine thought setting itself in opposition to rabbis, a tendency rebutted by detractors as purely "neo-Karaite." Jewish anti-Talmudic clandestine messianism was indeed a perceptible stream at this time, and its essence was a fusion of philosophical skepticism and rationality with neo-Karaitism.[59] Of relevance here are the early eighteenth-century admonitions of the London rabbi David Nieto (1654–1728), whose chief work, *Matteh Dan* (1713), extols recent innovations in science celebrating the telescope and microscope, and encouraging Jews to study Cartesianism and Newtonianism, but at the same time denounces the new Karraitas (Karaites), or Jewish deists, attempting to seduce Jews away from the Oral Law and rabbinic authority. Basically an attack on rabbinic interpretations and authority, this new threat, he thought, had become rampant in London as well as Amsterdam. Resort to philosophical arguments was encouraging the tendency but could not bring men to salvation because, however alluring, philosophy remains always uncertain and doubtful. There exist, after all, a great many modern philosophies, all in conflict with each other.

It was to the post-1715 French clandestine literature that Orobio's most enduring contribution to the radical tendency's subversive campaign was made. The 1720s and 1730s proved key decades for discovering and diffusing Orobio's openly anti-Christian, rationalizing Judaism. A key intermediary here was the notorious deist Jean Lévesque de Burigny (1692–1785), author of a celebrated account of ancient pagan thought, the *Histoire de la philosophie payenne* (The Hague, 1724) and leading member of a deist circle that included Thémiseul de Saint-Hyacinthe (1684–1746). Recalling a stay in Holland in 1720, in a letter preserved today in the Bibliothèque Nationale, Lévesque mentions encountering several "learned Jews in Holland,"[60] one of whom claimed to "possess a work of Orobio discussing Isaiah 53 to which the Christians were unable to reply" which Lévesque arranged to have copied. He procured too a copy of the *Dissertation sur le Messie* "where Orobio attempts to prove the characteristics the Prophets attribute to the Messiah do not fit the figure of Christ." Through Lévesque's mediation, both texts, reworked but still attributed to Orobio, were later clandestinely published together in Paris, in 1770, by Diderot's ally, the baron d'Holbach, a leading radical enlightener and crypto-republican, under the title *Israel Vengé, ou Exposition naturelle des prophètes hébraiques que les chrétiens appliquent à Jésus, leur prétendu Messie* [Israel Avenged, or Natural Exposition of the Hebrew Prophets Which the Christians Apply to Jesus, Their Pretended Messiah] by "Isaac Orobio."[61]

This vehemently anti-Christian material, claims d'Holbach's 1770 preface, had been rendered into French from Spanish, in Holland, by a Jew named "Henriquez" for a foreign man of letters residing in the Netherlands in 1720–22, an allusion to Lévesque de Burigny or Saint-Hyacinthe. This unnamed *érudit* "seems to have retouched or corrected the translation."[62] Attached to the Bibliothèque Nationale copy survives a note by the poet Eusèbe Baconnière de Salverte (1771–1839) commenting on the reworking, suggesting that while *Israel Vengé* possibly included passages by Diderot, "I know for certain d'Holbach reworked much of the text, if it was not entirely by him which is what I tend to believe."[63] No further French edition appeared until 1845. No English translation appeared until 1838, and even then it came out only in a restricted printed version "not published," guardedly labeled (wholly contrary to the original intention) "expressly for the use of young persons of the Jewish faith."[64]

Instrumental along with Lévesque in incorporating Orobio into French clandestine subversive literature was his friend Saint-Hyacinthe who probably introduced Lévesque to "des juifs savants" in Holland in the first place. Using the deliberately evasive, teasing phrases typical of early Enlightenment disseminators of clandestine philosophical literature, Saint-Hyacinthe contacted Des Maizeaux in London, in October 1737, recounting his failure to persuade a Dutch publisher to issue in English, and then French, two unpublished manuscripts—one a translation by a Jew "of an MS [manuscript] of Orobio that is very important to refute since this MS circulating among the Jews keeps them in their blindness regarding the Messiah, something neither charity nor piety should tolerate given this Jewish doctor construes the 53rd chapter of Isaiah in so seductive a manner that one does not recognize in it any more a reference to the Evangelical History which, however, is clearer there than in any other prophecy." "Until this exposition of Orobio *is* refuted we can hardly hope to see Jews open their eyes to the light." Churchmen would surely have disposed of Orobio long ago, added Saint-Hyacinthe insinuatingly, had only the manuscript been available in print.[65]

The comprehensive list of early Enlightenment French clandestine manuscript texts compiled by Miguel Benítez in 1988, and subsequently expanded, shows Orobio to be the chief source of a not inconsiderable slice of the total corpus of anti-Christian polemic circulating in French during the early and mid-Enlightenment. Of around 150 texts in this general category of irreligious underground literature listed by Benítez, no less than seven are reworkings of Orobio's texts, several surviving in substantial numbers of copies.[66]

Mostly, these manuscripts adapted to the subversive clandestine philosophical milieu gaining ground in France during the 1720s and 1730s purposely omit Orobio's vigorous defense of the Mosaic Law. Furthermore, they generally omit all mention of Orobio as their author, the goal now being to deploy Orobio's substantive arguments against Christian doctrine with maximum effect, the manuscripts' propagators assuming their objective would be more effectively achieved by omitting all mention of the texts' having a Jewish origin and Jewish objectives.[67] Openly conceding Judaic provenance could only diminish the manuscripts' standing, and hence impact and subversive power.[68] At the same time, the arguments of these touched-up French versions were manipulated in Orobio's favor. Thus, for example, one of these manuscripts, "Conférences d'un Juif avec un Chrétien," a partial translation of the Van Limborch–Orobio encounter, deliberately waters down Van Limborch's replies, sometimes, like Boulainvilliers's text, even entirely deleting his responses to Orobio's objections to further sharpen Orobio's case against.

Orobio's deployment as an anonymous French-language clandestine polemicist against Christian doctrine also affected and, in an equally biased fashion, manipulated, Orobio's secondary function, as a foil to Spinoza, into something quite different from what Orobio had intended. While manuscript versions of *Certamen philosophicum,* Orobio's rebuttal of Spinozism, in French and Spanish remained rare, this book was undoubtedly circulating in French early in the century, or earlier, and, from 1721, also in Spanish.[69] Yet, this, the only published text by a Jewish author rebutting Spinoza's challenge published in the century after the *herem* of 1656 prior to Mendelssohn's *Philosophische Gespräche* (1755),[70] was deliberately twisted to lead the reader in a different direction from that which Orobio intended, being likewise reworked to serve a subversive Radical Enlightenment function. It appears, for example, in the notorious *Réfutation des erreurs de Benoit de Spinoza par M. de Fénelon, Archevêque de Cambray, par le P. Lami Benedictin et par M. le comte de Boulainvilliers* ("Bruxelles" [Amsterdam], 1731), a compilation edited by Nicolas Lenglet Dufresnoy (1674–1755) and published in 1731, with the barely disguised aim of surreptitiously championing and disseminating instead of attacking Spinozism.

A diplomat and historian whose biting wit made many enemies, Lenglet Dufresnoy was a clever, somewhat disreputable literary intriguer on the Parisian scene figuring among the foremost connoisseurs of the clandestine literature.[71] According to The Hague's *Journal Littéraire*, his 1731 collection was as replete with "malice and deception as its title," being actually an exceedingly "dangerous" work, "the object of which, under a false title, is to establish Spinozism" [dont le but, sous un faux titre, étoit d'établir le spinosisme]. Although Orobio's was among the longest texts in the volume, here yet again, both his name and Jewishness are deliberately deleted while his attempts to combat Spinoza are blatantly distorted by this calculating manipulator of *clandestina* against Orobio's intention.[72]

Even earlier, indications abound that Orobio's chief published philosophical work, the *Certamen philosophicum*, was vulnerable to being reworked into a clandestine resource designed to draw attention to, rather than rebut, Spinoza's theory of substance and other key elements of his system. Orobio "wrote against Spinoza," Basnage points out, "being a philosopher who had thoroughly studied metaphysics," while at the same time refuting the Collegiant controversialist Johannes Bredenburg (1643–1691), who insisted on Spinoza's irrefutable philosophical cogency.[73] Orobio composed his *Certamen*, Leibniz later noted, after being drawn into debate with Bredenburg, who had long searched in vain for arguments capable of overturning Spinoza's naturalistic and atheistic conclusions. Having provoked uproar within the Dutch Collegiant community by sensationally publishing his thesis, arguing, not unlike the German thinker Friedrich Heinrich Jacobi, during the great Spinoza controversy of the 1780s, that there is in fact no philosophical reasoning able to overturn Spinoza's philosophy, such is its exceptional cogency, and that the only viable Christian response is either a leap of faith to escape it, abandoning philosophical reason altogether, or grudging acquiescence in the principle of "double truth." Bredenburg opted for the latter: revealed truth is unassailable but so is philosophical truth even where the two contradict each other. For Bredenburg, reason and Christianity do contradict each other at essential points, yet, both are true.

But "double truth" was hardly a robust defense of any revealed faith. Orobio designated Bredenburg a denier of a creator God and divine providence like Spinoza and Spinoza's jurist friend at The Hague, Abraham Johannes Cuffeler (c. 1637–1694). Cuffeler, in his *Specimen artis ratiocinandi* [Specimen of the Art of Reasoning] ("Hamburg" [Amsterdam], 1684), published shortly after Orobio's debate with Van Limborch, had joined Spinoza in holding that reason proves the universe cannot have been "created" and that there is no such thing as divine providence.[74] Orobio felt spurred to write against Spinoza in part because Bredenburg had rhetorically asked for help from whoever could provide it in constructing the viable refutation of Spinozism he was unable to find and partly because Bredenburg and Cuffeler together had powerfully renewed the Spinozist threat. Simultaneously rebutting Spinoza, Bredenburg and Cuffeler, Orobio's *Certamen* appeared shortly after Cuffeler's book, in 1684 (according to Bayle, in both Latin and Dutch, though no copy of the latter has been unearthed).[75] Appearing in a second edition at Amsterdam, in 1703,[76] it eventually appeared also in Spanish as *Defensa de la verdad divina y natural contra los principios de Juan Bredenburg*, translated by G. de la Torre (The Hague, 1741).

From the first, it was somewhat unclear whether Orobio's book acted to stem or accelerate Spinozism's spread. Yves de Vallone (c. 1666–1705), a subversive Huguenot writer known to have studied the *Certamen* during his exile in Holland (1697–1705), discovered from it everything he knew of Spinoza's doctrine of substance and modes which Orobio strove (albeit not very effectively according to many) to overturn. To many, Orobio's refutation seemed to consist more of dismissive rhetoric than robust argument. In attacking "one substance," for example, Orobio professed to eschew past authorities "since Spinozists disdain all authority both divine and human," relying instead on the irresistible power of "reason." But his demonstration of how reason contradicts Spinoza, merely reiterates empty scholastic-sounding categories. "These new philosophers," held Orobio, referring to Spinoza, Cuffeler and Bredenburg, "proclaim principles and doctrines they do not properly understand, nor do they know how to correct the "fantasies" they call "demonstrations."[77] Bredenburg had failed to analyze Spinoza's "substance" properly, failing to perceive the error in Spinoza's proposition that it "is impossible there should be more than one substance," when uncovering that weakness is crucial. For "this dogma is firmly rooted in the hearts of Spinozists and the chief foundation of their errors," the basis especially of Spinoza's blasphemous doctrine that God and the totality of being are one. But in battling Spinoza's one-substance monism and seeking to demonstrate the reasonableness of *creatio ex nihilo* [creation from nothing], Orobio offered little more than the discarded neo-Aristotelian classifications of multiple substances still prevailing in Iberian universities, and assurances that God can depart from the "fixed order of nature" which Maimonides as well as Spinoza had denied.[78]

Orobio's argument relies chiefly on undermining the axiom, fundamental to Spinoza, Cuffeler and Bredenburg, that "nothing can come from nothing" [ex nihilo nihil fit]. This maxim was incorrectly construed by his opponents, held Orobio, to open the door wide to "atheism." For "something" and "nothing" are incommensurable, not logically equivalent or opposite categories, being altogether unlike and non-comparable. "Nothing" cannot be defined in an absolute sense but only as the absence of what is created. In logic, therefore, "nothing positive can be affirmed about not being," it being requisite for a positive proposition that there exist a genuine equivalence and comparability between subject and object. As nothing can be legitimately asserted about "not being," it cannot be logically ruled out that something can come from nothing where what is created did not exist before.[79] Happily, once Spinoza's pernicious interpretation of this proposition is refuted, "Spinoza's entire machine of atheism is entirely overthrown."[80]

THE REVOLUTIONARY "ISAAC OROBIO" OF 1770

Despite its anti-Spinoza purpose, Orobio's *Certamen*, after appearing only slightly doctored in Lenglet Dufresoy's collection, came to be more widely deployed for spreading than combating Spinoza's ideas. The real Orobio was an incisive foe of Christianity, a less incisive adversary of Spinoza, and no enemy of Judaism. The French clandestine literature's fabricated "Orobio," by contrast, fought Christianity *and* Judaism and was a furtive agent fomenting instead of combating Spinozism. To promote this concocted legend, an elaborate construct, an imagined Sephardic *philosophe,* in effect conflating the real Orobio with Spinoza, emerged in the early eighteenth century underground philosophical literature deliberately crafted as a kind of synthesis of the two. Under the invented name "Moïse Aboab", this fictitious Jewish *philosophe* steadfastly assailing all revealed religion, appeared first in the *Entretiens sur divers sujets* (Amsterdam, 1711) by the deist orientalist, once a Catholic convert to Calvinism, Mathurin Veyssière de La Croze (1661–1739).

A pure literary fabrication, La Croze's "Moise Aboab" is an unrelenting rationalist unbeliever, supposedly from Amsterdam, mirroring Spinoza by starting his pilgrimage through "la philosophie nouvelle" by learning Latin and studying Descartes intensively while reading Spanish poetry for relaxation.[81] Unlike Spinoza, interestingly, he nevertheless remains within and helps steer his community. After spending six years running a sugar plantation, supposedly, in the Dutch colony of Surinam, where he acquires his vast reading and becomes impressed with the New Testament,[82] this curious configuration "Aboab" [Orobio] shadowing Spinoza was admired by many freethinkers including the marquis d'Argens. The book reappeared in fresh editions in 1733, 1740, and at "Londres" in 1770, with the specifically "Jewish" part being separately published in a curious Dutch "conversionist" version, deleting Aboab's rejection of Christianity, at Amsterdam in 1757.

La Croze's 1711 dialogue between "Aboab" and the English freethinker "Bolingbroke" unfolds in Amsterdam. Having immersed himself in philosophy, theology, Latin and Greek, "Moïse Aboab" embarks on a long intellectual pilgrimage from Surinam to and across Europe. Repelled by the narrowness of Jewish life which he encounters in Poland, a country some call "le Paradis des Juifs" where Jewish men of learning "apply themselves solely to the Talmud and the other books of our nation" and few know anything else, for a time he is attracted to Christianity and decides to convert.[83] But on further researching Christianity and its dogmas, he finds he is even more repelled by this religion's irrationality, bigotry and compulsion to persecute than by Judaism. Shocked by the "idolatry" and intolerance of the Catholic and Greek Orthodox churches, and by all Christians' hatred of Jews, besides the endless feuding and divisions among Protestants and between Protestants and Catholics, he informs "Bolingbroke," these defects "m'en a dégouté" [disgusted me with it].[84] Impervious to Bolingbroke's entreaties to reconsider, Aboab resolves to seek salvation elsewhere.

Much of the content of the debate between La Croze's fictitious "Aboab" and the erudite "Mylorde Bolingbroke" is lifted from a manuscript entitled *Dissertation sur l'athéisme et sur les Athées* that was in part a literary echo of the real Orobio's efforts to stem the tide of Spinozism. But "Moise Aboab" also includes a fictive strand of the Amsterdam Sephardi poet Abraham Gómez Silveira (1656–1740) whose poetry had been burned by the Inquisition in Cadiz and who, fleeing from persecution in Spain, spent some time in Italy before migrating to Holland in the 1670s. In the years 1698–1700, the real Gómez Silveira had entered into a prolonged controversy with the Huguenot theologian Isaac Jaquelot (1647–1708), in Berlin, where La Croze had become royal librarian, vigorously disputing Jaquelot's ardent conviction that Jesus Christ was indeed the Messiah. In contradicting this Berlin Huguenot preacher, Gómez Silveira regurgitates many of Orobio's arguments against Christianity.[85]

Veyssière de La Croze, originally from Nantes, was a famously obese ex-Benedictine monk long residing in the renowned Parisian abbey of Saint-Germain-des-Près. Filled with doubt about Catholic teaching, he fled France, in 1697, and converted to Protestantism in Basel. Appointed librarian at the Prussian royal library, and a teacher at the Collège français de Berlin, this internationally recognized expert on Socinianism, Islam, Judaism, pantheism, Spinozism, deism and atheism figured among the foremost *érudits* during the age of Bayle and Leibniz, with both of whom he corresponded. Jokes circulated about his massiveness in every respect. It was from around the start of the eighteenth century, several observers noted—that is, following La Croze's arrival—that clandestine manuscripts of Jewish origin gained a footing among uprooted Huguenot refugees settled in Prussia. No one nurtured this process more, or was more fascinated by the material, than La Croze.[86]

The immediate background of the *Entretiens* was an untitled anonymous Portuguese manuscript composed in Amsterdam surviving in Jaquelot's collection and presented to La Croze, in August 1709. Unlike La Croze, who was decidedly more ambiguous, Jaquelot was keen to combat Orobio and the Jewish clandestine polemical literature, and became increasingly embattled in polemics with Sephardic scholars over whether Jesus *was* the Messiah and with both Socinian and Jewish savants over whether Jesus was also divine. Remembered today as a critic of Bayle, he was a firm proponent of the view he shared with Le Clerc and Locke that Christian truth rests securely on "reason." Before arriving in Berlin to serve the Huguenot community as pastor there, in 1702, Jaquelot had spent many years in Holland. It was there that an Amsterdam Jew presented him with the anonymous Portuguese text presumably in response to Jaquelot's vigorous conversionist efforts. In 1698, Jaquelot had published his *Dissertations sur le Messie* [Dissertations on the Messiah], which included sections rebutting the Karaite Isaac of Troki and other Jewish polemicists attacking Christian teaching.[87]

Jaquelot believed the unknown author of the manuscript he entrusted to La Croze, in 1709, was Orobio while La Croze disagreed because the text was in Portuguese, not Spanish. "An impious work to be sure," this Portuguese text was also exasperatingly "erudite." Comparing versions kept today in the Ets Haim Library in Amsterdam, Martin Mulsow discovered it is actually a text by Orobio's mentor, Moseh Raphael d'Aguilar.[88] La Croze entitled it *Liber blasphemus contra sanctissimam religionem nostrum scriptus Amstelodami, a Judaeo Lusitanus, lingua lusitana* [A Blasphemous Book against Our Most Holy Religion, Written at Amsterdam in Portuguese by a Portuguese Jew],[89] but rather deviously added an explanatory comment, declaring: "I once translated almost the whole work into Latin, but afterward, considering the matter more carefully, destroyed my nearly completed version owing to the innumerable blasphemies it contained."[90] Perhaps La Croze did consider burning it, but he did not actually do so, instead slipping it into furtive circulation among a network of other *érudits* in Germany, thereby further complicating the escalating furor over the suddenly proliferating but previously unheard of scourge of Jewish clandestine manuscripts in Iberian languages. In 1700, Gómez Silveira replied to Jaquelot's book in a Spanish tract that remained unpublished in manuscript but likewise circulated among restricted circles in Germany and Holland. It was known under the title *Dissertaciones sobre el Mesias, donde se prueba a los cristianos que J.C. no es el Mesias* [Dissertations on the Messiah in Which It Is Proved to the Christians That J.C. Is Not the Messiah].

No text claiming Jesus Christ was not the Messiah could then be published. But such tracts exerted a disturbing impact on more than a few beside Jaquelot and La Croze including the English theologian, Richard Kidder (1633–1703), from 1691 bishop of Bath. Eagerly endorsing Jaquelot's rationalist Christian stance, Bishop Kidder published his *Demonstration of the Messias against the Jews* (3 vols., London, 1699) seeking to refute Isaac of Troki and the author of yet another recently surfaced Portuguese Jewish assault on the Christian view, entitled *Porta veritatis* [The Gate of Truth], a manuscript Menasseh ben Israel had left with the Cambridge Platonist, Ralph Cudworth, in 1655, the year before Spinoza's expulsion from the synagogue in Amsterdam, during his visit to London.[91] Horrified by *Porta veritatis*, Kidder had kept it securely locked up at home, regarding it as the "greatest effort against Christianity that I ever saw in any language whatsoever." Kidder stipulated in his will, that "it be not sold to any private person, for any price how great soever, lest by that means it should be printed, without an answer, to the prejudice of Christianity. I rather will that it should be burnt, or given to some public library upon sufficient caution." It was neither to be transcribed nor lent out except to such readers as could be fully trusted.[92]

La Croze long pondered what to do with his unknown but undeniably dangerous anonymous Jewish text. Among learned colleagues to whom he confided his possessing the piece was the Leipzig theologian Christian Theophil Unger (1671–1719), an expert on Jewish-Christian polemics who then also tried to discover something more about it. A still more renowned German Hebraist, Johann Christoph Wolf (1683–1739), professor at the Hamburg Gymnasium since 1712 (who also owned copies of several of the Jewish clandestine manuscripts) was another in whom La Croze confided. Unaware that Orobio's mentor, Rabbi d'Aguilar, was the author, La Croze consulted Wolf about the text's possible authorship, calling it an outstanding example of Jewish polemical writing where Christ's miracles are likened to the delusions of "monks and nuns who often deceive the superstitious women of Spain and Portugal." Wolf could not identify the author either, but showed keen interest in the text and its provenance. Finally, in 1715, La Croze confided to Wolf that he had translated most of the Portuguese into Latin but remained unsure what he should do next as "no one wants to publish this dangerous and blasphemous book, in which the divine name of the Lord Jesus Christ is dishonored and vilified with the most shameless and caustic blasphemies and insults."[93]

A decade later, in 1725, La Croze lent "his" copy of d'Aguilar's text to Wolf, who was eager to study it more closely and, like Jaquelot, concluded Orobio was the author. Eventually, La Croze gave Wolf his copy as a gift (housed today in the Hamburg University Library). But where Wolf, like Kidder, genuinely tried to block diffusion of d'Aguilar's treatise, retaining it for scholarly use only, to prevent the public hearing of its arguments, in La Croze's hands, seemingly, additional copies were made and diffused. While such manuscripts remained exceedingly rare, observed Wolf, in the third volume of his authoritative *Bibliotheca Hebraea,* of 1727, "various of Orobio's manuscripts were circulating in the hands of the Jews" and represented a deadly challenge to Christianity. An expanded account of the manuscript appeared later, in the fourth volume of his *Bibliotheca Hebraea*, in 1733.[94]

Among those acquiring a transcript was the Polish Socinian pastor Samuel Crell (1660–1747), a learned foe of Christian mysteries such as the Trinity who spent much time traveling across northwest Europe disputing with Trinitarians. When discussing Old Testament passages referring to God and the Messiah, explained Crell, in a book repudiating the doctrine of Christ's possessing two natures that he published in 1726, he cited, much to La Croze's indignation, "eruditus quidam Judaeus in tractatu Lusitanica lingua" [a certain erudite Jew in a Portuguese-language treatise], declaring the Messiah could not be man and God at the same time even professing to be following Jewish reasoning as set out by the unnamed Portuguese author. No better illustration of how Sephardic anti-Christian manuscript polemics during the early eighteenth century, the era of the clandestine literature, fed unseen into the growing Unitarian and deistic literature which then further amplified the wider impact, could be found. Crell's book was published in England with the help and financial assistance of Collins and Matthew Tindal, two of the most notorious English freethinkers of the age.[95] Jews, Unitarians and freethinkers were now jointly perverting the Gospel's pure doctrine, complained La Croze to Wolf, insincerely probably, "with doctrines of which not even Muslims would approve."[96] Ostensibly appalled by Crell's book, in 1727 La Croze finally felt impelled (or so he claimed) to destroy his Latin rendering.

But if he really did so, his reaction came too late: during the 1730s, copies of d'Aguilar's text prepared by La Croze, Crell and others, began circulating more widely in Germany thereby further inflating the underground status of the Jew "Orobio."

The foremost authority on Orobio, Yosef Kaplan, holds that the only connection between "Aboab" and Orobio is an entirely superficial one amounting to nothing more than the allusion to Orobio in the amended title of the fourth edition of La Croze's text published in 1770 entitled *Entretiens sur divers sujets d'histoire et de religion entre Mylord Bolinbroke et Isaac d'Orobio, rabin des Juifs Portugais à Amsterdam*. This was a title doubtless inspired by the recent appearance of the reworking of several texts of Orobio by d'Holbach and Naigeon, under the title *Israel Vengé*.[97] But there is perhaps something more to the connection than that, for besides Gómez Silveira's reliance on Orobio, there were also other, even if decidedly convoluted, ties between the real Orobio and "Aboab." It was when La Croze had just begun wrestling with the Jewish polemical manuscripts that he first published his *Entretiens,* back in 1711. The book's high point is an encounter between a Huguenot and a Portuguese Jew in Amsterdam amounting to a fictive rerun of Orobio's 1683 debate with Van Limborch except now, for the first time in modern literature, a fictitious Jewish philosopher becomes the voice of a deist spokesman represented as acute, wise and upright, a kind of "Nathan der Weise" *avant la lettre.* He emerges here as a bold and outspoken accuser of modern Christendom for its damaging and negative effects on society, echoing Orobio in rebuking Christians for their tyranny, intolerant zeal, persecution, corruption, repressive dogmatism, and bigotry.

Whatever the ex-Benedictine defector's real views about Christianity, La Croze was undoubtedly wracked by nagging doubts and perplexity and, by 1711, realized there was something perverse in the contemporary Christian view of the Jews as intellectually backward and irrelevant to contemporary erudition. Having rejected traditional Judaism and detesting the endless feuding among the Christian churches (as well as their collective persecution of the Jews), his "Aboab," declares himself disgusted with both religions and, like Spinoza, De Prado and "Orobio," pointedly seeks salvation in philosophy instead.[98] The figure of Orobio here fuses with the unknown "Judaeus Lusitanus" and the author of the *Porta veritatis* into an underground tradition that convinced La Croze the chain of major Jewish philosophers had not ended with Maimonides or Spinoza, and that the contemporary Portuguese Jewish intellectual world transplanted to

Amsterdam posed a fundamental challenge of formidable power and incisiveness to all Christendom, despite the complete failure of Christian contemporaries to realize it.[99]

La Croze's "Moise Aboab" is a literary-philosophical device for attacking religious intolerance and bigotry, and eulogizing calm, dispassionate and erudite discussion of religion. "Aboab" is also intended as a tool to weaken conventional theological assumptions embedded in Christian society. The centrality of Orobio in La Croze's construct only grew more pronounced in subsequent decades. His book reappeared in new editions in 1733 and 1740 and, and yet again in 1770 as we have seen, now tellingly styled *Entretiens* between *Mylord Bolingbroke et Isaac d'Orobio, rabin des Juifs portugais à Amsterdam*, for the first time making the multilayered allusions to Orobio explicit.[100] Not the least of its subversive ploys was its incorporating a long account of "athéisme de système" [systematic philosophical atheism] as a powerful threat to all revealed religion, attributing the first coherent statement of this early modern new and more sophisticated form of atheism to Giordano Bruno and then remarking that Bruno's principles show "une grande conformité avec ceux de Spinosa" [great conformity with those of Spinoza], God being equated with Nature, or rather the infinitely "extended being" that acts from necessity through all eternity.[101]

Another revealing insight into Orobio de Castro's increasingly merged real and fictitious presence in French clandestine radical thought by the 1740s, is provided by one of the foremost anti-*philosophe* attacks on the role of "philosophy" in the early eighteenth century, the Abbé Houtteville's *La Religion chrétienne prouvée par les faits* [The Christian Religion Proved by the Facts], a book first published in 1722. The earliest edition of what became an exceptionally widely diffused work features no discussion of Orobio whatever. But from the 1740 edition onwards, Orobio and the power of his unpublished manuscripts becomes a component of this Catholic apologetic work. "If it is necessary to take account of some of those who most directly rose up against us during the last century," adds Houtteville, in 1740, after discussing Hobbes and Spinoza, "I would particularly consider what the famous jurist Jean Bodin and the Jew Orobio opposed us with. Both were erudite; I do not wish to contest their merit. But both the one and the other had very little exactitude of mind so that it does not seem the art of reasoning was the principal, or even one of their main talents. In judging thus, I beg all my readers to believe I speak with candor and directness, without a controversialist's bias. This willingness I would not need to request if everyone could decide about this, as I myself can, after reading manuscript copies that are conserved in some cabinets."[102]

Like earlier reviewers, Houtteville argues that in their 1683 Amsterdam debate Van Limborch triumphantly defeated Orobio's arguments "with force." Christianity unquestionably conquered, Orobio being worsted at every step. Still, their dispute could hardly be said to be over. At several points Houtteville wished Van Limborch had been "encore plus pressant" [even more pressing]. What troubled him despite his confidence in Van Limborch's victory was that while Orobio's manuscripts all remained unpublished, precisely their being generally unavailable, found only in the "cabinets" of a few exclusive bibliophiles, their very clandestinity, was preserving, no matter how undeservedly, even amplifying Orobio's outrageous Jewish slights against Christianity. Plainly, the very fact Orobio's anti-Christian texts remained unpublished was helping the manipulated, reworked "Orobio" of the French freethinkers to usurp his real profile and inflate into the formidable fictitious force it had now become.[103]

La Croze's "Orobio" in turn became the chief inspiration for the marquis d'Argens's imaginary Jewish philosopher who severely rebukes Christendom in his *Lettres Juives*. Unlike Voltaire, who placed Judaism and Enlightenment in direct antagonism to each other and scorned modern-day Jews—though not Orobio, whose anti-Christian arguments he praised[104]—d'Argens considered Judaism in its potentially reformed, purged version (with its Talmudic and rabbinic baggage largely eliminated) not just compatible with a commendably enlightened attitude but an apt vehicle for advancing Enlightenment based on anti-theological "philosophy."[105] Like Leydekker, Bayle and Bolingbroke, d'Argens depicts the ancient Jewish Sadducees as a key element in the debate. He presents them as pure philosophical rationalists excluding all *supernaturalia* for whom Judaism functioned as a potent engine of reason readily turned against the anti-*philosophisme* and irrationality of Talmud, rabbinic authority and tradition, a group emphatically rejecting belief in the soul's immortality, angels, demons, Satan, and all spirits separate from bodies.[106] The Sadducees' successors, held d'Argens, were the medieval Karaites—Jewish rebels against rabbinic authority likewise much favored by the underground radical tendency he championed.

D'Argens reflected real trends present in the early Jewish Enlightenment, especially in Holland, and simultaneously envisaged a modern "reformed Judaism" *avant la lettre* that would prove philosophical and unremittingly anti-rabbinic. This construct he considered a powerful weapon against theologians, academics and polemicists defending the old order. It was a vision of Jewish modernity, of how to reform Judaism, that would benefit the Jews and all of society. This vision he propagated first in Holland, and then, following his move to Berlin, in 1741, at the court of Frederick the Great of Prussia. It was d'Argens who set the first substantive Jewish enlightener in Germany, Aaron Salomon Gumperz (1723–1769), on his path to philosophical Enlightenment, a move from which much followed: "it was through my association with Herr Aaron Gumpertz who later became a doctor of medicine (he died some years ago in Hamburg)," the foremost early figure of the Berlin Jewish High Enlightenment, Mendelssohn, later recorded, in an autobiographical note, "that I acquired a taste for secular higher studies [die Wissenschaften]."[107]

Gumpertz, possessing considerable knowledge of rabbinic learning and medieval Jewish philosophy, in or around 1742 began studying secular subjects and learning Latin. He came to the attention of d'Argens, who, having exalted purified "Karaite" Judaism as essentially a deistic creed appropriate for cleansing the eighteenth century of irrational nonsense, adopted Gumpertz as his Jewish representative, standard-bearer, "secretary" and protégé with the deliberate aim of rendering him an instrument of Jewish reform and enlightenment. Obtaining his doctorate in medicine from the University of Frankfurt an der Oder, in 1751, Gumpertz practiced medicine first in Berlin and then Hamburg. He was the first German Jewish example of a reforming enlightener who remained fully active in Jewish community life, eulogizing and pursuing modern science and secular learning and gaining a reputation among the Berlin public while preaching innovation and reform within the Jewish community, an example Mendelssohn always prized and venerated and that helped set him on his historic course.

Introduced by d'Argens to the Berlin "Monday Club," a select coterie dedicated to pursuing literature and Enlightenment, it was in this milieu that Gumpertz encountered the young German playwright Gotthold Ephraim Lessing (1729–1781). Sharing a common passion for the theater, they became friends. Both d'Argens and Gumpertz then in turn helped shape in Lessing's mind the ideal infusing his groundbreaking and soon notorious play *The Jews* (1749), a drama that openly promotes d'Argens's "Jewish" program. Owing to its unprecedented, undisguised philosemitic attitude, it was a piece bound to elicit protests from all sides when first performed. Objected to with particular indignation was its presenting Jews as exemplary instances of the highest moral caliber and conduct.[108] In 1753, Gumpertz produced an anonymous text, "A Jew Writing to a Philosopher with the Answer," examining the reasons for continuing exclusion of the Jews from civil liberties and arguing that because Christians and Jews possess the "same capacities of body and mind," denying Jews civil rights would only further entrench their narrowness, isolation and ignorance. Granting civil rights, on the other hand, would cause these undesirable negative traits to wither and disappear.[109] Here was the germ of the argument Mendelssohn and his ally, Christian Wilhelm von Dohm, were powerfully to revive in the German public sphere decades later, in the 1780s, when launching their public campaign for Jewish emancipation and equality. Theirs was a vision that owed more than a little to d'Argens's philosophical philosemitism, just as d'Argens's philosemitism can be traced back, in part, to the legacy of La Croze and "Orobio." In the end, though, having drawn a first sketch of the project, Gumpertz failed to live up to his own and d'Argens's expectations. Afflicted by various illnesses and becoming deeply depressed, he proved unable to carry his reform project any further and in his last years sank into obscurity.

The publishing *anno mirabilis* of the Radical Enlightenment was, without doubt, the year 1770, the year of d'Holbach's *Système de la nature* and Raynal's *Histoire philosophique des Deux Indes*, when the two most widely known and generally divisive radical texts of the later Enlightenment both burst onto the scene. The year 1770 proved Radical Enlightenment had ceased to be a mere clandestine underground unnoticed by all but a handful, and become the major shaping factor in the revolutionary consciousness of the later eighteenth century. And in that year too appeared the culminating recapitulation of "Orobio" and his attacks on amalgamated Judeo-Christian religious authority, supposedly at "London" (in fact at Amsterdam), as we have seen, under the title *Israel Vengé, ou Exposition naturelle des prophéties hébraiques que les chrétiens appliquent à Jésus, leur prétendu Messie.* Par ISAAC OROBIO (à Londres, 1770). Due to the touching up and imposture practiced by d'Holbach and his assistant, Naigeon, in producing this text, it tends to be dismissed as just an inauthentic literary fabrication. But this is to miss the point. For precisely due to the input of d'Holbach and Naigeon, it became one of the most sustained, vehement and detailed attacks on Christianity, its doctrines, conduct and clergy ever published, a major milestone in d'Holbach's career as a front-rank Radical Enlightenment crypto-republican,[110] as well as anti-Christian subversive and hence landmark of the eighteenth century. A key text of 243 pages, it appeared unambiguously under the name of "Isaac Orobio," and in the "Avis de l'éditeur" preceding the preface not only recounts the real Orobio's life story but reaffirms and expands many of his essential arguments as originally stated in the 1687 *Amica Collatio.*

The author, explains the "Avis de l'éditeur," was a "Spanish Jew named Isaac Orobio" who, having studied "scholastic philosophy" in Spain, grew so skilled philosophically that he was appointed to lecture at Salamanca, after which he became a physician in Seville. Suspected of Judaism, he was hurled into Inquisition dungeons and suffered three years of "torture worthy of the barbarism of that infamous tribunal." Escaping to France, he became a professor of medicine at Toulouse, but "tired of the need he was under to dissimulate the religion he deemed the true one, doubtless rendered even dearer to him by Christian ill-treatment," he finally transferred to Amsterdam where, after being circumcised, he could openly profess Judaism. Having composed his text in his own language, it was rendered into French by a Jew called Henriquez, using the author's original manuscript (which had never been published) "at the request of a literary man, living in Holland: this person appears to have retouched or corrected the translation."[111]

Christians, the book's preface states tersely, base their religion, their belief in Christ as the Messiah, on the 53rd chapter of the Book of Isaiah. Even though the doctors of the different churches disagree about almost everything else in their rival theologies, they all agree as to the clarity, certainty and completeness with which this chapter prophesies "everything that Jesus Christ has suffered to expiate the sins of the human race, everything that is contained in the Gospels."[112] D'Holbach's fictitious "Orobio" then recites in detail all the reasons the real Orobio de Castro set out in his unpublished work, and in the *Amica Collatio,* as to why no rational being can doubt that the Christian theologians, with their inadequate Hebrew and historical knowledge, all hopelessly muddled, misunderstood, misinterpreted and misused the crucial passages. Nothing could be more confused than to suppose the Messiah promised to Israel as the bringer of peace and unity to the world in the Old Testament, and as the transformer and reformer of the world, is one and the same being as God. Pouring scorn on the idea Christianity brought greater order, harmony and moral quality to the world, "Orobio" asks: "have the Christians been more united by seeking to usurp what did not belong to them, and appropriating the name of the people chosen by God? Do they dare say they enjoy the peace, tranquility and general union promised and that the Messiah they adore without question should have procured for them?"

After their Redeemer's death, Christians were oppressed by pagan Rome for three centuries. Christian martyrology relates the persecution and torments its believers had to suffer. But since then, the Greek Orthodox Church continued to be persecuted by the Turks. In the year 1770, all of humanity remains mired in misery, disorder and the violent dissensions unceasingly dividing the warring sects wracking the Christian world. Protestants condemn Catholics for idolatry and other abuses; if they are right, for 1,200 years "Christianity has been plunged in idolatry while submitting to the authority of the Pope." Catholics denounce the "error and blindness of the heretics," "detest Luther and Calvin" and pronounce Armenians and Muscovites "schismatics," while in Africa, "the only part of the world that at first generally embraced Christianity," today one finds scarcely any Christian vestige. In modern [North] Africa, Islam alone rules supreme. Muslims say they cannot understand how God can be put in the womb of a woman so as to become a man and that anyway it is impossible He should die; they rightly boast more believers than the Christians likewise in Asia. "Can one pretend, despite such incontestable proofs against, the true Messiah has really come while men enjoy none of the benefits temporal or spiritual his coming supposedly promised?"[113]

"Nothing is more wretched," concludes "Orobio," "in the eyes of all the nations than the people of Israel in its present state." Nothing could be clearer than that Isaiah 53 is a divine promise to the Children of Israel that God will end their misfortunes and sufferings. But the Jews, "far from being delivered from misery and their afflictions remain dispersed around the world; they are more dispersed at present than they were six centuries before the coming of the pretended Messiah of the Christians." In fact the Second Captivity following Titus's destruction of the Second Temple "has been much tougher than the first" one prophesied by Isaiah.[114] Christians themselves admit the "Jews have become the opprobrium of all the nations due to the sentence they pronounced against Jesus Christ." The coming of the pretended Messiah has brought no benefits. The notion the Messiah, the very symbol of innocence, died voluntarily to save mankind, to procure from God, at the cost of his own life, pardon for men's sins is not just "diametrically opposed to reason" but makes nonsense of the task of putting the world in better order. Killing the just to let the criminal go free would "overthrow the order of nature, authorize crime and fill the world with horror." If a just man offered to die to save a criminal would any tribunal on earth consider that at all reasonable?[115]

In short, concludes *Israel Vengé*, humanity and the world are in utter disarray, and for this hopeless disorder and moral decay the churches, together with kings and aristocracy, bear the chief responsibility. The "people of Israel is justly called 'the man of suffering' [l'homme de douleurs], because no-one could undergo more cruel sufferings and martyrdom than they have undergone since their captivity. Their misfortunes are great, they are scattered throughout the world, they scarcely have any place where they can observe in tranquility the Law the Lord delivered to them on Mount Sinai."[116] Their miseries are so manifest to all the world that it is useless to detail them. There are no more insupportable miseries than those which, in the name of Christ, the hatred and contempt of the nations heaped upon the Jews.[117]

FOUR

The Destabilizing Reverberations of the Early *Haskalah*

Mendelssohn, the presiding figure of the Jewish Enlightenment, in his youth called "Moshe Ben Mendel Dessau," was the son of a poor Torah scribe in Dessau named Mendel. As a boy, intended for the rabbinate, he followed his local rabbi David ben Naphtali Fränkel (1704–1762), when the latter was appointed chief rabbi in Berlin, in 1742, walking the entire way from Dessau to the Prussian capital. Traditional study of Torah, Talmud and rabbinics he combined thenceforth with Latin, philosophy, mathematics and modern languages. There were prospects for studious poor Jewish youth in Berlin, and Mendelssohn developed into a polished, sought-after tutor to sons of the wealthy Berlin Jewish elite. What proved harder and finally highly problematic were his tireless efforts to fuse Enlightenment ideas with Jewish tradition and build a viable, stable, modernized platform for Jewish religious modernity and post-ghetto identity.

Crucial to Mendelssohn's emergence as the first major modern Jewish thinker (aside from Spinoza) was his encounter, we have seen, as a youth, in Berlin, with d'Argens's Ashkenazic protégé, Aaron Salomon Gumpertz (1723–1769). Descended from a renowned Rhenish family of rabbis and likewise first entering into the world of eighteenth-century secular learning as an autodidact, Gumpertz took his own early steps researching in his father's extensive library. In Berlin, Gumpertz was instructed in mathematics and natural science, and inspired by Israel Zamosc (c. 1700–1772), from near Lvov, who had moved to Berlin after years at Zamość and after publishing a remarkable Hebrew text, *Netsah Yisrael* (The Eternity of Israel) (1741), exalting Maimonides and claiming revelation and belief stand above reason and science but, equally, insisting modern mathematics and science must be incorporated into Jewish erudition and tradition to correct often erroneous still prevailing assumptions (such as that the world is flat) abounding in the medieval Hebrew literature. In traditional Polish Jewish circles, his 1741 publication gained Zamosc the reputation of being a rebellious subversive, but this rendered him appealing to the studious element of Berlin Jewish youth.

By the mid-1740s Gumpertz had polished his spoken and written German and made contacts among the Berlin German and Huguenot intellectual elites. Attending formal medical courses at the Berlin Collegium medico-chirurgicum on Unter den Linden, Berlin's most prestigious street, he witnessed dissections in its *theatrum anatomicum,* made friends and spent years engrossed in the latest medical studies, intending a career as a physician among the Berlin Jewish elite. Steeped in up-to-date medicine, he enrolled as a student at the Prussian state University of Frankfurt an der Oder in May 1750, graduating in under year with an M.D., in March 1751.[1] He never practiced as a physician, though, but, instead, after preparing ritual calendars for the Berlin Jewish community for a time, served from 1751 to 1754 as personal secretary to Pierre Louis Moreau de Maupertuis (1698–1759), one of the foremost scientific writers of the age and president of Frederick the Great's Académie Royale des Sciences et Belles-Lettres. If Zamosc first stimulated aspiring young Berlin Jewish intellectuals to study mathematics, science and Leibnizian-Wolffian philosophy, it was Gumpertz who created a circle and encouraged the young Mendelssohn to acquire proficiency in French, Latin and philosophy and establish meaningful connections with non-Jewish *érudits* as a path by which to combine modernity with traditional Jewish learning, socially and culturally as well as intellectually.

Via Gumpertz, Mendelssohn made numerous contacts at venues like the Joachimsthaler Gymnasium, as the later French revolutionary leader Mirabeau relates in his eulogy of Mendelssohn, of October 1784,[2] and discovered the world of the Berlin's French philosophical celebrities—d'Argens, Maupertuis and La Mettrie. Most probably, it was also Gumpertz who, in 1753 or 1754, first introduced Mendelssohn to the already noted young dramatist Gotthold Ephraim Lessing (1729–1781), an encounter that would prove the most decisive of Mendelssohn's life.[3] Lessing and Mendelssohn became close friends and allies, and remained such for the rest of their lives. Among other reforms they discussed early on, was what became a joint venture to transform the public image of their soon common hero, Spinoza, to salvage what they considered his unjustly condemned philosophical legacy from general opprobrium and recrimination.

Gumpertz and Mendelssohn both suffered from and resented what the latter called the "most bitter hatred" of the Christians. Aged just twenty, the same age as Mendelssohn, Lessing proved a revelation to him, being already renowned, even notorious, throughout Germany for his comedy *Die Juden* [The Jews] (1749), a play rooted in conversations with d'Argens and Gumpertz, and reading such works as d'Argens's *Lettres Juives* directly challenging conventional assumptions and thinking. Lessing's play created a stir, outraging many, including such prominent figures as Johann David Michaelis (1717–1791), Germany's most renowned professor of Bible studies and ancient Judaism. By claiming the moral caliber of modern Jews, far from being despicably debased, is actually identical to that of Christians and, in individual cases not infrequently superior, Lessing's play, Mendelssohn soon grasped, though intended to assist, in a way rendered the Jews' position still more precarious than it was already. Discussing the play with Gumpertz by letter, in June 1754, Mendelssohn expressed anxiety lest Lessing had presented too glowing an image of Jewish integrity, posing an over-correction not wholly corresponding to reality that risked rebounding on the Jews by intensifying prejudice and hatred further.[4]

If Gumpertz introduced Mendelssohn to Lessing, Mendelssohn introduced Lessing to Spinoza.[5] In his first substantial text, the *Philosophische Gespräche* (1755), which Lessing helped get published, Mendelssohn sought to refashion Spinoza's image by presenting him not as the philosophical monster and universal threat routinely denounced by churchmen but as a key herald and precursor of the Leibnizian-Wolffian system, then the dominant philosophical orthodoxy in German and Swedish universities. By allegedly first formulating Leibniz's concept of "pre-established harmony," explaining how substances interact following fixed laws without inherently interacting, through divine direction, Spinoza supposedly performed a vital formative function in initiating Leibnizianism and hence in shaping modern German philosophy.[6] According to Leibniz's *harmonie préétablie*, made more systematic and applied across the board by Christian Wolff (1679–1754), turning it into a fixed institution of the German, Scandinavian and (at Petersburg)

Russian academic establishment, every "substance" affects only itself, but all substances, all spiritual entities and matter, including man's soul and body, function as if causally interacting, being pre-programmed by God to "harmonize" with each other. It was a novel way of explaining the world's apparent causal unity, harmony and order under divine direction. "Being not only the greatest but most prudent of philosophers," Leibniz borrowed this key idea, argued Mendelssohn, from Spinoza's parallelism but without admitting the fact.[7] Mendelssohn remained personally always convinced of the superiority of the Leibnizian-Wolffian philosophy over the other Western philosophical traditions reconciling reason and faith while integrating body and mind more closely than did Cartesianism.

Mendelssohn's own budding system likewise aimed to accommodate elements of Spinoza safely defused and embedded within a Leibnizian wrapping friendly to religion, resolving the age-old mind-body divide by explaining interaction of bodies and spirits in Leibnizian-Wolffian terms. From Mendelssohn's reconciling Spinoza with Leibniz,[8] Spinoza, it followed, had been unjustly treated by Jews and Christians alike, perpetuating a reprehensible injustice causing "impartial minds to regard [Spinoza] as the insulted party and magnanimously take his side." Of all Spinoza's innumerable critics and adversaries, contended Mendelssohn, "only the venerable Wolff, at Halle, was not subject to this reproach."[9] Reviewing his text, in March 1755, Lessing wholeheartedly concurred with his ally's innovative perspective on Spinoza's relationship to Leibniz and Wolff, agreeing Leibniz was not, after all, the "inventor" of the pre-established harmony, Spinoza having preceded him here by eighteen years.[10]

MENDELSSOHN'S ENLIGHTENMENT

It was a stance Mendelssohn subsequently always adhered to that fitted his own wider commitment to combining science and philosophy with natural theology and the need, as he saw it, to harmonize natural theology with empirical knowledge and, as an extension of this, Judaism with reason.[11] If one of Mendelssohn's aims was to salvage something of Spinoza's deeply mired reputation by suggesting that whatever his errors concerning God, Creation and the soul, he had provided an essential stepping-stone to understanding the relationship of minds and bodies, his intervention also meant Spinoza helped Leibniz and Wolff build their definitive, supposedly enduring philosophical canon, now dominating all German higher education, implying that what was best in German thought, Leibnitio-Wolffianism, in fact, fused Jewish and German elements. Declaring Spinoza integral to mainstream tradition of German thinking and modern Jewish thought alike, however indigestible to many, was a claim from which Mendelssohn never retreated: this modern Jewish-German intellectual tradition rooted in Spinoza and Leibniz, and the doctrine of pre-established harmony, he judged altogether profounder than both Locke's empiricism and French and d'Holbachian materialism.

Lessing, on the other hand, did not long stay satisfied with his initial response to the *Philosophische Gespräche* or Mendelssohn's accommodating perspective. Developing his concept of philosophy as a useful reforming tool in German culture, he resumed study of Spinoza's key philosophical texts during his years as secretary to the Breslau garrison commander (1760–65), reexamining the *Ethics* closely. Taking up the issue of Leibnitio-Wolffianism's relation to Spinozism again in his essay *Durch Spinoza ist Leibniz nur auf die Spur der vorherbestimmten Harmonie gekommen* [Only through Spinoza Did Leibniz Arrive at the Pre-established Harmony], he re-opened the question directly with Mendelssohn, in April 1763. "It *was* Spinoza," Lessing still agreed, "who led Leibniz to the *vorherbestimmte Harmonie*";[12] but he now qualified his former stance by adding that Spinoza's conception of body and mind, as distinct manifestations of the same single reality, obviates all need for a theory like Leibniz's of a pre-existing harmony established by God. Spinozism removes all requirement for a theory explaining the connection between minds and the physical world. It is the axiomatic separation of body and soul in Leibniz, urged Lessing, his and Wolff's need to create space for *supernaturalia* and immortality of the soul, that moved Leibniz to introduce his divine master-plan of pre-established harmony, and eventually indivisible monads, to explain how God's intentions synchronize body and spirit, permeating physical reality at every level.

"By means of his pre-established harmony, Leibniz seeks to solve the puzzle of how two such different things as body and soul can be unified; Spinoza, contrariwise, perceives no distinction between them [body and soul], and hence no [need for] union, and no puzzle needing a solution."[13] The gulf between Leibniz's and Spinoza's conceptions Lessing vividly conveyed with his simile of two primitive savages gazing for the first time at their own reflections in a mirror. Once over the initial shock, they try to explain this amazing phenomenon. As the mirror image makes exactly the same movements as a real body, and in the same order, sequences seen in reality and in the mirror must have an identical cause. But where one thinks the two things are separate but somehow synchronized by a higher mind, the other thinks body and image, despite appearances, are somehow one and the same.[14] Lessing's conclusion undercuts pre-established harmony implying the intrinsic superiority of Spinoza's unitary solution to the mind-body problem. Here Lessing and Mendelssohn began to diverge significantly in their respective approaches—at least on the surface.

At the same time, as emerges from the Mendelssohn and Lessing exchange of letters about Spinoza's theory of the affections, during the summer 1757, Mendelssohn admired also other aspects of Spinoza's thought, deeming (like many others) his analysis of the emotions unrivalled in penetrative power.[15] Through the early and mid-1760s, after first discussing it with Lessing, in Berlin, in 1760, Mendelssohn slowly composed the text that would win him renown across Europe, securing his reputation as a leading philosopher. His most successful book, his *Phaedon* (1767), built on Leibniz, Wolff and Alexander Baumgarten,[16] presented a theory rejected by Lessing (who continued to adhere to Spinoza's conflation of body and mind), that reverses Spinoza's monism (reduction of everything to one single substance, meaning that everything is subject to the same fixed, unchanging set of causal laws), pivoting on the separateness, incorruptibility and immortality of the soul. *Phaedon* received exceptionally high praise in published reviews and private discussion from celebrities such as Isaak Iselin (1728–1782), a leading Enlightenment figure in Switzerland and, initially, also Herder, whose own encounter with Spinoza's thought commenced in the late 1760s, first with the Bible criticism, then, in the early 1770s, with Spinoza's political thought, and finally, from the mid-1770s, the *Ethics*. Reprinted many times, esteemed as a bulwark against French materialism as well as Spinoza, *Phaedon* appeared in succession also in Dutch (1769), French (1772) and Danish (1779), becoming one of the standard tools of the age for reconciling natural theology and philosophy. With this, Mendelssohn seemingly nailed his colors unequivocally to the moderate Enlightenment, reconciling philosophy and science with religious authority and the social status quo. It soon transpired, though, that this was not the whole story.[17]

The existing moral order is indissolubly linked to the soul's immortality, insists Mendelssohn, arguing that "a thinking whole" cannot arise from "unthinking parts." "Immortality of the soul," though not central to traditional Judaism itself, and completely absent from the Hebrew Bible, remained an essential pivot of Mendelssohn's thought. It was through harmonizing religion and philosophy that Mendelssohn emerged as a front-rank champion of Germany's moderate mainstream, achieving a uniquely enviable status for a Jewish newcomer that he retained for the rest of his life and proved a major asset for German Jewry more broadly. "Moderation," reconciling religion and philosophy, was indeed indispensable to a leading Jewish intellectual figure at the time;[18] there was no other path to an acceptable profile in the public world of the Enlightenment. Nevertheless, there remained something slightly suspect, according to some, about Mendelssohn's strategy, resoundingly successful until the mid-1780s. Was his stance really one of "moderation"? *Phaedon* earned its author the sobriquet the "German Socrates" and made him the Jewish Enlightenment's foremost symbol in a seemingly uncontroversial non-divisive manner that may, however, have veiled a hidden underlay more aligned with Lessing, Spinozism and the underground radical tendency undermining religious authority than first appeared.[19]

Ostensibly, Mendelssohn repudiated Spinoza, La Mettrie, Diderot, d'Holbach and Helvétius. Yet his closest friend and public ally, the man who since d'Argens was the most active in salvaging the Jewish people's moral standing, defending them amidst a sea of hostility, in private discussion, placed Leibniz's doctrine of the soul under a question mark while rebutting the entire Leibnizian-Wolffian scheme of metaphysics and natural theology.[20] Others too, Herder among them, were growing doubtful about the Leibnizian approach's cogency. "With you and most philosophers and theologians liberation from sensual perceptions," he granted, writing to Mendelssohn, early in 1769, "is potential spiritual perfection from which the rewards of the future condition derive," and yet one must ask: "what is a soul liberated from all sensual perceptions, and what is a purely spiritual perfection" in a human soul? "I must confess: I do not know."[21] Like Lessing, and soon Goethe, Herder denied that a de-sensualized soul is a meaningful concept, or that it aids human happiness to attempt to conceptualize such a thing.

Mendelssohn may genuinely have believed in the soul's immortality along with a knowing God and divine providence,[22] though this is not certain, and did insist on the indispensability of Leibniz and Wolff for defending the respectability and viability of Enlightenment reform, including his plea for greater toleration and freedom for the Jews. Without the soul's immortality there was no philosophical basis for a natural theology acceptable to Christianity and Judaism alike. Leibnizian-Wolffian metaphysics robustly upheld shielded one from Christian theologians and rabbis simultaneously. As a

Jewish philosopher seeking to establish himself in the 1760s and 1770s and rehabilitate Judaism in a hostile world, his overall strategy would be implausible without adhering to a Leibnizian stance and opposing Lessing's and Herder's more accurate view of Spinoza's relationship to Leibniz. For an irenic spirit aiming at Jewish-Christian reconciliation and a respected Jewish Enlightenment combining orthodoxy and observance with emancipation and Jewish rights, nothing would be more fatal than being revealed by mainstream "Christian" Enlightenment antisemitism to be a subversive promoting an enlightened Judaism and Jewish aspirations and hopes while secretly advancing materialism and Spinozism.[23] Hence his unwavering insistence that Leibniz's system (and as he claimed, later), Lessing's, represented "purified Spinozism."[24]

Lessing, meanwhile, gravitated inexorably toward Spinozistic monism, as was further indicated by his 1763 fragment *Über die Wirklichkeit der Dinge ausser Gott* [On the Reality of Things outside God]. If "in the concept which God has of the reality of a thing, everything is present that is to be found in its reality outside him, then the two realities are one, and everything supposed to exist outside God exists in God."[25] Hence, nothing can be outside God. Rejecting dualistic conceptions of the God-world relationship, Lessing, while still speaking of "natural religion," by this time seems no longer to have been a positive deist in any meaningful sense; he no longer conceived "natural religion" like Voltaire, Turgot, Mendelssohn or Reimarus as a divinely created universal system of physical laws, species, spiritual entities and morality. Rather morality and natural theology for him were now anchored in the universal, unalterable, eternal laws of the nature of things.

Lessing's Spinozism hardened his thesis that there is no connection whatever between moral worth and theology, that faith in one creed rather than another contributes nothing to the true moral order. To assume a Christian belongs to a higher moral order than a Jew or Muslim by reason of his or her faith, he concluded, amounts merely to the crassest prejudice. His post-1760 radicalism was clearly connected with his growing dismay at how little in the way of social and educational amelioration was actually emerging in the Prussia of the 1760s and 1770s. If serfdom, noble privilege, intolerance, intrusive censorship, authoritarian ecclesiastical institutions and highly defective education were still everywhere the rule, so were Jewish disabilities and formalized discrimination against Jewish society. The Enlightenment was undoubtedly transforming central and eastern Europe in innumerable ways under the sway of the three most renowned "enlightened despots" of the age—Frederick the Great of Prussia (r. 1740–86); Catherine II of Russia (r. 1762–96); and the Habsburg Emperor Joseph II (r. 1780–90). But the net result, if far from minimal, was nonetheless glaringly defective and problematic. How is mankind to forge a just moral order underpinning legislation based on an authentic ethics anchored in a philosophically cogent universal system rather than belief, theology and priestly authority? Here Spinoza's perspectives seemed uniquely relevant to Lessing, as to Herder, Diez, Ewald, Knoblauch, Wekhrlin and Bahrdt, and perhaps also Mendelssohn even though he was publicly committed to the Leibnizian-Wolffian legacy.

Radical Enlightenment and modernizing Jewish aspiration most closely converged in Mendelssohn's world in his and the radicals' critique of Frederick the Great's *Aufklärung*. Reputedly the very acme of toleration, Frederick enjoyed a mostly if not wholly positive reputation in European enlightened circles until around 1770. But during the 1770s, the glowingly positive image of *le roi philosophe* began wearing thin. This was reflected especially in critiques propagated by the radical circles around Lessing, the future French revolutionary leader Mirabeau and also the German enlightener Christian Wilhelm Dohm (1751–1820) (behind the scenes), and Heinrich Friedrich Diez (1751–1817), the latter a Prussian diplomat, champion of press freedom and, at this time, Spinozist radical enlightener (he changed later), even keener on equal Jewish rights than Dohm.[26]

FIGHTING FOR JEWISH EMANCIPATION

A temporary French visitor in Berlin, Mirabeau could afford to be the most outspoken; the others were more muffled to begin with, but no less cutting. Frederick was unwilling to treat his subjects as independent-minded, mature individuals, explained Dohm publicly years later, but aimed to forge a hierarchical, noble-dominated and dependent society wholly subject not just to the crown but also the nobility, especially the military and diplomatic nobility.[27] A notably ugly feature to some, wholly at odds with his vaunted toleration, was his aversion and stringent policy toward the Jews. His unenlightened views in this regard were caustically commented on by Diderot, Dohm, Brissot, Cloots, Mirabeau and the radical-minded Spanish American revolutionary Francisco de Miranda while in Berlin, in 1785. Privately, nobody was more aware of Frederick's hierarchical mentality, arrogance and antisemitism than Mendelssohn.

Frederick cared little for Christianity or churchmen. But Jewish tradition had rendered the Jews so manifestly deficient in precisely the qualities he wished to inculcate into Prussian society—deference, military prowess, discipline, veneration of the army, loyalty to state and crown—that he deemed it impossible to integrate them usefully into Prussian society, and inadvisable to remove the rigorous discriminatory barriers long maintained against them.[28] Frederick strictly enforced the existing work and residence codes on the Jewish majority, marginalizing them within Prussia while rigorously restricting Jewish immigration from Poland and Lithuania. He continued the limited toleration, and business and residence rights, accorded to a small wealthy elite in his capitals—Berlin, Königsberg and Breslau (Wroclaw)—those amply contributing to state coffers, or in some other fashion, like prominent intellectual figures such as Mendelssohn and Markus Herz. But even that concession was grudging. Securing Mendelssohn's permanent right of residence as a *Schutzjude* [protected Jew], in Berlin, in 1763, required two obsequious missives from the applicant himself and personal interventions by d'Argens. When their initial approach failed, d'Argens waited three months before trying again, this time prodding his reluctant sovereign with a witty note from a "poor Catholic" [d'Argens] to a "poor Protestant" [Frederick] on behalf of a "poor Jew" [Mendelssohn]. Frederick relented but put his foot down regarding Mendelssohn's proposed admission to the Prussian Royal Academy of Sciences: he was definitely not having that.[29]

Emancipation meant admitting Jews into the crafts, retailing, public office, the learned professions and the academies, from all of which they remained rigorously excluded. If centuries of "Christian oppression," as Dohm called it, had severed the Jews from most ways of earning a living, Frederick's policy heightened this "oppression" and further aggravated the mounting problem of Jewish unemployment, vagrancy and criminality.[30] If successful, Jewish emancipation would inevitably entail economic and professional disadvantages for Christian neighbors, a "disadvantage," the Emperor Joseph only belatedly realized after introducing his most progressive measure—the Toleration Edict of 1781. Though less hostile to Jews than Frederick or Catherine, it was certainly not Joseph's intention that his expanded toleration should attract fresh Jewish immigration causing a significant increase of Jewish numbers in the Austro-Hungarian monarchy.[31] He soon felt obliged to resume restricting Jewish entry into retailing, the crafts and professions by introducing fresh exclusions and disabilities. Special taxes and occupational restrictions applying specifically to Jews stayed in force despite the Toleration Edict, even in Prague and Vienna, where Jews had dwelt in sizeable numbers for centuries. Yet, despite the inconsistencies of his legislation, Joseph treated the Jews, remarked Dohm, "as the Jews had thus far never been treated in any Christian state."[32] Joseph laid out a path for Jewish emancipation, followed prior to 1789 nowhere else, accompanying a profound social and cultural shift which simple justice and moral integrity, according to Mendelssohn, Herz, Dohm, Diez and Mirabeau, demanded should be adopted everywhere.[33]

But there was no such thing as greater tolerance for Jews, Joseph's reforms showed, without other far-reaching changes affecting all of society that would inevitably provoke a fierce backlash from substantial segments of society including merchants, shopkeepers, lawyers, academics and professionals and still more zealously, the devout and the Christian clergy. Frederick and Catherine had no intention of emulating Joseph's example. Freeing Jews from the restrictions to which they remained subject, Mendelssohn, Dohm and Mirabeau realized, was impossible without a bitter struggle with adversaries invoking "Christian values" as their justification.

Mendelssohn was stirred to action by a wave of antisemitic agitation in Alsace-Lorraine, but could move only behind the scenes. He could no more avoid hiding behind the royal official, Dohm, as his political *alter ego* promoting Jewish emancipation in the public sphere, than behind Lessing in their common drive to detach morality from religion, politics from theology, and rescue Spinoza. Dohm willingly assisted in promoting the project and, in 1781, in collusion with Mendelssohn,[34] published his *Über die bürgerliche Verbesserung der Juden* [On the Civil Improvement of the Jews], a soon famous brochure advocating equal civil status and rights for Jews which predictably provoked vehement protest and prolonged public controversy. Dropping the old argument regarding the economic usefulness of Jews, except in the reverse sense that emancipation would reduce Jewish involvement in finance, Dohm based his (and Mendelssohn's) case on common justice, the need to detach the state from theological wrapping, and the usefulness of equality of rights to society as a whole. The booklet paralleled the argumentation advanced by Toland except that it was less emphatic in proclaiming the unity of mankind and admitted, as Toland had not, that Jewish society and morality needed improving.[35]

A Halle graduate and close friend of Dohm, passionate bibliophile and expert in Turcology, Persian and Zoroastrianism, as well as noted enthusiast for diffusing radical literature, being particularly an admirer of Helvétius,[36] Diez helped prepare successive editions of Dohm's booklet, publicly championing Dohm's stance while, at the same time, privately expressing some dissatisfaction with his approach. Diez wanted to further radicalize Dohm's position by eliminating all compromise with residual restrictions on Jewish activity that, to a point, Dohm seemed willing to accommodate. Bolder than Dohm,[37] he flatly rejected Dohm's conceding that even if other disabilities were lifted, and Jews entered the professions, they should remain excluded from public and political office.[38] Why was it inconceivable Jews should be in positions of authority over Christians? Diez disdained all concession to prejudice, credulity, theology and tradition, the only "religion" he could accept being that of "pure reason." Spinoza's first sympathetic biographer, author of *Benedikt von Spinoza nach Leben und Lehren* (1783), Diez equally outstripped Dohm in fiercely repudiating demands that conversion to Christianity, as the clergy demanded, was in any way a desirable requirement or condition for full Jewish equality. Diez remained convinced the Germany of his time was a land in fetters weighed down by dismal credulity fostered by pernicious religious authority.[39]

By demanding full Jewish emancipation and equality, and an end to communal autonomy, Diez was following up his earlier tract of 1781, his today little-noticed *Apologie der Duldung und Pressefreiheit* [Vindication of Toleration and Press Freedom], the first text in central Europe proclaiming the need for full freedom of thought and the press as a fundamental benefit for society, and demanding an end to press censorship.[40] Diez's *Apologie*, like Carl Friedrich Bahrdt's better-known but later text *Über Pressefreyheit und deren Gränzen* [On Press Freedom and Its Limits] (1787), was unmistakably chiefly inspired by Spinoza, an added reason why people preferred not to discuss it. Here was "philosophy" looking forward to an entirely new era of open-mindedness and toleration opposing outright traditional thinking, Christianity and anti-Jewish bias, indisputably inspired by Radical Enlightenment ideas. Diez immensely admired Raynal's *Histoire philosophique*, which served as a significant source for both his and his friend Dohm's ideas about social oppression as well as colonial empires about which the latter later published an incisive critique.[41] Among Diez's connected projects was his translation of Alexandre Deleyre's *Tableau de l'Europe* (1774), an incisive summary of Raynal's *Histoire philosophique* which Diez sharpened further into a ferocious German-language assault on despotism, religious authority and colonialism and published in 1783 at Dessau, where the local prince, eager to turn his little court into a "Mecca" of Enlightenment, for the moment championed full press freedom.[42]

Diez's fifty-six-page booklet on Spinoza's life and teaching likewise appeared at Dessau and was warmly praised, in 1786, by the radical journalist Wilhelm Ludwig Wekhrlin (1739–1792), at Nuremberg, in his journal *Das graue Ungeheuer* [The Grey Monster]: "not easily can one find in so few pages so many partly unknown truths stated so freely and courageously or with such energy and majesty, as in this short text."[43] Lauding Spinoza's moral uprightness, Diez and Wekhrlin made little effort to conceal their animosity toward Christianity, preachers, theologians, conventional morals and all received opinion. Diez professed amazement that Christians could wonder that an "atheist" like Spinoza should live a morally upright life when they seemed utterly unperturbed that innumerable persons, including pastors, priding themselves on being pious "Christians" and flaunting their churchgoing, all too obviously, led morally despicable lives.[44] "Religious zeal so blinds the individual he never knows where to stop."[45] Religious enlighteners, unsurprisingly, denounced this "impertinent nonsense," Mendelssohn's friend Johann Albrecht Reimarus (1729–1814), a prominent figure at Hamburg, declaring Diez's Spinoza booklet "disgusting," especially in claiming morality has no genuine foundation in revelation or nature but is constructed by society and justifiable, as Spinoza argues, solely according to what improves and benefits society. Diez championed the cause of the Jews along with religious toleration, freedom of the press, and anti-colonialism and was not wholly lacking in support. The social and political power of the world's religions was mainly due to two things, agreed Wekhrlin, in 1786, "fear and ignorance of causes." Hobbes, Boulanger, Fréret, Hume and Helvétius had all grasped this, as had Lucretius in ancient times, but as yet, unfortunately for minorities and the independent-minded, most people had not.[46] How is mankind to rise to a higher moral order buttressing legislation not based on religious authority? Here Spinoza appeared uniquely pertinent.

Like Diez and Mirabeau, Dohm was privately no admirer of Frederick's enlightened despotism, especially not his social and education policies, which, he believed, during the king's last years, had gone from bad to worse. As a senior Prussian official, Dohm needed to tread carefully. Like d'Argens and Mirabeau, he inwardly rejected Christianity (he admitted privately to Georg Wedekind and other radical friends), but could not confess this publicly. Despite serving a monarch, he was also a crypto-republican, but could not admit that either.[47] Once again, indisputably, it was his radically enlightened approach, rejection of theology and aversion to monarchy and mainstream values that cemented his alliance with d'Argens, Mirabeau, Cloots and Diez, and enabled him to perceive the Jewish question as he did. Frederick's aversion to Jews, Dohm and Diez were convinced, was integral to his supposedly enlightened policy and efforts to restrict, in effect minimize, both their numbers and role in society.[48] Where Frederick viewed the Jews as people of low moral caliber, the opposite to the human material—"honorable, patriotic, courageous and fit for war"–he needed for Prussia, Dohm, like Toland, held that centuries of oppression, and enforced narrowness of occupation-structure was chiefly responsible for Jewish society's defective character, the root cause of Jewish finance, vagrancy and petty crime.[49] Dohm's brochure on Jewish emancipation was widely reviewed and, the following year, appeared in French.[50]

The controversy over it dragged on. Mendelssohn kept out of sight behind the scenes. With no small plausibility, conspiracy theorists might well rush in, purportedly uncovering a vile pro-Enlightenment Spinozist-Jewish-deist plot to subvert Christianity, and might well publicly denounce the circle within which Dohm and Mendelssohn were generating the drive for Jewish civil rights. But there was no denying that the publicity campaign Mendelssohn orchestrated rested on a theory of political rights and individual freedom separating church and state almost entirely, and reducing religious commitment to virtually a private matter.[51] God has no taste for religious coercion, he insisted, and no civil or ecclesiastical authority is ever justified in demanding submission to a particular creed. Only "atheists," declared Mendelssohn, with blatant inconsistency but in accord with the prejudices of the time, can fairly be denied freedom of conscience and religious practice. Unlike Dohm, he also claimed his stance fully accorded with the Hebrew Bible, a contention easily disproved, according to the controversialist August Friedrich Cranz (1737–1801), given that Moses regularly instituted religious laws prescribing stoning and death for Sabbath-breakers, blasphemers and other violators of divine commandments.[52] Early Judaism was undoubtedly a coercive religion tying politics and society together.

More moderate in tone in his Hebrew writings than in German, and veiling the Spinozist components of his thought, Mendelssohn forcefully presented his precarious synthesis of moderate and radical Enlightenment elements in his fifty-page preface to the German translation of Menasseh ben Israel's famous English text *Vindiciae Judaeorum, Or, A Letter in Answer to Certain Questions Propounded by a Nobel and Learned Gentleman: Touching the Reproaches Cast on the Nation of the Jews; Wherein All Objections are Candidly, and Yet Fully Clear'd* (Amsterdam, 1656). This historic text appeared for the first time in German, in April 1782, translated by Mendelssohn's friend Markus Herz (1747–1803), under the title *Rettung der Juden* [Vindication of the Jews] (Berlin and Stettin, 1782), at the Berlin press of Friedrich Nicolai (1733–1811), an enlightened editor actively collaborating with Dohm and Mendelssohn.[53] A Dutch translation followed the same year.[54] Mendelssohn's preface to the German version of Menasseh ben Israel is indeed the first German publication straightforwardly to proclaim the principle of "universal and equal" rights of mankind, expressly rejecting Locke's more traditional but now increasingly obsolete concept of hierarchically stratified "rights." His preface made the fundamental, yawning gap between moderate and radical Enlightenment, between *ancien régime* hierarchy and universal and equal rights, plainer to see while rendering Mendelssohn's own posture more than ever ambivalent.

Mendelssohn thanked divine providence for blessing his last years with a glimpse of something totally new in history, the glorious moment in which the older idea of "toleration" of minorities, such as Locke's now obsolete tentativeness, was finally ousted by the more fundamental, potent and valid concept of inherent "rights," with the "*Rechte der Menschheit* [The Rights of Mankind] embraced in their true breadth." The basic drift of Mendelssohn's social and political thought, as Leo Strauss noted later, follows Spinoza's *Tractatus Theologico-Politicus* in viewing individual happiness and the good of society as man's supreme goals, a stance pushing Mendelssohn to demand full Jewish integration into general society and participation in the common good.[55] Owing to his seeming moderation in other respects, it is often insufficiently realized how subversive Mendelssohn's political thought was with respect to Jewish community organization and government—too much so in his friend Dohm's opinion.[56] Well received by some, Mendelssohn's trenchant preface was publicly condemned by Protestant clergymen and some Jewish community elders due to its rigorous curtailing of all religious authority.[57]

Mendelssohn proved zealous for equal rights for all.[58] Severely limited, pre-1780 toleration in Germany focused mainly on according limited toleration to the two main Protestant churches and the Catholics: such fringe Christian sects as the Mennonites, Polish Socinians, Moravian Brethren as well as "heathens, Jews, Mohammedans, and supporters of Natural religion were either wholly excluded or, at best [brought into the discussion] only as grounds for rendering toleration more problematic."[59] Mendelssohn made no mention of the fact that the new wider concept of universal and equal rights, and hence universal toleration, originated partly across the Atlantic and had only surged up in Europe since the onset of the American Revolution in 1775–76; but contemporaries hardly needed having this pointed out. Equality was a concept seeping slowly into Germany, partly from the Jeffersonian (radical democratic republican) tendency in the American Revolution, partly from French radical circles. If the *Fragmentenstreit* (1774–78), the greatest clash between Christian theologians and secularizing Enlightenment in eighteenth-century Germany, brought the *Naturalisten*—a term chosen by Mendelssohn deliberately to include atheists and Spinozists with deists—for the first time into the picture, with their right to be tolerated championed by Lessing, Dohm and Diez, now all religious minorities and heterodox elements were being recognized, as they were not before 1775, as deserving the same equal rights. Locke's "moderate" restricted toleration, for so long debarring the Jews from equal status (along with Catholics and atheists), was visibly crumbling.[60]

SEPARATING RELIGIOUS LIFE FROM THE FUNCTIONS OF THE STATE

In his culminating philosophical work, *Jerusalem, oder über religiöse Macht und Judentum* [Jerusalem; or on Religious Power and Judaism] (1783), building on arguments introduced in his *Menasseh ben Israel* preface, Mendelssohn seconded Spinoza's assault on institutionalized religious authority (albeit refraining from pointing this out) by urging the need for total separation of religious life and the churches, as well as individual conscience and philosophy, from the functions and duties of the state.[61] No religious organization ever possesses any right to authority, temporal power or jurisdiction over citizens![62] All citizens, whatever their faith, share in the same obligations and duties with respect to society and the state and, by sharing the same rights and duties, share a common moral obligation to each other shaped by the legislation and requirements of the state, none of which should have inherent ties to religion. "Rights of the Church," the authority of religious leaders, are ruthlessly stripped out by Mendelssohn, diminished to the point, as in Spinoza (and Jefferson), where religious authority no longer possesses any sway over law, institutions, political processes, social morality or freedom of expression and the press. Churchmen of whatever stripe simply have no privileges, special status, precedence, right to censorship, jurisdiction of any kind, and must be stripped of all influence on legislation, lawmaking and enforcement of the laws. For Mendelssohn as for the 1660s *cercle spinoziste*, there exists no such thing as *ius circa sacra*, no authentic rights of clergy—rabbis included—to discipline communities by threatening dissidents with condemnation or banishment.[63]

Fundamental too in *Jerusalem*, and symptomatic of the radical strand in Mendelssohn's thought, is the pervasive anti-Lockean strain. Locke sought to establish a separate sphere of spiritual redemption and belief corresponding to his separating the sphere of *supra rationem* from the natural world subject to reason. This higher sphere of authority and guidance, concerned with saving souls, remains ultimately the responsibility of church doctrine and the clergy but one partly delegated to the state to guard and administer *for* theology and the churches. This schema, the essence of moderate Enlightenment, Mendelssohn deemed profoundly erroneous. He refused to grant that the eternal can be segregated from the worldly, or that churches should be entrusted by political sovereignty with directing consciences and shaping moral goals, which in Locke the churches must supervise but cannot undertake without the secular arm's support. In Locke, whenever a clash of basic values ensues, the state must ultimately defer to religious authority which, to Spinoza and Mendelssohn alike, was a recipe only for discrimination and tyranny.[64] The true divide, contends Mendelssohn, is not between worldly and eternal but between coercion and conviction. All citizens must be constrained to submit to the laws, but no one should be coerced in matters of belief or religious observance.[65] Locke's tentative toleration is inherently bad in effect if not intention and needs discarding *in toto*.

For dismantling all *Kirchenmacht* [religious authority] and forging a new philosophical dualism displacing the old familiar divide between temporal and spiritual, Mendelssohn was assailed from every side.[66] Under his dichotomy, jettisoning Locke and defining a more secular Enlightenment political philosophy rooted in *Moralphilosophie*, philosophical ethics becomes the vital theoretical sphere determining the correct relations between men and social groups, leaving religion and churches handcuffed to defining relations between the individual and God, tied to the level of the purely personal.[67] The state thereby becomes more of a moral agent with wider ethical goals than the churches, being the superior body in the social and moral sphere instead of subordinate, and hence, so far as this world is concerned, the supreme moral agency. Where the state can coerce, religious authority can only exhort the individual to strive for redemption, possessing no jurisdiction over social relations, no right to direct or coerce.[68] With this strategy Mendelssohn sought to emancipate the Jewish people, but, by the same token, effectively emasculated rabbinic and congregational authority and that of the Jewish elders.

Desire to convert the Jews to Christianity, basic in Locke, had indeed receded since Locke's time; purely religious objections to Jewish equality now counted for less than they once did. Yet, in Prussia and most German states, as in France, Italy and Poland, restrictions and disabilities confining Jewish society persisted as before. "We continue to be excluded from all arts, sciences, and other useful human occupations and crafts," complained Mendelssohn, and prevented from striving for "useful improvement," and our "lack of culture" is then cited to justify our continuing exclusion. The result was a dismally narrow occupation-structure and lack of participation in general culture, education and law. "They bind our hands, and then accuse us of not using them."[69] Mendelssohn acknowledged his own good fortune in being joined in the fight for Jewish rights by an official as prominent as Dohm.[70] Dohm's and Diez's recriminations, laying the blame for the Jewish society's inadequacies squarely on the churches and society's long-standing bias, prejudices and oppression of the Jews, he eagerly endorsed, diverging from Dohm only in one respect—rejecting his proposal that churches and Jewish communities alike should retain the power to expel and ban as a way of residually enforcing religious authority with respect to belief and conduct within the community, a point where, alluding unmistakably to Spinoza's expulsion, Mendelssohn rejected the prevailing position outright.[71]

Jewish equality, if potentially among the Enlightenment's most significant projects, was so bitterly resented throughout Europe as to figure prominently among the reasons why commentators like Lessing, Dohm and Mendelssohn remained pessimistic as to the Enlightenment's ultimate prospects. At the close of his life, Lessing increasingly felt defeated, tucked away in the great library at Wolfenbüttel where he was director, under unremitting siege from indignant theologians and the press. In declining health, he completed his three great culminating works—*Die Erziehung des Menschen Geschlechts* [Education of the Human Race] (1777), *Ernst und Falk* (1778), and *Nathan der Weise* [Nathan the Wise] (1779)—that together formed an impassioned parting swipe at prevailing cultural and social attitudes. If the first pronounces Revelation a form of "education" delivering "nothing that human reason left to itself could not also arrive at" but instilling it faster and more readily than it penetrates by reason alone, he nevertheless viewed Revelation as an inferior, narrower path while, like Mendelssohn, seeking unambiguously to demolish ecclesiastical authority.[72] All three works powerfully re-articulated their joint general reevaluation of all values right across the German cultural and educational scene.

Nathan der Weise, the best-known exemplar of the Enlightenment literary cult of the "upright and wise Jew" first introduced as a core radical notion by d'Argens, was the work, Mendelssohn affirmed, after Lessing's death,[73] that he valued above all the rest of his oeuvre. Among the Enlightenment's most eloquent pleas for toleration, it has ranked among the peaks of classical-era German literature ever since. Set in twelfth-century Jerusalem and based on an ancient tale, this moral-philosophical drama strove to promote a more equal, "enlightened" relationship between Christians, Jews and Muslims. On the surface, the play's central theme, the parable of the "Three Rings," proclaims toleration and mutual respect among the three revealed religions—Judaism, Christianity and Islam. But deeper down, the work is less concerned with minimizing differences between faiths, or preaching indifferentism, than with promoting the idea that champions of each of the Three Rings cannot possibly know which, if any, of the three is the true Revelation. Accordingly, all three can confirm the legitimacy of the irreconcilable doctrines they profess only via their moral actions—by fostering virtue, charity, usefulness to others, devotion and goodwill. For Lessing, as Spinoza, the real meaning of "true religion" can never be encased in doctrines formulated by theologians.[74] Indeed, the play, as Lessing himself acknowledged, clearly reflects aversion to "positive religion." On publication of *Nathan der Weise*, in 1779, few critics failed to notice the Spinozistic thrust of Nathan's remarks about miracles, his dismissing what ordinary folk believe, and the play's implication that none of the great monotheistic religions represents "true religion,"[75] or that Lessing enthusiasts interpreted Nathan as a "noble Mendelssohnian character."[76]

Not only is *Nathan der Weise* no "Christian" play, except in Spinoza's sense, but an insinuatingly anti-Christian play as not a few realized. It dramatized for all to see the collision between enlightened despotism (here symbolized by "Saladin") allied to conventional religion and what Lessing deemed the Enlightenment's authentic moral values. In the encounter between "Saladin" and "Nathan" occurs a clash of worldviews framed by Lessing's insight that true enlightened values and political despotism perennially stand in irresolvable conflict. For all his talk of "justice" and dislike of religious intolerance,

"Saladin," much like Frederick, possesses little grasp of true human values, morality or respect for others, and is motivated, we glimpse during the last act, again not unlike Frederick or Catherine, chiefly by appetite for power, military dominance and money. For all his skill and intelligence, this professedly enlightened despot ultimately sacrifices what is best to insatiable greed for mastery.[77]

First performed in Berlin just three years before Frederick's demise, in April 1783, *Nathan der Weise*'s opening performances received a predictably frosty reception, marked by the conspicuous absence of Jews, who reportedly stayed away through prudent apprehension. The Lutheran clergy were furious and far from alone in their indignation at the play's message. For many years the drama proved divisive throughout German-speaking central Europe and also Scandinavia, the Danish version being banned from the stage outright (in Denmark and Norway) until 1799.[78] Lessing's philosophical outlook clashed fundamentally with what was commonly felt, believed and thought not just by the orthodox but in official circles and the common people. The controversy aroused left Lessing's overall legacy even more engulfed in bitter recrimination than before.[79]

If the German Enlightenment's successes were considerable, so were its failures. Among its hindrances was the widespread academic and theological opposition its triumphs generated, provoking the clergy and arousing the suspicion of princes and monarchs. Toleration, nowhere complete, in the long run became less and less so in Prussia, Bavaria, Bohemia, Hungary, Poland, Russia and Austria alike. Equality before the law, abolishing serfdom, unshackling the press, all made only halting, modest progress. The state of education remained highly unsatisfactory from an enlightened perspective. Social and legal integration of the Jews, like marriage and family law reform, ending persecution of homosexuals, unmarried mothers and the suicidal, had all scarcely begun. Curbing older forms of superstition in rural areas looked effective on the surface, but fighting credulity, irrationality, superstition, and prejudice, having reached a certain point, seemed now to slide back into reverse. Consequently, the rising opposition of the traditional and ordinary dialectically provoked still further intensification of Radical Enlightenment zeal denouncing middle-of-the-road positions, prevarication and Frederick's legacy besides older entrenched attitudes. This in turn then generated a sharper popular reaction against moderate as well as Radical Enlightenment.

The rise of new, wildly fashionable fads discarding "reason" for feeling and enthusiasm, Mesmerism, wonder cures, Masonic rituals and the exorcisms of the Bavarian Father Johann Joseph Gassner (1727–1779) stoked a tide of furious emotion, gripping the upper classes too, that proved deeply characteristic of the 1780s and 1790s, a trend everywhere encouraged by the growing Rousseau cult and some leading theologians. No fleeting mood of the moment but a growing cultural force fervently embraced by a swelling army of mystical, throne-loving *Anti-Aufklärer*, as of Tory "church and king" Loyalists in England, and love of secret "mysteries," drove a general Counter-Enlightenment reversal vowing restoration of the sacred, mysterious and veneration of noble rank. Far from exterminated, traditionalist anti-intellectuals like those Wekhrlin dubbed the "Hottentots" of Glarus, daily amassed fresh adherents and support with which to draw society more and more toward Rousseau's purity of "simple souls," and across the Atlantic to America's "Great Awakening," under the sway of the pulpit, the venerated and the irrational.

Mainstream and Radical Enlightenment voices alike shuddered at these new trends. But moderate Enlightenment philosophers, Wolffians and Lockians, through reserving space for theology and the *supra rationem*, could not, on purely philosophical grounds, cogently deny belief in wonders of any kind, not even magic, witchcraft, werewolves, fairies and demons.[80] Conceding the veracity of miracles, held Carl von Knoblauch (1756–1794), a jurist, critic and journalist ally of Wekhrlin who, like him, Diez and Lessing, asserted the impossibility of miracles and figured prominently among Gassner's detractors, means ultimately that one possesses no antidote to the overwhelming challenge of popular zeal, no way of showing all wonders, mystery and "magic," and claims to the protective power of prayer, are deception. The sole solution, urged Knoblauch, was comprehensive repudiation of Mesmer and Gassner using arguments of a kind Leibnizians and Lockeans could not offer: what was required was a redoubling of the philosophical assault on credence in *supernaturalia* and supernatural forces of any kind, to fight all prejudice, credulity, mystery, thaumaturgy, wonder-works, exorcism and, in the case of "Poland, Hungary, Silesia, Moravia, Austria and Lorraine," tenacious belief in vampires.[81]

Only philosophy proving the will cannot arbitrarily change physical things could stem the craze for wonders, mysterious theology and miracle cures; and the only philosopher whose philosophy is sufficiently cogent and categorical to rule out every supernatural manifestation from thaumaturgy to vampires and Gassner, held the dying Lessing of the early 1780s, is the author of the *Ethics*, now more than ever "der konsequenteste von allen

Philosophen" [most consequent of all the philosophers], as Knoblauch called him.[82] For Lessing's following there exists no true supernatural explanation for anything. If popular superstition, credulity, ignorance and enthusiasm are to be beaten back in the interest of human amelioration, existing obsessions, creeds and philosophies must be challenged and overcome. In the 1780s, it struck not a few of Germany's acutest minds that only one cogent answer offered itself. "If the world still exists in some future incalculable point in time," concluded the most admired scientific mind at Göttingen, the physicist Georg Christoph Lichtenberg (1742–1799), "the universal religion will certainly be a modified Spinozism. Reason left wholly to itself leads to nothing else and it is impossible that it should lead anywhere else."[83] A sufficiently prominent coterie of such minds was now at hand to provoke a widening uproar of theological outrage and condemnation.

Gassner and Mesmer, "conjurors" fueling the uproar, charged Knoblauch, were especially adept at mobilizing women and the illiterate.[84] That most of the untutored, as well as the clergy, courts and academics adamantly denied philosophical reason is mankind's exclusive universal guide, does not mean the radical views of Lessing, Herder, Thorild, Diez, Forster, Bahrdt, Weishaupt, Wekhrlin, Knoblauch, Maimon, Cloots, Lichtenberg and Dohm depicting the social world they inhabited as inherently oppressive and defective, judged from an authentically enlightened perspective, were untimely or ineffective. Rather, surging belief in incomprehensible divine and diabolic powers, preference for wonders and the miraculous, only further stiffened the views of those seeing the general adoption of science, legal science and social science as the uniquely valid paths to a broader general overhaul of politics, law and legislation based on universal and equal criteria. Recognizing the need for more enlightenment as the indispensable precondition for ameliorating the human condition, inevitably spelt a reactive resurgence of radical zeal.[85]

The 1780s hence simultaneously witnessed an intensification of modish "enthusiasm" allied to mystical fashions *and* escalation of philosophy's war on "superstition" and credulity. Fighting the tide of fanaticism, sorcery, and Gassnerism, radical *Aufklärer* strove to convince the more highly educated, including those professionally engaged in defending faith in wonders, revelations and miracles, that it was they who were legitimating and authorizing the growing fervor behind Europe's and Britain's surging Counter-Enlightenment.

Besides *Anti-Aufklärer*, enlightened despotism, theologians, and moderate enlighteners with a taste for Locke, Mendelssohn found himself pitted against conservative Jewish orthodoxy. The open breach between pro-Enlightenment *maskilim,* his supporters in the Jewish world, and the conservatives began with the publication, in 1782, of a key Hebrew text, *Divrei shalom ve-emet* [Words of Peace and Truth] which later reappeared during the revolutionary era in French (1792) and Italian (1793). It was composed by Naphtali Herz Wessely (1725–1805), a Hamburg poet and scholar steeped in Hebrew and familiar with rabbinics and Talmud. Mendelssohn and Wessely had been allies at a distance since 1768, when the latter started to translate the *Phaedon* into Hebrew. This was a project Mendelssohn had considered undertaking himself but abandoned, and which Wessely too failed to complete.[86] Wessely, actively engaged in business, shifted his domicile between Copenhagen, Amsterdam and Hamburg before moving to Berlin, in 1774.[87] *Divrei shalom ve-emet,* his ringing manifesto demanding the introduction into standard Jewish schooling of science, geography, history and legal studies and less stress on Talmud and religious studies, with Hebrew now being studied like a classical language, with special attention to grammar, set off a far-reaching commotion within numerous leading Jewish communities.

Wessely, writing exclusively in Hebrew, addressing a Jewish public only, became a key adjunct to Mendelssohn's overall strategy. His pamphlet expressed immense enthusiasm for Mendelssohn's plans for reforming Jewish schooling while roundly denouncing the traditional approach with its neglect of biblical Hebrew, Hebrew poetry and text criticism, and overemphasis on Talmud studies. Loudly deploring conventional teaching methods, he also underlined the shortcomings of Yiddish as the main language of instruction in Jewish schools in Germany, Poland-Lithuania, Bohemia-Moravia, Hungary-Transylvania and Russia, regretting Hebrew was no longer a spoken language. Mendelssohn deemed Wessely a model exemplar of the modern Jew such as Gumpertz and he himself had aspired to forge. But where Mendelssohn applauded, conservative rabbis reacted with fury to Wessely's demand for combining modern sciences and languages with rabbinic learning and purer Hebrew, Rabbi David Tevele (d. 1792) of Leszno (Lissa), in western Poland, charging Wessely with shamelessly "trampling on the glory of the Torah."[88]

Wessely warmly lauded Joseph II's toleration, eulogized Mendelssohn's German translation of the *Pentateuch,*[89] and, like Solomon Maimon, summoned Jews to take advantage of the opportunities opened up by the emancipation process, demanding they reform their education system fundamentally. Wessely's sentiments were bound to aggravate relations between Jewish traditionalism and Berlin *Haskalah* reformism. In early 1782, following publication of Wessely's pamphlet in Hebrew, appeared a still harder-hitting German rendering (and later that year also in Dutch), entitled *Worte der Wahrheit und des Friedens* [Words of Truth and Peace] prepared by another of Berlin's *maskilim*, David Friedländer (1750–1834), after which full-scale civil war within the Jewish world erupted between Enlightenment and Counter-Enlightenment. Urging Jewish support for Joseph II's reforms as they affected Jewish communities and education throughout central Europe including southern Poland and Lemberg [Lvov], and Austrian Italy, Wessely's and Friedlander's brochures generated a new activism and militancy, the German version using a sharpness of tone many felt would have best been avoided.

Jewish enlighteners, Friedländer most of all, strenuously disparaged the inward-looking narrowness of traditional teaching methods used in Germany, Poland and Bohemia. Their proposed synthesis of religious teaching with secular knowledge and the sciences placed such stress on the latter and the proper teaching of modern German, that it was interpreted by leading rabbis in key Jewish centers like Prague, Vienna and Vilna as an outright attack on Jewish tradition, observance and learning.[90] Friedländer's version of Wessely's tract, though not as vehement in denouncing rabbinic traditionalism as Solomon Maimon, in his less noticed autobiography published in 1793,[91] became far more widely known, indeed became the most renowned Berlin *Haskalah* publication after Mendelssohn's main works.

Orthodox rabbis, including the influential Rabbi Ezekiel Landau (1713–1793) of Prague, openly accused Mendelssohn and his following of Epicureanism, deism and crypto-Spinozism. A traditionalist trained in Polish yeshivas, Landau, like Tevele, became an active adversary of Jewish Enlightenment in general, though there was no way a formal ban, or *herem*, like that imposed on Spinoza could be contemplated at this time when communal autonomy was being drastically cut back by the Emperor Joseph and neighboring rulers with Mendelssohn's blessing.[92] While Mendelssohn and Wessely had no wish to inflame the internal Jewish quarrel more than necessary, Friedländer joining the fray with his sarcastic German rendering, more abrasively promoted his and Mendelssohn's rationalistic, philosophical "Judaism," eager to dismantle what he viewed as the outdated unenlightened superstitious Talmud-based folk religion of most rabbis.[93]

Not unreasonably, observers often viewed Mendelssohn as the guiding hand behind Wessely's and Friedländer's efforts. Successfully linking Jewish Enlightenment to German culture, Mendelssohn stressed, depended on effectively defending divine Providence, immortality of the soul and the integrity of Scripture philosophically. His own *Jerusalem* (1783) reaffirmed his general repudiation of Spinoza's substance monism and Bible criticism; yet, on another level, even though Spinoza is referred to by name only, *Jerusalem* was undeniably a sanitized reworking of the *Tractatus Theologico-Politicus* aimed at bolstering toleration and personal liberty, and promoting equal rights for all, while insisting the Hebrew Bible supported such a libertarian stance.[94]

Philosophically, however, the Mendelssohnian stance posed a major problem: Spinoza and Lessing directly contradicted Mendelssohn's and Friedländer's claim that the Hebrew Bible's teachings fundamentally accord with reason, proclaiming the chief points of universal morality, religious freedom and the essence of rational natural theology, including immortality of the soul. A thesis Lessing (and the older Reimarus) expressly rejected, it was indispensable to Mendelssohn. In *Jerusalem*, Mendelssohn retreated somewhat from his earlier bold claim that the Hebrew Bible's core doctrines are identical to those of philosophical natural religion, but resolutely retrenched behind the weaker tenet that what God revealed to the Israelites prompts incipient awareness of those truths, a problematic construct of a fragility so obvious the leading Counter-Enlightenment critic, Johann Georg Hamann (1730–1788), suspected him of encouraging subversion of religion and "atheism."[95]

FIVE

Maimon's Rebellion and Mendelssohn's Dilemma (1770–1800)

During the 1780s, Europe's and America's vigorous Counter-Enlightenment opposition caused *Aufklärung* advocates and educators to fight back with fresh determination, mobilizing "philosophy" more robustly than ever to combat what to them was socially and morally backward theology and prejudice. Against this backcloth of a fraught, deeply divided central European culture arose an incipient, more militant Jewish secularism alongside the greatest of all the late Enlightenment German intellectual controversies, the *Pantheismusstreit*, or "Pantheism struggle," of 1785–90, a philosophical drama that dragged on for five or six years but continued to echo powerfully right through the years of the French Revolution, and after. Some of those who initially viewed the French Revolution enthusiastically, placing it in a positive philosophical context, like the young Hegel, Hölderlin, Fichte and Schelling, began claiming a connection between the philosophical revolution of the seventeenth century and the revolutionary dawn of universal and equal rights.[1]

Timing and context explain not just the peculiar intensity and ramifications of the great German "Spinoza controversy," reaching to the heart of the literary and journalistic, as well as the academic, philosophical and theological worlds, but also how and why an intellectual quarrel could exert a considerable impact on cultural life generally, leaving a lasting stamp on the careers and legacies of many of the greatest figures of Germany's classic age, especially Lessing, Mendelssohn, Kant, Goethe, Lichtenberg and Herder, but also many second-rank figures such as Jacobi, Rehberg, Thorild, Diez, Wizenmann, Maimon, Herz, Heydenreich, Knoblauch and the younger Reimarus.

Far from being dramatically new, as it seemed to the public, Goethe pointed out (like Heine later), in essence the *Pantheismus* controversy merely brought to the surface in more conspicuous fashion, a tangle of previously veiled intellectual encounters that all principal participants in the public drama had privately wrestled with for decades. Prior to the 1780s, though, they had grappled with the fundamental issues it posed practically always in the isolation of private pondering, in the corners of taverns or privacy of friends' lodgings.[2] What was essentially new in 1785 was the sudden revealing for all to see of subterranean tensions fundamentally reshaping German intellectual life and philosophy ever since Leibniz first acknowledged, in 1671. the centrality of Spinoza and the *cercle spinoziste* for philosophy, religion, hermeneutics, morality and politics.

Of those embroiled in the *Pantheismusstreit*, a good many, like Lessing, Herder, Goethe, Lichtenberg, Diez, Ewald, Wekhrlin, Knoblauch, Forster, Heydenreich, Thorild and Maimon, and somewhat later, Hegel, Schelling, Fichte and Hölderlin, were powerfully attracted to Spinoza's system. Others, like Mendelssohn or Wizenmann, favored selected strands but with major reservations; still others aligned broadly against, like Kant, Reinhold, the younger Reimarus, Jacobi, Rehberg, Biester and Hamann. Many had been privately immersed in this struggle since long before—Lessing and Mendelssohn since the early 1750s, Herder since the late 1760s; Hamann, doyen of German Counter-Enlightenment, first closely studied Spinoza, he assured Jacobi, in November 1784, more than twenty years before, but all now felt the compulsion to resume that study and open up the debate.[3]

Among younger scholars sucked into the great imbroglio gripping German philosophy, Solomon Maimon (1754–1800) was arguably the most striking autodidact and audacious rebel. Having lived his early life within the confines of east European Jewish tradition and Talmudic studies, for him, *Aufklärung*, we learn from his autobiography, was the dawn of truth after an interminably long night of darkness.[4] This was so even before he departed the southeast Lithuanian region of Mirz on the River Niemen linking Kovno to Alytus and Grodno, where he grew up. Foremost Jewish Enlightenment philosopher after Mendelssohn, Maimon played a highly idiosyncratic role in the *Pantheismusstreit,* one differing profoundly from that of the others, resulting in his becoming the most radical Jewish thinker of the age. Besides contributing to reshaping Germany's post-Kantian philosophical scene, he aspired to help revolutionize much else. Already a Spinozist of a sort well before the public controversy, by the time of his second stay in Berlin (1779–82), he had long shared a view of God as the material cause infusing everything and inseparable from the totality of all being, hence Spinoza's substance-mode pantheism. His approach connected him not just to Spinoza but also to the greatest figure of medieval Jewish philosophy, Maimonides, the anchor of his earlier thought-world back in Lithuania, and the Polish-Ukrainian Cabbalists he had encountered at the "court" of the Maggid of Mezrich (or Mezhyrich), in northwestern Ukraine, who had marked his outlook years before his migration to Germany.[5]

The "darkness" against which Maimon rebelled was partly intellectual but still more cultural and social in the widest sense. For he considered the east European Jewish culture from which he sprang to be stiflingly constricting in every way, as depriving individuals of the reality and opportunities of the world. He passionately rejected and denounced, in an objective spirit he claimed, the learning and entire edifice of rabbinic culture. In eastern Europe, he held, rabbis and their entourages formed an "aristocracy" lording it over the uneducated and middling non-learned by overlaying the true moral principles, the essence of Judaism, with an elaborate Pharisaic superstructure serving as a buffer between them and the non-learned, as well as those few grasping the "reality of things." It was a buffer designed to concentrate power and prestige in the hands of those directing their vast edifice of superficial statutes, requirements and observances. Rabbis, admittedly, were no hereditary aristocracy. "Every Polish Jew is destined from birth," he remarks at one point, "to be a rabbi, and only the greatest incapacity can exclude him from that office."[6] All parents aspired to the rabbinate for their sons, which was precisely why few could ever succeed in life. In Maimon's revolutionary social-cultural philosophy, virtually the entirety of Jewish history needs interpreting and being rewritten as a ceaseless struggle between a constricting rabbinic Phariseeism and Jewish society's middle and lower orders that had repeatedly rebelled against their rabbinic oppressors but so far always unsuccessfully.

A second dimension of Maimon's projected revolution was against what he deemed the crass and brutal ignorance of the typical Jewish school, or *heder,* like that where he himself imbibed Hebrew, Torah and Talmud, at

Mirz. Unlike the Lithuanian, Ukrainian and Polish peasants around them, all male Jews needed to read their prayer books and follow the reading of Torah portions, with the boys taught by despotic teachers in grimy surroundings under an iron discipline. Their Hebrew, according to Maimon, they learnt by rote without any attention to grammar, levels of meaning or language development, or the language's relationship to Aramaic (Syriac) and other ancient languages reflected in Talmudic era Jewish texts. Everything was imbibed in the most superficial manner, exactly as Wessely and Friedländer afterwards complained. Instruction, moreover, was exclusively in Yiddish, a language Maimon came to disdain, being a language lacking proper dictionaries, language rules and attention to grammar.[7] Talmud study formed the core of Jewish education and general culture in Poland-Lithuania-Ukraine, an arid study without philology and dictionaries forging a social reality in which the ordinary man, he claimed, dared not undertake anything not consonant with the Law according to "the learned."[8]

A third and not the least of Maimon's key rebellions was against arranged early marriage. If Dov Ber Bolochów (1723–1805), a Polish Jewish memoirist and wine merchant, married at the age of twelve, Maimon's marriage was arranged whilst he was still eleven, his first son being born in 1767, when he was fourteen. Aside from the severe disadvantages for personal development such early marriages entail, and resulting heavy economic dependence on parents and uncles, eleven- and fourteen-year-olds being in no position to support their families themselves, early arranged marriage meant the inescapable despotism of mothers-in-law over child brides and grooms to a degree Maimon found insufferable. In his mid-twenties, he deserted his wife and children, rebelling against his wife's family, which he detested, and a practice he regarded, however powerful a tool of social discipline in the hands of heads of households and the community, as chronically and intolerably constricting.[9]

FORSAKING THE *SHTETL*

Maimon came to view his own deeply emotional personal rebellion against the backdrop of repeated attempted revolutions by the Jewish uneducated and semi-learned, against their Jewish "aristocracy," the rabbis and *parnasim*, or governing council elders. He himself had briefly participated in the last major mass rebellion, that of the "new" Hasidism arising in the northwest Ukraine in the mid-eighteenth century in the wake of Baal Shem Tov. Around 1770, he had made his pilgrimage to Volhynia, to the "court" of the next head of the Hasidic movement, Baal Shem Tov's successor, Rabbi Dov Baer of Mezrich (d. 1772), whom he first glimpsed clad from top to toe in shining white silk. He soon grew contemptuous of Hasidic encouragement of belief in wonders and signs, especially Dov Baer's assumption of special holy status, his claims to supernatural powers and crude manipulation of his followers, exhorting them to experience the divine through his person as the *Tsadik* [righteous one], their subservience to him and his entourage. But in their moral outlook, love of music and joy in life and reaction against traditional rabbinic authority, he recognized elements with which he wholeheartedly sympathized. The appeal of Hasidism to ordinary folk lay in its insistence the path to the divine lay not in study, or accumulation of knowledge, but experience of life through heartfelt recitation of prayer and performance of good deeds performed with feeling and joy. This subversion of the established rabbis and community leadership provoked a mighty rift between the so-called *Talmudisten* and the new Hasidic culture, a contest intellectual, moral and social set to rage for decades.[10]

Maimon developed a unique perspective on the history of Jewish revolt against tyranny, rebellion both internal and external to Judaism, viewing its core as a triangular struggle over the centuries between Talmudism, Cabbalism and Maimonidean-Spinozist rationalism. Throughout the Jewish world, the unenlightened—that is, the greatest part of Jewish society—was so dominated by "rabbinic prejudices" that all study of the sciences and humanities, "even if in the Hebrew language," was traditionally "held to be forbidden fruit."[11] While the Jews of eastern Poland, Lithuania, White Russia and the Ukraine enjoyed much broader economic freedom and scope than the Jews of Warsaw, Cracow and Prague, or Germany, he still conceived of them as a wretched donkey laden with the terrible double burden of their own "ignorance" and rabbinic narrowness on one side and the crushing ignorance and superstition of Poland's Catholics with their hatred of Jews on the other. The degree of enlightened revolutionary force required to dissolve this double burden of combined Jewish and Polish "ignorance" seemed to his mind almost unimaginably colossal.[12] If Hasidism was the latest mass "revolt" against rabbinic narrowness and arid legalism,[13] it was preceded by the wider rebellion of Jakob Frank in the 1750s and 1760s, and back in the 1660s by the fervent movement of Sabbatai Zevi, the "false Messiah." These were all rebellions against Talmudism seeking "to abolish the whole ceremonial law and especially the rabbinic decrees."[14]

One might laugh at the ignorance, love of wonders and zealous superstition of Sabbatianism and Frankism, observed Maimon, but the Sabbatian frenzy came shortly after Spinoza's personal revolt against the rabbis in 1656, and there was a connection here, "given the deeply rooted prejudices of the nations," evident at any rate to the truly discerning: for "a moral system based on reason, a wholesome Reformation, was at that time impossible." Without "Enlightenment" no true revolution, sweeping aside abuse and wrong morality, and replacing it with true morality, is ever possible anywhere. "Consequently, prejudices and irrational fervor" until his own time "had to be fought with prejudices and irrational fervor"; then there *was* no other way to fight tyranny and aristocracy. Long before Sabbatai Zevi, the first founders of Christianity, added Maimon, similarly rebelled against the Pharisees, seeking to restore true morality and meaning to human life. They too initiated a huge rebellion of the untutored that quickly became just as fertile in "aristocracy" and power-thirsty ecclesiastics avid for control and statutes, in unquestioning veneration for fake wonders and miracles, and distortion of true morality, as the Pharisaic system they rejected.[15]

But if every previous attempt at revolution by mass action failed dismally, held Maimon, subsiding into superstition and ignorance governed by "aristocracies" of "holy men" and churchmen, the Jewish world, like the world more generally, had nevertheless edged gradually toward reason, propelling the advance of philosophy, preparing that future Enlightenment that alone can engineer a genuine revolution in human conditions for the better. The Averroist esoteric tradition of medieval philosophy had given birth to the radical rationalism of Maimonides which, while still living in Lithuania, had been Maimon's intellectual mainstay and chief lever of hope. Maimonides forged a subversive underground intellectual tradition within Judaism, continued later in parts of Spain by the likes of Moses Narbonne (or Narboni; d. 1365) who went still further than Maimonides in envisaging Judaism as merely a rough guide to the universal core of philosophical and moral truth, the path to supremacy of reason and philosophy over religion, religious law and ecclesiastics. Narbonne was also a great admirer of the radical rationalist autodidacticism Maimon considered his particular salvation, however solitary his own exit from the "darkness." For him, autodidacticism had been the only way out of what he saw as the "Talmudist" prison. Nor did Maimon fail to notice precious strands of convergence between this underground medieval Jewish philosophical tradition and the Lurianic Cabbala of the sixteenth and seventeenth centuries, a mystical tradition, he rightly observed, that had fed into Sabbatai Zevi's messianic revolt. He himself had embraced Cabbala early on as a refuge from rigid Talmudism,[16] while the Lurianic concept of *ruah ha-olam* [world soul], he later realized, encouraged notions of God as permeating, or even identical with, nature, rendering the individual mind an "organ of the Godhead," uniting the human mind with God, as Maimonides too had expressed it.[17] Here was the Jewish intellectual tradition Maimon was the first to comprehensively view as culminating in Spinoza and in *his*, that is Maimon's, Enlightenment.

The Hebrew word for "Enlightenment," *Haskalah*, is an abstract noun derived from the Hebrew and Yiddish term for intellect and good sense, namely *seychel*; and from *seychel* would arise the true revolution, Maimon's "Radical Enlightenment" against rabbinic and all tyranny. Teasingly *Litvaks*, as Polish Jews termed their Lithuanian co-religionists, were later perennially recommending "good sense" [*seychel*] against Polish superstitious unworldly meandering, which *Litvaks* thought typical of *Polaks*, but in Maimon *Litvakism* assumed a highly idiosyncratic form. While his repudiation of Lithuanian Jewish life and culture, his own early background, was never total, and he always remained something of the Talmudic genius he had been as a boy with vestiges of pride in his Lithuanian roots, his denunciation of rabbinic "aristocracy" and schoolroom tyrants along with Hasidic personality cults, together with his own ever-restless individuality caused him to rebel, eventually, not only against rabbinic authority, but also the *Haskalah*'s publicly acclaimed leaders, including Mendelssohn, whom he came to see as a philosophical hypocrite afraid to acknowledge his own secret Spinozism.[18]

Fiercely unsympathetic to "most of the rabbis," though himself steeped in traditional Jewish learning and far from wholly estranged from the Hasidic ethos he imbibed as a youth, Maimon, having acquired some German in Lithuania, migrated in stages, from around 1778–79. He stayed first in Königsberg with which his father, a minor merchant, had traded along the rivers, then Stettin, and after trying to enter and being turned away from Berlin, spent many months as a wandering beggar, or *Betteljude*. During the early 1780s, he had been a teacher for two years at Posen, in Prussian Poland, a period he later called the "happiest and most honorable of my life." Here, he composed his *Hesheq Shelomo* [Wisdom of Solomon] which, though never published, was the first text where he develops his subversive Maimonideism spiced with his irrepressible wit and progressively less disguised freethinking impiety. Returning to Berlin in 1783, this time successfully, he experienced his life-altering encounter with Mendelssohn while discovering Wolff and then Locke (Mendelssohn too had begun with Locke in German translation), quickly mastering the systems of "Spinoza, Hume and Leibniz." Before long, he felt ready to examine Mendelssohn's own project, progressing to Kant only much later.[19]

Still bitterly railing against the dismal "darkness" of orthodox Judaism and Polish-Lithuanian Catholicism, he continued his odyssey in modern philosophy by composing a critique of Wolff's metaphysics that coaxed him into further exploring Spinoza. Especially during 1783, Maimon debated extensively with Mendelssohn, who, to an extent, took him under his wing; but their initial intellectual harmony proved brief. The positions Mendelssohn championed, and publicly adapted to later eighteenth-century conditions, charged Maimon (and Lessing), were merely a halfway house on the road to Spinozist awareness of the "reality of things." Mendelssohn remained blind, willfully or unconsciously, he objected, to Spinoza's superior coherence.[20] For his part, Mendelssohn tried to restrain Maimon's boundless Maimonidean-Spinozist defiance without success, though it was less this that produced their speedy final rupture than Maimon's unruly lifestyle miring his reputation in Berlin, his growing reputation as an *apikoros* [Yiddish for hedonist] and "heretic," his visiting brothels and refusal to take a steady job—the Berlin *Haskalah* circle suggesting he was more suited to be an apothecary than a teacher. Maimon later freely admitted being not just a rebel against all conventional norms but temperamentally averse to steady paid work.[21]

By late 1783, disorderly lifestyle led to his expulsion from Berlin (under Frederick the Great's Jewish regulations), endorsed by Mendelssohn or, as Maimon sarcastically jibed, under sentence of Mendelssohn's "excommunication."[22] Some months later, his incorrigible disorderliness resulted in ejection from the Amsterdam Jewish community, brusque departure from Hamburg, and, after further wandering in Germany and a spell in Dessau, a longer stay at Breslau. At Breslau, during the height of the *Pantheismusstreit* (1785–87), Maimon still in various ways collaborated with the *Haskalah*. Not yet a Kantian or post-Kantian, his system at this point was a blend of his hero Maimonides with other medieval Jewish sources plus Spinozist pantheism. But eventually he found himself boycotted in Breslau too by the local Jewish community leaders, who learnt he was propagating "schädliche Systeme" [pernicious systems], that is, Spinozism, among young people, and was expelled yet again.[23]

There was scant sign of reconciliation between Maimon and Mendelssohn at the end of the latter's life. Anything apt to bring discredit upon the budding *Haskalah*, of which Mirabeau and others proclaimed Mendelssohn Europe's chief figure,[24] was anathema to Mendelssohn. During the *Pantheismusstreit*, Spinoza's legacy could be perceived everywhere emerging from the shadows of private debate to become again, as in Holland after 1670, a menacing as well as pervasive presence. The first German writer to claim openly that, when judged purely philosophically, ignoring the mountain of recrimination heaped on him for over a century, Spinoza was more consistent and "consequent" than Leibniz, Wolff or any other major thinker occupying German philosophy's center ground was the Humean conservative skeptic August Wilhelm Rehberg (1757–1836), responding to the Berlin Academy's prize competition of 1779. Yet, Rehberg, a court official and dogged defender of the royal and aristocratic social status quo, as well as Hume's skepticism, did not really believe such a universal, irrefutable philosophical system actually existed, but only that if such a system could exist, then Spinoza's was the closest thing to it.[25] Rehberg's disturbing avowal preceded the full-blown controversy erupting in 1785, when Spinoza's allegedly incomparable cogency was reaffirmed by Jacobi, Herder, Goethe, Diez, Lichtenberg and Knoblauch, developing "into a kind of fashion in German philosophy."[26]

Many found it profoundly disturbing that despite all the efforts of churchmen, universities and governments for over a century, Spinozism appeared to be gaining, instead of losing, ground. Diez's biography of Spinoza was followed by the first German translations of Spinoza's *Improvement of the Human Understanding* and the *Tractatus Politicus*, the latter entitled "On Aristocracy and Democracy," published at Prague in 1785 and 1786,[27] editions sympathetically introduced by Schack Hermann Ewald (1745–1824), secretary to Ernst Ludwig II, duke of Saxe-Gotha (r. 1772–1804) and, according to Lichtenberg, "one of our most enlightened [aufgeklärtesten] princes."[28] Disputing whether or not Spinoza was an "atheist," objected Ewald, in his 1785 preface, so overshadowed all else in this discussion that readers had quite lost sight of the fact that Spinoza has much of significance to say about citizenship, legislation and the form of the state.[29] Ewald's Spinoza translations were intended to encourage not just engagement with Spinoza's ethics and metaphysics but also investigation of his politics and the best form of state, an initiative clearly implying, in the wake of the American Revolution, that issues of democracy, and the relationship of democracy to aristocracy, had become a reasonable, even essential, topic of enlightened debate.[30] In 1787, Ewald published the *Tractatus Theologico-Politicus* in German (also for the first time), at "Gera," as the "first volume" of Spinoza's "philosophical writings," followed in 1790 and 1793 by a second and third volume, containing the *Ethics*.

The great German Spinoza debate was shifting from whether it was permissible to read Spinoza's books and ponder his arguments about miracles, divine providence and religion to what exactly were the practical, moral and political consequences of Spinoza's revolutionary conception of God and recommendations for statecraft, legislation and society. All "consistent philosophy," complained Friedrich Heinrich Jacobi (1743–1819), "is Spinozist, hence pantheist, fatalist and atheist;"[31] and such thinking was being surreptitiously diffused and encouraged by the leading spokesman (Mendelssohn) of modern Jewish thought. Denouncing the consequences, not the reasoning, Jacobi mobilized opinion against Mendelssohn's project, rejecting especially the providential theist rationalism and defense of natural theology Mendelssohn tied to the cause of Jewish emancipation. Like Maimon (and Leo Strauss later), Jacobi viewed Mendelssohn's combining divine providence and immortality of the soul with Spinoza as an unworkable fix, a puny façade utterly incapable of fencing out Spinoza's central claims. For this reason, Maimon had some sympathy for Jacobi's scheme to rock the entire German cultural arena and weaken all philosophizing partially or tacitly rooted in Spinozistic perspectives via his revelations about his 1780 debate with Lessing.[32] Jacobi's objective, though, was to defeat Spinozism with an expressly Christian strategy. Spurred on by his ally Hamann, Jacobi roundly lambasted the entire Berlin radical "enlightened" circle, including Maimon, Dohm and Diez, whose activist, reformist *Aufklärung* he pronounced non-viable, anti-Christian and philosophically inextricably linked to Spinozism.[33]

German philosophical debate had become more than ever precariously entwined with theology since the earlier *Fragmentensstreit* [Fragment Controversy] (1774–78) had set Germany's theologians in arms against Lessing.[34] As the Jews were the prime beneficiaries of Lessing's intervention and toleration, and the main focus of *Nathan der Weise*, and as Mendelssohn was Lessing's close ally, Jacobi's success in stirring public anxiety and indignation over Lessing's alleged "Spinozism" confronted Germany's leading Jewish thinker with a dangerous threat.[35] Since his ejection from Breslau, even

Maimon, the fearless prophet of "critical thinking," scornful of Mendelssohn's evasiveness regarding Spinoza, believing the entire Leibnizian-Wolffian philosophical tradition was just Spinozism dressed up to appear theologically and politically respectable, shrank from publicly endorsing Lessing's "Spinozism."[36] Presumably obvious to Mendelssohn privately for two decades, he could not publicly admit that Lessing (to whom he remained close during the latter's last years),[37] was a "Spinozist" as this would ruin his deceased friend's reputation and literary legacy and wreck his own (and Maimon's) schemes for building robust bridges between Judaism and German thought. Public vilification of Lessing, they realized, must severely harm, if not ruin, the campaign to advance toleration and ameliorate the Jewish condition, exposing Jewish emancipationist goals to denunciation as anti-Christian, atheistic Jewish subversion.

Since Jacobi considered the Leibnizian-Wolffian system "no less fatalistic than Spinoza's philosophy, to whose principles it inevitably leads one back, if a persistent search is made,"[38] Mendelssohn experienced great difficulty in evading the snare Jacobi and Hamann had laid for him. Nor was it only philosophers who sensed the vast pitfall the new "Spinoza controversy" represented for Mendelssohn's Enlightenment project. Many key figures well understood what the assault on Lessing's standing signified. The Lutheran pastor and biblical fundamentalist Johann Melchior Goeze (1717–1786), Germany's leading voice denouncing Lessing's toleration since the *Fragmentenstreit,* and renowned foe of liberal Protestant theologians, had for decades, since arriving in Hamburg, in 1755, striven to raise opposition to all extension of Jewish rights, prevent synagogue construction and impose Hamburg's existing disabilities and restrictions on Jews more stringently.[39] The attack on Lessing could lead on to a broader offensive to discredit Mendelssohn, block Jewish emancipation, and tighten restrictions confining Jewish life and activity, and synagogue building, in Germany.

Jacobi's 1785 campaign was an assault not just on "reason" in defense of faith, against the Enlightenment's radical tendency, but also on the entire philosophical tradition seeking to reconcile "Spinozistic" reason and Revelation, and the hegemony of the Leibnizian-Wolffian system as a basis for a secularizing moderate Enlightenment conceived as equally Christian, Jewish or Muslim, to which Mendelssohn linked his own philosophy. As Jacobi and Hamann perfectly grasped, Lessing's natural religion and Mendelssohn's rational Judaism were, despite Mendelssohn's assurances to the contrary, more closely entwined than he and other Leibnizians could admit, with neither being grounded in Revelation, Christian teaching or church-approved faith. Morality, human integrity and goodwill were converted by Lessing and Mendelssohn alike (and Maimon) into duties of society and the state while religious authority was being eliminated, leaving Christianity reduced to a private set of obligations confined to the solitary individual's relation to God and Christ, and hence socially, legally, politically and educationally powerless.[40] Mendelssohn aspired to rescue Judaism and the Jewish people from oppression and integrate them into the emancipated world of the Enlightenment, but in doing so menacingly equated Judaism with reason, and, without admitting it, allied it with secularism and Spinozism, ruthlessly stripping out society's entire investment in faith, clergy, prayer, miracles and wonders.[41] By proclaiming Judaism a religion devoid of dogma and belief in the Christian sense,[42] and Jewish tradition no obstacle to laws rendering Jews citizens like others, subject to the state and its laws, not a "state" within the state, Mendelssohn struck out in a direction repudiated by rabbis while simultaneously generating a new form of conflict between Jewishness and "Christian" values.[43]

MENDELSSOHN'S TRAGIC PREDICAMENT

Mendelssohn had based his hopes for Judaism's shift to respectability and philosophical acceptance on the now threatened Leibnizian-Wolffian foundation of natural theology and natural law (also under threat from Kant's and Hamann's critiques). Jacobi's intervention proved unsettling for Mendelssohn, *Aufklärung* and the future of German-Jewish relations in several ways. It placed the earlier *Fragmentenstreit* in a more menacing perspective and, in the eyes of some, confirmed that hidden allegiance to Spinozist anti-Scripturalism, irreligion, libertinism and rejection of theologically based morality is what lay behind Lessing's alliance with Mendelssohn and the Jews—much as Goeze and Lessing's other preacher adversaries contended. Fallout from the earlier uproar had already turned the reforming liberal Lutheran theologians, the Neologists, headed by Semler, Teller and Eberhard, firmly against Lessing.[44] Tarring Lessing with "Spinozism" would cast Mendelssohn and Lessing's much vaunted friendship in a sinister new light vindicating those convinced that at the heart of *Aufklärung* lay a fatal clandestine mix of Jewish scheming, Spinoza and rejection of Christ.

Mendelssohn could best extricate himself from this knot of difficulties, salvaging his project, the younger Reimarus and his sister, Elise, suggested, by publishing a full-length treatise definitively refuting Spinoza's philosophy and again unequivocally reaffirming God's existence and the soul's immortality. Pleading age and ill-health, initially Mendelssohn declined, suggesting it was the younger Reimarus who possessed the insight and stamina for such an undertaking and the affray bound to follow. By early 1784, though, filled with a renewed sense of urgency and awareness of how profoundly his project for Jewish emancipation and educational reform was menaced by Jacobi's and his allies' assault on Lessing, as well as the advance of Kantianism and mounting rabbinic opposition to *Haskalah*, Mendelssohn had changed his mind. He set furiously to work on his last major text, *Morgenstunden*, his treatise against the "Spinosisten" and *Naturalisten*.[45] In August 1784, Mendelssohn sent Jacobi a list of objections to Spinoza's metaphysics, commencing with the claim, already foreshadowed by Leibniz and Voltaire, that it is self-contradictory to allocate the attribute of thought to God while denying him conscious will and "intellect."

In 1785, Mendelssohn published his *Morgenstunden oder Vorlesungen über das Dasein Gottes* [Morning Hours, or Lectures on God's Existence] demonstrating God's omnipotence and providence, and repudiating Spinoza while refraining (as he had promised Jacobi) from discussing the private correspondence between them or Jacobi's conversations with Lessing. It was his valiant last throw at papering over rifts, salvaging the Leibnizian-Wolffian legacy and restoring stability to the philosophical arena while defusing the danger posed by public perception of Lessing as a "Spinozist" and himself as a wavering, inconsistent tool of a deviously impious Lessing and the "Spinozists." A new bridge between the Enlightenment's moderate and radical wings was the result: Lessing had indeed championed natural religion and is best classified, maintained Mendelssohn, as propounding a modified or "purified Spinozism."[46]

Morgenstunden examines Spinozism from all angles, acknowledging Spinoza's thought had always boasted many adherents among contemplative minds while noting too its appeal to zealots and "enthusiasts," reminding readers of Wachter's "insight," corroborated by Leibniz (and Maimon), that Spinozism's origins lay in Jewish Cabbalistic mysticism. The two greatest threats of the age, materialism and blind fanaticism, urged Mendelssohn, paradoxically converged in Spinozism.[47] Maimon, meanwhile, then still at Breslau, among other *Haskalah* projects espoused that of translating Mendelssohn's *Morgenstunden* into Hebrew (a manuscript now lost); by then, and after his departure still more, he could hardly any longer disagree that being tarred with the brush of "Spinozism" meant inevitable entanglement in severe difficulties. Ejected from Breslau, he too subsequently cloaked his Spinozism with an outward show of Leibnizianism, almost as much as he had accused Mendelssohn of doing, if more superficially. Following Mendelssohn and Lessing in adopting the idea that Leibniz had borrowed his pre-established harmony from Spinoza, Maimon claimed Leibniz had carefully concealed his system's underlying "Spinozism."[48] In interpreting Spinoza's metaphysics, meanwhile, Maimon was introducing an important twist that established a novel approach to Spinoza, afterwards popular with Hegel, Schelling and the early nineteenth-century Romantics: when identifying God and Nature as one, he contended, Spinoza was not actually building a system of "atheism," as Bayle claimed, but rather of "acosmism," that is, in Spinoza's system, it is not God that is unreal but the world, all reality outside of God lacks independent existence.[49]

It is illogical, asserts *Morgenstunden*, reworking Mendelssohn's ontological proofs of God's existence and providence, to locate thought in God without assigning to Him will and intelligence, the power to choose between alternatives, hence intelligent design. "Without this unifying subject the parts of the whole, always many, remain isolated and unattached; only through all-embracing thought [as Leibniz held] can they be united."[50] "Spinozism" can be a force for good, held Mendelssohn, but only where "purified" as Lessing and he himself had striven to show. God's will and power are assuredly the basis of divine providence. Spinoza had tragically strayed from this essential truth but still remained "this great man" whose errors are not just reparable employing Leibniz's and Wolff's principle of "sufficient reason" but, as the noble Lessing recognized, worthy of being cultivated and amended to yield the precious fruit of rational religion reconciled with great and true philosophy.[51]

Morgenstunden includes a curious dialogue in which an imaginary "Lessing" expounds his "verfeinerte Pantheismus" or "geläuterte Spinozismus" [refined or purified Spinozism].[52] Mendelssohn's "Lessing" one by one concedes the force of Mendelssohn's proofs of God's existence, beneficence and providence and the irrefutability of his objections to Spinoza's uncorrected metaphysics. "Purified Spinozism" is shown to blend admirably with the Leibnizian-Wolffian system, as Maimon too argued.[53] Corrected "Spinozism" hence combines consummately with true religion and morality, Lessing reportedly concedes, via Leibniz's principle that "das einzige vollkommenste Wesen hat sich von Ewigkeit her mit nichts als mit der Betrachtung des Vollkommensten beschäftigen können" [Throughout eternity, the sole most perfect Being could concern Himself with nothing but the contemplation of what is most perfect].[54] Some viewed Mendelssohn's text also as a counter-blast to Kant, something many then deemed urgently needed. But the stress throughout was on defending positions Christians too had a stake in—God, providence and the soul's immortality—without pressing Mendelssohn's earlier claim that the most essential truths proved by reason are found already, or are implicit, in biblical Judaism. *Morgenstunden* continued Mendelsohn's "Jewish project" but more guardedly than before, urging the philosophical convergence in reason of Judaism with Christianity.

Hearing nothing for months, suspecting Mendelssohn had violated his promise not to publicly discuss their exchanges without consulting him first, Jacobi hurried to forestall Mendelssohn's effort to thwart his exposure of Lessing as a pernicious "Spinozist." To counter what he construed as Mendelssohn's breach of faith,[55] he published his exchanges with him under the title *Über die Lehre des Spinoza in Briefen an den Herrn Moses Mendelssohn* [On Spinoza's Teaching, in Letters to Herr Moses Mendelssohn] (1785), which appeared in September 1785, almost simultaneously with *Morgenstunden*.[56] Besides correspondence with Mendelssohn and others, the book's appendixes included responses to Mendelssohn's objections to his Lessing interpretation and Goethe's still unpublished odes "Prometheus" and *Das Göttliche* [The Divine], both appearing here for the first time without the poet's permission (which Goethe greatly resented).

Both books had a powerfully divisive effect. Mendelssohn's eloquent appeal was driven by dread of seeing "natural religion"—belief in God, providence and immortality, and the Leibnizian-Wolffian legacy pulverized between rival extremes—Spinozism, on one side, and Jacobi's and the Rosicrucians' anti-Enlightenment, anti-rationalist effusions on the other. In the preface to *Morgenstunden*, Mendelssohn concurs with Jacobi, Rehberg, Feder, Kant and the younger Reimarus on the need to stem society's dangerous drift toward the "*Materialismus* that threatens to become so general in our time," a serious menace to everyone but one causing an equally undesirable drift to zealotry, irrationality and Counter-Enlightenment. Counter-Enlightenment was ruinously wrongheaded. Contemporaries would do far better to ask: how, then, should thinkers rationally respond to the resurgence of materialism, the "allgemeine Umwälzung" [general revolution] in philosophy so as truly to defeat the interventions of Diderot, d'Holbach, Raynal and their circle, now threatening the world?[57]

Angered by Jacobi's accusation that his lifelong friend had not confided his true opinions to him, Mendelssohn was greatly distressed in his last months at seeing Lessing heavily compromised.[58] In an emotional missive, of October 1785, he complained to Kant of Jacobi's shabby conduct in publishing private correspondence "without having asked for and obtained the correspondents' permission" and misrepresenting Lessing's opinions by turning him into a "declared Spinozist." Jacobi's text he called a "monstrous" blend of rationality and zealotry: "the head is Goethe's, the body Spinoza's, the feet Lavater's," the last a reference to Johann Caspar Lavater (1741–1801), a Swiss Counter-Enlightenment pastor and anti-philosophical fundamentalist vehemently critical of Mendelssohn who figured among Jacobi's heroes.[59] Defying rapidly waning health, Mendelssohn hurled himself into a final bout of work, composing a fierce last rebuttal of Jacobi, convinced he must at all costs avert the public discrediting of his friend, Germany's "admired defender of theism and rational religion" and halt Lessing's calculated transmogrification into a "Spinozist, atheist and blasphemer."[60]

Delivering his finished text personally to his publisher in Berlin in freezing weather, on 31 December 1785, on foot and too lightly clad, Mendelssohn caught a fever, leading to coughing fits and rapid debilitation. Deeply distraught, he died five days later. His last text, *An die Freunde Lessings* [To the Friends of Lessing: An Appendix to Mr. Jacobi's Correspondence on the Doctrine of Spinoza], appeared posthumously just three weeks afterwards. Lessing *had* been drawn to *Pantheismus* in his youth, he conceded (this time without denying Lessing's anti-Christian stance); but what the mature Lessing professed, as *Nathan der Weise* attests, was a "purified Spinozism" uniting Jews and Christians, Judaism and Christianity, in belief in a knowing God. "Was Lessing a Spinozist?" Simply posed, the question is meaningless. First one must define what Spinozism is and is not.[61] Spinoza's relation to Judaism and to Christianity was complex. Spinozism, he affirmed, approaches closer to traditional Jewish teaching than the "orthodox teaching of the Christians," hence the distance to be covered to get from Spinozism to natural religion and theism, the degree of "purification" needed, in the case of Judaism is less than with Christianity.[62] Judaism Mendelssohn differentiated from Christianity in fairly broad terms: "Judaism requires faith in historical truths, in facts on which the authority of our positive ritual law is based. The existence and authority of the Supreme Lawgiver, however, must be acknowledged by reason and here, in the case of Judaism, revelation and faith are not required: "Judaism is not a revealed religion but a revealed law."[63] As a Jew, Mendelssohn claimed special justification to "seek conviction through rational arguments" without jeopardizing the essentials of his religion.

Kant, for his part, disapproved of both Mendelssohn's *Morgenstunden* and Jacobi's reply, both reaching him in Königsberg, in September 1785, sent by Hamann, who, along with the *Berlinische Monatsschrift,* was urging Kant to intervene publicly. With polite bows to Kant, Mendelssohn acknowledged his colleague's superior acuteness and insight while observing cuttingly that, despite everything, the "all-crushing" Kant had not yet shown the same capacity for building new foundations for authority and belief as demolishing the old ones.[64] Were Jacobi and his allies justified in claiming rational knowledge of God and his providence is impossible because Spinoza's system cannot be overturned philosophically?[65] Given that Counter-Enlightenment "fanaticism" and systematic atheism (of Diderot, Helvétius and d'Holbach) were both advancing, philosophers of standing must speak out and help guide the public. If Kant stayed silent, urged Markus Herz (1747–1803), earlier one of Mendelssohn's closest allies, and other disciples, Jacobi's claim that he had the great man of philosophy on his side would surely have harmful consequences for Kantianism. Some hoped Kant would intervene to back Mendelssohn. But Kant, while rejecting Jacobi's claims, was equally irritated by the public's perception of the relationship between himself and Mendelssohn. From his main professorial ally at Halle, Ludwig Heinrich Jakob (1759–1827), he learnt that readers there viewed *Morgenstunden* as Mendelssohn repudiating and scoring a "triumph" over Kant (to which, however, Mendelssohn himself made no claim).[66]

For Kant too the *Pantheismusstreit* had become a convoluted personal dilemma exposing his reputation and philosophy to new pressures, making it difficult for him to stand aside as he would have preferred. But if Hamann hoped Kant would join him and Jacobi against Mendelssohn and Lessing, he too was disappointed. Germany's chief enlightener resolved to be cautious and aloof: he had no desire to align with Lessing's Spinozism, or his former, now estranged student Herder, or Jacobi and Hamann, or indeed with Mendelssohn and the Jews, since he strongly disagreed with Mendelssohn that Judaism was a religion of rationality and tolerance par excellence. Outwardly polite toward Mendelssohn, he openly despised Herder and soon also Jacobi, who, he suspected, was out merely to make a name for himself and whose book, he told Herz, "was not worth a serious refutation."[67] The sage of Königsberg was especially exasperated that his philosophy was being buffeted from all directions at once.

After first proposing (to Hamann's delight) to rebut *Morgenstunden*, as publicly reported in Ewald's journal, on realizing Mendelssohn was chiefly attacking Jacobi's arguments, not his own, Kant changed tack.[68] The furor, Kant felt, unhelpfully entangled two different questions he believed needed separating: first, the question of whether Lessing was a "Spinozist" *tout court*, in Jacobi's sense or, as Mendelssohn claimed, a "purified Spinozist." This was a dispute of little concern to Kant, who had long since repudiated "Spinozismus" and its exponents (though Jacobi, he notes in parenthesis, had convinced him Lessing probably did incline to "atheism"). Second, and more important, was the issue posed by the threatened crumbling away of every philosophical demonstration of God's being, the growing "praise and almost deification of the incomprehensible Spinozistic chimaera" [die Lobpreisung und fast Vergötterung des unverständlichen Spinozistischen Hirngespinstes] empowering Jacobi's ridiculous summons to embrace faith and positive religion as the sole exit.[69] Kant's answer, *Was heisst: Sich im Denken orientieren*? [What Does It Mean: To Orient Oneself in Thinking?], appeared in the *Berlinische Monatsschrift*, in October 1786.

Distancing himself from Mendelssohn and Jacobi, Kant adeptly stepped in as the *Pantheismusstreit*'s principal arbiter of the middle ground in Mendelssohn's place, the "third force" between Radical and Counter-Enlightenment. Diplomatically styling Jacobi "an acute author" and Mendelssohn a dogged seeker after truth, he dismissed Mendelssohn's text as adroit an exemplum as one could find of the philosophical genre to which it belongs, but now wholly obsolete.[70] "All the proofs in the worthy Mendelssohn's *Morgenstunden* [. . .] accomplish nothing by way of demonstration." For the task he set himself, grounding God, providence and immortality, is impossible for any philosophical system; his book was just an exercise in reason overreaching itself, futile metaphysical speculation. The greater menace, though, was that of "enthusiasm," the "dethroning of reason." Mendelssohn and Jacobi alike he rebuked for "arguing dogmatically," using "pure reason in the sphere of the supersensible," opening doors to both confusion and mindless zeal.[71] If the primacy of reason properly deployed in metaphysical questions within the correct epistemological bounds falters, then "a wide gate is opened to all 'enthusiasm' and superstition, even atheism."[72]

Kant broadly succeeded in putting down both sides. Rejecting Mendelssohn's approach out of hand, he equally brusquely dismissed Jacobi's "double truth" contention "that the Spinozist concept of God is the only one agreeing with all the principles of reason and yet must, nevertheless, be rejected" in favor of religious truth.[73] Jacobi's parading Spinoza's concept of God as the only correct outcome of philosophical reasoning he attributed to a desire to debase philosophy itself. "Have you thought what you are doing," he reprimanded Jacobi and Hamann, "where your attacks on reason will lead?" With their irresponsible conduct Mendelssohn's adversaries were simultaneously endangering faith and "freedom of thought." His rebuke resounded again in the preface to the *Critique of Pure Reason*'s second edition, in 1787.[74] Reason properly delimited epistemologically alone can ground men's notion of God. All men committed to enlightened progress must champion philosophical reason and freedom to philosophize: all must be free to determine their own convictions. But whatever individuals decide, "do not dispute that prerogative of reason which makes it the highest good on earth, the prerogative of being the final touchstone of truth."[75] Whoever does so is unworthy of this freedom and will "surely forfeit it too." Here, besides Jacobi and other Counter-Enlightenment mystics and Rosicrucians, Kant, without directly saying so, deftly targeted also official repression, especially the recent crackdown on the Bavarian *Illuminati* and ban on teaching his own system at Marburg, where, following polemical attacks by opponents, his system had been judged morally pernicious and conducive to skepticism.[76]

"THERE IS NO SUCH THING AS "MODERATE ENLIGHTENMENT" (LEO STRAUSS)

Following his death, Mendelssohn's philosophical legacy was sidelined by Kant and left precariously placed also within the Jewish world. Mendelssohn's unyielding rationalism projected Christianity as a revealed religion depending on unreliable reports and miracles rather than on confirmed historical facts, as Judaism supposedly did. There are no "mysteries" in Judaism, he maintained, and nothing relating to the power, majesty and providence of God not attested by the power of reason alone. "Thus the report that Lessing was a Spinozist could, for me, be neither astounding nor alienating."[77] By projecting a Lessing championing "purified Spinozism," Mendelssohn walked a tightrope around radical thought, detractors deeming his attitude to Christianity highly offensive, and Jewish critics, including some "enlightened" Berlin Jews, increasingly worried by his aligning Judaism closely to Enlightenment "reason" and "purified Spinozism."[78] His Jewish legacy appeared trapped between Lessing, Jacobi and Kant almost as if he embodied in his own person and philosophy the clashing *Haskalah* impulses championed by Wessely and Friedländer, one rooted in religious tradition and Hebrew, the other in secular reason and philosophy.[79] In the Jewish world after 1786, it was this profound, disturbing ambiguity in his stance that prevented Mendelssohn's subsequent reputation and legacy retaining their exalted status of the early 1780s.

Maimon, like Kant, rebuked both sides in the vast public "Spinoza controversy," disagreeing with Mendelssohn *and* Jacobi. Jacobi, whose philosophical astuteness he too recognized, had rightly discerned an inherent tendency to Spinozism in Mendelssohn's stance, and Lessing's, which both refused to publicly acknowledge down to their deaths. Maimon still begrudged Mendelssohn's attempts to present himself to the public as the champion of the Enlightenment and *Talmudisten* at the same time; his allegiance to Leibniz and Wolff he styled a "political dodge and piece of hypocrisy." Mendelssohn's evasiveness he attributed to what he saw as his mediocrity as a philosopher rather than the conscious Jewish strategy it was.[80] But equally, Jacobi's Christian bias, manipulation of the public and devious use of texts were anathema to Maimon.[81]

Plunging into Kant's *Critique of Pure Reason* only after Mendelssohn's death, in 1786, in the late 1780s, Maimon was fleetingly an out-and-out Kantian; after that, he became more lastingly a "post-Kantian," or rather philosopher synthesizing Maimonideism, Spinozism and Kantianism.[82] Swiftly mastering Kantianism's finer points, by early 1789, he had completed his *Versuch über die Transcendental-philosophie* [Essay on Transcendental Philosophy], a lofty, difficult text shown to Kant by his Jewish friend, the physician-philosopher Markus Herz. This Lithuanian Jew, Kant acknowledged to Herz, in May 1789, was among the "most eminent disciples" his "critical philosophy" had garnered, even if he remained unclear exactly what the significance of Maimon's notoriously difficult, even opaque, commentary on his epistemology actually was.[83] It was published in 1790.

Initially, Kant was enthusiastic, in May 1789 praising Maimon as one of the few fully to grasp the significance of his system. Briefly, it was assumed

Maimon was endorsing Kantianism as the much-needed "third way." But Maimon wrote obscurely, and at first, through the early 1790s, few grasped the exact significance of his commentary on Kant. When he did see it, it struck Kant's former disciple Johann Gottlieb Fichte (1762–1814) as a thunderclap: "I firmly believe," he assured one of the leading Kantians, Carl Leonhard Reinhold (1757–1823), in March 1795, that Maimon "has completely overturned the entire Kantian philosophy as it has been understood by everyone until now, including you, and am prepared to prove it. No-one noticed what he had done; they looked down on him from their heights; I believe that future centuries will mock us bitterly."[84] Kant's throwing in a dash of Humean skepticism to help distance us from metaphysical and theological concepts like truth, God, soul and redemption was all very well. But notwithstanding Kant's fundamental distinction setting *a priori* concepts like "space" and "time," intrinsic to how we think, which we cannot remove from our minds, against our minds processing *a posteriori* sense experience, Kant, argued Maimon, was unable to demonstrate how two such different things, intrinsic concepts and impressions received by our sensibility, ultimately meet and interact to produce knowledge. How do innate concepts like space and time organize our *a posteriori* sense impressions?

Maimon convincingly showed that Kant's formal dualism between concepts and sensibility presents an intractable obstacle to accommodating the very dualism Kant's system establishes, a problem he felt *he* could resolve with his "acosmic" Maimonidean-Spinozist monism tinted with Hasidism, removing the barriers and gaps between metaphysical concepts like God, our minds and things-in-themselves, which Kant fails to do.[85] Reinhold and other "Kantians," he maintained, had it all wrong. Kant was merely a late, albeit not the final stage in the evolution of philosophical truth with Maimonides and Spinoza the crucial preceding steps. Maimon's grand synthesis, or "Koalitionssystem," as he called it, synthesizing God and the world, was a remarkable cumulative concoction commencing with medieval Averroism and Maimonides, proceeding next through Bruno, Spinoza and Leibniz, and culminating in Kant slightly modified, the overarching scheme tinted with Cabbalism and Hasidism.[86]

But if Maimon correctly stressed, like the German Jewish philosopher Leo Strauss (1899–1993) later, that Mendelssohn's attempt to reconcile reason and revolution was ultimately fragile and bound to unravel, he erred in not seeing that it was Mendelssohn's veiled radicalism that rendered the *Haskalah* universally viable. Still, Maimon, again like Strauss later, did see that it was

Mendelssohn who first initiated the Enlightenment's and Judaism's "vindication" of Spinoza, the second stage of the West's judgment of Spinoza. It was eventually to be followed, added Strauss, by a third stage—Spinoza's "canonization" by Heine and Hess. Hence, Mendelssohn in the end contributed decisively, certainly more than Maimon, to converting Spinoza into the supreme icon of Jewish "modernity" and secularism.[87]

Had Mendelssohn known Strauss's maxim that "There is no such Thing as Moderate Enlightenment" which Maimon so memorably pre-echoed, he might well have demurred publicly but silently agreed. And if Mendelssohn never recovered his former prominence in German philosophy, he remained an abiding epoch-making proponent of modern Jewish thought, the unrivalled principal figure of the *Haskalah*. He was the first too, with Gumpertz, to introduce a model into the Jewish world as to how, through *Bildung*, planned self-development and self-education, Jewish individuals could escape the cramping bounds of tradition and observance and develop their capacities freely, thereby entering the world of Enlightenment and Western intellectual debate. Mendelssohn's success in elevating himself toward the upper echelons of German intellectual life inspired Maimon and many who followed on the path of what has aptly been termed "autodidactic self-formation" through reading, discussion and the pursuit of intellectual excellence, in quest of emancipation from rabbinic authority and "superstition."[88]

As is perhaps hardly surprising, the later stunned and helpless passivity with which German Jewry contemplated the rise of organized mass antisemitism after 1880, and, later still, the horrific nightmare of Nazism, prompted some in the post–World War II era to claim Mendelssohn in some way led German Jewry onto a disastrously wrong path, that he was ultimately a false guide leading his co-religionists toward loss of identity as Jews, assimilation and destruction. Maimon being long forgotten, Leo Strauss did much to re-expose the inner contradictoriness of Mendelssohn's publicly proclaimed "moderate Enlightenment" and what he considered its propensity to collapse into its own half-acknowledged underlying Spinozism. To Strauss, Mendelssohn's "purified Spinozism" amounted to just a convenient myth with no real existence.[89] Hannah Arendt scathingly attacked Mendelssohn's strategy, viewing the German-Jewish quest for *Bildung* that resulted as the enterprise of an "obsequious bourgeois *Kulturmensch*" far too addicted to German acculturation. She deplored the loss of Jewish awareness, identity and loyalty among the innumerable German Jews subsequently drawn to assimilation, but was surely wrong not to recognize the positive aspects of Mendelssohn's veiled Spinozism for the subsequent achievement of a meaningful Jewish modernity. For there was no other way Mendelssohn could have smuggled in the indispensable Spinozist elements into his German-Jewish synthesis and plans for a general Jewish Enlightenment.

Maimon was the great rebel of the Jewish Enlightenment and, though largely forgotten later, dying unmourned of ill-health made worse by alcoholism in a Silesian village, in November 1800, in a way a rebel with even wider ambitions than Mendelssohn. For despite his vagaries and rumbustious humor, Maimon was an *Aufklärer* and metaphysician of formidable ability who genuinely believed the "fundamental principles of morality, politics and even of taste, must bear the stamp of reason if they are to be of any use at all," as he exclaimed in the dedication of his *Versuch* to the Polish king, in December 1789, just as the French Revolution was gaining momentum. He had aspired to help the Jews escape their "darkness" while also contributing "something to giving the noble Poles an advantageous opinion of my nation, that is of the Jews living under their protection, to convince them that the Jews, if they have not been useful to the state that has been so patient with them, have lacked neither capacity nor good will, but only a purposeful direction for their powers." The Jews he hoped to alert to their true situation and its drawbacks, "encouraging their boldness and enthusiasm for the task of making themselves, via enlightenment and honesty, ever worthier of the respect of the nation under which they live [whether Poles, Lithuanians, Germans, Russians or Ukrainians]."[90] They must raise their moral level, adapt to the states under which they live, but also preserve the core of their ancient heritage.

Maimon aspired too to serve as a bridge between Kant and Spinoza by clarifying the workings of "reason." If, in 1789, Kant complimented him on his rare grasp of his system, by 1795 he had come to realize Maimon's pretensions extended considerably further than that. He noted too that despite Maimon's hiding behind a screen of Leibnizianism when discussing "intellect," his understanding of the human intellect as "Einschränkung" [limitation] is essentially Spinozism. Even accepting Kant's revised conception of "truth," Maimon pointedly underlined, accepting "truth" consists not in the matching of a definition or representation to the thing-in-itself, but rather in conformity of sensations to the *a priori* rules basic to our minds, Kant still provides no basis for explaining how his dualism of concepts and sensibility coheres, how our intuitions do correspond to the *a priori* rules. He ended by totally ruling out any plausibility for Kant's "synthetic" judgments in physics and dismissing Kant's "practical reason" as a false path for ethics.

On realizing his former disciple had uncovered what Maimon (and later Fichte and others) considered an irresolvable difficulty in his philosophy, Kant, writing to Reinhold, in March 1794, haughtily commented: "Jews always like to do such things, acquiring a semblance of importance at other people's expense."[91]

SIX

David Nassy's New World Vistas (1770–1790)

During the seventeenth century, driven by oppression and persecution, trickles of mainly Sephardic Jews found their way to Dutch Brazil (1630–54), several Caribbean Islands, New Amsterdam (from 1664 "New York") and the plantation colony of Dutch Guyana, or Surinam. Jewish settlers in all these regions, later including also Charleston and Savannah in the Carolinas and Georgia, and Philadelphia, found themselves, despite (or owing to) their relative isolation and the fewness of white settlers of all kinds, considerably more advantageously placed than they had been in Europe, where the great bulk of their co-religionists remained more oppressed.

Yet, despite the unparalleled freedom and toleration they enjoyed in the Dutch and British trans-Atlantic colonies, toleration growing with the advance of the Enlightenment, most of early New World Jewry still remained a separate, narrowly educated and strictly religious subculture. Rigidly enclosed and marginalized, as critics saw it, they stayed passively within the confines of traditional Jewish observance, custom, and language (Portuguese, Spanish and increasingly also Yiddish). During the seventeenth and eighteenth centuries, New World Jewry became firmly established and prospered, chiefly in the Caribbean and on North America's East Coast, as a widely dispersed but far from inconspicuous community, left alone even if still often giving rise to complaints. In the later eighteenth century, this *de facto* social-cultural segregation eroded considerably, especially owing to the impact of Enlightenment ideas, the Revolution that gave birth to the United States (1775–83), the decline of the Dutch seaborne empire, and, not least, reverberations of the French Revolution in the Caribbean.

When the American Revolution began, in 1775–76, there were scarcely more than two thousand Jews in the entire territory soon to be transformed, after a long, bitter struggle, into the United States, a country then with some two and half million inhabitants. Most of its Jews were concentrated in just five centers—New York, Philadelphia, Newport in Rhode Island, Charleston and Savannah. Yet, despite their small numbers, there were revolutionary sectors where Jews, even if on a minute scale compared to the far more numerous Irish, nevertheless played a disproportionate, distinctive role sufficient to make them occasionally noticed as an identifiable subversive category. This happened, for example, in Georgia, the southernmost British mainland colony, where the local community, Mikveh Israel, was founded, in 1735, in the port of Savannah, the colony's capital established two years earlier. Mikveh Israel's founders were a group of forty-two Jews who arrived together on a vessel from London, twenty-five of them Sephardic newcomers only recently arrived in England as refugees. The latter were fleeing from the Inquisition in the Iberian Peninsula, escaping the intensified persecution of "New Christians" that swept Spain and Portugal in the 1720s and 1730s, and in Portugal persisted through the 1740s. It was the Inquisition's last major push to crush the incomprehensibly tenacious crypto-Jewish underground. In Savannah, more Sephardim and Ashkenazim soon joined the first group.

The most prominent family in Savannah's mixed Sephardic-Ashkenazic community, the family that established the community's permanent cemetery, in 1773, was that of Benjamin Sheftall, a merchant of German background who, with his wife, figured among the original founders. His merchant son, Mordechai Sheftall (1738–1797), emerged during 1775 as the leader, in Georgia, of the boycott movement against British and British Caribbean imports, the man who took the lead in turning away British vessels without permitting them to unload their cargoes, and, before long, became the main organizer of armed resistance to the crown in the colony. Although his role throughout the Revolutionary War was principally civilian, financing and organizing supplies for the Continental Army, he was so pivotal to the local effort that he was promoted to the titular rank of "colonel." As early as August 1775, the British governor of Georgia, Sir James Wright, reported to London that "the conduct of the people here is most infamous," singling out for special mention "one Sheftall, a Jew" as the leading figure of the resistance and chairman of Georgia's boycott committee. It was "this fellow," he explained, who "issues orders to captains of vessels, sending them away without letting them unload."[1]

British troops occupied Savannah, in 1778, causing most of the town's Jews to flee into the interior, or to Charleston, in South Carolina. Savannah then remained in English hands for around five years (1778–82), a period when royal control was reasserted and locals were kept under close surveillance. "I judged it also necessary," reported Wright to London, on 9 March 1781, "to prevent the Jews who formerly resided here from returning, or others from coming to settle here. For these people, my Lord, were found to a man to be violent rebels and persecutors of the king's loyal subjects." This hardly fitted, admitted Wright, with Britain's tradition of imperial toleration but, he assured his superiors, "the times require these exertions."[2]

Sheftall remained a lifelong, observant Jew along with several others who distinguished themselves as officers in the American Revolution, including Frances Salvador (1747–1776), son of a prominent London Sephardic family, a South Carolina landowner and revolutionary, and the first unconverted Jew to sit as a representative in any American state legislature. He was killed in August 1776, in the South Carolina interior, fighting Native Americans allied to the British. Several such individuals felt inspired by the new revolutionary ideals and had an impact on the struggle locally and on their religious communities. But these figures were not attempting to transform Jewish life as such, or redeem the Jews worldwide from their age-old status of degradation and marginalization. Nor were they trying to elevate Jews generally to any envisioned new status as citizens sharing in equal rights and as equal participants in the Enlightenment. Still, very occasionally, one ran into an individual who did nurture such a broader revolutionary outlook, seeking the path to an enlightened Jewish future. Notable here was the Sephardic writer and revolutionary David Nassy (1747–1806), or to give him his full synagogue name, David de Ishac Cohen Nassy, a descendant of one of the first Jewish colonizers in the Dutch zone of South America's northeastern coast.

Nassy typified the fringe of enlightened Jewish *érudits* whom the marquis d'Argens labeled "Spinosistes" owing to their exceptionally wide reading, radical outlook, dislike of clergy of all stripes and appetite for wide-ranging reform.[3] Among the numerous non-religious works proliferating in Nassy's impressive personal library, housed at Jodensavanne in the tropical interior, and later at Paramaribo, Surinam's chief port and capital, beside works of Hobbes, Bayle, Montesquieu, Voltaire and a plentiful stock of Spanish literature, were the six volumes of an early 1738 edition of d'Argens's *Lettres Juives* (6 vols., The Hague, 1736–40). It was here that d'Argens first sketched his imagined Sephardic elite of intellectuals and reformers transforming all Judaism and Jewry in Spinoza's wake.[4] Prominent among those orchestrating the clandestine myth of the subversive Jewish thinker and reformer, the concocted "Orobio" who overturns all accepted religious authority and repression, Christian and rabbinic equally, d'Argens, not unlike La Croze earlier, and d'Holbach later, materially contributed to encouraging the rise of this new breed of philosophically powered Jewish revolutionary.

Jesuit and other critics denouncing d'Argens for his *Lettres Juives* claimed he had fabricated it all, offering the world a ridiculous myth. These erudite, discerning Jews, men of high moral integrity exalting Spinozism and detailing a heady list of Christian failings, actual or virtual *Spinosistes* disdaining what most people believe, they argued, simply did not exist. D'Argens mires our world with a lurid, destructive, absurd fiction. To this, d'Argens answered that these "Orobio"-like Jewish *Spinosistes* were no fiction or myth concocted by him but actual, real Jews of wide reading, genuine learning and high moral stature he had personally met earlier in life and conferred with at Amsterdam, The Hague, Constantinople and Venice.[5] Given the strongly French-language orientation of his books and intellectual interests, Nassy was clearly familiar early on with the "Orobio" role model encountered in the clandestine philosophic literature and hence with the iconic Sephardic philosopher figure deploring Jewish society's inadequacies and rabbinic Judaism's defects, along with Christian and Islamic theology's alleged fallacies, viewing all humanity "avec un oeil philosophe" [with a philosophic eye], as d'Argens expressed it. The foremost intellectual of Caribbean Sephardic Jewry during the revolutionary era, Nassy was indeed a classic instance of a Jewish *philosophe* nurtured on French radical freethinking blended with the Iberian crypto-Jewish underground heritage. He evolved into a revolutionary aspiring to help free not just a particular country from a distant sovereign, or support local resistance to unpopular imperial measures, but contribute to emancipating all humanity from the entire range of its worldly and spiritual shackles.

By reaching out to the non-Jewish world through their wide secular interests and reading, Nassy and his small circle at Paramaribo and the Jewish township of Jodensavanne entered the wider trans-Atlantic cultural world and became eager reformers while simultaneously sliding into conflict with the Law of Moses and rabbinic authority as well as the West's general structures of thought and prejudice. Rigid observance, tradition and law, and indifference to the world beyond Judaism, became for Nassy an insufferable barrier to individual development, a focus of ever-sharper enlightened critique. Over the centuries, it seemed to him, intolerance and unrelenting repression had caused the Jews to be squeezed into a pitifully restricted ghetto of the mind, adding to the ghetto of social reality. Consequently, Jewish community elders and congregations in the New World had conserved the same restricted outlook blighting the Old World, severely hampering those striving for freer, more secular perspectives in defiance of rabbinic authority.

Victims of a merciless oppression, fleeing the flames of the "hideous tribunal of the Inquisition" still raging in Portugal in the 1730s and the 1740s, were the very men, admonished Nassy, who instituted "le despotisme religieux," darkening New World Jewish life ever since its seventeenth-century beginnings. The same old loathsome spirit of persecution and fanaticism relentlessly oppressing Jews for centuries in Iberia had impelled Holland's tragically misguided Sephardic community to oppress Uriel da Costa and Spinoza even "avant que leur athéisme eut éclaté" [before their atheism burst out], and their narrow-minded repressiveness still gripped the economically flourishing Sephardic congregations of the eighteenth-century New World.[6]

New World "Pharisaic," that is, rabbinic "passion dangéreuse" stifling freedom of thought and expression, was a Jewish failing no less malicious and reprehensible, in Nassy's view, than the prejudiced, persecuting spirit of practically all churches. Despotic community control and repression sanctioned by colonial authorities characterizing New World Jewry, held Nassy, was sustained by the same profound ignorance and lack of understanding hampering the rest of the Jewish world of his time. European Jewish society's excessive preoccupation with retailing, peddling and usury may have stemmed partly from lack of alternatives due to social exclusion, but arose also from lack of awareness of the "common good" (understandable in its context though this was), and rigid communal separateness and discipline. Jewish communal organization and educational separateness accentuated defects originating in external repression, which then enabled Voltaire and other supposedly "enlightened" detractors to present these as innate in the Jewish people. The root cause of this malaise was a deplorable lack of secular education and enlightenment constricting the Jewish majority's outlook in the New and Old World alike. New World Jewish credulity and "ignorance" fomented ceaseless theological wrangling, perverse preoccupation with "céremonies superstitieuses," and a deplorable *bigotisme* [bigotry] as rife among Jews as among Catholics and Calvinists. Before finding themselves driven to the tragic extreme of "atheism" by such *bigotisme*, Uriel da Costa and Spinoza, argued Nassy, found themselves at an intermediate, balanced, more positive stage steering toward an outward-looking, enlightened secularized Judaism that should have been encouraged, not crushed.

That Nassy enjoyed already a reputation for exceptional erudition in philosophy, languages and history, all aspects of the trans-Atlantic Enlightenment, including its clandestine texts, well before the age of thirty, hence prior to the American Revolution's commencement in 1775, emerges plainly from the memoirs of a high-ranking French official (and later royalist leader during the Revolution) Pierre-Victor Malouet (1740–1814). A senior figure in Saint-Domingue (Haiti), he owned sugar plantations and numerous slaves but also led the local (moderate) Enlightenment. He met Nassy during a seven-week trip to French Cayenne, in 1776 (not 1777 as sometimes stated), the same year United States Independence was proclaimed and the revolutionary drama intensified, to survey local conditions and discuss the problem of slave insurrection and flight. Malouet toured Paramaribo, Jodensavanne and Surinam's sugar plantations on French royal official business, gathering information.[7] In Surinam, he encountered two Jews "dont l'érudition et les lumières m'ont fort étonné" [whose erudition and enlightened views greatly astonished me], Joseph Barrios and "Isaac Nassy [*sic*]." Nassy was an "extraordinary man considering that he had succeeded by the age of thirty, never having left Surinam where he was born and without any other support than his own genius, in elevating himself above the errors of his sect, researching deeply into its history, correcting Boulanger's mistakes in his writings on antiquity, and learning Arabic as well as Chaldaean and rabbinic Hebrew methodically, and most modern languages which he speaks and writes correctly."[8] Nassy indeed possessed excellent French and Dutch besides Spanish and Portuguese (then still the first languages of Dutch Caribbean Jewry), and in 1776, aged only twenty-nine, was master of an astoundingly wide range of Enlightenment literature.

The "Boulanger" here was Nicolas-Antoine Boulanger (1722–1759), an atheist *philosophe* and republican-minded ally of Diderot and d'Holbach who died young but was long remembered for his subversive *L'Antiquité dévoilée dans ses usages* [Antiquity Unveiled by Its Usages] (1766), a classic of eighteenth-century anti-theological radical thought. That Nassy took to correcting Boulanger's "errors" in the latter's history of antiquity at a young age corresponds with what we know of his energetically irreverent outlook. Nassy proved not just knowledgeable about Judaism ancient and modern, accomplished in languages and well-read in antiquity and later history generally, but by 1776 was already an aspiring reformer steeped in radical ideas.

Joseph Barrios, exceptionally gifted too, died young, much regretted by friends, in 1786, after being entrusted by the colony's governor with supervising supplies for the cordon of inland military outposts guarding the plantations from runaway rebellious former slaves south of Jodensavanne. Jews had served in the Surinam militia since 1671, a fact later vividly recalled in Holland in the 1790s and opening decade of the nineteenth century, during disputes over whether Jews were fit for military service.[9] Nassy left the military side to others. Singularly studious, a lifelong, obsessive intellectual, for Nassy, as for Maimon, philosophy was less a means of diversion from worldly troubles, though it was consolation too, than a tool for transforming the world around him. Consolation he needed, having experienced only failure and frustration as a sugar and coffee plantation owner, during the early 1770s, leading to bankruptcy and loss of his estate. Laden with debts, in the late 1770s, he worked in Jodensavanne as an apothecary.[10]

Actually, not only Nassy, but the entire Surinam Jewish community from the 1770s endured a steadily worsening economic plight and other setbacks to its narrowly based plantation economy dependent on slaves. Though now more slowly than those of Jamaica, the number of Sephardim in Surinam was still increasing, rising from 790 souls, in 1778, to 852 in 1789.[11] But where, in 1730 Jews possessed 115 out of Dutch Guyana's total of 401 flourishing sugar and coffee plantations and, in 1760, 115 out of 591, the colony's sugar and coffee output, contracting especially since the disruption of the Fourth Anglo-Dutch War (1780–84), was rapidly overtaken by British Jamaica boasting, by the late 1780s, over three times as many slaves working its plantations and, still more dramatically, by French Saint-Domingue (Haiti) with nearly five times as many.[12] By 1788, moreover, the specifically Jewish plantation economy producing sugar and coffee had for various reasons lost ground even faster than Surinam's plantation system overall. By 1788, the number of Jewish-owned plantations in the colony had declined to a mere 46.[13] In sugarcane and coffee output, Surinam was less and less able to compete with either the French or British Caribbean.

It was painfully obvious that the whole Jewish community faced a socioeconomic emergency, and was sliding into "dire poverty and decay," contraction reflected in the community's communal tax on congregants' incomes, the *finta*, which shrank disastrously between 1770 and 1790 by over two-thirds.[14] Such was the post-1775 Surinam Sephardic economy's shrinkage that among communal leaders and militia captains on guard duty at Jodensavanne, to give one instance, the patrician Abraham Rafael Curiel, descendant of the renowned Curiel family of Amsterdam, found his *finta* assessment dropping from 246 guilders, in 1770, to only 80 in 1778, and 83 in 1787. Yet, at the same time, because his income contracted more slowly than most of the rest, by 1778, he had ascended from twenty-fourth- to eleventh-wealthiest of the Surinam Sephardim, and fifteenth, in 1787.[15] Worsening economic conditions caused many Jews to abandon the colony at this time, some returning to Europe, others migrating elsewhere in the Americas. Nassy, by contrast, remained his entire life in Surinam apart from a three- to four-year interval, from 1792, in the nascent United States and several months on the Danish Caribbean island of St. Thomas.[16]

CARIBBEAN ENLIGHTENMENT AND THE QUEST FOR EMANCIPATION

Surinam Jewry, tiny by European and Near Eastern standards, was large by New World standards, huge as a proportion of Dutch Guyana's total white population. For some years departures of Jews were more than compensated for by poorer new arrivals, mostly Ashkenazim, from Europe and elsewhere in the Caribbean, so that total Jewish numbers in Surinam were still increasing until the late 1780s despite the economic recession. In 1791 Surinam's Jewish population reached 1,281, comprising 834 Sephardim and 447 Ashkenazim, the latter now accounting for over a third of the total and steadily growing as a proportion of the whole. Beginning with the smallpox epidemic of 1789, however, through the 1790s, the demographic curve suddenly reversed. While the Ashkenazic segment continued to grow slowly, it was the Sephardic segment that contracted, between 1791 and 1817, from 834 to 691, after which the position stabilized. By 1849, when Surinam Jewry was only half Sephardic, the corresponding figures were 683 Sephardim and 681 Ashkenazim.[17] Even so, Surinam remained throughout a major outpost of Jewish New World settlement and of cultural ferment caused by the trans-Atlantic revolutionary wave.

Already an ardent enlightener before the American Revolution, Nassy became a revolutionary step by step. His Enlightenment's secular thrust was fully reflected on his library shelves in Paramaribo, which held (when inventoried in 1782) 433 books. By 1776, Nassy's collection, that of possibly the most widely read Jew in the Americas, was defiantly secular, with a strikingly small number of Hebrew and prayer books, or other religious literature,[18] heavily dominated by shelves of French philosophy and literature capped above by portrait prints of Voltaire and Rousseau. He had copies of Bayle's *Dictionnaire*, a seven-volume set of Montesquieu, all of Rousseau in thirteen volumes, Hobbes's *Leviathan* in Dutch, Fontenelle, Hume's philosophical works in a two-volume French version published at Amsterdam, in 1764, with Voltaire the best-represented author. Naturally, he possessed too a copy of the most influential of all eighteenth-century works discussing the world beyond Europe—the *Histoire philosophique des Deux Indes* (1770), the most renowned "philosophique" late-Enlightenment work on the Indies East and West and a text notoriously radical in content. Its most subversive sections, composed by Diderot and his circle, included a fierce denunciation of British policy in India and, in later editions, a plea to readers to support the American Revolution. Appearing in numerous editions through the 1770s and 1780s, Nassy repeatedly cites the *Histoire philosophique* in his own early Geneva edition of 1771.[19]

The *Histoire philosophique* was also the most authoritative Enlightenment work arguing that in the future, Jewish emancipation must become a reality, and to be real, must obtain some secure, designated spot beyond Europe, perhaps Jamaica or another Caribbean island, where the Jews, free at last from Christian hatred and oppression, would finally be left alone, unmolested to rule themselves "enfin libres, tranquilles et heureux dans un coin de l'univers" [finally free, tranquil and happy in one corner of the universe].[20] Historians often underestimate the *Histoire philosophique*'s impact on the Enlightenment and especially for fomenting anti-colonialism and general revolutionary attitudes, but also its role in re-orienting and reshaping the (Radical) Enlightenment's stance toward Jews and Judaism. It is assuredly no accident that the *Histoire philosophique* is cited more often, and more centrally, than any other text in Nassy's *Essai historique sur la colonie de Suriname* (1788), his own chief work and the Surinam Enlightenment's chief literary adornment. Completed in 1786, though not published until 1788, this chronicle was chiefly composed by Nassy but with the collaboration of friends, all erudite Sephardics, notably Moseh Pereira de Leon and S. H. de la Parra. The

Histoire philosophique calls for the emancipation of all humanity, universally, citing the Jews as deserving no more but also no less than the rest.

Nassy's *Essai historique* cites verbatim a passage where the *Histoire philosophique* discusses the, thus far unheard of, free status of the Jews in Surinam: "there is not perhaps any other dominion in the world where this unfortunate nation (the Jewish) is so well treated; not only have they been given freedom to practice their religion, own landed property, and decide themselves concerning disputes among its members, but in addition they enjoy the right of all the citizens to participate in the general administration and in choosing the public magistrates." The *Histoire* suggests this illustrated how commerce "silences all the prejudices of peoples and religion before the general interest that should link men together," concluding: "qu'est ce que ces vaines dénominations, de Juifs, de Luthériens, de François, d'Hollandois? Malheureux habitants d'une terre si pénible à cultiver, n'êtes vous pas tous des hommes?" [What are these vain denominations of Jews and Lutherans, of French and Dutch? Unhappy inhabitants of a land so difficult to cultivate, are you not all men?][21] Nassy could only applaud "la philosophie impartiale," the spirit of Diderot and the French Radical Enlightenment pervading this fundamental work, lamenting only that this memorable passage was afterwards deleted from many subsequent editions—so vehemently did some object.

Other notable works about Europeans in the Indies in Nassy's library were French renderings of Bartolomé de Las Casas and William Robertson, Marmontel's *Les Incas,* Raynal's account of the American Revolution, and Anquetil Duperron's *La Législation Orientale*, a major work championing Hindu, Zoroastrian and other Indian and Persian learning and traditions, fiercely critical of European colonialism in India. Besides d'Argens's *Lettres Juives,* also among his numerous books of secular Jewish interest, were Isaac Cardoso's *Excelencias de los Hebreos* (1679), Isaac de Pinto's *Précis des arguments contre les matérialistes* and *Essai sur le luxe,* and, no. 235 in the catalogue, d'Holbach's reworking of Orobio de Castro and La Croze—*Israel Vengé.*[22] In a remote tropical haven, remote from Europe's cultural life, Nassy was in no way cut off from rare, clandestine, illicit books that Europeans, Christians and Jews alike, including the Dutch, were then strictly forbidden to read. Although we do not know exactly when he first obtained such items, he possessed some at least when the American Revolution began. If we cannot be sure when the idealized cosmopolitan "Orobio" fashioned by La Croze, d'Argens and d'Holbach first penetrated his imagination, it did and must have helped implant in his mind a vision of the idealized Jewish reformer and *philosophe* of surpassing secular erudition, robustly anti-Talmudic and tradition-shattering, who grasps the "reality of things" and strives to reshape our world while most of society, including the secular governing authorities, as yet possesses little inkling of what is required.

Nassy eventually owned a spectacular stock of Radical Enlightenment texts, seething with anti-religious sentiment and materialism,[23] including, besides Boulanger, a 1770 French edition of Toland's *Le Nazaranéen*, d'Argens's *Philosophie de Bonsens* (1737), Fréret's *Oeuvres*, d'Holbach's *La Morale universelle* (3 vols. Amsterdam, 1776), d'Holbach's *Éthocratie*, Richard Price's *Observations sur la nature de la liberté civile* (Rotterdam, 1776), and Voltaire's not especially convincing refutation of d'Holbach, *Dieu, Réponse au* Système de la Nature (1770).[24] Also among his library representing the Enlightenment's radical thrust were the anonymous *Bekeerings-Geschiedenis van den Graaf J. F. Struensee uit het Hoogduitsch vertaald* (Amsterdam, 1772), recounting the tragic story of the clash of Enlightenment reform with Protestant repression in Denmark-Norway during the 1770–71 Struensee episode.[25] Before briefly revolutionizing government, laws and education, and working to widen toleration and freedom of expression in Denmark-Norway, Struensee, the man whose life ended on a scaffold in Copenhagen jeered by an immense crowd urged on by the clergy, had, while a physician in Altona, proposed municipal healthcare on an equal basis for all, including Altona's Jews.[26]

Belonging to a remote, relatively tolerant society deep in the tropics, Nassy had little need to be overly reticent about his revolutionary creed. For the rest of his career he continued collecting French philosophical literature and discussing texts with his small group of like-minded Enlightenment devotees. The quest for full toleration, freedom of thought, civic equality for Jews, ejecting religious authority from public debate, politics, and law, and support for the American, French and Batavian revolutions permeated Nassy's approach throughout: "philosophes aimables," he urged the like-minded, during the 1780s democratic ferment in Holland, "réunissez-vous pour implorer l'Être des êtres pour le salut d'un gouvernement qui sans perdre de vue les égards dus à son culte, scut mettre en vogue, et protéger le contraire de ce qui a fait verser des ruisseaux de sang en Europe. Que l'intolerance civile, et le préjugé national puissent être bannis de la terre à perpétuité!" [Well-meaning philosophes unite to implore the Being of beings for the salvation of a government [in the Netherlands and Dutch Caribbean] which, without shelving the respect due to its public religion, knows how to put into common use and protect the opposite to what has caused rivers of blood to flow in Europe. May civil intolerance and national prejudice be banished from the earth for ever!][27]

The American Revolution had introduced a new standard of equality and civic integration which stood in striking contrast to the continuing situation in the Dutch, French and British colonies. Yet, at the same time, instituting Jewish equality remained far from complete, and glaring inconsistencies were still prevalent, even in the United States despite the fact that individual Jews, from Georgia to Canada, had undeniably played their part in the long and bitter struggle against the British crown. When an American rebel force captured Montreal, in 1775, but found itself in great difficulties due to the French Canadian population siding with Bishop Briand of Quebec and the clergy against the Revolution, boycotting the rebels and denying them supplies, one of the few local figures who intervened for the Revolution, against the bishop and local opinion, was a locally prominent Jewish merchant, David Salisbury Franks (1740–1793). Unlike most of the Jews in the Montreal area who were generally as Loyalist as the French-speaking Catholic majority, Franks helped supply and finance the beleaguered rebel force from early 1776 until June, when he, along with the remnants of the invasion force, had hastily to evacuate Montreal. As the struggle raged on, Franks rose to became a major and aide-de-camp to the revolutionary commander Benedict Arnold (1741–1801), prior to the latter's defection to the British in 1780. From 1778, Franks used his proficiency in French as a liaison officer assisting communication between the Americans and the French force sent to support the revolutionaries against Britain. Finally, during 1782–83, he assisted Benjamin Franklin during his ambassadorship in Paris.[28]

The names of Hyam Salomon (1740–1785), a leader of the Philadelphia Jewish congregation newly arrived in America, in 1775, from Lissa, in Poland, of Solomon Bush, a Philadelphia militia captain, by July 1777 one of the commanders of the Pennsylvania state militia, whose sister married Sheftall's son, Moses, and others devoted to the Revolution, likewise became fairly widely known. But the new North American paradise was not yet quite what the Jewish revolutionaries wanted and what some Jews elsewhere were tempted to suppose it was. In fact, in nearly all states of the Union, the American Revolution initially made strikingly little difference to the continuing exclusion of Jews from office, political participation and equal civic rights. Apart from New York State, where there was an early shift, all other states retained strict "religious tests" for officeholders requiring avowed allegiance to Christ, thereby wholly debarring Jews from office until well into the nineteenth century. This was the case likewise in early nineteenth-century Canada: despite the strict Loyalism of most of Canada's Jews—in contrast to their co-religionists in the United States and much of the Caribbean, equality as regards land purchases, officeholding and qualifying for election as representatives to the regional assemblies was effectively denied to Jews in both Upper and Lower Canada, until 1833.[29]

Naturally, continuing debarment was resented. In December 1783, at the close of the Revolutionary War, the Philadelphia Jewish community headed by Rabbi Gerson Seixas, "their parnas or president Asher Myers, Bernard Gratz and Haym Salomon," petitioned the State Council of Censors, in Philadelphia, the nation's then capital, about the continuing anomaly. "The Jews residing in Pennsylvania, most respectfully showeth," began their petition, they had a definite grievance because "it is ordered that each member of the General Assembly of representatives of the freemen of Pennsylvania, before he takes his seat, shall make or subscribe a declaration which ends in these words: "I do acknowledge the Scriptures of the Old and New Testament to be given by divine inspiration" since this clearly infringed the Revolution's supposedly sacred principle that no man could be deprived of his civil rights "on account of his religious sentiments."[30] Pennsylvania used different wording than Maryland or Delaware, the latter's state constitution, revised in 1776, requiring unequivocal avowal of "belief in the Christian religion" from whoever was elected to and accepted public office. It was less coercive than Massachusetts, which besides debarring Jews from public life required all citizens to pay the state church tax to whichever church predominated in their neighborhood.[31] Still, Jews found themselves no less systematically excluded from public office in Pennsylvania than virtually everywhere else in the nascent United States and British Canada.

Jews had forthrightly supported the Revolution, the petitioners reminded the Philadelphia assembly, while their "brethren of St Eustatius, for the same cause, experienced the most severe resentments of the British commanders." The second point referred to the events of February 1781, when Admiral Rodney's fleet captured the Dutch island of St. Eustatius so as to sever the foremost single artery by which powder, munitions, arms and artillery reached the rebels from abroad, mainly Holland which, from 1775 until 1783, was the Revolution's principal foreign source of supply. Rodney's landing force of three thousand men had assailed the St. Eustatius entrepôt, that "nest of vipers that preyed on the vitals of Great Britain," as a leading contemporary historian of the Revolution put it, because that base and especially its Jews had "done England more harm than all the arms of her most potent enemies, and alone supported the infamous American rebellion." St. Eustatius Jews, after decades enjoying exceptional freedom even by the standards of other Caribbean colonies, had become "objects of particular resentment." In retaliation for their "infamous" collusion with the Revolution, Rodney ordered the expulsion of all 101 Sephardic menfolk from the island: they "were ordered to give up the keys to their stores, to leave their wealth and merchandize behind them, and to depart the island without knowing the place of their destination."[32] Britain's seamen then plundered the island's warehouses. That was all very well, replied the Pennsylvania state assembly, but their gathering could and would not lift the restrictions on Jews and all non-Christians.

Theology's grip on society and politics, backed by prejudice, experience showed, was not so easily broken. Hence, a more robustly anti-theological form of Enlightenment was needed to justify the demand that society concede Jews equal status as intellectually independent men of integrity, and as citizens. Nassy, Montel, Franks and the Jewish New World Enlightenment clique had every reason to embrace the Radical Enlightenment, the only uncompromising emancipatory universalism available. In contrast to the moderate mainstream, Radical Enlightenment provided New World—like Old World—Jewry with clear conceptual tools opposed to existing structures of authority, sufficiently opposed to the political and social status quo, sufficiently anti-theological and revolutionary in short, to advance their cause against the edifice of prejudice and bigotry rooted in centuries of discrimination.

Among obstacles hindering Surinam Jewry's progress and freedom, held Nassy, in a memorandum urging extensive reform of the Sephardic community regulations, or *Haskamoth*, and especially the education system, submitted to the community board of elders, the *Mahamad*, in 1785, was "ignorance," poor Dutch and an insufficiently Dutch-oriented vernacular culture to enable them to become adequately integrated into society. The community's present economic predicament, he argued, was worse than it would have been, had not ease of living and abundance lured the Jewish plantation owners of the more prosperous first half of the eighteenth century into complacency and neglecting their offspring's education, and the need for modern languages and science.[33] Beyond basic literacy and numeracy most, Sephardic and Ashkenazic alike, were chronically deficient in languages, science and culture and prone to hide behind constricting, narrow rabbinic horizons keeping them immersed in credulity and superstition.[34] Nassy's strictures applied to the womenfolk too. In his *Essai historique*, he compliments Surinam's Jewish women on their good looks while stressing the lamentable ignorance characterizing, he thought, especially the Ashkenazic Caribbean female, though this was their sole serious shortcoming: "These women lack only education and knowledge of the outside world for them not to be inferior in any way to the most distinguished European women." Especially, they were handicapped by "l'ignorance des langues."

Over many years, Nassy reiterated the need for a new kind of Jewish schooling geared to general enlightened principles, the sciences and vocational preparation rather than old-style religious studies. Surinam Jewry's chronic educational deficit had to be swiftly reversed: "we consider it our duty, in order not to leave our nation in blind ignorance, to establish a public school here in Paramaribo."[35] The post-1770 drift from the inland rural plantation settlement of Jodensavanne where Jews dwelt as a self-sufficient Portuguese-speaking autonomous mini-society, separate from other whites, to the busy port of Paramaribo where more integration with the rest of the colony's society and its occupations was unavoidable, led others too among Surinam Jewish society to question the traditionally tight control the *parnasim*, or governing council elders, exerted over communal life and organization.

Sephardic settlers in the Caribbean during the seventeenth century may have enjoyed exceptionally advantageous conditions compared to most Old World Jewish communities and had the initiative and energy to take advantage of it. But Jewish New World settlement also maintained the full apparatus of Sephardic community governance driving the *bigotisme* of which Nassy complained. Sephardic community structure and attitudes more generally originated in his view in the deeply repressed Portugal of the Inquisition. As in Europe, from early on New World Jewish Enlightenment therefore called for curtailment of religious authority and a general transformation of Jewish lifestyle and attitudes.

RELIGIOUS AUTHORITY AND THE PUSH FOR EQUAL RIGHTS

Tension between tradition and enlightenment in Surinam Jewish society was notably stoked by a protracted dispute between two Jews quarreling over a financial transaction. In 1761, Aaron de Fonseca tried to retrieve part of the interest on a five-thousand-guilder loan that the colony's civil court had ruled, in August 1750, he must pay in full but he deemed excessive. Finding he could appeal to the rabbinic court to discount some of the interest due under Dutch colonial law, De Fonseca petitioned the *parnasim*, who backed his appeal and directed his creditor, Nassy's friend Salomon de Montel, to return some of the interest already paid. Under the community's privileges and regulations, the *parnasim* charged Montel with unlawful usury and, when he refused to comply, threatened him with the community ban, or *herem*. Montel then appealed over the heads of rabbis and *parnasim* to the colony's governor, complaining of being subjected to religious coercion incompatible with Dutch law. "Under the appearance of privilege, the *parnasim* seek to introduce religious coercion and an inquisition contrary to all liberty."

Montel's quarrel with the community elders and rabbis proved long and bitter, causing him to grow ever more adamant in rejecting rabbinic and communal authority: "Yes, even should they want to excommunicate him daily," he reportedly retorted, "he could not care less." The congregation, for its part, kept up the pressure, the *Mahamad* explained, less due to the financial dispute itself than his scornful, defiant attitude toward rabbinic and communal authority. Where Nassy's *Essai historique* designates Montel a reasonable old man, "a Portuguese Jew and great lover of French literature," renowned for virtues that cost him dear, "aussi aimable par ses vertus, que malheureux par ses bontés" [as kind by his virtues, as unhappy through his good deeds], the synagogue governing board considered him a deplorable exponent of freethinking and insubordination inclined to mislead Jewish youth. Montel's fight with the synagogue authorities dragged on for decades.

Accused of flouting rabbinic and communal authority in the most overt, disrespectful manner, Montel fought back, depicting the affray as a war of reason against religious obscurantism. Among the most affluent of the Surinam Sephardic elite, Montel was also among the most erudite, and a noted connoisseur of Enlightenment books. For years, "Monsieur de Montel," records Nassy's *Essai*, conducted "a steady correspondence with Marc-Michel Rey (1720–80), publisher and book-seller in Amsterdam, who furnished works to all the book-lovers of Surinam."[36] Marc-Michel Rey as it happens, was also the chief publisher of illicit radical works in the Dutch Republic, specializing in texts officially banned in France, including those of d'Holbach and Rousseau. A Genevan deist who had transferred to Amsterdam in 1744, Rey had married Elisabeth Bernard, daughter of the radical enlightener Jean-Frederic Bernard (c. 1683–1744), the first *érudit* to compile an encyclopedia of religion, treating all faiths on a neutral, equal basis and presenting Judaism in a relatively dignified light.[37]

The escalating clash over the role of Jewish religious authority in Surinam spurred the *parnasim* to pursue Montel relentlessly in the governor's council, the colony's consultative body, the *Politieke Raad*, from which Jews *qua* Jews were legally excluded from representation, but to which they could submit petitions.[38] Should Surinam's governor back the *Mahamad*, complained Montel, he would be restoring "the Auto-da-fé whose flames would be kindled once again and could spread to other persuasions." The governor did indeed back the *parnasim,* ruling that Dutch law indisputably approved of the use of formal excommunication by all recognized religious communities as a means of enforcing religious authority and social discipline including judgments about financial disputes.[39] By threatening their miscreant with the *herem*, the *Mahamad* were acting wholly within their community's rights and privileges. With Montel still recalcitrant, *Mahamad* exasperation seethed to the point the *parnasim* petitioned the governor to banish Montel from the colony unless he submitted and repaid the disputed amount to Fonseca. The governor agreed to do so.

Ritually excommunicated from the synagogue, expelled from the colony, Montel departed for Holland and spent three years presenting his appeal directly to the States-General in The Hague. On 20 July 1764, after long hesitation, the States finally ruled in his favor and directed Surinam's governor to readmit him to the colony and "effect a speedy reparation for the injustice done."[40] Montel returned in triumph, reducing Jewish religious authority in the New World to tatters, a humiliating setback from which it never fully recovered. This was bound to encourage efforts toward freeing individuals from Jewish religious oversight in a manner that henceforth became a central theme of the New World Jewish Enlightenment.

Montel's three years in Holland coincided with a lively discussion among the Sephardic Jewish intellectual circle there over how to respond to Voltaire's fierce aspersions and indictment of Jewish society.[41] In ancient times, held Voltaire, in his *Sermon du Rabbin Akib* (1761), and other writings, the Jews had been "un peuple barbare, superstitieux, ignorant, absurd." That the great *philosophe* himself maintained that over the centuries Jewish tradition had, through its "Pharisaic narrowness" and "fanaticism," inflicted immense harm not only on the Jews themselves but humanity generally, spread intense dismay in Jewish enlightened circles. Since 1762, the Dutch Portuguese Jewish intellectual leadership, especially Isaac de Pinto (1717–1787), sought to counter this antisemitic onslaught with vigor. De Pinto, the foremost Jewish economist before Ricardo, and assiduous analyst of the problem of Jewish poverty in the Netherlands, saw this poverty, like Toland earlier and Dohm later, as primarily due to disabilities and restrictions on Jewish economic activity.[42] In his *Apologie pour la Nation Juive, ou Reflexions critiques*, of 1762, De Pinto, to many young Sephardim of Nassy's generation the very exemplar of a modern enlightened Jew, powerfully berated the great Voltaire for holding a blatantly prejudiced and unjustified attitude.

To achieve the Surinam Jewish Enlightenment's chief objectives, civil equality especially, many of the same things were required as were needed to solve the problem of Jewish poverty in Europe. The Jews must fight existing restrictions and laws, insisted De Pinto, combat religious authority Jewish and Christian, and build an armory of enlightened argument against disabilities reinforced by prejudice and bigotry now made even more formidable than before by Voltaire's flagrantly unjust anti-Jewish aspersions.[43]

Aspersions on the Jews spiced with Voltaire's remarks had indeed by the 1760s become characteristic of the Western moderate Enlightenment—a new, sophisticated form of prejudice stripped of theological underlay, propagated by what Nassy deemed the wrong sort of Enlightenment. Indeed, Voltaire's antagonistic remarks had become a specific threat to the position of Caribbean Jewry. The magistrates of Demerary and Essequibo, in western [later British] Guyana, still at this time subject to the Dutch Republic, had recently endorsed an account of their colonies containing an unprecedented attack on the Jews' standing and reputation under the title *Brieven over het bestuur der colonien Demerary en Essequibo, tusschen Aristodemus en Sincerus* (12 vols., Amsterdam, 1785–89). The pseudo-enlightened antisemitism pervading this text Nassy and his Sephardic friends considered a veritable scandal.[44] Like Struensee, Lessing, Dohm and Diez, and the French radical enlighteners committed to Jewish emancipation, the Paramaribo Sephardic reading circle deemed genuine Enlightenment and still more Enlightenment the only effective antidote to this newfangled non-theological trans-Atlantic, partly

Voltairean, anti-Jewish campaign denying Jews entry to public offices and the professions.

Gradually, others too began sympathizing with Nassy's and Montel's approach. Gatherings in Montel's house resulted, on 16 February 1785, in the founding of the Jewish literary and learned society *Docendo Docemur* [By teaching we are taught], with the newly arrived governor of the colony, J. G. Wichers (earlier "First Fiscal" in Surinam, in the years 1772–80) as chief patron.[45] The Sephardic society's prospectus, drawn up in Montel's library, was signed by all the leading figures of the Surinam Jewish Enlightenment—Montel, Nassy, Moseh Pereira de Leon, Isaac de la Parra, Immanuel de Anaria and others such as S. G. Soares and Samuel Hoheb Brandon.[46] The aim of this "collège de littérature" was chiefly to counter the "crasse ignorance" typifying both the youth and older generation of the Surinam Jewish community.[47] Among its "modern" features and innovations, *Docendo Docemur* admitted women to its meetings. Sessions were held alternately in French and Dutch with interjections allowed in Spanish and Portuguese, where passages were not readily understood. The society began with lectures and a debate about ancient Rome with Montesquieu's *La grandeur et la décadence* as set reading.[48] An early course on "philosophy in general" analyzed several French texts, rather daringly including d'Argens's *La philosophie du bons sens*, and *De la philosophie de la nature, ou traité de morale pour l'espèce humaine* (1770) by the freethinking Jean-Baptiste Delisle de Sales (1741–1816).[49] The society, attended mainly by Jews, successful for a time,[50] gathered, according to its prospectus, twice weekly on "Sundays and Wednesdays from six in the afternoon until nine o'clock" in the evening, at the home of Montel, who had generously offered the use of his house and splendid library, which included many rare works.[51] As Marc-Michel Rey, Montel's chief book supplier, was a leading publisher also of Radical Enlightenment texts, the collection housed some of the most daring clandestine texts then available anywhere.[52]

In 1786, a broader, more inter-confessional group, Jewish and Christian, the Paramaribo library and reading society, according to the *Essai historique* another main seedbed of the Surinam Enlightenment, was likewise founded by Montel, who principally built up its library. Under Montel's and Nassy's leadership, the group amassed a "library that was so large and filled with works on all subjects that it yields in no respect to any other in all the Americas and equals several large libraries in Europe."[53] Dutch colonial administration officials and senior army officers joined together with the physicians Van Wiert and Godfried Willem Schilling (1725–1799), and a fringe of young cultivated Jews interested in Montel's reading circle's lectures and debates. Schilling, another friend of Nassy's, ran Paramaribo's military hospital and was a noted expert on leprosy, about which he had published a treatise, *De Lepra commentationes*, at Leiden, in 1778. Another participating non-Jew was the later Dutch revolutionary Abraham Verheul (1770–1817), who while still young, in Surinam, was decisively formed by this surge of Enlightenment enthusiasm.[54]

Inspired by the American Revolution, Nassy declared himself, in the *Essai historique*, a particular admirer of the chief spokesman for Jewish emancipation in Europe, Christian Wilhelm Dohm, whose text on Jewish rights Nassy had encountered in its French version over a decade before. The *Essai* itself had originated, we learn from its opening pages, in a lively discussion among Surinam Jews precipitated by a French *précis* of Dohm's *Über die Verbesserung der Juden* (1781), in the *Gazette Littéraire* issue of May 1784. Only in February 1786, after a frustrating wait, did the first copy of Dohm's booklet itself, in its French version, reach the colony.[55] Finding it full of "raisonnemens solides, et d'une impartialité lumineuse" [solid reasoning and luminous impartiality], from early 1786 the Paramaribo enlightened circle closely examined Dohm's thesis, giving it a close reading "dans notre College de Littérature connu sous le nom de Docendo Docemur" [in our literary college known as Docendo Docemur].[56] Dohm thereby gained a trans-Atlantic reputation as the first enlightener to seriously investigate how to overcome the stigma of millennia and, in a practical fashion, integrate Jewish society into general society in a viable manner. Despite his reservations about Judaism, and Jewish society's excessively narrow occupation-structure, in the Sephardic Caribbean Dohm was considered a staunch champion of the Jewish cause beside Mendelssohn and such French radicals as Brissot, Cloots and Mirabeau, the men who took the lead in disseminating Dohm's message throughout the French-speaking and trans-Atlantic world and carrying it through, during 1789–93, in the French revolutionary context.

Dohm's intervention gained a prominent place alongside the *Histoire philosophique* in the thinking of the New World Sephardic diaspora's secularists. The thesis central to Dohm's approach that Jewish society's truncated economic profile stemmed from systematic oppression beyond the Jews' control, religious and legal discrimination to which they had been subject for millennia, signally reinforced the emancipatory universalism of their radical thought. So grateful for Dohm's pathbreaking initiative were Nassy and the Paramaribo community's other intellectual leaders they petitioned the *parnasim* for permission to send him a collective letter of gratitude in the name of the entire Jewish community. Dated 10 March 1786, this missive was signed by Nassy first, styled "David de I[saac] C[ohen] Nassy," followed by De la Parra, Moseh Pereira de Leon and others.[57] Touched to receive it, Dohm replied from Cologne, in January 1787, his letter arriving in Paramaribo the following June. He was delighted to learn that his booklet about "your nation so unjustly wretched" had reached as far as Surinam, and that "your situation" in the New World confirmed his thesis that the Jews "are capable, like us, of being good citizens as soon as they are permitted to be," and through enlightenment could rise from the degradation oppressive circumstances had thrust on them.[58]

Jews, Sephardic and Ashkenazic, everywhere in the Americas just as in the Old World, needed a comprehensive revolutionary rationale and agenda measuring up better than did the American Revolution to the new principle of "universal and equal rights." Voltaire's antisemitism was challenged by De Pinto, Montel and Nassy, who loudly denounced this aspect of his writing, accusing him of seeking to "écraser la Nation Juive et de la rendre hidieuse aux yeux de l'univers" [crush the Jewish nation and render it hideous in the eyes of the universe], not least in his widely read *Traité de la tolerance* (1763) of which Nassy's personal library featured two copies—a tract Nassy deemed highly reprehensible, "un traité complet de fanatisme philosophique."[59] For progressive-minded New and Old World Jews alike, the adversary their revolution had to confront turned out to be a four-headed hydra consisting of theology, traditional Jewish communal authority, popular ignorance and, where deeply prejudiced, as in Voltaire's own writings, Voltaire's mainstream Enlightenment.

For achieving the level of integration and "emancipatory universalism" that would render all equal on the basis of universal and equal human rights and equal opportunity, the ambitious goal set by the likes of Nassy and those who thought like him, Radical Enlightenment perspectives and arguments were obviously apt to prove far more useful and relevant than the social and moral relativism of Montesquieu and Hume, Rousseau's exaltation of the ordinary, Voltaire's caustic wit or the aristocratic conservatism of Ferguson or Burke. Mainstream Enlightenment in the tradition of Voltaire, Montesquieu,

Hume, Ferguson, Adam Smith and Burke, by contrast, could offer them comparatively little. Indeed, it looked positively hostile and unwelcoming, like the mainstream Enlightenment reading societies in the Netherlands, the best known among which expressly excluded Jews from membership and refused to support Jewish equality, justifying their stance by insisting their religiously inspired principles firmly committed them to defend "Christian" values. Any stance such as Locke's, Hume's or Burke was not just inadequate but virtually useless for promoting any kind of comprehensive program of Jewish emancipation such as was now in prospect.[60]

SEVEN

Zalkind Hourwitz (1751–1812) and the "Great Revolution"

The fight for Jewish emancipation during the revolutionary era 1775–1848 was long, bitter and inconclusive. What historians broadly term the "emancipation of the Jews" was in fact a highly complex intellectual, social, cultural and political process presenting challenges to others but also new dilemmas for the Jews themselves not least by accelerating the rise of the secular, revolutionary Jew. The convoluted process exerted a wide-ranging impact at every stage, as much perhaps from the attendant delays and frustration as its gradual successes.

The Western world's mainstream Enlightenment, as the writings of Leon Poliakov and Arthur Hertzberg show, often encouraged antagonistic or ambiguous attitudes toward Jews and Jewishness. Hertzberg's thesis that "modern, secular antisemitism was fashioned not as a reaction to the Enlightenment and the [French] Revolution, but within the Enlightenment and Revolution themselves" is doubtless justified in part,[1] but his approach involves some oversimplification and underlines the need to distinguish between different Enlightenment streams. Anti-Jewish rhetoric where employed by radicals, like d'Holbach, was frequently just another way to discredit Christian Revelation and the Church Fathers. Thus, the *Bréviaire philosophique ou Histoire du Judaïsme, du Christianisme et du Déisme* (1792) by the Piedmontese ex-Jesuit revolutionary Joseph-Antoine Cérutti (1738–1792), lambasted "Jewish" religious authority but did so to tie it historically to post-Jewish ecclesiastical sway. It was the intolerance and rigidity of the "lois judaïques" [Jewish laws], held Cérutti, that prepared the ground for "l'atrocité des lois chrétiennes" [the atrocity of Christian laws]. Papal government was merely "la théocratie juive" [Jewish theocracy] reconfigured, Christianity itself just "un second judaïsme." Little of this vituperation applied to actual Jews or Jewish life. If the true Original Sin is man's own unremitting credulity and stupidity, all biblical Revelation, for Cérutti, including the Jewish, is an eternal "charlatanerie anti-naturelle."[2]

In 1789, the call not just to tolerate Jews on a broader basis but to transform Jewish existence, according Jews equal rights to freedom of expression, happiness, participation and prosperity, was something dramatically new. Here, one might consider Montesquieu a precursor to an extent. Despite disdaining Judaism and rabbinic learning like most enlighteners, he was willing to draw Jews more broadly into society while seeing no reason for Jews to abandon their faith. But he by no means advocated anything like civic equality. A defender of noble privilege, he had no desire to integrate most of society into political life. His aristocratic style of naturalism and institutional conservatism effectively precluded sweeping change based on universal principles. Montesquieu, whom Diderot's and d'Holbach's assistant Naigeon classed among those *philosophes* like Helvétius and Buffon who minced their words through dread of prison and the theologians,[3] took some hesitant steps but came nowhere near rejecting ecclesiastical authority or proclaiming a general emancipation of non-Christians.[4]

Urging universal and equal rights, whether in France, Germany, Britain or anywhere in Europe, was definitely a rarity among enlighteners. One encountered it solely among one particular stream amidst the vortex of the age's conflicting ideological currents. Wherever the debate over the Jewish question intensified, as at Berlin, the Rhineland or Alsace-Lorraine, locals often showed greater hostility to lifting Jewish disabilities than the rest of their countrymen.[5] The driving force behind Jewish emancipation in Western society and culture was thus extremely narrow, the exclusive motor being Radical Enlightenment and its dogged commitment to confronting religious authority and common prejudice along with all previous philosophy, existing laws and systems of government.

The French Revolution eventually accorded full equality and civil rights to the Jews with the expectation Jews would become "useful" to society and align their attitudes and educational practices with the secularizing, soon openly republican state, and serve in the militias and armed forces supporting the Revolution. In short, Jewish emancipation was an integral, publicly proclaimed feature of the French Revolution—not just early on (1789–92) but also, with far-reaching consequences, during its post-Thermidor expansion into the Low Countries, Rhineland, Italy and parts of Greece. It was a process that advanced rapidly especially in the years 1796–1800 following the setting up of revolutionary republics in Italy under the auspices of Napoleon (then still outwardly an ardent republican), as well as briefly on Malta, the Greek Ionian Islands and, fleetingly, Napoleonic Egypt.

Even so, opposed by long-standing religious norms, doctrines and discrimination, Jewish emancipation after 1789 continued to be impeded by numerous obstacles. Securing equal citizenship status and rights for Jews required in the first place a tremendous intellectual reorientation, undermining ancient, long-standing structures of authority, law, economic practice and theology, a great effort of innovative political and social theorizing accompanied by wide diffusion of revolutionary ideas. In localities like Metz, in Lorraine, and the Alsace region, where Jewish communities were sizeable and conspicuous, it also meant thwarting fiercely resurgent local popular antisemitism fuelling opposition, resistance marked by repeated outbreaks of anti-Jewish violence often combined with more general anti-revolutionary agitation. Countered by religious authority and long-standing sentiment, there was, assuredly, no other plausible mechanism for Jewish emancipation than a sweeping general social and political revolution driven by a comprehensive new revolutionary consciousness. Where no revolution occurred as in Britain or Canada, and in even the United States after the, in some respects, more conservative revolution there, constraints imposed by the post-revolutionary "blasphemy laws" meant, as we have seen, that Jewish civil equality there was postponed for decades, until deep into the nineteenth century albeit not as long as black emancipation, universal voting rights for white males and equality for women.

The 1770s and 1780s have rightly been considered a crucial threshold—the point at which key minds began to "seriously contemplate the transformation of Jewish status." But attempts to explain this decisive transition as due to long-term shifts engineered by the Enlightenment in general, encouraging readers to view history as progress and something chiefly mutable in response to broad social trends,[6] hardly accounts for so transformative and divisive a phenomenon. It might explain why Jewish emancipation powerfully gained momentum at that particular moment hand in hand with sweeping rejection of many other prevailing social, institutional and theological structures, invoking, for instance, a "gradual increase of religious toleration toward Protestants and Jews which the royal authorities supported."[7] But the mass cultural history approach, given its vagueness and undifferentiated applicability, amounts to little more than the optimistic assumption that the Enlightenment was a broad sociocultural process that gradually transformed sentiment overall in a positive direction, a view impossible to defend in the light of the evidence, given the strength and breadth of opposition and of Counter-Enlightenment sentiment.

Following the American Revolution, fundamental reform including the "project to naturalize the Jews in Germany," as the journalist disciple of Diderot, Wilhelm Ludwig Wekhrlin (1739–1792), called it, the issue of Jewish citizenship was suddenly very much in the air. Like many Enlightenment reform initiatives, however, the idea of Jewish emancipation reached back, he stressed in 1779,[8] much earlier, in France especially, to the contributions to the *Encyclopédie* of Wekhrlin's hero, Diderot. Although Diderot shared in the "underlying ambivalence characterizing Enlightenment responses to Judaism," his attitude toward Jews, unlike Voltaire's, was innovative and predominantly positive.[9] Where the expanded *Dictionnaire de Trévoux* (9 vols., Paris, 1752), the encyclopedia of the Jesuits, repeats traditional reproaches, dwelling on alleged Jewish responsibility for crucifying Christ and "Jewish" moral deficiencies while dismissing the entire topic in a single column as entirely unimportant and marginal, the *Encyclopédie* of Diderot and d'Alembert devotes a massive fifty-four-column entry to the immense festering problem of modern Jewish society, penned by Diderot in person, an article ruthlessly stripping out all theological criteria from the discussion, insisting the question be judged solely in terms of philosophic reason and the Jews' uniquely complex role in history.

THE "ANTI-JUDAISM" OF THE *PHILOSOPHES*

If only slightly less hostile to Judaism as a religion than Christianity, Diderot never singles out Jews for special antipathy and in several passages evinces unmistakable sympathy for them as victims of Christian oppression and persecution.[10] In Diderot, there is little of the tendency of some deistic and atheistic writers of the age to assign to Jews as a people inherent defects such as inordinate love of money, inbred hatred of others and addiction to superstition, fanaticism, demonology and obscurantism. Despite his scorn for Talmud, Pharisaic legalism and rabbinic law and divisive post-biblical Jewish religious disputes, Diderot envisaged the Jews as normal humans, much as

Toland and Bernard and Picart's encyclopedia of religion, the *Cérémonies et coûtumes religieuses de tous les peoples du monde* (1723–44), had earlier. Diderot's main focus was the Jews' continuing entrapment in segregation and oppression. That Jewish civil emancipation for Diderot was more than just a theoretical stance is shown by his taking the matter up, on arriving in Russia, in 1772, with Catherine the Great. Among his first interventions in Petersburg was his presenting a set of questions about the status of the Jews of her empire, among other points asking why Jews were not tolerated in her capital, Petersburg.[11]

Diderot's *Encyclopédie* article helped establish a tradition of Enlightenment analysis of Jewish marginality, degradation and isolation and suggestions for amelioration and tackling the problem of institutional, theologically justified discrimination. His reforming perspective remains today an unfortunately neglected aspect of the general Enlightenment, pivoting on the principle, soon widely embraced, that Jews are men with characteristics in all essentials identical to everyone else and that, judged as a people, they possess no innate characteristics differentiating them from, or rendering them worse than others. To those claiming avarice, commercial greed and desire to separate from others were irredeemably ingrained features of the Jewish character, Diderot answered that Jews, contrary to what was widely assumed, had not been shunned or scorned in pre-Christian times. Predominance of finance and commerce in later Jewish society stemmed from particular circumstances during the late Roman Empire, namely systematic persecution by Christians. Before Constantine, Jews were full citizens, not a Roman underclass. Christian dominance, theology and repression alone grounded Jewish marginality.[12] Diderot's stance became the classic Radical Enlightenment "take" on the Jewish question that in the 1780s and later principally battled the obstacles to Jewish emancipation and integration.

Other radicals diffusing this subversive message included Wekhrlin, Diez, Dohm, Mirabeau and the Franco-German materialist-atheist Anacharsis Cloots (1755–1794). In his *Lettre sur les Juifs à un ecclésiastique des mes amis* (Berlin, 1783), Cloots, more vehemently than the discreet Dohm, deplored Jewish society's being boxed in over the centuries by an excessively narrow range of economic occupations, marginalization he considered the fault and moral responsibility of the churches exclusively. Commencing with unremitting pressure by late Roman Christian emperors, theology, credulity, fanaticism and intolerance created the perverse imbalances that characterized modern Jewish society.[13] Had the power-hungry Emperor Constantine opted for Judaism instead of Christianity, then that religion would have domineered over Christianity as the late Roman world's universal creed.[14] The anti-Jewish decrees of the emperors following Constantine steadily reinforced the tendency for Jewish life to organize around commerce, the sole path to survival in an increasingly intolerant, theologically defined late Roman imperial world.

Unlike other radical *philosophes*, Cloots, son of an Amsterdam merchant-banker, did not view Jewish aptitude for commerce and finance as a negative trait in itself but rather as a "source of prosperity for those states that welcomed them." "So useful, so necessary" were Jews in Spain and Portugal, that their expulsion initiated an era of decline and desolation.[15] So "useful" was this people's industriousness that in some specialized sectors of commerce and finance they were indispensable: "all business languishes on the London and Amsterdam stock exchanges during Jewish religious festivals."[16] More than other radical *philosophes,* Cloots was inclined likewise to commend Jewish intellectual capabilities. Despite sharing Diderot's abhorrence of Talmud and rabbinic law, Europe's Jews, he thought, showed undoubted capacity for scholarly erudition and "philosophy" not just in the isolated case of Maimonides but also with "Abrabanel, Pilzaro, Mortera, Menasseh-ben-Israel, et Orobio dont les noms seuls," he suggested, "font trembler la théologie chrétienne" [whose names alone make Christian theology tremble].[17] Cloots felt only contempt for the Abbé Grégoire's pious hope that once more humanely and equally treated Jews would finally see the light and convert *en masse* to Christianity.[18]

Incontestably, as with Diderot and Wekhrlin, it was Cloots's fierce *anti-christianisme* that grounded his *philo-judaisme*: to him emancipation of the Jews was simply part of the process of emancipating humanity generally from deadly entrapment in ecclesiastical sway and imposture. What he called "le philosophisme moderne" alone could finally end the age of the Wars of Religion, the hateful power of "superstition" to divide men and pit them against each other to underpin a social order enabling churchmen to join with emperors, princes and aristocrats in grabbing for themselves vast lands, privilege and influence in law, government and education while everywhere propagating prejudice and hatred. Ending theological dispute and confessional strife which priests deliberately exploit to extend their unholy sway, he alleged, would benefit all the world's citizens who could finally reunite in "le temple de la Religion naturelle."[19] By the early 1780s already fiercely radical, Cloots later figured among the leaders of the violent de-Christianization campaign unleashed in France during 1792–93. While applauding Voltaire's war on intolerance, Cloots shared neither his deism nor antisemitism, preferring like his revolutionary Jewish ally, Jacob Peyrera (together with whom he was to be guillotined by the *Robespierristes*, in 1794), the atheism of Meslier, Boulainvilliers and Fréret.[20]

Cloots's text diffused far and wide, reaching such remote corners as the Paramaribo Sephardic group pursuing Enlightenment studies headed by Nassy.[21] Other contributors to such literature before 1789 were Mirabeau, who in the mid-1780s collaborated with Dohm, in Berlin, and Jacques-Pierre Brissot de Warville (1754–1793), who, like Mirabeau, would assume a prominent role in the French Revolution.[22] Brissot had been a radical enlightener through and through long before the Revolution. His *L'État civil des Juifs* (1784), reviewing the English translation of Dohm's booklet "on the civil improvement of the Jews," appeared in the second issue of his *Journal du Lycée de Londres* (1784–85), a year after Cloots's essay, and followed Diderot, Wekhrlin, Diez, Dohm, Cloots and Mirabeau in seeing Jewish defects not as inherent, repugnant separateness and economic narrowness but as acquired characteristics originating in eighteen centuries of "Christian" persecution and oppression. Jews needed integrating into society on the same basis as everyone else.[23]

Where "Jewish" defects remained a problem for Dohm, Brissot minimized talk of the Jews' supposed universal unprepossessing traits. Discussing Jewish rights to him exclusively meant underlining "Christian" defects and *ancien régime* society's general defectiveness, the overall repressiveness of monarchical, aristocratic and ecclesiastical tyranny. "How can one be surprised at the hatred Jews feel for all sects, all nations?" Brissot's solution was that Jews must learn to conquer their isolation after receiving equal status, eligibility and rights, which should be accorded to them without delay. Where Dohm proposed widening their range of occupations without conceding Jewish eligibility for public office or authority over Christians, Brissot, like Diez, eager to curtail society's "Christian" base as much as possible, did not hesitate to demand also their access to office.[24]

Mirabeau, another fierce oratorical scourge of the *ancien régime*, was equally sweeping in rejecting priestcraft and mysteries. While denouncing all philosophy "contre la raison" including everything Locke considered "au-dessus de la raison" [above reason] and Christian responsibilities of the state, he eulogized Lessing as an outstanding spokesman for toleration, secularization and demystification. Like Diderot, Dohm, Diez, Wekhrlin,

Cloots and Brissot, Mirabeau held that Jewish society's deficiencies stemmed exclusively from oppression, degradation heaped on them over the centuries by "Christian bigotry and hatred."[25] The humiliation to which churchmen subjected the Jews was simply part of the world's wider machinery of theocratic repression and imposture.[26] Hardly original, borrowing heavily from, while also sharpening, Dohm, Mirabeau's pamphlet presents Mendelssohn as a great Jewish thinker in the tradition of Maimonides.[27]

Although Brissot had earlier introduced Dohm to the French, in October 1784, it was Mirabeau's pamphlet *Sur Moses Mendelssohn, sur la réforme politique des Juifs* (1787) that chiefly drew the French reading public's attention to the international struggle for Jewish rights. Like Brissot, Condorcet and Cérutti, Mirabeau already evinced strong republican proclivities well before the onset of the Revolution, his 1787 pamphlet illustrating once again how closely crypto-republicanism and anti-aristocratic attitudes had become allied to proclaiming universal and equal rights, rejecting all theological criteria and religious authority and—following Spinoza and Toland—dismissing Locke's (and the Religious Enlightenment's) pivotal distinction between what is against and what is "above reason." For radical enlighteners, rational philosophy is the exclusive basis for "universal morality" and social reform. For all men, held Mirabeau, following d'Holbach, there exists "only one reason so that the universal morality [la morale universelle] of peoples and sovereigns is founded on nature and this eternal order cannot change" with the consequence that Christian salvation is entirely irrelevant to man's true destiny.[28]

Appearing in several versions, in Berlin, Amsterdam and Strasbourg, with "Londres" on the title page, Mirabeau's pamphlet, rejecting Locke's dualism and Montesquieu's relativism, did more than any other publication to promote progressive attitudes to Jewish emancipation across the trans-Atlantic world. "How should moral corruption not be very great," demanded Mirabeau, among a people for whom the sole permitted occupations are those "les plus capables de dépraver toute morale" [most capable of depraving all morality]?[29] "Never has any people suffered such cruel, sustained and prolonged persecution."[30] But change was coming. There were incipient signs of improvement though the process had not yet gone far: "for the enlightened men the Berlin Jewish community boasts in considerable number, thanks to the venerable Mendelssohn's efforts, have not yet had sufficient time to instil enlightened principles into the common people." Mirabeau, like Dohm, Diez, Brissot, Cloots and Grégoire, admired the "enlightened" Berlin Jewish leadership's approach and expressed confidence in their *Aufklärung* transforming Jewish life and assisting a general "improvement": "Eh! Quel plus heureux prognostic de leur amendement, que tant de changements utiles dans leur colonie de Berlin par le seul exemple de Mendelssohn!" [Eh! What happier prognosis for their improvement than so many useful changes in their Berlin community by the sole example of Mendelssohn!][31] It was thanks to this "soberly written plea for racial tolerance," among Mirabeau's best tracts, that Mendelssohn's name resounded loud and positive in National Assembly corridors between 1789 and 1791 while Jewish rights were being furiously proposed and contested.[32]

For Mirabeau, as for the first Jewish writer to publicly debate the issue in France, Zalkind Hourwitz (1751–1812), securing Jewish rights was inseparable from recognizing that meaningful public morality means elimination of all confessional distinctions from the public sphere and drastic curbing of religion as a force in government, law, education and society. "Qu'ils soient d'ailleurs Juifs, Chrétiens, idolâtres, Déistes ou Athées peu importe. Les vrais fidèles, les vrais saints, sont les bons citoyens" [whether men are Jews, Christians, idolaters, deists or atheists matters little; the true faithful, the true saints, are the good citizens] affirmed Diderot's and d'Holbach's assistant, Jacques André Naigeon (1738–1810), when addressing the National assembly in 1790.[33] In their *Dictionnaire des Athées,* the atheist *philosophes* Sylvain Maréchal and Jerôme Lalande echoed Mirabeau's dictum that "la pratique du bien moral est la seule religion obligatoire à laquelle l'homme puisse être contraint avec justice" [the practice of moral good is the sole obligatory religion to which man can be justly compelled].[34]

Hourwitz, an erudite Polish Jew from a village in southeast Poland near Lublin, among the chief centers of Polish Jewish cultural life, commenced his life in France, at first reportedly as an impoverished Parisian peddler vending textiles, in the mid-1770s.[35] After long obscurity amidst the small Ashkenazic community of the French capital, in 1789 Hourwitz secured a minor post as an interpreter, translator and Hebraist at the Bibliothèque du Roi, enabling him to become a professional librarian, critic and eventually language theorist. Professing to be the son of a Polish rabbi,[36] he became the Ashkenazic personage who most fully articulated the new trans-Atlantic secular Jewish revolutionary identity in France and most conspicuously participated as a Jew in the struggle for Jewish emancipation.

Hourwitz's campaign against discrimination and anti-Jewish rhetoric commenced with an ironic reply, in October 1783, to a "Letter from Warsaw" by an anonymous Polish writer published in the London-based French journal *Le Courrier de l'Europe*. Begrudging Joseph II's toleration decree, this critic asked whether it is fitting to incorporate into the Polish nation an element so different—"enemies in commerce, robbers by principle and by taste, a swarm of usurers incessantly occupied with calculating what they can gain from the private and public misfortune of others." Presenting himself as a "Polish Jew," Hourwitz replied that this "good Pole," an ignorant "monk," he assumed, abhorred not only Jews but the enlightened Habsburg Emperor Joseph II too. He resented the new toleration and also Joseph's measures beneficially introduced throughout the Austrian monarchy against the monasteries and to disempower ecclesiastics. Stubborn and credulous, this "monk" was so backward as to resent the Jews' emerging from the darkness to which they had for so long been confined through the machinations of benighted monks like himself, progress eminently pertinent to the wider advancement of mankind. Devout our "good Pole" undoubtedly was, but he had a chronic disability: a medieval mentality, a retarded, superstitious mind shaped by books claiming Jews desecrate the Christian host to extract "Christian" blood.[37]

Deriding antisemitic opponents as crass obscurantists, pitiable *ignorants*, superstitious products of medieval thinking characterized Hourwitz's unapologetically pungent style throughout. In Hourwitz few signs survive of traditional Jewish reticence, quite the reverse; his attitude is pugnacious, his tone outspoken and savagely anti-clerical. Strongly oriented toward historical explanation, he scorns everything savouring of popular prejudice. To insist on the Jews' collective culpability for some particular occurrence in the past, calling them "Christ-killers," was totally illogical. Jews are no more collectively responsible for the crimes of a few than are Poles, the English or Portuguese for regicides, or whatever vileness perpetrated by their basest rogues. "Even the animals in La Fontaine's *Fables*," he quipped, with typical Hourwitzian humor, are "less unjust: for they would never [be so illogical as to] hang all the donkeys for the Epicureanism of one."[38]

Hourwitz's second letter to the *Courrier de l'Europe*, discussing Voltaire and Rousseau, acknowledged that some great writers, "modern apostles of tolerance[,] are also intolerant toward the Jews, but a celebrated writer, like everyone else, is susceptible to error and to passion." If the recurring anti-Jewish rhetoric of Diderot, d'Holbach and Cérutti is not antisemitism in any basic sense, Voltaire's oft-expressed antagonism to modern and ancient Jews, and Judaism, was another matter, a rooted antipathy evident and notorious by the 1760s. Unfortunately, Voltaire offers a ready resource, Hourwitz added later, in 1787, for all those opposing the efforts of the "bons esprits" to improve the lot of the Jews, and Rousseau too occasionally depicts Moses and ancient Judaism in a manner detrimental to Jewish emancipation.[39] While his own efforts might look puny against the "seductive eloquence of Voltaire and so many other celebrated writers who were avowed enemies of all those among their fellow men who pray to the Supreme Being in Hebrew,"[40] he had no intention of shirking the fight. Here, Voltaire and Rousseau were reprehensible and needed firm rebutting. Their claiming Moses's legislation rendered the Jews misanthropic, hostile to their fellow men and prone to separate themselves from the rest of mankind was simply offensive nonsense: Moses, on the contrary, was the "most tolerant and charitable of all legislators."[41] The Hebrew Bible does *not* encourage Jews to hate other peoples and "Rousseau and Voltaire in asserting the opposite cruelly malign an oppressed nation, the first from *esprit de paradoxe*, the second private resentment."[42]

Perhaps Voltaire intended his sallies to be understood as directed less against "modern Jews" than Old Testament Judaism, the "tronc du Christianisme" [trunk of Christianity]. But no matter how malicious Voltaire's remarks, the "Jews pardon him for everything malignant he utters, considering only the good he did them—even if this good he delivered unwittingly." Jews had become less subject to hostile pressure in recent years than in pre-enlightened times, improvement they owed to the Enlightenment's progress and weakening of religious bigotry. For this receding of persecution the Jews "en sont redevables au progrès des lumières" [are indebted to the progress of the Enlightenment], which Voltaire with his many works against "fanaticism" advanced more vigorously than anyone else.[43] Radical writers often expressed such divided, partial veneration for Voltaire. Diderot once confided to Condorcet his having long kept a bust of Voltaire beside his writing desk but removed it one day on meeting his gaze and suddenly feeling "Voltaire" was mocking what he wanted to write.[44]

As for Rousseau, radical *philosophes*, Hourwitz among them, followed Diderot and d'Holbach in pronouncing him always "paradoxical," brimming with contradiction, a thinker conflating a few radical strands with conservative and traditionalist views to forge an immensely popular but incoherent cult. Some readers wished to know why, if such strictures about Voltaire and Rousseau were correct, the Jews had stayed silent in the face of such brutally unjust charges for so long? Hourwitz shared their question and impatience. Jewish religion, Talmud and rabbinic writings were largely irrelevant, in his view, to explaining the distinctive features and peculiarities of Jewish society. Jewish behaviour and culture had their imperfections needing improvement, but these stemmed almost entirely from prejudice and oppression, Christian and Jewish.[45] Where permitted to participate in the normal procedures and processes of society, contended Hourwitz, by and large Jews were honest, happy and useful. On Jews and Judaism the Enlightenment remained profoundly divided throughout and Hourwitz devoted himself to doing all he could to tilt the balance.

It was decidedly not gradual shifts in the general outlook, in *mentalités*, then, that lay behind the invention of "universal and equal rights," or behind Jewish emancipation. Rather than due to mainstream shifts, social forces or social practice, Jewish emancipation was widely resisted in society and by churchmen, drawing its effective impetus almost exclusively from the same revolutionary vanguard that forged the revolutionary consciousness of the age more generally. Attributing Jewish emancipation to gradual, broad cultural change in society misses the fact that those advocating Jewish equality and integration were almost exclusively uncompromising adversaries of the existing order, and foes of traditional religious authority (which most people and most enlighteners, indubitably, were not). What counted was *not* broad cultural shifts, or the mainstream Enlightenment's dissemination, but the advance of a particular radical strand within the Enlightenment encompassing such key Jewish revolutionaries as Nassy, Montel, Hourwitz and Hartog Lémon.

THE METZ ACADEMY COMPETITION (1785–1789)

Shortly before the Revolution, in 1787, Hourwitz already enjoyed some renown in France thanks to the latest hotly contested prize competition staged by the prestigious Royal Academy of Metz. First proposed by the Academy in August 1785, and publicly announced on 1 September, the competition was for the best essay answering the question, "Are there ways to render the Jews more useful and happier in France?" The prize was a gold medal worth four hundred livres.[46] Both the choice of topic and wide publicity it received were due to a notable figure, Pierre-Louis Roederer (1754–1835), a leading light of the Metz Academy, prominent in local commerce and industry, an expert on legal issues and later a leading revolutionary and ally of the Brissotins against Robespierre and Marat.

Roederer, a member of the *parlement*, or judicial high court, of Metz, occupied a position of influence from which he could criticize both the *parlement* and, as a firm disciple of Beccaria, most civil and criminal law currently in force in Louis XVI's France.[47] His view of the Jews, their potential contribution to society, and the significance of the topic for society as a whole, was considerably more positive than was usual.[48] Dissatisfied with what *philosophes* had written on the Jewish question thus far, Roederer initiated the prize competition and ensured it remained among the Metz Academy's prime concerns over the next four years down to the commencement of the Revolution. He echoed the call to emancipate the Jews proclaimed earlier in Germany by Mendelssohn, Dohm and Diez and, from 1784, in France, by his future revolutionary allies, Mirabeau, Brissot and Cloots, being passionately committed to the Enlightenment and especially that stream demanding sweeping social, institutional, legal and political change. Like Mirabeau, Brissot and Cloots, he thirsted especially for an Enlightenment drastically reducing church sway and theology's influence.

Having selected the essay competition topic, Roederer served as the Academy's *rapporteur*, meaning the presiding figure charged with summing up the proceedings for the jury, in effect chairing the jury of five local dignitaries evaluating the essays. Aspiring to engineer a revolution in Jewish *and* Christian life, Roederer planned a concerted attack on conventional thinking and prevailing religious ideas, initially in Alsace-Lorraine, secondly in France and thirdly the Western world generally. Designating himself and his allies "disciples de la philosophie moderne," he openly clashed with *philosophes* like Voltaire, Montesquieu and Rousseau as regards the scale and type of changes French society required. His, Mirabeau's and Brissot's Jewish strategy was thus an integral part of a more generalized revolt, the "revolution of the mind" preceding the Revolution, squarely aimed against ecclesiastics, *parlements*, the legal system and royalty—the *ancien régime* as a whole.[49]

The Metz Academy's question for the prize competition seemed a perfectly serious inquiry to most, but on first hearing of it, claims Hourwitz, he could hardly believe his ears. How could such an offensive way of expressing the matter be taken seriously? How would his fellow Frenchmen feel, asks his entry essay, if the Stockholm Royal Academy posted the question whether there are ways to render the legally discriminated against Catholics of that realm "more useful and happier in Sweden?" The question reminded him, he says, of the episode when Charles V's troops besieged and were about to ruthlessly sack the papal capital, Rome, in May 1527, and the Emperor ordered public prayers for the Pope's deliverance. "How to render the Jews happy and useful?" Nothing could be simpler. Cease oppressing them, excluding them and rendering them useless "by granting them, or rather returning to them, the rights of the citizen of which you, the French, stripped them contrary to all divine and human laws," and contrary to society's own interest.[50]

Whatever others thought of Hourwitz's feigned stupefaction, there was an appreciable response to the Academy's announcement. Nine competitors submitted full-length entries during 1785–87, four ecclesiastics, three jurists, an academy secretary and just one other—Hourwitz, the "Polish Jew of Paris"—who, however, missed the initial deadline, June 1787, submitting his entry a month late.[51] As principal *rapporteur*, Roederer chaired the proceedings. The jury selected as the two best submissions thus far those of Claude-Antoine Thiéry (1764–?), an *avocat* of the *parlement* of Nancy (who had consulted with the local Jewish leader Berr Isaac Berr (1744–1828), and the soon renowned Catholic priest, the Abbé Henri Grégoire (1750–1831). Both were sympathetic to the Jewish cause. Grégoire, then still an ordinary *curé* [priest] at Embermesnil, near Lunéville, had conferred with another local Jewish leader at Metz, Isaiah Cerf Bing. However, in August 1787, Roederer decided none of the essays were satisfactory as a solution to the problem since none offered much in the way of practical answers in law, education, economy and politics to the concrete difficulties Jewish emancipation would inevitably present. Deeming all entries thus far abstract musings and rhetorical outpourings rather than coherent plans of action, Roederer presented some penetrating criticism of the 1787 entries, including those of Grégoire and Thiéry.

No-one, he objected, had examined whether the changes they proposed were compatible with Jewish religious and community law, "with their prejudices," or whether a political revolution in Jewish circumstances might be detrimental to whatever in their present moral constitution was praiseworthy, or asked whether existing French laws and prejudices would admit the changes proposed. No entry pondered the effect of conferring full civil rights on Jews on French economic life, or "the effects of recent laws in their favour introduced in neighbouring countries and what can be inferred from these," this last referring to Joseph II's toleration decrees in Habsburg lands. Jewish emancipation Roederer sought to advance in a manner compatible with "the traditions of their community," with new legal structures appropriate for Jewish society that would not harm French society.[52] Given the prize competition's international as well as national resonance, Roederer wanted something more comprehensive and concrete from the competitors. The jury he urged to postpone awarding the prize and re-advertise the competition since its usefulness to society mattered more than the formality of a previously announced deadline. The competitors were exhorted to revise in response to Roederer's criticism, and resubmit.[53]

Hourwitz's effort had hitherto attracted no attention and failed to reach the short-list.[54] In the resumed competition, from the autumn of 1787, he took Roederer's strictures seriously and substantially revised, this time submitting before the new deadline in 1788. A competition of this kind, given the topic, should be entered, he thought, by at least one Jewish competitor.[55] Seeing he had much to learn, having only recently discovered the relevant publications of Mirabeau, Mendelssohn, Dohm and Diez, and the German controversy's significance for Poland, France and generally, he scrutinized Dohm's arguments, broadened his perspective and recast his essay.[56] Dohm's pamphlet did him honor, he commented, but in one way hardly accorded "with our century." Why was it still necessary, at such a late stage, for a publicist of Dohm's stature to show "Jews are men like all other peoples" and "not responsible for the crimes, real or imagined, of their ancestors" as the prejudiced unenlightened believe. Dohm's efforts, he suggested with his usual irony, could be compared to Saint Augustine arduously battling paganism, using reason and all his eloquence to demonstrate its "absurdity."[57] A resident of Paris without office, ties or official responsibilities within the Jewish community, he remarks in his preface, he felt better qualified to pronounce on the issues with "perfect impartiality" than certain other Jews infiltrating the proceedings—a dig at the Metz community *parnasim*, Berr Isaac Berr and Isaiah Cerf Bing.[58] These two, Hourwitz believed, had a vested interest in steering Jewish emancipation in a particular direction to suit existing community structures and elites.

The Metz Ashkenazic community and Alsatian Jewish village communities were less segregated from their Christian neighbours than Jews in Hourwitz's native southeastern Poland. Nevertheless, Alsace-Lorraine too segregated Jews from the rest to a marked extent. Metz's sizeable Jewish community of between three and four thousand, around five hundred families (not much smaller than Lublin's), comprised around 10 percent of the city's total population of thirty-six thousand, with the community concentrated in the quartier Saint-Ferroy, an overcrowded quarter under the restrictive ordinances of an *ancien régime* crown closely allied to church and guilds, which meant constriction by a host of disabilities, of economic and legal debarments. Forbidden to own or rent land, excluded from virtually all crafts, Jews were hindered too by numerous other marks of institutionalized discrimination.[59] While fiscal and property regulations curtailed Alsace-Lorraine's Jews' economic "rights," and they were shut out of most professions and all public offices, other regulations ensured the continuing dominance of a community organization designed to keep Jewish life firmly under the thumb of rabbis and a small affluent lay oligarchy of merchant-financiers.

Metz figured among the foremost French frontier garrison towns. Jewish business in the region specialized in supplying grain and horses to the royal army and its garrisons. Exclusion from guilds, retailing, the military, public office, teaching and most professions, even if less tight than in Warsaw or Cracow, left most of the Metz Ashkenazic community and those of the surrounding villages permanently impoverished, living from street vending, peddling secondhand goods, and not infrequently organized petty crime. Vagrancy was rife. Within their segregated religious and social sphere, these communities possessed extensive judicial autonomy, but had to pay additional taxes to the crown specific to their community to which no-one else was subject. In France, as everywhere in continental Europe at the time, settled Jewish life outside the vagrancy sector, Ashkenazic and Sephardic alike, remained under tight supervision of Jewish boards of elders or syndics (*parnasim*).

These boards strictly enforced conformity with rabbinic law and tradition, overseeing almost every aspect of everyday life, communal existence, marriage and education, leaving any Jew personally not fully observant or sceptical, like Hourwitz, subject to ceaseless harassment from rabbinic authority within as well as the "Christian" world without. To a self-proclaimed self-consciously enlightened, "philosophic" critic knowing Yiddish perfectly but preferring French, Jewish emancipation meant not just wider toleration and release from discriminatory fiscal and legal constraints but emancipation from repressive religious supervision and community control.

The Academy judges delivered judgment and awarded the prize finally on 23 August 1788. More impressed this time with Hourwitz's effort, and doubtless prompted by Roederer, the judges opted to "crown" all three leading entrants as the winners—Thiéry, Grégoire and Hourwitz—with the monetary prize split equally between them. Like Roederer himself, all three urged comprehensive Jewish emancipation, equality and integration,[60] making the event indeed a significant turning point in modern history. A "revolution" was occurring among Europe's educated minds regarding the Jews, stressed Thiéry, a lawyer of Protestant background. The principal factor driving the change, he agreed with Roederer and Mirabeau, was neither the public nor religious leaders, but "la philosophie." "Philosophy" had transformed the situation by discrediting every theological argument aimed at bolstering prejudice and discrimination. Although Mirabeau was the *philosophe* to whom most credit was due for this shift in French educated sentiment, Thiéry professed to have independently reached the same conclusions as he.

Thiéry unreservedly urged Jewish emancipation, insisting like Mirabeau, Diez, Brissot and Cloots, that the whole burden of responsibility for the centuries-long persecution and oppression of the Jews, their degrading marginalization since the first Christian centuries, lay with the churches and the common people. Bigotry encouraged by monks and priests exploiting the most deplorable ignorance was the core problem.[61] Jewish society, argued Thiéry, *was* defective, corrupt and given to usury. It needed reform. But this was scarcely different from the rest of French law, institutions and society, all of which he deemed in urgent need of fundamental reform.[62] His tone fitted the revolutionary character of his argument and his awareness of the great difficulty society faced in stomaching such a message. Successful Jewish emancipation and integration required among other things, he held, an end to separate Jewish dress and education rooted in rabbinic sway, a shaving off of beards and eliminating Jewish institutional autonomy. If obstacles weathered by centuries of prejudice were to be conquered, the crown must initiate secularizing education enabling Christian and Jewish children to mingle and imbibe enlightenment, morality and civic values together. Progress required a huge joint Christian-Jewish effort,[63] regulated by a religiously neutral, secular, enlightened state as envisaged by Dohm, Diez, Brissot and Mirabeau.

Grégoire equally wanted the Jews integrated into French society as equals but thought they needed "improving" before the process could proceed far and, ultimately, must convert to Christianity. Where Grégoire and other ecclesiastics wanted Jews to reform first before removal of disabilities, and Brissot thought improvement was eventually needed but should not be a prior condition, Hourwitz insisted the Jews had not degenerated morally but simply been oppressed by church, state and society.[64] Like Brissot, he demanded emancipation forthwith without preconditions, while claiming it was Christian society, not the Jews, that chiefly needed reforming and remodelling.[65] Far from having characteristic vices and being more corrupt than other peoples, Hourwitz, having witnessed Jewish life in London and Amsterdam as well as Paris and Poland, felt able to guarantee that they are the "most peaceable, sober and industrious of all peoples while capital crimes are practically unknown amongst them." Emancipating the Jews should proceed forthwith albeit be just a strand of a much wider revolutionary process necessary to ameliorate general society and elevate mankind as a whole.[66]

Defending Jewish moral integrity, Hourwitz angrily rejected also the ancient Christian charge of obstinacy. It is not easy for Christians to accept that their arguments for their faith look exceedingly weak to anyone with the slightest knowledge of the Hebrew texts; but eventually they must accept this. Whereas the clandestine, unpublished manuscripts of the Jews perennially represent a dire threat to Christian belief, Christian arguments cannot possibly look convincing to anyone genuinely knowledgeable about the Hebrew Scriptures. All "Jewish converts" to Christianity, he argued, are invariably scoundrels and hypocrites converting from some insincere motive, usually to obtain some post or other gain otherwise denied them, like a Jew he knew in London who embraced Methodism to "marry a rich widow of that sect whom he then abandoned three months after their marriage." Since such conversions are thoroughly base, "one never sees a Jew becoming a Christian at Constantinople, a Catholic at Amsterdam, or Protestant at Paris."[67] Hence, when the Amsterdam reading society "Voor den Godsdienst, en het Vaderland" [For Religion and the Fatherland] proposed a thirty-ducat prize for the best answer to the question, "what are the reasons preventing modern Jews from openly embracing Christianity?" and several Jews, including Hourwitz, submitted entries, no prize was awarded. Instead of announcing the winner by the agreed deadline, February 1784, this worthy society lapsed into the most impenetrable silence. The society's librarian and secretary, the publisher Willem Holtrop, though well-disposed toward Jews, and friendly with the Jewish reformer Hartog Lémon, refused to provide any reason for this curious "literary bankruptcy" despite Hourwitz's repeated efforts, through contacts, to extract some explanation. But the real reason is simple: there *are* no cogent text-based arguments in favor of Christianity.[68]

Admittedly, conceded Hourwitz, "rabbinic severity" rendered Jews unable to offer military service away from home on campaign; but nothing prevented their recruitment in defensive units at home (he himself served in the revolutionary militias, in Paris, from 1789),[69] to help guard their country's interior security. On Saturdays, they "would put Christians where *they* should be" and, on Sundays, muster up and take *their* place "as practiced in Surinam and other Dutch colonies."[70] Nassy later reaffirmed this argument in his *Lettre Politico-Théologico-Morale,* citing the Surinam white militia and Caribbean Sephardic Jews serving in the naval force based at Curaçao and in the wider Caribbean during the Fourth Anglo-Dutch War (1780–84).[71] As for Jews shunning farming and the countryside, that arose entirely from oppressive disabilities and exclusion. One *did* find Jewish *cultivateurs* of the land in eastern Poland, Turkey and Persia and even some in the villages of Pinache and La Bastide, near Bayonne; but certainly more Jews should engage in farming.[72] Remove unjustified repressive restrictions and the Jews would revert to the land.

Hourwitz's reform agenda in some respects resembled Thiéry's but was far from identical. His viable integration into French society required not the Jews' assimilation, or erasing their separate identity and character, but their becoming "more enlightened" and studying Talmud less. One criticism he wholeheartedly embraced was that they did indeed, aside from Mendelssohn and one or two others, insufficiently devote themselves to the sciences and Enlightenment studies.[73] "By improving the lot of the Jews," society would benefit not only them "but also letters, humanity and the French state, since nearly all French Jews, besides knowing French, possess German or Spanish too, with some knowing Biblical and rabbinic Hebrew, and Aramaic."[74] They can therefore more readily than others learn Arabic and other oriental languages analogous to Hebrew and Aramaic, and be usefully employed in letters or commerce on the coasts of the Levant, Persia, India and North Africa. Later, in his grammatical work, Hourwitz would insist that there was nothing sacred or divine about the Hebrew language, which he saw as the daughter of ancient Phoenician (Punic) and closely related to Syriac and Arabic. "If one day [the Jews] penetrate to China, they could provide, aided by their confreres settled there since time immemorial, much light on the history of that empire and the history of their own nation." First, though, the Jews needed rescuing from the Christians' "éternelle et cruelle oppression."[75]

Jews must enjoy the same economic freedom as others and mix freely with non-Jews. For this to happen, their familiarity with French and French society needed broadening, and everyday use of Yiddish and Hebrew lessening. The mixed Sephardic-Ashkenazic community of Paris, consisting of around five hundred Jews in 1789, in its scattered, undisciplined state, relative lack of rabbinic supervision and detachment from community control, while representing only one-eightieth part of the roughly forty thousand Jews now in France, was nevertheless in this respect a signpost to the future.[76] The crown should forbid use of Hebrew and Yiddish when Jews draw up business contracts and agreements. Jews must be required by law to maintain their records of dealings, whether with Christians or their own people, exclusively in French, with legal deeds drawn up in Hebrew characters disallowed, so that all can be equally subject to French law and jurisdiction. To achieve this, public schools must be opened to Jewish children, enabling them to learn French adequately—from which, argued Hourwitz, a double advantage would follow: being schooled together with Christian children "will facilitate enlightening their conduct and make them familiar with Christians from their childhood onwards; they will develop ties of friendship with them strengthened by being neighbors and by convergence of language and usages."[77]

That the "honnête homme" [honest man] is eternally worth more than the religiously devout was the basis of Hourwitz's moral code, as that of Radical Enlightenment generally. Accordingly, like the ecclesiastic Grégoire, who first became widely known through the Metz competition, Hourwitz was antagonistic to rabbinic and communal authority over the individual Jew, in particular outside the synagogue. Integration on the basis of equality, he thought, necessitates forbidding rabbis and synagogue elders to exercise any authority over co-religionists in their extra-synagogue activities, in society generally.[78] Rabbis and Jewish community elders must also be stripped of the power to impose communal bans on congregants and forbidden to prevent dissident persons appearing in synagogue. Nor must they be allowed to refuse communal "honors" in synagogue services to those who shave off their beards, dress like Christians, attend the theatrer or neglect "some other usage totally unrelated to religion introduced solely through superstition to distinguish them" from everyone else.

Jews must learn to place a higher value on an honest Christian or Muslim than the most punctiliously observant Jew who is less honest; equally, the honest Christian must learn to esteem the honest, patriotic Jew more highly than even the most zealous churchgoer imaginable who is less honest. "In a word, love God and your neighbor."[79] France's judges and courts must end the "barbaric practice" when passing criminal sentences on individual Jews of designating persons to be "of the Jewish nation," since the current usage "serves only to render the entire nation odious through the misbehavior of an individual."[80]

Pronouncing all three winners to be of equal merit and to share the prize, the Metz Academy declared this outcome a triumphant vindication of the power of reason to transcend prejudice, tradition and confessional bias. Despite the three competitors' differences of professional and social background and religion, all three had reached broadly the same conclusions, offering much the same analysis and (prompted by Roederer) approximately similar solutions.[81] This point was echoed the following year by the Abbé Grégoire in his address to the revolutionary French National Assembly presenting his motion in favor of Jewish rights. When he, a Catholic priest, published his work "on the regeneration of this people," the public was much struck by seeing "the same cause defended" by two others, a jurist from Nancy and a rabbi's son, M. Zalkind Hourwitz, a Polish Jew, attached to the Bibliothèque du Roi.[82]

Hourwitz in this way emerged as the most outspoken, best-known standard-bearer of a new, anticlerical secular Jewishness making its first appearance at this time and taking permanent shape during the revolutionary era. He became equally a leading Jewish propagator of a new kind of *philosophique* political ideology that emerged more forcefully during the 1770s and 1780s, especially in France, Holland, Italy and Germany, than it had earlier. Hourwitz's revolutionary fervor drew on the wider emancipation effort gaining impetus from 1780 through the efforts of Mendelssohn, Friedländer, and such German *Aufklärer* as Dohm and Diez, as well as the anti-Jewish ferment rife then in Alsace-Lorraine. Dohm's claim that state and church had together perverted and deformed Jewish existence and that only a basic shift in policy, separating church and state, could solve the underlying problem was doubtless hard to stomach for anyone embracing traditionally pious attitudes but music to the ears of the radically enlightened fringe of Jewish society.

REVOLUTION AND JEWISH EMANCIPATION (1789–1792)

Jews had been shamefully oppressed over the centuries, Grégoire agreed with Thiéry and Hourwitz, and suffered great wrongs inflicted by society that needed putting right. But rather than lay the main blame on Church and Church Fathers, like the radicals, Grégoire attributed the age-old oppression to "une politique barbare" [barbarous statecraft] of medieval monarchs, feudalism and an ignorant populace.[83] One must not measure the Church's true moral integrity by the Inquisition: "generally speaking, no one was more moderate toward the Jews than the clergy."[84] But caught between the papacy's opposition (and that of most clergy) and the anti-church stance of the radicals, Christian radicals like Grégoire, Lamourette and Fauchet pursuing a genuinely church-compatible universalist ideal during the Revolution, striving to combine religious authority with "universal and equal rights," grew perilously isolated.

Grégoire's efforts to combine Catholic zeal with Enlightenment in the end earned him little thanks from theologians and not much from radical enlighteners.[85] Unqualified support for the Jewish cause among non-Jews without demanding their conversion remained largely confined to irreligious secular radicals, known from 1789 in German lands as *Revolutionsfreunde* [Friends of the Revolution], the small handful of intellects active and articulate in supporting the Revolution's human rights ideals. Championing the Jewish cause against the tide, they did so essentially because emancipating Jews from *ancien régime* oppression seemed part of the same process as emancipating men generally from kings, popes, aristocracy and priestcraft. Anti-Montagnard, staunchly anti-*Robespierriste* champions of "universal and equal rights" invariably envisaged the Revolution as the necessary outcome of "philosophy," the true fulfilment of the Enlightenment's goals.[86] Among enlighteners a radical minority, they too were eventually marginalized.

Among those notably striving to improve the condition of Jews in France was Antoine Joseph Gorsas (1752–1793), a former tutor, and from 1789 editor of the *Courrier de Versailles* as it was first called, later the *Courrier de Paris*. A prominent revolutionary journalist championing Jewish emancipation, Gorsas helped diffuse in France the new ideas regarding the Jewish question emanating from Germany and Metz. A passionate democratic republican reviling credulity, superstition and despotism, and detesting priests and aristocracy (and later Robespierre and the Montagne), Gorsas was among the first pro-Revolution journalists to forcefully back Grégoire's emancipationist efforts in the National Assembly, rejecting the calumnies against the Jews disseminated by substantial sections of France's now unbridled press.[87] On 21 November 1789, his paper reported that some "poor Jews of Paris" had organized a collection among themselves to support the Revolution, "being filled with a fervent desire to assist a *patrie* that has become theirs, and rally their brothers, the Christians, to less unjust ideas [about the Jews]." When a group long deplorably marginalized by general opinion, he urged his readers, "seeks to eliminate the bigotry of which they are the victims, should we not, can we not, aid them in conquering this wretched prejudice?"[88]

Shortly after the National Assembly's crucial vote, of late August 1789, passing the *Declaration of the Rights of Man and the Citizen*, Gorsas's paper promptly supported the motion to accord the estimated "50,000 Jews" (actually closer to 40,000) living in France full equality of rights.[89] In this effort, Gorsas collaborated with Hourwitz and may possibly have employed him for a time.[90] Gorsas dreaded the common people's ignorance and prejudice, their susceptibility to being manipulated and stirred up. Scorn for popular thinking was among the factors that later made him a target of the Montagne. Inside the National Assembly itself, there were a few other energetic supporters of Jewish emancipation besides Mirabeau and Grégoire, including the legislature's most radical Protestant spokesman, the former Huguenot pastor Jean-Paul Rabaut de Saint Étienne (1743–1793). Rabaut's address to the Assembly, on 28 August, urging full and equal rights for Protestants pressed for emancipation of the Jews on identical grounds: "I demand for the French Protestants," as Gorsas enthusiastically reported his words, "for all the kingdom's non-Catholics what you demand for yourselves—liberty and equality of rights."[91] "I demand it also for that people torn from Asia, always wandering, always proscribed, always persecuted for eighteen centuries who will adopt our morals and usages, if by our laws they are integrated together with us, a people we should not reproach for [defective] morality this being the consequence of our own barbarity, the humiliation to which we have unjustly condemned them."[92]

Grégoire presented his motion for Jewish equality on 1 September 1789. On 24 September 1789, the National Assembly formally admitted France's Protestants to full rights of citizenship of the now constitutional monarchy, but unmoved by the oratory of Mirabeau, Rabaut and Grégoire, and several Jewish petitions calling for exclusion from the arts and crafts to be lifted, the Assembly, finding itself deeply divided over this issue, decided to postpone further consideration of Jewish status for the moment. Deliberation of the issue resumed only in December. A lively debate then ensued in which the "moderate" Bishop De La Fare of Nancy, the Abbé Maury and Jean-François Reubell, "the pitiless enemy of the Jews" as Brissot called him, took the lead in presenting arguments against making the Jews Frenchmen and citizens.[93] Despite support in and outside the Assembly, in the final debate on 23 December, Mirabeau, Grégoire, Rabaut and the republican democratic Left advocating Jewish equality and full citizenship were defeated narrowly, by 408 votes to 403, those opposing equal Jewish rights comprising a broad spectrum of "moderates," monarchists, and churchmen.

The opposition was headed by Anne-Louis Henri De La Fare (1752–1829), the same bishop of Nancy who, in August 1789, led the Assembly's Sixth

Bureau's unsuccessful effort to water down the *Declaration of the Rights of Man and the Citizen* by diluting freedom of expression and the right to criticize the Church. The Sixth Bureau, recent research demonstrates, intervened in the human rights debate trying to defend Catholic conservative interests and, as far as possible, dilute the "universal and equal rights" urged by Mirabeau, Sieyes and Brissot.[94] If less "medieval" than Arthur Hertzberg claimed, De la Fare *was* a declared monarchist and energetic adversary of "universal and equal" rights principles generally and most of all of Jewish rights. Staunch for king and Church, he was to flee France in January 1791, becoming an émigré counter-revolutionary. Royalist gratitude for his strenuous efforts to resist universal human rights and Jewish emancipation, led after Napoleon's downfall to his elevation, under the Restoration, to the exalted rank of Cardinal-Archbishop of Sens.[95]

Admittedly, not every prominent backer of Jewish equal rights was a radical enlightener. In the National Assembly, the key motion advocating Jewish rights was formally presented by an aristocratic "moderate," Comte Stanislas de Clermont-Tonnerre (1757–1792), an enthusiast for British-style constitutional monarchy and aristocratic precedence. However, the arguments he utilized on this occasion, to further Jewish equality, were decidedly radical. As the papers reported, it was malign laws, he argued, that had turned the Jews into "bad citizens."[96] He opposed separate status and representation for Jews as for all religious and social groups, but his demanding the Jews be integrated into the French nation, contrary to what is sometimes suggested,[97] did not mean he sought wholesale dissolution of Jewish community structures and erasure of Jewish cultural and religious identity. Like Hourwitz, what he called for was an end to legal separation and extra-synagogue communal jurisdiction.

Clermont-Tonnerre was apparently won over to support the Jews by reading the arguments of "the Polish Jew" Hourwitz.[98] Hourwitz's Metz prize essay may have been the last to appear, being published after Grégoire's and Thiéry's essays, but under the title *Apologie des Juifs* came out at the crucial moment, April 1789, just when the Revolution was beginning. It was widely discussed and reviewed. Its favorable reception in the *Mercure de France* highlighted the symbolism of an erudite, unafraid Jew sallying forth to "défendre sa nation" and reclaim "pour elle ces droits imprescriptibles et communs à tous les hommes" [for them these imprescriptible rights common to all men].[99]

After Clermont-Tonnerre's memorable speech in the National Assembly, the ecclesiastics Maury and the bishop of Nancy vigorously countered his claims, but in Clermont-Tonnerre met an unyielding defender of individual liberty, press liberty and separation of powers. Most French clergy and the papacy opposed not only Jewish equality but the Revolution's universal and equal rights program generally, creating a situation which developed into a profound tragedy for the brave Grégoire and such fellow committed revolutionary Christian egalitarians and "constitutional" prelates as Antoine-Adrien Lamourette (1742–1794) and Claude Fauchet (1742–1793), who eventually became dangerously isolated and vulnerable within the Revolution.[100] Lorraine Jews had performed some useful services in his own diocese of Nancy, granted De la Fare, nevertheless, Jewish equality made little sense since Mosaic and Talmudic religious law separates Jews from the rest of society and ordinary folk detest the Jews. Should this group of eternal "étrangers" [strangers] be accorded equality and civil rights against the episcopate's advice, the bishop predicted "great disasters": the Christians of Alsace-Lorraine "les a en horreur" [hold them in horror]. Partly, he agreed, this stemmed from prejudice: "les préjugés du peuple contre les juifs ne sont que trop connus" [the prejudices of the people against the Jews are only too well-known].[101] But one could not simply ignore the fact that bestowing rights of citizenship on Jews could "allumer un grand incendie" [light a great conflagration].[102]

Since chairing the Assembly's Sixth Bureau, back in August 1789, opposing freedom of speech and freedom to criticize Church, theology and clergy by diluting the *Declaration of the Rights of Man* as much as he and his following could, resisting Jewish rights likewise had become integral to De la Fare's stance.[103] Blocked in December 1789, the battle over Jewish rights resumed in January 1790, backed by the Paris city government's radical faction headed by Brissot and Condorcet. On 29 January 1790, a Parisian Jewish delegation including Hourwitz called on the city government to intervene with the National Assembly on behalf of Jewish equality, which the municipality promptly agreed to do.[104] It was not, therefore, the "French Revolution" as an undifferentiated whole, or the National Assembly, and still less public opinion, that supported Jewish integration into society, Jewish equality and the right to live free of restriction wherever they chose (Jewish residence under *ancien régime* law remained legally restricted to Alsace-Lorraine, Avignon, Bordeaux and Bayonne). Rather, Jewish emancipation resulted principally, almost exclusively, from the anti-theological tendency propagated widely through the 1770s and 1780s by the Radical Enlightenment vanguard with Mirabeau, Brissot, Cloots, Roederer, Gorsas and the Metz prize winners well to the fore, a crucial distinction which historians have mostly failed sufficiently to underline.

Meanwhile, the threat of antisemitic disturbances loomed larger. Since July 1789, peasant unrest gripped large parts of rural France, leading to frequent attacks on noble chateaux. The disorder in Alsace and Lorraine, from mid-July 1789 assumed an emphatically antisemitic as well as anti-aristocratic character with anti-Jewish disturbances during early August, at Lixheim, Hegenheim, Hagenthal, Buschweiler, Blotzheim and Durmenach. Witnessing numerous ugly scenes, Gorsas dutifully reported this harassment of Jews and surging hostility to Jewish emancipation,[105] an expression of bitter social resentment, frustration and violence sweeping France. Many Jews at this stage fled the violence in the countryside, seeking refuge in Metz, Nancy and Basel. The yawning gap between the French Revolution as a powerful social eruption of the people expressing numerous widely felt grievances, and the Revolution as "esprit philosophique," of radical ideas in action, was becoming ever more glaringly obvious.

During 1789–90, this contradiction between popular antisemitism and the Jewish question as conceived by radical Enlightenment revolutionary ideology, increasingly impressed itself on Gorsas and Hourwitz. Gorsas's journal, among the most attentive of pro-Revolution papers to the agitation permeating provincial France during the autumn of 1789, powerfully denounced the unreasoning "hatred of the people" against both Jews and Protestants, high-lighting the pillaging of Jewish homes at Lixheim, in Lorraine fifty miles east of Nancy, at Hagenthal and eighteen other villages in Alsace, and the dire menace the peasantry's unrelenting Catholic piety posed for the Revolution in its entirety. The ignorance and credulity of disadvantaged elements, admonished Gorsas in October 1789, not the French people overall, was the core problem; popular credulity menaced the Jews, and equally menaced the Revolution itself. Like the Abbé Grégoire, he publicly urged the National Assembly to take special measures to protect this particularly vulnerable, exposed minority: "great danger surrounds in particular the Jews in Lorraine and Alsace."[106]

With its substantial Ashkenazic population, approximately thirty thousand Jews,[107] roughly six thousand Jewish families, Alsace-Lorraine remained at the heart of the surging drama. As De la Fare and Gorsas both emphasized, the region seethed with burgeoning antisemitic resentment. For the immediate outcome of the Revolution, and eventual 1791 emancipation decree, was an expanding Jewish role in local commerce, retailing and peddling. Jewish traders' increased visibility in Nancy, Metz and the countryside around proved highly unwelcome, stiffening resentment and providing fuel for both hardened counter-revolutionaries and pro-Revolution "moderates" and populists opposing civic rights for Jews. Prominent here was Jean-François Reubell (1747–1807), a Colmar lawyer and Estates-General deputy who, after Thermidor, would become a member of the Directory. The Jews, contended Reubell, worked contrary to ordinary folk *and* revolutionary values, being men who think only of profit and moneymaking. A leading detractor of Jewish morality, Reubell himself was notoriously corrupt, among the worst of the Montagne's impressive array of unscrupulous populist demagogue leaders. During the French occupation of Mainz (1792–93), he was fiercely denounced by the great German radical and revolutionary Georg Forster, for his utterly scandalous conduct and chicanery.

Disagreement over Jewish rights prompted both sides to exploit oratory and the press to the utmost. Another leader opposing Jewish rights was the famously eloquent Abbé Maury, who implored the National Assembly to heed the common people.[108] Jews did not engage in agriculture, the French people's primary economic sphere, but stuck to finance and commerce of a kind threatening, if further expanded, to gain a stranglehold over peasant society even far beyond Alsace-Lorraine.[109] After an ill-tempered debate, on 28 January 1790, the National Assembly, patching up a compromise voted by 374 votes to 224 to accord civil equality to the less execrated Sephardic Jews of the southwest (Bordeaux, Bayonne and Peyrehorade) and the ancient community of formerly papal Avignon and Carpentras, leaving the issue of equal rights for France's largest Jewish community, the *Ashkenazim* of Alsace-Lorraine and Paris, once again aside. Disgusted, Mirabeau absented himself from the vote.[110] A precarious "fix" devised, reported the Venetian ambassador to the Doge, in defiance of all logic, it was totally unsustainable as a principle, a "monstrosity" violating all common sense: "a Jew of Bordeaux will enjoy the Rights of Man, but not a Jew of Lorraine or Alsace."[111]

The Sephardic communities of the southwest and Avignon in January 1790 now finally became French citizens.[112] The first legislation proclaiming the equal citizenship rights of any Jews anywhere, Clermont-Tonnerre scathingly denounced it as a ramshackle compromise blatantly inconsistent with the *Declaration of the Rights of Man* and the Revolution's essential values—a "blasphemy" against the National Assembly's own decrees.[113] Almost at once, the growing Jewish community of the capital, now estimated at over eight hundred, backed by the revolutionary Paris city commune now under Brissotin control, and the Jewish communities of Alsace-Lorraine, renewed their demand likewise to be declared citizens with identical legal rights to everyone else. But such was the clergy's opposition, that of Metz, Strasbourg and the Alsace-Lorraine delegates headed by Reubell, that the January 1790 stalemate dragged on inconclusively still for many more months.

Most of Paris's Jews including many who, since the onset of the Revolution had only recently arrived from Alsace-Lorraine or the southwest, dwelt in the shabby Saint-Martin quarter of the Carmelites, soon to be renamed the revolutionary section "Réunion," a district where, as in Paris generally, Jewish community discipline remained markedly looser than elsewhere.[114] With fewer than a thousand Jews in Paris at this juncture, it was striking, Gorsas pointed out, that no fewer than one hundred of them were serving in the National Guard patrolling the streets for the Revolution.[115] In February 1790, Gorsas cited Hourwitz as his model of a selfless "revolutionary Jew" reportedly donating a quarter of his modest Bibliothèque salary, his sole source of income, to the cause of the Revolution.[116] Hourwitz himself published several open letters at this point in Gorsas's *Courrier*, the *Chronique de Paris* and other revolutionary papers, claiming denial of equal rights for Jews would be a disaster depriving the Revolution of all claim to principled integrity and moral foundation. Answering Maury's contention that the "Jews have never been farmers," he suggested in Gorsas's paper, on 24 April 1790, that the good Abbé had forgotten his Scripture. Swayed by prejudice, "you appear not to know the principles of your own religion": "love your neighbor as yourself, and your *patrie* more than your ecclesiastical position, and treat the Jews as your brothers."[117]

Another protest letter, published on 12 January 1791, nearly two years after the start of the Revolution, sizzled with Hourwitz's biting humor, a weapon he regularly blended with careful erudition in pursuing his fight for Jewish rights. "I have the honor of being your relative," he addressed the *Chronique de Paris*'s editor, "like you being a direct line descendant of Adam, albeit a very distant one. Despite our kinship, unlike you I do not possess rights of citizenship, the reason for this being that the man and woman who produced me (without consulting me) prayed to the Supreme Being in Hebrew and lived in Poland, hence beyond the boundaries of Bordeaux and Avignon." A long-term Parisian resident without rights of citizenship, he possessed only the meagre status of "a foreigner."[118] Was it not astonishing, he demanded, in another letter to Gorsas's *Courrier*, of 24 January 1791, tying the delayed emancipation of France's Ashkenazic community (delay even Brissot deemed unavoidable for now) to the Revolution's disgraceful evasion thus far of the issue of black emancipation, that France's National Assembly had shelved the "business of Jews of all colors, and the men of color of all religions, while simultaneously allowing directors and secretaries of gambling-casinos to enjoy full rights of citizens?" To be a citizen, even a legislator in France today, "this land of equality and liberty," concluded Hourwitz, requires only "a white foreskin and just enough honesty to avoid being hanged."[119] For this travesty, the Revolution's so-called "moderates" were responsible among them Maury, De La Fare and the centrist leader Antoine-Pierre Barnave (1761–1793). Hourwitz particularly denounced Barnave's lack of principle and his colluding (during 1789–92) with the French Caribbean white planters in their efforts to defend slavery and block equal rights for free blacks.

If all this was disturbing, how astounding to find in the latest public announcement of the appointment of a senior Paris police official that the latter's revolutionary surveillance responsibilities covered "cafes, taverns" and all categories of persons lacking French citizenship, namely "foreigners and Jews!" Such wording differentiating between French Jews and French "citizens," suggested Hourwitz, reminded one of Cicero's witticism distinguishing "Julius from Caesar," but it should not be supposed the city government was joking. Hence, he felt obliged to protest in the papers: why is the municipality treating "us like a species of amphibian?" How could France's capital justify using such odious terminology, emulating the *ancien régime* police directly "contrary to the Rights of Man?" Such miring of revolutionary principle was especially galling in that all the capital's electoral sections had "generously" declared in favor of Jewish citizenship, in their representations on the subject to the National Assembly.[120] Hourwitz's letter stirred the official Jewish representatives in Paris, A. Asur, Mordechai Elie and D. Silveyra, to join in pressing his protest, albeit in more deferential tones. A few days later, the city government shamefacedly apologized issuing a brief statement, in the same journal, that the municipality had indeed made an unfortunate "error": Jews should not be referred to in such a manner, or in any way "distinguished from other citizens or subjected to any particular inspection."[121]

During the years of unimpeded revolutionary press freedom (1789–93), prior to the Counter-Enlightenment ascendancy of Robespierre and the Montagne, France's monarchist press remained in business and continued denouncing Jewish emancipation along with the other sweeping changes projected by the National Assembly. Ordinary folk, France's reactionaries tirelessly reiterated, detested Jews and bitterly resented what was proposed.[122] Not until 27 September 1791, however, did the National Assembly finally overrule Maury, Bishop De La Fare and the combined "moderate" and conservative opposition, proclaiming all the Jews of France full citizens with equal rights.

By no means all of Hourwitz's letters to the Paris papers during the early revolutionary years concerned Jewish rights and the status of the Jews. Other revolutionary topics interested him too, provoking his typically incisive responses. These included the procedures and organization of the National Guard of which he was a proud member, and the efforts to dismantle the wealth and power of the Church. A letter to Gorsas, published in the *Courrier de Paris*, in early December 1789, discussed how to protect the secrecy of orders issued to the capital's National Guard patrols.[123] Hourwitz also regularly joined in the denunciation of "aristocracy," the "aristocratic" vice of duelling and other social ills such as the "scoundrels" running gaming-houses as well as, later during the Napoleonic years, longed to change all the names of the "streets, squares, fountains, and sewers" of Paris to more logical and meaningful names.[124]

HOURWITZ AND THE POLISH-LITHUANIAN DIMENSION (1789–1794)

Aside from the Jewish question, Hourwitz intervened most significantly in support of black emancipation and political manifestations, asserting the unity of mankind and universality of equal rights. On the evening of 19 June 1790, he appeared before the National Assembly deputies among a "delegation of foreigners," thirty-five selected representatives of the peoples of the world, led by the universalist revolutionary Anacharsis Cloots, with each participant wearing their "native attire" aimed at displaying the solidarity of all nations and peoples. No doubt savoring the humor of the situation, Hourwitz chose to represent "Poland," dressing and presenting himself as a typical "Pole." But fraternity of peoples, universality of mankind and the occasion itself, he treated with great seriousness. The delegation expressed hope that the great revolutionary "fête of the Federation" due to be celebrated on the Champ-de-Mars in Paris on the first anniversary of the fall of the Bastille, the following month, would prove a celebration genuinely by and on behalf of all the peoples of the world.[125]

As in world history generally, the revolutionary struggle for equal rights for all citizens proved one of the greatest turning points in Jewish history. Grégoire rightly called it a "revolution."[126] Hourwitz's *Apologie* contributed chiefly in France, but did not go unnoticed in the rest of Europe. At the time, the revolutionary summons to free the Jews and bestow on them equal rights had an electrifying effect throughout the Jewish world, especially among the small intellectual elites of Jewish enlighteners of Berlin, Königsberg, Hamburg, Amsterdam, the Italian cities and the Caribbean, on figures like Nassy, Hartog Lémon, Peyrera and Friedländer, criticizing and rejecting restrictive rabbinic authority and community leadership. Thus, Hourwitz's *Apologie* appeared in extracts and was discussed in the long-enduring Hebrew Enlightenment journal *Ha-Me'asef* (1784–1811), inspired especially by Mendelssohn's and Wessely's ideals, a monthly which had begun in Königsberg but latterly transferred to Berlin and which included articles by Polish as well as Prussian *maskilim*. Consequently, Hourwitz's essay soon exerted a noticeable impact in eastern Europe too.[127] In Poland, where the ferment surrounding enlightened reform was in full swing during the so-called the "Sejm Wielki" [Great Sejm], or Four Years Assembly (1788–92), Jewish emancipation, including Hourwitz's perspective on the issue, now became a topic of public debate and dispute.

At this point, Polish legislators were under severe pressure from the threatened disintegration of what remained of the kingdom, the looming threat of Poland-Lithuania being finally partitioned out of existence by the grasping ambitions of the crowned heads of Russia, Prussia and Habsburg Austria. The Sejm could no longer avoid urgent, serious deliberation of far-reaching political, social and economic reforms and began promisingly by voting through proposals for Poland's first standing army.[128] Amid much else, this general debate led to intense discussion of proposals for a "reformation of the Jews," even the possibility of "granting equal rights," though in Poland the latter was an extremely embattled concept which even the looming Russian menace could not carry far. Reflecting recent developments in Germany and France, Poland's legislators pondered a plethora of proposed changes regarding the Jews. At first, this discussion was mostly rhetorical without provoking much resonance from below. But by late 1789, with the impact of the French Revolution mounting, many people were being drawn into the discussion, with the small but wealthy Jewish urban elites of Warsaw and Cracow clamoring for equal rights almost as vociferously as those of German and French Jewry.[129] But that was out of the question. In Poland-Lithuania even the most liberal spokesmen in the legislature distanced themselves, when publishing their views, from the approach of the *philosophe* reformers in France heading the assault on religious authority and tradition.

The most influential of the Warsaw reforming faction's left wing in 1789 was Hugo Kołłątaj (1750–1812), a churchman from a minor noble family who had studied in Vienna, Naples and Rome, nurtured a broader vision than most Polish nobles and headed the commission that in the 1780s had reformed the universities of Cracow and Vilna. He viewed the various fiscal levies and burdens and the legal disabilities segregating Jews from the rest of the population as a serious barrier and urged reform to place the Jews in a more equal, less degraded position. But even Kołłątaj did not think it feasible to accord full equality, especially not political rights, eligibility to public office, or even full burgher status in principal cities such as Warsaw and Cracow where Jewish equality was fiercely opposed.[130] Kołłątaj did seek, though, further curtailment of Jewish communal autonomy. Back in 1764, the Sejm had already suppressed Polish Jewry's general assembly [Sejm Żydowski], the "Council of the Four Lands," and the Council of Lithuanian Jewry, forbidding them to convene again.[131] But on most points, Kołłątaj and his circle were less amenable and, in some instances, even urged additional disabilities, in particular for excluding Jews from selling alcoholic spirits and leasing taverns, inns and distilleries, then among the most controversial roles characterizing Jewish life in noble-dominated Polish-Ukrainian society. Finally, though the principal rift in Poland at the time, the friction between the towns and the *szlachta* [nobility], beside holding up much else, prevented any major reforms affecting the Jews from materializing.[132]

Conservative commentators and the reformist wing alike were anxious to defend the existing highly stratified system of Polish social classes, or "estates," ecclesiastical, noble, burgher and peasant—and, along with this stratified system of differentiated "rights" and privileges, also Jewish separation and local autonomy. The radical egalitarian vision set out in the shortened Polish translation of Hourwitz's *Apologie* published at Warsaw in late 1789 as *The Justification, or An Apology of the Jews*, and the full-length French-language version of Hourwitz's brochure, advertisements for which also appeared in the Polish papers at the time, was rejected by all shades of Polish opinion.[133] Convinced Jewish society had numerous moral and social defects, and was chiefly responsible for the scourge of drunkenness afflicting Poland's peasantry, the reform committees had little sympathy for Hourwitz's thesis that these defects all resulted from "Christian" oppression.

Resistance to even partial local civic rights for Jews grew month by month.[134] Worried by the steady increase in the Polish Jewish population, there was one point, though, where Poland's noble reformers proved entirely amenable to suggestions for far-reaching change. They were eager to curb the Polish-Lithuanian Jewish custom of early marriage so denigrated by Maimon and other Polish-Lithuanian Jewish reformers such as Dr. Salomon Polonus, a physician at Vilna known as the "Amsterdam doctor" in reference to his training (later among the community leaders in Lithuania who helped mobilize Jewish support for the Kosciuśzko "revolution" against Czarist Russia, in 1794). Polonus urged that Jewish boys should be at least eighteen and girls sixteen before being permitted by law to marry.[135] Like Hourwitz, Polonus also proposed that Jews be made "citizens" on an equal basis to Poles and Lithuanians, be made liable for military service, learn Polish in school and that their impoverished should be directed to agriculture, their courts restricted to religious matters alone, and rabbis educated in modern studies and the sciences as well as Talmud,

Polonus's tract was one of seven or eight brochures advocating far-reaching reform of Polish Jewish society published and discussed at this juncture, including one by Szymel Wolfowicz, another known opponent of the traditional Jewish community structure, likewise representing the views of the enlightened clique at Vilna. Much distressed by the problem of Jewish poverty, he proposed schooling Jewish children in Polish to assist their integration into society, and opening up handicrafts to Jewish artisans. But, strikingly, where Polonus also wanted all the crafts opened to the Jews and other major changes, Hourwitz's tract was the only text by any author, Polish or Jewish, demanding complete equalization of rights in every respect including abolition of Jewish communal judicial autonomy.[136]

Meanwhile, Germany appeared a less promising scenario in the 1780s for Jewish advancement than France or Poland-Lithuania. While some Berlin Jews were conspicuously "affranchis" [emancipated], notes Mirabeau's key radical work *De la monarchie prussienne sous Fréderic le Grand* (6 vols., "Londres," 1788), hardly any non-Jews in Prussia, only a "très-petit nombre d'avocats de la cause des Juifs" [very small number of advocates of the Jewish cause]—that is, the likes of Dohm, Diez and Wekhrlin—displayed any willingness to emulate Lessing and speak or write in favor of Jewish emancipation.[137] Mendelssohn, as he confided to Lessing and Gumpertz, had felt profoundly shocked by the disparagement of Dohm and vehement antisemitism expressed by the renowned orientalist Professor Johann David Michaelis

(1717–1791), a Halle Pietist and leading professor at Göttingen. Among the foremost representatives of "Religious Enlightenment" in Germany, Michaelis opposed equal rights for Jews, seeing them as an innately inferior people and religion, and because so many were religious skeptics.[138] Few central European non-Jewish savants shared Mendelssohn's sense of shock. Many preferred to see a refashioned anti-Judaism penetrating enlightened circles. Frederick the Great had granted residence rights only to a small Jewish elite in Berlin, Breslau and Königsberg while retaining strict work, marriage and residence restrictions on most of Prussia's Jewish population and severely limited Jewish immigration. If roundly denounced by Mirabeau and his collaborators in *De la monarchie prussienne*, the king was barely criticized by enlighteners adhering to more pro-court moderate positions. Rather, in moderate "enlightened" circles, if more politely than in reactionary circles, Mirabeau, Dohm, Mendelssohn and their Berlin friends committed to Jewish emancipation, the Jewish enlighteners around Friedländer and Herz, found themselves bitterly mocked as Berlin's "Aufklärungssynagoge" [Enlightenment synagogue].[139]

Non-Jews discussing the Jewish problem in his day, protested Hourwitz, seemed bizarrely willing to praise Michaelis's pseudo-academic "expertise" in Hebrew, Bible and Judaism, regarding him as a learned authority with profound erudition on the subject. Supposedly among the foremost practitioners of modern historical-critical biblical scholarship, Michaelis's writings, insists Hourwitz, invoking his own training, offered scant grounds for anyone to respect him or any of his academic colleagues as genuinely knowledgeable about Jews and Judaism. Rather, all contemporary *érudits*, hostile or sympathetic alike, oozed an astounding ignorance of the entire subject of biblical Hebrew and ancient and modern Judaism, as they did, he claimed in his post-1800 writing, about linguistics and the origin and evolution of languages generally. This applied not least to the philosemitic d'Argens, author of the *Lettres Juives,* who despite knowing nothing about Jews figured among the best-known writers of the day on the topic.[140] All Michaelis proved with his heap of "ridiculous lies and gross contradictions" was his own crassness and the indescribable depth of academic ignorance and bigotry.[141]

Hourwitz pointedly cites Mirabeau's astonishment at German theologians' lack of "curiosity" about the arguments objecting to Christian claims the "celebrated Mendelssohn, to get rid of the annoying fanatic Lavater," threatened to publish. Mendelssohn had merely threatened to uncover this still concealed repository of truth, but otherwise adhered to traditional

Jewish reticence, so that his and other Jewish anti-Christian arguments remained veiled from both the public and the academic sphere, confined to carefully restricted unpublished manuscripts. Rousseau grasped at least that Jews may possess arguments "against Christianity" of which Christians are wholly ignorant and can never learn about while it is not "permitted for them to dispute freely on this topic."[142] A striking difference between radical enlighteners like Hourwitz and church reformers like Gregoire and Fauchet striving to fuse "universal and equal rights" and democratic republicanism with Catholicism, and introduce radical ideals of equality and emancipation into Christianity, was in their attitudes to the Jewish *clandestina*. Where atheist and deist radicals avidly espoused Jewish arguments conserved in unpublished Spanish and Hebrew manuscripts, so far absorbed only into the underground literature, the likes of Grégoire, Lamourette and Claude Fauchet, France's leading revolutionary Christians, wholly ignored Jewish critiques of Christian Bible exegesis.[143]

Opposition to Dohm's and Mendelssohn's emancipatory proposals, by prominent Polish as well as German, French and Dutch enlighteners, was indeed a striking feature of the wider Enlightenment and one on which Hourwitz felt obliged to comment.[144] During the 1780s, outside Austria-Hungary, Dohm's campaign for the civil improvement of German Jews had largely stalled. "Moderate," and especially "Religious Enlightenment," geared to compromise with the existing social order and allied to religious authority, kings and aristocracy, remained firmly negative in response. Disturbingly for some, moderate Enlightenment was also becoming a portal for a new racial approach to disparaging Jews, a tendency exemplified by Michaelis. Prominent among "enlightened" opponents of Jewish emancipation seeking new arguments and rhetoric, the internationally renowned Bible expert and Hebraist Michaelis had led the outcry against Lessing's play *Die Juden* in 1749 and, figured prominently among those developing the growing penchant for racial classification as a new form of social hierarchy.[145] A renowned "enlightener," Michaelis adamantly rejected Jewish emancipation and all notion Jews should, or could, be considered equivalent in moral status to "Germans"—or any "Christians," Jews being "incapable," as Grégoire expressed Michaelis's view "of regeneration being intrinsically *pervers*."[146] Michaelis's approach became a source of a remodelled, secularized antisemitism, a so-called "enlightened" antisemitism based not on theology but supposed racial traits that was to culminate later, in the 1830s and 1840s, in the fulminations of the otherwise radically rationalist philosopher and Bible critic, Marx's mentor, Bruno Bauer.

At the heart of this newly devised "enlightened" antisemitic ideology was Michaelis's notion, going beyond Voltaire, that Jewish moral degradation and unwillingness to participate in the norms, activities and duties of society, stem principally from unalterable characteristics ineradicably ingrained in Jewishness through ethnic inheritance as well as separate religious beliefs and tradition, hence flowed from their "innate character."[147] Reprimanding Mendelssohn, Dohm, Diez and Lessing, Michaelis opposed Jewish emancipation on the ground of Jewish ethnic difference *and* the cultural effects of their forms of religious observance including refusal of military service, which of itself, he contended, ensured unalterable Jewish separateness.

Making scant use of his reputed mastery of biblical Hebrew, Michaelis placed heavy emphasis on the "fact," as he called it, that in modern society Jews were much likelier to be complicit in crime than "the Germans." This soon widely taken-up thesis, that Jews are innately more criminally inclined and of lower moral caliber than Christians, Michaelis partly substantiated by misusing several phrases from Dohm's booklet. Dohm had indeed drawn readers' attention to the problems of Jewish vagrancy, criminality and petty thieving in central Europe (and the Netherlands and England). Michaelis greatly enlarged on this theme, sensationally adding firm "evidence" that despite Jews comprising only a minute fraction of Germany's population, less than 1 percent, no less half of all convicted thieves in Germany were Jews. To substantiate this stunning statistic, protested Hourwitz, Michaelis "invokes all the criminal registers" over several centuries without citing any, and with this fanciful mass of "evidence" supposes readers learn for certain that the "proportion of Jewish to Christian malefactors is not less than twenty-five to one."[148] Taken seriously by the ill-informed, such misinformation Hourwitz derided as the most preposterous prejudice and nonsense.

Rebelling against "Christian" bigotry and Jewish tradition alike, Hourwitz always remained loyal to his vow to fight for emancipation and the Jewish people's amelioration. His revolutionary secular identity focused on defending Jewish moral integrity while loudly repudiating traditional Jewish passivity and deference: Jews, boxed into their marginal status everywhere, not least Poland-Lithuania, must cease their dreaming of solace and consolation in remote places, must forget their messianic longing for some distant future via an imagined ingathering of exiles to their ancient Holy Land and work to positively ameliorate their circumstances where they are—in Poland-Lithuania, France, Germany, and Russia alike. "They await the Messiah but await death with still more certainty. Exit the Messiah! The Messiah! Let us be him ourselves!"[149]

Hourwitz's role as "Jewish revolutionary" during 1789–90 was thus a distinctive and significant one, and not just in France. Not much of an activist, and certainly no revolutionary leader, he has been described by one scholar as a "rebel son of the world of Ashkenaz," dwelling "in the same precarious zone of isolated individualism as had Spinoza."[150] Untypical he undoubtedly was; but invoking "isolated individualism" is to miss the point. For Hourwitz was undoubtedly among the chief archetypes and founders of a new kind of moral and social Jewishness rooted in the dilemmas of modernity, rejecting entirely the degradation of the past along with rabbinic and all religious authority. A thoroughgoing radical enlightener, he deployed the philosophy of the Enlightenment and, like Börne and Heine later, excoriating wit, to fight for a broader, secularized democratic vision of justice and equality militantly opposed to tradition, theology, rabbis and common prejudice alike.

EIGHT

Jewish Revolutionaries and the Terror (1793–1794)

Militant secularists like Hourwitz helped forge a new kind of Jewish revolutionary consciousness and redefine Jewish identity. He celebrated his own emancipation of mind and lifestyle—release from the internal Jewish and external "Christian" double repression of the past—and aspired to help engineer that of his people.[1] Not just a French citizen, he desired to be a citizen free to express himself as someone different from most, a cosmopolitan "other," yet sharing in the revolutionary "common good" of society as a whole. Gathering his rhetoric and insistence on free expression specifically from Radical Enlightenment principles, he battled for the Revolution *and* the Jewish people, joining eagerly in France's insurrection against kings, aristocracy and clergy, Christian and Jewish, while pointedly criticizing Voltaire and Rousseau.

"Le fameux Hourwitz," the best-known Jewish member of the Paris revolutionary National Guard,[2] sought to help remake the world on a more elevated basis social and moral, which inevitably entangled him in bitter conflict with the "universal and equal rights" Revolution's adversaries. During the Revolution's early stages, until late 1791, Hourwitz's targets were relatively few, comprising essentially the counter-revolutionary Right and the less extreme "constitutional monarchist," aristocratic bloc still present in the National Assembly allied to the Catholic "moderates," with the formidable Bishop De la Fare and Abbé Maury among their leaders. This faction wanted the Revolution watered down to the point that it could be effectively reconciled with the principles of monarchy and aristocracy while salvaging much of the authority and property was well as the independence of the Church.

Hourwitz regularly denounced the Revolution's out-and-out enemies, among them the so-called "Non-Juring" (or refractory) clergy refusing the oath of allegiance to the national legislature as against the "constitutional clergy," who did swear. After July 1790, increasingly forced to hide, Non-Jurors strove to stoke reactionary sentiment against the Revolution among the illiterate peasantry, having greatest impact in Brittany, the Lower Loire and Alsace-Lorraine.

Indeed, Non-Juring priests, whether they stayed in France or fled abroad as many did during 1792–93, were the Revolution's most tenacious foes. Fervent for pope and king, solidly opposing all secularizing reforms, their much-touted consistency and loyalty to the papacy, suggested Hourwitz, far from heroic as some supposed, was paper-thin. They resisted the revolutionary regime, demanding unbending obedience to Church and papacy from their parishioners. But when it came to their own loyalty to the papacy, they seemed more erratic: did they not immediately acquiesce without murmur when ordered by the Assembly to cease sending remittances of money collected from the pious out of the country to Rome?[3] Meanwhile, Hourwitz sniped at the "constitutional clergy" too. Among his humorous newspaper sallies was one appearing under the initials Z.H.P. [Zalkind Hourwitz Polonais], dated February 1791, teasingly playing on his alien status as a non-citizen "foreigner" supposedly unfamiliar with France, jocularly inquiring why French prelates, all sworn to celibacy, under the *ancien régime* were usually accompanied by "very pretty nieces" but, no sooner had the Revolution begun," unfathomably, than these "nieces vanished all at once."[4]

The picture changed dramatically, though, following the Paris rising of 10 August 1792, which marked the final overthrow of the monarchy and opened the way to inauguration of the First French Republic. On that day, the crowds stormed the Tuileries palace and the remnants of monarchy and the Revolution's Center-Right were swept away together with the royal Swiss Guard, and whatever remained of court life and ritual, along with the remaining "moderates" and constitutional monarchist opposition. By then, the Abbé Maury and De la Fare had already fled abroad and the moderate-radical struggle of 1789–92 was at an end. After that, Hourwitz chiefly dreaded and abhorred the intolerance, lies and ruthlessness of the *Robespierriste* and other Montagnard populist blocs responsible for suppressing all dissent and, from the autumn of 1793, for imposing the Terror, although he still made occasional jabs at churchmen, aristocrats, casino-directors and all the other "rascals" betraying the core values of the Revolution.

From late 1792, the core ideological conflict within the Revolution was henceforth between republicans and pseudo-republicans supporting dictatorship. It was a fight now to the death between champions of "universal and equal rights" and basic freedoms, including liberty of the press—that is, the authentic democratic republicans advocating equality, individual liberty and freedom of expression, the groups backing Brissot and Condorcet, with Roederer, Rabaut and Gorsas among their ranks—on one side, and the authoritarian populism of Marat and the *Robespierristes* with their demagoguery, populism and ruthless Counter-Enlightenment ideology, on the other. It was the latter who were behind the Terror and who forged the crushing 1793–94 tyranny of the "ordinary," of Rousseau's "simple souls" so emphatically eulogized by Robespierre and his supporters—the grip of intolerant, despotic power rooted in the frustration, intolerance and aggressive prejudices of the illiterate and ill-informed.

Both kinds of ideological Counter-Enlightenment tearing at the Revolution, Non-Juror and *Robespierriste,* specialized in mobilizing militant ignorance and illiteracy. But unlike the Counter-Enlightenment Non-Juring clergy, *Robespierristes* and other Montagnard factions rallied their support chiefly in the big cities, among the urban mobs, rather than in remote conservative rural areas, infusing their populism with brutal displays of vandalism as well as the anti-*philosophique* fury and anti-intellectualism they directly shared with the Non-Juring clergy. Above all, the Montagnards used their street power to shut down France's free press and overpower and wholly crush the revolutionary republican democratic Left.

From August 1792, radical enlighteners, non-Jewish and Jewish, including France's leading Jewish revolutionaries, Hourwitz, Pereyra, Furtado and the Brothers Frey, willingly or unwillingly found themselves dragged into conflict with Robespierre's tyrannical faction. Before long, all were hounded and became victims of the ever-more-encroaching and oppressive Montagne.[5] Practically all those propagating Radical Enlightenment views maintaining the enlightened democratic revolutionary values of 1789–92, and hence criticizing Robespierre and his allies, were publicly denounced as "enemies of the Revolution" and the people, and forced into hiding or executed, mercilessly crushed under the heel of *Robespierrisme.*

Prior to the Terror, the rising of 10 August 1792 that ended the monarchy, sometimes called the "second revolution," ushered in a brief period of hopeful, ecstatic optimism, surrounding the declaration of the Republic, and the proclaiming of the revolutionary Year 1, in September 1792. Until May 1793, the Brissotins precariously retained the upper hand in the Convention and most major city governments outside Paris, including Lyons, Marseille, Bordeaux, Toulouse, Montpellier and Caen. But if August 1792 swept aside all vestiges of monarchical and aristocratic forms (until 1814), the dramatically changed situation quickly, generated a sea of seething conflict as to the true principles of the Revolution, bitter strife over how the future Republic's constitution, laws, institutions, education and cultural life should be restructured. The division and turmoil soon threatened to plunge the nascent revolutionary republic into irreparable disarray.

FROM POLISH "FRANKISM" TO REVOLUTIONARY EGALITARIANISM

In his passionately anti-*Rousseauiste* and anti-Lockean treatise on the theory of the democratic republic, the *Philosophie sociale, dédiée au peuple françois,* penned in August 1792 but published some months later, the Revolution's second-most-notable Jewish publicist after Hourwitz, "Sigmund Gottlieb Junius Frey," or simply Junius Frey (1752–1794), as he became known, memorably deplored the tragic consequences of this descent into discord, confusion and Terror. Such furious and bitter internecine intellectual and political strife, observed Frey, in turn rendered the entire French public easy prey for the worst and most unprincipled elements among the revolutionary leadership and press.[6]

Junius Frey, his brother Emmanuel and their sister Leopoldine were siblings with a remarkably idiosyncratic Jewish background. Though, since 1775, no longer a Jew by religion, Frey, a native of Brünn (Brno) in Moravia, where he was called "Moses Levi Dobruschka," possessed a good knowledge of Hebrew, rabbinics and medieval Jewish philosophical literature, his father having originally intended him for a rabbinic career. Through his mother, Schöndl, he was a cousin and former ally of one of east European Jewry's most notorious sectarians, the famed Sabbatian mystic Jacob Frank (1726–1791), leader of the eighteenth century's foremost Ashkenazic heretical movement. Frankism formed an important strand in Frey's own remarkable background and intellectual formation.

Born to a family with Sabbatian links, in a village of Polish Podolia, today a region of southwest Ukraine bordering Romania, Frank spent his childhood and youth in the Danubian provinces of Moldavia and Wallachia and, later, in Ottoman Lands proper. As a young man, Frank wandered from Czernowitz to Bucharest, Smyrna, Sofia, Salonika and Constantinople.[7] A rebel against rabbinic authority, he traveled extensively in the Balkans, visiting Salonika several times, imbibing the doctrines and traditions of the Sabbatian movement descended from the seventeenth-century "false messiah" Sabbatai Zevi, whose sect was compelled to convert outwardly to Islam under pressure from the Sultan in Constantinople, in 1666. Known in Ottoman lands as "the Dönmeh," those who remained loyal to Sabbatai Zevi after his conversion formed a secretive Judaeo-Muslim sect based in Salonika which nominally venerated Mohammed but remained principally steeped in Sabbatai's revelations, a tightly knit group shunning marriage with both mainstream Muslims and Jews. While in Salonika, Frank himself, moved by the "holy spirit," converted and was anointed a Sabbatian leader.

Leaving Salonika, he returned to Poland, in 1754, to spread his spiritual message there. This preceded by some twenty years Junius Frey's [Dobruschka's] abandonment of Judaism.[8] Meandering among Podolia's Sabbatian centers—Korolowka, Jezierzany, Podhacje and Bursk—Frank built a movement that grew distinct from Sabbatianism proper, holding secretive gatherings in furtive defiance of rabbinic authority, characterized by psalm-singing, dancing, flaunting Christian-type crosses, symbolic transgressions of orthodox observance and fresh revelations recorded in heretical Hebrew texts. It seethed too—and not just according to rabbinic detractors—in flagrant extramarital erotic activities.[9] Frank's mystical Messianic resurgence soon convulsed all Jewish Poland, appealing especially to the Jewish impoverished and less educated, who were won over in their thousands.[10] A handsome, imposing man with a resounding voice whose surviving portrait shows him wearing flowing Turkish garb, from 1756 Frank stood under a general rabbinic ban, the great *herem*, like those imposed on Uriel da Costa, Prado and Spinoza. His adherents were often termed "anti-Talmudists" because release from the burdens of Talmud and normative Jewish observance pervaded their conduct and tenets. The strands of Judaism Frank retained he infused with the mystical tradition of Cabbala. Collective violation of Jewish fasts and heavy vodka consumption likewise figured among the movement's conspicuous features.

In this way, Frank established a tradition of Polish-Ukrainian Jewish emancipatory radicalism, political as well as religious, remnants of which survived down to, and supported, the Kościuszko armed rising against the Russian invasion of Poland in 1792–94 and remained identifiable even down to the Polish rising against Russia of 1863–64.[11] Among Frankist vestiges no more passionate emancipationist anti-Talmudists and foes of Jewish orthodoxy could be found than the Brothers Frey.

To expand his following, freedom of action and sway over his followers, Frank and his entourage convinced the Catholic bishop of Kamieniec Podolski, a Polish fortress town bordering the Ottoman Empire, that they wielded Christian crosses as a precious symbol and by repudiating the Talmud sought to erase the gulf between Judaism and Christianity, reuniting the two faiths. In so doing they intended to award preference to Catholicism over Protestantism and the Ukrainian Orthodox Church. This moved the bishop to stage a weeklong anti-Talmudist disputation between Sabbatians and Frankists, on one side, and Jewish orthodox, on the other, at Kamieniec, in June 1757, under Catholic supervision, designed to impress both the Catholic and Jewish public with a display of theology's power. This was followed in the autumn by a series of public burnings of condemned sacred books, especially as many copies of the Talmud as could be found. From 1759, now based at Lvov, Frank, the self-proclaimed spiritual emancipator and unifier of faiths, urged his adherents to convert formally to Catholicism, albeit only in token fashion as Sabbatai's followers had to Islam.[12]

Frank orchestrated a movement of mass baptism, often with members of the Polish nobility acting as godparents, in which thousands, including many in Warsaw and the Lublin area, converted, in places generating great fervor, a movement scattered throughout Poland-Ukraine and soon into the Habsburg lands.[13] On 17 September 1759, Frank himself outwardly embraced Catholicism, at Lvov. Nevertheless, he governed his mystical sect as an entirely separate spiritual empire, erasing all established theological boundaries, proclaiming himself the living bridge between Judaism and Christianity and the true messianic revelation and reincarnation of Sabbatai Zevi. A mystical current stressing spiritual renewal, his movement evolved into a disturbing heretical mix, fusing Torah with the cross, which, already the following year, precipitated his arrest in Warsaw, a city where hundreds of Frankists now held tenaciously to his syncretism. In late eighteenth-century Warsaw Frankist "neophytes" abounded, especially among the tavern-keepers, but were regarded with growing hostility by Poles, Jews and royal authorities alike—not least for being free of the special disabilities applying to Jews. An official inquiry, in 1763, identified between seventy and eighty Frankist tavern-keepers just in the villages, including Chmiel and Jankowice, around Lublin. Scorned as "unaffiliated people," neither Jews nor Christians, such persons were deemed deeply suspect by Catholics and as apostates by Jews.[14]

Deciding he was a dangerous heretic, the Polish authorities confined Frank to a monastery at Czestochowa from which he was released only after twelve years (1760–72), by Catherine the Great's invading troops, in 1772. Frank claimed to have predicted Poland's dismemberment by Russia colluding with Prussia and Austria, her sudden drastic truncation via the vast First Partition (1772). He envisioned the ensuing vast loss of Polish territory as divinely ordained and linked to his movement. Choosing Catholic Austria in preference to Orthodox Russia or Protestant Prussia as his future political base, Frank transferred his spiritual headquarters, family and following to Brünn (Brno), the regional capital of Austrian Habsburg Moravia, long already a center of Sabbatian sentiment. Frank's mother, Rachel Hirschl of Rzeszów, was a sister of Löbl, the Sabbatian leader in Moravia.

For eleven years, from 1773 to 1784, Brünn remained the hub of the entire Sabbatian-Frankist Jewish Polish-Ottoman-Moravian heresy over which Frank presided with the aid of two forceful women, his daughter, Eva Frank, and his cousin, Schöndl Dobruschka, daughter of Löbl Hirschl, mother of the Frey siblings and wife of Zalman (Solomon) Dobruschka, son of the local Sabbatian leader in Brünn.[15] Christ and the Trinity for Frank and Schöndl were not doctrines to be rejected but precious emblems folded into their broader mystical, anti-Talmudist Jewish-Christian-Sabbatian mix. Contacts in Vienna helped persuade the devout Empress Maria Theresa and her advisers that Frankist support was indeed a useful way to advance Christian belief among the Jews, a people and faith she detested, and also Catholicism among Orthodox Ukrainians and other non-Catholics. This enabled Frank's politically adroit circle of "believers" to gain privileged access at court and win the Empress's lasting support, even though at this stage most of Moravia's Frankists remained outwardly Jewish in lifestyle.

Brünn was a town from which Jews had been legally excluded for centuries. There the Frankist community put down firm roots, a community over which Junius's father, Zalman Dobruschka, much immersed in local affairs and now effective head of the Moravian Frankist movement, established an ascendancy adeptly blending Christian themes with adherence to a selection of Jewish tradition and rites.[16] Zalman's own father had built a flourishing business empire on money-lending, jewelry and taverns, and from 1750, extended it by securing the lease on the imperial tobacco monopoly for all Moravia. Combining family business with community leadership and

Viennese court favor, Zalman was aided by his famously beautiful, domineering and clever wife, Schöndl, the Freys' mother. The Brünn community was henceforth Europe's chief focus of Sabbatian-Frankist heresy and of the semi-secret links they established between Judaism and Christianity. Their superficially Jewish external façade and Sabbatian-Frankist allegiance were regularly denounced by orthodox rabbis, notably Jacob Emden (1697–1776) and his circle in works such as their fiercely anti-Sabbatian compilation *Sefer hit'abbekut* [Book of Struggle] (Altona, 1762), where Schöndl is portrayed as a pernicious propagator of Sabbateanism and mystical eroticism, the "ha-zonah-mi-Brünn" [the prostitute of Brünn].[17] When Zalman died, in May 1774, Schöndl, now mother of twelve children, became effective head of the huge Dobruschka clandestine mystical financial-religious empire.

All but two of Schöndl's children formally converted to Catholicism, the eldest, Carl, in 1761, the youngest, Leopoldine, thirty years later, in 1791. Schöndl's most talented son, Moses, married the daughter of a wealthy Viennese Jewish financier and, in 1775, eight months after their "Jewish" wedding, then twenty-three, publicly renounced Judaism together with his new wife. Baptized at Prague, he assumed the name "Franz Thomas" to which he attached the surname Schönfeld, that of their "godfather," the adopted surname also of his brother Carl, now an Austrian officer. Their younger brother David (Emmanuel) converted later. Conversion was the prized ticket to full emancipation, but "Franz Thomas" remained, notwithstanding, privately hostile to Catholic ecclesiastics and doctrine, a consistent feature of his subsequent fervent revolutionary ideology. In July 1778, Maria Theresa raised the energetic young convert to the Austrian nobility as "Franz Thomas Edler von Schönfeld."

Raised at Brünn amidst an anarchic Jewish sectarianism nurturing secret beliefs and practices, subsequently a Viennese courtier, Moses Dobruschka, now styled "von Schönfeld," steeped himself in German literature and wrote plays and poetry, including admired German renderings of the Psalms of David. Like other Moravian Frankists, he also acquired a taste for exotic underground masonic movements. Moravia happened to be a focus of Habsburg noble secret masonic societies mystically inclined to promoting the unity of mankind. One keen participant in their activities visiting Brünn in 1784, was Casanova. "Franz Thomas" first demonstrated his appetite for sweeping revolutionary transformation, and gift for organization, by linking Frankist elements to a circle of Habsburg secret society enthusiasts and Rosicrucians to forge a highly unusual new masonic order that, unlike most

Masonic lodges on the Continent, admitted Jews as well as Christians.[18] Among other rituals designed to blur the ancient rift between Judaism and Christianity were his ritual feasts of pork and milk. Displacing the bogus Cabbalism some lodges liked toying with, Schönfeld incorporated into his circle genuine Cabbalistic elements.

Celebrating Christmas and the Day of St. John the Baptist alongside Shevuot and the anniversaries of Moses's birth and death, this new order was originally called the "Die Brüder des Lichts" [Brothers of Light], but afterwards renamed "Die Ritter und Brüder des heiligen Johannes aus Asien in Europa" [Brothers of the Holy Johannes from Asia in Europe]. Their several lodges, bitterly opposed by most German and Austrian Freemasons, were found in Brünn, Vienna and the Silesian town of Troppau.[19] Shunned by most, there was no denying, though, that the movement sought not just a fusion of religions but to bring Christianity back to its original, "pure Jewish" origins steeped in Hebrew, the "Christianity" of Jesus's time. A campaign mounted by leading Austrian Freemasons to denounce these outrageous "Asiastic Brethren" as an assault on true "Christian values" (which in terms of that age it was) eventually succeeded. Under Joseph II's *Freimaurerpatent* of December 1785, all Austria-Hungary's "undesirable" lodges, including theirs, were suppressed.[20]

"Franz Thomas" next transferred permanently to Vienna, concentrating on commerce and furnishing supplies to Austrian military garrisons in the Balkans. He also found employment for a time in the Imperial Library as a translator, orientalist and expert on manuscripts and Hebrew books. While Schöndl, their mother, at Brünn, stayed outwardly within the Jewish fold, her elder sons, after transferring to Vienna, ranked as courtiers, prominent "Christian" noblemen and ardent adherents of the reforming emperor, Joseph II. Nothing, though, in this arrangement prevented Schöndl and "Franz Thomas" continuing to collaborate for many years, overseeing the family business empire. They jointly pulled off a stunning coup, in 1788, on obtaining the imperial contract, in exchange for a down payment of one-tenth of projected value, for sorting, appraising and selling on the crown's behalf, all the jewels encrusted in ritual objects confiscated from those Austrian monasteries the Emperor suppressed. (Between 1781 and 1790, Joseph II dissolved virtually half of all the monasteries in Austria-Hungary.)

Schöndl's contract remained operative until Joseph II's death, in 1791. In high regard under the deceased emperor but finding his position at the imperial court less promising under Joseph's successor, the adroit young Baron Franz Thomas Edler von Schönfeld forsook Vienna, leaving his wife and daughters behind, and after some months exploring Berlin, and some other parts of Germany, suddenly proclaimed his conversion from Frankist-tinted Freemasonry to French revolutionary values. Changing his name yet again, this time to "Junius Frey," and now urging abolition of all courts and "nobility," he defected to revolutionary Strasbourg, arriving there in mid-March 1792, bringing Emmanuel and Leopoldine with him. This was shortly after a bitter schism had opened up in the Strasbourg Jacobin society with 137 dissatisfied, mostly more affluent, members, led by the city's controversial Protestant mayor, the mineralogist Pierre-Frédéric, baron de Dietrich (1748–1793), breaking away to form a separate society, the "Friends of the Constitution." The Freys aligned with those adhering to the old club, some 286 members siding with the Paris Jacobins.[21]

The press arm of Dietrich's faction, the *Feuille de Strasbourg*, was opposed by the pro-Montagnard *Courrier de Strasbourg*, a journal ranking among the best-known Jacobin provincial papers, conspicuous for providing better coverage than any other single revolutionary paper of developments in Germany.[22] It was edited by an outstanding Germanist and orientalist, Jean-Charles Laveaux (1749–1827), originally from Troyes, a scholar with unusual fluency in German, having earlier taught at Basel and Berlin. At Strasbourg, Frey made it known that the new Austrian emperor, France's enemy, had seized his formerly extensive assets in Habsburg lands. Signing his name "Junius G. Frey" and immersing himself in the local revolutionary struggle, he was initiated into the Revolution working for Laveaux's Jacobins. The Strasbourg press wars were indeed the ideal training ground for Frey as for other *Revolutionsfreunde* ejected by German princes seeking position and influence in France while plotting revolution in central Europe. At Strasbourg, Frey could reinvent himself imbibing revolutionary rhetoric and polishing his French. He carefully explored the intricacies of the rival revolutionary factions as reflected in the province's German-language Jacobin debates, especially the Strasbourg society's twice-weekly meetings which Laveaux chaired, German still being extensively used by all sectors of society in Alsace. Once accustomed to Yiddish, later a master of polished literary German, from early 1792 Frey remodeled himself as a prominent revolutionary publicist in French and German.

Denouncing *feullantisme* (pro-constitutional monarchy revolutionism) and *Barnavisme* (Barnave's following), the Freys backed the core

Jacobins against all revolutionary "moderates" and monarchists. By May 1792, with Laveaux released from the imprisonment to which Dietrich had confined him, the Jacobins had gained the upper hand in Strasbourg. Thrilled by the republican gains during the spring of 1792, among other pro-Jacobin gestures, the Freys paid for the commemorative medals struck to celebrate Laveaux's eventual triumph over Dietrich and their Feuillant foes.[23] Dietrich was afterwards guillotined in Paris, in December 1793.

Once more confident of their French, the Brothers Frey transferred next to Paris, in June 1792, establishing their conspicuously affluent household in the rue'd'Anjou, Saint Honoré (no. 19), in a private "hotel" rented from the comtesse de Mun, a daughter of Mme. Helvétius, where they hung portrait prints of Franklin, Rousseau and Voltaire alongside busts of renowned Roman republicans Brutus and Cicero. Donning revolutionary cockades and bonnets, they soon emerged as regular participants at meetings of the Paris Jacobin Club and, in Junius's case, as a prominent republican ideologue and revolutionary theorist. Both brothers participated in the 10 August 1792 mass assault on the Tuileries palace that finally overthrew the constitutional monarchy, in which Clermont-Tonnerre among hundreds of others was killed.[24]

From September 1792 the Freys joined the entourage of National Convention delegate François Chabot (1756–1794), an ex-Capuchin monk and powerful orator representing the department of Loire-et-Cher, now a front-line *sansculotte* leader notorious throughout France for his vehement animosity toward Brissot and his following. Chabot figured among the foremost proponents in the national legislature of graduated "progressive" taxation, the policy of taxing the rich heavily to support the poor, as well as a vigorous advocate of de-Christianization and sponsor of equal rights for the illegitimately born. He had his good points. But Chabot was also deeply corrupt, a strange blend of doctrinaire Jacobin and *bon vivant*, a perfect target for the machinations and ambition of the Brothers Frey. Churning out torrents of egalitarian rhetoric, presenting himself as champion of the *sanculottes* and downtrodden, Chabot simultaneously exhibited an unquenchable thirst for luxuries, wine, delicacies and expensive décor, and was a notorious womanizer. He also professed to be greatly impressed by Frey's intellectual virtuosity, skill in philosophical debate and talent as a publicist expounding republican ideas.[25] The brothers were doubtless glad to gain a powerful ally and reassuring protective shield.

DEMOCRATIC REPUBLICANISM VERSUS MONTAGNARD POPULISM

Unfortunately for the Frey Brothers, paranoid xenophobia regarding "foreigners," stirred by the likes of Marat and Hébert, at this point became a significant factor in the Montagnard leadership's infighting, intrigues and plotting. In late October 1792, nearly three months after the downfall of the Feuillants and the monarchical constitution but nine months before the Montagne definitively seized power with their *coup d'état* of June 1793, Hourwitz, alarmed by the paranoia and xenophobic agitation against "foreigners" permeating Montagnard ranks in Paris, published a letter in the *Chronique de Paris* recalling the dangerous gush of rumor earlier when Brissot's ally at the interior ministry, Roland, had announced that some "Hebrew documents" had been discovered and sent to the Bibliothèque Nationale for scrutiny. Nothing more was heard about this from official quarters for months, but insidious "agitators" began spreading rumors that this "concealment" concerned the secret correspondence of a fiercely denounced and vilified Jewish traitor known as "Ephraim of Berlin."

The furor surrounding "Ephraim of Berlin" had first seized public attention in the summer of 1791, during the fierce Feuillant repression of the anti-monarchist democratic republican radicals following Louis XVI's flight to Varennes. The then anti-republican revolutionary leadership under Barnave claimed Prussia and England aimed to destabilize France by distributing cash payments to unruly elements through the hands of an insidious Jew, "Ephraim of Berlin," undermining the Revolution by stirring disorder on all sides. The "Jew Ephraim" did actually exist and *was* in fact a Prussian crown agent; even the tale about disbursing funds among the unruliest Parisian elements to destabilize the Revolution may have had substance.[26] On being seized, though, Ephraim's papers were found to be a mix of mundane, inoffensive German and French with about one-third in suspiciously incomprehensible Hebrew.

A case already convoluted grew still murkier after a fresh stash of Hebrew documents turned up that proved useful additional ammunition against virtually anyone the Montagnard leadership chose to target, that is, anyone criticizing or opposing them. Although this second batch had nothing to do with Ephraim, explained Hourwitz, who was entrusted with examining the Hebrew for the authorities, *sansculotte* agitators "spread it around that these papers were clandestine political correspondence" of Ephraim with one of Louis XVIs trusted advisers, Armand-Marc, comte de Montmorin. The allegedly treacherous Brissotin minister Roland had supposedly secreted away this fatally damning evidence since it compromised the entire Brissotin faction. Having duly inspected the suspect Hebrew cache at the Bibliothèque du Roi (now called the Bibliothèque Nationale), Hourwitz pronounced the files entirely harmless commercial correspondence dating from the 1780s concerning a plea for financial assistance from a Jew of Livorno to co-religionists in France. He announced this news publicly, explaining he was an official translator at the Bibliothèque Nationale and had thoroughly examined all the Hebrew papers in question, on 13 November 1792. For some, this was frustratingly disappointing. "Because this accusation, absurd as it is, finds dupes among those who naively trust in the virtue of the Apostle of murder and anarchy [i.e., Marat]," protested Hourwitz, "I thought it necessary to deny it emphatically" before the public.[27]

The Feuillants by this time had long since been eliminated. The "Jew Ephraim" affair was being revived basically as a Montagnard ploy against the democratic republicans, the Brissotins. Not wholly coincidentally, Hourwitz's letter appeared just a week after the today famous champion of women's rights, Olympe de Gouges (1748–1793), shortly to be guillotined by the Montagne, placarded central Paris with her withering *Prognostic sur Maximilien Robespierre*. Her protest poster derided Robespierre's pretensions to be a man of virtue, sincerity and integrity, declaring him deceitful and his conception of "virtue" perfidious and abysmal in every respect. "You, the friend of your co-citizens, of peace and order? I will cite this maxim for you: 'when a wicked man acts as a good one, he is preparing great mischief.'"[28] Most shocking about the trumped-up affair of the Hebrew documents, declared Hourwitz, were the unmistakable signs of dishonest misrepresentation and manipulation behind the scenes, clearly intended to mislead the public, a deeply shocking "malevolence" manifest in certain [Montagnard] political quarters. The true menace of the "Jew Ephraim" affair was certainly not the Jew but the unscrupulousness of the purveyors of the "Jew Ephraim" tale. Days later his Montagnard opponents retaliated by getting Hourwitz's position abolished, leaving him jobless at the age of forty-one.[29]

French Jews as such were never singled out by the revolutionary authorities as a suspect group during the Terror.[30] Still, as conspicuous outsiders, individual Jews prominently participating in revolutionary activity were increasingly at risk from the mounting public xenophobic paranoia stirred up by the admirers of Marat, Robespierre and other Montagnard leaders, and through being readily linked, by association, to revolutionary factions condemned by the Montagne. A true champion of the Revolution of free expression and universal human rights, by 1793 Hourwitz was decidedly skating on thin ice, as were Pereyra and the Brothers Frey. The latter stood out among the tiny batch of foreign Jews sufficiently attracted to the Revolution to have migrated to France from abroad to directly participate. While Hourwitz, Pereyra and Frey plunged into the increasingly fraught infighting and intrigues in Paris, the leading Jewish figure in the southwest, Abraham Furtado (1756–1817), was prominent in the Revolution there.

Prior to the Revolution, Furtado had served as one of two "syndics," or principal representatives of the southwest French group of Portuguese-Jewish communities, a position to which he was appointed by the Bordeaux *Mahamad*, in March 1787. Together with Brissot's future allies, Vergniaud and Gensonné, Furtado helped found the Girondin "Société des Amis de la Constitution," which, until June 1793, led the Revolution in Bordeaux. Furtado's original base, the city's prosperous Sephardic community, had long exuded a sense of being different and superior to the Ashkenazim of Alsace-Lorraine and Paris. Elected onto the Bordeaux *conseil général*, Furtado, fiercely anti-Catholic and anti-clerical, hostile to institutionalized religious authority generally, and supporting the democratic republic, became prominent in the Girondin (Brissotin) city government and, as such, energetically opposed the Montagnard tide in the southwest, soon drawing their ire.[31]

Jacob Pereyra (d. 1794), likewise a prominent Sephardic figure, was a former Bayonne tobacco merchant, later a merchant at Bordeaux. Moving to Paris in the summer of 1790, he rose from being a local section delegate to being named one of the revolutionary commissioners representing the French legislature in the occupied parts of the Low Countries. A reputed "atheist" on bad terms with rabbis and the syndics of the French Sephardic communities, he appears to have had no particular ties with the Jewish community in Paris.[32] Appointed by the Convention as one of three *commissaires* accompanying the French military commander, Charles-François Dumouriez (1739–1823), during the first French revolutionary occupation of Belgium (1792–93), he participated in a crucial meeting at Tournai, on 28 March 1793, following several shattering defeats that (temporarily) drove the French armies out of most of Belgium and the Rhineland. In this secret conference, Dumouriez, a moderate monarchist outraged at being vilified by the Montagne, having berated Danton, then on inspection tour of the French troops in Belgium, confidentially tried to persuade Pereyra and the two other *commissaires*, Pierre-Joseph Proly (1752–1794), a natural son of the Austrian minister Kaunitz, and the Belgian revolutionary Pierre-Ulric Dubuisson (1748–1794), of the need to jettison the Republic and democratic republicanism, and revert to constitutional monarchy.

While conferring with the three *commissaires*, Dumouriez, then France's leading general, contended that the Jacobins had created a disastrous situation. During this crisis meeting, he grew so exasperated as to ill-advisedly rage that he alone could save France from the revolutionary government's mismanagement, corruption and ineptitude. Only monarchy could stabilize the country and the Revolution. He planned to use the army, he hinted, to restore the king and rescue France from the scoundrels and ignoramuses of the Convention. He denounced the entire pending new democratic constitution as "stupid," claiming Condorcet understood nothing. Should the present fiasco continue, he would come in person to Paris, seize power and end the disastrous current setup. With the democratic republicans (Brissotins) hopelessly at odds with the Montagne, he would resolve the deadlock by dissolving the legislature even if France's republicans denounced him to the entire world as "Caesar," "Cromwell" or "[General George] Monck." The three *commissaires,* Pereyra, Dubuisson and Proly (all to be guillotined by the Montagne in 1794), rebuffed him, staying loyal to the Revolution's democratic principles and becoming the first prominent revolutionaries to alert the National Convention regarding Dumouriez's pending betrayal, defection and treason.[33]

But in terms of ideas and political theory, the outstanding Jewish participant in the mounting revolutionary affray was Moses Dobruschka, subsequently "Franz Thomas von Schönfeld," now Junius Frey. Written originally in German, rendered into French and published in Paris, Frey's book of revolutionary theory not only nailed his ideological colors firmly to representative democratic republicanism but included a scathing critique of the political ideas of Robespierre's and Marat's ceaselessly adulated and publicly exalted hero, Rousseau. Unscrupulous financially and perhaps politically, Frey nevertheless still ranks among the Revolution's more perceptive democratic commentators, an observer deeply disturbed by the negative role of direct popular participation in the political process, at how populist appeals were destabilizing the already highly unstable, fluctuating situation in the Paris sections (political wards). In his own "section," named République française, where he lived and spent lavishly on republican gatherings and dinners which he attended attired in his liberty bonnet, briefly he enjoyed everyone's esteem—as Robespierre himself later observed. (Robespierre, typically, insinuated this proved only Frey's adroit, despicable hypocrisy.)[34]

As the democratic republican Brissotin ascendancy progressively crumbled, and the populist Montagne built their support among the least informed and educated, including in the neighboring Paris section Mauconseil (soon renamed Bon-Conseil) where Hourwitz and Gorsas resided, Frey's standing and prospects initially looked bright. While Mauconseil figured among only four Paris sections sufficiently penetrated by Marat's supporters and *Enragé* elements to openly back the failed attempted *coup d'état* against the National Convention of 9 and 10 March 1793, opinion there remained fiercely divided, with substantial support for the Brissotin faction that Gorsas and Hourwitz championed.[35] As the months passed, strife and confusion poisoned all corridors of the Revolution, hopelessly sullying its more edifying values, paving the way to dictatorship, repression and Terror. The struggle between Brissotins and the Montagne was unrelenting. When, in June 1793, the Brissotin, or "Girondin," faction was finally purged from the national legislature, provincial France descended into a brief but chaotic civil war engulfing Bordeaux, Toulouse, Caen and Montpellier, the struggle proving particularly ferocious and bloody in Lyon. Bordeaux and Lyon took the lead in resisting the ruthlessly authoritarian power usurpers. Furtado too fought the repression, participating in the armed resistance to the Montagnard takeover in Bordeaux, which continued through the summer.

With civil war tearing the Revolution's vitals asunder, in Paris the Terror proper commenced in the late summer. The essential purpose of the Terror was to consolidate the new regime's grip by eliminating all prominent opponents, critics and dissidents, first and foremost all authentic libertarian revolutionaries, the democratic republicans. With Paris now firmly under the pro-dictatorship faction, Frey seemingly strode diametrically opposite to Hourwitz, Pereyra and Furtado, drawing closer than ever to Chabot, who, for a time, appeared to be successfully leading a major wing of the victorious Montagnard coalition. Frey publicly took sides by publishing a violent seventy-two-page anti-Brissotin propaganda tirade entitled *Les Aventures politiques du Père Nicaise; ou l'Antifédéraliste* (Paris, 20 July 1793), a vehemently condemnatory tract requested by Chabot and lauded by the new ruling faction which the *Comité de salut public* voted to disseminate in quantity, twenty thousand copies reportedly being produced and distributed.[36] *Les Aventures politiques du Père Nicaise* is an appeal to the armed Brissotin insurgents of Bordeaux, Lyon, Marseille and Calvados denounced by the Montagne as "fédéralistes," to abandon their resistance to the triumphant Jacobin core, the Montagne.

Frey's tract was also a blistering assault on the principle of federal republicanism, whether in America or Europe, a doctrine the Montagne tirelessly but inaccurately attributed to the Brissotins in their propaganda. Brissotin insurrection, argued Frey, was dividing France, tearing society asunder at a time of war with other European powers. This proved the Brissotins were "patriotes hypocrites," deceiving those believing their declarations while secretly angling to overthrow the Revolution and bring back royalism and the people's foes. If the populace of the rebel regions persisted in following such perfidious "conspirators," they would, through their own naive gullibility, drown their own country in blood and clap chains of slavery on themselves.

The Girondin "rebels" opposing the Montagne, held Frey, were really declared or covert royalists, not republicans at all. The Girondin-Brissotin bloc he divided into two main categories, one innocent—the "feeble and blind instruments" of the "traitors destroying the Revolution—the other vilely guilty, "their insidious leaders exhorting the people to march on Paris" and overthrow the people's glorious Montagne. The Brissotin leaders claimed to be republicans but were really allies of the English, Prussians and Austrians. Amongst this allegedly pernicious pseudo-republican leadership, Frey cited by name Gorsas, Pétion, Buzot, Rabaut, Barbaroux, Lanjuinais and the Huguenot republican and regicide Marc-David Lasource (1763–1793).[37] Having studied theology at Lausanne and become a Reformed minister at Castres, Lasource had become a fervent revolutionary democrat instrumental in securing the unification of Nice with France. A National Convention delegate for Tarn and leading opponent of Danton and Robespierre, he was outlawed in June 1793 and guillotined three months after Frey's pamphlet appeared, on 31 October.

Frey summoned the allegedly misled ordinary men and women of France to embrace, as their "nouvel évangile," the Republic's "new constitution" drawn up by the Montagnard leadership and proclaimed in June 1793 (albeit still based on Condorcet's February 1793 democratic constitution).[38] The Montagne alone, he declared, will establish "our happiness and felicity," unite France and be genuinely "populaire."[39]

Fédéralisme, asserts Frey, totally contradicts the Revolution's true goals, the authors of the famous *Federalist Papers* (1788), published in New York, having hatched a political theory pernicious and damaging in every way. The United States was "an association of several states under one government," the worst contradiction in political thought imaginable; Federalism was a cauldron of artifice, fraudulent politics, and deception based, like the doctrine of the Holy Trinity, on consummate incomprehensibility purposely designed to befog the ignorant, a malevolent, deceptive mystery designed to confuse so profoundly as to ensure men's being easily misled.[40] "Worse still, *le fédéralisme* represented a pernicious plot to divide France into fragments," carve her up to resemble the "hotchpotch of the German Empire," rendering both entities prey to the interests of arrogant royalty, ecclesiastics and aristocracy.[41]

"Federalism" as a concept and tradition in fact had scant relevance to the Brissotin faction and their goals, and their prime theorist, Condorcet, the figure who played the leading role in compiling France's first democratic republican constitution, the Girondin-Brissotin democratic draft constitution of February 1793 consistently repudiated the concept. Despite this, among a largely illiterate public who mostly had no notion what this perplexing new term signified, vilifying *fédéralisme* proved an enormously effective means of impressing and alarming the public with a dreadful-sounding menace and for mobilizing support against the Montagne's foes both during the struggle of the summer of 1793 itself and throughout the subsequent Terror. Among a group of city councilors and local leaders guillotined at Nîmes in July 1794 as a "federalist" "trying to weaken and even destroy the national authority" was a local Jewish trader, Jassé Carcassonne.[42]

REJECTING *ROUSSEAUISTE* POPULISM

Not only the populace, however, but also many sincere revolutionaries, like Frey himself, soon discovered that it was they who were being manipulated and misled, or at least had miscalculated. Frey's polemical tract appeared just weeks before the "constitution populaire" he praised to the skies for grounding France's revolutionary liberty and glorious future was suddenly indefinitely suspended on Robespierre's orders. Over the next months, most newspapers were shut down and, during the autumn, the Terror and general repression of personal liberty and the authentic standard-bearers of the Revolution, the ultimate betrayal of the Revolution's basic values, commenced. On 7 October 1793, Gorsas, among the early Revolution's principal journalists, was the first outstanding, upright democratic republican advocate of free expression and universal and equal rights to be guillotined. Dozens more quickly followed, among them Brissot, Rabaut de Saint-Étienne and Olympe de Gouges, executed by the same unscrupulous populists wielding dictatorial power in defiance of the Revolution's basic principles, seeking to extinguish the democratic republican voice. Mercilessly hounded, Condorcet was outlawed and forced into hiding.

Not long after the Montagne secured all of Bordeaux, in late summer, a guillotine appeared in the city center, the "Place nationale," and systematic repression began there likewise in October, earlier (albeit less massively) than at Lyon, which was totally devastated as punishment for supporting the Montagne's enemies, in November.[43] Outlawed on 27 September 1793, Furtado went into hiding in extremely cramped quarters, perilously crouching for 135 days with only a small aperture providing him a glimpse onto a Bordeaux street and of the signs of terrifying repression written "on the faces of passers-by the imprint of the Terror."[44] Later, Furtado managed to hide more comfortably on a small property he owned near Bayonne.[45] Whatever side they had chosen, every prominent Jewish participant in the Revolution was now exposed to immanent risk.

Dread and suspicion gripped every nook of France and every crevice of the French Jewish community. The attacks on churches throughout France and destructive vandalism of sacred objects that also commenced during the autumn soon spread likewise to the synagogues. With the *sansculottes* implementing the dictatorship's bidding and the Sephardim especially known to be pro-Girondin-Brissotin in sentiment, in Bordeaux, Bayonne, Paris and other cities all the silverware and other ritual objects were pilfered from the synagogues and larger devotional objects unceremoniously carted away.[46]

Robespierre inaugurated his sustained drive against subversive "foreigners" in France two days after Gorsas's execution, on 9 October 1793, by backing a National Convention Montagnard deputy, Fabre d'Églantine, who proposed the arrest of all British subjects (including declared republicans) presently on the Republic's territory and seizure of their possessions. On 10 October 1793, Junius and Emmanuel Frey were denounced to the Paris police as spies "of the first order" by a German Jacobin, Johann-Baptist Wilhelm: during their eighteen months in France these "two Jews" of Austrian origin who "had changed their names several times," passed themselves off "as *archipatriotes*." Moved by ambition, they had earlier repudiated Judaism and hypocritically converted to Christianity following which Maria Theresa elevated them to noble status, bestowing on them the title "Edle von Schönfeld."

"Highly intelligent" intriguers, their "words and writings exude the purest patriotism and they frequently invite members of the Convention to dinner," while perniciously spying for Austria, or Prussia, or both.[47]

Since arriving in France, Frey had added impressively to his skills, developing his oratory and formidable grasp of modern political theory and Enlightenment texts, becoming adept in debating Locke, Montesquieu and Rousseau. Strikingly, his principal work, the *Philosophie sociale dediée au peuple françois*, published in the early summer of 1793, during the brief civil war, and later republished as a valuable re-affirmation of republican values under the *Directoire,* in 1797, with a slightly altered title, as the *Philosophie sociale, dediée à tous les peoples par un citoyen de tous les pays,* powerfully projected the universalism and cosmopolitanism the Robespierre faction denounced so vehemently. It revealed no trace whatever of the repressive Rousseauist anti-intellectualism promoted by Marat and Robespierre, let alone Moravia's Germanic secret masonic societies and their occultism, but did reflect something of the sweeping anti-Talmudism of east European Jewish Frankist and Sabbatian sectarianism and mysticism.[48] Infused with intense revolutionary awareness, the work is essentially Radical Enlightenment *philosophie moderne*, anti-religious and comprehensively libertarian. Evincing fierce antagonism to Moses's religious legislation, Frey claimed Moses, like Mohammed later, but unlike Christ, merged politics and religion in a disastrous fashion empowering a priesthood which had then oppressed all the Jews for millennia and from which they now urgently needed emancipating.[49]

Another feature of Frey's *Philosophie sociale* that derived in part from his Sabbatian-Frankist heritage was the intense quasi-religious utopianism of his social vision, presenting Jesus Christ as just a man with nothing at all supernatural about him but, rather, as an outstanding social and political agitator, an icon of revolutionary consciousness much preferable to Moses, embodying a great step forward in humanity's progress. Here was a thesis that fitted well with Chabot's Montagnard populist maxim that Jesus was a *sansculotte,* the people's *philosophe.* Christ proved superior to Moses, held Frey, especially in proclaiming his spiritual empire to be not of this world, his requiring total separation of religious authority and doctrine from the legal and political sphere.[50] What mankind chiefly needed emancipation from, contended Frey, was not Christ or Christ's authentic message, but the vast deception and falsity practiced on humanity by churchmen, churches and all Christian theology. Mankind requires emancipation from the perversion of Christ's teaching, the power-seeking blend of theology with law and politics of which practically all churchmen are comprehensively guilty, the papacy most of all.

Another key feature of Frey's democratic republicanism was the vehemence of his anti-*Rousseauisme*, as fierce as that of d'Holbach, Condorcet, Volney or Destutt de Tracy. Rousseau's particularist conception of the "general will" he totally rejects, especially his affirming, in chapter 12 of book 2 of the *Contrat social*, that every people is always entitled to change its laws, "même les meilleures" [even the best] since, if it wishes to harm itself, there is no-one possessing the right to prevent it.[51] Such claims Frey considered deeply characteristic of Rousseau and his deviationist conception of popular sovereignty, to his mind a ruinous, deplorable, even fatal departure from Enlightenment principles and true "general will," especially the principle that no-one has the right to challenge sound laws formulated by the people's delegated representatives in the national legislature in accord with proper constitutional procedure. Such laws constitute the true "general will," never to be confused with the majority bullying minorities. His understanding of "general will" Frey expounded very much in the spirit of Diderot, d'Holbach, Condorcet, Volney and Destutt, thus wholly contrary to Rousseau. "General will" for Frey signifies what best serves the public welfare and common good when the worldly concerns of all are approached equally and exclusively judged by the criterion of philosophic reason, a conception clashing head-on with Rousseau (and Robespierre).

The direst danger menacing the Revolution, contended Frey, was precisely the unruly mob stirred by rabble-rousers invading the big city sections, and here Rousseau's theories, crowned by his perversely anti-Diderotian, anti-Condorcet theory of *volonté générale* [general will], could only confuse, endanger and aggravate further, rather than assist. If one embraces the profoundly mistaken stance of J. J. Rousseau, objected Frey, "on peut dire affirmativement que les peuples seront encore, comme ils l'ont toujours été, le jouet de l'ignorance ou de mensonge" [one may state emphatically that peoples will still be what they have always been, the plaything of ignorance and lies]. Frey's political theory and *philosophie sociale*, if not his public expressions of allegiance, though mistakenly sometimes affirmed by scholars to "follow Rousseau," in fact collide with Rousseau and Rousseauism in the most significant fashion and especially with Robespierre's and Marat's cult of Rousseau.[52]

The "people is sovereign no doubt," concurs Frey, reaffirming the authentic Spinozist tradition of "general will," but must also remain subject to just laws undeviatingly "fixed by principle."[53] That is what true "freedom" is. If "gouvernement démocratique" alone sustains true liberty and equality, it is unfortunately also the form of government most susceptible to risk via "agitations intestines" [internal disturbances]. Frey's Jewish and Frankist background shows through perhaps most in his emphasis on the need for genuine "gouvernement démocratique" to safeguard the safety and happiness of all those belonging to minorities. Democratic government must above all shield minorities, particular groups, and especially protect them from a popularly wrongly conceived and defined Rousseauist *volonté générale*, cruelly encouraging a merciless "tyrannie d'une majorité oppressive."[54] Democratic rule can justifiably suppress a particular group but only where such a group threatens the basic principles on which democratic well-being is based, and never because it is loathed and despised by larger groups. The majority can overrule minorities only when doing so safeguards what matters most to society as a whole, and to every individual making up society, namely protecting the equal rights for all, in the sense of protecting the worldly happiness and interest of everyone equally. By this criterion, Frey thought the existing (Brissotin) laws against France's aristocratic and Non-Juring ecclesiastical *émigrés* were perfectly justified.[55]

"Individual conservation is thus the eternal principle, the fundamental basis of all justice and injustice." [La conservation individuelle est donc le principe éternel, la base fondementale de toute justice et injustice.][56] No-one can deny Rousseau's importance in preparing the Revolution, granted Frey. Nothing is truer than his dictum, "man is born free but is everywhere in chains."[57] But since his theories provide no antidote to the looming peril of tyranny of the majority, "J.J.," as he calls [Jean-Jacques] Rousseau, is also a perennial headache. Rousseau's political theory requires comprehensive rejection as not just fatally flawed but unworthy, more obstacle than aid to the revolutionary democratic republicanism Frey repeatedly proclaims infinitely the best of all forms of government. "C'est ainsi qu'après avoir brisé le joug de la royauté, Rousseau, le père de la Révolution française, le bienfaiteur du genre humain, devient son plus grand ennemi." [It is thus that having broken the yoke of royalty, Rousseau, father of the French Revolution and benefactor of the human race, becomes [the Revolution's] greatest enemy.][58] Here, according to Frey (not without justification), was the surpassing paradox of the French Revolution in the sphere of political theory.

Furtado's pre-1789 veneration of Rousseau, like Frey's, evaporated during the Terror, changing into deep loathing of the all-destructive sway of ignorance, militant populism and Robespierre.[59] In Furtado's case, though, unlike Frey's, it meant also reverting to a guarded, aristocratic admiration for Locke and Montesquieu. Rousseau's wrongheaded *volonté générale* posed the overriding ideological menace, but according to Frey's conception of human well-being Locke and Montesquieu too need to be firmly rejected. Locke defines "liberty" in the last analysis as the "power" to fulfill one's individual aspirations, which Frey deemed yet another fundamental error, a means of laying the basis for aristocracy and subjection of the masses to elites. Genuine liberty, he maintains, is that which pertains equally to the entire body of society free of all privilege, that does not accord more weight or rights to one part than another, or to vested interest, as Locke's system blatantly does in favor of property and aristocracy—the class that in England dominated all of society and politics. "La liberté est l'égalité des droits [liberty is equality of rights]" ran Frey's favorite revolutionary refrain.[60] Hence, it was wrong to insist on wholly unlimited, unrestricted liberty of the press and freedom of expression. The press must be free and open but not be allowed to erode the basic principles on which the constitution rests through unrestricted liberty of opinion and churning out lies and misinformation, as Marat's paper had: society must not turn lies, hatred and deception into "un droit saint et sublime" [a holy and sublime right].[61]

Toleration and freedom of expression, held Frey, require carefully defined limits: "to suffer the exercise of a religion that shocks [basic democratic and egalitarian] principles" is consequently freedom pushed too far. There should be no "tolérance contre les principes." While true Christianity, as he characterizes it, teaches that its empire is not of this world, the organized faith of the churches oversteps the mark and the claims of other religions, like orthodox Judaism, likewise represent a "usurpation manifeste sur les droits de la société, un assassinat du principe" [a manifest usurpation of society's rights, the destruction of principle].[62] A genuine democratic constitution, he argues, requires a carefully calibrated, fixed order of priorities—the basic moral and social principles on which democratic society rests being laid down first and only afterwards worked into the specifics of particular forms and procedures. Among major thinkers, Kant—then still largely unknown outside Germany—alone receives Frey's full approbation. (Later, Kant was among those who read Frey's text in its 1797 edition after receiving a complimentary copy from the publisher).[63]

Junius Frey, the universalist theorist of *Philosophie sociale*, the man who had sought to unify Judaism and Christianity in Moravia, and return to

Christianity's authentic origins free of church theology, maintained that human reason had been sadly trapped ever since, in an ever-deepening malaise. For eighteen centuries, despite the philosophical-theological attempted "revolutions" of "Luther, Zwingli, Melanchthon, Calvin, Huss, Spinoza, Hobbes, Leibniz, Locke and others," the defeats "reason" suffered had left the world in ever-greater darkness, with heavier and heavier chains being imposed by kings, aristocrats and churchmen, until, finally, "a new revolutionary giant in philosophy, the destroyer of the two principal barriers, skepticism and dogma, wrecker of all useless philosophical systems," dispelled the swirling fog, at least in theory.[64] This was the "immortal Kant."

Freeing mankind in theory and in practice had only just begun. Frey consistently and, as far as one can tell, sincerely, to the end adhered to his democratic republican egalitarian creed and anti-Rousseauist concept of *volonté générale*, underpinning his vision of humanity's future "constitution universelle." The only impeccably valid, correct and eternal political principles, held Frey, are those of liberty and equality defined, as he defines them, expressly in opposition to Rousseau's "general will" and pernicious notions of education and "virtue," and also against Locke's and Montesquieu's reprehensible theories of aristocracy and property. Aside from claiming the relevance of Kant's political thought, a feature unparalleled in the writings of other participants in the French theoretical debates of the era before Thermidor (Kant otherwise arriving on the scene of French political debate only in the late 1790s), the principles Frey expounds in his *Philosophie sociale* parallel most closely those of Condorcet's democratic republican constitution of February 1793 and the modified version of the same produced by Herault de Seychelles and his committee in June 1793.[65] His was an approach certain to infuriate Montagnard sentiment and provoke Robespierre's enmity.

DISILLUSIONMENT, READJUSTMENT AND THE GUILLOTINE

The Terror challenged France's Jewish revolutionaries and their pre-1793 outlook in multiple respects. Hourwitz, less elegantly attired and elitist than Furtado or Frey, had less difficulty in lying low for the interim and veiling his allegiance to the Girondin-Brissotin faction.[66] Still, any normal sense of discretion would have involved wholly suspending his career as a revolutionary publicist and commentator for the interim between June 1793 and Thermidor (July 1794), withdrawing into total silence. Remaining as inconspicuous and submissive as possible was the only way to survive. But this hardly fitted Hourwitz's fiery nature; he still took occasional risks courageously, if sporadically, speaking out despite the obvious danger. Yet, unlike his equally secular-minded Sephardic neighbor, Pereyra, and the Frey Brothers, he *did* in the end survive the Terror.

Where Furtado and Hourwitz remained staunchly anti-Montagnard, Frey and Pereyra threw in their lot with the Danton clique and hence, indirectly, the Montagne. Both fully participated in the onslaught on the Brissotins in the Paris sections and town hall during May and June 1793. If Frey denounced the Brissotins' *fédéralisme* and monarchism,[67] Pereyra, active in the Paris Jacobin Club, during the autumn of 1793 participated prominently in the public de-Christianization campaign, figuring among those involved in the intimidation of the ex-Jesuit "constitutional" bishop of Paris, Jean-Baptiste Joseph Gobel (1727–1794), on 9 November 1793 resulting in the latter's forced recantation of Christianity before the National Convention along with eleven other renouncing priests, and the ex-bishop's public adoption of [atheistic] *philosophie*.[68] But Pereyra's anti-Christian revolutionary zeal did little to shield him, any more than his fervent republicanism did Junius Frey, or his brother, from Montagnard paranoia, vindictiveness and xenophobia. All three became targets of Robespierre and his aides. Ominously, Pereyra was suddenly expelled from the Jacobin Club late in November.[69]

In the autumn, Robespierre began vigorously backing his trusted ally Saint-Just's proposal, emanating from the *Comité de salut public*, to widen detention of suspect foreigners to all foreign citizens originating from countries at war with France or involved in international networks. Nothing could have been more menacing to Jews actively participating in the Revolution. Over the winter of 1793–94 Robespierre and Saint-Just assiduously worked to persuade the Convention and people that foreign powers were insidiously at work, employing foreign agents to "divide Paris against itself, and spread immorality here," identifying Pereyra, a close associate of Danton's circle, as a useful tool with which to attack Danton and others now being targeted. They also put their spotlight on the Brothers Frey and Hourwitz's and Pereyra's associate Cloots (of Dutch and Prussian background). Allegedly linked to foreign subversion and treachery, all these figures were soon accused of sowing "a new fanaticism," as Saint-Just designated their democratic theories, which, in the case of Frey, whose anti-Rousseauism undoubtedly also represented an annoying theoretical irritant to *Robespierrisme* and the Montagne.[70]

Robespierre initiated his drive against the Paris "de-Christianizers" at the Jacobins, on 21 November (1st Frimaire), less than two weeks after Archbishop Gobel's public humiliation, with Proly, the Belgian Dubuisson, and Pereyra—three "foreigners," one a Jew—among the principal culprits denounced by name for "atheism" and disruptive ideas and conduct. All three had already been accused the previous month of being foreign agents.[71] Speaking at the Jacobins, Robespierre did not hesitate to link their "treachery" of overreaching de-Christianization and atheism with their supposedly also being "secret agents of Pitt" and other hostile European governments.[72] Pereyra, charged with misconduct political and financial, was arrested together with Cloots, a few days later. With the Girondin-Brissotin faction decimated during the early months of the Terror, Robespierre, Saint-Just and their henchmen strove next to eliminate all remaining opposition blocs, in part by smearing them as "secret allies" of the Brissotin "traitors." This was most conveniently done by insinuating far and wide that Robespierre's new foes, the Hébert faction and Danton's following, were all complicit in cultivating insidious secret links with their earlier adversaries, the Brissotins, while simultaneously involved in "foreign" plots aimed at overturning the Revolution and restoring monarchy.

Saint-Just's notorious summons to the French, orchestrated by Robespierre, to shut "all the nobles, all the foreigners" out of Paris and France's fortified strongholds represented a shift in policy of obvious peril to foreign-born citizens like Hourwitz, the Moravian Brothers Frey, and even Furtado, who, though raised in a prominent Bordeaux Portuguese Jewish family, had actually been born in London.[73] Pervasive xenophobia powerfully contributed, along with complex intrigue, to the Freys' downfall. Since January 1793, Chabot had developed intimate ties with the Frey Brothers and regularly frequented their apartment as a guest at their dinners. In October he married their now sixteen-year-old sister Leopoldine, receiving an enviably large dowry in exchange, a marriage conspicuous politically and socially. Despite the introduction of civil marriage and full freedom to marry earlier in the Revolution, remarkably few "mixed marriages" between Jews and non-Jews had yet been recorded in Paris, or elsewhere in France. The wedding of Chabot and Leopoldine, celebrated just a few weeks before Robespierre's sweep against foreign "scoundrels," in early October, was one of the few notable exceptions.[74]

On 16 November, Chabot, beset by scandal, was denounced by a Montagnard spokesman in the Jacobin Club for disgracefully defying public opinion "by marrying a foreign woman." Chabot's career and high standing in the Revolution had begun to unravel almost immediately following his marriage, commencing with a convoluted affair relating to shares in the main French East India trading organization, the Compagnie des Indes. Wild rumors had caused huge oscillations in the share price followed by massive manipulative buying and selling. At the highest levels of government, the public interest had been sold out by corrupt profiteering. Chabot was implicated along with other prominent Convention deputies, including Fabre d'Églantine and other Danton associates.[75]

Detractors later explained Chabot's marriage as part of the Frey Brothers' supposedly malicious behind-the-scenes plan, partly instigated by the royalist Baron de Batz, to render Chabot susceptible to their wiles, employing their sister's charms as a conspiratorial tool against the Republic on behalf of Britain and other hostile powers. The Frey Brothers were accused of seeking to overthrow the Revolution and destroy the Republic by miring it in financial, sexual and legal corruption with the eventual goal of restoring the monarchy. Despite energetic searches, Saint-Just could find no evidence to support any of this but was hardly disposed to be embarrassed by that. As Jews, it would readily be assumed in populist circles and among Chabot's Montagnard foes, that the Frey Brothers cared only about money and treachery, and that, specializing in base wiles, must assuredly be devious agents of the Viennese court.[76]

Following the execution of the nationally decried and loathed "Austrian" Marie Antoinette, the previous month, the populace were being furiously stirred against "foreigners." Chabot had profiteered at the people's expense and vilely "contracted a[n advantageous] marriage with an Austrian woman!" When accused in these terms in the Convention, Chabot reportedly broke down and burst into tears. Arrested on 27 Brumaire (16 November 1793) together with Dubuisson, Chabot was duly incarcerated awaiting trial. A week later, on 3 Frimaire An II (23 November), his brothers-in-law, the "barons étrangers" [foreign barons] the Freys, were likewise expelled from the Jacobin Club, arrested, and imprisoned. They too were held behind bars over the winter of 1793–94.[77] "Foreigners" were now decried on all sides. Even foreign-born prominent revolutionaries who were elected deputies of the National Assembly, like Cloots and Tom Paine, decreed the National Convention, on 25 December 1793, were henceforth forbidden to attend the legislature's deliberations.[78]

If the Dantoniste *commisssaire* and munitions supplier Pereyra was in reality French-born,[79] this could not save him. Beside other trumped-up charges, Pereyra, Proly and several others were perversely accused of complicity in Dumouriez's monarchist conspiracy, the very plot they had taken the lead in uncovering and defeating.[80] With the consummately twisted populist double logic perfected by Robespierre and Saint-Just, the Freys were charged with being "ultra-révolutionnaires" advancing democratic ideas too zealously (i.e., maliciously intending to divide the Revolution), while simultaneously acting as counter-revolutionary spies, agents and traitors betraying the Revolution to foreign courts. These vile reprobates, reported the journalist Desmoulins before he broke with Robespierre and the group dictatorship, embodied in themselves the double menace of *modérantisme* [moderation] blended with democratic extremism, the "heinous" two-faced menace threatening France. Absurd though such brazen balderdash was for anyone with any knowledge of the facts, Robespierre and his aides had again hit upon a handy populist stratagem. The alleged twin menace of seeming opposites, the indicted men's being simultaneously "*Exagérés*" and "*Indulgents*," parading "extremism" and "moderation" at the same time, however nonsensical, worked wonders with the scantily informed.[81]

To crush this entirely fake double menace, Robespierre, Saint-Just and their circle opted to liquidate the Hébert faction, the *Exagérés* first. During March 1794, several leading *Hébertiste* figures were showcased in a four-day trial (21–24 March 1794) staged by three of Robespierre's most ruthless henchmen, Amar, Barère and Saint-Just. In this procedure more than two hundred witnesses were called to falsely testify. France's supposedly despicable "ultra-révolutionnaires" were charged with being secret royalists, simultaneously propagating extremism and *modérantisme* while steeped in corrupt dealings with foreign courts, charges implicating Pereyra further, as well as the Freys. Two principal figures now linked to Hébert were Chabot and Cloots, both denounced by Robespierre in person and with both of whom Pereyra as well as the Freys were associated. Then, in April, it was the turn of the *Dantoniste* adversaries of the *Exagérés*, the *Indulgents* [*Dantonistes*] to be hauled before the revolutionary court.

Their show trial turned in part into a resumption of the March proceedings against Chabot. While the assets of his brothers-in-law, the Freys, had been confiscated by the imperial authorities as possessions of "Jacobins," and in Vienna they were burnt in effigy, he and they, Chabot "admitted" in court, had illicitly profiteered hugely at the expense of the people, in Paris and in French-occupied Belgium. The Freys, confessed Chabot under duress, had given him their sister's hand in marriage (together with a dowry of 200,000 livres) as political cover, to gain a false "reputation for patriotism."[82]

The indictment engulfing Chabot, Fabre and the others implicated in the Compagnie des Indes scandal, as well as the Freys and Pereyra, mixed their allegedly wallowing in corruption with seeking to undo republican government in league with monarchs. Their concocted fusing of corruption and extremism with undercover royalism masquerading as patriotism was initially kept separate from the other "conspiracy" Robespierre, Saint-Just and Amar cooked up engulfing Danton, Desmoulins, Philippeau and Herault des Seychelles, the jurist who finessed the Montagnard revision of Condorcet's 1793 constitution, "suspects" all arrested and imprisoned in the Luxembourg on 30 March 1794. But elated by the success of their intoxicating *modérantisme* wedded to extremism construct, their accusers took increasingly to presenting the *Exagérés* and *Indulgents* as the closest of allies. To accelerate the destruction of their rivals, Robespierre and Saint-Just merged the two sets of indictments and trial procedures, those against the Hébert and Danton blocs respectively, conflating the Chabot affair with *Dantoniste* crimes down to the smallest touches and details by contriving the fabrication of yet more charges, false testimony and highly dubious evidence.

Using Robespierre's notes, Saint-Just, on 1 April, laid his *réquisitoire* [indictment] before the [Convention, demanding Hérault's and the others' trial and execution. They were charged beside the earlier accusations with being secret allies of the Brissotins, whose downfall they supposedly viewed "avec horreur." Pereyra and "the Prussian Cloots," having already been dispatched together with Hébert and his circle, on 24 March 1794, the trial of the Dantonistes, from 2 to the 5 April, conducted in an exceedingly intimidating and biased manner, ended with fifteen *Dantonistes* headed by Danton and Desmoulins, and including Chabot and the Brothers Frey, being likewise sentenced to the guillotine. On 5 April 1794, transported in the usual charrettes, Chabot and the Freys along with Hébert's foes—Danton, Desmoulins, Fabre, Philippeaux and Hérault—were brought to the guillotine in the Place de la Révolution (today the Place de la Concorde) and guillotined before large crowds.[83] If it was any consolation, not many enjoyed the privilege of being guillotined alongside Danton.

Vilified and disgraced by Robespierre, executed as a betrayer of the Revolution, in reality Frey seems to have remained loyal to the cause of the democratic republican Revolution which Robespierre and Saint-Just so despicably betrayed, to the very end. On the eve of his execution, he left a moving last testament for his teenage son who had accompanied him to Paris, together with a copy of his *Philosophie sociale*. Dated 19 March 1794, his last statement read: "sache que mourir n'est rien, mais qu'il est cruel d'être méconnu et de ne pas pouvoir continuer à travailler pour la liberté" [Know that dying is nothing, but it is cruel to be misrepresented and not to be able to continue to work for liberty].[84]

Leopoldine, Frey's sixteen-year-old widowed sister, left on her own, fled with her nephew, Frey's son, and a few belongings from Paris for Boulogne, and then England. When Saint-Just introduced a further decree in the Convention claiming "Paris has become the target of foreign designs," stipulating fresh security measures targeting foreigners from lands at war with France, Hourwitz and numerous other Jews residing in Paris found themselves under increased threat. Since the "downfall of liberty can only be achieved by the loss of Paris," admonished Saint-Just in his xenophobic speech introducing the measure, any "noble or foreigner" found in Paris or the garrison cities, ten days after enactment must be deemed "outside the law" and subjected to automatic arrest and execution.

By early April 1794, with Peyrera and the Frey Brothers dispatched and Furtado in hiding, Hourwitz alone, mostly unseen but still occasionally sallying forth, survived among the French Revolution's leading Jewish revolutionaries as a declared republican democrat fighting the lies and hypocrisy of Robespierre and the Montagne. Astoundingly, at the height of the Terror, he dashed off a protest letter to the president of the Committee of Public Safety, on 16 April 1794, demanding Saint-Just provide the Convention with a clear "explanation" for his draft decree further inflating Paris's now absurdly overblown paranoia about "foreigners:" the regime was deliberately whipping up irrational fear in the capital, one could only presume, for certain persons' own devious purposes.[85]

After the Terror finally ended, late in 1794, with Robespierre's sudden downfall and execution freeing everyone from the worst of nightmares, nothing could again be as it had been before 1793. The elation of the early Revolution had evaporated for good. Within a few months, as relief from dark menace spread, carefree pleasure-seeking wholly replaced the stark austerity of the Terror. Furtado, a permanently scarred survivor, once back in circulation, his youthful optimism and early confidence transformed into a detached, wary skepticism, still adhered to the basic standpoint he had kept to throughout—a republican vision aligned with that of the hounded, now dead Condorcet and the guillotined Brissotins but one now less democratic than it had been. While reserving his sharpest disparagement of religious authority for the Catholic Church and its clergy, Furtado, like Hourwitz, Pereyra and Frey, whether deistically or atheistically inclined, continued to regard all religions with *philosophique* "indifference" and suspicion. This remained the case also subsequently when, under Napoleon, he resumed a prominent leadership role within the Bordeaux Sephardic community and became a tool of Napoleon's Jewish policy.[86]

NINE

Remaking the New World (1790–1820)

Emancipating the Jews, held radical enlighteners, required a double strategy—demolish the barriers and restrictions while simultaneously commencing the process of economic normalization, hence change the orientation of Jewish society—penalizing the usurers as Furtado urged, curbing excessive preoccupation with trade, money and business, and open up the Jewish occupation-structure. This would lead of itself to the required rectification of the Jews' social and moral character. Economic normalization, shifting attitudes through secular education and inculcating a more meaningful, positive sense of citizenship and respect for the common good were hence all requisite along with demolishing rabbinic and communal religious authority.[1]

David Nassy, feeling hemmed in at Paramaribo, a widower since November 1789 and desiring a change of scene and opportunity to broaden his horizons and experience, in 1792 requested a three-year furlough from his position as secretary to the *Mahamad* to spend that period in the political, cultural and scientific capital of the new United States, still then (prior to the move to Washington) at Philadelphia. Both Surinam in general and its Jewish community were now in evident decline.[2] The plantation economy's diminishing profitability practically everywhere in the Caribbean outside the British sphere of dominance, at a time of overwhelming British naval superiority and, from 1792, with almost continual warfare disrupting seaborne trade, rescuing Surinam Jewry more than ever meant creating fresh opportunities. What was needed above all, in Nassy's view, was re-education, reorienting New World Sephardic youth toward fresh skills, professions and occupations. But any such solution faced formidable obstacles given Dutch Caribbean Jewry's diminishing affluence and the Dutch Protestant settlers' growing tendency to block efforts to diversify Jewish activities by reinforcing the barriers excluding Jews from the law, administration, medicine and other higher professions.[3]

Those apt to lose from Jewish admittance to the legal and medical spheres, and into retailing, resented Jewish aspirations and some, including influential personages among officialdom, aimed to refurbish the partly lapsed disabilities and barriers of the past. As the *Essai historique* testifies, Nassy fiercely resented the traditional institutionalized discrimination against Jews in the political and legal establishment of the Old World, not least in the *ancien régime* Dutch Republic (revolutionized in 1795), and resented too the remaining barriers in Holland's New World colonies. His indignation at discrimination and resentment at the continuing inferior Jewish status in the Netherlands, Guyanas and the Caribbean is reflected in several passages, including one where he recounts the decision of Surinam's governor and council not to appoint his "enlightened" friend and ally Moseh Pereira de Leon to the position of Surinam's senior legal procurator. A lawyer with exceptional experience as a lower advocate in the courts and pillar of the local Surinam Enlightenment, as well as a Paramaribo *parnas*, or governing council elder, Pereira de Leon was outstanding, felt Nassy, but scandalously debarred from the higher reaches, after considerable prevarication at the governor's mansion, because there was no precedent anywhere in the Dutch colonial empire for appointing Jews to higher judicial functions in the administration.[4]

Among the growing opposition were those deploring Jews entering retailing, law, medicine and pharmacy.[5] Of the eight qualified practicing physicians in Surinam, in 1786, before Nassy emigrated temporarily to Pennsylvania, already no fewer than half, four, were (Ashkenazic) Jews working alongside four Christian colleagues. Of the colony's eight apothecaries, one was an Ashkenazi and another a Portuguese Jew.[6] But if it was partly for economic reasons that Nassy left, in April 1792, to reside for a time in Philadelphia, accompanied by his adult, disabled unmarried daughter, specifically to redirect his own professional career, from pharmacy into medicine, his goals were much wider than that. Inspired by the ideals of the American

Revolution, he was eager to sample the heightened intellectual opportunities Philadelphia offered, to learn about the new American reality and to advance his plans for reforming Surinam education and society. Admitted as a practicing physician in January 1793,[7] becoming by the same token Philadelphia's first practicing Jewish physician, he was also the first Jew elected to the renowned American Philosophical Society of Philadelphia created by Benjamin Franklin, now presided over by Jefferson and the French radical Volney. Nassy, in effect, was the first Jew to win standing in America in medicine and, at the same time, for achievement in antiquarian learning and ancient languages.

Residing in Philadelphia (1792–95), corresponding almost exclusively in French, Nassy soon found himself among the medical men heroically battling the city's great yellow fever epidemic of 1793.The yellow fever epidemic also landed Nassy into the midst of a bitterly divisive controversy among the Philadelphia medical fraternity starting in September 1793, when the renowned "Founding Father" Benjamin Rush (1746–1813), a key promoter of hospital and prison reform in the city, and professor of medicine and clinical practice at what later became the University of Pennsylvania, and his following clashed with another leading medical professor, Adam Kuhn (1745–1813), a son of German immigrants trained at Uppsala and follower of Linnaeus and his circle. For Rush, blood-letting and mercurial purges were the indispensable answers to the fever. Kuhn protested in the Philadelphia papers, rejecting blood-letting as a remedy and recommending instead bark, wine and cool baths. Rush replied that Kuhn's method, "if persisted in," will result in "desolating three fourths of our city. The almost universal success with which it hath pleased God to bless the remedies of strong mercurial purges and bleeding in this disorder," read his public statement of 12 September, "enables Dr Rush to assure his fellow citizens that there is no more danger to be apprehended from it, when those remedies are used in its early stage, than there is from the measles or the influenza." The same day, Rush assured the "College of Physicians," his Philadelphia colleagues, that indeed "he had found bleeding to be useful" and had "bled twice in many, and in one acute case four times, with the happiest effects" and accordingly was much distressed by "the contrariety of opinion among the members of our college upon the remedies proper to this disease."[8]

A French military surgeon, Jean Devèze (1753–1829), newly arrived among the refugees fleeing the upheaval in Haiti, who, like Nassy, had earlier witnessed yellow fever epidemics in the Caribbean, led a third faction, partly agreeing with Kuhn, recommending stimulants, quinine, cleanliness, rest and a light diet. "Two fifths of all the sick that were sent to Bush Hill," the infirmary where Devèze and other opponents of Rush's approach were based, retorted Rush, in early November, sadly departed this world in a few days. Expressing criticism of the physicians' public quarreling in the newspapers, which he remarked was increasing rather than allaying confusion and alarm, and rejecting Rush's use of mercury cures, Nassy, who relied on his own experience of such epidemics (Surinam also suffered further outbreaks of yellow fever in 1793 and 1795–96) and who took almost two hundred patients under his care during the epidemic's first six weeks, took up an in-between stance, engaging in blood-letting but cautiously, only in some cases and never more than twice while wholly avoiding mercury cures; later, in November 1793, he published in a bilingual French-English edition at Philadelphia his own twenty-page *Observations sur la cause, la nature, et le traitement de la maladie épidémique, qui règne à Philadelphie* [Observations on the Cause, Nature and Treatment of the Epidemic Disorder Prevalent in Philadelphia] (Philadelphia, 1793). In his text, he went out of his way to be calming, practical and to avoid taking sides.).[9]

Rush first encountered Nassy apparently at a Philadelphia circumcision party, shortly after the latter's arrival. He described him as an "ingenius physician, a Jew" who assured him, as they chatted about circumcision, that "Jews in consequence of the loss of the foreskin were less subject to venereal disease," and in addition, "escaped all the troublesome symptoms which were connected with the foreskin, as phimosis, paraphimosis, chancres. Etc." Soon after this meeting, Nassy visited Rush at home to present him with a copy of his history of Surinam. A fervent Christian, Rush asked him "what he thought of the present state of the world, and whether the favors largely shown to his nation by public bodies" since the advent of the American and French revolutions "did not indicate the speedy fulfillment of certain prophecies relative to them." He agreed "with Dr Franklin," Nassy answered evasively, "that it was best to believe, but that it seemed very improbable that the Supreme Being should give a preference to any one nation such as it was said He has given to the Jews." Like Furtado, Nassy did not think the Jewish future should be envisaged as the outcome of any messianic project particular to Jews as a separate nation. Rather, the Jews should integrate their future in the republics of which they were already, or soon hoped to be proclaimed citizens, as in the United States, the Dutch colonies, Holland and France.[10]

Nassy, like his ally Montel, was not a religious man. But it was never part of his reform agenda to detach himself from the social and political predicament, or the future destiny, of the Jewish people, quite the contrary.[11] In Philadelphia, he joined the Mikveh Israel synagogue, where he met other prominent Jewish revolutionaries (and where he encountered Rush) and supported its efforts and charities. Overall, he remained deeply committed to his people. It was demolishing ignorance, obscurantism and prejudice, including what to him was the serious hindrance of rabbinic and synagogue authority over the individual, that stood at the core of his Enlightenment reform ideology.

Meanwhile, the years of his stay in Philadelphia enabled Nassy to witness a crucial turning point in the history of the nascent American republic and its attitudes to the fast-changing world outside. For these were years when the basic ideological split within the American Revolution intensified, pitting the legacy of Franklin, Jefferson and Paine—the democratic republican tendency issuing from the Radical Enlightenment—increasingly against the "aristocratic republicanism" of John Adams, Alexander Hamilton and the so called "Federalist" faction headed by President Washington, with its veneration of the British "mixed government" model and growing antipathy toward revolutionary France. Until the latter end of Nassy's stay, the years 1795–96, American public opinion remained broadly favorable, as it had since 1789, in its attitude to the French Revolution and the spread of "universal and equal rights" internationally. But precisely during those years occurred a marked shift in sentiment, caused partly by revulsion against Robespierre and the Terror, partly by the 1793–94 upheavals in Haiti, and partly by the growing influence of evangelical preachers via the "Great Awakening," away from support for the French Revolution toward increased sympathy for the "British model" and hostility to French "godlessness."[12] For Nassy, the chief question was how all this should and would impact on the wider revolutionary process in the Caribbean, Latin America and Europe.

THE SEPHARDIC "CARIBBEAN REVOLUTION"

For at the same time, Caribbean Jews found themselves similarly increasingly split between supporters of the Revolution as an ongoing international project and Orangist opponents determined to reverse the process. Many Caribbean Jews looked sympathetically on the continuing progress of the trans-Atlantic

Revolution. But in Surinam and on Curaçao, as in Holland, most of the merchants and also the community rabbis and *parnasim* supported the Prince of Orange and the British alliance.[13] Since 1750, when around 1,500 Jews, mainly Sephardim, dwelt on Curaçao, the community had declined in numbers, falling to 1,200 by 1785, and then to only around 1,000 by 1795. Demographic decline, however, hardly reduced their prominence in the region since the shrinkage was due largely to increased dispersal to neighboring parts of the Caribbean and the Carolinas. Tensions both on the island and all around remained acute. Jews still represented a considerable slice of Curaçao's white citizenry as a whole, which was likewise increasingly bitterly divided between Orangists and "Patriots."[14]

On Curaçao and the other five Dutch islands, as in Surinam, (but not Dutch western Guyana, now under British occupation), festive commemorations and banquets were laid on to mark the advent of the 1795 "Batavian Revolution," which triumphantly ejected the House of Orange and British military presence from the Netherlands. The Batavian Revolution followed the French Revolution in proclaiming democratic republican values, and the requirement for government to be devoted to the well-being of society as a whole, ideals supporters and opponents alike considered jointly "American" and "French" in inspiration. The Surinam banquets celebrated in particular the 1795 military alliance between revolutionary France and the new Dutch Republic, and the Dutch adoption, at French prompting, of the principles of the 1789 *Declaration of the Rights of Man and the Citizen*.

At one of these festive gatherings in Paramaribo glasses were raised by all present to Abraham Verheul (1770–1817), a Surinam enlightener now figuring among the revolutionary leadership in Holland who, within days of the arrival of the French army of invasion, delivered a famous speech about human equality, the *Redevoering over de gelijkheid der menschen* [Speech on Human Equality], on 11 February 1795, in the Amsterdam Club *Felix Meritis* exalting "equality" and the transformed "new Fatherland that presents itself before our astonished eyes." His *Redevoering* made no direct mention of Jews or blacks, but loudly denounced monarchy, aristocracy and all privilege, fiercely condemning the reactionary and aristocratic views of Edmund Burke, proclaiming the general principle of *de gelijkheid* [equality] as universally valid, "the soul of freedom and my particular principle: the more people are equal, the more they enjoy the same rights, the more they are free—equality is the foundation of political and civic freedom."[15]

The Dutch and English already enjoyed a considerable measure of civil freedom before 1795, but now, in the Dutch case, this was notably enlarged. Dutchmen could at last stop the old ruling patrician oligarchy, the Holland town regents, continually sidelining the common interest, the well-being of the citizenry as a whole to serve their own narrow interests, including in the colonies. Supposedly, Dutch citizens were now to enjoy full democratic republican freedom. Later that year, Verheul became president of the Batavian Republic's committee for colonial affairs, the *Comité tot de zaaken der coloniën ende bezittingen op de kust van Guinee ende in Amerika*, responsible for bringing his democratic Enlightenment program and legal expertise to bear on the far-reaching political, social and educational reforms planned for the colonies.[16]

Among key unresolved issues raised but left undecided following the Batavian Republic's establishment on the basis of popular sovereignty, democracy and the principles of the revolutionary French Republic, in 1795, was the question whether Jewish citizens now possessed full civic rights and equality or not. This was a highly topical issue both in Holland and the colonies. The newly convened Dutch National Assembly of 1795 initially failed to reach any definite conclusion. Should the Jews too enjoy full citizenship status? The issue remained a major internal controversy within the Jewish communities of the Netherlands and its western colonies through 1795–96, dividing a pro-Revolution minority of secularists from Orangist traditionalists dominating the Jewish majority.

Disagreement about Jewish emancipation and rights remained intense in Dutch society, much as in France and Germany. Various pamphlets for and against appeared in 1795–96, among the fiercest against being that of the (unconsciously) ironically named Dordrecht Club "Tot Behoud van Vrijheid en Gelijkheid" [For the Maintenance of Freedom and Equality].[17] Voltairean Enlightenment new-style antisemitism helped sway opinion against the Jews. Jews had always strictly segregated themselves from the rest of humanity, argued the Dordrechters, neither marrying non-Jewish women nor participating in non-Jewish society, thereby ensuring Jewish society remained permanently deformed by numerous innate defects. "Jews have always been suspect and, even if they turn Christians still hide their Judaism, converting only for the advantages this gives them, as they did in Spain and Portugal." An additional factor fueling opposition was fear that emancipation would stimulate a further wave of immigration of poor German and Polish Jewish immigrants, often vagrants, peddlers or criminals.[18]

On the other side, prominent voices like Nassy's demanded an equivalent change to that achieved in revolutionary France, a charter of universal rights that would genuinely transform society on the basis of republicanism, democracy and equality. It was a call emanating most vigorously from the French National Assembly both prior to the overthrow of the democratic republicans in France, and likewise after the fall of the *Robespierriste* Counter-Enlightenment reaction, the Montagnard reign of Terror based on misinformation and the prejudices of the illiterate, lasting from June 1793 to July 1794. The renewed summons propagated from early 1795 by the restored neo-Brissotin democratic republican revolutionary regime, loudly echoed in the, since 1795, revived, re-generated and re-invigorated French press, also exerted a massive impact on France's republican satellite states bringing about rapid change in Jewish life in much of Europe.[19] Already tentatively proclaimed earlier, in 1792–93, by the revolutionaries in Belgium and the Rhineland, Jewish emancipation became a key feature of the 1795–99 revolutionary campaigns, under the *Directoire* (1795–99), in the Rhineland and Netherlands, and under Napoleon—then still a staunch republican—in Italy. Following the renewed advance of the French revolutionary armies, the Jews of Frankfurt, Venice, Livorno, Rome and the other Italian communities were swiftly liberated from the chains of the past, the papacy and the ghetto. In 1797–99, the Jews of Corfu, the other Greek Ionian islands, Malta and Egypt under French occupation were similarly emancipated.

The now trans-Atlantic movement to emancipate the Jews and bestow on them equal rights exerted an electrifying effect throughout the Jewish world, especially the "enlightened" intellectual elites already emancipated in mind and socially flourishing on one side of the Atlantic, in Paramaribo, Curaçao, St. Thomas, Charleston and Philadelphia, and, on the other, at Berlin, Königsberg, Hamburg, Paris, Amsterdam and Venice. But stiff opposition to this aspect of the "General Revolution" continued right through the 1790s, notably within republican France's newest and now most important ally, the supposedly egalitarian, revolutionary and emancipated Batavian Republic. Jewish enlighteners, among whom the secularized, enlightened intellectual fringe of the Dutch New World Sephardic communities stood out,[20] understandably felt frustrated and indignant. Often scandalized by the failure to advance more swiftly toward full emancipation, they were aggrieved too at the stubborn refusal of the rabbis and most communal authorities to support the reformers' efforts.

It took four whole months for news of the French conquest of the Netherlands to reach the Caribbean. Once the Batavian Republic was proclaimed in Surinam, Curaçao and the other islands, French revolutionary troops, often freed blacks, occupied parts of Curaçao with ambiguous intent, while the rump of the island capital, Willemstad, remained garrisoned by Caribbean-based Orangist troops opposing the Revolution and allied to Britain. With white and black French revolutionaries occupying enclaves on the island, on 17 August 1795 erupted on the Curaçao plantations one of the biggest black insurrections of the age outside Haiti. Within days, as many as two thousand of the island's twelve to thirteen thousand slaves (and approximately 3,700 free blacks), spurred by the Haitian Revolution and France's revolutionary decree freeing the slaves in the French Caribbean, rose in armed revolt, a rebellion lasting nearly a month. It was brutally suppressed by Orangist troops and militias (some black), under the command of the island's governor, suppression followed by dozens of executions.[21]

Amidst the usually overlooked but stupendous Caribbean conflict of the later 1790s swirling around the French and Haitian Revolutions, emerged the most important late literary undertaking of David Nassy, physician, historian and leading light of the New World Jewish community—a text begun in Philadelphia—his *Lettre-politico-théologico-morale sur les Juifs* (1798). A brochure today still relatively little known owing to its rarity, it is certainly among the foremost New World egalitarian texts and emphatic pleas for Jewish equality and emancipation of the age. Composed in French, mainly in 1795–96, Nassy intended it as a bilingual publication, which involved some delay before it was rendered also into Dutch, and ready for the press. The work of a "patriot" who loves "my native country despite its injustices towards me," it finally appeared as a bilingual Franco-Dutch edition, dated Paramaribo, 10 December 1798.[22] Continuing discrimination in the Batavian Republic and its colonies Nassy pronounced hypocritical, shocking and totally unacceptable.[23] Apart from rejecting the arguments of the moderate Enlightenment on this topic, and the Dordrecht Club's notion of "Freedom and Equality" in particular, the tract's prime feature was a passionate appeal to Juriaen François de Friderici (1751–1812), the intrepid soldier and reforming governor-general (1790–1802) of Surinam responsible for steering the colony through the political whirlwinds of the tumultuous 1790s, a figure with whom Nassy was on good personal terms.[24] Though Friderici was previously an Orangist and moderate enlightener, in the dedication Nassy appeals to him to take his stand beside bolder, more forthright Enlightenment reformers like Dohm and Mirabeau, in championing and promoting Jewish rights.[25]

Discrimination, physical and moral, against Jews, Nassy, the unbeliever, resented enormously. Both the *Essai historique* (1789) and *Lettre-politico-théologico-morale* (1796/97) confirm his passionate commitment to Verheul's "universal and equal rights" formula in principle and Dohm's recipe as the means to realize them with respect to the Jews. Freedom of the press and expression were equally essential principles in his eyes: like all radical enlighteners without exception, he utterly loathed Robespierre and *Robespierrisme,* as the worst of political evils.[26] From 1789, Nassy and his friends subscribed to what by 1795 had evolved into a comprehensive trans-Atlantic political ideology proclaiming equality, democracy, full freedom of expression and ending religious authority's hold over social organization, law and education. Nassy tags on also Raynal's (and Diderot's) principle that less protectionism and colonial restrictions, a shift to free trade, especially with the newly independent United States, would benefit the Caribbean and its peoples generally, the Jews included, and the Dutch homeland.[27]

Instituting the new Batavian Republic and its military alliance with revolutionary France did not mean an end anytime soon to Orangist conservative opposition, Jewish disabilities or black slavery in the Dutch, as distinct from French, Atlantic colonies. It created a strange contradiction that in the neighboring territory of Cayenne (French Guyana), as in Haiti, Martinique and Guadeloupe, the revolutionary regime formally abolished black slavery in 1794 whereas in adjoining supposedly revolutionary Surinam nothing of the kind occurred in the mid-1790s.[28] To begin with, the Dutch trans-Atlantic Revolution of 1794–96 changed little on the ground in the Netherlands and less still in the Dutch New World, apart from the now generally seething turmoil and uncertainty. In the Dutch colonies it remained entirely unclear what the Batavian Revolution really entailed for minority groups, white Catholics and Jews, as well as free blacks and slaves. Meanwhile, the 1794–96 dramatic advances of the combined Franco-Dutch Revolution, along with the specter of advancing black emancipation in the Caribbean, caused great, unprecedented consternation in London and Madrid and, to a degree, Philadelphia.

So menacing did the prospect of resurgent Franco-Dutch democratic-revolutionary arms, privateering and the rhetoric of black emancipation throughout the Caribbean seem to British ministers, that despite the relative failure of their 1793–94 offensive, a renewed, still larger British counter-offensive was now mounted, developing during 1796 into a vast military reinforcing expedition comprising nearly one hundred ships and thirty thousand troops. The French and Dutch Atlantic revolutions combined had to be checked and defeated if crown, aristocracy and British imperial domination were to survive, the British government believed, and should be repulsed first in their trans-Atlantic outposts. This huge new armada joined the substantial British and Spanish royalist forces already entrenched in the Caribbean, battling the Revolution in the islands, first and foremost Saint-Domingue (Haiti), which both Britain and Spain now invaded from opposite sides, striving to stop black emancipation in its tracks.

Yet despite overall naval and military superiority and massive resources committed, Britain's Caribbean counter-revolutionary offensive, aside from recovering Grenada and Saint Vincent and occupying western Guyana and Curaçao (in 1800), only sporadically succeeded. Revolutionary France's National Convention dispatched much smaller expeditions to Guadeloupe and Saint-Domingue, but these managed to hold the line in both, especially owing to emancipated and willing black and mulatto troops and militias. Yellow fever and malaria, moreover, exacted a staggering toll on Britain's seamen and troops. Altogether, opposing the Franco-Dutch-Haitian Caribbean Revolution between 1796–1800, cost the lives of some forty thousand British troops and sailors estimated to have died or disappeared, through fighting, disease and desertion, many breathing their last in makeshift hospitals, including churches in Jamaica, the hub of the British Caribbean.

Faced by such a mighty counter-offensive, the immediate outlook for Caribbean revolutionary transformation looked more doubtful than ever. The evidence of the mid- and late 1790s proves those primarily propagating egalitarian ideas around the region were as a rule not black Haitian rebels but, more often, operating on sea and land, white French republicans together with mulattoes from Guadeloupe and the lesser Antilles. Nevertheless, where local colonial regimes resisted or only embraced the new revolutionary order reluctantly, that is, in the Caribbean beyond Haiti, Cayenne, Martinique and Guadeloupe, extensive subversive conspiracy was afoot among both whites desiring wider resort to genuine revolutionary principles and aggrieved, disaffected blacks. A string of major and minor conspiracies and revolts shook the region at this juncture.

On Curaçao, in December 1796, occurred a popular pro-Patriot *coup d'état* that replaced the previous governor with a supposedly more "Patriot"-minded successor, Johan Rudolf Lauffer (1753–1833), who turned out, however, to be a firm moderate and, for some, a disappointment.[29] Along with most other supposed pro-Batavian Caribbean Dutch dreading a renewed black uprising, Lauffer soon abandoned all pretense of championing revolutionary principles. Most Curaçao whites concurred; a handful passionately disagreed. In this tense atmosphere, the official French agent on the Island, Urbain Devaux (1767–1836), under orders of the *Directoire*'s representative on Saint-Domingue (Haiti), Philippe Roume de Saint-Laurent (1743–1804), quietly organized renewed revolutionary ferment angling to oust Lauffer and install a more forthrightly pro-French revolutionary regime. Anonymous pamphlets circulated. Secret meetings were held. Roume's and Devaux's man-on-the-spot was a remarkable young Jewish revolutionary born at Cap Français (today Cap-Haïtien) in northern Haiti, a roving *commissaire* of the *Directoire*, Isaac Jessurun Sasportas (d. 1799).

The Haitian capital, Cap Français, in the 1780s featured a small but affluent Sephardic community, mostly consisting of recent arrivals from Bordeaux and Bayonne, or else from Curaçao, in which the Sasportas family were prominent.[30] Isaac, twenty-three years old at this point, belonged to a well-known mercantile family with close ties to Curaçao, Jamaica, Cuba and St. Thomas; he also had a merchant uncle at Charleston, South Carolina. Fluent in French, Spanish and English, an idealist with money, trans-Atlantic connections and fondness for gambling at cards, elated by the French Revolution's decrees emancipating the Jews, he spoke as ardently for black as for Jewish emancipation. The planned renewed rising on Curaçao was nipped in the bud, however, in September 1799; Lauffer arrested Sasportas and another leading conspirator. When news of the conspiracy got out, the Curaçao *Mahamad* were shocked to find this Sephardic interloper from Cap Français, Sasportas, had drawn several local Sephardic Jews into active complicity with the French, including Elias Brandon, Jacob Athias and Moseh Frois d'Andrade, the latter identified as someone actively stirring anti-Orangist and anti-British sentiment with subversive oratory.[31] Sasportas and Athias were hurriedly expelled.[32]

JEWISH EQUALITY AND THE FIGHT FOR BLACK EMANCIPATION

Ejected from Curaçao, Sasportas continued receiving orders from Roume, who, under pressure from the *Directoire* in Paris for vigorous action in the Caribbean, switched to an alternative plan concocted by Sasportas and himself, an effort to re-ignite escaped slave insurgency in the Jamaican interior. Since 1793, Jamaica's Blue Mountain maroons, or escaped slaves, had been in insurrection in the hills for several years but, by 1798, had been forcibly suppressed by British troops. Sasportas was now commissioned to gather information and, if possible, rekindle resistance among the Blue Mountain maroons. He made his way to Jamaica from Curaçao with a former slave of his father's and another French agent. This second conspiracy concocted by Sasportas sought to spur black insurgency in the Blue Mountains in concert with subversion and sabotage by Irish dissidents in Kingston, creating enough turmoil and confusion to open the way to the projected conquest of Jamaica by four thousand black troops standing ready who would be quickly shipped across from Haiti, a hundred miles away, under the mulatto general Martial Besse (1759–after 1805). The invasion force would bring with them separate edicts simultaneously proclaiming both slave emancipation in the British colonies and the liberation of Ireland. A substantial black slave revolt on Jamaica would hopefully destabilize British rule there, open the way to French conquest of Jamaica and generally wreck Britain's mounting war effort in the Caribbean.

Roume discussed Sasportas's scheme with the black leader who had done most to establish virtual black independence in the interior of Haiti, the famed Toussaint Louverture (1743–1803), who, however, while feigning support for the *Directoire*'s revolutionary abolitionism for the moment, preferred to exploit the situation to secure British and American backing for his own permanent control of Haiti and, for this reason, wrote secretly warning the governor of Jamaica and providing the details of Sasportas's revolutionary scheme.[33]

Arriving at Kingston purporting to have come to trade, Sasportas was arrested, imprisoned and then tried in November 1799 by special military court-martial. Quickly discarding his alibis, Sasportas made no secret of his being a revolutionary "enthused with the idea of liberty." The sixteen officers who heard his case found him guilty of "entering the Island of Jamaica, during war as a Spy, hired and employed by the enemy for hostile purposes." He was sentenced not just to be "hanged by the neck until he be dead," reported the *Royal Gazette of Jamaica*, but to execution in a fashion as "public and disgraceful as possible," to highlight "the enormity of the crime" and "render the example most striking and effectual to those concerned in like practices."[34] He was to be "marched to execution," secured in irons, surrounded by a double guard with a "label fixed on his breast and the word SPY wrote in large characters." Marched out for his public hanging, on 23 December 1799, Sasportas, reported eyewitnesses among the assembled crowd, looked calm and undaunted beside the black coffin for which he was destined. He even managed to cry out as they were stringing him up: "Vive la Liberté, vive la République!"[35]

On Jamaica, Sasportas's lonely stand against slavery and oppression of the blacks was soon buried in oblivion. What was remembered was his public disgrace as a base "scoundrel." Jamaica's black rebels and fugitives continued to attract no sympathy either. The moral, psychological and social adverse effects of prolonged oppression, justified by theology, to which all the world's Jews had been subjected, are what enables oppression, argued Mirabeau, much like Diez, Cloots and Dohm, to continue over the centuries. Regarding the Jews it acquired fresh bogus justification, as Voltaire's disparagement of the Jews illustrated, from the very degrading consequences of its impact. Pressing an entire people down into misery, humiliation and age-old legalized oppression inevitably forges the marks of degradation and inferiority, apparent inborn negative traits and a defective outlook which then, in turn, appears to legitimize among the great mass of society, including many who should be more enlightened, the very hatred and repression nurturing the disabilities, intolerance and moral disfigurement. This ugly truth was still more vividly illustrated by the white planters' subjection of the blacks throughout the Caribbean region. For an even more crushing and humiliating combination of factors had kept the blacks enslaved to white masters for centuries, locked in debasing subjection entrapping their offspring too for generation after generation in brutal oppression justified by bigotry, law and theology.

Nassy was both conscious of, and perplexed by, the parallels between Jewish and black degradation. His plea for Jewish equality was clearly based on the principle of universal and equal rights: "All men must have equal rights, equal privileges; birth, religion, wealth, and rank taken together do not justify inequality; only virtue, talents, character, whether this be useful or dangerous to the state, vices and inability, can form the base of inequality among individual members of the state." So passionate was he in demanding equality before the law and equality of opportunity that Nassy could hardly have been oblivious to the glaring contradiction between the glowing principle the American and French Revolutions proclaimed to the world and the dismal reality of slavery in the United States, Spanish and Portuguese America, and the Caribbean, with which he, Montel and Sasportas were all too familiar.[36]

Besides a total of 1,311 white Jews (including the Ashkenazim), there were also some eighty Jewish mulattoes and free blacks within the Surinam Jewish community, and another black Jewish community on Curaçao.[37] Nassy himself had owned slaves and early on converted at least three of these to Judaism; but Surinam's half-caste black Jews, though admitted as congregants, were confined to a markedly subordinate status, and Nassy's own notes about this, dating from 1791, show he had little desire to alter this racially based hierarchy.[38] In 1790, a mulatto named "Joseph de David Cohen Nassy," possibly an illegitimate son of his, was tried in Surinam for convening a mixed-race Eurafrican Jewish prayer meeting. Still, Nassy, the *Essai historique* indicates, did feel deeply troubled by the fraught relationship of whites and blacks, and had long been acutely conscious of the moral predicament, the social and political trap this generated, albeit for the moment could discern no solution to which he could commit himself.

When touching on the pre-1789 French royal Code Noir in his history of Surinam, the laws relating to slavery and the blacks throughout the French Caribbean colonies prior to 1789, with their focus on repression and religious indoctrination rather than betterment of living conditions, Nassy remarks cuttingly that "jamais ouvrage n'a reçu un titre plus analogue à son contenu que celui-ci. Il semble qu'il désigne plutôt la noirceur du fanatisme et de l'intolérance religieuse, que la couleur des Nègres qui lui a fait donner ce titre" [never did a text receive a title corresponding more closely to its content than this. It seems rather to describe the blackness of fanaticism and religious intolerance than the color of the negroes that gave it this title].[39] In Surinam, Nassy had long acknowledged that when countering tropical diseases both the blacks and local Amerindians had discovered plants and devised treatments unknown to the whites that undoubtedly helped; a comprehensive dictionary of tropical medicine for the Guyanas should, he felt, include the significant contributions of both ethnic groups to medicine.[40] Still, he refrained from calling outright for an end to slavery, or supporting the Haitian Revolution and wider drive to emancipate the blacks, while proclaiming an egalitarian ideology in stark conflict with the reality of subjugation, degradation and hierarchical race relations prevailing throughout the Caribbean except, from 1793–94, in the French colonies, where slavery was now formally abolished.

In his passages on general equality in the *Lettre-politico-théologico-morale*, Nassy still abstained, as he had in the *Essai*, from condemning slavery and subjugation of blacks in principle. He confined himself, as with his Code Noir remarks earlier, to condemning, and expressing sympathy, solely by hint and implication. Steeped in the *Histoire philosophique*, the work that signaled the real beginning of modern anti-colonialism, as also in Mirabeau's writings, and all texts that helped prepare the ground for the *Declaration of the Rights of Man* and war on slavery as an institution, as well as the Brissotins' drive to emancipate free blacks during the early and middle stages of the French Revolution, he was more familiar with the burning issue of black equality than many, or than his brief comments on the topic might suggest. At Philadelphia, as in London and Paris, he cannot have failed to notice that considerable effort had already gone into calling for slavery's abolition. Since several leading enlighteners Nassy knew and admired in Philadelphia, including Benjamin Rush and family members of the leading Jewish revolutionary among the Mikveh Israel congregation, Solomon Bush (1753–1795), the sole Jew belonging to the Philadelphia Abolition Society,[41] were committed abolitionists, Nassy could hardly fail to feel the force of American and British as well as French Brissotin and other abolitionist arguments. Bush, a local hero, a veteran of the Battle of Long Island (1776), badly wounded in a skirmish in September 1777 (in which his brother, a militia captain, Lewis Bush, was killed), had risen to the rank of "lieutenant-colonel" in the Pennsylvania militia. The Pennsylvania Society for Promoting the Abolition of Slavery, set up in 1787, at that moment the principal abolitionist organ in the New World, boasted the recently deceased Benjamin Franklin as its first president and Rush as its secretary.[42]

"In Pennsylvania," Rush had reported, in 1791, to Granville Sharp (1735–1813), a leading abolitionist in London, rather optimistically, "our laws have exterminated domestic slavery, and in Philadelphia the free blacks now compose near 3,000 souls. Their men are chiefly waiters, day laborers and traders in a small way. Their women are chiefly cooks and washerwomen." Though deemed entirely reliable in such occupations, "under these circumstances they are still in a state of depression, arising chiefly from their being deprived of the means of regular education and religious instruction."[43] Most of Philadelphia's black community were indeed now freemen, many only recently freed. Nassy witnessed the problem of black illiteracy and lack of education further through his involvement in battling the 1793 yellow fever epidemic, when he must additionally have been conscious of the blacks' crucial, widely noted contribution to fighting the epidemic, as nurses and attendants in the hospitals, or, as Rush put it, "what my African brethren have done for the city."[44]

It was the lack of education among the blacks, their illiteracy, that remained for Nassy, as for all radical enlighteners, the main attendant difficulty. In Philadelphia, Nassy, with little English to begin with, worked closely with Devèze and other French refugees who had fled for their lives from Haiti, where they had lost everything. Doubtless, he frequently heard their hair-raising firsthand accounts of the terrible massacres of whites and dispossession and flight of the whites that the Haitian Revolution brought in its wake. During 1793–94, the reports generated a wave of profound shock and horror throughout the Caribbean, South America and United States, not least in the mind of Thomas Jefferson.[45] It was this dark, frightening background which explains the profound hesitation and glaring contradiction in Nassy's thinking—his undeniable sympathy for the plight of the blacks combined with his equally profound conviction, contrasting with Sasportas's approach, rooted in Surinam's no less than Haiti's experience, that black emancipation cannot come all at once but must be a staged, gradual process.

Nassy had often commented on the periodic violence overshadowing relations between whites and blacks in Surinam and the rest of the Guyanas, and what he saw as its consequences. Even the male slave, Mattheus, he brought with him to Philadelphia, and manumitted there, in August 1792, Nassy afterwards kept at his side in a condition, as Pennsylvania law then permitted, of semi-servitude. Given the black population's total lack of education, he believed the revolutionary, emancipating notions of liberty and equality now sweeping the New World plantation economies must certainly "throw them into a kind of drunkenness" [espèce d'ivresse] that he dreaded would not pass until the blacks had destroyed everything. Given this terrible potential for slaughter and wrecking, releasing the blacks too soon from slavery, before they attained a certain level of awareness and culture, to his mind would be the most disastrous present one could possibly give them.[46] He wholeheartedly concurred with Raynal's remark that "with the mind of a slave, one is not far from slavery itself."[47]

In 1796, planning his new, enlightened school system for Paramaribo, influenced by his experience in Philadelphia, Nassy tellingly envisaged no color bar. He conceived rather a future with white and black Christians and Jews receiving their schooling together, with poor students receiving financial support from society as a whole.[48] It does not seem, though, that Nassy ever formulated a more concrete, broader plan of action regarding black emancipation, even with respect to education. He did elaborate, however, on how black resistance in the Caribbean impacted on white Christian attitudes toward the Jews. Large-scale flight of runaway slaves into the Surinam forests and establishment of maroon communities living in open rebellion, a growing problem since around 1750, was frequently blamed by Christian whites in the Guyanas, complains the *Essai historique*, on the alleged innate cruelty and harshness of Jews toward their slaves, a charge Nassy rejected as despicable calumny.[49] There were no grounds for accusing Jews "of greater tyranny toward their slaves than attributed to other inhabitants of the colony." But neither did Nassy lay particular blame, as a few did, on badly behaved "Christian" plantation owners who supposedly aggravated black suffering and grievance by drinking heavily and becoming thereby more despotic.[50] Jews in the tropics were attested to be less given to alcohol than their Dutch Protestant neighbors, but they too were equally complicit in tyrannizing over the blacks. This Caribbean antisemitic myth that slaves running away from plantations and ensuing slave insurgency were due to the Jews' innately malign character remained an abiding trope in the Guyanas until well into the nineteenth century.[51]

JEWS AND SPANISH AMERICA'S STRUGGLE FOR LIBERATION

Despite Nassy's attraction to "the great principles of liberty and equality of which the United States gave the first example to the world," he kept his promise to return to Surinam after three years. Heading back to the Caribbean, he departed Philadelphia extolling the new American reality. He sailed by way of St. Thomas, a Danish island where he next spent several months getting to know local conditions and the Jewish community there.[52] Whilst there, Nassy found himself confronted and on all sides surrounded by the greatest contest between major European powers ever to occur in the Caribbean region as revolutionary France and its new Dutch ally pressed on with their relentless war of principles and arms against the opposing efforts of Britain allied to Bourbon royalist Spain, which strove to stem the Haitian Revolution by invading from Puerto Rico and to check the occasional overspill of revolutionary ferment from Curaçao and neighboring islands onto Venezuela. Nassy finally reached Surinam in January 1796, a year after the French revolutionary conquest of the United Provinces. On arriving back, he found himself amidst a tide of optimism in the Dutch colonies, the wider Caribbean, and with increasing impact also in the neighboring parts of Spanish America—at least among those with views resembling his own; for some, it was a moment of almost messianic expectation of the redemption of mankind. Nassy and his friends celebrated the birth of the revolutionary new age, warmly embracing the principles of liberty and equality in full expectation of a period of intense constitutional debate and reform, of drawing up plans for revising virtually every aspect of colonial public life, administration, education and law.[53]

Nassy and those like-minded active in the late eighteenth-century New World Jewish Enlightenment were eager enough to celebrate the Batavian together with the American and French Revolutions, sharing as they did the fervor of Condorcet, Priestley, Price, Jefferson, Franklin and Paine in outright opposition to Robespierre and the Montagne on the one side, and America's "aristocrats" opposing the democratic tendency (and the French Revolution)—Washington, Hamilton, Adams, Gouverneur Morris and America's political Anglophiles—on the other. To those who thought like Nassy and the American Jeffersonians and Paineites opposing the "Federalists," the fundamental principles of the two great revolutions, those of America and France, were indeed one and the same with democratic republican equality the unifying and overriding thread.[54] Nassy's 1798 pamphlet, indebted especially to Dohm and Mendelssohn for its political and moral arguments, urges Jewish emancipation not on the basis of economic usefulness but for the purpose of transforming Jews into equal citizens fully participating and integrated into society.

In addition, Nassy hoped the Jewish contribution to the sciences and general learning, to improving the wider world, would increase once the heavy burden of prejudice and restrictions finally lifted: "if, despite the abject state in which it finds itself, this nation has the honor of having given to the world the likes of Spinoza, Orobio, Uriel da Costa, and Zacuto," how much more could it contribute to the world if the legalized wretchedness in which it had long languished were lifted?[55] Given the still highly negative image of Spinoza among most Jews and Christians, this was certainly a remarkable choice of names for a leading Caribbean Sephardic voice to use in expressing his point.

Written in 1796, Nassy's *Lettre-politico-théologico-morale* has a long preface added two years later, shortly before publication, in December 1798, introducing some significant new thoughts and considerations. As scholars have noted, the element of disillusionment is more marked in this later text than in the *Lettre* itself. Nassy never rejected the French Revolution as a model in favor of the American, or came to view the two revolutions, as did for example Washington's successor as President, John Adams (1735–1826), as representing two entirely distinct, essentially conflicting models of revolution.[56] It is quite wrong to conceive the revolutionary era, as American conservatives often still do, in terms of a clash of a supposedly American-style "New World perspective" versus a quite different, more violent and socially orientated French perspective. The *Droits de l'homme et du citoyen* [The Rights of Man and the Citizen] as proclaimed in France, in 1789 and reaffirmed in 1792, remained still very much the core of Nassy's revolutionary ideology, in 1798 no less than before.[57] He continued to oppose the principles of "nobility" and hereditary privilege and, unlike Adams, Hamilton or Morris, held as strongly as ever that those brought up in poverty, or belonging to a different religion, or of "obscure birth," should not be disdained or formally excluded from public office once they possess the requisite education and talent.[58] Republics, in his eyes, remained still broadly superior to monarchies in their potential for human well-being, albeit now in a more qualified fashion than earlier.

Nassy was writing in a corner of South America, the subcontinent where within a staggeringly short space of time, a mere quarter century, the majority of the world's republics (with nearby Venezuela the first) would soon be situated. But already then, in 1798, he no longer viewed republics as automatically superior to all other forms of government but improvement on what humans had had before only when profound restructuring of institutions and law occur along the right lines. Like all radical enlighteners he had all along rejected the aristocratic republicanism on the British model that so appealed to Adams. He scorned oligarchic Switzerland and had long dismissed the pre-1795 oligarchic Dutch Republic with contempt. He felt the same about all other oligarchic republican models run by narrow and corrupt elites. Venice, controlled by a more formal, legalized nobility than the Dutch and Swiss republics, in his eyes was perfectly dreadful, its citizens even more oppressed, he says, than those of the Ottoman Empire.[59] The United States, very soon to be the model for a great many of the Spanish American revolutionaries,[60] too now looked somewhat disappointing to Nassy, becoming distinctly more oligarchic during the 1790s under the domination of the "Federalist" party than it had been earlier. But what chiefly changed to darken his outlook since 1795–96, we see, were the string of setbacks, of which the Terror in France was the worst, strengthening his conviction that the basic frame of government—oligarchic or democratic republic, constitutionalist or absolute monarchy—in the end is less important for human well-being than levels of awareness, integrity, education and overcoming ignorance that a given society achieves.

Above all, Nassy abominated *Robbespierrisme* and the Terror, and worried more than he had earlier about the anarchic conditions punctuating the different phases of the French Revolution and especially about how changes very much for the worse can be swiftly engineered by demagogues. The root cause of the setbacks the Revolution suffered, the basis of Robespierre's pernicious and detestable tyranny, he did not doubt, were not errors of principle or in the model but exclusively the effects of popular credulity, prejudices and lack of awareness: "the entire nation let itself be subjugated by Robespierre" without understanding at all how he mastered them, without grasping why ignorance and crassness encourage the sprouting up of so many "démagogues ambitieux."[61] Both the French and the "Dutch" Revolution of 1795 revealed for all to see that every revolution's greatest vulnerability are the beliefs and errors of the illiterate untutored mind, a terrible vulnerability as evident in relation to white as to black emancipation. In France, the people were seduced into bowing their heads under the repulsive "yoke of the Jacobins" by a notion of "perfect equality" wholly utopian and impossible.

Nassy was just as opposed to Rousseau's political thought as Furtado or Frey. True "liberty" means following the path of reason, a basic principle of Spinoza and the Radical Enlightenment tradition and the prime basis for its wholesale rejection of Rousseau. "Le bien de la société veut que les citoyens les plus utile à la chose publique, soient les seuls employés au service de l'état, les plus honorés et les plus récompensés." [The well-being of society requires that only the citizens most useful to the public interest are employed in the service of the state, and are the most honored and best recompensed.][62] Like Frey and all radical enlighteners, Nassy rejected outright "pure democracy" in the sense of "direct democracy" of the people. He could not have been more contemptuous of Rousseau's abjuring representation by elected delegates, or Rousseau's and Robespierre's deeming "simple souls" morally superior by virtue of their very ordinariness. To locate true legitimacy in politics in the outlook of ordinary people Nassy considered, rather, a grotesque, terrifying error. In the early stages especially, it cannot be the opinions of ordinary folk that sustain the democratic republic based on the common good because they lack education and receive such ideas as they have from the clergy, or other manipulators which automatically disqualifies them from judging anything correctly. In this way, his outlook remained an unremittingly "Enlightenment" conception: the good of society is upheld only when "reason" and the "common good" are promoted which means led by those most able to grasp them and see how to promote the "common good." Hence, the Revolution's true goals are achieved only where ignorance is pushed back, prejudices curbed and popular thinking elevated by education.

To claim, as one scholar has, that for Nassy "the single positive outcome of the French Revolution was the emancipation of the Jews" and that, apart from that, the Revolution triggered only anarchy, lawlessness and a misconstruing of "equality,"[63] is seriously inaccurate. To argue that, by late 1798, Nassy projected a characteristically American perspective on "revolution," or set up a typically New World perspective against the Old World model offered by the French and Dutch Revolutions, is very much to miss the point. Nassy's revolutionary aspirations extended far more widely than just a quest for Jewish emancipation, as was equally the case with his fellow prominent Jewish revolutionaries striving to end Jewish cultural and social semi-ghettoization in the Dutch and Dutch colonial context, his Jewish allies, Sephardic and Ashkenazic either side of the Atlantic whom he lists as "Bromet, Asser, Lemon and Sasportas," even if he is less than altogether happy with how these fellow revolutionaries conducted themselves in the fight for "la liberté batave" [Dutch liberty].[64] Even if his enthusiasm for it remained alive to an extent, the American Revolution was never a separate or exclusive model for Nassy, any more than for Simon Bolívar (1783–1830), Spanish America's great liberator, who later came to have still greater reservations about the American Revolution in the context of Spanish America and the Caribbean than did Nassy.[65] Nassy grew more cautious and had more reservations regarding the French and Batavian revolutions than Sasportas and Hartog Lémon, but remained no less committed than they to far-reaching revolutionary change either side of the Atlantic based on the joint democratic republican American-French-Batavian model.

At vast cost in money and lives, Britain not only prevented the Revolution spreading during the late 1790s and the first decade of the new century but in part reversed its successes. In 1799, Surinam was overrun by the British. In July 1800, despite French revolutionary troops from Guadeloupe briefly occupying much of Curaçao in the name of the two republics, France and the Netherlands, with some support among Curaçao's slaves (though not much from the whites),[66] the British (with American support) within three months succeeded in ejecting the French and their black troops, and occupying Curaçao too. Slavery was thereby vigorously reaffirmed.[67] The British-occupied Dutch colonies were returned to the Batavian Republic under the short-lived "Peace of Amiens" (1802), but when war between Britain and France (and the Dutch) resumed in 1803, it was not long before the British returned. After a brief battle, they retook Surinam, in May 1804, having by then reoccupied the rest of then Dutch (later British) Guyana—Berbice, Demerara and Essequibo.

Britain faced stiff resistance, however, on attempting to reoccupy Curaçao, in 1804, being opposed by many anti-Orangist Dutch Patriots, Jews and free blacks alike. This opposition delayed Britain's re-occupation of this key Dutch island until 1807. The militia force repelling the British landings on Curaçao between 1804 and 1806 was led by a young merchant, Luis Brión (1782–1821), a fervent republican revolutionary educated in the Netherlands, baptized as a Catholic as a child, but who apparently was, and was universally assumed to be, "a Jew," though the full details of his background remain unclear.[68] With Curaçao again under British control in the years 1807–16, many of the island's whites, certainly including some Jews, remained anti-Orangist republicans at heart and continued looking for subtle ways to oppose the occupation, while also showing a degree of sympathy for the efforts of the nearby Venezuelan insurgents against Spanish royalist rule in 1810–12. Down to 1812, allied to Spain's royalists, Britain successfully blocked French ambition, black emancipation and Jewish emancipation alike throughout the Caribbean except for Haiti and Cayenne. But after Napoleon's catastrophic defeat in Russia, the British government's attitude toward the efforts to topple Spanish rule and the Spanish crown in northern South America, grew more ambiguous.

Where Britain firmly blocked the further advance of the Revolution in the Caribbean, Bourbon Spain, despite initial success in 1812–16, was decidedly less successful in blocking the Revolution in South America. When the temporary victory of the royalists in Venezuela and the fall of the "First Venezuelan Republic," of 1811–12, forced the insurgent leader, Simón Bolívar, to seek temporary refuge on British-occupied Curaçao, in September 1812, the British governor stripped him of his vessels and other assets and possessions on arrival but then refused to have anything further to do with him, despite efforts by sympathizers of the Spanish king to get him tried for treason. The British governor preferred to leave him free to quietly recoup the losses his army had suffered and reorganize his subversion of Spanish colonial rule. Some Curaçao Jews assisted his efforts. Whereas in the Netherlands itself formal Jewish equality was introduced in 1796 and consolidated in subsequent years, in Surinam and Curaçao the same measure remained wholly in abeyance, due to the British occupation, and there it stayed until 1825, while Jews as "Jews," remained officially excluded altogether from residing or trading with neighboring Spanish America.[69] This generated a notable restlessness and resentment among some Caribbean Jews, a factor not without a certain significance for the future of the Revolution in South America. The Spanish crown and Inquisition (with its tribunals in Lima, Cartagena de Indias and Mexico City) remained (as the eloquent Bolívar well knew how to remind his Curaçao hosts), their unforgotten symbolic and ideological enemy.[70]

Bolívar on Curaçao in late 1812, found himself temporarily wholly without means. At a time when he could get no help from anywhere else, he was provided with lodgings by one Curaçao Jew, Abraham de Meza, while another, the lawyer Mordechai Ricardo (1771–1842) from Amsterdam, a cousin of the famous economist, who defended him from local efforts to get him indicted for treason on behalf of the Spanish crown, also lent support in several other ways, among other things placing a striking octagonal observation tower near the seashore, overlooking the harbor, at Willemstad, at his disposal, a building where Bolívar's two sisters were lodged.[71] More importantly, local Curaçao Jews provided the *Libertador* with vessels, money and supplies. Should he ultimately succeed, they undoubtedly hoped for access and rights of settlement in neighboring Venezuela, which indeed they did acquire in the 1820s. At least four Curaçao Jews became senior officers in Bolívar's army, including Benjamin Henriquez (b. 1784), a republican anti-Orangist who served as one of the *Libertador*'s cavalry captains, and Lieutenant-colonel (as he became) Juan (Isaac) de Sola (c. 1795–1859). From 1818, for some years De Sola was a leading editor of the revolutionary newspaper, the *Correo de Orinoco*, which survived until 1822, and remains famous in Venezuela even today, a paper seeking to widen support for the revolution among the local population, published at Bolívar's temporary post-1817 headquarters, at Angostura, deep in the Venezuelan hinterland.[72]

Still more prominent was the aforementioned Luis Brión (1782–1821), a young and fervent republican anti-Orangist who, having shown his revolutionary convictions on Curaçao during the late 1790s and fought the British in Holland, in 1799, sided with the French revolutionary troops and rebellious slaves against the British on Curaçao in 1800, and fought the British again, on Curaçao in 1804–7. He commenced his long-standing support for

Bolívar, in 1812, by putting just a single frigate at his disposal. But over the next nine years, during the first five or six of which Bolívar was still receiving no financial or other support apart from volunteer soldiers from Europe or North America, Brión emerged among the *Libertador*'s most important suppliers and backers financially and militarily. He recruited seamen for the Venezuelan revolutionary cause, at first purely locally, from Haiti, and elsewhere in the Caribbean, and purchased large quantities of arms and munitions investing all his own fortune in the enterprise, apparently never receiving anything much back by way of repayment. He built up a Curaçao-based revolutionary naval force which loyally performed Bolivar's naval and supply operations off the Venezuelan and Colombian coasts, a long, rugged coastline that, by 1817, he largely controlled. Bolívar made him "admiral" of his "navy," and later had him officially appointed commanding admiral of the "Gran Colombian navy."[73] Brión participated in numerous significant strategic discussions with Bolívar.[74]

Later, in 1817, when Bolívar established his base on the Orinoco in eastern Venezuela, at Angostura, it was Brión who commanded the armed river vessels, enabling him to secure strategic control of the river mouth, an estuary vital to Bolívar's securing his then only foothold in Venezuela and the South American mainland, and to Brión's shipping in the North American and British arms and supplies he had purchased on Bolívar's behalf and then transporting them upriver to where they were needed.[75] Later he contributed notably also to Bolívar's conquest of Colombia, and the founding of the "Republic of Gran Colombia" by securing the coastline and the prosperous ports of Riohacha and Santa Marta, a region where loyalty to Spain remained strong but which was vital to Bolívar's strategy and communications.[76]

Brión remained attached to Bolívar's army of liberation for the entire span from 1812 until he died of tuberculosis on Curaçao, in September 1821, soon after Bolívar's greatest triumph, the Battle of Carabobo (24 June 1821), the Spanish crown's most decisive defeat in Spanish America, the battle which secured Bolívar's control of Colombia. After that Bolívar "destroyed the Inquisition," as a contemporary traveler put it, in Colombia, as he had in Venezuela and would soon do in Ecuador. De Sola, now a lieutenant-colonel in the army of "Gran Colombia," fought in the battle of Carabobo and afterwards participated in the storming of the last major Spanish royalist stronghold in Venezuela, Puerto Cabelo, in November 1823, where he was wounded. De Sola was also a prominent participant in the moves, before and after Bolívar's death in 1830, to dissolve the republic of "Gran Colombia" and separate what is now Venezuela from Colombia.[77] It is indeed amazing not that Bolívar's grand republican vision failed but how low his prestige and reputation suddenly fell in all the republics he had created (Venezuela, Colombia, Ecuador, Peru and Bolivia) at the end of his life and in the immediate aftermath of his demise.

Known as "The Jew," the first admiral of two republics, Venezuela and Colombia, Brión was certainly "Jewish" in the eyes of contemporaries. Braving Caribbean storms and shipwreck, and in the end suffering personal ruin in Bolívar's cause, Brión made quite a splash for a time, though by no means all the comment was favorable. When a notorious mutiny of Irish volunteers disrupted Bolívar's hold on Riohacha, in northeast Colombia, in 1820, and Brión intervened to block the mutineers' path on Bolívar's behalf, thwarting a large group of Irishmen, the *Dublin Evening Post* afterwards published a private letter from Jamaica denouncing that despicable "piratical coward, Admiral Brión, formerly a Dutch Curaçao Jew and by birth a haberdasher of that settlement."[78]

Bolívar by contrast was extravagant in his praise. When he learnt of Brión's death in 1821, he wrote from Quito, where he then was, that "all Gran Colombians [i.e., Venezuelans and Colombians] should set up an altar in their hearts dedicated to gratitude to the Admiral. I myself shall be the first to convey to posterity, so far as I can, an eternal memorial to the good that he did to my fatherland, and to his elevated, magnanimous character."[79]

TEN

The Dissident Jews of *Felix Libertate* (1787–1800)

With the outbreak of the French Revolution in 1789, the possibility arose, for the first time, of Jewish entry into European political arena via the new political societies, groups and clubs avowedly dedicated to transforming the political order, ameliorating society, attacking race prejudice, emancipating the non-privileged and rescuing discriminated-against minorities ranging from fringe religious groups to illegitimate children. The trans-Atlantic "General Revolution" opened up fresh opportunities for organizing, intensifying and redoubling the publicity and political pressure for Jewish emancipation and breaking down resilient barriers and the segregation of old.

But the barriers were not so easily dismantled. Jewish sense of solidarity and identity was certainly a matter of choice to a degree. In France, during the Revolution predominantly Jewish districts in several neighborhoods produced predominantly Jewish revolutionary clubs. Not wholly secular and broadly aligned with the general revolutionary culture of the moment, the Bayonne Saint-Esprit district Jacobin club established by two young Jewish traders, Isaac Pereire and Mardochée Lopes Fonseca, added a certain distinctive Jewish twist as did the Metz Jewish quarter—singing the Marseillaise in Hebrew, and throwing in Torah quotes during festivals even whilst celebrating the Supreme Being during Robespierre's ascendancy.[1] There was also, though, often considerable local opposition by the non-Jewish majority to Jewish participation in reading societies and clubs, as at Mainz during the

1792–93 revolution. In the Netherlands, especially Amsterdam, where a substantial Jewish population was concentrated, Jewish revolutionaries had to battle an array of obstacles, tenacious resistance to Jewish integration, Christian and Jewish, rallying around the conservative Orangist faction, existing law, tradition, churches and rabbis.

A particular problem confronting Jewish revolutionaries was that gentile allegiance to the "General Revolution," throughout Europe, frequently signified less than wholehearted support for all its core principles including Jewish emancipation. If support for the Revolution in the Netherlands, for instance, was sometimes ardent, it was more often tepid or half-hearted. Sometimes a selective approach was deliberately adopted by leading thinkers and writers who hesitated to consider the Mendelssohn-Dohm-Diez extension of civil rights to the Jews desirable, or else, like Fichte, though broadly amenable to the Revolution through the 1790s, rejected Jewish equality as such out of hand.[2] Meanwhile, stiff opposition persisted among the traditionalist Jewish majority, the rank-and-file of the communities under rabbinic leadership. While the trans-Atlantic movement to emancipate Jewish life and bestow equal rights on Jews had an electrifying effect throughout the Jewish world, especially among small "enlightened" coteries already intellectually emancipated, as found in Paris, Amsterdam, Berlin, Königsberg, Hamburg, London, Venice, Philadelphia, Paramaribo and the Caribbean, where Jewish intellectual fringes clashing with rabbinic control already existed, strict observance and community leadership, tradition, community institutions and religious orthodoxy everywhere remained a formidable barrier. Whichever aspect one considered—political, religious or philosophical—virtually only radical enlighteners, non-Jewish and Jewish, displayed unqualified enthusiasm during the revolutionary years for comprehensive emancipation of Judaism and the Jews including admittance to public schools, universities, professions and politics.

In cities and regions with sizeable numbers of Jews, support for Radical Enlightenment equality, including Jewish equality, gained momentum but, even where formidable, remained mostly confined to a small, untypical intellectual fringe. Jewish resistance stemmed predominantly from established tradition and religious commitment, but not altogether. There were additional social and institutional pressures. Other factors too bound the Jewish masses to the *parnasim,* rabbis and old elites presiding over synagogue affairs. Only a proportion of Amsterdam Ashkenazic heads of household, for example, were financially fully independent synagogue "members" with corresponding status.[3] Some estimates put full memberships of family heads in Amsterdam as low as two or three thousand.[4] Much of the Dutch *Ashkenazi* main body was so impoverished, that it depended on regular communal aid from community revenues, income partly deriving from the ubiquitous communal monopoly on kosher meat sales. But such poor relief was assigned only on condition of strict, unquestioning conformity to rules set by community elders. Contemporary Jewish society was hence a profoundly differentiated, oligarchic structure, or system of "slavery," as one Jewish revolutionary put it,[5] itself the outcome of restrictive, socially distorting discriminatory *ancien régime* policies. These had been in place for centuries, maintained by Europe's ruling elites, princely courts and "aristocratic" republics, with Amsterdam, papal Rome and the ghettos of Frankfurt, Prague and Venice among the most glaringly stratified and autonomous such entities.

Consequently, realistic appraisal of the direst problems affecting European Jewish life in the 1780s and 1790s could not focus just on the Jews themselves, or rely on gradual or "moderate" solutions. Effective criticism could arise only from a radicalism rejecting the wider social and political status quo and proposing more sweeping change. Jewish communal hierarchy and dependence were, hence, part of the seedbed of the modern "revolutionary Jew" greatly contributing to the magnetic force of the new revolutionary consciousness among those resenting entrapment in such stifling, restrictive structures.[6] Well over half the Jews of Germany, Austria-Bohemia and the Netherlands led economically marginal lives based on petty trade, peddling, secondhand goods, community handouts and thieving. Accordingly, if one contends "Radical Enlightenment" was the sole shaping cause of the upsurge of revolutionary principles in the era 1775–1848, this is not some form of historical "idealism" as some object, but rather predicating a wide array of legal, social and economic conditions prompting social revulsion and resistance, even if response projected first on the level of ideas. *Ancien régime* oligarchic structures were an oppressive social reality that could ultimately be dismantled and replaced only by a process of revolution in thought *and* action. Only as conceptual rejection at all levels of the existing status quo could comprehensive emancipation be envisioned in 1789.

The old, established wealthy Jewish financial elite and community leadership, even where well disposed toward a mild variant of the Enlightenment thinking, found themselves, wherever faced with the rising challenge of revolutionary forces, under mounting pressure to fall back on the bulwark of tradition, rabbinic authority and existing communal and educational institutions. In Germany, Italy and Holland, pressure mounted on Jewish authorities and long-existing institutions also to endorse the anti-revolutionary efforts and armies of the royal and princely courts. Existing Jewish financial and social elites consciously aligned with the royal and aristocratic interest (and the London Stock Exchange, where much of their money was invested) to fight revolutionary and then Napoleonic France. In major communities this circumstance inevitably deepened further and embittered the split between the divergent and soon opposed Jewish Enlightenment streams, moderate versus radical, a phenomenon discernible first, foreshadowing the later more general rift, at Bordeaux, Bayonne, Avignon and Metz.[7]

In the Netherlands, an additional complicating factor was the lingering memory of the bitter clashes of May 1787 in Amsterdam when bands of anti-Orangists roamed Amsterdam, attacking homes of magistrates and others known to back the conservative Orangist cause. This had provoked great anxiety in the Jewish quarter (traditionally Orangist in sympathy), prompting both the Portuguese and Ashkenazic congregation elders to authorize the forming of armed groups of vigilantes, batches of a few dozen men each, to guard synagogues, community buildings and specified private homes deemed at risk including at least one non-Jewish Orangist magistrate.[8] These May clashes were resentfully remembered, in October 1787, when Prussia invaded (with British backing) to thwart the looming victory of the democratic republican "Patriots," overthrow the democrats and restore the House of Orange (and British hegemony). Especially on 11 and 12 October 1787, renewed clashes occurred driven by local Patriot fury at seeing the Jewish leadership and most ordinary Jews applaud the downfall of the Patriots, openly displaying support for Prince, Prussia and Britain. At least one sizeable street fight was provoked by Jews cheering the House of Orange and sporting orange cockades, an unfortunate incident resulting in several dead and injured.

Bad feeling generated by Jewish traditionalist Orangism during the upheavals of 1780–87 lingered on after the founding of the Batavian Republic under French auspices, in 1795. Jewish Orangism remained a significant theme in the publicity and sloganeering of revolutionary clubs avowedly devoted to "freedom" and "equality," such as the Dordrecht society that so angered Nassy by refusing to allow Jews to belong or participate: "the history of Holland in the years 1784–1787," the Dordrechters objected, "discloses their [the Jews'] unpatriotic behavior; for they sided with the Prince of Orange."[9] With the 1795 Batavian Revolution, Jewish Orangist armed guards again tangled in brawls with Patriot demonstrators and looters. On the worst day, 11 October 1797, three Jews and several Patriots were killed.[10] The Patriot leadership in Amsterdam, a city unique at that time in western Europe outside Germany and Italy for having a large proportion of Jewish inhabitants, a proportion higher even than Metz, amounting to over 10 percent of the total, were convinced the Jews, rich and poor alike, defying principle and people, had thrown in their lot with their traditional protector, the Prince and his court, against the pro-French republican revolution.

DUTCH JEWRY DIVIDED

In the new circumstances, from 1795, strict neutrality, Dutch synagogue authorities decided, was their sole viable option. Following meetings with Patriot leaders designed to defuse the local furor, the *parnasim* of the Amsterdam Portuguese and Ashkenazic congregations issued ordinances strictly forbidding Jews to demonstrate, participate in street gatherings or in any way join in the political conflict.[11] Before long, the synagogue elders went a step further, prohibiting Jewish community members, under threat of communal bans, not just from participating in parades and demonstrations for or against the House of Orange, but even from informal small group discussion of the political crisis.

Dutch Jewish radicals hence found themselves clashing head-on with their community's prevailing Orangism, while most of their co-religionists, under rabbinic tutelage, grew steadily more hostile to the revolutionary tide. This further impacted in curious ways on the wider intellectual and political arena, notably broadening the rift between moderate and radical Enlightenment in the Dutch social and cultural spheres. While numerous reading societies and associations dedicated to promoting Enlightenment ideas and amelioration had arisen during the 1770s and 1780s, in provincial cities such as Dordrecht, Groningen, Utrecht and Middelburg besides Amsterdam, The Hague and Haarlem, these mostly reaffirmed their "Christian" character as an amalgam of different Protestant Dissenter elements, laying down what they considered the only desirable and respectable form of Enlightenment. "Christianity" in this way became an affirmed and defined collective red line separating moderate from radical Enlightenment. But while in principle deists, atheists and materialists were all excluded from these local reading and reform clubs too, in practice they were rarely actually shut out as there was no obvious way to identify such persons as non-Christians. More readily identifiable categories contravening the required criteria, however, especially Jews, *were* systematically excluded under explicit written rules enshrined in their constitutions, by the clubs' expressly "Christian" self-conception and credentials.

Amsterdam's most prestigious Enlightenment club, the *Felix Meritis* founded in 1777, like the famous North Holland society *Maatschappij tot Nut van 't Algemeen* [Society for Advancing the General Welfare], founded in 1784, adamantly refused to relent. Their procedures fixed originally by liberal Mennonites and other Protestant Dissenters long rejecting the theology and traditions of the Dutch Reformed Church, indeed all the main churches, nevertheless insisted, like the Freemasons' lodges in Germany and Holland, as Lessing noted derisively, on their "Christian" character, piety and intentions, which, to their way of thinking, meant unbending exclusion of Jews from membership, meetings and activities.[12] Much the same story applied in Groningen, Deventer and other Dutch cities with sizeable Jewish communities. In some cities, such as Utrecht, Leiden and Deventer, exclusion went together with a long-standing, traditional policy on the part of the city governments, still barely breached, to exclude Jews from settling at all within their civic bounds. To rejection by clubs and societies, Jewish enlighteners responded in the only way possible—by setting up their own reading, book lending and debating societies. The first such in Amsterdam, *Concordia crescimus*, established in 1789, despite conducting its debates in Dutch, reaching out to the *Ashkenazim* and stressing the need for Jews to assimilate to contemporary Dutch culture, nevertheless remained largely Sephardic in character.[13]

Moderate Enlightenment was altogether more mainstream, acceptable and entrenched in society than its radical rival Enlightenment tendency. Yet, by 1795, historians estimate at most only around 5 percent of the Dutch people participated in any way in the enlightened culture of clubs and reading societies, or read enlightened texts.[14] The great majority remained immersed in the religious narrowness of the past, showing little understanding or sympathy for the (relatively) more tolerant and broader new attitudes. Ancient animosity toward Jews was further fanned by a growing influx of poor Jewish immigrants from Poland and Germany. In March 1795, following a riot at Kollum blamed locally on "pernicious radicals" and their following, local Frisian judicial authorities identified forty-seven-year-old Salomon Levy, a

German immigrant, as an objectionable intruder organizing subversive agitation and had him executed.[15] Promoting Jewish emancipation in Holland in the 1780s and 1790s, in other words, could only mean adopting a revolutionary attitude and opposing mainstream conventional thinking, hence as being perceived as actively opposed to "Christian values." It was a context bound to intensify anti-Jewish sentiment but also, among Jews, anti-Christian feeling beside hostility to existing judicial structures, religious authority and rabbinic tradition and control.

The 1780s and 1790s thus marked a fundamental divide in modern Jewish history—the commencement of a deepening rift, ceaseless and often bitter, between modern secularism and orthodoxy, a rift later hesitantly bridged by a few compromising trends struggling to devise middle-of-the-road positions of the kind that evolved into nineteenth-century Reform Judaism. The appeal of "philosophy" in Dutch Jewish life, and pressure to adopt broader perspectives, accordingly, grew both stronger and yet more divisive. Jewish radical response injected also an urgent impulse to close the linguistic and cultural gap separating the neighboring but culturally very distinct Sephardic and Ashkenazic milieus. Jewish emancipation and Enlightenment in the Netherlands and its colonies, as in France, Belgium, Italy and Rhineland Germany, in the end had little choice but to become aggressively subversive regarding their own religious traditions as well as prevailing structures of authority and "Christian" attitudes.

In January 1795, following the French invasion over the frozen rivers, the undignified flight of the Prussian and British troops sent to prop up the Stadholder, and the collapse of the Orangist regime, optimism briefly surged among the relatively small group of Dutch Jewish enlighteners eager to participate actively in, and align with the Revolution. Those keen to break with the past and integrate into Dutch society on the basis of universal and equal rights, the revolutionaries, non-Jews and Jews together, could now set the wheels of an effective general and Jewish emancipation in motion.[16] The two great driving principles of the Batavian Republic, created in 1795, after all, were democratic elections for the national legislature and the supposed access of all religious denominations to the political sphere and office on an equal basis.[17]

At this point, several Jewish leaders emerged into the limelight, notably Mozes Salomon Asser (1754–1826), a coffee merchant who had studied law, Herman Leonard (Hartog) Bromet (1724–1812), a former importer of coffee from Surinam with a Sephardic wife, and the high-minded physician Hartog de Hartog Lémon (1755–1823), Dutch Jewry's leading enthusiast for radical ideas and the French Revolution, along with the latter's brother-in-law, Judah Littwak, who had lived in Berlin and known Moses Mendelssohn,[18] and the physician and publisher, also from a highly cultured Ashkenazic family, Joachim van Embden (1741–1826). These enlightened activists had been in contact with each other as committed opponents of the House of Orange for some time, especially during the tense months, in late 1794, just preceding the Orangist regime's collapse. Filled with optimism fired by the French entry into the Netherlands, and the British exit, they helped usher in the Batavian Republic (1795–1806), proceeding politically, intellectually and religiously diametrically against the wishes of the rabbinic and Jewish communal authorities, who remained staunchly pro-Orangist and anti-Patriot in line with their earlier allegiance during the 1780s.

The revolutionary Batavian Republic forged in 1794–95 was supposedly grounded on popular sovereignty, democracy and the principles of the French *Declaration of the Rights of Man and the Citizen*, a text published, slightly modified, in Dutch translation, on 31 January 1795, purportedly as the official creed of the Batavian Revolution.[19] Allied with revolutionary France from the outset, among the fundamental challenges facing the new republic was the issue whether the Jews of the Netherlands and the New World colonies now possessed full civic rights as a consequence, or not. A major practical result would be that Jews, until 1795 officially debarred from living in Utrecht, Haarlem, Leiden, Deventer, Dordrecht and most Dutch towns, having become Dutch citizens would henceforth enjoy the same right as everyone else to live wherever they chose. Equally, Jews would no longer be excluded as "Jews" from key organizations. So at the outset, in January 1795, groups of emancipated Jews applied to join the Amsterdam civic militia, as also the militias of other main towns, and support the Revolution in arms on the basis of equality, citing the principle of universal and equal rights. In Groningen, The Hague and some other places, this was readily accepted, as was Jewish conscription into the hastily reformed Batavian army and navy. But much to their dismay, the Amsterdam emancipationist Jewish pressure group found themselves blocked not just by the militia itself, and the city burgomasters, but also by rabbis and Jewish community authorities unwilling to see the barriers separating Jewish life from the general community dismantled by revolutionary change pushed for by Jewish dissenters.[20]

Besides prejudice and Orangist opposition, a major factor slowing progress of Jewish emancipation in the Netherlands during 1795–96 were the wider divisions and confusion among the political elites, at The Hague, nominally now supporting the Republic, over the Revolution's goals, especially between centralizers and federalists. Of itself, removing Orangists and strict Calvinist orthodox from the scene hardly sufficed to produce an effective working consensus. Rather, general disarray hindered progress toward fundamental reform of whatever kind. Even formal separation of church and state in the Republic, on which all groups other than the Calvinist Orthodox agreed in principle, to end the privileged position the Reformed Church had enjoyed since 1579 as "the public church," failed to be formalized by the new democratically elected *Nationale Vergadering* [National Assembly] until 5 August 1796, over a year and a half into the Revolution.[21]

Most Dutchmen backing the Patriot democratic movement, rejoicing at seeing the British and Prussian troops sent to help the Stadholder beat a hasty retreat, in 1794–95, were shopkeepers, retailers and artisans. They supported the Batavian Revolution but remained largely impervious to the increasingly tolerant attitudes infusing the national legislature and some of the press and clubs. Rather, as those most exposed to increased Jewish competition in business and the crafts, and most resentful of poor Jewish immigrants, they doggedly adhered to their old anti-Jewish (and anti-Catholic) prejudices.[22] Relations were particularly tense in Amsterdam, where Jews remained excluded from nearly all craft guilds. Street brawls and attacks on Jews occurred on 1 April, 18 May, 9 and 25 August and 25 September 1795. From the Amsterdam National Guard, Jews remained officially debarred until 1807.[23]

Delegates to the national legislature hesitating to accord full Jewish equality were readier to agree to compromises and some softening of the exclusions. But such was the nature of revolutionary rhetoric, the terminology of universal rights, and the new Jewish revolutionary consciousness, that qualifying loopholes and let-out clauses diluting "universal and equal rights" were difficult to formulate and stomach. The result was divisive debate feeding deadlock. With moderates opposing democratic radicals and the new Dutch National Assembly at The Hague unable to agree as to whether Dutch Jews should have full citizenship status with voting rights or not, the deadlock became a major political and social controversy punctuated by furious disagreement and clashes of opinion. Meanwhile, throughout the Jewish communities in the Netherlands and its colonies, the trans-Atlantic coterie of Jewish enlighteners, David Nassy prominent among them, stepped up their denunciation of rabbinic authority and community leadership.

For the moment, deadlock meant the restrictions on Jewish residence were retained in practice, and most craft guilds remained closed to Jews. Equally, the traditional system of Jewish communal autonomy over congregants, applying since the early seventeenth century, stayed for now intact. Legally, Jewish residence remained largely confined, as before, to specified towns where organized congregations had long existed, principally Amsterdam with around 23,000 Jews, The Hague, with the second-largest Dutch Jewish community, which would grow to 5,358 by 1840, Rotterdam, the third-largest community with around 2,000 Jews in 1800, Amersfoort and Groningen.[24] The range of towns where Jewish communities, large or small, were found in the Republic had notably increased during the century down to 1795, yet many towns still excluded or stringently restricted Jewish residence. There was no general accepted right to reside, own property or conduct business. During 1795–96 the now expected general right of settlement, with the right to establish synagogues and organized communities, remained still unresolved. This left exclusions in place at Utrecht, 's-Hertogenbosch, Gouda, Maastricht, Tilburg and briefly also Deventer, where the first modern synagogue was established only in 1798.[25]

In 1777, 's-Hertogenbosch, in Dutch Brabant, had refused citizen status [the *burgerrecht*] to Hartog Simon, a German Jew tenacious in attempting to secure this privilege.[26] Under the new republican order, from 1795, in theory such discrimination violated the Republic's declared principles and lapsed. But, after long deliberation, the city council again refused Hartog Simon and generally debarred Jewish residence and business activity in the city, emboldened by the strength of local "Christian" sentiment. The citizenry, the local debate, of May 1795, reveals, were convinced Jews ply their trade and peddling deceitfully using unfair and underhand methods that would damage local shopkeepers and the whole populace. Even admitting a single family, like that of Simon, was considered inadvisable, "a bridge over which probably a whole army of 'Israelieten'" would plague the town.[27] Real change in Jewish status, it turned out, was impossible without wider revolutionary change effectively curbing local civic and ecclesiastical as well as Jewish autonomy.

For the present, Jewish status and rights in the Netherlands and the Dutch colonies remained highly uncertain and unstable, as well as detached from the main political clubs, movements and institutions. The sole unifying thread effectively linking the Jewish communities were religious institutions and a social hierarchy whose pattern, structure and authority was authorized, where such congregations were permitted, by local civic authorities. Consequently, the coterie of Jewish enlighteners, those most scandalized and disgruntled by the failure to move more rapidly toward comprehensive emancipation, and by the rabbis' and communal authorities' resistance to their efforts, found themselves at odds with the entire existing Dutch legal, administrative and institutional system, as well as Jewish tradition.[28] Shocked and frustrated by the political, legal and psychological deadlock in both the European and colonial contexts, Nassy was increasingly angered by what to him was disgraceful, hypocritical backsliding from the Revolution.[29] Activist and radical Jewish leadership in both the New World colonies and the Netherlands were bitterly disillusioned that Jews were still prevented from serving in the Amsterdam civic militia as they served in the North American state militias, and in Paris since 1791–92, and that the principal reading societies, even the new "Patriotic" clubs, continued excluding Jews from their ranks.[30]

ORGANIZING THE PRO-REVOLUTION JEWISH BLOC

Rabbis and elders did not want traditional barriers separating Jewish life from the general community removed.[31] In 1795–96, in flat contradiction to the French revolutionary principles of 1789, enlightened Dutch Jews found themselves still expressly excluded from all formal political participation and the political clubs. Having no alternative, a clique of aggrieved enlightened activists established their own separate Jewish revolutionary club and enlightened forum, *Felix Libertate* [happy by means of Liberty], in Amsterdam, on 6 February 1795. This combined Sephardic-Ashkenazic Jewish counterpart to "Christian" *Felix Meritis* was dedicated to exerting political and cultural pressure in support of Jewish emancipation.[32] Proclaiming their equal right to existence, happiness, schooling, participation and prosperity, it aimed to integrate the Jews into the rest of society and fundamentally transform Jewish life by securing full civil rights including unrestricted access to the professions, militias and all academic and public positions. An offshoot society with similar goals was established in Rotterdam, in 1797, with, as one of its leading members, Leonard (Levie) Salomon Davids (1771–1820), municipal physician to the poor since 1793, among the pioneers of vaccination in the Netherlands. Davids had clashed with the local rabbinate ever since his student days, when he was stigmatized and fined by the Rotterdam Jewish congregation, in 1788, for attending a theater performance on the Jewish Sabbath.[33]

Proclaiming the *Declaration of the Rights of Man and the Citizen* its core revolutionary creed, *Felix Libertate* had Asser, Bromet and Hartog Lémon as its chief spokesmen, the last being its secretary. Strikingly, the club had a marked Ashkenazi majority of over two-thirds of its sixty-five to seventy members.[34] Confronting prejudice (Dutch and Jewish), and aiming to instil patriotic, egalitarian, revolutionary virtue into traditional Jewish minds, the club tried also to enlist the help of non-Jews in its quest for full Jewish emancipation, but very few non-Jews joined. Prominent, initially, was a certain Jacob Sasportas; but he and others of the Sephardic minority stayed only briefly, disagreeing with Asser and Hartog Lémon about the society's objectives. Sasportas urged political and juridical equality only without wanting to mobilize the Revolution and its political rhetoric to reform Jewish society itself, change its general character or seek to mitigate the Jewish masses' economic plight.[35]

Daunted by the radical tide, Amsterdam's established Jewish community elite grew apprehensive and, at this point, several wealthy Dutch Sephardim migrated to Hamburg and London to escape the Revolution. The *parnasim*, even though firmly forced onto the defensive, obliged to moderate their rhetoric and more and more endeavour to avoid trouble and minimize friction with the new regime, still refused to abandon their traditionally Orangist stance. Under their ordinance of 20 January 1795, combining caution and alarm, the community elders redoubled their insistence on forbidding Jewish community members to gather in groups in the streets, parade or discuss politics. The advent of *Felix Libertate* on the scene inevitably meant escalation and intensification of the now divisive ideological war within the community over rabbinic authority, freedom of expression, human rights, education and the principle of equality.[36]

Felix Libertate acquired its own building and meeting hall, and set to work to exert political and cultural pressure within and outside the Jewish community for attainment of its emancipationist goals. The club demanded full religious toleration on a broader, more equal basis than before, the overcoming of the "hydra of prejudice," removal of all disabilities and comprehensive equality of legal status, including equal rights of residence and bringing the Jews into the artisan crafts and the professions which together meant transforming the whole character of Dutch Jewish existence. Equally, its leadership aimed to reform Jewish communal institutions and education using as their tool the secularizing and soon openly republican state. For Jews, this agenda became an essential component of the "General Revolution," the summons to transform mankind on the basis of republicanism, democracy and equality issuing from the French National Assembly in 1792–93.[37]

Among *Felix Libertate*'s opening revolutionary moves was having the French 1789 *Declaration of Rights of Man* translated into Yiddish and Portuguese. They then petitioned the Amsterdam city government's new revolutionary standing committee to compel the *parnasim* to have these declarations read out to the entire Jewish community in synagogue. The city's steering committee agreed to this, producing a directive to the *parnasim* that provoked bitter opposition in both the Ashkenazic and Portuguese congregations.[38] Even the stated principle of individual freedom of conscience and practice in religious matters posed a direct challenge to rabbinic authority and the community elders, who, much like the Protestant pastors and heads of the Catholic hierarchy, flatly denied that individuals possess any right to follow their own consciences in matters of belief and religious observance or freedom to criticize religious authority. Nor should Jews be seeking to integrate into any existing state here and now when they were praying for a messianic return to their own state in the Holy Land. A tussle ensued in The Hague and Rotterdam as well as Amsterdam in which the *parnasim* eventually triumphed, first by reminding the Amsterdam city government that no other church or religious sect was similarly required to read out such a declaration to their congregations and, secondly, by collecting signatures of congregants for a petition requesting exemption from the *Felix Libertate* inspired directive. More than six hundred adult male members of the Amsterdam community signed the petition demanding the city government release the congregations from the obligation to proclaim the *Declaration of the Rights of Man* in synagogue, though many of these, according to the reformers, were "ignorant bumpkins" unable to read.[39]

Felix Libertate retaliated, on 26 March 1795, by plastering the streets of Amsterdam's Jewish quarter and the synagogue doors with posters in Yiddish and Dutch denouncing the *parnasim* for obscurantism and anti-Enlightenment reactionary attitudes. Yiddish, significantly, remained still heavily dominant amongst the Ashkenazic community, full fluency, even adequacy, in spoken and written Dutch remaining fairly infrequent among Jews—a potent factor and perhaps the principal one for the still considerable, albeit not unbridgeable, cultural distance, the striking lack of mutual sympathy and understanding, observers noted, dividing Amsterdam's Jewish and Christian populations.[40]

Under the changed circumstances, it proved impossible, though, for *parnasim* and rabbis to long keep up a united front against universal rights and the Revolution. A few religious leaders, most notably the remarkable Rabbi Yizhak Graanboom (1739–1807), belonging to a Swedish, originally non-Jewish, family that had moved to Amsterdam in 1749 (to convert to Judaism), eventually, in March 1797, broke away, contributing to the evolving ideological-religious schism by helping set up a new pro-Revolution (slightly) reformed congregation.[41] This *Naye Kille* [New Community], a Dutch-language joint Ashkenazic-Sephardic pro-Revolution synagogue set up in Amsterdam, known subsequently as *Adath Jesurun* [Community of Righteousness], inaugurated with Hartog Lémon as president on 23 June 1797, was linked from the outset to *Felix Libertate* and shared its creed.[42] The *Naye Kille* constituted a complete new Jewish community with its own separate cemetery and rival kosher meat hall, although there was considerable delay before the city government permitted it to publicly announce and organize separate religious services, the burgomasters worrying lest the widening schism exacerbate the public wrangling among Jews and foment still greater disarray and disturbance. Although Rabbi Graanboom introduced shortened services and a few other changes to liturgy and synagogue ritual, these were limited in character. But the new community severed all links with the old congregations, fostering a quite distinct intellectual and social orientation. It was this, one presumes, rather than the minor departures from established Jewish tradition and observance, that moved Jewish traditionalists to denounce Rabbi Graanboom as a despicable "convert" and the "red-bearded priest."

In their early efforts, *Felix Libertate*'s delegates in The Hague, Asser and Bromet, despite the backing of prominent radical enlighteners and enthusiasts for French Revolution principles like Gerrit Paape, suffered only setbacks. During 1795, "moderates" managed to get Jewish spokesmen excluded from participation in high-level National Assembly discussion and key decision-making on the grounds they represented a "Jewish club."[43] Still, declaring the Jews the "unhappiest part" of Dutch society, "trapped, oppressed and scorned," *Felix Libertate* exerted enough impact to set in motion the process that eventually did produce the long-awaited decree of emancipation declaring Dutch Jews to be citizens on the same basis as the Republic's other citizens, ending the city governments' oversight over Jewish life, residence and congregational institutions.[44] The society demanded in the name of the Jews of the Netherlands a decree modeled on that of the French National Assembly expressly ruling that no Jew "should be excluded from any rights or privileges set out under the Batavian *Burgerrecht*" [civil rights code]. Still, it took over a year and a half from the Batavian Republic's founding for their petition to be formally presented in the new National Assembly, by *Felix Libertate*'s spokesman, Asser. Presented in August 1796, the proposal prompted further divisive debate and resistance in the legislature, and from most rabbis and churches. Despite majority Dutch and Dutch Jewish opinion being opposed, it passed unanimously in the end, in early September, mainly owing to a reinforcing boost given by the French minister at The Hague, François Noël.[45]

On paper, *Felix Libertate* succeeded, but only owing to heavy pressure from revolutionary France without which Dutch Jewish emancipation would probably not have materialized at this point even in theory. Jewish emancipation had by this time been vigorously propagated in the French revolutionary press for over five years, and in the press of all France's republican satellite states. Espoused by revolutionaries in Belgium and the Rhineland earlier, Jewish emancipation was integral also to the 1796–97 revolutionary campaigns under Napoleon—then still presenting himself as a republican leader—in northern Italy. Nevertheless, it faced continued stiff opposition throughout Europe's revolutionary zone, both town and country folk frequently resenting the prospect of Jewish entry into retailing and the professions on the same basis as everyone else.

The Batavian Republic's 2 September 1796 decree, "On the equality of the Jews with all other citizens," in theory conferred full legal equality and citizenship rights on Dutch Jewry. Yet, still there persisted a yawning gap between theory and practice. For many members of the National Assembly, the decree was a half-hearted concession to the logic of the Revolution internationally, made under pressure in parallel with developments in France, the Rhineland and Italy. The network of democratic revolutionary republics created during the late 1790s in the Italian peninsula, the so-called *Triennio giacobino* (1796–99), certainly brought about the immediate de-ghettoization of the Jews of Venice, Mantua, Ancona and the other Italian communities, extending in 1798 even to papal Rome where for centuries the Jews had been shut in, degraded more humiliatingly than anywhere else. The revolutionary shift meant real moves toward lifting the restrictions of the past, bringing Jewish emancipation in one fell swoop, in 1796–98 not just to Italy and Holland but also, in 1797–99 to the Jews of Corfu, the other Greek Ionian Islands, Malta and then Egypt under French occupation during 1798–1801.[46]

After 1800, during the new century's opening decade, Jewish emancipation gained impressive added impetus, especially from 1808, due to the policies of Napoleon and his brothers, Joseph, Louis and Jérôme, after their installation as kings of Spain, Holland and Westphalia respectively. Despite retreating steadily from republican ideology, after Brumaire (9 November 1799), Napoleon and his brothers still pressed on with their program of dismantling the ghettos, ending separate Jewish education, removing discriminatory bars and ending Jewish disabilities, seeking to integrate the Jewish communities into state, society and the armed forces on an equal footing with the rest.

Yet, at the same time, this dramatic, impressive progress lent additional tools to those mobilizing prejudice and hatred, helping incite the lurking, sporadically resurgent counter-revolution never far below the surface. During 1799, anti-Jewish demonstrations and incidents provoked by a furious *popolaccio*, a mix of artisans, shopkeepers, peasants and many others, occurred in Rome, Verona, Modena and numerous other places in Italy. In the Arezzo region of eastern Tuscany, in May 1799, erupted a particularly fierce rebellion of fervent faith, the "Army of 'Viva Maria!,'" fiercely anti-French and pro-Austrian, which succeeded in capturing Siena in late June. On 28 June, led by a priest, Giuseppe Romanelli, holding aloft the miraculous image of the "Madonna del Conforto," sworn to put faith above everything, the crowds massacred several French, pillaged the ghetto and synagogue, and finally burned alive three Jews and a French soldier in Siena's great square, the Piazza del Campo. "*Furor populi, furor Dei*!" [The fury of the people (is) the fury of God], the bishop, Monsignor Zondadari, reportedly shrugged when declining to intervene.[47] There was a powerful backlash against the Jews, even more than against the French, likewise on Corfu.[48]

From early 1795 until June 1798, radical ideas noticeably gained ground in the Low Countries, Germany and Italy in parallel with the French Republic's military advances; yet, Dutch Jewish access to their accorded rights hardly did. In the Netherlands, there was as much or more opposition behind the scenes to removing long-standing barriers and prejudice and turning emancipation theory into practical reality, as compliance. The 1796 emancipation decree officially placed Dutch Jews on the same basis, providing the same freedoms as were enjoyed by the rest of society, stating unambiguously that "no Jew shall be excluded from any of the rights or privileges accruing under the Batavian *Burgerrecht*."[49] But in the immediate aftermath, between 1796 and 1798, tenacious continuing local opposition, popular and theological especially, but also Jewish, greatly impeded these sweeping provisions' implementation.[50] If Dutch Jews were now equal in constitutional law, in terms of status, education, the professions, shopkeeping and holding public office, they remained, at the local level particularly, a largely separate and discriminated-against segment of society.

This applied not least to Jewish status in Dutch "enlightenment" societies. The proposal to admit Jews to Amsterdam's *Felix Meritis*, moved in March 1798, aroused Holland's enlightened "moderates" and was overwhelmingly rebuffed.[51] Residual cultural and mental "ghettoization" remained starkly obvious in the political clubs as in the reading societies prominent in the Netherlands at the close of the eighteenth century and advent of the nineteenth. Meanwhile, the revolutionary secessionist congregation at Amsterdam conspicuously failed to detach the Jewish masses from their loyalty to the old congregations and the *parnasim*. In October 1798, a few months after their Dutch-language breakaway synagogue adopted its revised community laws (March 1798), *Adath Jesurun* informed the Amsterdam city government that its membership had now risen to 105 families, totaling 445 persons. The new initiative thus achieved some success at the communal level but conspicuously failed to win the support of the pious majority. At this point, the Old Ashkenazic community counted around 21,000 souls, equivalent to over two-thirds of Italy's entire Jewish population of 30,000.[52]

Deference to religious authority stood firm. An additional obstacle, noted by Asser, was that Holland's wealthiest Jews often kept most of their riches deposited in English banks, stocks and funds which of itself guaranteed Jewish social elite loyalty to Britain and a resolutely pro-Orangist, pro-aristocratic and anti-Revolution stance.[53] Defection to *Adath Jesurun* from the *Oude Gemeente* [Old Community] was further discouraged by constant admonitions of the *parnasim,* or domineering "enslavers" as Hartog Lémon called them, warning those severing themselves from the traditional community they would face multiple sanctions. Defecting pro-Revolution dissidents had their names recorded on a special list of "infamy" kept within a "cage" adjoining the main Amsterdam Ashkenazic synagogue. Strikingly, even though the bulk of Dutch Jewry had an economic interest largely at odds with that of the community's financial elite, especially as regards opening up retailing, crafts and the professions to Jews, potentially a massive gain for a largely impoverished population, this nevertheless exerted less weight on

Jewish opinion, or at least appeared to, than obedience to communal authority and old-style messianic hope. This was partly due, of course, to the Jewish masses' continuing limited ability to read vernacular languages other than Yiddish, Spanish and Portuguese and consequent inability fully to keep up with political news and debates. If Orangism and tradition stayed embedded in the communal mentality, adequate reading knowledge of French or Dutch remained rare among the poorer segments. Hartog Lémon who as the Old Community "poor relief" physician (*armendoktor*)—a position of which the Old Community now relieved him—had a detailed knowledge of the misery, distress and illnesses of Amsterdam's Jewish poor, was exceptional in constantly emphasizing the eventual economic benefits that would accrue to the less well-off from the revolutionary institutionalization of equality he so passionately advocated.[54]

Marginal status in terms of numbers and mass support did not deter the *Naye Kille* from persevering with its propaganda war against old-style rabbis and unreformed Judaism, among other methods producing challenging pamphlets expounding democratic republican and universal rights principles in Dutch and also German, not just for recent and not so new arrivals from central Europe but deliberately deploying German as a principal international language, together with French, as the prime language of Jewish Enlightenment debate, of Mendelssohn and the Jewish *Aufklärung*.[55] Yiddish, though, remained indispensable too. During the July 1797 election campaign for the Second National Assembly, preceding the first democratic elections in which Dutch Jews ever participated as voters and candidates, held on 1 August, *Adath Jesurun* stepped up its journalistic efforts against the "Old Community," assailing the *parnasim* as reprehensible allies of Britain, aristocracy and monarchy, and spreading radical notions among the Jewish majority in Yiddish, as Ashkenazic enlighteners with less challenging new ideas had done earlier, even though Dutch *maskilim* wanted Holland's Jews to forsake Yiddish and adopt Dutch, the language of their country, as their everyday tongue.[56]

Especially noteworthy in the revolutionary campaign in Yiddish was a series of twenty-four folksy *Diskursen* [dialogues] printed cheaply on rough paper and brimming with satirical and humorous remarks, including some decidedly coarse invective (answering equally coarse orthodox polemics against Graanboom and Hartog Lémon). Thanks to the Revolution, public offices, crafts, retailing and the professions, the Yiddish-reading poor were assured, would soon be opened to Jews, after centuries of repression, which meant opportunities for earning one's livelihood would burgeon. The first of the new congregation's popular Yiddish *Diskursen*, immediately preceding and linked to the 1 August 1797 elections, was entitled *Diskurs gehalten tvishn yehudem in shif fun Itert nakh Amsterdam* [Discourse Held between Jews on a Boat between Utrecht and Amsterdam]. Decrying the Old Community leadership's despotic character while placing Asser, Bromet and Hartog Lémon in a venerable light, it made great play of the issue of which community kosher butchers provided the cheapest meat and which of the communities' rival suppliers was the more strictly *kosher*.[57]

Crucial was the fight to abolish social hierarchy within. The community elders were accused of co-opting themselves to preside over Jewish life, choosing only from among their circle without the larger community having any say in selecting *parnasim*.[58] In the *Naye Kille* "at the calling up [to the reading of the Torah, in synagogue] no difference is made between rich and poor. Who has heard of any special pew for *parnasim*?"[59] But for many Ashkenazim it remained a reprehensible feature of the New Jewish Community that Dutch was used in synagogue for communal announcements and as the language of instruction in its notoriously reform-minded school. Both were intended as main tools for integrating Amsterdam Jewry into Dutch society and instilling patriotic ideas and a secular conception of "virtue" proclaimed common to Jews and Christians alike.[60] Adoption of Dutch was in every way basic to the *Naye Kille*'s strategy, being the language of politics, integration into society and higher education. Yet, Yiddish too remained crucial as the chief language of the less educated, impoverished and marginalized. Many read and some were influenced by these pro-Revolution Yiddish tracts; many Jews participated for the first time in the 1797 elections for the *Nationale Vergadering*, in which two prominent Jewish reformers, Bromet and Hartog Lémon, succeeded, despite the opposition of many Jewish orthodox, in getting elected as "national" delegates representing Amsterdam in the legislature while a third Jew, M. Moresco, became the first Jew ever elected to the Amsterdam city government. It was a resounding success for the secessionists, a landmark especially significant on an international level since Hartog Lémon and Bromet were the first two Jews ever elected to any national representative political assembly anywhere in Europe.[61]

Progress was slow and arduous. Bromet and Hartog Lémon strove to advance the fortunes of the radical democratic republican faction in The Hague and rally Jewish support behind it. But Jewish conservatives, deploying their own Yiddish pamphlets, had considerable success in outflanking charges of domineering, despotic oligarchy instilling "prejudices" by highlighting the secessionists' drifting from strict religious observance and accusing them of violating the Sabbath and *kashruth* [Jewish food law], of opening the door to libertinism and mixed marriages. All this was deeply disillusioning for ardent Jewish revolutionaries, the most earnest and energetic in pursuing the Revolution's goals remaining throughout Asser, Bromet and Hartog Lémon, the latter a political activist whose outlook was particularly rooted in Enlightenment thought. Reading German, English and French besides Dutch, steeped in the thought-world of Lessing and Mendelssohn, having lived for a time in Germany at Emden,[62] he was well aware the Dutch were failing to live up to their own principles, that most of the revolutionary rhetoric flooding The Hague was little more than hot air. "Since the French Revolution and since that of 1795," he averred pessimistically, speaking before the *Nationale Vergadering*, in November 1797, "I have got to know so many 'friends of the people' who make a great show of support for the people, love of the people, and pure *Patriottisme* but who, when better acquainted with, prove to mean by this nothing but their personal interest, that I am not amazed by anything anymore."[63]

Brimming with genuine revolutionary ardor, Hartog Lémon was directly complicit in the radical conspiracy at The Hague leading to the French-backed *coup d'état* of 22 January 1798, headed by the Dutch "Patriot" general Herman Willem Daendels (1762–1818).[64] *Adath Jesurun* was virtually the only religious organization in the entire Netherlands immediately and publicly to endorse the 1798 radical republican regime and its revolutionary initiatives with enthusiasm, the breakaway Amsterdam synagogue issuing an announcement signed by Asser, five days afterwards, publicly proclaiming the oath its leaders had taken in synagogue in support of the new regime and vowing "inexorable aversion to the Stadholdership, aristocracy and feudalism."[65] Briefly, the 1798 coup meant closer alignment between revolutionary France and Holland, opening the door to more vigorous measures implying among much else, an immediate positive impact on Jewish rights and by no means only at Amsterdam and The Hague. Following the radical *coup* of January 1798, Jewish radicals for a short time gained the upper hand in their fight with Jewish orthodoxy. Many changes followed, including, in February 1798, that Hartog Simon finally won his citizenship at 's-Hertogenbosch.

Holland's Jewish revolutionaries, armed with enhanced leverage at The Hague, dominated the Jewish scene for the interim and secured the dismissal of the old *parnasim,* replacing them with members of the Old Community considered less antagonistic to Graanboom, the new congregation, and to *Felix Libertate* and its principles. But in Dutch society below the level of the radical vanguard, opposition to revolutionary radicalism had now acquired yet another reason for viewing the Jews with aversion. In ensuing months, in several places, this produced confrontations with Jews being specially targeted by conservatives as treacherous militants backing French interference, subverting "Christian values," and disloyal to the House of Orange which was supposedly loved by all true Dutchmen. Increased antagonism to Jews during 1795–98 was paralleled by a similar increase in anti-Catholic sentiment in the Netherlands likewise stoked by removal of formal barriers to inclusion and incipient emancipation.[66]

The victory of revolutionary principle and universal and equal rights in the Netherlands proved short-lived. Only half a year later, the pro-French radical faction, whose support base was always narrow, were ousted in their turn by the "moderate" coup of June 1798. Hartog Lémon was among the prominent revolutionaries arrested and imprisoned, but only very briefly.[67] From June, adherence to revolutionary principle and "universal and equal rights" were once more thrust aside and the Jewish national representatives at The Hague and the Jewish representative on the Amsterdam city government, soon again removed from the scene. Although Moresco was briefly followed by another Jew, Isaac da Costa, there were subsequently no more Jewish members of the Amsterdam city government prior to the establishment of the modern Dutch monarchy, in 1813. Given the size of Amsterdam's Jewish population, approaching 11 percent of the city's population, for sympathizers this was a conspicuous, ugly anomaly: during the entire revolutionary period in the Netherlands, from 1795 to 1813, a combined total of no fewer than 254 representatives were elected to, and served on, the Amsterdam city council of whom only two, or well under half of 1 percent, were Jewish in the city with the highest proportion of Jewish population of any major city in western Europe![68] The Republic's Jews, like the Catholic segment, were unceremoniously pushed back at this juncture into a humiliatingly subordinate position lacking all representation at national level and deprived of many of the rights to which they were now nominally entitled.

Attempts were made by various community leaders to soften and negotiate an end to the nagging, festering schism dividing Dutch Jewish society and attitudes. But this too proved difficult to achieve. The schism simply dragged on unresolved. The Amsterdam of 1800 and following years, consequently, continued to exhibit three culturally and educationally quite separate Jewish community organizations—the Portuguese, Ashkenazic and the *Adath* with the community overall deeply split between conflicting, irreconcilable political and social ideologies.

ELEVEN

Napoleon and the Jews (1796–1815)

Napoleon, having conquered Italy while still presenting himself as a republican general, from 1799 not only conquered much of western, central and east-central Europe as France's autocratic "First Consul," and from 1804, as "Emperor of the French," but also engineered decisive changes in Europe's political, administrative and legal framework, of which some aspects were never subsequently reversed. He and his (often underestimated) brothers made the most of their opportunity to sweep away the debris of the past, setting about the task with gusto. Under the Napoleonic code of law and government, merit and efficiency were the overriding criteria for choosing men for positions of rank, responsibility and influence, and sole path to meaningful reform. The Bonaparte Brothers were the last great "enlightened despots."

To the Bonaparte Brothers few things mattered less in the wider scheme of things than religious allegiance. In the Netherlands, Belgium, Italy, Germany and France itself, it was under the Napoleonic regime that Jews for the first time began to be appointed more than transitorily to positions of responsibility and influence, acquired the right to settle wherever and however they wished, and, for the first time in European history, enter the legal, medical and military professions in significant numbers. For all these reasons, for Europe as a whole, the twenty-year Napoleonic hegemony proved one of the most decisive turning points in modern Jewish history, effectively shattering the social, cultural and educational mold of the past.

Napoleon's sweeping re-organization of the European state system, especially the German Empire, during 1803–6 transformed the political map and provided the essential frame for many of the far-reaching reforms that ensued. Numerous former *ancien régime* principalities and republics were eliminated altogether: all German ecclesiastical states, which by the eighteenth century often had somewhat larger Jewish minorities than the non-ecclesiastical states, disappeared except for the electorate of Mainz which meant that nearly all their Jewish populations were now under new territorial princes. Of the fifty-one Imperial Free Cities of the German Empire before 1800, only six survived in 1806, and, of these, only four still figured in Restoration Europe, after 1815. The four largest German states after Austria and Prussia—Bavaria, Württemberg, Baden and eventually Saxony—were all expanded and raised to the status of kingdoms, converted into separate sovereignties for the moment entirely non-dependent on Prussia and Austria, under the French emperor's "protection" for as long as Napoleon's hegemony lasted. In principle, all the German states, large and small, were freed from ties to the Austrian Habsburg ruler, who, in August 1806, Napoleon compelled to abandon the ancient title of "Holy Roman Emperor."[1]

Under the new German framework—the so-called "Confederation of the Rhine," established on 17 July 1806, from which Austria and Prussia were excluded—sixteen confirmed, newly enlarged western, southern and central German states formed a loose pro-French confederacy headed by Bavaria, Württemberg, Baden and Hesse-Darmstadt. Not without reason, even if the extent of rationalizing actually implemented has sometimes been exaggerated, Napoleon was justly styled by some German reformers, educationalists and administrators as "the regenerator" of Germany much as he was by their Italian, Dutch and Spanish counterparts. Politically, Napoleon created a large and vigorous "Third Germany," a bloc designed to function as a counterweight to Austria and Prussia in central Europe and ensure French mastery overall, constituting an effective alliance of middle-sized states sufficiently well-organized to raise substantial armies and financial contributions. Meanwhile, Germany's western edge, the Rhineland, was directly incorporated into Napoleon's French Empire while a separate, middle-sized northwestern segment, misleadingly named the "Kingdom of Westphalia"—in practice comprising less of Westphalia than territory absorbed from the former duchy of

Brunswick-Lüneburg, Hesse-Cassel and from Prussia's western fringe hived off under the Peace of Tilsit (1807)—formed an entirely new and artificial "kingdom" ruled by Napoleon's youngest brother, Jérôme (1784–1880). Planned as a model "kingdom" of two million inhabitants, the first German state ever to possess a modern published constitution, based on the latest administrative concepts and the principle of equality, it survived for six years (1807–13).[2]

Annexation of the Rhineland, the new "kingdom of Westphalia" and emergence of the other new kingdoms meant massive administrative, social and legal adjustments, more substantial than any attempted pre-1789 "enlightened" improvements. The same applies to the new order introduced in Belgium from 1792, Italy from 1796, and in Spain by Napoleon's brother Joseph Bonaparte (1768–1844), from 1808. Despite the immensity of these changes, historical accounts, influenced by the demands and pressures of "national" history, often suggest that pre-1789 and post-1815 German princely rule, sanctioned by Britain and the conservative powers fighting Napoleon, was somehow more legitimate, "national" and authentic than the highly artificial, imposed Napoleonic order. As a result, the traditional historiography is prone to frown on and understate how extensive, modernizing and fundamental the changes actually were and how profoundly many aspects of life were altered, if not always then often for the better. In Jewish history, the changes represent a basic divide and crucial acceleration of the secularizing and enlightening process in motion since the mid-eighteenth century. At the time, Jewish opinion was deeply divided, but the more progressive-minded tended to view Napoleon (even after the so-called "infamous laws" of 1808), as a kind of secular savior, a true *Helek Tov* ["good part," or Bonaparte, in Hebrew].

Germany outside Prussia became a new kind of society. Before 1800, Germany was a hierarchical, profoundly stratified society built on privilege and specific rights with a powerful nobility largely exempt from taxation consisting of highly confessionalized states where, invariably, either Lutheranism, Calvinism or Catholicism locally predominated as the official confession of state. Everywhere, Jews stood out as the most oppressed and marginalized of a vast array of legally subordinated and discriminated-against religious minorities ranging from Mennonites to Moravian Brethren and Polish Socinians, and in Hamburg even Quakers. Law and institutions everywhere radiated *ancien régime* social hierarchy, parading the subservience of the main body of society to joint princely, noble and ecclesiastical dominance. Even if the chief motive for the Napoleonic transformation was resolve to ensure smoother, easier administration, communication and French military control, many dividing lines and debarments cementing the old pre-1789 German fragmentation and princely confessional mosaic vanished in breathtakingly rapid succession. Noble and civic privileges, church authority and "rights," ecclesiastical control of high schools, colleges and universities, many guild restrictions, and numerous key fortress complexes within and around Germany designed to fortify interior and exterior borders, including Breslau (Wroclaw), where the famously formidable town fortifications were blown up as soon as the French seized the city, in January 1807,[3] permanently disappeared, clearing a host of barriers.

Distributing a mass of ecclesiastical lands to a drastically reduced number of politically and territorially enhanced secular princes (mostly with their avid collusion) amounted to a much larger transfer of power, resources and cultural assets than incorporation of the fertile, thickly populated Rhenish west bank with its 800,000 inhabitants into France. Indeed, nothing counted more in sweeping away Germany's old fragmentation into rigidly separate confessional blocs than Napoleon's abolition of the ecclesiastical states. Transfer of former ecclesiastical lands from prince-bishops and abbots involved no fewer than two and one-third million inhabitants along with huge quantities of monastic and other ecclesiastical buildings, books and other property to the new secular entities, thereby strengthening these and putting an end to local church dominance where it had existed since the early Middle Ages.[4] In this wide-ranging reorganization, the simultaneously political, religious, cultural and social liquidation of Germany's ecclesiastical states, all the major German secular states, including Austria, were to a greater or lesser degree complicit.

Deep confessional divides remained but were fundamentally transformed. Instead of a vast patchwork of contrasting spiritual hegemonies with one of the three main confessions (Lutheran, Calvinist and Catholic) subordinating the rest, the entire patchwork of confessional fragments gave way to larger multi-confessional states based on an imposed toleration. Religion was suddenly reduced to being chiefly a private matter of limited concern to prince, city governments or judiciary, beyond a residual role in education and poor relief. All confessions, Protestants, Catholics, deists and Jews, now found themselves administered by state employees and representatives in much the same way throughout, a confessional revolution of incalculable implications. In much of the country, all formal legal disabilities and discrimination relating to Jews swiftly disappeared in theory, though in practice the old restrictions actually receded, as it has been aptly put, "in direct proportion to the degree of French control."[5]

On the Rhenish left bank, directly annexed to France, the transformation was especially far-reaching. Where prior to 1792 a small enlightened Jewish fringe, often in conflict with Jewish community authorities, urged reform in their capacity as individual petitioners or writers, or as reading circles, now, as in France, Jewish community organization was absorbed into the fabric of the Napoleonic state: as a result, individuals gained access to an array of new career opportunities and whole communities benefited as expanded scope for Jewish commerce and shopkeeping reduced Jewish poverty, in exchange for which the state expected military service and fiscal integration with the rest of society. The Jewish community of Trier, where Karl Marx was born, in 1818, was in this respect a classic example. Something of the pre-1800 conflict between traditional Judaism and the reforming tendency of the *Haskalah* persisted, often as friction between small surrounding village communities and the Jewish leadership in the city, but large segments of the old oligarchic community leadership had by 1815 reinvented themselves as "enlightened" secularizing professionals allied to the Napoleonic state. Marx's father, Heinrich Marx (1777–1838), for example, younger brother of Samuel (Shmuel) Marx (1775–1827), rabbi of Trier, was an Enlightenment zealot who became an official of the Napoleonic state in Trier and dignitary of the newly created Jewish consistory, performing various fiscal and administrative functions relating to both city and the Jewish community (including paying his brother's rabbinic salary).[6]

One consequence of this social transformation was that German antisemitism both intensified and broadened, the theological aspect tending to (superficially) recede while the social and economic dimensions inflated into a much wider range of contexts than before. "Christians" were wholly unwilling, complained the Trier Jewish *consistoire* to the Napoleonic prefect, in 1811, to accept Jews as equals, so the old implacable hostility and rejection continued as before, only now assuming a more general social and cultural character than formerly, with new strands of envy and resentment reinforcing older aversion.[7] A few non-Jewish enlighteners in Germany continued championing the cause of Jewish emancipation. In 1809, Wilhelm von Humboldt (1767–1835), a frequent participant in the now famed Jewish salons of Berlin, composed a detailed memorandum proposing comparable extension of the new equality and full citizenship rights for Jews, prevailing in the French Empire including the Rhineland west of the Rhine, also to Prussia's Jews.[8] But broadly, a more ominous shift occurred, later readily exploited by nationalist voices. In Germany, the Jews' rapid rise to prominence enabling them to extract more favorable group status for their communities even from the most resistant bodies, as the financier Mayer Amschel Rothschild (1744–1812) did when supposedly extorting equal civil rights for Jewish citizens from and humiliating the Frankfurt city government, in 1811, their suddenly markedly strengthened position was widely perceived to arise directly from the French invader's policies and Enlightenment ideas trampling on "Christian values."[9]

German state re-organization during 1801–7, consequently, meant the emergence of larger, less stratified secularized entities far more religiously diverse than their pre-1800 heavily confessionalized and mostly much smaller predecessors. Fulda's Jews, for example, until 1806 subjects of a minuscule Catholic ecclesiastical state under "prince-abbots," after a period under the enlarged Duchy of Berg were re-assigned by the Congress of Vienna in 1814 to the predominantly Protestant principality of Hesse-Cassel. This left Fulda's Jews in a middle-sized state predominantly Calvinist (55 percent of the population) rather than Catholic, but under a hegemony now balanced by large religious minorities, over a quarter of Hesse-Cassel's population being Lutheran and 15 percent Catholic. One and a half percent were Jewish, rendering the state truly multi-confessional.[10] Eliminating hundreds of small principalities with widely varying toleration rules while adopting Napoleonic codes of practice entailed not just greater mingling of confessions, but also, for the first time, standardization of minority religious status on a roughly equivalent basis throughout, with the surviving greatly expanded principalities usually finding themselves with disproportionately larger Jewish minorities than they had tolerated earlier. Thus, the Grand Duchy of Baden grew five times in area under Napoleon's reorganization while its Jewish population, by 1808, had grown nearly seven times, from 2,265 to 14,200; the Jewish population of new "kingdom of Württemberg" grew in just five years (1805–10) by no less than fourteen times, to 7,000.[11]

THE NEW "EUROPEAN ORDER" AND JEWISH EMANCIPATION

Napoleon, then, powerfully renewed, indeed represents the culmination of the old alliance of absolutism and Enlightenment that played so central a role in Europe from the 1740s onward. Regarding the Jews, the Napoleonic state system adopted almost exactly the recommendations and admonitions of *Aufklärer* such as Dohm, Diez, Cloots, Mirabeau, Brissot, Von Humboldt and Wekhrlin in their approach to building a non-discriminatory integrated European modernity accommodating all religions. In his thinking and negotiations about Jewish emancipation, Dohm boldly "went beyond the views of the Prussian absolutist state that employed him" and contrived "to integrate his view" within the established agenda of the enlightened absolutist state. In Germany, between 1799 and 1814, his program was substantially accomplished, with the state vigorously intervening in the reorganization of civil society, imposing by decree a new near equalized relationship between Jews and non-Jews and, in return, Jews were expected to integrate as far as the essential rules of their religion would permit. As Napoleon and Von Humboldt both intended, the change, accomplished via civil rights, new institutions of education, reduced rabbinic authority and promoting Enlightenment, in principle rendered Jews equal subjects undertaking equal civic duties participating in the functioning of a new kind of state system based on merit and service rather than aristocracy, privilege and hereditary status.[12]

Whereas in Italy, emancipation in the allied republics was pushed through earlier, in the years 1796–98, simultaneously with the Rhineland (following annexation to France, in 1798), in most of Germany, emancipation came only after imposition of the Napoleonic system in the years 1806–11. From 1806, formal local decrees of Jewish emancipation with partial to near full political and legal rights followed in rapid succession in the German satellite states, in Württemberg (1807), Westphalia (1808), Baden (1809) and likewise Frankfurt (1811). In Baden, where the issue had hovered under discussion at the prince's court since the 1780s, and reemerged in 1797 following a memorandum based largely on Dohm's arguments, the Jews were largely emancipated, in 1809, under the enlarged Grand Duchy's founding constitution. Bavaria, formerly intractably Catholic, proved more reluctant, introducing a limited Jewish emancipation only in 1812–13. Responding partly to the wider trend, and partly to internal pressures for self-renewal, Prussia, following her devastating defeat at Jena, in 1806, and Mecklenburg produced their own enactments in 1812 and 1813, though here too the shift conspicuously failed to provide full rights of citizenship.[13] Dohm had urged "political and moral" regeneration of Jewish society via state intervention, stressing the need for reform of education, as was now espoused by Napoleon's policy. This too was reflected, albeit to a lesser extent, also in Prussia's limited Jewish emancipation.

After crushing Prussia at the Battle of Jena and drastically diminishing Prussia in size, Napoleon partially resurrected Poland in the shape of a small independent rump called the "Grand Duchy of Warsaw" which survived six years (1807–13). The Emperor's Jewish policy was now having implications also for eastern as well as western Europe. The Austrian envoy in Paris warned his superiors in Vienna, on 23 October 1806, that Napoleon's ambition was to "present himself as the liberator of the Christian population of Poland and also as a messiah of the large Jewish population there."[14] In the summer of 1806, Napoleon convened a general Assembly of ninety-five Jewish Notables from across the Europe he now controlled, to further standardize Jewish religious law and organization, a convention presided over by Abraham Furtado and active for several months, until March 1807. This preliminary Napoleonic convention wrestled with several thorny questions posed by the regime, notably whether Jews considered themselves a separate nation or as belonging to the nations among which they resided.[15] The Assembly's drafts were afterwards reviewed by a larger, more formal body, the so-called "Grand Sanhedrin" of February and March 1807, summoned under an October 1806 proclamation issued in Hebrew, French, Italian and German. This "Grand Sanhedrin" comprised seventy-one delegates, forty-two rabbis (including Shmuel Marx) and the rest lay leaders, with a "president," Joseph David Sinzheim (1745–1812), chosen by Napoleon's interior ministry for being the premier Talmudist in France, fluent in German, Yiddish and French, and in addition a publicly declared admirer of the emperor.

Sinzheim, like Furtado and Hartog Lémon, aspired to purge the world's unjust perception of Jews and Judaism fomented by centuries of prejudice, rejecting the notion that the Law of Moses encourages hatred and financial cheating of non-Jews.[16] Conducting its sessions in a mixture of Hebrew, Yiddish, German and French, the "Grand Sanhedrin" was directed, like the *Consistoire Israélite* set up to oversee French Jewish life in March 1808, to bind Europe's and the Near East's Jews and their communal organizations more closely to Napoleon's empire.[17] Equal religious status with other confessions under the state, and equality of individual rights, were the core principles along with reducing communal autonomy and expanding commitment to the goals of the Napoleonic state-system now incorporating part of Poland as well as Germany, Italy, the Low Countries and, from 1808, much of Spain. The Sanhedrin's delegates, however, hardly reflected the overall distribution of Jewish population: nineteen, or over a quarter of the assembly's seventy-one members, wildly overrepresented Italy, where dwelt a mere 31,000 Jews out of a total population of nearly eighteen million,[18] the rest mainly represented France, Germany, central Poland and Holland. For the Netherlands, Hartog Lémon, Mozes Salomon Asser and Judah Littwak attended on behalf of *Felix Libertate* while a rival delegation represented Amsterdam's "Old Community."[19]

As the attending Dutch, Italian and German deputies and rabbis frequently understood little or no French, numerous sessions were held in Hebrew, a language that by this time had undergone extensive reform and renewal as a literary culture in Holland and Germany over several decades,[20] and that under Sinzheim's presidency consolidated as a modern language and political tool employed for public affairs, becoming a political and administrative language for the first time in modern history at the Paris Grand Sanhedrin. If some leading personalities found in Hebrew a barrier to following the debates, the greatest difficulty facing both gatherings was the unrelenting clash between tradition, communal autonomy and rabbinic authority on one side, and the secularizing, integrating drive of the state and Jewish *Aufklärer* on the other. It was the very same split dividing the Dutch leadership since 1795 writ large and was never resolved. On many disputed points a great deal of time and energy was expended without any sign of progress. Furtado, chairing many sessions of both gatherings on Napoleon's behalf, found the whole business exceedingly frustrating.[21] Still, adjusting Jewish law and community organization to conform to the Napoleonic civil code figured among the assembly's principal functions, and here some progress was made. On 19 February 1807, the Sanhedrin ruled that henceforth no Jewish divorce could occur following the "forms of the Law of Moses" until after the marriage was dissolved by the relevant local government secular tribunal under "the forms fixed by the [Napoleonic] Code civile."[22] As marriages between Jews and non-Jews were now normalized under the *Code civile*, another ruling, while acknowledging that such "mixed marriages" could not be sanctioned in synagogue, forbade rabbis to pronounce any kind of disapproval, anathema or ban against such unions (which now became noticeably more frequent). The new central *consistoire* and rabbinate set up to administer the entirety of "French Jewry" was entrusted with overseeing thirteen regional *consistoires* among them Trier, Koblenz, Mainz and Krefeld, in the annexed zone of Germany, and Turin and Casale in the annexed part of Italy.[23]

Jewish communities retained some legal autonomy, but not much. The request of the central *consistoire* of French Jews, in 1809, to establish publicly supported separate Jewish primary schools, was refused in the interest of national integration and equality.[24] Jewish children's attendance in France's regular public schools noticeably increased under the Napoleonic system but slowly and markedly unevenly in different French departments, as was true also for Germany and Italy.[25] In Alsace, around 10 percent of Jewish children attended the public schools; in some *departements* the proportion was higher, rising to around 20 percent.[26] The wealthiest mostly continued having their sons tutored at home. While inclusion and participation were resisted by the wider society, issues where synagogue authorities themselves championed separation, autonomy and the traditional patriciate's sway proved equally contentious. Educational reform everywhere involved a dramatic change in theory but a slow, grudging one in practice.

In the Netherlands, under pressure from France, the 1796 decree had in theory already established Jewish equality in law, but hardly in reality. However, significant change in Dutch Jewry's organization and status did come finally with the end of the Batavian Republic, in 1806, when Napoleon converted the country into a kingdom as part of his European state system, under his brother, Louis Napoleon, or "King Lodewijk," as the Dutch called him, who moved the Dutch capital from The Hague to Amsterdam, and appropriated the former grand city hall of Amsterdam as his new "royal palace." Louis Napoleon emulated his brother's approach to Jewish affairs in France, setting up a *Opperconsistorie* [High Consistory] for all Dutch Jewry, reuniting *Adath Jesurun*, and the Jewish enlighteners of *Felix Libertate* with the old Ashkenazic community while simultaneously linking the Sephardim with the now much larger, more scattered Ashkenazic community with their substantial congregations in Rotterdam, The Hague, Amersfoort and Groningen. The *Opperconsistorie,* from March 1807 projected as the governing organ of all Dutch Jewry, functioned under the new, non-confessional "royal" ministry for religious affairs becoming the channel through which the newly imposed Napoleonic crown could routinely interact with the Jewish community and vice versa.[27]

Inaugurated in December 1808, with Hartog Lémon among its key functionaries, Leonard Davids representing Rotterdam Jewry, and another eager reformer, Marcus Edersheim, representing The Hague, the *Opperconsistorie* ensured Dutch Jewry's affairs were henceforth regulated at national level greatly reducing in the process the traditional power and authority of the *parnasim* and rabbis. It marked a considerable step toward the modernization of Dutch Jewish life. The *Opperconsistorie* also tried to get the community's administration to function exclusively in Dutch, deliberately demoting use of Yiddish by arranging for congregations to be served by rabbis fluent in speaking and writing Dutch, though with many originating abroad this goal proved elusive, as did reform of Jewish schooling.[28] Another of the board's functions was to ensure numbers of freshly arriving poor foreign immigrant *Israëlieten* without definite occupation or regular means of earning their bread were kept to a minimum and did not further swell the lists of registered Jewish poor and vagrant. Poor immigrant Polish and German Jews were now allowed to wander and beg as before, receiving community support, but henceforth only for a maximum of three months. All Dutch congregations had to regularly report their lists of such people to the *Opperconsistorie*.[29]

Institutional change accompanied wider change in society and culture. Between the 1796 decree and 1807 little had changed on the ground. Admitting Jonas Daniel Meijer (1780–1834) as the Dutch Republic's first practicing Jewish lawyer, in November 1796, was significant symbolically but until 1807 proved an isolated exception—and even he was largely boycotted by non-Jews. From 1807, though, the process gained momentum, helped by the continual barrage of memoranda and petitions that Asser, Hartog Lémon and other *Felix Libertate* leaders mounted at court, their reports frequently landing on the desk of King Lodewijk himself. Hartog Lémon and Asser stressed the adverse effects of discrimination, including by learned societies and pro-Enlightenment clubs like Amsterdam's *Felix Meritis* and the famous society *Maatschappij tot Nut van't Algemeen* which still persisted in formally excluding Jews from their ranks "out of principle."[30] Hartog Lémon and his colleagues likewise intensified their earlier campaign against the *parnasim* and synagogue secretaries for exercising tyrannical authority over their congregations "fondée en grande partie," protested Jonas Daniel Meijer, "sur la superstition."[31]

Louis Bonaparte, continually reminded by Hartog Lémon of *Felix Libertate*'s pro-French attitudes and of the aristocratic pretensions, Orangism and "anglomania" of the *parnasim* and Jewish plutocracy, proved responsive to this Jewish Enlightenment pressure group's pleas. Both lingering separation from gentile society and Jewish community autonomy were steadily chiseled away at. It was owing to the monarch's direct intervention, sending a royal intermediary for the purpose, that the Amsterdam *schutterij* [city militia] was finally forced, from January 1807, to admit Jews on an equal basis.[32] Several Jews were now chosen for influential public positions in "royal" service and the public domain, acquiring influence and authority over "Christians." Jacob Belinfante, a Sephardi with excellent Dutch and knowledge of general affairs, was appointed editor of the *Staatscourant* [Government Gazette] in 1807; he remained editor until 1837. In 1808, Carel Asser (1780–1836), son of Mozes Salomon Asser, a Leiden graduate in law, was promoted to a senior post in the ministry of religious affairs; he later figured among the chief legal commentators on the Napoleonic Dutch and French civil codes.[33]

Napoleon's fourth brother, Jérôme—Joseph was the oldest of the five, Napoleon himself second, Lucien and Louis next, with Jérôme the youngest—introduced a comparable framework, complete with consistory, in his transitory "Kingdom of Westphalia." In 1808, Jérôme's highly artificial new "realm" was 72 percent Lutheran, 14 percent Reformed (Calvinist), 13 percent Catholic and 1 percent Jewish, with Judaism placed on an equal basis with the other confessions, as in Holland under direct supervision of the state via a new overseeing council, or *Konsistorium der Israelieten*. An assembly of co-opted notables, established in March 1808, this body henceforth appointed the rabbis, paid their salaries, and supervised their obligatory German-language sermons.[34] As in France and Holland, the *Konsistorium*, convened in the kingdom's capital, Cassel, albeit, in the case of "Westphalia," was dominated by a single figure, Israel Jacobson (1768–1828), a wealthy court financier zealous for the educational and civil amelioration of Jewish society, instrumental earlier in the duchy of Braunschweig-Lüneburg-Wolfenbüttel, in 1803, in notably securing abolition of the notorious *Leibzoll,* the early modern body tax on Jewish subjects, historically among the chief fiscal markers separating German Jews from others.

Jérôme's *Emanzipationsdekret* [Emancipation Decree] of 27 January 1808, wholly broke with German tradition and the past, according equality and equal civil rights to Jews resident in his kingdom. It was the first "complete emancipation" of the Jews ever in Germany beyond the Rhine. All historic disabilities and special taxes, long-standing restrictions on rights of residence, property ownership and movement, were abolished.[35] All subjects,

Jews included, being now placed on a basis of legal equality, schools henceforth were obliged to accept both Jewish and Christian children. The kingdom's Jewish religious life Jacobson entrusted to the most enlightened rabbis and teachers he could recruit. Besides regular sermons in standard German, innovations introduced into the synagogue included shortened services and using choirs, innovations intended less to make rabbis resemble Christian clergymen than expose synagogue congregations to moral and social exhortation of the kind approved by the Napoleonic enlightened monarch and leading Jewish reformers elsewhere.[36] As in Holland and Italy, the changes encountered stiff resistance from the non-Jewish population but likewise from Jewish orthodoxy denouncing alterations to services and rituals, use of German in Jewish schools, and Jacobson's plans to introduce schooling for girls.[37]

Ties between the Napoleonic Enlightenment and the rise of early Reform Judaism were close. The first emphatically innovative German Jewish Reformed services originated during the later Napoleonic years in Berlin and in the new Westphalian kingdom, with Israel Jacobson, early in 1810, inaugurating his Jewish "chapel" built for his school for poor Jewish boys, at Seesen. Jacobson's reformed "temple" moved the reader's platform (*bimah*) from its traditional position at the center of the synagogue to the front, before the ark, to facilitate its use for public announcements, exhortations and sermons. Its inauguration, to which he invited Christian as well as Jewish notables, and at which he himself spoke, was used, like Hartog Lémon's inauguration of the Amsterdam *Nieuwe Joodsche Gemeente* [New Jewish Community] earlier, to eulogize enlightened toleration and the ideal of Jews and Christians being brothers joined by common devotion to God and to reason, without either group needing or desiring to rival or impinge on the other.[38] When the Westphalian kingdom and its Jewish consistory were abolished following Napoleon's downfall, in 1814, Jacobson transferred to Berlin where he re-established his regular Sabbath services complete with organ accompaniment, German sermons and simplified ritual that rapidly attracted a sizeable proportion of the Berlin community, his "temple" being the ancestor of the mid-nineteenth-century Berlin Jewish *Reformgemeinde*.

Imitating the Napoleonic reformers, Prussian bureaucracy's reform party likewise promoted the idea that Prussia's subjects needed energizing and being rendered more supportive of the state via a secularized, non-confessional system of education like that proposed by the great education reformer Wilhelm von Humboldt (1767–1835), focusing on modern subjects, sciences and individual formation, or *Bildung*. Some of the Prussian reformers, including von Humboldt, also urged, as part of this schema, full Jewish emancipation on the basis of natural rights. But, after delays, this was ultimately rejected by the crown. Prussia's monarch preferred the partial emancipation enacted under the 11 March 1812 Emancipation Edict which was subsequently drastically cut back, after 1815.[39]

Cast in the form of a royal concession, the Prussian edict, unlike those coming earlier in western, central and southern Germany, acknowledged no basic rights and offered few new freedoms. Access to the professions remained restricted. The question of Jews teaching in Prussia's universities and *Gymnasien* was deliberately shelved, until, in 1822, the now overtly anti-Enlightenment, reactionary Ministry of Education firmly opted for "Christian values," refusing Jews the right to teach in Prussian state institutions. Though nevertheless enthusiastically welcomed by Prussia's Jewish community organizations and the *maskilim,* poorer Jews mostly regarded the decree as just another nuisance providing no obvious advantages since registering with the police as Jewish "citizens" required fees and other obligations such as fixing family surnames in standard German fashion.[40] In 1817, the Berlin Ministry of the Interior deferred their decision as to whether Prussia's newly acquired Polish Jewish subjects, inhabiting the post-1814 recently annexed and re-annexed areas of Prussian Poland (Posen), enjoyed the same civic rights accorded to Prussian Jews under the 1812 edict; deferral in practice, it eventually emerged, meant outright denial of those rights.[41]

The Italian republics Napoleon created during the 1796–99 *Triennio giacobino* [Jacobin Triennium], he consolidated in 1802, into a single (northern) Italian Republic and then, in 1805, having entirely discarded his republican cloak, this unitary Italian Republic into the *Regno d'Italia* [Kingdom of Italy] with himself as "king." Most crucial changes in law and social organization affecting Italian Jewry had therefore already occurred some years before they began in most of Germany. The ghetto at Reggio Emilia was the first in Italy to be abolished, in October 1796, that of Ancona followed in February 1797, Venice in May 1797, Modena in July 1797 and Mantua's ghetto with its six synagogues, in 1798. In early 1798, the French drove the Pope from Rome, established a republic there and freed the Jews from the many centuries of oppressive papal ghetto restrictions for the first time. Two prominent Jews, Moise Beniamino Foà, of Reggio, and Moise Formiggini, of Modena, served as deputies in the congress that constituted the first of the Italian republics, the

Repubblica Cispadana [Cispadanian Republic] of 1796–97, both supporting plans to introduce new Jewish schools combining Jewish education with the new enlightened concept of general education, including the sciences. At the *Consulte de Lyon*, the Lyon gathering convened to set up and organize the new "Republic of Italy," in January 1802, no fewer than six of the 441 notables and delegates appointed to participate were Jews.[42]

Dohm had expressed no clear preference as between reform of Jewish education in their own schools and educational change through attending non-Jewish schools, nor did the Napoleonic state. The Jews themselves had been deeply divided since the 1780s over whether their schooling required refashioning in any direction whatever. Most Jewish enlighteners following the path mapped out by Moses Mendelssohn and, in Amsterdam, by *Felix Libertate*, demanded a new type of specifically Jewish school combining traditional Judaism with learning modern languages, general history and science. The chief advocate of this approach, Mendelssohn's disciple Naphtali Herz Wessely (1725–1805), pious and traditionalist in many respects, keen especially to modernize the Hebrew language, in his 1782 open letter in Hebrew, *Divrei Shalom ve-Emet* [Words of Peace and Truth], to the Austrian Jewish congregations, urged community schools teaching both Jewish and modern subjects, especially German, and teaching Hebrew as a modernized, living literary and debating language.[43]

Wessely's tract, the manifesto of the educational *Haskalah* across Europe and first discussion of modern Jewish education in Hebrew, had immediately provoked a barrage of furious negative responses from rabbis in Prague, Posen and Vilna, offended especially by his implication that without a broad secular culture and general education, one is simply not equipped to study or fully grasp Torah and revealed divine law. Wessely's formula proved still more controversial in its French, Dutch, Italian and especially its (somewhat altered) German rendering, more of a free paraphrase than strict translation by David Friedländer (1750–1835), a prominent *Haskalah* figure stemming from a higher stratum of Berlin Jewish society and straying further than Wessely from rabbinic authority and traditional orthodoxy. In 1781, Friedländer, together with other leading Berlin Jews, had initiated the Berlin Jewish Free School as a platform for his and Mendelssohn's educational schemes. It was the first Jewish boys' school to mix instruction in Judaism and Hebrew with German, French and the sciences while at the same time equipping poor boys with vocational skills like bookkeeping and accounting, useful for obtaining future employment.[44]

If Wessely too clashed with Jewish orthodoxy, he and Friedländer manifestly understood the *Haskalah*'s aims differently and were moving in different directions. Their divergence was initially papered over by shared rhetoric and phrases, but during the later Napoleonic years, when Friedländer was a leading voice in the effort to reform synagogue services and cut back community support for Talmud study, as well as reform the community's other charities and institutions, the growing rift between orthodoxy and the surging Reform tendency became deeper and clearer, developing into a full-scale crisis in Berlin Jewish life. Friedländer strove for a philosophical religion of reason, a moral system of eternal truths marginalizing tradition, observance and orthodoxy, and largely eradicating rabbinic sway, whereas Wessely had aimed to modernize at the edges while strengthening the traditional core with improved Hebrew study. The changes he urged, like his substituting Sephardic for Ashkenazic pronunciation of Hebrew, were more than minor but hardly disturbed the basic content and character of Jewish services.[45] This divergence was not the old contradiction of radical versus moderate Enlightenment left implicit and unresolved in Mendelssohn's thought, but rather a tussle rather between a greater and lesser dose of traditional observance and traditional Torah and Talmud text-centered preoccupation within the new modernized, secularizing Jewishness.

Wessely's and Friedländer's conflicting approaches and recommendations became more divisive when more widely applied and discussed during the Napoleonic era. What exactly were Jewish schools for and how did they relate to the purposes of general society's public schools? The correct balance between reforming Judaism and replacing religion with philosophy and reason was clearly no easy matter to resolve. In principle, Napoleonic officials preferred Jewish boys to attend the newly organized regular open public schools where they would mix with non-Jewish children and study only secular subjects learning nothing about Judaism and no Hebrew. Napoleon's state general schooling system was introduced in the Italian Republic, from 1802, with elementary schools, middle (*ginnasio*) and high schools (*liceo*). In towns such as Mantua and Modena, some Jewish boys did attend these schools, but, as in Amsterdam, where the Jewish and Christian schools remained entirely separate, in Italy most Jewish parents preferred sending their sons, where possible, to synagogue schools, fearing they would otherwise face a hostile environment and pressure to convert.

Thus, the preferred option was to follow Wessely's recipe and the Amsterdam *Nieuwe Joodsche Gemeente* formula with a revolutionary new type of specifically Jewish school subject to the requirements of the Napoleonic state geared to studying modern languages and the sciences while remaining traditionally religious in orientation. However, in France, Italy and Germany alike, very few Jewish schools of this type actually materialized. German Jewish pupils aiming to proceed to university had to attend ordinary state public schools as a matter of course. Three major exceptions were the Berlin Free School; the famous *Philanthropin* at Frankfurt-am-Main, established in 1804, an exploratory new species of Jewish school attended by a high proportion of the city's Jewish children; and Cassel, in the new realm of Westphalia, where Jacobson's Jewish public school flourished, from 1809, offering a balanced curriculum of Hebrew and Jewish studies alongside German, French, mathematics, history, geography and science. The head of the Frankfurt *Philanthropin* for many years, from 1806, Michael Hess (1782–1860),[46] though equipped with a traditional religious training at the yeshiva of Fürth, was an eager advocate of Jewish education based on universal principles and axioms, the new enlightened concepts of *Bildung*, moral individualism and teaching morality on a non-confession basis, a project he viewed as implementing Wessely's ideas.[47]

In Napoleonic Italy, only one specifically Jewish *ginnasio* materialized, in the northern town of Reggio Emilia, second city of the former duchy of Modena, and even this sole exception emerged only very late, during the last two years (1812–14) of the Napoleonic regime. The school plan was drawn up, in fourteen articles, by affluent local citizens led by Jacob Israel Carmi (1767–1849), who had represented Reggio Jewry in the 1807 Paris "Grand Sanhedrin" and later became Reggio's chief rabbi, and by Foà, former chief librarian of the duke of Modena, someone long immersed in the book trade and Enlightenment ideas. Their plan was readily approved by the authorities. Eighty guests gathered for the inauguration ceremony, on Sunday, 29 November 1812, in the school hall packed with teachers and children's parents, and decorated for the occasion with a huge portrait of "Napoleon, our great, most merciful sovereign." Funding the school with private fees, its three directors, including Carmi, duly combined general secular studies of the kind preferred by the government—Italian, French, science and history—with Hebrew and Jewish studies to minimize risk of the boys coming under Catholic influence and losing their "Israelite" identity. Much emphasis was placed on discipline and "virtue," and much attention given to awarding prizes, silver medals specially inscribed *La scuola Israelita* [The Jewish School]. (Among the striking features of the Napoleonic revolution in European Jewish life was the widespread replacing of the designation "Jewish" with the epithet "Israelite," or in Dutch *Israëlietische Hollanders*.)[48] In October 1813, the Reggio Jewish secondary school's student body comprised twenty-three paying students and several poor children exempted from fees. The school survived, though, only through its first two academic years.[49]

General cultural and social forces, broad *mentalités*, yet again, as with the Enlightenment more widely, played little or no part in furthering the impact of the Napoleonic Enlightenment on Jewish life and Christian-Jewish relations. Christian reaction in society beyond the context of Napoleon and his state system exerted a largely negative counter-pressure. Popular sentiment everywhere tended to be outraged by the emancipating of Jews. Churchmen were almost invariably hostile. Freemasonry contributed nothing positive: in Frankfurt-am-Main both main Masonic lodges continued excluding Jews. In Berlin, where the Jewish population reached 3,400 by 1790, and there were many affluent, highly educated and enlightened Jews, all three masonic organizations strictly debarred Jews.[50] The same was true, complained Ludwig Börne, of the Frankfurt reading societies and museum boards. In Frankfurt, prominent Jews responded like their co-religionists in Amsterdam by setting up their own separate societies, founding their Masonic lodge, in 1807. Certainly, efforts were made to support the *Philanthropin* and turn it into a forum for Jewish-Christian collaboration for local philanthropic purposes, but virtually no "Christians" joined, stripping it of the ability to fulfill any function other than furthering local Jewish causes.

EMANCIPATION REVERSED

The real driving force behind the late Enlightenment's transformation of the European Jewish reality promoting a profoundly innovative but mostly also highly unpopular set of ideals was the Napoleonic state system, along with the Napoleonic press, strongly supported by men like Carmi, Jacobson, Furtado, Asser and Hartog Lémon, and backed by such political clubs and associations as adopted Radical Enlightenment ideology, as the way to advance a genuinely egalitarian, secularizing political and social agenda. Orthodox Jewish resistance to Enlightenment and the Napoleonic reforms as they affected Jews was led by rabbis and *parnasim* but drew added momentum from social factors often hardly connected with Judaism, or religious issues as such, stemming from defensive cultural traditions of separation and distrust.

A troubling instance was a riot occurring in the Amsterdam Jewish quarter, on 11 April 1811, when a group of "oisifs Israélites" [idle Israelites], as the city police chief called them, assailed a squad of soldiers accused of roughly manhandling a Jewish girl for embracing her brother whom she spotted among a column of freshly recruited conscripts, Jewish and non-Jewish, being marched out of the city. Some conscripts were forcibly set free in this affray, causing the escort to open fire on the protesting demonstrators, leaving one dead and several wounded, and dispersing the crowd, but also causing it to spread out and launch fresh assaults on isolated policemen and Frenchmen elsewhere in the city.[51]

Unlike the Jewish majority, veteran Jewish revolutionaries and radical enlighteners firmly supported but were by no means wholeheartedly in sympathy with the Napoleonic regime due to its autocratic authoritarianism and heavy drain on resources and manpower, and heavy taxation, to support the Napoleonic armies. In 1812, after Napoleon's debacle in Russia, what Hartog Lémon most dreaded was not Napoleon's overthrow but a renewed English invasion of the Netherlands and restoration of the House of Orange.[52] In February 1813, not long before Amsterdam's synagogues were decked out for the last time in celebration of Napoleon's birthday (11 August 1813), Hartog Lémon let slip some indiscreet remarks indicating his preference for a revived "Batavian Republic," rather than a restored Orangist prince, a republic he would have liked to see headed by the ardent republican Johan Valckenaer (1759–1821), a Frisian former university professor at Franeker dismissed in 1787 from his chair by the Stadholder for democratic leanings.[53] Arrested by a now acutely nervous French military command in Amsterdam fearful of popular unrest surging up, Hartog Lémon was repeatedly interrogated, being suspected of involvement in one of the numerous plots afoot to oust the French and negotiate terms with the Orangists, and found himself suddenly under threat of execution for his staunch republican sympathies. Pleading innocence of involvement in any anti-French conspiracy, he was sentenced, owing to lack of concrete proof of treason, to two years imprisonment instead of execution. Barely a month after Napoleon's decisive defeat at Leipzig (16–19 October 1813), before allied units had yet reached the Netherlands, a violent uprising against the French did erupt in Amsterdam.

The French evacuated. On 30 November, the Prince of Orange, returning in triumph from England, landed at Scheveningen. By then, Amsterdam's synagogues had already jettisoned the *Opperconsistorie*'s rules for worship and communal procedure and dropped Dutch for public announcements.

There is no doubt that Dutch Jewry's traditional Orangism was actually strengthened rather than weakened, during the Napoleonic era. One might have expected the reverse, given the organizational improvements and implementation for the first time of the emancipatory measures reaching back to the Batavian Revolution. But for most Dutch Jews the positive effects of the reforms were more than counterbalanced by the collapse of commerce and sudden steep increase in poverty levels resulting from Napoleon's "Continental Blockade" of Britain and British retaliatory measures against the Dutch and seizure of the Dutch colonies.[54] From 15 November, the Prince was acclaimed in synagogue prayers throughout the Netherlands as "His Royal Majesty, the Prince of Orange and Nassau, sovereign prince of the United Netherlands." The community soon received a visit and expressions of gratitude for their loyalty from the Stadholder in person. But despite most Dutch Jews being now more than ever enthusiastically Orangist and vehemently anti-French, their hopes of seeing the new organizational structure for their community, headed by the hated *Opperconsistorie,* abolished were by no means wholly realized.

Following strenuous protests and demonstrations, in Amsterdam even with riots against it, the *Opperconsistorie* as such was abolished and, in appearance at least, extensive modifications were made to Lodewijk's arrangements for the Jewish communities. In addition, the Portuguese community was allowed to separate itself once more. But in substance the *parnasim* never regained their old authority, nor the congregations their former autonomy. *Parnasim* and rabbis had permanently lost the power to supervise the private lives and lifestyles of their congregants, as well as to issue bans against dissidents. An overall structure remained in place under a central "Consulting Committee" meeting in the national capital, now transferred from Amsterdam back to The Hague. This body, on which "enlighteners" and Sephardim were overrepresented, soon renamed the *Hoofdcommissie* [Head Committee] for "Israelite affairs," operated as before, firmly under royal supervision, with Dutch *de rigueur* as the entire community's legal and administrative language. "King Willem I" (r. 1815–40), as the returning Prince was soon accepted by the Dutch, and recognized by the Allies and their Vienna Congress as being, proved to be, in a more monarchical manner, scarcely less "enlightened" in attitude than Louis Napoleon.[55]

Seven months previously, in April 1813, shortly before Valckenaer too was briefly arrested, imprisoned, and—on its emerging that he was fiercely anti-Orangist—released by the French, Hartog Lémon had been transferred to a castle prison in France. He was released only a year later, on the same day, 6 April 1814, that the Emperor Napoleon finally surrendered to the allies. Having suffered imprisonment in France for his republicanism, on returning to the Netherlands, Hartog Lémon was investigated by the newly installed "royal" police on account of his known anti-Orangism. They had him correctly listed in their records as not just a former Batavian activist and anti-Orangist but the most anti-monarchical Jewish revolutionary to be found in the Netherlands. They tried to discover whether during 1812–13 he had actively conspired to incite popular resistance to the Prince, Britain and the Orangist Restoration.[56] On his release under severe warnings, Hartog Lémon avoided all further political involvement.

With post-Napoleonic reaction inevitably came a general reaction to Jewish emancipation. As with many other aspects of enlightened reform, mainstream opinion remained generally negative right across the continent. Powered by traditional Christian society and values, it was equally a response of traditional Jewish society and culture. In some places, notably the Netherlands, the ensuing reversal was mostly a question just of nuances and gentle *de facto* distancing rather than explicit legal and political enactments reversing what had occurred. King Willem I, bowing to opposition from "Christian" circles, did, though, appoint noticeably fewer Jews to political, administrative and honorific positions than had Louis Napoleon.[57] In Napoleonic Poland, Jewish emancipation had never been implemented in practice at all, on the grounds that the Jewish population was not yet ready for integration, so the Grand Duchy's re-incorporation fully into Czarist Russia, with parts going to Prussia and Austria, left little to reverse.[58] More generally, within the bounds of the former Napoleonic state system, reversion to discrimination, disabilities and institutionalized subordination and marginality of Jews was consciously sustained and vigorously enacted.

Aversion to the Napoleonic system in Germany was indeed far-reaching; but the claims of generations of historians that this reflected a powerful upsurge of "nationalism" is misleading. What surged up powerfully was popular traditionalist sentiment tinged with local enthusiasm for the returning *ancien régime* authorities, strongly laced with antisemitism, usually without any thought of a united German state or people. Occasional appeals for German unity were heard, but these referred to the league of principalities militarily and logistically allied in the fight against Napoleon rather than national feeling or desire for unification. Where applicable, kings, princes and the old civic oligarchies were, like the Prince of Orange in Holland, warmly welcomed back by the man in the street as well as the clergy, nobility and merchant class. Where the *ancien régime* did not return owing to Prussia's British-backed massive territorial rewards, the mood was hardly one of exhilaration. When the Swedish flag was hauled down for the last time in Greifswald in former Swedish Pomerania, in 1814, rather than joyful celebration of their reversion to (German) Prussian rule, the local Pomeranian population wept, displaying undisguised sorrow. But everywhere without exception support was robust for canceling French reforms and laws and reverting to the old rules and corporations.

Canceling Jewish rights and equality in particular was decidedly popular, newly acquired Jewish rights being reversed with exemplary zeal and energy at Hamburg and Lübeck where the old elites had temporarily been largely ousted, until 1813, by Napoleonic, often foreign, administrators.[59] Buoyed by the Restoration, the revived Free City of Lübeck, where French interference had enabled Jews to settle for the first time, rather than introduce disabilities did not hesitate to re-expel the entire community, in March 1816, by decree of the city senate—albeit due to the ensuing long legal battle over this, it took another eight years, until 1824, for re-expulsion of Lübeck Jewry to be fully implemented.

Emblematic of the fate of Napoleon's transformation of Jewish life was the quashing of Reggio's Jewish *ginnasio*. Carmi and the school's other directors appealed to the newly restored duke of Modena, Francesco IV, in June 1814, for their "glorious institution" to be permitted to continue. But before long it became obvious that there was little point in trying to salvage it since preparation of Jewish pupils for high school and university, its essential purpose, was now firmly blocked: Jews were no longer being admitted. The restored ducal government also ordered the removal of all Jewish pupils already studying in the duchy's public schools, including the Napoleonic *licea* which, with appropriate changes of nomenclature, were continued. This was part of a broad process of re-segregation of Jewish life in the Italian states during the Restoration era. In post-1814 ducal Modena the Jews were ordered back to the ghettoes and to re-submit to the now resurrected old work restrictions, though nighttime closure of ghetto gates and other re-imposed ancient regulations remained less strict than before 1789. Once again, Jews had to wear a distinctive emblem outside the ghetto, pay special taxes not levied on others and found themselves debarred from public service, the professions and military service. Once restored, the papacy likewise reconstituted the ghetto in

Rome; true to papal tradition, the Roman ghetto was the very last to survive in Europe, remaining in force until 1870![60]

Until the 1830s, Jewish emancipation was still some way off, in the New World as well as the Old, and staunchly resisted still in many quarters. Hardly anywhere beyond the United States and France was the issue even approximating to being settled. In 1838, the now elderly Swedish king, the former French marshal Bernadotte, attempted to introduce full, unqualified Jewish emancipation in Sweden but in doing so provoked ugly antisemitic riots that led him to adopt a more modest outcome, retaining some disabilities.[61] In Canada, advocates of social and political equality in the 1830s and 1840s supported the Act of the Legislative Assembly of Lower Canada, in 1831, inspired by the French Canadian radical republican leader, Louis-Joseph Papineau (1786–1871), "to declare the equality of persons professing the Jewish Religion." This act (with royal assent the following year) did finally proclaim the Jews' full legal and political equality, making Canada the first part of the British Empire to pass such legislation.

When the new rabbi of Montreal, the famous Abraham de Sola (1825–1882), who had grown up in London and keenly resented British society's reluctance to remove the last lingering restrictions affecting British Jews, arrived in Canada, in 1846, he was delighted by the difference he found there with conditions in Europe. Jews in England at this point still found themselves in the humiliating position of being unable to stand for election to Parliament or hold higher office and restricted by other political and higher education disabilities that "still disgraced," as De Sola put it, "the political code of Great Britain."[62] Certainly, the position in Britain was relatively benign compared with that in Germany, Austria-Hungary, Russia and Poland. Still, Jews were denied access to degrees at Oxford and Cambridge, the only universities existing in England and Wales until University College London (UCL) opened its doors, at the end of the 1820s which meant that, until then, there were no English universities at all which Jews could attend. Founded on uncompromisingly secular Benthamite Enlightenment principles, refusing even to have a theology department, UCL long represented a unique breach in the wall of English higher education discrimination.

Counter-Enlightenment zeal and anti-Jewish feeling were conspicuous features of the 1813–14 offensive to overthrow the Napoleonic system and replace it following Napoleon's defeat. But while popular backlash contributed to reversing major strands of the Enlightenment, it also served to frustrate and antagonize the most emancipated section of Jewish society, powerfully reinforcing the Radical Enlightenment tendency now more than ever entrenched in their midst. Ludwig Börne, Heinrich Heine, Moses Hess and Karl Marx were all products of this post-1813 vigorous Jewish response to the anti-Jewish reaction and general reversal of the late Enlightenment's transformation of the Jewish world.[63] Pan-European dismantling of the legacy of the French Revolution and Napoleonic reforms soon bred an angry new generation of revolutionary Jews.

TWELVE

Heine, Börne and the Post-Napoleonic Jewish Revolutionary Tradition (1810–1840)

Post-Napoleonic repression (1814–48) occurred during a turbulent time, a seething intellectual and moral ferment culminating in two great revolutionary waves of 1830 and 1848. Presided over by a European so-called "Holy Alliance" led by Russia, Prussia and Austria, in international affairs closely allied to a domineering British aristocracy, the papacy and the restored French Bourbon monarchy, the Restoration was constantly vigilant for the slightest sign of underground republican, anti-aristocratic subversion of crown, hierarchy and altar. The era from 1814 to 1848 was suffused with unrelenting officially backed anti-republicanism, anti-secularism and antisemitism, as well as anti-cosmopolitanism, anti-Americanism (conspicuous in upper-class Britain) and antipathy to representative democracy. However, the Holy Alliance, supporting ecclesiastical oversight of the monarchical-aristocratic order, on one level also needed a dash of enlightened toleration since its formal essence was political "Catholic," "Protestant" and "Orthodox" collaboration, devout monarchs joining hands to repress via their political and cultural collaboration every sign of protest or subversion from below.

Since after 1814, popular grievance and economic distress remained just as widespread in Europe (including Britain) as in pre-1789 Europe, the Holy Alliance faced an unceasing challenge on every side. But while grievance was ubiquitous, discontent was not easily welded into a coherent conceptual framework of rationalized opposition formidable enough to seriously threaten this internationally concerted triumphant conservative reaction. Contrary to the older historiography, politically conscious national feeling hardly existed anywhere as yet beyond fringe elite circles. It made scant difference how great was the majority's grinding poverty, deprivation and degradation: without an effectively mobilized ideological framework no alternative could be envisioned or concerted. What prevailed in the rhetoric of the day was neither "nation" nor "people," nor any revolutionary scheme. What counted now in public discourse was predominantly revived monarchy, aristocracy and "Christian values," or what was termed "Christianity," a socially, politically and militarily victorious joint Protestant-Catholic-Orthodox social and political ideology, unremittingly reactionary and repressive. If Napoleon swept the Holy Roman Empire away for good, majority sentiment helped the 1814–15 Vienna Congress restore, if not its former state boundaries, then many trappings and frills embodying the old Empire's spirit and character, its princely, aristocratic and ecclesiastical essence. Whether artisans, wage-laborers, peasants or middle class, the common people faced many pressures and difficulties, with bouts of intensified hardship, but rarely dreamt of rejecting the existing order, indeed mostly evinced basic deference to "kings and priests," courts and princes and deep instinctive aversion to irreligious, radical ideas. In Germany, observed the veteran radical Arnold Ruge (1802–1880), common understanding languished as if the "old Holy Roman Empire still haunts it."[1] This remained the case despite harsh economic conditions generating not just disaffection but sporadic outbreaks of inchoate unrest. Popular sentiment thus cemented the quiescent, time-honored passivity of what Heinrich Heine called Germany's "Winterschlaf" [winter sleep] and Ruge the "old petty-bourgeois consciousness," but also punctuated it with occasional violent outbursts.

What mattered when fomenting serious subversion and planning revolutions, after 1814, was once again not cultural shifts, *mentalités,* or general attitudes, but alienated professional elites, especially the thousands of purged officials, academics, lawyers and army officers, along with aggrieved intellectuals and journalists. In the post-1814 era, until the 1848 revolutions, aside from the occasional brilliant autodidact, Europe's revolutionary-minded democrats consisted almost exclusively of highly educated university students, literary men, artists and professors, persons like Heine, Börne, Stendhal, Büchner, Shelley, Quintana, Compagnoni, Michelet, Lamartine, Foscolo and Angeloni. Their narrow social base reflected democratic republicanism's withdrawal into the submerged world of an alienated, aggrieved trans-Atlantic intelligentsia and literary coterie. This confirms that post-1814 developments not only failed to bridge but widened further the already yawning gap between late Enlightenment and the common people, a divide no less significant than that pitting the radical intelligentsia against churches and princely courts. It was the old pre-1789 original dilemma of the Radical Enlightenment now writ large.

Following the Vienna Congress and post-Napoleonic Restoration, the appeal of radical ideas for secularized Jews in the early nineteenth century was much enhanced by—indeed in part the direct consequence of—reverses suffered by the emancipation process. Until 1814–17, groups of enlightened advisers at princely courts, notably in Berlin, continued urging equal or at least improved civil rights for Jews. But never more clearly than between 1814 and 1848 did the Enlightenment demonstrate that, far from being rooted in mainstream opinion, broad-based cultural trends, or "sociability," its impetus derived predominantly from an intellectual vanguard challenging the predominant mind-set of most social segments, including aristocracy, clergy, shopkeepers, teachers and artisans.

While growing anti-Jewish sentiment during these years, especially marked in Germany, and reversal of previous steps toward emancipation, stemmed primarily from social and economic factors, the justifications offered by the restored monarchies—the post-1814 "Holy Alliance" of Catholic, Protestant, and Orthodox empires (Russia, Prussia and Austria), plus Britain and post-Napoleonic France, sworn to uphold a joint monarchical-ecclesiastical hegemony across the world—stressed the responsibilities of the "Christian state" and need to reverse Enlightenment "godlessness" and irreligion. If in France, the Low Countries and Denmark, Jewish disabilities were not restored between 1814 and 1818, in central and east-central Europe (and Sweden), this was the case.[2] Theologically tinted ideological rhetoric, bolstered by the post-Napoleonic years' prevailing anti-Enlightenment mood, encouraged cultural segregation and a purging of publishers and bookshops, schools and universities that lent reactionary conservatism new momentum among the pious and impious alike. Emphasis on and defense of "Christian values" and their generally assumed inherent antagonism to Judaism and

Enlightenment decisively shaped this profound change of course. After 1814, reading societies reacted more strongly than earlier against the secularizing, deistic spirit of *Aufklärer* like Lessing, Dohm, Mirabeau and Diez advancing the cause of Jewish emancipation.

A few novel ideological ingredients also made an appearance. German university *Burschenschaften* [student societies] justified devising so-called *Judenparagraphen* debarring Jewish entry partly on the ground that Yiddish-speaking Jewish culture and customs were an intractable impurity threatening to adulterate "our folk character" that needed to be kept out. Reversing emancipation in accordance with such a logic was a serious undertaking, but it was taken to such lengths that at times it risked appearing petty and trivial, rendering its agenda a little ridiculous even to supporters and the genuinely devout. A "considerable sensation amongst the Jews of Prussia," reported the British envoy in Berlin, William Russell (formerly aide-de-camp to Wellington), to Lord Palmerston, in London, in October 1836, was caused by a "late ordinance prohibiting them from adopting Christian Names, and directing that in all official reports they should be designated only by the appellation of "Jews." Uncertain exactly which first names were now proscribed, the Berlin Jewish community asked for "a list of the names which they are prohibited to assume, but the Government experiences some embarrassment in specifying them."[3]

The general reversal, politically and socially driven, infused with the staged piety of right-wing Romanticism, generated fresh frustration and tensions within society generally and also, much having changed in Jewish society since 1789, renewed friction between Jews and the majority. The Berlin youth group the *Gesellschaft der Freunde*, founded by Mendelssohn's son, Joseph, and Jewish friends, in 1792, to promote emancipation and function within Jewish society as a reforming pro-*Aufklärung* pressure group, seethed with exasperation. After 1814, for any Jew eager to dedicate him or herself to advancing the Enlightenment, the "common work of humanity," protested one member, no greater obstacle, no greater nuisance, was at hand than these touted "Christian values," the alleged "Christian character" of German and European society.[4] "You gentlemen of the Frankfurt Museum for Art and Science," complained Ludwig Börne indignantly, in 1821, "answer me: why do you admit no Jewish friend of art and science, no Jewish scholar or artist? You gentlemen of the Frankfurt reading societies, answer me: why may no Jew sit among you and read the *Allgemeiner Anzeiger*?"[5]

Ludwig Börne (formerly Loeb Baruch) (1786–1837), son of a banker, and like his Rothschild contemporaries raised in the Frankfurt ghetto, the walls of which had been smashed down by the French in 1796 and were never rebuilt, received a traditional Jewish upbringing and education. Aged twenty when Napoleon shattered Prussia's military might at the battle of Jena (1806), he studied medicine and afterwards law and administration at Giessen, Heidelberg, Berlin, Halle and, again, Giessen, from where, in 1809, he obtained his doctorate in administrative law. A minor official, working through the latter part of the Napoleonic era in the Frankfurt city police administration, as a *Polizeiaktuarius* [secretary in the police department], his career in officialdom's lower echelons in a fast-changing city looked assured. Then came the "Christian" reaction. Frankfurt joined with Hamburg and Lübeck in systematically reversing Jewish rights. Across much of Germany, during 1813–15, Jews were dismissed from all official positions and responsibilities. Börne was just one of many Jewish officials who lost their positions as a result.[6] Compelled to seek another career, he turned to journalism and never subsequently wavered from his vehement hatred of the new order and the hypocrisy of "Christian values."

Remaining in Frankfurt, from 1813, he confronted post-Napoleonic Germany's conservative, refurbished "Christian character" head-on with pen and incisive wit. But with reactionary authoritarianism the order of the day, Börne found that if he wanted to get anywhere in life he simply must change religion outwardly. In 1818, at the relatively advanced age of thirty-two, he was baptized as a "Lutheran" and de-judaised his name. Before long, he won fame via the shrewd, incisive social satire characteristic of his writing, and as a discerning theater and literary critic. With his distinctive *Judenwitz* [Jewish wit] as a prime tool of social critique, he emerged among the foremost early nineteenth-century revolutionaries of the mind.[7]

"Christian Johann Heinrich Heine" (1797?–1856), born Harry [Chaim] Heine to a Jewish family in Düsseldorf, then a small town occupied by French revolutionary forces, likewise belonged to a generation benefiting from the far-reaching education reforms following Napoleon's victories. He too had a decidedly non-traditional Jewish upbringing. While still a schoolboy at the Düsseldorf Lyceum on the banks of the Rhine, already steeped in Spinoza, Toland, d'Holbach and other freethinking authors, Heine learnt early to associate Spinoza with battling ignorance, obscurantism, prejudice, injustice and oppression, and the prevailing reality surging all around him.[8] At his now secularized former ecclesiastical secondary school, he befriended Joseph Levy, a timid, socially awkward classmate, bullied by the others, with whom he had long discussions about philosophy. On leaving the Lyceum at around nineteen (confusion persists as to his exact birth date), Heine exhorted a younger schoolmate to "befriend poor Levy." "It is the voice of humanity you hear. I implore you by everything you hold holy to help him. He is in the direst straits. My heart bleeds. I can't say much; the words burn in my flesh." Heine's hatred of bullying, the mean, coercive and oppressive, his loathing of commonplace prejudice, lay deep.[9]

Like Börne, Heine remained unconverted until well into adulthood, reluctantly receiving baptism and changing his name from "Harry" to "Heinrich," only in June 1825 at around twenty-eight. His father, Samson Heine (1764–1828), a small businessman who, Heine later claimed, never read any of his writings, failed in business. For years his parents depended for financial support on a successful but domineering relative in Hamburg, a paternal uncle, Salomon Heine, who, observing Heine's unsuitability for business at his banking firm, offered means for university study but with strings attached. His uncle stipulated law, envisaging for Heine a prosperous legal career which, under the changed circumstances, could only mean conversion. Starting in 1819, at an unusually late age—nineteen, twenty or, possibly even twenty-one—Harry studied for six years at Bonn, punctuated by a period in Berlin. Neither uncle nor father held literature or philosophy in much esteem.[10] But "philosophy" and literature were Heine's escape path from what to his mind were the insufferable philistinism and constraints of business, family and the mundane. He paid only desultory attention to his legal studies.

Already earlier, by 1821–22, Heine's student efforts to win a literary reputation, negotiate philosophy's recent turns and navigate his social situation, began bearing fruit. During 1822, several newspaper reviewers acknowledged his precocious poetic talent; by then, he had also discovered Hegel, whose lectures he attended and genius he admired. Hegel's philosophy he considered conservative only on the surface, attributing to it a clandestine radical essential core.[11] On 4 August 1822, Heine joined Europe's most advanced circle for research into Judaism and Jewish history, the Berlin *Verein für Cultur und Wissenschaft der Juden* [Society for the Culture and Learning of the Jews], which deeply influenced his subsequent outlook.[12] Although his knowledge of Judaism always remained sparse, and his relationship to his Jewish past ambivalent, his sense of spiritual belonging to a meaningful group identity, and sympathy for the Jews' unhappy history and sufferings was repeatedly demonstrated, most eloquently in a moving, unfinished novella, *The Rabbi of Bacherach* (1824), composed a decade after the Prussian government's quashing Jewish equality. Fond sentiments about medieval Jewry were distinctly unusual among semi-assimilated and fully assimilated Jews alike; indeed, converted Jews aspiring to pass as "Germans" in everyday life rarely avoided imbibing something of the prevailing antisemitism permeating what contemporaries called "Christian values," with their absolute presumption of being of a higher moral order than all other values. This figured among the many factors complicating Heine's straightforwardly embracing his cultural "Germanness."[13]

Besides Jewishness, bullying and forced conversion, another deep preoccupation, this one traditionally underestimated, occupied his thoughts and feelings from his school days on, creating an unbridgeable psychological wedge between him and mainstream society—immersion in eighteenth-century Radical Enlightenment clandestine literature. Forbidden texts like Toland's *Pantheisticon*, Meslier's *Testament* and d'Holbach's *System der Natur*, he and a few fellow subversives cherished in deliberate defiance of official Prussian school and university prohibitions. Already an "atheist" of Spinozist stripe prior to his forced baptism, he recalled later, it was his early embrace of forbidden thought, especially Spinoza, that shaped his lifelong conception of the French Revolution as a tragically interrupted process, yet still thus far the most meaningful step in a "General Revolution," the hoped-for universal transformation that radicals everywhere dreamt would elevate humanity to a higher plain. This underground ideology he would, in turn, help transmit to Moses Hess, one of the first German exponents of socialism, though Heine was somewhat less inclined than Hess to assign Jews a special role in his "world revolution" in stages.[14]

Shortly after joining the Berlin *Verein*, Heine had set off for Prussian Poland, where he stayed as a guest on estates belonging to the family of a young nobleman, Count Eugene von Breza (1802–1860), with whom he had become friendly. Touring western Poland in August and September 1822, he garnered impressions about what, at the time, was a topic German writers tended to avoid, given Poland's conquered, divided and degraded condition. His first serious essay, "On Poland" (1822), though still immature, expresses sentiments about Poland's nobility, peasantry and Jews that typified his basic stance toward Europe's general predicament for the rest of his literary career. The aristocracy seemed politically and culturally the sole intellectually aware class, the only segment in their society prepared for revolutionary insurrection against Russian tyranny. Though not unsympathetic to the Polish peasantry, he was aghast at their staggering ignorance, superstition and prejudices, as also their poverty, and what to him was their vile servility to Church and nobility. For Heine, Polish peasant ignorance embodied the very core of the social and cultural paradox impeding full-scale genuine revolution.

Heine was struck too by the limited horizons and backwardness of Polish Jews. Prussian western Poland was a region where Jews evinced an astounding lack of enthusiasm for the 1812 Prussian Emancipation Decree, and scant interest in becoming Prussian "citizens."[15] Finding their Yiddish abhorrent, he scorned also (western) Polish Jewry's narrow range of occupations, believing they should become less oriented toward petty trade, especially running taverns at the behest of and rented from nobles and selling alcohol to peasants, which he deemed "very damaging" to Polish society *and* the Jews. They should revert to agriculture.[16] Yet, he admired the Jews' sense of continuity with their past, the authenticity of Polish Jewish culture, which he contrasted with the much-diminished Jewish awareness of now increasingly assimilated German Jewry.[17]

Never religious in any conventional sense, Heine was a revolutionary secularist from the outset, a radical enlightener, atheist, Left Hegelian and, like Börne, implacable foe of the 1814–15 Restoration. The *ancien régime* and Restoration he scorned in every sphere, even poetry, where he defied numerous conventions including Goethe's uncontested towering stature. Despite his kinship with Goethe's deeply un-Christian pantheism steeped in Spinoza, his readiness to call Goethe "the Spinoza of poetry," he considered Goethe's "Spinozism" too passive socially, culturally and politically, as verging on *Indifferentismus*.[18] An aspiring young poet, he begrudged too how completely the great man overshadowed all his generation's poetical and literary efforts.

Later, during the Weimar Republic, German-Jewish exaltation of Spinoza's "Jewish secularism" and universalism became closely linked to the figure of Goethe, whose literary greatness, acknowledged by all Germans, was undeniably pervaded by Spinoza's thought—much as Heine had stressed. Accordingly, it became a cultural priority of the antisemitic nationalist Right to decouple Goethe from Spinoza and from Heine's perceptive analysis of Goethe's Spinozism as emphatically as possible, if only by outright falsifying of the truth. Their eternally pure, exclusively German "Goethe," explained Houston Steward Chamberlain, a leading forerunner of Nazi-style racial antisemitism, in his book *Goethe* (1932), was totally remote from Spinoza, as all proper Germans would expect; yet, tragically, Goethe to an extent, had been lured [*hineingelockt*] into Spinozism in "philosophical matters" by the misguided Herder. Had Goethe heeded Jacobi's impeccably German and upright admonitions denouncing Spinozism as fatal to all true "Germanness" and "Christianity," he would never have sunk into so deplorable an error.[19]

Heine's "Spinozism," in part akin to Goethe's and Herder's, but less purely personal and literary, differed in being more social and political. Rhetorically at least, his "Spinozism" was noticeably more engaged and activist.[20] Even so, Heine felt sufficiently close to Goethe and appreciative of his greatness to reprimand the "resentment," even "hatred," toward him he later accused Börne of exhibiting due to Goethe's patent distaste for revolutionary action and far-reaching reform.[21] A "Spinozist" revolutionary Jew, Heine diverged from Hess, Marx and the revolutionary socialists in believing world history and humanity have no pre-ordained structured destiny or goal, that "God or nature" is strictly non-teleological and progress to better things far from guaranteed; a better humanity needs striving for but may not be achieved. He trusted in no materially determined, inevitable social and economic transformation for which humanity is destined by the logic of social development. Rather than capture and change the economic system, Heine's goal was to elevate and enlighten humanity. He was no proto-socialist but a radical enlightener in a way Börne, Hess and Marx were not. His "revolution" exalted individual liberty and general emancipation from social oppression, constricting illusions and falsehood. He wanted "the emancipation not just of the Irish, Greeks, Frankfurt Jews, West Indian Blacks, and other oppressed peoples but the emancipation of the whole world." His vision was of a liberation of body and spirit together rooted in an ethical stance, a quasi-religion rejecting both Christianity and rabbinic Judaism (albeit suffused with deep allegiance to Jewish tradition and peoplehood), advocating "rehabilitation of the flesh" and oneness of matter and mind.[22]

Uninterested in social reorganization, collective emancipation planned on a pre-constructed basis, Heine eventually found himself caught in inescapable friction with the rising socialist revolutionary consciousness of his time. At the same time, though, there was no escaping his deep sense of alienation from, and being in constant conflict with, the existing status quo. In 1825, Bonn University authorized his doctorate but, in accord with Prussia's laws precluding Jews from higher degrees and professions, ruled that he could receive his doctorate only if he first obtained the required baptism into the "Christian" faith.

ENLIGHTENMENT, POPULISM AND THE "COMMON MAN"

For Jewish revolutionaries like Börne, Heine, Hess and many another alienated intellectual male and female,[23] the problem of estrangement from ordinary folk grew especially acute after a major wave of popular anti-Jewish violence, the "Hep! Hep!" riots, erupted across Germany during 1819.[24] Between 1789 and 1814, temporary removal of the restrictive barriers had enabled western European Jewry to rapidly move upwards, ameliorate their economic lot relative to the rest, and often, as with the Rothschilds, discard their old pre-1789 reticence about showing it, a conspicuous change that greatly intensified active "hatred against the Jews." Börne, who had more reservations about the Rothschilds than Heine, detesting their role in financing and propping up princes and kings, emphasized, with his usual insight into such things, the envy and indignation arising from the Jewish bankers' and wealthy entrepreneurs' increased visibility.[25] The cry H-E-P, according to some, was the acronym for "Hierosolyma est perdita!" [Jerusalem is lost!] shouted in the Crusades, an emotional Crusader battle cry expressing murderous hatred of non-Christians, especially Muslims and Jews.

Commencing on 2 August, in Würzburg, with pilfering of Jewish shops by shopkeepers and artisans, shouting allegiance to "our dear Frankish land," bitter fury against Jews setting off pogroms spread swiftly first through Franconia, then more widely, continuing into October.[26] Several Jews were killed, many injured and much Jewish property looted. The ugliest scenes occurred in Bamberg, Bayreuth, Darmstadt, Karlsruhe, Mannheim and, most notoriously, Frankfurt, where the old restrictions, abolished by the French in 1796 but restored in 1814, were tighter and more degrading than in Berlin, Vienna, Mainz or Munich, but over 10 percent of the population was Jewish. Subsequently, the riots spread also to Heidelberg, Leipzig, Dresden, Cologne, Bremen and Hamburg. The trauma was indescribable. Memories of the window-smashing, pillaging and beating up of Jews on the streets persisted for decades, jolting many a formerly Jewish newly converted "Christian" out of the reassuring convention, then widespread among those clamoring for conversion, that "Christians" are morally superior to "Jews." Only the lower orders were involved in these disturbances, reassuringly reported the British envoy at Berlin to London, knowing his superiors, like their counterparts in Paris, Berlin, Vienna and Petersburg were continually on edge lest revolution again be rearing its head. The upper orders could relax because these riots were definitely not "excited by the revolutionists," even though in general, the "revolutionists" too "are decided enemies of the Israelites."[27]

Spurred by harsh economic circumstances and deprivation, the enraged rioters railed furiously against those they held responsible for their wretchedness. But instead of directing their fury against kings, priests and noblemen, as radical enlighteners recommended, they misdirected their rage, encouraged by Church tradition and a modish, misty anti-Enlightenment "Teutonism" dear to the Romantic literary Right, against Germany's 270,000 Jews (including those of Prussian western Poland), a tiny proportion of the population. "The enmity to the Jews" pervading many towns in Germany, reported another British envoy, in September 1830, exemplified by the "Hep! Hep!" disturbances, "for which no rational, or at least sufficient cause can be assigned, exists to a certain degree here at Frankfurt, and is not entirely confined to the lowest dregs of society."[28] Börne, present in Frankfurt in 1819, disagreed with this, discerning an all too rational cause: hatred of Jews, he claimed, was a tool of elites and princes useful for deflecting popular fury away from themselves, rendering the common people "prison guards of the Jews" and keeping them thoroughly intimidated.[29] A predictable psychological consequence of the trauma was heightened Jewish antipathy to Christianity as a faith. A more paradoxical result was increased Jewish self-esteem, notably in Berlin, where revulsion against "Hep! Hep!" helped stimulate renewed research into the history and significance of Jewish culture and history. The future woman novelist, friend of Heine, and revolutionary Fanny Lewald (1811–1889), only eight when the antisemitic cries and smashing of windows were first heard, but a convinced "Spinozist" when "Hep! Hep!" returned during the 1830 revolutions, and already somewhat unsure about and tending to discount "Christian values" while submitting to conversion to Christianity, in 1829, now began asking herself who, then, *was* "aufgeklärter und besser" [more enlightened and better]?[30]

Romanticism, including Heine's powerful nostalgic leanings, in some respects diluted the pre-1814 Enlightenment's stress on "reason," placing new emphasis on emotion, feeling and symbolism suffused with melancholy. But the late Enlightenment did not cease promoting philosophical reason as mankind's true savior, and no writer of the era so effectively satirized and derided

Romanticism's irrational strain rejecting the Enlightenment as Heine. He especially scorned religionizing right-wing Romanticism venerating the Middle Ages. While assuredly setting the lone, isolated individual starkly against both authority and the crowd, Romanticism mostly proved a cultural filter and intensifier rather than a separate Counter-Enlightenment ideological trend. Eschewing the middle ground, reconfiguring and re-invigorating both Left and Right, Romanticism's effect, broadly, was to sharpen rather than bypass the Enlightenment's characteristic split—separating comprehensive reform from "moderation"—and pitting both radical and moderate Enlightenment more emphatically against a reinvigorated Counter-Enlightenment pinning all ills on irreligious Enlightenment "philosophy" and insidious intellectual notions and undergrounds.[31]

Feeding on disillusionment, alienation, nostalgia and the distressing aftermath of defeat and foreign exile following the Revolution and Napoleonic era, Romanticism basically reaffirmed and deepened existing ideological rifts in more literary and artistic terms. The revolutionary and Napoleonic experience hence steered Romanticist yearning into both resurgent revolutionary *and* revived reactionary fervor. Backward-looking apparently, even conservative Romanticism with its staged religiosity and resort to continent-wide concerted measures was, as Stendhal stressed, in fact a profoundly "modern" phenomenon. Both reactionary-religious Romanticism and the Romanticism of Heine and the radicals were highly charged responses to the challenges of an age of profound cultural and social inner strife.[32]

To the dismay of those unseated or blocked by the canceling of Jewish equality, the reversal won the applause of much of society. Admittedly, most of the rest of Germany's populace equally lacked political rights and freedom of expression and were frequently more deprived of educational opportunity and money for basics than many Jews. But at this point the Jews were swiftly demoted to an exceptional extent legally, socially and politically, finding themselves stripped almost overnight of recently acquired rights of residence, citizen status and ownership of fixed property, of eligibility for university degrees and the higher professions. Until the 1860s and 1870s, discrimination on religious grounds, though gradually receding after 1848, remained a force, even in Switzerland, Sweden and at England's top universities, Oxford and Cambridge, a disconcerting scenario drawing numerous intellectually inclined young Jews from backgrounds affluent enough to enable them to study at university, to radical ideas.

By 1830, intellectualized resentful alienation and anger rendered Börne and Heine models for a whole generation of aspiring young revolutionary Jews.[33] Ardor for the defeated but not extinguished revolutionary Enlightenment, Heine recognized more than most, lived on chiefly in the minds of the intellectual, literary and artistic fringe. Radical thought was certainly a form of elitism but provided the perspective basic to Heine's conception of man's pursuit of happiness and fulfillment, a product, to his mind, of the best of France, Holland and Germany. His and his friends' radical counter-culture, he knew, must necessarily remain a fringe phenomenon, fundamentally non-national, non-popular, non-Christian and irreligious; but that counter-culture could, even so, perhaps one day shepherd the rest. It was France's "philosophers, their immortal writers," agreed the "Young Hegelian" philosopher and revolutionary Ruge, who, from 1789, "engendered for the French the new, world-shaking consciousness" enabling men to break free, for a time, from the stifling fetters of monarchy, aristocracy and clergy. It was Montesquieu, Rousseau, Voltaire, Sieyes and Mirabeau who prepared the Revolution. When would the Germans discard unthinking deference, demanded Ruge, their dismal, infinitely constricting conventional piety that did nothing but misconstrue the world around them, the contemptible parochialism blocking pursuit of a better society? Sweeping away the old political structures, comprehensive rejection of the past alone could bring liberty and justice: but such change is impossible without a prior "reform of consciousness" gained through study, literature and effective analysis, that is, "philosophy."[34]

Arguing the people were not the motor or guiding force behind post-1814 European subversion, and could not be, is far from denying the power of social forces or popular discontent. Where mobilized, the populace showed abundant capacity to make their feelings felt, to destabilize and reshape. Since 1789, the populace had vented their frustration in huge mass protests in Ireland, Spain, Greece and Italy no less than France and Germany, even, if less violently, in Britain. With Europe's anti-French "liberation" movements of 1808–9 (especially in Spain and Portugal), and 1813–15 (especially in Germany), the common people, seized emotionally by great waves of religious and patriotic (but not national) sentiment essentially regional in character—Aragonese, Navarrese, Andalusian, Saxon, Bavarian, Prussian and in West Pomerania even "Swedish" rather than "German"—had risen with great vigor. During 1812–14, townsmen, artisans and peasants often felt passionately motivated in driving the French out. The same was true of the Netherlands.

But no matter how popular, deeply felt and vigorous were these uprisings, whether in Spain, Germany, Holland, Greece or Italy, the populace rose without any notion of transforming the political and religious system only to find that the 1814–15 Vienna settlement delivered all its rewards and recompense to princes, nobles and ecclesiastics, according nothing whatever to the common people.[35] "In 1813 and 1815," lamented Ruge, in his article "A Self-Critique of Liberalism" (1843), the Germans "did not think at all, and we still must pay for our thoughtlessness." As the hugely disillusioning outcome proved, "in our perverse, deeply and unspeakably confused Germanness," the people just blindly opted for tradition, monarchy and faith.[36]

Distress, degradation and poverty, then, no matter how vast, is not of itself a revolutionary force, no tool of social transformation when not effectively marshaled behind a thoroughgoing reform project, which rarely occurs. Rather, it is a force readily diverted to bolster all manner of conflicting tyrannies. By its very nature oversimplifying and unjustly generalizing, populism remains an unreflecting menace easily deflected in damaging ways. The rousing *Wartburgfest* [Wartburg festival], of 18 October 1817, near Eisenach, in central Germany, stirred patriotic fervor among the scantily informed, introducing into German political culture for the first time a vehement new political ideology—fiercely antisemitic "Teutomania." Orchestrated by students and professionals steering sentiment to the right, it was no spontaneous occurrence.

Potentially, widespread economic discontent could become a threat to princes and courts, a revolt against the prevailing status quo, but only where established values were consciously challenged, which the presiding "Holy Alliance" vowed should never be permitted to occur again. The serious threat to Restoration-era royalty, aristocracy and churchmen, the policing regimes were acutely aware, stemmed not from deprivation and exploitation of the masses but the clandestine ferment of subversive intellectual opposition. The repressive Carlsbad Decrees, jointly imposed by Austria and Prussia, in September 1819, to head off the dreaded "revolutionists," reflected the courts' clear perception of the situation, by focusing almost entirely on tightening surveillance of universities and student societies, and strengthening press restrictions. Philosophy alone, held radical reformers, can transcend the mundane, elevate "the ordinary" to a state of mind and awareness, capable of securing meaningful change; the courts fully acknowledged the accuracy of this. It was the only point on which princely courts and "revolutionists" wholeheartedly agreed. In a word, to achieve real change, the "Germans need the dissolution of liberalism," as Ruge expressed it, by means of radical ideas "into democratism."[37]

The German Confederation's later resolutions equally concentrated on the reality that organized political and social subversion derived chiefly from a fringe of discontented *Akademiker*, student organizations,[38] jobless graduates and independent writers, since the late 1820s most notoriously the *Junges Deutschland* [Young Germany] literary movement with Heine and Börne well to the fore. Since discontented Jews formed a conspicuous element of this fringe, conservatives hit back by jeering at "Young Germany" as really "Young Israel" and "Young Palestine."[39] In December 1835, with the politicization of its literary preoccupations obvious, "Young Germany" was banned outright by the courts of Prussia, Austria and the lesser states, forcing the group to eke out its subsequent existence as a furtive underground with which Heine and Börne both remained closely associated.[40] It was his being raised as a Jew in the Frankfurt ghetto, Börne had no difficulty in admitting, that made him love freedom more ardently than others, to dream of "liberty as a nightingale with the voice of a giant." The antisemitic jibes of his foes, reminding the world his real name was "Baruch," only made him still more aware of this, as he sallied forth to bludgeon conventional German thinking and society with cutting sarcasm.[41]

Heine and Börne, the two pre-eminent revolutionary Jews of the 1820s, both fighting political reaction, prejudice and conservatism, first met and debated their revolutionary project and its difficulties during a harmonious three-day encounter at Frankfurt, in November 1827, when Börne showed his new companion round the old ghetto. Between 1827 and 1830, they saw much of each other. Both were passionate fighters for press freedom. Initially, Heine admired Börne almost as an older brother teaching subversion, expression and wit. If Heine was the more antagonistic to churches and religion, Börne was the more hostile to aristocracy.[42] To an extent, Börne, always a more hands-on political activist, broadened and radicalized Heine politically. According to Heine, though, even on first meeting they agreed only about politics, both quickly realizing they were less in harmony about philosophy and literature.

Post-1814 France was the weak link in the reactionary chain forged by Vienna, the Czar, Germany's princes, Britain's aristocracy and Spain's exemplary "throne and altar" tyrant, the pillar of the Inquisition in its final years, Fernando VII. Restored French Bourbon monarchy (1814–30), with its grudging compromises with constitutionalism, press freedom and

Enlightenment, struck Heine, like Stendhal, Shelley and other literary radicals of the day as no authentic reversion to monarchy, aristocracy and religious authority but a precariously artificial charade, hypocritically parading courtiers and ecclesiastics. Unlike post-1814 Germany, Metternich's Austria, Czarist Russia, Wellington's Tory Britain, Restoration Italy and Fernando's Spain, lands where royalty and aristocracy regained their former sway, in Spain like Prussia gained even increased powers,[43] facilitating repression of dissident political and religious publications, post-1814 France seethed still with enlightened ideas, moderate and radical, pullulating through the press, literary groups and student associations without serious hindrance. To the distress of writers like Chateaubriand, Bonald and Joseph de Maistre yearning for solidarity with Europe's monarchical-religious Right, for a purer, more forceful general reaction against irreligion, constitutionalism, abolitionism and all insubordination, in post-1814 Bourbon France popular sovereignty survived residually in Louis XVIII's 1814 "royal charter," leaving royal ministers partially responsible to the legislature. Liberty of conscience and near equality of cults was scarcely cut back at all, and worse still, considerably more press freedom persisted, against royal and episcopal wishes, even than Napoleon had permitted. Though it succeeded to a modest extent, the restored crown seemed completely unable to come anywhere near making good the tremendous losses in revenues, properties, personnel and authority which bishops, secular clergy, seminaries and religious orders alike had suffered since 1789. To uncompromising reactionaries, Restoration France was not just a missed opportunity but a thoroughgoing disaster lacking effective clerical dominance over education and society, stringent restrictions on the press, even obligatory church tithes, never mind outright subordination of other faiths.[44]

Under the impact of the 1830 "July Revolution," the conspicuously weak French Bourbon "show monarchy" collapsed all at once. After "Three Glorious Days" of barricades and street fighting in Paris, the royal troops were repulsed by insurgents and the last Bourbon king, Charles X (r. 1824–30), forced to flee the country. Initially, both Börne and Heine were immensely elated. This renewed upheaval, they did not doubt, marked the long-awaited resumption of the great Revolution of 1789–95 and, with it, resumption of the German republican revolutionary tradition of the early 1790s established by Georg Forster and the Mainz republicans of 1792–93.[45] Intoxicated, Börne, still in Germany, greeted the first news as "sunbeams packed in printed paper," envisaging "bold hopes rise up impassioned like trees with golden fruit." But it was not long before Börne, Heine and a mass of other revolutionary enthusiasts became utterly disillusioned. In the July Revolution, Parisians rose magnificently against the Bourbon monarchy, with Lafayette at their head, but with no plan beyond seizing the capital. And soon enough, the people were misled down a false path. By November 1830, only six weeks after arriving in an elated Paris, Börne had abruptly changed his tune and turned to denouncing the new regime (accurately) as the tool of the Paris *Finanzbourgeoisie*.[46]

The "Gallic Cock" may have "crowed for the second time," observed Heine, but within weeks Paris and all Europe's intelligentsia were plunged again in dejection. Exploiting the people's efforts, a small clique, headed by financiers, seized power, establishing a supposedly "liberal," "moderate," British-style monarchy with Charles X's cousin, Louis-Philippe (1773–1850) as France's last king, that quickly revealed its repressive nature and, from 1834, increasingly met protest by restricting the press, imposing curbs on freedom to gather and demonstrate and repudiating every democratic republican principle outright. It was the old story, sighed Heine: the people rose, bled and suffered not for themselves, or their own benefit, but the profit of others. "Armes Volk! Armer Hund!" [Poor people! poor dog!]. "The people gained nothing from their victory, except still greater distress." Disillusionment led Heine sometimes to underestimate the people as an active force, to assume the ordinary man thinks only about petty cash, the here and now; but he never underestimated their dangerous capacity for fanaticism, superstition and faith.[47]

During the late summer of 1830, the revolutionary tide flowed from France and Belgium into Germany, first reaching Aachen where modern industrial techniques had recently been adopted and workers were resentful, then Hamburg, the Rhineland, southern Germany and Switzerland. But the popular thrust in Germany and central Europe, as in Paris, remained conspicuously undirected, reflecting piecemeal local discontents rather than fundamental reform agendas.[48] In Belgium and Switzerland, renewed revolutionary turmoil did produce solid, permanent gains. At Zurich, the *Neue Zürcher Zeitung*, founded in 1821 by Paul Usteri (1768–1831), led the progressive papers in demanding press freedom. Soon, in other cantons too, the long-standing strife between "aristocrats" and "democrats" for control of the Swiss federation intensified, from November with lively demonstrations at Freiburg, Aarau, Schaffhausen, Basel and Lausanne. The Swiss "aristocrats" (town patricians), whom Börne deemed "worse and more dangerous than the kings," battled to stem the tide of republicanism and democracy, but in Switzerland, unlike

Germany, a long tradition of democratic republican allegiance helped generate a more genuine revolutionary impulse. By 1831, no fewer than ten cantons, including Zurich, Bern and Luzern, had been forced into extensive concessions, heavily revised constitutions and extended freedoms.

Swiss press freedom, secured in 1830, proved an appreciable gain for all Europe, as did Zurich's new function as a haven for exiled revolutionaries fleeing Germany. As in Paris, defeated revolutionaries arrived in droves, by 1833–34 greatly contributing also to the founding of several new higher education institutions at Zurich and Bern, of high quality and emphatically secular character, further weakening traditional Swiss patrician and theological influence.[49] All this buoyed Börne's early enthusiasm for the July Revolution, for Lafayette and Louis Philippe: Switzerland's newly strengthened democratic tendency and enhanced freedom of opinion, he hoped, would help breach the repressive walls of German reaction and censorship too. But if the 1830 French revolution proved a giant deception, the 1830–31 Swiss Revolution, despite Zurich's new freedoms, proved inconclusive, patrician resistance receiving support from the peasantry and clergy, leaving a legacy of strife between urban and rural interests, guaranteeing further conflict in the future.[50]

The wider Revolution scored a few successes also beyond Switzerland and Belgium, such as in Baden, where Grand Duke Leopold (r. 1830–52) granted freedom of the press, in 1831, and other legislative reforms. Occasionally, it even happened that the real culprits were targeted. On 7 September 1830, crowds occupying the center of Brunswick attacked and burned down the early eighteenth-century *Residenzschloss* [residential palace] of the unpopular Duke Karl, who, in 1827, had suspended the Brunswick constitution. Börne and Heine, contemplating the revolutions engulfing Germany, both briefly wondered whether their compatriots were, after all, outstripping France in fundamental reform, but soon discarded this fleeting notion. Wherever the 1830 revolutionary upsurge assumed a more organized, coherent character, it was, as in 1792–93 and 1798–1806, the work of reading societies, intellectuals, writers and journalists. Where briefly successful, the 1830 German revolutions, like those of France and Belgium, scarcely conformed to Hannah Arendt's scenario of "professional revolutionists" watching and analyzing without doing "much to advance and direct it." The reality was the exact opposite. It was their initial success that made eventual failure so distressing to Heine, Börne, Ruge, Bauer and all the German radicals of the era, non-Jewish and Jewish. Wherever, as in the Grand Duchy of Hesse-Cassel, well-directed strategies enabled committees of constitutional monarchists and democratic republicans to coordinate sustained, targeted pressure in state capitals, they briefly succeeded in twisting the arms of the German Confederation's princes, though, too trusting, only enough to extract incomplete concessions.[51]

In Hesse-Cassel, the rioting forced the Grand Duke to concede a constitution some judged the most progressive adopted in Germany thus far, massively widening the suffrage and, on paper, eroding privilege. This elaborate 160-article constitution, very grudgingly accepted by the Grand Duke, in January 1831, was principally drafted by a Marburg professor, the enlightened Austrian jurist Franz Sylvester Jordan (1792–1861).[52] However, Hesse-Cassel's revolutionaries soon faltered due to their "moderation" insufficiently weakening prince and nobles: Hesse-Cassel's new single-chamber legislature not only conceded substantial influence to the Grand Duke but of fifty seats assigned only thirty-two for election by independent householders, deferentially reserving eighteen for nobles, clergy and Grand Ducal relatives. This was to show how sensibly they imagined they were compromising, balancing the democratic tendency against the steadying principles of monarchy, aristocracy and church. Trumpeted by supporters as true compromise in the English spirit, Börne drenched it with derision for safeguarding court dominance instead of advancing constitutional freedom, proclaiming press freedom while retaining newspaper restrictions, and declaring equality of cults while retaining disabilities on Jews.[53] Börne was soon vindicated: step by step, from 1832, Elector Wilhelm II strengthened police powers and neutralized the *Landtag* [state parliament]. With the legislature emasculated, Professor Jordan was placed under police surveillance and, in 1839, imprisoned.

Overall, less coherent than in Switzerland, France or Belgium, Germany's revolutionary movement fast fragmented in every direction. At Leipzig, it was impossible to see what the agitation sought to achieve. In Hamburg, as at Breslau, Munich and other cities, the popular fury quickly degenerated into the renewed "Hep! Hep!" antisemitic riots that profoundly shocked Heine and Börne, Fanny Lewald and many another. The windows of Heine's wealthy uncle, Salomon, were among those smashed in. The one common feature, yet again, was the revolution's undirected popular, unruly character.[54] Aghast at the revolution's incoherence and chaotic fury, Börne's *Briefe aus Paris* (1830–31), though devoted to furthering the struggle for freedom, expressed bitter scorn for the anarchic, bigoted German revolt against "tyranny," with still greater derision than his scorn for France's dismal failure and Belgium's bowing to monarchy. Heine, equally disgusted by the general fiasco, in May 1831, reviling the stifling German censorship, fearful of police spies, and longing for personal liberty and peace, also transferred to Paris as a permanent expatriate.

"WARTBURG" VERSUS "HAMBACH"

Radicals now felt disillusioned and sometimes deterred; "moderates" felt torn between the perceived need for constitutional, religious and educational reform and a mounting dread of social unrest.[55] Deflecting where not outright suppressing the 1830 revolutions (outside Belgium, Baden and Switzerland at least) in the end the upheaval proved an outright victory for financiers, courtiers, clergymen, *antiphilosophes*, the pious and tradition. Veteran revolutionaries Jewish and non-Jewish, *Freiheitsfreunde* [Friends of Liberty] like Heine, Börne, Ruge and Wirth, sank into still greater dejection than before. Struggling to conserve their old revolutionary zeal and optimism, "teaching the Marseillaise to children," as Heine sarcastically expressed it, they rotted away "at home, in prison, or in a garret in exile" like the worthy Georg Forster, who had helped inspire the 1792–93 Mainz Rhenish revolution and miserably expired, in Paris, in 1794, during the Terror.[56]

For radicals, the one bright spot was the *Hambacher Fest* [Hambach Festival] of May 1832, the culminating moment of pre-1848 German democratic republicanism. Heine savagely contrasted the 1817 *Wartburgfest*'s narrow, bigoted "nationalist" razzmatazz with the genuine democratic spirit at the more edifying *Hambacher Fest*, uniting radical intellectuals and segments of the people impressively, if briefly, in a rousing commemoration of previous revolutionary effort, and announcement of plans for the future. This uplifting occasion, which took place at Neustadt, in the Rhenish Palatinate, enthused huge crowds with its stirring rhetoric but, despite greatly alarming the authorities, proved isolated, temporary and ultimately unsuccessful.[57] Organized by Rhineland journalists who, in February 1832, had founded a Freedom of the Press Society that grew rapidly to boast 116 branches with five thousand members, chiefly in southwestern Germany, it proved a great milestone in freedom of the press history. Banned by the Bavarian authorities, the dissident journalists, calling for the "rebirth of Germany," retaliated by using their wide network to rally support from over a large area."[58]

The *Hambacher Fest*, Germany's national freedom festival, was staged on an unprecedented scale from 27 May to 1 June 1832, reportedly attracting twenty-five thousand people, mostly artisans and students with a sprinkling of Polish exiles figuring prominently in the opening procession from Neustadt marketplace to the castle ruins.[59] Among principal organizers was the radical journalist Johann Georg August Wirth (1798–1848), editor of the *Deutsche Tribune,* chief organ of the *Presse- und Vaterlandsverein* [Press and Fatherland Union] banned by the Bavarian authorities in March 1832, that had led in clandestinely inviting reading societies and organizations to attend. Among celebrities invited to speak, Börne was a prominent figure on the rostrum, his speech enthusiastically cheered by the multitude with shouts of "es lebe Börne" [long live Börne]. Right through the 1830s Börne was lionized by radicals in a manner Heine would never be, and that, for a time, rendered him an icon for younger aspiring revolutionary Jews filled with anger against the status quo.[60]

The Hambach agenda was in no way traditional, national, popular, socialist or religious. The goal of the freedom festival, insisted Wirth, was not nationhood or unification, nor "moderation" or some vague "liberalism" (although he did later drift toward a more nationalistic stance from around 1840). Aside from an occasional anti-Catholic slur (being staged in a predominantly Protestant district), it was a good-humored affair.[61] Participants were there to celebrate democratic values, human rights and republicanism based on "Freiheit, Aufklärung, Rationalität und Volkshoheit" [Freedom, Enlightenment, Rationality and Sovereignty of the People].[62] The gathering celebrated representative democracy and press freedom, the people's principal shield against rapacious rulers and the path to triumph over oppression. The speakers extolled the cosmopolitan fraternity of all peoples, and the Germans' fraternal support for Polish, Italian, Hungarian and Spanish liberty.[63] Their standard, a tricolor in black, red and gold, was later adopted by the Weimar Republic and is the present-day German flag. Wirth summoned the Germans to rise against the "Holy Alliance" crowns and their contemptible ally, Louis-Philippe, and fight for their sister nations of "Spain, Italy, Hungary and Poland," as well as Germany. In France, the July Revolution had been shamefully betrayed to "liberal" vested interests, especially bankers, using Louis-Philippe to extend their wealth at the expense of democracy and the people's happiness. Misled, France had embraced a contemptible "moderation," compromise with monarchy and aristocracy, utterly scorned by all true *Republikaner.*[64]

Wirth concluded his oration by urging three rousing cheers for the peaceful, brotherly "conföderirte republikanische Europa" of the future! In part a folk festival, accompanied by music and jollification over large beer-mugs in taverns, there was, despite some among the crowd sporting the old Phrygian liberty cap, doubtless less fervor for radical principles and European union and more traditional deference than the leadership liked to suppose.[65] The Bavarian court, breaking with its pro-French Napoleonic legacy, opting now for outright reaction, nevertheless sent in half the Bavarian army, 8,500 troops, to occupy the Hambach locality. Bavarian, Austrian and Prussian authorities subsequently pursued every organizer the police could identify.[66] Börne hurried back to Paris. Wirth was caught in hiding and tried at Landau. By "republic," he declared, in a defiant eight-hour speech before the judges, he meant "the empire of reason, justice, humanity, freedom and happiness."[67] Sentenced to a long spell in prison, he escaped in 1836, first to France, then Switzerland, spending the rest of his life in exile apart from a brief return during the 1848 Revolution.[68]

Memories of 1830 and the 1832 *Hambacher Fest* helped keep commitment to basic rights, democracy and revolution in southwest Germany alive, especially among reading societies and student networks.[69] But post-Hambach German democratic republicanism, driven from Germany, had more than ever to regroup in exile, retrenching its publishing and intellectual effort among the refugees at Zurich, Bern, Geneva, London, Paris and Brussels. Heine, meanwhile, to Börne's annoyance, having urged Germans to abandon their old "cosiness" and spring into action, loudly demanding the "Rechte der Menschheit" [Rights of Mankind], and that Germany's woods be turned into "barricades for the liberation of the world,"[70] by his own conduct showed his summons was just a personalized fantasy. No genuine activist, just a remote observer, he merely watched from afar.

As the revolutionary fury of 1830–31 subsided, both Heine and Börne chose to remain permanently in Paris, still the headquarters of revolutionary excitement and activism. Heine preferred France for his refuge to England or America, he later explained, from love of its cosmopolitanism and, like Börne, attachment to the great Revolution. It was France that had initiated the world process of modern emancipation. Heine did briefly consider England as an alternative but decided against it in view of its philistine loyalism, aristocratic social dominance and the "Church and King" mania he so detested. "Or should I go to America," he had asked himself, "that gigantic freedom-prison, where the invisible chains would press on me even more painfully than the visible ones at home, and the most annoying of all tyrants, exercises its rough despotism!" Heine ruled out America, convinced nothing is worse than the tyranny of the commonplace, everyday notions backed by popular religiosity, even though the United States boasted no nobility or princes and everyone was deemed equal—apart that is, he added sarcastically, from a few million humans with black or brown skins "who are treated like dogs."[71]

Lafayette, despite failing in 1830, remained a great hero to Heine and Börne—"Lafayette the incomparable," who had done more than most to remake the world on the basis of the *Declaration of the Rights of Man and the Citizen*,[72] the "Ten Commandments of the new world creed whose like could be produced only once by nature which, in her economical way, had tried to share him across two worlds and two centuries."[73] For both Heine and Börne, like the older Percy Bysshe Shelley (1792–1822), the French Revolution was indeed the "master theme of the epoch in which we live."[74] But unlike Börne, Heine did not choose Paris as a base for future activism or commitment to organized subversion. An uncompromisingly radical Left Romantic poet, Heine stood out, not unlike Shelley, as a hugely subversive figure combining literature with the revolutionary spirit of the age. A self-proclaimed "democrat, philanthropist and atheist" with a mechanistic, deterministic concept of nature as a set of immutable laws moved by necessity, Heine embraced "the truth" as expounded by Spinoza, d'Holbach and Condorcet, whose texts Shelley too lauded for demolishing superstition and faith, and reorganizing Bible study, scholarship and science around the politically and socially critical tool of reason.[75] Of all relevant texts, for Heine as for Shelley, Spinoza's *Tractatus Theologico-Politicus* remained the foremost defining reality and the path to a better future.

Both Heine and Shelley viewed human motivation and inspiration, the capacity to grasp reality, as elusive and complex, remaining always in some sense beyond precise definition in scholarly or scientific terms. The French Revolution, like everything else, for them had only material causes; yet, both felt a need to qualify this by insisting that poetical insight can intensify, elevate and perpetuate the commitment and exhilaration of revolutionary consciousness.[76] Men can be persuaded to embrace democratic Revolution step by step by rigorous argument, but poetic imagery can assist by inducing intuitive jumps helping readers penetrate more spontaneously and directly to the truth. The "oppressed, having been rendered brutal, ignorant, servile and bloody by long slavery," held Shelley, can be awakened by poetically expressed images and notions to rise up against the whole ruling construct and exact a "dreadful revenge."[77] Adopting a stance bearing striking resemblance to Shelley's parallel view, Heine likewise accorded poetic genius special powers to discern reality's true direction and character from subtle, unobvious signs.[78]

No such parallelism, though, alleviated the increasingly strained relationship between Börne and Heine. Where the miserable failure of the July Revolution, in Börne's opinion, was due to the bourgeoisie capturing the Revolution and using it to further their own selfish interests so that the future Revolution must be a struggle of the poor against the rich,[79] Heine refused to visualize the path forward as a class war. Heine later also claimed never to have held Börne's taste or literary criticism in much regard, though this cannot be strictly true as Heine concurred in part with Börne's scathing criticism of Goethe for his Olympian aloofness.[80] While Heine avoided the crowded, smoke-filled German artisans' gatherings Börne occasionally frequented, his aristocratic aloofness and seeming ambivalence toward mass movements and democracy increasingly exasperated and antagonized Börne.[81]

Börne, while living in Paris, had surprisingly little contact with Frenchmen of any sort, intellectuals, socialists or workers, but did confer with the numerous German revolutionary exiles milling in throngs around Lafayette, Benjamin Constant, the Spaniard Quiroga and other renowned *Revolutionshäupter* [revolutionary leaders], captivated like him by the mystique of "Revolution" and the aura surrounding these republican celebrities. Ultimately, though, the *Revolutionshäupter* of 1830 too, dismayed by the wretchedly disappointing outcome in France and generally, seemed baffled as to what kind of Revolution they should strive for and how to attain it.[82] But where Börne attended German artisan and other subversive gatherings showing *engagement* of a kind, Heine chose the cultural limelight, loving the cafés and museums, regularly attending the theater, salons and high-society gatherings of a kind Börne avoided. Börne hence grew more isolated in Paris socially but remained better connected with German protest and the international revolutionary underground than Heine.[83]

An additional factor deepening disillusionment among revolutionary Jewish intellectuals like Heine, Börne, Hess and Gabriel Riesser, was the lack of any positive outcome regarding equal civil rights for Jews even where constitutions were liberalized in 1830 and basic freedoms fleetingly or permanently established. Only after Hesse-Cassel was absorbed into Prussia, in 1866, did full civil rights devolve on the Grand Duchy's Jews, finally reversing the cancellation of rights long before temporarily secured under Napoleon. The decades-long debate preoccupied German culture to a remarkable extent. There was hardly any other issue over which so much ink was spilt. Between 1815 and 1830 alone, approximately 2,500 books, brochures and pamphlets by authors Jewish and non-Jewish debated this convoluted issue.[84] Yet, for decades after 1830, despite increasing pressure for liberalization and mountains of printed debate, deep-rooted *Antijudaismus* and Jewish disabilities remained as solidly entrenched as before.

Jewish emancipation in mid-nineteenth-century central Europe remained generally a failed cause. Antisemitic outbreaks and restrictions persisted, not least in Hamburg, where Germany's most eloquent advocate of Jewish rights, Gabriel Riesser (1806–1863), untiring in his efforts and devotion to benevolent gradualism, led in seeking to overcome the barriers through oratory and the press. No revolutionary, Riesser criticized Börne for being too militant, too extremist in pursuing Jewish rights, as everything else, for being a "revolutionary" showing insufficient confidence in Germany's future, princes and legislatures;[85] but, as late as 1850, Riesser had precious little to show for his gradualist efforts. As far as Jewish rights were concerned, the same dismal picture applied to Switzerland, where the 1830 and 1848 revolutions achieved considerably more than in Germany but Jewish rights proved just as unattainable in the face of public opposition. In Canton Geneva, where the Napoleonic era's equal Jewish civil rights lapsed in 1816, along with the general conservative reaction, Jewish rights were restored in 1842. But Zurich only finally accorded Jewish equality in 1862, while in Basel Jewish disabilities remained so constricting not even a proper synagogue could be built until 1868. Full Jewish equality arrived in the canton of Bern finally only in 1876.[86]

Riesser, a brilliant orator, both of whose grandfathers were rabbis, after studying law at Heidelberg and Kiel, had aspired to an academic career, but despite exceptional abilities was denied a university chair. Unlike Börne, Heine and later Marx (all having the same ambition), he was unwilling to accept baptism as the price. Without baptism, he was also prevented from practicing most of a lawyer's functions. By the late 1820s, Riesser had become Europe's foremost advocate of Jewish emancipation by non-revolutionary means, a leading voice within German Jewry and, unlike Börne, who disliked his stress on Jewish identity, also a prophetic voice warning against assimilation, holding that Jews have an equal right, as Jews, to be German "citizens" and should remain "Jews" building a common historical and cultural rather than religious understanding of their collective identity. He rejected the post-1789 trend designating the Jews as "Israelieten" instead of Jews, preferring to call a "Jew a Jew" in his own publications.[87]

Through the early 1830s, Riesser published articles and tracts fiercely denouncing the assumptions and style of the public debate over Jewish rights in Hamburg, Baden, Hesse-Cassel, Bavaria, Switzerland and Prussia. Tirelessly exposing the hypocrisy and bigotry of press and popular attitudes, he also abjured Börne's approach, regarding him as too extreme in opposing princes and aristocracy, more given to hatred than love with his unbending egalitarianism and lack of sympathy for Jews as Jews.[88] Riesser's most promising target was the Grand Duchy of Baden, where greater press freedom pertained than elsewhere and where, in 1831, the legislature devoted much time to deliberating Jewish rights. Finally, though, despite extensive support, his efforts flopped even there.[89] He was additionally hindered by his preferring the Hamburg Reformed Temple to orthodoxy, which meant he incurred Jewish orthodox hostility as well as Christian, assimilationist and radical opposition.

Riesser deserves attention for tirelessly fighting for emancipation and also for being among the first to reject religion as the criterion for defining Jewish group identity. Following Heine rather than Börne (for whom the prime Jewish legacy was cosmopolitanism), Riesser construed modern Jewish identity and sensibility as cultural and social rather than religious. Whether Jews had converted to "Christianity" or not, were observant or not, mattered less than their general outlook. "The Jews have never recognized Heine," he complained in 1840. They "have never considered him except with indifference, no more admiring his poetic and stylistic talents than others; never have they shown sympathy for his views or his satirizing Jewish and Christian religious notions."[90]

Yet, however one defines Jewishness and Jewish identity, without devoting oneself to the demoralizing grind of gradualism boxed into endless "liberal-legalistic" legislative wrangling, the fruitless legislative slog Riesser sank his energies into, the only credible path to emancipation, for the nonobservant, was to embrace Börne's cosmopolitanism and comprehensive revolution. If freedom of expression, and Jewish rights were to be secured, princely tyranny, aristocracy and the "Christian" and "Jewish" ecclesiastical authorities, backed by popular attitudes, had to be confronted, and this was conceivable only via a subversive intellectual underground promoting an imminent revolutionary denouement promising sweeping change for all. Intellectuals, Jewish and non-Jewish, following this path, Börne and Heine prominent among them, were acutely aware that building such a unified revolutionary consciousness was no simple matter. Existing philosophical systems opposing kings, aristocrats and ecclesiastics presented a scene more of fragmentation and internal doctrinal turmoil than unified effort.

Philosophy culminating in Hegel was scoffed at by many as a peculiarly German addiction distracting minds from political reality. Heine disagreed, predicting the envisaged "philosophische Revolution" would prove far from the harmless mystification the pragmatic-minded supposed. It was the "philosophical revolution" that *was* effectively preparing the ground for the actual revolution, he argues in his *Zur Geschichte der Religion und Philosophie in Deutschland* [On the History of Religion and Philosophy in Germany] (1833–34), a subversive work that provoked a general pan-German ban on Heine's entire oeuvre and much of the rest of the output of "Young Germany."

Heine judged it impossible to predict the ultimate outcome of revolutionary movements arising from the philosophical input he deemed the key to meaningful revolutionary conspiracy. Briefly, disillusionment with 1830 heightened his sense of revolutionary expectation and commitment: "I am busying myself now greatly with the French Revolution," he assured a friend, on 22 May 1832, and also with German *Saintsimonismus*, meaning the first stirrings of international socialism. "I will write books about both," he promised, though it was not long before he became disenchanted with Saint-Simonianism.[91] Far from signifying the collapse of revolutionary impulse into cloudy metaphysics, post-Hegelian philosophical effervescence meant that the republican-socialist revolution Heine saw looming would be far-reaching, ruthless and implacable in ideological fervor, "filling the world with horror and admiration." "The German Revolution will not be milder, more gentle than the French [Revolution]," he averred, "for being preceded by Kantian criticism, Fichtean transcendental idealism, and *Naturphilosophie*." "Do not take my advice lightly, the advice of a dreamer who warns you about Kantians, Fichteans and *Naturphilosophen*. Do not take lightly the fantastic poet, who expects in the realm of appearance the same revolution now transforming the realm of the spirit."[92] Rather a "drama will be enacted in Germany that will make the French Revolution look like a harmless idyll."[93] While less prescient than commentators sometimes suggest, and only vaguely relevant to the 1848 revolutions, rise of Marxism or anything subsequent, Heine's premonitions about Germany's philosophical ferment preparing future vast events are not insignificant.

DIVERGENT JEWISH REVOLUTIONARY SCHEMES

Heine's *Zur Geschichte der Religion und Philosophie* projects his (and Hess's) philosophical hero, Spinoza, as humanity's great champion, the emblem of a higher, more exalted revolutionary tradition than that of other republican activists or socialists toward whom he was briefly attracted but from whom he soon felt more and more estranged. Spinoza's legacy, still officially shunned by the entire Jewish world, had, from the early nineteenth century onwards, commenced its astounding reversal in standing. Secularization, revolution and emancipation was slowly transforming the old picture. Orthodoxy had begun its long migration to the periphery while a wholly new Jewish secular culture slowly emerged, with Riesser and, later, Hermann Cohen (1842–1918), "the last great thinker of the German idealist tradition," as leading voices. Among the consequences were new perspectives on the Jewish-Christian relationship, on earlier eras of Jewish history, and a growing need for secular icons with a social and moral message. Spinoza's reputation perceptibly benefited from a shift already hinted at earlier in Mendelssohn, Maimon and Nassy. Rescuing Jewish identity from the narrow corridors of orthodoxy, gradually transformed Spinoza into a morally, politically and culturally positive manifestation, a hero of the German Jewish world first, then of eastern Europe's secularizing Jews and finally a stock fixture of early twentieth-century Yiddish literature.[94]

Accustomed to view history as a ceaseless struggle between ascetic spiritualism and sensualism, "Jerusalem versus Athens," Heine aimed to synthesize spirit and body. "Even in their earliest beginnings, the Pentateuch shows, Jews veered to abstraction, their whole religion being nothing but a feat of dialectics whereby matter and spirit are divided, and the Absolute recognized only in the form of the spirit."[95] This is where Mosaic tradition went wrong. In Spinoza, according to Heine's conception, a truer Jewish tradition is restored—God manifesting himself in all things and human perfection becoming fulfillment of body *and* "Geist" [spirit]. Heine provisionally joined forces with Saint-Simonians and socialists in demanding "rehabilitation of the flesh," but only via a pantheism rooted in Spinoza, differing greatly, it turned out, from socialist aspirations, being closer to the "pantheism" of some Cabbalists.[96] Heine's two warring absolutes, "Athens versus Jerusalem," could be transcended only by reuniting body and spirit, restoring the whole through finding the mean, as Spinozistic (and Cabbalistic) pantheism reunites God and the world, and as Schelling advocated "when still a philosopher," and "did not differ in the least from Spinoza."[97]

Spinoza drew a line "just as distant from the materialism of his brother, Locke, as from the idealism of his brother Leibniz," reconciling the two antitheses.[98] His dialectical clash of categories, Heine employed to contrast what he called "Nazarenism" (Judaism subsumed into Christianity) with "Hellenism," sometimes setting Nazarenism against the true Jewish spirit, which, to him, was in some sense a subterranean current at odds with rabbinic strictures, Jewish orthodoxy and Christianity. A giant, Moses was the immediate predecessor of Christ, but one who affixed Judaism unhealthily to a personal God demanding ascetic obedience and ritual compliance.[99] The overweening lawgiver and denier of the "Hellenic spirit," Moses, with his obsession with rigid codes of observance and "hatred of all imagery, and of sculpture," repelled Heine as he had Frey. Over the centuries, a perverted Pharisaic orthodoxy and its heir, Christianity, ceaselessly strove to drive body and spirit apart. Heine's aesthetic-moral philosophy, first developed between 1817 and the mid-1820s, and, he initially believed, such movements as Saint-Simonian socialism, alone could reconcile and harmonize body and spirit and effectively fight the theology of sin and perdition, and following Spinoza, clinch the ultimate synthesizing victory.[100] Hence, Heine's poetic battle-cry: "Spinoza ist der Philosoph der Zukunft" [Spinoza is the philosopher of the future]; for Börne, in stark contrast, Robespierre was the man of the future.[101]

Heine's schema was essentially a modified form of *Linkshegelianism* [Left Hegelianism], a radical idealism seeing the meaning of events in their supposed underlying "true motion" of spirit, conceiving past and present, the philosophy of history, as a working out of fundamental ideas. This guided his approach not least to the French Revolution's achievements and failures. "Take note of this, you proud men of deeds," he exhorted in 1833, "you are nothing but unconscious servants of those men of thought, who, often in modest silence, plotted all your doings in advance. Maximilien Robespierre was nothing but the hand of Jean-Jacques Rousseau, the bloody hand, which pulled out a body from the womb of his time for the soul that Rousseau made." Rousseau's restless, troubled personality was a premonition of "what sort of midwife his thoughts required to come bodily into the world."[102] Bonaparte, a still more towering figure than Robespierre, despite the carping of "German freedom-lovers with too much republican orientation to venerate [him]," had done more than anyone else to rescue German philosophy, literary studies and critique from persecution and ruin when everyone with republican sympathies in Germany reeled under the assault of aristocracy and "insignificant clerics." "Without him, our philosophers would have been eliminated on gallows and the wheel, along with their ideas."[103]

But if the format was Hegelian, Heine's conclusions differed dramatically from Hegel's. "Jew" and "Greek" to his way of thinking were no longer ethnic or theological terms, but diametrically contrasting ways of interpreting the world, pitting the ascetic against the sensual, the dogmatic and theological against the real and rational. In his major prose texts, Heine evinced an unshakable conviction, later shared by Hess, that Judaism and Jewishness embody the central continuity in relation to both Hellenism and Christianity, defining the principal creative current of Western history, being a living, organic force vital to the development of the whole. Heine and Hess thereby sought to reverse the (by them bitterly resented) topos, entrenched in the German mind by Kant and Hegel, that the Jews are a marginal, irrelevant remnant, a mere lingering vestige running counter to what truly matters, the essential thrust of [Christian] history.

"Spinozism," held Heine, supersedes materialism by elevating mankind, transcending the rift between "Athens and Jerusalem." Assuredly, revolutionary materialism and Spinozism alike work toward democratic revolution. In preparing for the future revolution, Spinozists and French materialists were allies, as they were with the socialists. But where socialists, like the revolutionary materialists of 1789–99, aim to reduce society to categories essentially economic, the lowest common denominator in Heine's schema, Spinozism aspires ultimately to elevate everyone into a godlike superhuman, combining knowledge, liberty and equality in a richer, more inspiring manner than revolutionary materialism or socialism: "we want to be neither *sans-culottes*, nor frugal citizens nor mean political leaders; we shall found a democracy of gods, equally glorious, equally holy, equally joyous."[104]

Philosophical insight and ethics, commencing with the Enlightenment, held Heine and Hess, were slowly displacing religion as the true basis of the moral and political order. "Spinozism," the starting point and core of Enlightenment, had slowly gained acquiescence helped by Mendelssohn, a process culminating, contended Heine, in the pantheistic naturalism of Lessing,

Goethe, Schiller, Fichte, Schelling and Hegel. What Heine, Hegel's as well as Spinoza's disciple, claimed was an "open secret," that "pantheism is the clandestine religion of Germany," was in fact more or less true of Lessing, Goethe and Herder—and to an extent Hegel, though Hegel himself publicly denied being an irreligious pantheist.[105] With some plausibility, Heine could project onto the entirety of German philosophy at its peak the two-tiered structure he had long recognized in Spinozism and eighteenth-century Enlightenment *clandestina* [illicit texts] since his schooldays. It grounded his claim that German philosophy maintained a bogus Christian front to veil its true character from churchmen, repressive authorities and a brutally ignorant people, a still largely hidden duality of public and secret permeating even Hegel's political theory, which, for readers of discernment, veils the secret key to Revolution, but as taught in universities constituted the grand philosophy of the Prussian state.[106]

Though sympathizing with the poor, Heine, far more than Börne and Hess, dreaded and disdained the "thoughtless multitude" and its populism, nationalism and antisemitism. Repudiating contemporary German culture and attitudes wholesale, he also considered Germany Europe's most fertile soil for building on Spinoza's legacy, nurturing the fruit of his philosophy. Whatever most people thought, Spinoza's way of thinking, pantheism, was the "religion of our greatest thinkers, our best artists, the clandestine religion of Germany—as was predicted fifty years ago by those German writers who campaigned so vigorously against Spinoza [i.e., Jacobi and Hamann]."[107] Established, official culture Heine viewed as an unholy alliance of Christian counter-revolutionaries, antisemitic Voltairean *philosophes* and scheming "moderates," a "pandemonium" of thought traditions arraigned against mankind's principal enlighteners, headed by Spinoza and the latter's heroic disciple, the worthy Lessing.[108]

Christian alignment with populism, nationalism, aristocratic dominance and Voltairean anti-Spinozism could, however, not long obstruct the underlying, anti-Voltairean, anti-Rousseauist true Enlightenment; the "true" revolution forged by philosophers and literary men like himself would eventually triumph.[109] Central to Heine's "Spinozism" stood the idea that "morality is independent of dogma and legislation, the pure product of healthy human sensibility," man's "true morality" is the reason of the heart, that will preside eternally over a perfected mankind in the future.[110] Goethe's courtly aloofness and aligning with princes, his refusal to embrace revolutionary politics, Heine deemed counterbalanced by his Spinozistic pantheism. If Schiller never discusses the fraught topic of Jewish emancipation, despite one of his closest friends, Wilhelm von Humboldt, figuring among the framers of Prussia's 1812 emancipation decree that briefly preceded reversion to Jewish disabilities after 1814, Heine ranked Schiller among the great cultural heroes, perceiving him too, like Nietzsche later, as propagating Spinoza's "God or nature" against Moses's miracle-working personal God and the rigid monotheism of the ancient Hebrews.[111] "Spinoza's teaching hovers around us," contends Heine's *On the History of Religion and Philosophy in Germany*, "like a Goethian song."[112] No easy position to promote, it conduced to ever-growing social and ideological isolation.

The setback of 1830 bitterly disappointed Heine and Börne alike and, at the same time, proved a turning point in their relationship. Resuming contact in Paris, in the autumn of 1831, both still an inspiration to "Young Germany," they still shared important common concerns. Like Hourwitz earlier, both wielded their famed *Judenwitz* as a tool for deflating contemporary society's complacency and bigotry, while hostile critics denigrated their cutting wit as proof of their supposedly un-German, typically Jewish character.[113] Neither ceased resenting antisemitism or feeling solidarity with the Jewish people. "The best among the assimilated Jews," Hannah Arendt once called them, Heine and Börne "never lost their awareness of necessary solidarity with the underprivileged in general."[114] For Heine and Börne, like Ruge, it was not just princely courts and clergy that were contemptible, but also the entire mystique of what Ruge called the "*Philisterthum* [Philistinism] of debased Romanticism," student right-wing *Teutomanismus* [teutomania], nationalism, and antisemitism along with vaguer xenophobic attitudes and book-burning, and despite the many students, professors and professional men drawn to this noxious mix, they agreed too that this was all absurdly anachronistic, a yearning for an obsolete Germanness, true "Christianity" and "old Reich" now all pitifully irrelevant vestiges of the past.[115]

Yet, from the outset there was also tension between them, a clash of principles and temperaments. As early as 1831, the Paris police (following their movements closely) noticed Heine's lack of ideological fervor was causing estrangement between him and more activist, revolutionary *patriotes*.[116] When Börne once asked Heine what he did on his first day in Paris, and Heine answered that he had visited the Bibliothèque-royale to examine medieval manuscripts, Börne found this incomprehensible and outrageous: how can anyone spend their first day in Paris poring over medieval manuscripts rather than proceed directly to the Panthéon to venerate the tombs of Rousseau and Voltaire, or the Place Louis XV to witness the scene of great revolutionary events! To Börne, that "first day" symbolized Heine's anti-social remoteness, reprehensible ideological and political *Indifferentismus*.[117]

After the *Hambacher Fest* (which Heine failed to attend) they saw little of each other and drifted increasingly apart. By 1833, Heine resented the Left's criticizing his far from wholly negative view of Napoleon and Louis-Philippe's post-1830 liberal monarchy, especially the progressive education policy of the latter's chief minister, Guizot. He begrudged too the Left's scorning his aversion to Jacobin tradition. Despite sympathy for the laboring poor, he had faulty ideas, it was rumored, about Jacobins, Robespierre and Napoleon, smacking of disloyalty to the authentic revolutionary attitude, a slur with which Börne concurred. If Heine was as indignant as any revolutionary exile about the German Confederation's joint decrees of 28 June 1832 negating the concessions conceded under pressure in 1830–31, and the princes' banning all political organizations, public meetings and demonstrations, and reassertion of stringent book, pamphlet and newspaper censorship, his opposition remained purely rhetorical. Börne's pronouncements were more directly linked to opposition circles, more specifically republican, more emphatically democratic and hostile to the July monarchy. If Heine and Börne had been allies in the past, once ensconced in France, Heine proved less and less willing to participate in organized subversion, and, Börne found to his dismay, wanted less and less to do with him personally. Heine came to regard Börne as raucous militant; Börne decided Heine was not serious in his principles.[118]

The June 1832 ordinances were Metternich's reply to the *Hambacher Fest*, which, consolingly for revolutionaries, continued to reverberate throughout Europe. All the way until 1848, it remained perfectly feasible to view the early 1830s democratic republican upsurge in southwestern Germany and Switzerland as the assured future general path to a well-grounded, universal democratic republican modernity. Until the devastating setback of 1848, radical observers, including Heine, Börne, Riesser and also the non-Jewish Ruge who regularly met Heine in Paris during the years 1843–45, could all view the common project into which they sank their efforts as the authentic, inevitable European destiny, even if Heine evinced a stronger sense of lurking menace than the others.[119]

What Germany needed, held Börne, was hard-nosed political writing and incisive polemics, advancing plans for the next revolution which he eagerly anticipated. Where for Börne, "only the religion of nature, only the Republic can save us," Heine agreed the people need emancipation from oppression but felt more attracted to towering reformers like Lafayette and Napoleon, and, despite his criticism, perhaps even Moses, figureheads capable of single-handedly altering the frame of society. He would have liked to have been a powerful leader or speaker moving the masses too. Where Börne deemed Bonaparte a traitor to true revolutionary principles, Heine hero-worshipped Bonaparte. If both abhorred monarchy, ecclesiastics and the old hereditary aristocracy, Heine now viewed what he saw as the harshness of Börne's revolutionary zeal, along with his thirst for economic equality generally, with something close to aversion. Börne's *Briefe aus Paris,* a work widely read that had a huge impact,[120] he styled *Sansküllottismus* [sans-culotteism] of thought and expression such as one has never encountered in Germany."[121]

While acknowledging, like the others, Hambach's stirring effect, Heine disliked the intoxicating fervor it had aroused. "Poor Börne could not stop talking about Hambach," he remarked later, "and the pleasure he took from being there."[122] At Hambach, genuine revolutionary values, elevating philosophical, cosmopolitan and French principles had indeed predominated: philosophical "reason," not the misty, bigoted rigmarole of Wartburg, "was acknowledged as the highest authority." But precisely there was the tragedy of the German predicament. Despite praising Wirth and his republican high-mindedness in 1832, Heine later reappraised the episode as, after all, rather flawed. Unlike Börne, he stood aloof from Wirth's and Ruge's further efforts.[123] At Hambach, one could imagine the faction proclaiming the healthy principles of "French freedom" as uppermost in German revolutionary conspiracy, but the signs showed unmistakably this was delusion: not the words "humanity," "world citizenship," "reason" and "truth" but the quasi-religious fanaticism of contemptible Teutonists, populists and nationalists, the words "Fatherland," "Deutschland," "faith of our fathers," etc., all the crasser slogans were those that would electrify the unenlightened, the great majority. In revolutionary times, one must kill or be killed: "I hereby announce," prophetically averred Heine, diverging sharply from Börne, Ruge and Wirth, indeed the entire radical democratic republican mainstream Left of his day, "that these representatives of nationality have much deeper roots in German soil than the representatives of *Cosmopolitismus*," and that in the coming struggle, the cosmopolitans will probably find themselves at the losing end. Teutomaniacs offered a "mix of primitive superstition and demonic power that would prove stronger than all the arguments of reason." Here Heine proved far more prescient than in his predictions about German philosophy.[124] Abhorring demagoguery and demagogues, Heine in the last analysis construed Hambach and Wirth's heroic stand as a fading lamp in a sullen sky.

Börne was emphatically more of a *Volksfreund*, a proto-socialist showing decidedly greater willingness than Heine to mix with, as well as show sympathy for, artisans. Börne also showed greater sympathy for the surging early 1830s neo-Jacobin veneration for Marat and Robespierre, whom Heine, Ruge and all Enlightenment radicals and moderates alike publicly repudiated.[125] Where Heine scorned Robespierre as the "Napoleon of the petit bourgeoisie," Börne considered Robespierre the Revolution's towering peak, a tenderhearted, good man, practically "virtue" personified, the ultimate symbol of justice, equality and rights.[126] The great French Revolution had inaugurated modernity and, for Heine and Börne equally, remained a halfway interrupted, unfinished story. By 1832, Börne, now in steadily declining health due to his worsening lung illness, felt more enthralled than ever by the drama of 1789–94 and began researching into aspects of it, contemplating the possibility of writing a full-length history of the Revolution.[127]

Börne saw his own revolutionary ideology as neo-Jacobin and based on "French principles." But here, partly enticed by Philippe Buonarotti (1761–1837), the former co-conspirator of the supreme egalitarian of the great Revolution, Gracchus Babeuf (1760–1797), let his instinctive egalitarianism mislead him. A sworn egalitarian, Buonarotti did more to refurbish Robespierre's reputation and tarnish the "Girondins" as the friends of bankers than any other post-revolutionary writer. In the wake of the 1830 Revolution, he was free for a time to convene meetings and propagate his neo-Jacobin ideology and did so with considerable success, helped by the general disillusionment at the outcome of 1830 and, soon, the growing repressiveness of Louis Philippe's regime. Buonarotti's vision of the Jacobins, Marat and Robespierre as a social-ethical ideal, and Robespierre's veneration for Rousseau, both strongly appealed to Börne, even if he was not wholly blind to the ruthlessness of the Terror.[128] Perhaps Robespierre did seek dictatorship, he grants at one point, but does that really matter when, like a high priest called by

Heaven, he believed in ordinary people and "virtue" more strongly than anybody else?[129]

The future Revolution would indeed be a war of the poor against the rich to demolish existing property relations. "There is something higher than the law—justice; something higher than general well-being—universal morality; more beautiful than freedom—virtue."[130] Until Robespierre's downfall, the Revolution advanced, held Börne, "from then until today it has been on the defensive." "The future Revolution must resume" from where Robespierre left off.[131] The reason why history, philosophy, politics and experience have so far failed to establish a perfect state, is because it is never based on "justice, virtue and morality"; these have never been the aims except briefly, during the French Revolution. Yet, without these there is no harmony or stability. The people are often misled by demagogues, but the instinct of the masses does not miss the right path for long. France needed to revert to the "dictatorship of the people."[132]

That the veritable Robespierre was a fanatical tyrant who ruthlessly suppressed freedom of thought, freedom of expression, the best revolutionary newspapers and journals and, politically, was monumentally corrupt and given to systematic lying, Börne could not accept for a moment. Robespierre's cheating his ignorant audience had cost the French dearly, observed Heine, rendering their Revolution bloodier and more anarchic than necessary, undoing thereby its best achievements. "That the French had to pay such expensive tuition was the fault of pre-1789 despotism so stupidly afraid of the light, that [. . .] it tried to keep the people in intellectual immaturity, barring all instruction in the science of the state while entrusting censorship to Jesuits and Obscurantists of the Sorbonne and, in the most foolish way, suppressing the periodical press, the most powerful means of promoting the intelligence of the people."[133] Passionate for freedom of the press, Heine cared more for individual liberty, especially his own, than collective salvation through political action, or relieving the destitution of the poor, and occasionally his antagonism toward the popular was almost pathological.

Börne had long recognized in Heine what he called (echoed later by Hermann Cohen) his "great Jewish anguish."[134] It must be conceded, though, that Börne showed little real grasp of the great Revolution's essential paradox with which Heine constantly wrestled: the people, unjustly exploited and hungry, justifiably felt aggrieved and deserved their Revolution. But "the people" were also ignorant, prejudiced and repressive, given to simplistic answers and to trusting untrustworthy leaders, so how was one to square the circle?[135] The last meeting of Heine and Börne occurred on 9 January 1833; from February 1833 onwards, Börne began publicly denouncing what he saw as Heine's weak, unreliable character, idleness and political timidity. Unlike other prominent men caught in the turmoil of the time, mused Börne, Heine "possessed two backs" receiving regular thrashings, one from the radical, the other from the aristocratic side.[136] In elegant circles, Börne struck Heine as taciturn and monosyllabic, a man engaging in meaningful discussion only with the like-minded.[137]

While Börne was certainly the more isolated of the two in France, he at least ploughed through heaps of newspapers, closely following the detail of the latest developments. Heine read more widely, remaining deeply preoccupied with art, history and literature, cultivating a much wider, more philosophical and literary perspective. Disliking his single-minded focus, Heine rather unfairly styled Börne "ein Sklave der nazarenischen Abstinenz" [a slave of Nazarene abstinence].[138] Irritated by his literary and aesthetic aloofness, by 1832, Börne regularly vented his criticism of Heine's character and condescension in Parisian German café society, and at meetings of exiles, denigration that got back to Heine, rendering their relationship ever worse. It became an open rift unlikely to be mended. Even so, deeming their quarrel unhelpful to what he still saw as a joint wider project, Börne confined his fiercest disparagement to private letters and unpublished manuscripts.

A clash of temperaments and of revolutionary ideologies, at the core lay their powerfully conflicting visions of the French Revolution. The French Revolution, Börne grasped perfectly, was really three conflicting revolutions, three totally irreconcilable rival ideologies locked in permanent struggle.[139] The Revolution of the "moderates," like Louis-Philippe's backers in 1830, aimed to keep king and aristocracy and reproduce something like the "British model." It was totally at odds with the Revolution of what Börne terms France's *Geistesaristocracy*, that is, the intellectual elite, the Revolution of the (Radical) Enlightenment, of the *Encyclopädisten* culminating in Condorcet, Brissot and the Girondins, which was undoubtedly republican and devoted to freedom of expression, equality of rights and representative republican government, but being, as he saw it, the work of intellectuals backed by the bourgeoisie, stuck to spheres and deployed ideas beyond the comprehension of ordinary folk. Finally, there was the outlook of the common people who carried the Revolution through to the, in his view, higher Revolution of Rousseau and Robespierre. This superior, people's revolution was based not on intellect and concepts but instinct, sentiment and the ordinary. How could anyone truly identifying with the people not opt for the last? Here was why even the socialistic Catholicism of De Lamennais with its appeal to ordinary folk also came to appeal to Börne in his last years.[140] "Virtue," sentiment and Rousseau's "simple souls" matter infinitely more than enlightened ideas.

Börne understood perfectly that the Radical Enlightenment's revolution of ideas, universal rights and the intellectuals, clashed fundamentally with the ethos of Marat's and Robespierre's following, the *sansculottes* and the cult of the populist ordinary, and was indeed in bitter conflict with it. Few understood the logic of the French Revolution's internal conflict so clear-sightedly. "The Girondins fought for the intellectual aristocracy," he noted, "and that is why they had countless supporters among both contemporaries and those that came later."[141] But the only ideological impulse that counts for ordinary folk, is that of Rousseau, the rhetoric of "virtue," which is what drew ordinary men in droves to Robespierre, who ceaselessly exhorted the "virtue" of the people and in Börne's eyes was the Revolution's supreme emblem, the "Martyrer der Wahrheit" [martyr of truth].[142] Where Börne followed Rousseau, genuinely believing in the goodness of unspoiled human nature, Heine, after 1831, dismissed Börne as an "argwöhnischen Kleingeist" [suspicious, small-minded character] *à la* Robespierre spouting a ridiculously naïve notion of "virtue."[143] Radical enlighteners, like Condorcet, and in the German context Forster, Ruge and Heine, utterly scorned Robespierre's "Counter-Enlightenment"; Börne the proto-socialist, like the French socialists then, and later the Marxists, embraced it.

Börne and Heine had their ideological, political and literary differences, but at bottom the clash was perhaps ultimately between incompatible temperaments. No Nazarene or philistine, Börne was far from being just a shrewd organizer and journalist; his formidable literary gift and scathing wit, remarked Ruge, penetrated not just to the heart of matters political but, piercing defensive armor, sometimes even the hearts of hardened opponents. Heine, by contrast, needed quiet, time for himself and to resonate through his writing, a requirement clashing with Börne's impatient taut activism. After Börne died of his lung disease, on 12 February 1837, Heine even neglected to attend his old comrade's funeral six days later—as was swiftly relayed back to Germany by the underground radical gossip factory—despite the funeral taking place close to where both men lived. He had never been Börne's friend (or enemy), claimed Heine loftily, but his non-attendance left a notably unfavorable impression on the large German expatriate community residing in Paris.[144]

More scandalous still, to many, was the publication, in 1840, of Heine's beautifully written if long-winded polemic against the deceased exiled revolutionary. Their escalating quarrel during Börne's last five years had assumed a sadly obsessive role in Heine's thinking. His scathing critical assessment of Börne's life and achievement, his political activity, writing and wit, his *Ludwig Börne, Eine Denkschrift*, was widely deemed malicious, unbalanced and unfair at the time. The book appalled fellow radicals but is eminently revealing about Heine's general view of the world. Decrying Börne's "Nazarene narrowness," his "Robespierre brand" of demagogic republicanism, and eagerness to curry favor among society's lowest strata, the publication was indignantly reviewed by Riesser, Ruge and many others. So offended was Heine by Riesser's furious review, he reportedly challenged him to a duel.[145]

Ruge interviewed Heine himself on the subject, in September 1843. Heine explained that he was really attacking Börne's milieu and circle rather than Börne himself, and in deriding an acclaimed hero of the fight to emancipate Europe's peoples was by no means abandoning the revolutionary struggle itself. Ruge remained unconvinced.[146] The mature Heine, suggested Ruge, deluded himself into believing he was some sort of arch-revolutionary among all the exiled and non-exiled German revolutionaries, all of which was some kind of fantasy. A radical subversive, at once drawn to and repelled by Heine, Ruge viewed him as a would-be presiding figure withdrawn within himself, timidly holing himself up in Paris, afraid to return to Germany lest he be arrested and locked up (Ruge had spent six years in royal prisons 1824–30) while, in private conversation presenting himself as Germany's ultra radical. For a time, indeed, he had been, in a way, but so far as Ruge could judge, only in a purely rhetorical sense. Splendidly witty at the expense of others, he manifested neither wit, nor judgment, when it came to himself.[147]

However useful a scourge of anti-Enlightenment right-wing Romantics in the 1820s, the post-1830 Heine, Ruge concurred with Börne, had indeed retreated into *Indifferentismus,* aloofness and literary snobbery, passively trapped in the old social and political system.[148] After his death, Börne was commemorated by the radical-minded public very differently from how Heine would be remembered after his demise. During the 1840s, Börne's grave in Paris became well known as a commemorative site to drivers of Parisian taxi cabs, a place of pilgrimage for freedom fighters and revolutionaries from all over. It would be hard, mused Ruge, for those fighting for universal rights across the globe, to venerate Heine's future grave in comparable fashion.[149] Börne, in Ruge's eyes, was a courageous freedom fighter, trusting more fervently than anyone that the international democratic republican fight was not for any one nation or people but a common struggle of all peoples against universal tyranny. Even less sympathetic to Heine and warmer toward Börne, Engels later dubbed the latter the "John the Baptist of the new era."[150]

Radicals rejected where "moderates" basically accepted the existing social, political, religious and institutional order. Though not necessarily men of action, the first were by definition revolutionaries of the mind expounding ideas entailing far-reaching change while moderate Enlightenment reformers broadly sought to legitimate the existing aristocratic and courtly order. Of course, the dividing line was unclear or ambiguous at times, obliging the historian to take account of circumstances, the radical underground's clandestine character and the pressure to mask intellectual radicalism so prevalent in Europe beyond the zone conquered by French revolutionaries after 1789. Kant and Hegel, like Mendelssohn, could well be considered a baffling mix of radical and "moderate" elements. "Thus Kant never openly declared his republicanism," remarked Ruge, "and Hegel never admitted his atheism. Why?"[151] As a mask to preserve their respectability; but not everyone endorsed such an analysis. Hence, unfortunately for their long-term subsequent legacies, their attitude to the existing Prussian state, to social, political and religious reform, appeared to most contemporaries more conservative and respectable than it actually was.

Many veiled their more radical tendencies from the public, like Kant and Hegel, for decades, and there is a sense in which Heine, beyond his own self-image, did so too. This exasperated Börne but cleared the way for Heine to become an icon of the German Jewish middle class in a later era, something Börne could never be. Despite the crushing setbacks of 1830 and 1848, Heine's quieter, more sophisticated radical vision survived and began exerting a widening appeal. The young Hermann Cohen in his essay "Heinrich Heine und das Judenthum" (1867) [Heinrich Heine and Jewry], published long before he was appointed to his philosophy chair at Marburg, in 1875 (the first unconverted Jew to become a full professor in Germany), warmly eulogized Heine's perspective on modernity and world Jewry. He also enthusiastically absorbed Heine's approach into his own philosophical perspective. For Cohen too, positive personal religion, Judaism especially, underpinned that "great democracy where each person should be not just king but also bishop in his household."[152] Endorsing Heine's pantheism and destruction of dogmatic religious authority—while exhibiting none of the antagonism to Spinoza and Spinozism he became notorious for in later life—the young Cohen celebrated Heine's reconciliation of Germanness and Jewishness as a form of ethical idealism rooted in individual liberty and French Revolution ideals, delighted by Heine's overturning the age-old historical opposition of Judaism and Christianity such as embedded in Kant and Hegel, with its generally accepted assumptions to the detriment of the former.[153]

Until a decade or so after his death, however, Heine was not emblematic for any segment of Jewry, let alone a quintessentially representative German Jewish icon. Hence, in the wider Jewish consciousness, Spinoza's most vocal admirer, among the acutest, most prescient commentators of the nineteenth century's first half, for some forty years after first gaining status as a German poet, as a cultural critic and intellectual voice likewise needed rescuing from total marginality in the German-Jewish outlook. He only began to be publicly eulogized as a major cultural representative of the secular Jewish world in the 1860s, emerging almost in parallel with Spinoza, first salvaged by the very same prominent, much-admired young philosopher, Hermann Cohen, who, later, toward the close of the nineteenth century, turned emphatically against Spinoza, to become the modern Jewish intelligentsia's fiercest antagonist of the steadily emerging "Jewish" Spinoza cult.[154]

Yet perhaps Heine's greatest contribution as a specifically "Jewish revolutionary" was not so much his contribution to modern Jewish cultural identity as something rather different: was he not the true founder of the historiography and study of the Radical Enlightenment as a clandestine tradition? It was Heine who effectively first recognized, as Bruno Bauer did likewise but only from the later 1830s, the further development of the hidden underground philosophical networks of the late seventeenth century, in Germany as throughout Europe, as a working out of Spinoza's ideas deep in the underground of European culture, a clandestine intellectual ferment marking out the path, and sketching the necessary legislation, for curtailing religious authority, secularizing the Western mind, and forging the revolutionary democratic republic based on the "common good." He was the first to recognize this underground transition as a revolution in thought carried through in the face of censorship, repression and persecution, the veritable hidden history of intellectual and conspiratorial opposition to the privileges and power of kings, aristocracy and clergy. Heine's was a vision of a dichotomous Enlightenment of radicals versus publicly applauded moderates that Leo Strauss subsequently revived with his researches on the relationship of Spinoza to the Enlightenment in the 1920s.[155] Strauss's work then in turn marked the twentieth-century starting point of the present-day Radical Enlightenment historiography.

THIRTEEN

Moses Hess (1812–1875) and "The New Jerusalem"

More deeply imbued with traditional Judaism than Heine or Marx, Moses Hess (1812–1875), was raised in an observant household, at Bonn, mainly by a pious grandfather on whom he looked back with deep affection. His mother died when he was fourteen, his father, Moritz Hess, owner of a successful sugar refinery, in Cologne, was frequently away. Born when the Rhineland formed part of Napoleonic France, Hess's traditional *yeshiva* education after a time aroused in him a vehement reaction against religious orthodoxy, leading, from the age of sixteen onwards, to a prolonged estrangement from both religion and his father.[1]

The young Hess, permanently at odds with his observant father, refused to involve himself with the family business in any way. Instead, he studied at Bonn University, from 1836 to 1839, but left without a degree. An autodidact in philosophy and general culture, working, insofar as he had a profession, as a journalist, Hess was a gentle, dreamy type lacking that polemical gift and incisive wit Heine and Marx shared with Hourwitz and Börne. Long before meeting Heine in person, Hess imbibed the heretical "Spinoza ideology" of Heine's *History of Religion and Philosophy in Germany,* along with Hegel's conception of history as spirit and physical nature unfolding in dialectical stages toward the perfection of civil society.[2]

In Hegel, Heine and Spinoza, especially the latter's doctrine unifying spirit and matter, along with the republican fervor of 1830 and the *Hambacher Fest,* the young Hess found his inspiration and what he considered the true basis of modern materialism and socialism, the quintessence of modernity. Spinozist monism, to his mind, underpins everything, from reconciling physical nature and soul to what he later conceived as a "Jewish national renaissance" which he hesitantly began to ponder in the 1850s and to which he contributed in an important way in his last book (1861).

His concern with Jewishness as a modern problem Hess himself afterwards dated from the Damascus scandal of 1840. This ugly international affair erupted when Hess was twenty-eight: Capuchin friars accused local Jews, in Damascus, of secretly murdering one of their number and another man, to utilize their blood for ritual purposes at Passover, evoking a tremendous upsurge of pent-up Christian antisemitic hatred in and far beyond Syria, causing Western antisemitic fervor for the first time to merge also with powerful Muslim anti-Jewish sentiment. Waves of fury extended as far as France, where, already a little earlier, antisemitic sentiment was powerfully blending with early socialism, especially in the thought of Fourier and Proudhon.[3] The "Damascus affair" impacted strongly on Hess, Heine and many others.[4] It was then "that it dawned on me for the first time," remarked Hess later, "that I belong to my unfortunate, slandered, despised, and dispersed people."[5]

As regards social revolution, by the late 1830s Hess had already ventured well beyond Heine and, though closer to Börne's stance, had gone beyond him too. His militant social reformism, which he and his small circle later dubbed "True Socialism," he first introduced in his *Die heilige Geschichte der Menschheit* (1837) [The Holy History of Mankind], the earliest substantial socialist text to appear in German, and the first Young Hegelian book with a clear socialist tendency. Never particularly erudite or highly educated, Hess composed his initial effort while still a university student in his mid-twenties, immersed in quasi-religious elation, jotting down shortly after publication: "Spinoza raised my consciousness fully to that level on which I wrote the "holy history of mankind," with the 'Bible in one hand and *The Ethics* [of Spinoza] in the other."[6] He subtitled his work: "From a Young Disciple of Spinoza" [Von einem Jünger Spinozas].[7]

The book was by no means based on economic analysis or anything remotely like a theory of class warfare. Rather, Hess's opening attempt to present socialism as the necessary, inevitable result of general social development reworks Hegel's schema and Heine's Spinozistic pantheism into a social revolutionary philosophical creed teaching universal human brotherhood and the eventual reconciliation of those possessing wealth with those without possessions, an ideology, he maintained, that transcended both Judaism and Christianity. An early strain of what Marx and Engels later scorned as "Utopian Socialism,"[8] Hess pronounced his vision morally and intellectually superior to Saint-Simon's, Fourier's and Proudhon's approaches, leading mankind to a higher level of moral thought and social theory.

Dividing history into a sequence of fourteen eras, he presented each as characterized by "the spiritual leadership of a great personality" heralding fundamental social change, as, for example, the Christian communities of the Roman Empire, who, he believed, initiated a new phase of mankind's development toward maturity and modernity.[9] Hess's fourteen eras he organized into three main defining phases of history, the introductory epoch culminating in the first great turning point, the coming of Christ; the second climaxing with the second great turning point, the coming of Spinoza, the "prototypical figure of modern times"; with the third main stage being the revolutionary era ushering in mankind's post-Enlightenment class conflict–resolving effort that will culminate, supposedly, in a richly harmonious and enhanced social future.[10]

What ties human history's three overarching epochs together in Hess's quasi-Hegelian schema is what he conceived as a progressive drive toward unification in all spheres—social, moral and cultural evolution—producing economic harmony, social equality and finally full freedom of the individual. The Hegelian element was conspicuous. Isaiah Berlin later objected, not altogether wrongly, that while Hess's title "claims the inspiration of Spinoza, apart from a vague rationalism, and belief in the unity of all creation, the text has little to do with the great seventeenth-century master." Spinoza's system, devised a century and a half before, *is,* however, Hess's chief thread tying all together, revealing the ultimate "common good" cementing all humanity under the single seal of a new universal civic religion based on knowledge of the unity of God (or Nature).[11] Spinoza, the thinker, retains his presiding significance throughout, above all other men except Jesus who, in Hess's eyes, was morally his equal but not his superior. Spinoza's philosophy is inherently more valuable than deism, Judaism and Christianity, argues Hess, all of which he considered to be subsumed within it.

Sniping at Kant, Hegel and the German Idealists, Hess reaffirms Heine's provocative notion that Christianity always remained in essence Mosaic Judaism's junior offspring, that Moses's laws and Jesus's teaching remain closely linked, albeit both are today now dead, turned to dust.[12] "Just as Christ did not want his teaching to overturn the Old Law so far as it was divine, but rather to widen it, so Spinoza repudiated neither the Christian nor Jewish religion as far they were divine." Rather, the master (Spinoza) showed "theology and philosophy, faith and knowledge, can dwell peacefully alongside each other."[13] This was a way of reconciling the core message of Spinoza's *Ethics*, that reason and knowledge are the path to true freedom and the "summum bonum" [highest good], with the *Tractatus Theologico-Politicus* basic message that most people are unable to rise to true insight and freedom so that to secure general "obedience," a mythical civic religion, is required. This civil religion, abstracting from Judaism and Christianity, must be entirely under the republic's control, not that of priests. In his subsequent works, Hess regularly drew on the parallel between Christ and Spinoza, first introduced by Heine styling Spinoza Christ's "divine cousin" and comparing the "world's rejuvenation following Christ" to the "world's rejuvenation following Spinoza."[14] With this astounding parallel, Hess was not trying to shock readers with outrageous blasphemy so much as convey how profoundly the Enlightenment, seconded by its direct and natural heir, the Great Revolution of 1789–99, transformed the entire human reality and its future prospects.[15] Borrowing Christianity's ethical principles while dispensing with Christian dogma, mysteries, priests and churches, Hess artfully merged strands of Spinoza, Hegel and Heine.[16]

Belief in God in any conventional sense plays no part in his schema. Implacable foe of commerce, money and paternal dominance, along with revealed theology, rabbis and priests, Hess, from the outset, long before reading Feuerbach's *Das Wesen des Christenthums* [The Essence of Christianity] in 1841, was an uncompromising atheist. At meetings with illiterate workmen at clandestine gatherings in Cologne and thereabouts, he answered the recurring question, "what religion should we all confess?" by replying following his schema, "the religion of love and humanity." When asked, "is this common human religion unChristian?" he answered, "no, it is all the more [Christian for omitting God, theology and priests], being the fulfillment of the Christian religion."[17] It is insufficient for philosophy to remove revelation, miracles, faith, priests and churches without also, as Spinoza showed, filling the moral gap.

Like Rousseau, an early inspiration in Hess's youth prior to discovering Spinoza, Hess conceived mankind as everywhere in chains, trapped in subjection and oppression. In mankind's wretched predicament, moreover, organized revealed religion had long functioned as a facilitating agent, sanctioning and smoothing social repression while forming a barrier to human progress.

All Young Hegelians adopted a perspective of this sort. But in Hess stress on the potential benign side of religion was stronger than with the others: there remains an urgent need for a secularized, purified, future world "religion" raised to a higher level and stripped of its old role as barrier. Religion without God will be a key agent of human liberation, and always necessary as long as there is no other way to introduce comprehensive social and political transformation and freedom, or emancipate ethical life, rendering mankind happy, without men's consciousness being raised first. This in turn requires not just terminating the repressive functions of traditional faith and belief but also generating a new religious sensibility for the masses.[18] Meanwhile, to soften the existing repression and harsh social circumstances traditional religion sanctions, existing religion, provisionally indispensable to suffering man, should remain in place as the "opium" of the people—as Hess foreshadowed Marx in designating it (though he too probably borrowed this telling simile from Heine, who had already used the image).

Much the same socialistic-messianic doctrine, with Adam again the prototype of pre-Christian antiquity, Christ the God-man prefiguring the Middle Ages and Spinoza the prototype of emancipated human modernity,[19] reappears in Hess's somewhat better-organized and -informed second book, *Die europäische Triarchie* [The European Triarchy], published at Leipzig in 1841. Existing religion occupies the moral vacuum philosophy alone cannot fill but eventually will need replacing with a modernized civil quasi-religion. Communism is history's logical outcome and should be conceived as the mediated life of God [Nature], just as "Nature is the unmediated life of God." Spinozism again outranks Hegelianism, he sticks to Heine in insisting, as Hegelianism is "Christian" and "Nazarene" and mistakenly places "spirit" [Geist] above Nature, enhancing repressive spiritualism whereas Nature, as Spinoza taught, "is not the handmaiden of spirit but its equal wife."[20]

Hess, like Heine and Marx, follows Hegel and the Hegelians in searching for history's meaning in great events, especially the French Revolution, which for Hess too was a world-historical event of universal significance, its ideas prefiguring the great changes in the real world on the level of "Geist" [spirit]. Spinoza's radicalism remained for Hess, as for Heine, a higher realm than eighteenth-century *philosophique* materialism or the new schemes of French socialism. Like Heine, Hess considered French materialism reprehensibly one-sided, the counterpart and antithesis to "Nazarenism," the most pejorative term in his and Heine's idiosyncratic vocabulary, something strictly confined to one aspect of substance, a repressive spiritualism antagonistic to

Spinoza's *natura naturans*, which is the synthesis of "Jerusalem and Athens," Heine's fulfilled sensualism.[21]

At the commencement of the modern era, Spinoza established the absolute unity of all being; and it is Spinoza who showed that while "Nature is itself pure necessity," man is nevertheless free in a philosophically specific sense rendering both morality and liberty meaningful and possible, even though he could not foresee all the consequences of the philosophical and ethical revolution he introduced.[22] His second book Hess envisaged more as a call for action, a "Philosophie der Tat," or fusion of philosophy and action into a synthesis, than a summons to further reflection. Recent German philosophy, culminating in Feuerbach, had now fulfilled its historic mission and propagated "the truth" understood philosophically. What was required now was not intellectuals but active collective involvement with the future, inspired leaders guided by the past and present, transforming truth into reality through revolutionary schemes promoting mass action: "we must build bridges that again lead from heaven to earth."[23] Again, Hess firmly disapproved of mainstream Hegelianism, viewing it as a constricting intellectual phalanx besieging universities from without while instilling quiescent philosophizing within. Still, the Left Hegelian school deserve applause for starting the current shift of attention from "philosophy of history to philosophy of action."[24]

As a communist revolutionary selecting strands of Spinoza, leaving aside others, Hess retained Spinoza's division of humanity between the philosophically minded and the multitude, but in his system the democratic republic and Spinoza's "great councils" largely disappear from view. "True democracy is social equality," held Hess's redemptive messianism, the mass reconciliation of rich and poor by the effort of the people on the basis of communism.[25] To promote his communist vision, he deliberately employed the term "socialism" to mean "communism," much as communists frequently did later, even though previous French usage employed the label "socialism" chiefly to denote work reorganization and employment reform while, in Germany, the term had not yet entered regular usage. "Communism" carried, for most, an unfamiliar and soon decidedly alarming ring.[26] Essential to emancipation culminating in "communism," admonished Hess, will be "emancipation of morals," meaning dissolution of formal marriage, introduction of open partnerships, heterosexual and same gender, together with free love generally, leaving civil justice to focus attention exclusively on "useful laws."[27]

Transforming the world through universal action, reaching toward emancipation of all mankind and universal free love would, he envisaged, be initiated and directed by Europe's principal "Triarchy" of political and cultural powers—Britain, France and Germany—each people bringing to fruition a different aspect of mankind's quest for freedom, helping remake humanity according to its distinctive cultural capabilities. England would provide up-to-date industry, technology and ways of mastering resources, thereby contributing materially to universal equality; France, where socialism and social reform had progressed furthest, would provide the laws of social-ethical freedom and forms of labor reorganization grounding universal political freedom. Germany, meanwhile, philosophically more advanced, would propagate the profound grasp needed to underpin true social-spiritual freedom. "First prophet" of Europe's unification, as of German communism and, later, Jewish nationalism, the final reconciliation of Britain, France and Germany for Hess offered the inestimable blessing of a general unification of wills and the end of all war, establishing permanent peace (with tripartite protection against irredeemably despotic Russia), nurturing union and human stability.[28] Education of the young would proceed under the direct supervision of the state. Hess's "New Jerusalem" would be an era without contradictions in which all men will be "free and equal," "woman will enjoy the same humane education as man; and man and woman will be united through the bond of free love." Freeing women from the bondage of marriage arranged by families, especially their fathers, was entirely indispensable to his scheme.[29] Having added the dimension of full erotic emancipation to his thought, Hess married a non-Jewish German girl, in 1840, whose previous lifestyle as a prostitute had left her with a lowly reputation. They lived happily together in harmony until his death.

Hess first met Heine in person at the age of thirty, when visiting Paris as correspondent for the *Rheinische Zeitung*, in December 1842; this was shortly after he had first met Friedrich Engels (1820–1895), in Cologne and converted him from something like Börne's Jacobinism to communism. But it was during the preceding decade, during the late 1830s, that he felt closest to Heine and when he most ardently reworked Heine's notion of Spinozism as a world-redeeming force. If his viewing atheism and communism as logically linked also distanced him from Heine's worldview, this did not prevent Hess's communism from remaining, at bottom, an ethical project requiring an uplifting and transformative "religious" sensibility, changing the people's existing consciousness. These features would conspicuously clash, a few years later, with Marx's and Engels's more uncompromisingly materialist and secular communism anchored in a determinism requiring no prior change of consciousness and viewing religious history as simply the outcome of social and economic forces.[30]

HESS'S JEWISH REVOLUTIONARY MESSIANISM (1837–1848)

Despite Hess's emphasis on moral elevation rather than capturing the economic system, on changing the way men think as the key to ameliorating the world and ending human misery, he cannot altogether be aligned with the Radical Enlightenment, even during the 1830s and 1840s when still an active revolutionary (1837–48) less given to the mystical proto-Zionism he adopted later. True, in Hess's idiosyncratic vision, it is only by discrediting and suppressing theology, "miracles" and religious mysteries that human history, paradoxically, can for the first time become genuinely "holy." Hess did approximate closer than the post-1844 Marx—that is, following Marx's conversion to economic determinism and preaching class warfare—to being a radical enlightener, seeking to emancipate mankind by changing how men think. But there remains the issue of how far Hess envisaged humanity's future elevated moral outlook, and human freedom, as an outcome shaped by and conforming to philosophical reason. In Hess, "reason" seems less than pivotal, indeed decidedly vague compared to his messianic longings and dreaming. In some respects, he seems closer already in the 1830s and 1840s to the mystical messianic yearnings of Frank or Sabbatai Zevi with their emphasis on the common people and spontaneity than the sophisticated revolutionary schemes of Maimon, Hourwitz, Nassy, Furtado, Hartog Lémon, Börne, Heine or even Frey.

Throughout his life Hess remained convinced the "messianic age is the present age which began with Spinoza and reached its world historical existence in the great French Revolution. With the French Revolution begins the rebirth of the nations—and it is to the Jewish national religion in history that the nations are indebted for it."[31] His first post-Christian phase of human redemption was the Enlightenment: "a spirit grew in the innermost entrails of the [Enlightenment] period, ready to create new forms once the old ones had collapsed. This was the Holy Spirit of truth, justice and love. And in the last half of this period it announced its future life through joyful leaps and all kinds of movements in the womb of the mother, the symptoms of its life became undeniable. At that time, a true quest for Enlightenment reigned supreme, everyone feeling the new era's electrical spark could not imagine being less than zealous in carrying it further." Enlightened despots like Napoleon in particular helped push it forward.[32]

Hess first encountered Heine in person late in the latter's life, ten months before Marx too transferred to Paris, in October 1843. Paris, however, tended to accentuate the socialist rather than "Spinozist" features of Hess's outlook, hence was not likely to bring Heine and Hess closer. Getting to know the French capital, Hess lost no time in familiarizing himself with the budding socialist, anarchist and communist movements proliferating in its midst, becoming quite friendly with Proudhon for a time and quickly becoming expert on the different socialist cliques and factions of German exiles. It was Hess who first introduced Marx, in late 1843, to French socialist groups and showed Ruge around when the latter arrived for his two-year stint in Paris (1844–46), introducing him to diverse French socialist leaders and testing him on the current state of the world's revolutionary movements while seeking to convert him too, as he had Engels, to his own idealistic communist brand.[33] During his stay, Ruge, a declared anti-nationalist (and soon declared anti-socialist and foe of communism) found himself encountering issues of labor organization and economics, and the challenge of socialism and communism, in ways he had not previously needed to in Germany, learning under the guidance of "this likeable and good man," the "Kommunistenrabbi" [Communist Rabbi], as Ruge jokingly called Hess, echoing the designation "Rabbi Moses of the Communists" that the Young Hegelians (as Hess himself later noted) had bestowed on him.[34] But before long Ruge pulled away, breaking with both communists and socialists. Remaining resolutely "radikal-demokratisch" rather than socialist, Ruge emphatically distanced himself from Hess.[35]

Hess helped Marx and the others convene meetings of thirty, a hundred, sometimes even two hundred German exiles and workers in a rented hall attached to a wine tavern in Paris. But sustaining revolutionary socialist unity proved exasperatingly difficult. After a short collaboration in 1843–44, Ruge and Marx fell out over class conflict and economic determinism. As a radical enlightener, Ruge viewed emancipating the proletariat as essentially a question of transforming its ideas and consciousness.[36] By abandoning Enlightenment altogether, socialism and especially its new currents, Ruge and other democrats warned, were re-opening the gates to popular ignorance and prejudice; and here certainly they were right. Socialism not only ignored

Radical Enlightenment's insistence, using philosophy as the tool, on transforming the people's thinking before trying to change political and social reality but, in the case of Pierre-Joseph Proudhon (1809–1865), actually sought regeneration by Rousseauist reversion to ordinary thinking and traditional piety, demanding everything authentically popular including, mainly in his private notes, an exceptionally vehement antisemitism.[37] Proudhon's socialism directly clashed with the radical vision of reason and progress toward equal rights. In effect, all socialist theorists except Hess wholly diverged from the radical enlighteners in concentrating solely on economic reality, seeing the proletariat as the focus of their efforts, and trying to instill what amounted to quasi-religious new authoritarian dogma spurning both individual and collective liberties.

Hess's ethical emphasis and visionary thinking in fact elicited a negative reaction among most of the Leftist luminaries he encountered, especially within the international socialist revolutionary movement itself. As a socialist thinker Hess went very much his own way, gradually becoming more and more isolated. During the early and mid-1840s, as their revolution gathered intensity, dynamism and recruits, European socialism, with its first base in France and second foothold in the Rhineland, grew impressively while simultaneously becoming spectacularly divided. If pre-1848 atheism, republican humanism and revolutionism reached their zenith in Germany, the expatriate German communities in Paris, Zurich and Brussels, heavily reinforced with revolutionary expatriates ejected from Germany in 1830, 1832 and subsequently, added to the heady mix: they threw social democratic Radical Enlightenment and socialist revolutionary theorizing together, briefly trying to blend and become the avant-garde of both but soon bringing the two increasingly into division and strife. Among the networks of exiles, surviving principally as an overheated intellectual-literary fringe, festering splits soon became pervasive—especially between democratic radicals and socialists. The close-knit Paris German community exerted an intensifying effect in particular through the paper *Vorwärts*, posing queries ideological and organizational that it transmitted to the radical and socialist underground networks fanning out in all directions across France, Belgium, Switzerland and Germany.

Meanwhile, Hess continued pondering the phases of history. In his essay "Socialism and Communism" (1843), he examined the intractable difficulties in the bizarre but sustained parallels Heine drew, following Hegel, between the different phases of modern German philosophy and the French

Revolution, placing alongside each other as dialectically corresponding phenomena eminent personages drawn respectively from the spheres of ideas and action. Though "it is far too great an honor for Maximilien Robespierre," he asserts, "to be compared to Immanuel Kant," he still retained that baffling parallel, even suggesting Kant "the great destroyer in the realm of thought, far surpassed Maximilien Robespierre in terrorism," and that "we find in both [Kant and Robespierre] the same unrelenting, cutting, unpoetic, and sober honesty," the "same aptitude for distrust," the same "petit-bourgeois" mentality.[38] Heine was by no means the only observer to discover in Kant a hidden crypto-revolutionary, a private non-believer and republican; this was Ruge's view too, and one by no means wholly implausible.[39] Heine drew extended parallels likewise between Fichte and Napoleon, between (the later) post-Spinozistic Schelling, toward whom Heine and Ruge evinced fierce antipathy, and the post-1815 Restoration, and, finally, between Hegel and the 1830 July Revolution, implying Hegelianism is a narrative of "moderation" masking fraud, betrayal of philosophy, modernity and the people. To be fair to Hess, much of Heine's grand schema of parallels struck him as eccentric fantasy, a poetic genius's fanciful analogies. Still, he found Heine's parallel between Kant and Robespierre compelling to an extent, seeing both in some fundamental sense simultaneously great positive and retrograde steps, dangerously negative not least in compromising with traditional morality and religion—much like Rousseau. "Kant is erroneously considered the founder of German philosophy," Hess pontificated, for the "true founder of German philosophy" is "none other than [the great thinker] whose world view lies equally at the foundation of French social philosophy, namely Spinoza."[40]

Convinced that "after Napoleon, little remained of the old nobility beside the name, its pride and power having been shattered," Hess, like Engels, and later also Marx, remained curiously confident the old "nobility is no longer the enemy who can destroy our future." The universal harmony history tends toward "must necessarily come to naught in the end wherever there is aristocracy appropriating the collective force of society, on one side, while pushing the majority into humiliation and servitude. By this we do not mean that [old] aristocracy whose power is already broken, the aristocracy of nobility which was attacked first because it stood in the way. We mean the aristocracy of money."[41] Justified with respect to France, and his native Rhineland, this inference hardly applied to Britain, most of Germany, Russia or Europe more generally, and least of all Prussia and Austria. Unlike

France, most of Europe and in part even the United States, remained under the old landed aristocracy rather than new money derived from trade and industry—even if in America it was a landed elite without titles. In Britain, then by far the world's leading technological, industrial and commercial as well as maritime and imperial power, the landed aristocracy remained throughout the effective ruling class. Hess's conviction, like that of Marx and Engels later, that the capitalist manufacturing and commercial elite had ousted the old hereditary aristocracy and become the chief obstacle to progress and the people, led him to mistake the real character of Europe's nineteenth-century development. But in one major respect he was justified: the "moral as well as physical misery which starts to dominate now is caused by the growing wealth of one part of society and increasing poverty of the other. This disharmony, this inequality will increase even further."[42] In Hess's mind the dialectic of social inequality could only finally be resolved in communist equality.

Ascendancy of the new "aristocracy" of money, insisted Hess, meant growing polarization between rich and poor, increasing pauperization of society, and contraction of the middle class, as economic power became increasingly concentrated in the hands of bigger and bigger enterprises. But the capacities of modern industry and technology, he also believed, like traditional religion offered possibilities and resources that would ultimately help the populace resolve the mounting social crisis. For Hess, Marx's inexorable class conflict was simply not "desirable," as Isaiah Berlin put it, "or inevitable."[43] Spinoza's goals are ultimately achievable: the state can serve the "common good," protecting the weak from the richest and strongest while equalizing the arena of individual striving for happiness. Peace can ultimately reign in society, replacing the dismal history of rebellion and endless wars with states associated in a stable and universal league of nations. Women will receive civil rights equal to those of men based on the same education; and education can be universalized and provided for all.

France and the United States, he declared, were already more equal societies than Britain and Germany, but they too were experiencing intensifying pressures that would end in pushing equality further. More than most revolutionaries, Hess passionately longed for resolution of the festering social contradictions he saw generating wretchedness and poverty on all sides, resolution in fulfillment of the logic of history, harmonization as massive revolutionary change, but a resolution that would skip the ugly revolutionary violence, terror, *Robespierrisme* and suffering of 1789–94. The new technology he judged an instrument of providence, an agent driving the growing gulf and antithesis between wealth and poverty for the moment but that will ultimately help restore wholeness and harmony, a contrary process of equalization which in Hess's view must inevitably come. Resolving the growth in inequality he considered inevitable. "But woe betide us if this contrast will not be mediated peacefully but instead will be adjusted through [another violent] revolution!" Hess hoped passionately that his "New Jerusalem will be founded" by collective effort, in effect general revolution but without immense turmoil and bloodshed.[44]

CAUGHT BETWEEN THE RIVAL FACTIONS

In January 1845, the French Ministry of the Interior, spurred by an increasingly exasperated Prussian court, ordered the expulsion from France of an impressive list of leaders of the murmured "Revolution in the making," including Heine, Marx, Ruge and the renowned Russian revolutionary anarchist Mikhail Bakunin (1814–1876). The expatriates responded by appealing to the French liberal and radical press, which kicked up a considerable furor over what they denounced as Louis Philippe's disgraceful and humiliating servility toward Prussia. Uproar in the papers sufficiently embarrassed Louis-Philippe's ministers for them to reduce the scale of the planned expulsion. Ruge and the now permanently sickly Heine were exempted, Marx and Bakunin ordered to leave. Marx departed on 1 February 1845 for Brussels; Bakunin transferred to Dresden. Hess evaded expulsion, having already moved back temporarily to Cologne, at first working closely with Marx and especially Engels, before he and his wife likewise transferred, in 1845, to the same Brussels neighborhood where Marx and Engels settled, the city now emerging as the organizational center of the incipient Communist movement. But the clan, once firmly established in Brussels, aiming to form a "party," was immediately riven by implacable quarreling, in particular between the Hesses and Engelses.[45]

Yet, the internecine factionalism within communist socialism, however bitter, was one thing; more significant for mankind in the historical long term was the rift between Radical Enlightenment and socialism (including communism). As democratic republicanism and socialism—the two main rival underground ideological blocs fighting the status quo—grew more mutually antagonistic, Hess and Marx opted for socialism while adherents of Ledru-Rollin, Michelet and (later) Lamartine, including Heine and Ruge, stuck to their literary and philosophical radicalism championing democratic principles, universal rights, and the freedom of expression of the great French Revolution, emphasizing above all the need to transform how men think. If, in France, both democratic republicans and socialists, noted Heine, gained ground for their respective theories by loudly denouncing the July Revolution's "fraudulent character," its being pirated by vested interests, their paths now decisively diverged, and they went from being potential to actual adversaries. The same rift emerged before the 1848 revolutions in Germany, widening there too with communists and socialists battling the democratic republican *Radikalismus,* the waning Radical Enlightenment of Ruge, Wirth, Bauer, Fröbel, Struve and Hagen. Julius Fröbel (1805–1893) was a geologist and enthusiast for science among the editors of the Zurich paper *Der schweizerische Republikaner* [The Swiss Republican] in the 1840s, a radical democrat prominent in both the Leipzig and Vienna revolutions of 1848.[46]

The fraught atmosphere embittering the revolutionary intellectual fraternity in Paris and Brussels during the mid- and later 1840s was the hothouse generating the early emergence of Marxism as a separate organized ideological current. Where Heine and the democratic republicans, like England's Benthamite philosophical radicals, adhered wholeheartedly to the Enlightenment in its radical mode, emphasizing their enlightened lineage and the need for political, legal and constitutional solutions, the new socialist Left repudiated the Enlightenment legacy, opting for a materialism stressing the primacy of the economic dimension of man. Where Ruge and Bauer claimed the Revolution was above all a striving for collective and individual "freedom" by changing the ideas and raising the consciousness of the people while rejecting religion for its damaging social consequences, socialists and Marxists took scant interest in changing the people's beliefs and opinions by propagating enlightenment, or even in weakening religious authority, insisting the correct way to engineer a new, improved society is to capture and transform the economic system. They fixed their gaze on labor organization and wages, wealth distribution, the facts of class warfare and how to reorganize the proletariat and ultimately economic life itself. It was a rift ultimately irreconcilable. Hess alone seriously tried to blend socialist economic millenarianism with a canon of great teachers of mankind and the centrality of amelioration by raising mankind's educational and moral level. An in-between transitional figure, Hess displayed a shrewd enough grasp of how profoundly individual liberty and the push for equality could collide to the detriment of both, as they had under Robespierre's dictatorship and the

Terror. He strove to avoid precisely that disastrous mire by envisaging true emancipation as combining elevated collective consciousness *and* economic reorganization.[47] Here lies Hess's chief significance as a Jewish revolutionary.

The injustice of gross economic inequality must indeed be corrected, democratic radicals concurred, but this requires first establishing democratic republics empowered to change how society is governed so that primogeniture and aristocratic privilege can be ended, inheritance laws reformed, educational opportunity widened, church property confiscated, and a rigorous system of progressive taxation adopted, as Condorcet, Chabot and others had urged during the great Revolution, establishing fiscal systems ensuring the heaviest tax burden falls invariably on the wealthiest and progressively less on each descending level, weighing least on those with modest means and the poor. Absolute equality of possessions and wealth, though, they rejected as a false principle, much like Frey back in 1793: true equality is "equality of rights" and opportunity.[48] Waging class war was hence no solution; rather, society must become more unified.

Where Hess broke ranks with the democratic radicals was not in his ardor to redress unremitting economic inequality per se, but rather the extremism, the lengths to which he took his vision of economic reorganization and his placing less stress on reason bolstered by intellectual debate as the supreme guide to humanity's better future. Abolishing private property and ending economic freedom, argued the radical enlighteners, can only confine, permanently clamp individual rights and freedom since it means abolishing economic freedom and vesting overweening power in the state, and for this reason such a program could not be part of any enlightened agenda based on freedom, free expression and rights.

Socialist switching of goals and targets meant in effect not just slackening the attack on religious authority, and ending the drive for adult re-education in the humanities and sciences, but powerfully re-affirming old-style Judaeophobia. Jewish emancipation Proudhon judged among the principal errors of the 1789–94 French Revolution, "doubly impolitic in that it opens the door to the parasites and unproductive people" devoted to trade.[49] It will be necessary, wrote Proudhon of the Jews in his private journal, in November 1847, to "require their expulsion from France, except for individuals married to French women, abolish the synagogues, not permit them to enter any employment, to work *enfin* toward abolishing their religion. It is not for nothing Christians have called them deicides. The Jew *is* the enemy of the human race. It is necessary to send this race to Asia, or exterminate it.

H. Heine, A. Weill, and others are just secret spies; Rothschild, Crémieux, Marx, Fould, are malicious creatures, bilious, envious, sour etc., who hate us. By iron or by fire, or by expulsion, it is necessary that the Jew should disappear." He ended this astounding tirade by remarking: "what the peoples of the Middle Ages hated indistinctly, I detest with reflection and irrevocably. Hating the Jew, like hating the English, should be the first article of our political faith."[50] (Heine, curiously, nurtured a similarly eccentric antipathy toward the English.)

Proudhon's anti-Judaism and Rousseauist love of "simple souls," unlike Fourier's, was disturbingly racial but of a specifically socialist type, albeit in his case bizarrely focused on intellectuals even more than traders and financiers in believing genuine socialism, as he understood it, was particularly threatened, perhaps even already fatally poisoned, by the "Jewishness" infusing modern philosophy. The antisemitic, theological tendency which gradually became more pronounced in Proudhon's socialism, prompting him to declare the Jews "the enemy of the human race," stemmed from viewing Jews as a distinct nation who are ordinary people's eternal enemy; but, bizarrely for a socialist, he felt less enraged by Rothschild and the Jewish financial elite than Marx, Heine, Börne, Hess and Adolphe (born Isaac Moïse) Crémieux (1796–1880), son of a Carpentras silk merchant who as a young lawyer won renown in Nîmes defending Protestants and Jews against local discrimination. In Proudhon's eyes, university-trained Jews, Hebrews like Heine, Marx and Hess "with doctorates in philosophy" (Hess had no doctorate but had only followed philosophy courses, including Bauer's, at Bonn) are more pernicious for society than even the wealthiest, best-connected pseudo-aristocratic Jewish bankers. The Jewish revolutionaries collecting in Paris viewed as a clique Proudhon abhorred more than any businessmen.

Here, Proudhon's views clashed with those of the indomitable socialist militant Louis Auguste Blanqui (1806–1881), who, though no less antisemitic and authoritarian than Proudhon and Fourier, remained more preoccupied with how to advance the revolutionary process itself than worrying about the role of intellectuals or the kind of society that would eventually emerge. A doughty fighter recruiting tough proletarians for acts of group violence, Blanqui was imprisoned for his terror exploits at least nine times between 1839 and 1871, but agreed with Proudhon, Fourier and Marx in considering the Enlightenment as such irrelevant. So uninterested in enlightened thought was Blanqui that he cheerfully revived the Babeuf-Buonarroti legacy, abandoning all thought of re-educating, inspiring or mobilizing the masses. He put his trust in small clandestine para-military revolutionary organizations like his own, designed to capture power by armed force, imposing a temporary tyranny that would forcibly change work relations and redistribute property.[51]

Blanqui's aggressive revolutionism leaning to violence formed the exact antithesis of the "True Socialism" of the gentle "rabbi" Hess. Of course, in the circumstances of the 1840s, Proudhon needed to mask his virulent antisemitism and outwardly appeared willing enough to debate amicably with Marx about differences, not all of which were small ones. In Paris, during the summer of 1844, Marx and Proudhon engaged in a series of philosophical encounters, often lasting deep into the night. Marx taught Proudhon Hegelianism and tried to impress him, not entirely unsuccessfully, with the power of German philosophy and its relevance to human liberation and the socialism to which Marx at that point was only just becoming converted by Engels among others. Marx and Proudhon failed to agree, but were not yet publicly at war.[52] But the divisions between the rival blocs vowing to overturn the status quo steadily deepened through the 1840s.

In the end, after a fiercely fought and protracted Europe-wide struggle which ended by blighting the hopes of all revolutionaries, what resulted in the rest of Europe in the triumph of kings, aristocracy and the papacy, in France led to the crushing of both revolutionary factions by something new, the force of populist autocracy. After months of dogged fighting, the 1848–49 Revolution was decisively suppressed by reactionary forces in Vienna, Budapest, Berlin, Dresden, Frankfurt, Cologne, Milan, Venice and Naples; but the French Second Republic (1848–51) was trodden under in a different fashion. With the outbreak of the French Revolution of 1848, the French monarchy had been swept away this time for ever, and the Second Republic established. Within months, the two revolutionary blocs dominating Paris, democratic republicans and socialists, after collaborating uneasily for months, fell to blows, especially in the bitter fighting of the so-called 1848 "June days." From the autumn of 1848, the Second Republic was then progressively eroded by the triumphant Louis Napoleon (1808–1873), who proved for all to see that neither socialists nor democratic republicans enjoyed the confidence of the truly ordinary man. The latter desired neither socialism nor enlightenment.

What the common people (outside Paris at least) wanted, rather, was a great leader, a figurehead of imposing authority, pointing out the nation's enemies that needed obliterating and publicly vowing to support the Church, a strong figurehead promising charisma, simple straightforward answers and faith. To begin with, Napoleon's nephew, Louis Napoleon, nominally went along with the Second Republic emerging by December 1848, with his promises to restore France's glory and support religion, as its "president." Looked on by most Frenchmen with genuine enthusiasm, he quickly consolidated his power until he was in a position to dismantle what remained of the Republic. Genuine republicans opposing him were swept aside, with Crémieux among those arrested and imprisoned. In December 1852, he proclaimed himself Napoleon III, "emperor of the French." Thus, the veritable victor of the revolutionary struggle of 1848–49, no-one could deny, was a pompous, bombastically Catholic would-be dictator caring little or nothing for republicanism, philosophy, history, equality, human rights, improving educational opportunities, social justice or even genuine religion. His crushing victory over the democratic radicals and socialists alike taught a ringing lesson: overwhelming victory goes to he who can most effectively rally the ill-informed. However dispiriting for radicals and socialists alike, it was a reality they had to face.

Once in power, Louis Napoleon employed the French army to help extinguish by force the last vestige of insurrection, republicanism and freedom of religion in Italy, the short-lived but heroically defended Roman Republic of February–July 1849 headed by Mazzini and Garibaldi. With Louis Napoleon's intervention in central Italy, and restoration of the papacy to power in Rome on the ruins of republican freedom, the direct consequence of the French people's choice, all republican hope was finally extinguished. During 1849, large numbers of demoralized, beaten "Forty-Eighters" streamed from France, Germany, Austria-Hungary and Italy, seeking refuge in Switzerland, England, South America and especially the United States. Julius Fröbel was among the revolutionaries defeated in Vienna who settled in New York. Europe's revolutionaries henceforth dwelt in often permanent exile both literally and often also within themselves, disillusioned frequently to the point of abandoning their revolutionary hopes. In this respect, even Marx was not altogether an exception.

Devastating defeat in 1848–49 did little, in any case, to mitigate the mounting bitterness poisoning relations between socialists and democratic republicans. To radical enlighteners the socialists' continuing call to arms, summoning the proletariat to rise against the rest of society, was another attempt to rally the least educated and informed against not just aristocracy, clergy and capitalists but against the professions, the middle class and the true revolutionary traditions of 1776, 1789, 1830 and 1848 without regard to democratic and secular "principles," a dangerous, authoritarian assault which, moreover, meant directly assailing the very Enlightenment whose direct heirs they were and which their socialist adversaries, all too glaringly were not.

RELOCATING THE "NEW JERUSALEM"

For the so-called "radikaldemokratische Reformpartei" that Ruge headed in 1848, with allies like the radical publisher Fröbel, who only narrowly escaped his death sentence in Austria after the defeat in Vienna, emancipation of the masses remained a feasible if formidably difficult project. But, for them, in striking contrast to the approach adopted by Marx after 1844, it was a question of reshaping consciousness and re-education.[53] What Bruno Bauer (1809–1882), Marx's former mentor, most fiercely denigrated in the socialist ideologies of Hess and Marx was the idea that a largely illiterate proletariat could ever be a progressive class, much less be the main agent of emancipation, the revolutionary instrument that would free mankind from despotism and oppression.[54]To Bauer, viewing the European spectacle from Bonn, the chief characteristic of the masses was their inability to understand their own predicament and misery, their clinging to prejudices (though no-one remained more steeped in antisemitic prejudice than Bauer himself).[55] To revolutionary socialists and Marxists, by contrast, democratic republican philosophical radicals were weak-minded, feeble tools of the "bourgeoisie" incapable of seeing that they themselves had now become a major obstacle to humanity's progress by rejecting class warfare, full-scale redistribution of property, and the inevitability of ending economic freedom. In their eyes, the democratic radicals were helping prop up a detested social system that they themselves condemned and agreed was oppressive.[56]

It was hard to discern any means to bridge the gap between Marxist socialism and Radical Enlightenment. The great and towering leader of the 1848 republican revolution in France, Lamartine, like Heine and Shelley, thought of himself as a Spinozist pantheist.[57] Like Ledru-Rollin, Lamartine in 1848 had summoned the French to renew their Revolution on the Brissotin model of 1792–93, venerating the "true spirit" of the great Revolution while roundly rejecting Robespierre, the *ultra-radicaux* of the Montagne, and their heirs, Babeuf and Buonarotti, as well as their more distant heirs, Proudhon, Blanqui, the socialists and communists avid to abolish private property and money and impose absolute equality. The universally acknowledged early leader of the 1848 Revolution in France, Lamartine briefly enjoyed vast trans-Atlantic prestige, commanding veneration as far as the United States, but his standing and efforts to rehabilitate the "Girondins" of the great Revolution disintegrated within months with disastrous speed due not least to the ruinous strife between radicals and socialists from which only Louis Napoleon profited.

Heine, going it alone as always, initially figured among those eulogizing the Revolution and especially Lamartine, only to despise him utterly a few weeks later—much as he had first eulogized, then belittled, the *Hambacher Fest*.[58] Socialism, having gained ground slowly during the 1830s and early 1840s, from 1848 advanced more rapidly, soon displacing the democratic republican Radical Enlightenment tendency almost completely. The failure of 1848 brought about effective permanent displacement of the Radical Enlightenment as a meaningful movement and process, and the start of the ascendancy of socialism in its various formats as the chief adversary of the monarchical-aristocratic-clerical status quo.

Hess, meanwhile, "dreamy and indecisive as ever," having in 1846 first submitted to Marx's leadership and shown some willingness to plunge into economics and adopt Marx's view of the proletariat and generally repair his bridges with them finally become estranged from Marx and the Marxists, finding himself sweepingly repudiated by them during 1847 and 1848.[59] By 1849, Hess's dream of the 1830s and 1840s lay utterly shattered. His moralistic fervor and vision of a fairer, socialistic future for mankind, the organized collective human quest for the best social and political outcome, originating in Spinoza's conflation of a worldly actuality transcending the purely spiritual concerns of Christianity and replacing Christianity with new and sounder universal values grounded in pantheism had withered. To understand humanity's situation under the post-1814 Restoration, we must "consider ourselves," Hess still agreed with Heine, "the child of the great Revolution that originated in France and has rejuvenated the continent! It is up to us to build on what it started." He had less time than ever for "weak souls, who always swim on the surface because they lack breath for deep diving," who "tearfully lament the horrors" of the great French Revolution. The "split between the lower and higher nature of man, between fantasy and reason," had now forever been overcome, he had predicted. "Once we have understood Spinoza and North America in their world-historical significance," that is the epoch-making significance of the revolt of the American colonies against Britain for which, he believed, Spinoza forged the spiritual basis that brought about its actuality (as, likewise, the actuality of the French Revolution), "no doubt can remain among us as to what our era wants in general—wants and will achieve."[60] By this Hess meant the promise of a revolutionary outcome without class warfare that would transform and ameliorate society by achieving basic equality. If he still believed it was what was needed, he was inevitably less confident that it could be achieved in the near future. Not only had no such revolution materialized, it was not even faintly perceptible on the horizon.

In 1849, deeply disillusioned by the failure of the revolutions and the directions taken by socialism and Marxism, Hess moved from Brussels to Zurich, then other towns, wholly abandoning activism and becoming more and more isolated from socialist and revolutionary circles. After the *coup d'état* by which Napoleon III suppressed the Second Republic altogether, seizing absolute power, in 1851, Hess quietly withdrew from active politics altogether.[61] Disillusioned and quiescent, less emphatic with respect to abolishing property, marriage and money, he continued delving for his true redemptive creed. Messianic commitment to Spinoza and Spinozism notwithstanding, while becoming politically disengaged he also diverged more and more from the Radical Enlightenment tradition owing to the mystical, messianic dimension increasingly infusing his deflated system.

To his bitter disappointment, socialism had fragmented in all directions and engendered only warring factions. Hess eventually returned to Paris for some years, taking advantage of an amnesty, before finally settling once again in Cologne, in 1861. The following year, immersed again in the fraught milieu of German Jewry, he published his prophetic *Rome and Jerusalem*. "Religious" in a non-theological ethical sense and Hegelian in its dialectics, Hess's thought still diverged radically from Enlightenment thought, being more than ever centered around a secular messianic vision. If his decades-old belief that Spinozism is the ultimate source of both French materialism and German Idealism continued, his conviction that it was from the blending of these, along lines prophesied by Heine, that modern socialism would prove the triumphant outcome, had considerably eroded.[62] Hess, though, was not one to abandon hope entirely. If Sabbatai Zevi was Judaism's "false prophet," he still believed "its true prophet was Spinoza."[63]

In his last book, *Rome and Jerusalem*, Hess again presents Spinoza as the anchor of modernity's emancipated consciousness. Spinoza had exploded "Christian dualism."[64] By so doing, Spinoza had also initiated the promised emancipation that, prior to its tragic interruption, had reached the verge of actualization in material life with the great French Revolution.[65] If from 1848, Radical Enlightenment found itself permanently ousted by socialism as the main oppositional force in Europe, Hess's response was to stray ever further off on his own. What was new and prophetic in his final visionary stance was his embrace of Jewish nationalism, his taking Spinoza's suggestion that the restoration of a Jewish state in their homeland was a real possibility if the Jews could "recover their courage," his proposing an early form of Zionism which he fused with his doctrine that the "Jews never possessed any desire for race mastery [unlike the Germans]." Hess believed in the continuity and distinctiveness of the Jewish race but rejected all notion of superior and inferior races, all races being equal in rights and capacities. "The Mosaic constitution definitely guarantees equality for all the inhabitants of the Land."[66]

Combined with his idea that there could and should be a Jewish national renewal on the basis of a return to agricultural labor with shared property in the Holy Land, his *Rome and Jerusalem* inspiringly planted the first seed of the Kibbutz concept and movement, the ideal of a shared collective of work, education and freedom. Theodor Herzl, the founder of modern Zionism, was so uplifted by Hess's book when he first read it, in May 1901, that he jotted down in his diary: "Wonderful, the Spinozistic-Jewish and nationalistic elements! Since Spinoza, Jewry had brought forth no greater spirit than this forgotten, faded Moses Hess!"[67]

FOURTEEN

Karl Marx and the Socialist Revolution

Born at Trier, on the river Moselle, on the extreme western edge of Germany, on 5 May 1818, Karl Marx (1818–1883), six years younger than Hess, belonged to a family boasting a long line of rabbis on both sides. Marx's father, Herschel Mordechai Marx (1777–1838), son and brother of local rabbis, made his way as a respected lawyer in the Rhineland city of Trier while under French occupation and, later, when the area was temporarily formally annexed, from the mid-1790s until 1814, in Napoleon's France. Owing his career, broad secular horizons, and success in the world as a Jew, to the Revolution, especially its anti-clerical, anti-religious thrust, and hence to the French Enlightenment without which neither the Revolution in the form it took, nor anything he accomplished would have been possible, Herschel Mordechai venerated the Enlightenment's achievements and great figures, Voltaire and Lessing especially.[1]

Napoleon's defeat and Prussia's annexation of the Rhineland created pressing problems for Herschel Mordechai and his family, as for Börne, Heine and numerous others. In 1814, Prussia annexed the Rhineland provinces with the blessing of the Vienna Congress and Holy Alliance proclaiming itself a "Christian" state. At once, followed by most smaller German states, and with considerable public support, the Prussian crown began reversing basic changes introduced since the French occupied the Left Bank of the Rhine, in 1794, among others canceling the equal status granted the Jews twenty years before. The new, greatly enlarged post-1814 Prussia also canceled the emancipatory measures ameliorating the status of the Jews under the edict of 1812 both in the newly annexed western areas and within Prussia's former borders as well as newly annexed Prussian Poland. Renewed exclusion of Jews from equal rights at this point became general throughout Germany, leaving the Jews once again automatically debarred, as Jews, from all higher professions, especially all state and judicial posts and any posts entailing jurisdiction, authority or status above "Christians."

For Jews in the higher professions, the pressure to submit to "conversion" was unremitting. Making exceptional efforts to avoid the, to his mind, obnoxious dilemma into which the Prussian crown thrust him, it was only after repeated applications to the Prussian interior ministry for exemption and permission to retain his post while remaining "Jewish," that Herschel Mordechai eventually gave in. With undisguised repugnance, he converted to "Christianity" for the sake of family and career.[2] Though submitting under duress, he did so only several years after Prussia's vast post-Napoleonic enlargement, in or around 1817, deliberately choosing the Lutheran Church, not the Catholic confession to which practically all the rest of Trier's Christian population belonged, enhancing thereby his position within the Prussian state even if simultaneously becoming more than ever an outsider locally. Paradoxically, he joined a regionally even smaller religious minority than that he had belonged to before, acquiring the Christian name "Heinrich" along with a lasting grudge, passed later to his son, against the imperious new Prussian monarchy, state, nobility and church. For several more years, moreover, Herschel, now Heinrich Marx, disdaining his new "Christian" duties, pointedly kept his wife and children outside the church, within the synagogue, while remaining close to his brother, Rabbi Samuel Marx. Only much later, in 1825, after the death of his rabbi grandfather on his mother's side, and with Heinrich now needing to consider his son's education and prospects, did Marx and the remainder of the family yield to the pressure to convert, seven years after Börne's conversion and two after Heine's. This was the same year Eduard Gans (1797–1839), the young Marx's future mentor who first introduced him to Hegelianism, likewise surrendered as the price exacted for his not being stripped of his professorship. Gans was then twenty-eight, an academic keenly interested in Jewish history and identity who, like Heinrich, wiggled and squirmed for years using every conceivable ploy to avoid conversion.

Initially raised as a Jew, Karl Marx was baptized a "Lutheran" at the age of six. In October 1836, aged eighteen, he commenced his university studies at Bonn, reading law, as had his father at Coblenz. But even before his father's death, a year later, Karl, abandoning law, his original vocational direction which repelled him, had transferred to Berlin devoting himself henceforth to his intellectual passion—philosophy. In Berlin, he recalled later, "I broke off all the connections I had hitherto contracted, made rare and reluctant visits, and tried to steep myself in learning and art." He initially embraced "Idealism," becoming a follower of Kant and Fichte, then, under Gans's guidance, immersed himself in Hegel. Gans, who knew Börne and Heine personally, had succeeded to Hegel's old chair, in 1831, and did much to establish Hegelianism in its more conservative format as a force in academe, while also tying Hegelianism to a positive view of Spinoza and showing other alleged "Judaic" tendencies, provoking detractors to deride his seminar as a "Jewish den" (Hegel had been a supporter of Jewish equality of rights). Marx's passionate embrace of philosophy was from the outset characterized by estrangement from both Judaism *and* Christianity, a hardly surprising aversion, in his circumstances, to organized religion generally. Meanwhile, police notes confirm, he also eschewed student secret societies and active subversion.[3]

Gans died aged forty-two, in 1839, when Marx was twenty-one and just plunging into *Neuhegelianismus*, the Young Hegelian tendency. Marx's next principal mentor (and soon close friend) in Berlin with whom he chiefly worked during 1839–41, was the highly controversial young professor Bruno Bauer (1809–1882). Steeped in theology, until recently figuring among the "Right Hegelians" intent on reconciling Hegel with Christian values, religion and loyalty to the Prussian state, Bauer had, just before encountering Marx, performed a sudden dramatic *volte-face*. From 1838, he embraced atheism, materialism and, by 1840, also (theoretical) anti-monarchism. With his *Kritische Darstellung des Alten Testaments* (1838), a work emulating Spinoza in explaining all biblical "miracles" in naturalistic terms ruling out the supernatural, Bauer broke with Christianity and the Right, immersed himself in Radical Enlightenment and with his incisive writing assumed a position of leadership among the so-called "Young Hegelians." Driving their further intellectual radicalization, he soon acquired the derisive epithet the "Messiah of Atheism."[4]

Following Gans and Bauer, Marx, like other aspiring young philosophers of his generation, venerated Hegel, envisaging him as a behind-the-scenes atheist and naturalist who, out of caution, in his books and lectures did not openly detach nature, politics and history's course from Christian values and theology, as he supposedly did in private conversation, and as Bauer,

Feuerbach, Stirner and others, including Marx, now did. Like other Young Hegelians, Marx thought Hegel more subversive of convention and religion in reality than appears on the surface, advancing this claim by invoking an "esoteric" Hegel who allegedly contradicted the exoteric Hegel. Still, in Hegel, theology and Christian values are formally retained, even if only superficially, and (constitutional) monarchy's superiority over all other political forms asserted, along with the superiority of aristocracy, the Prussian state and "Christianity" over Enlightenment irreligion and democratic republicanism. This soon barely sufficed to satisfy Marx.[5]

In Marx's intellectual development Radical Enlightenment decisively preceded socialism, which at this stage played no part at all in his thinking. This crucially significant point is nearly always overlooked by traditional "Marxology" and other modern scholars. Critique of organized religion, miracles, and especially religious authority, and adoption of Bauer's post-1838 vehement anti-theologism and animus against theologians, as well as his characteristic tendency to tie this to a generalized "Spinozistic" notion of democracy—a political stance rare among Young Hegelians but passionate in the "pre-Marxist" Marx—decisively preceded, by some four to five years, Marx's later abrupt change of path, his turnaround toward socialism and communism, and repudiation of Radical Enlightenment principles. From 1838 to 1843, prior to his move to Paris, Marx's intellectual development was exclusively that of a late Enlightenment radical and in no way that of a socialist. What later became known as "Marxism" during this formative period was only very remotely in the making. Karl's subsequent transmogrification into a "Marxist" guided initially by Engels, began only in 1844, in part through friendship and collaboration with Engels, whom he first met in November 1842, and partly through Hess and other socialists he encountered in Paris.

Marx's doctoral dissertation under Bauer's supervision, presented at Jena rather than Berlin where, from the late 1830s, reactionary tendencies intensified, focused on post-Aristotelian Hellenistic philosophy and its relation to Aristotelianism, specifically on the difference between the Democritean and Epicurean philosophy of nature, Epicurus (341–270 BC) being Bauer's favorite Greek thinker whom Bauer and the young Marx considered an epoch-making founding figure in the philosophical self-emancipation of man. As a doctoral student during 1839–40, Marx filled his notebooks with extracts from texts from ancient Greek thought, as yet rarely referring to Spinoza, but fully subscribing to Bauer's detaching all positive meaningful thought and ideas, all truth, from theology and religion to the utter discrediting of the latter. By 1840, with these points basic to his outlook, the young Marx thought it amazing anyone could take seriously the alleged analogy between Socrates and Jesus Christ, who, in his eyes, were total opposites and adversaries.[6] "If there is an analogy between Socrates and Christ, this could only be in the sense that Socrates is philosophy embodied while Christ is religion personified." "Philosophy, as long as a single drop of blood pulses in her world-conquering and totally free heart," affirms Marx's doctoral thesis, "will continually hurl the cry of Epicurus at her opponents: the profane man is not the one destroying the gods of the multitude, but he who foists the multitude's doctrines onto the gods."[7]

Thoroughgoing rejection of conventional notions and religion was already systematic in Marx's mind by the time he completed his dissertation, in April 1841. Driven by youthful philosophical zeal, hoping to transfer to Bonn, where Bauer had now taken up a new chair and continued directing Marx's studies by letter, the young radical submitted his doctoral thesis partly hoping to secure, with Bauer's assistance, a university teaching post.[8] While reading up for the oral examination, at Jena, Marx heeded Bauer's advice that, on these occasions the questioning "turned principally and regularly around Aristotle, Spinoza and Leibniz," and that he should prepare by steeping himself in these three.[9] In March and April 1841, accordingly, Marx studied and extensively annotated Spinoza's *Theological-Political Treatise* and *Letters*, compiling a montage of sections and notes with a particular political emphasis that clearly played a formative role in his subsequent intellectual and political development. Tying his first three basic planks—materialism, naturalism and rejection of Christianity—to democratic republicanism would define his basic stance throughout the key years from 1841 until 1843. Study of Spinoza and compiling his "Spinoza extracts" facilitated and deepened this development, especially by introducing him to Spinozistic democratic republicanism and the idea, powerfully revived by Mendelssohn in his *Jerusalem*, that the Mosaic state, unlike the Christian state, required not dogmata or beliefs but only obedience to laws governing outward conduct for the "common good." This lent the Mosaic state a distinctive, special status in the thought world of the pre-Marxist Marx.

Following Bauer's advice, Marx filled his notebook with forty-three pages of lengthy Latin extracts and quotations from Spinoza's *Tractatus Theologico-Politicus* (*TTP*) and *Letters*, focusing especially on Spinoza's (and now Marx's) viewing the course of history as the only divine providence that exists and history itself, like Spinoza, Hegel, Heine and Hess, as consequently identical to God's will. Since "God or nature" determines and fixes all laws of nature and all history, there exists no sin and no evil in the religious sense, or, as Marx copied the words, from Spinoza's letter of January 1665 to Willem Blyenburgh, "vel nulla dari peccata, nullumve malum, vel Deum ea peccata, atque illud malum efficere" [either there are no sins and no evil, or else God Himself is the author of sin and evil].[10] Several historians have previously pointed out the striking reluctance of modern scholars, Marxist and non-Marxist alike, not least in the Anglo-Saxon world, until very recently to acknowledge links between Spinoza and Marx during the early stages of the latter's intellectual development (especially between 1841 and 1843). Even in late twentieth-century France and Italy, where a rigorous "Spinozist Marxism" arose, impelled by figures such as Antonio Negri and Louis Althusser, the latter going so far (with some exaggeration) as to regard "Spinoza, du point de vue philosophique, comme le seul ancêtre direct de Marx" [from a philosophical point of view, the sole direct ancestor of Marx],[11] remarkably scant effort was made, as one scholar put it, "to relate Spinoza and Marx to one another in a direct, explicit and sustained manner."[12]

Given Marx remained a vehement radical totally uninterested in economic history, socialism, communism and class warfare for no less than six or seven years before converting to socialism, the generalized refusal of the entire Marxist world and most of the scholarly non-Marxist sphere to ponder the Spinozist tint of Marx's pre-1844 intellectual radicalism is not just a gap in the historiography but a true curiosity of modern intellectual history, illustrating inability to grasp the crucial centrality of the Radical Enlightenment in the European early nineteenth century.

By the time he reached his doctoral examination, Marx had grappled for months with Spinoza's political and social thought, amassing extracts from the 1802 Jena Latin edition of the *TTP* edited by H. E. G. Paulus, amounting to 170 excerpts in all. In compiling his selection, Marx chose especially—and often reordered—fragments concerning miracles, politics and the true nature of biblical prophecy, adding another 58 extracts taken from the 1841–42 Berlin edition of Spinoza's *Letters*.[13] His selection, not insignificantly, noticeably changes the order of, and reorganizes, the logic of Spinoza's argument, rearranging Spinoza's political thought into what, at the time was, for Marx, a kind of secular personal "Bible." Concentrating on chapters 6 (on Miracles), 14 (on faith) and 15 (on the relationship of reason to theology,) Marx, like Bauer, focused on separating all theology and Revelation from truth and reality, drawing the consequences for politics, law and Bible criticism, albeit *not* for morality, a dimension in which Marx, very differently from Hess, took notably scant interest. His very first quotation is from the first page of chapter 6 of the *TTP*: "et ex nulla re clarius existentiam Dei probari posse existimat [vulgus], quam ex eo, quod natura, ut putant, suuum ordinem non servet" [The multitude supposes the existence of God is proven by nothing more clearly than what they perceive as nature failing to follow its normal course].[14] For the young pre-socialist Marx, God, religion, churches and the supernatural in whatever sense, including Hegel's "Christian" monarchy, lack all meaning and validity. Divine governance of the world, for Marx, as Spinoza, signified only "fixum illum et immutabililem naturae ordinem, sive rerum naturalium concatenationem" [that fixed and immutable order of nature, or interconnection of natural things].[15] Insisting on the universal invalidity and inapplicability of theology of whatever description in all contexts, he followed Bauer and (to a considerable extent) also Feuerbach in construing theological doctrines as organized, systematic social and political deception.

FORMATION OF A DEMOCRATIC RADICAL (1841–1844)

Marx's early thought, deeply indebted to Bauer, was Spinozist-Hegelian materialism, naturalism, anti-providentialism and anti-Scripturalism, emphatically detaching morality from religion. But during this formative early period, it was arguably also Spinoza who most decisively shaped Marx's general view of man as being, in body and mind, purely a product of nature and then political outlook, his separation of all theology and religion from politics and society, his self-awareness as an active, committed democratic republican revolutionary.[16] Marx's early 1840s stance on politics was far more unusual among Hegelians than his earlier imbibed fierce atheism and hostility to churchmen and churches, though Bauer too, it should be noted, having emerged as a leading philosophical atheist by 1838, began actively promoting democratic republicanism during the early 1840s, which he had not done previously.[17] Savoring the universal determinism of Spinoza's Latin, Marx proceeded step by step to eliminate monarchy and attack princes and aristocracy.

The young Marx edged toward a conception of democracy as conservation of collective "natural right" with equalization through law, of basic freedoms. The more any given state conserves that "right" for the benefit of all equally, the more it conforms to nature, is stable and resolves inner contradictions. The less it does so, the further it deviates from nature and the more aristocratic, ecclesiastical and hierarchical, and the more theological, hence, more despotic, it becomes. It hardly matters whether one prefers to think this schema arose from Marx's own insight, aided by Bauer, merely finding subsequent confirmation in Spinoza, or whether Marx more directly "owed" his pre-1844 powerful democratic thrust, his then philosophical-political democratic stance, broadly to Spinoza. The point is that Marx's early radical posture, until 1844, was typically Radical Enlightenment, democratic republican and Spinozistic, and in no way whatsoever proto-socialist. If already earlier Marx rejected Hegel's claim to have completed and transcended Spinoza's philosophy by "Christianizing" and "Prussianizing" it while redefining divine providence as history conceived as the course of nature, between 1841 and 1844 Marx steered closer to Spinoza's "common good" as essentially a democratic republican construct geared to the "salus populi," than any of his immediate predecessors—Hegel, Fichte, Schelling, Feuerbach—except Bauer. But he kept to this path only until plunging into the worlds of economics, socialism and communism in 1844.

Wielding Spinozist democratism in one hand and Hegel in the other, by mid-1841 Marx had already gained renown in radical circles. A declared ally of Bauer, an academic rebel abjuring Kantianism and mainstream Hegelianism, like Spinoza viewing the essential purpose of the state to be "freedom," he figured prominently among a burgeoning group, a kind of philosophical Jacobin "Montagne" of subversive Left Young Hegelians alarming the universities, clergy, police and crown.[18] Among those impressed was Hess, who, having just met him, wrote to his friend Auerbach, in September 1841, at a time he too was immersing himself in the Young Hegelian "new German philosophy": "He is the greatest, perhaps the only true philosopher actually now alive [. . .]. Dr. Marx, as my new idol is called, is still a very young man (at most around twenty-four years old)." But it was Marx, he predicted in September 1841, "who will give medieval religion and politics the last push, as he combines a cutting wit with the deepest philosophical seriousness; imagine Rousseau, Voltaire, Holbach, Lessing, Heine and Hegel united in one person—I mean 'united,' not blended—then you have Dr. Marx."[19]

Berthold (Moses Baruch) Auerbach (1812–1882) was a noted author, estranged from Judaism and rabbis less by his university studies at Tübingen, Munich and Heidelberg, than reading Spinoza. His novelistic biography, *Spinoza* (1837), followed by his German edition of Spinoza's texts and biography of Spinoza, probably did more to familiarize the German public with Spinoza, and popularize his image, during the nineteenth century than any other single intervention. Auerbach's *Spinoza* was a guide out of the ghetto into a largely secular, multi-faith modernity where the Jew could integrate via equal rights while adhering still to his own religious tradition privately. He was at one with Heine, Hess and Marx in admiring Left Young Hegelianism and rejecting Kant's and Hegel's notion of Christianity as a higher spirituality than Judaism. Unlike Hess (at this stage) and Marx, though, he also shared Heine's aversion to Börne's militancy and violent *Antijudaismus*. At the same time, he rebuked all four—Börne, Heine, Hess and Marx—for seeking in place of Judaism a new philosophical quasi-religion. While turning "Spinozism" into a cult as ardently as Heine or Hess, he was less willing to see Spinoza as the outright foe of Christianity *and* Judaism.[20]

Marx's early non-socialist democratic radicalism was passionate but also obliterated whatever prospects of a university career this brilliant young converted Jew set out with. On completing his studies, he discovered, much to his disgust, that in princely, noble-dominated Restoration Germany, due to his views, all paths to a university career were permanently closed to him. Blocked from the higher professions, compelled to seek an alternative career, like many Jews, unconverted and converted,[21] he opted for journalism. Continuing his studies privately, and in an increasingly subversive fashion, he entered the treacherous, murky world of opposition journalism.

In Bonn during the summer of 1841, Marx planned to collaborate with Bauer on a projected journal, the "Atheistic Archives," that never appeared, and a book, the *Last Trump over Hegel, the Antichrist*, written teasingly, as if by a devout Pietist, alerting co-religionists to the atheistic menace hidden behind Hegel's apparently innocent verbiage. Marx, though, failed to get his sections ready in time and Bauer, losing patience, went ahead and published without his contribution, one of several episodes causing a cooling of their originally amicable collaboration. Bauer, in any case, was dismissed from his university post, in 1842, as an undesirable influence, ending Marx's hopes of academic patronage for good. With few alternatives, Marx stuck to journalism, showing his mettle early on. In October 1842, he was appointed chief editor of a new paper, the *Rheinische Zeitung*, based in Cologne (until banned by the Prussian government in early 1843). There he collaborated with several allies, including Hess, who had founded the paper and attended its weekly editorial meetings. A fervent socialist, Hess quickly found himself distinctly out of step with Marx and the other (predominantly Young Hegelian) contributors, who, at that stage, were all remote from socialism (besides Hess's ethical idealism). Turned down for the editorship by the investors and trustees in favor of Marx, who was then considered less radical, Hess by the autumn of 1842, fervently parading his ardent communist ideology, was becoming alienated from his own creation.[22]

As chief editor of the *Rheinische Zeitung*, Dr. Marx was unmistakably an avowed "atheist," foe of monarchy and churches and veiled revolutionary activist, a young philosophical guru exerting a great impact on those he met, already a leading figure in radical circles but, as yet, not even a beginner in the sphere of socialism toward which he remained, for the time being, mildly antagonistic rather than indifferent.[23] Like Gans, Bauer, Hess, Börne and Heine, Marx reviled every aspect of Restoration "Christian" Germany's princely culture, aristocracy and ecclesiastical authorities (including the public Hegel) while nurturing his lifelong generally favorable view of the French, the Enlightenment and French Revolution. A sullen, implacable revolutionary who already believed Germany ripe for revolution in 1842–43, Marx still viewed philosophy and radical thought, not social and economic forces, as the primary driver of revolutionary change. In short, until the age of twenty-six Marx remained a classic adherent of democratic Radical Enlightenment still not even remotely an economist, socialist or proto-Marxist.

Willing to promote anti-Catholic attitudes in the traditionally Catholic Rhineland, initially the Prussian authorities proved relatively lenient toward Marx's guardedly anti-clerical paper.[24] Marx's strategy (with which Hess disagreed) was to exploit this elbow room by masking the paper's political radicalism while concentrating on assailing bigotry and religious authority. Marx's first article in the *Rheinische Zeitung*, published in July 1842, was a scathing attack on a rival reactionary paper, the *Kölnische Zeitung*, that disparaged the Young Hegelians, denouncing the anti-Christian tendency of the "new philosophical school" and the *Rheinische Zeitung* as treason against philosophical reason itself. "Of course, from the beginning you only recognize as scholarly research what is merely your way of looking at things," Marx rebuked the rival paper, "it is easy for you to prophesy; but how is your affirmation more valid than that of the Indian Brahmin proving the Vedas' sanctity by reserving to himself alone the right to read them!" What sense did it make to call the secularized post-1814 Prussian monarchy of 1840 a "religious state?" His rival Cologne editors had forgotten that the existing Prussian civil code, like the Code Napoleon, was forged by philosophy, not religion, "not from the Old Testament but from the ideas of Voltaire, Rousseau,

Condorcet, Mirabeau, Montesquieu and the French Revolution. Ignorance is a demon; it is to be feared that it will yet cause many a tragedy."[25]

Marx's critique of organized religion he combined with rejection of monarchy (masked to a considerable extent in his paper) in favor of democratic republicanism, a stance he shared with Bauer and Ruge among other prominent Young Hegelians but not the rest. "The monarchical principle in general," he agreed with Ruge, writing from Cologne, in March 1843, "is the despised, the despicable, the dehumanized man; and Montesquieu was quite wrong to allege that it is honor. He evades the difficulty by distinguishing between monarchy, despotism and tyranny. But these are all names for one and the same concept, and at most denote differences in customs, though the principle remains the same." Like Spinoza, but contradicting Hegel, Marx argued that democracy is the primal and most natural and comprehensive form of state however much submerged by princely, aristocratic and ecclesiastical oppression. "All other constructions of state are a certain, definite and particular form of the state. With democracy alone is the formal principle also the material principle." For Marx, only democracy unites the universal and the particular in politics, resolving all contradictions; monarchy, despite Hegel's claims, remained just a truncated variant fed by invalid theological dogmata.[26] It is the democratic republic that is the most "natural" form of state, insists one of the *TTP* passages Marx annotated, the form that "accords the maximum of individual liberty to all men."[27]

At this stage, Marx also shared with Spinoza (and Bauer), indirectly or directly borrowing, a deep preoccupation with the idea that organized religion is, in essence, a political ideology imposed on society to foster submission and obedience functioning by deluding believers into accepting conjured-up fantasies that it is actually contrary to their own interest to believe.[28] Organized "priestcraft," Spinoza and the pre-Marxist Marx alike contend, is indispensable to despotism and inherently the majority's prime enemy despite being venerated by most people. It was hence more to Spinoza's system topped up by Bauer, rather than Hegel and Feuerbach, as most historians claim, that the early Marx owed his basic framework, his refusal to assign theology any validity and insistence on morality and religion being wholly separate, that the laws of nature govern everything so that "natural right" rules not only individual behavior but formation of society and the state, as also his idea that the more the state conserves the "natural right" of the masses, the more it is "democratic" and hence the more it fulfills its original and true function. No other Young Hegelian so conspicuously reworked and reaffirmed Spinoza's principle that "democracy is the truth of democracy; monarchy is not the truth of democracy," as Marx expressed it, meaning monarchy is ultimately merely democracy betrayed, perverted and inconsistent with itself.[29] "It goes without saying," noted Marx in 1843, reaffirming his profoundly un-Hobbesian, Spinozist insight foreign also to Kant and Hegel, "that all forms of state have democracy for their truth and are false insofar as they are not democracy."[30]

The young Marx keenly anticipated "the Revolution," that is, renewal of the Great Revolution, that he, like Börne, Heine and Hess, believed was gradually charging up its batteries to resume its sadly interrupted course. All monarchs and their following opposed Germany's new "idealists who want only the consequences of the French Revolution," as he put it, "and, therefore, in the final count, always a republic and an organization of free human beings instead of the system of dead objects," as he called what Spinoza termed "slaves." But Marx was also convinced the coming upheaval would bring no benefits whatever, just as the 1830 revolutions had not, unless based on a new general consciousness, an entire new way of thinking stemming from oppressed humanity taking stock and becoming enlightened. Authentic revolution occurs only when human self-confidence and freedom are "aroused again in the hearts of the people. Only this feeling that vanished from the world with the Greeks, disappearing under Christianity into the blue mist of the heavens, can again transform society into a community of human beings united for their highest aims into a democratic state."[31]

Slightly ironically, given his subsequent conversion to socialism, Marx, during his five years of close preoccupation with Bauer, Epicurus and Spinoza (1838–43), nurtured a distinctly aloof, almost contemptuous view of the masses resembling Bauer's, and not far distant from Spinoza's, distrust of "the multitude." Writing in March 1843 from Holland, Marx assured Ruge whom he met the previous year and with whom he agreed on plans for a future working relationship, that abroad the reputation of the "Prussian despotism" (which had obliged Ruge to leave Prussia and move to Dresden) was becoming increasingly disapproving and unfavorable. Free men outside Germany, he observed, invoking the "impending revolution" to which they eagerly looked forward, "even the dull Dutch," now considered Prussia's monarchy and its oppressive, despotic ways abysmal, and this encroaching low esteem and "shame is actually the victory of the French Revolution over the [even duller] German patriotism that defeated it in 1813," though unfortunately "in Germany even shame is not yet felt; on the contrary, these miserable people are still patriots."[32]

The "pre-Marxist" Marx conceived the democratic republic as the fittest mechanism for resolving social contradictions, raising men to their highest level of fulfillment, and ensuring the state avoids conventional thinking, policies and laws serving minority vested interests, especially of kings, courts and clergy, exploiting the majority. Pursuit of the "general will" based on the democratic republic shielding society from particular interests was undeniably a central feature of Marx's early political radicalism that in no way derived from Hegel, Hess or Feuerbach or, in this form, Rousseau. Hence, restoring emphasis to what has been termed "the occluded relation between Spinoza and Marx," enables us to see why Marx's notes, rearranging the order of ideas infusing the re-arranged extracts from the *TTP*, looks uncannily like the prime source of Marx's early political orientation, and especially his "radical critique of Hegel and the Left Hegelians."[33] His gradual shift from a positive to negative view of Hegel was not straightforward and among the key factors one must certainly include Hess. But Hess too, one must remember, when collaborating with Marx during 1841–43, always oriented himself chiefly by Spinoza rather than any other thinker despite being markedly less drawn to Spinoza's democratic theory than was "Marx before Marxism."

Catholic and Protestant bigotry and mass ignorance, felt Marx, at this time, were the chief barriers to the coming revolution. As it happened, 1842 proved a significant year in the revolutionary underground's evolution in central Europe. It was then, following publication, at Leipzig, of Lorenz Stein's widely read *Der Sozialismus und Kommunismus,* that the German public and Prussian authorities first paid attention to, and became alarmed by, the rise of socialism and communism, for them a disturbing, wholly new revolutionary impulse.[34] The next year, written between March and August 1843, Marx's *Zur Kritik der Hegelschen Rechtsphilosophie* (published in 1844) marked a further transition in the evolution of his early thought and what by 1843 was becoming his open break with Bauer. Leaning toward Feuerbach and Hess, Marx here rebukes Hegel for compromising with "Christian" values, monarchy and aristocracy, and joins Hess in promoting the idea that most existing recipes for changing the world anti-theologically, including Bauer's radical vision, revolutionize men on an excessively individual basis, producing a secularized version of Christian salvation focusing on individual re-education rather than collective transformation of society. It is here too, stressing the need for collective as opposed to individual salvation, that

Marx first mentions the proletariat. Still, for now, Marx kept within the Radical Enlightenment's boundaries. What was at stake was still collective enlightenment, the march of progress, with *Philosophismus* deemed the prime agent of change, leaving class pressures and economic conditions essentially absent: "today when theology itself has foundered," he asserts in the "Introduction," the "most unfree thing in German history, our status quo, will be shattered by philosophy." "Just as philosophy finds its material weapons in the proletariat, so the proletariat finds its spiritual weapons in philosophy; and once the lightning of thought has struck deeply into this naïve soil of the people, the emancipation of the Germans into men will be accomplished." Although by early 1844 the proletariat is thus beginning to emerge as the chief driver of revolutionary change, his thought is still quintessentially democratic, undogmatic, geared to the advance of philosophy and republican.[35]

In his *Zur Kritik*, contradicting Hegel, Marx identifies not just absolute monarchy but also constitutional monarchy and the British "mixed government" model as the perennial enemy of both intelligentsia and common people, "a hybrid," as he called it writing to Ruge in March 1843, "which from beginning to end contradicts and abolishes itself." For the Marx of 1841–44 "democracy is the solution to the riddle of every constitution. In it we find the constitution founded on its true ground—real human beings and the real people."[36] For the early Marx, democracy was more than a form of state: it was rather the essence of politics, the ultimate triumph of the "general will," where "democracy is the truth of monarchy, monarchy is not the truth of democracy." Monarchy, for Marx still, is necessarily democracy in contradiction to itself. Monarchy cannot, while democracy can, be understood in terms of itself, and while "democracy is content and form; monarchy amounts merely to a form that adulterates the content."[37] Here, once again, he expounds a characteristically Spinozist position. But while Marx's "Spinoza extracts" reflect his interest in the idea that God or Nature rules over men most crucially through political sovereigns, not religious authority, and insisting the collective good is the highest law, throughout this period he still only rarely mentioned a closely related key Spinozist idea, namely, that the only valid ethical values embodied in state policies and laws, and only "religious" concepts possessing moral validity, are "justice" and "charity."[38] Contrasting strikingly with the relative moral aridity of Marx's pre-1844 democratic approach, for Hess love of truth, justice and charity form the very core of Spinoza's, to him, infinitely precious message to humanity. Where Marx did bring up the subject of morality, in his paper, his "morality" public and private was strikingly at odds with organized religion and the policies of the state.

Marx's newspaper's veiled radicalism quickly became unacceptable to the Prussian government. "The specifically Christian law-giver cannot recognize morality as a sphere sacred in itself and independent," wrote Marx in February 1842, in an article "by a Rhinelander," banned in Germany, eventually published at Zurich, in 1843, by Ruge, "for he appropriates its inner universal essence for religion. Independent morality violates the universal bases of religion, and the particular concepts of religion are contrary to morality. Morality knows only its own universal and rational religion, and religion only its particular positive morality." Hence, the new press censorship laws proclaimed in Germany in the name of Christian piety and kingly authority, "must reject the intellectual heroes of morality—Kant, Fichte, Spinoza, for example—as irreligious and violating discipline, morals and exterior responsibility, as these moralists start from a contradiction in principle between morality and religion, for morality is based on the autonomy of the human mind whereas religion is based on its heteronomy [i.e., subjection to others]."[39] By late 1842, the Prussian crown, ever more allergic to intellectual rebellion, began harassing all publications emanating from Left Young Hegelian circles.[40] All of Germany joined in the crackdown, the famous *Leipziger Allgemeine Zeitung* being shut down by the Saxon government in December 1842. Already before that, Marx had alerted Ruge, from Cologne, that "it is impossible for me to write under Prussian censorship or live in Prussian air." Marx's and Hess's *Rheinische Zeitung* was obliged to cease publication in March 1843.

MARX'S AND HESS'S 1840S IDIOSYNCRATIC "ANTI-JUDAISM"

Editing the *Rheinische Zeitung*, Marx was a flag-bearer of Radical Enlightenment, as he was consistently between 1838 and 1843; and it was this that forced his exile from Germany. During 1842–43 he was basically still edging not toward socialism or communism but rather to closer alliance with Ruge and the democratic radicals.[41] At the point he stopped publishing the *Rheinische Zeitung*, he had agreed, at the request of the "president of the Israelites here," to support the petition of the local Jewish communities to the region's provincial parliament "on behalf of the Jews." He complied "although I find the Israelite faith repugnant; yet Bauer's opinions [his judging Christianity a higher form of consciousness than Judaism and Jewish rights an irrelevant "particularist" distraction] seem to me too abstract." Despite rejecting Judaism as a religion, and, like Hess, identifying Jews with the "money system," Marx played a small but positive part in the fight for Jewish emancipation, affirming his support for equal Jewish rights, and rebuking Bauer over this question, in Paris, in 1844, in the *Deutsch-Französische Jahrbücher*.[42] He chose to support the Jewish cause if only because rising Jewish resentment was useful to the Revolution and because, for him, punching as many holes as possible in the "Christian state" and "smuggling in the rational as far as we can," remained the central objective. "At least it must be attempted—and the embitterment [of the Jews] grows with every petition that is rejected [by the Prussian crown]."[43]

Publication of Bauer's articles on the "Jewish Question" in 1843 posed a challenge to Marx and the Left Young Hegelians generally, just as they were becoming a political force, because the fervent antisemitism of this defrocked ex-professor nicknamed the "Robespierre of theology" denounced Jewish emancipation across the board. On the Jewish question, Bauer reaffirmed Kant's and Hegel's idea that Judaism is a historically primitive vestige, irrelevant once superseded by Christianity, a vestige incapable of usefully influencing the course of history. The Jews, held Bauer, are unconducive to modern liberty because their religion and narrow focus on observance obstructs progress to modernity, which Bauer understood as the dissolution of all creeds into a universal secular consciousness.[44] His own highly prized second mentor after Hegel, namely Spinoza, may have been of Jewish extraction, but was assuredly no Jew when developing his precious philosophical system. Striving for such subsidiary, "particular" reforms as Jewish rights, therefore, would merely further hamper progress toward modernity's chief objective which was to demolish theology and theologians' sway.[45] During 1843–44, Marx drifted into outright conflict with Bauer personally, while starting to learn about socialism from Hess.

A leading figure of the oppositional, revolutionary movement in Germany, until 1843, aside from his visceral antisemitism, Bauer still belonged with the Radical Enlightenment. Ameliorating society depended, for him, on first effectively changing the popular consciousness through spreading radical ideas. If *philosophisme* remained, for Bauer, the principal revolutionary agent, his now estranged former disciple, Marx, for the present still took a more or less identical view. Bauer tied his systematic attack on religious authority and theology to democratic republicanism, identifying Robespierre as the enemy of all Enlightenment, highlighting not just Robespierre's crimes and the Terror, but equally condemning, like all radical enlighteners, *Robespierriste* repression of *philosophisme* and antipathy to atheism and cosmopolitanism. Robespierre had set his face entirely against the "correct" revolution that he should have promoted. By December 1792, Robespierre had altogether betrayed the great French Revolution by failing to enthrone "*Philosophismus* in the place of [mere worthless] political revolution."[46]

By 1843, Marx was publicly berating Bauer not for his *Antijudaismus*—he had scant objection there[47]—but for being too abstract and intellectual, too narrow in his approach, focusing on "political emancipation" alone when he should be calling for "human emancipation" liberating society in a far broader sense. Hess fiercely criticized Bauer for exactly this same alleged deficiency. In *Die letzten Philosophen,* a critique of Bauer published in 1843, Hess classifies Bauer and Stirner disapprovingly as both insufficiently rooted in social reality, as basically secularized "Christian philosophers" too abstract and too concerned with reducing human individuals to intellectual atoms with no real social binding, rendering them secularized Christian "souls" without realizing it. Tied to freeing the individual, they were forgetting society, uninvolved in reshaping the community. Here Marx appears to have borrowed from Hess and his "True Socialism" circle, without acknowledging it, especially when accusing Bauer of confusing general "human emancipation" with mere "political emancipation."[48] This social stress was something new in Marx's thought. In his *Rheinische Zeitung* articles, readers found as much emphasis as in Bauer on the role of ideas shaping the course of history and the human condition, on the need to elevate minds, hearts and human consciousness if the existing world of misery, slavery and oppression was to be transformed into a better one. But now Marx began stressing the vital significance of the whole, of society overall. Still, for the Marx of 1842–43, "philosophy" remained the primary agent in changing men's consciousness and ideas, and the state the chief tool of legal, institutional and social change, the instrument with which, as in Spinoza and Hegel earlier, legal, moral and political freedom must be realized. It is the state that educates its members, Marx wrote, in July 1842, "by converting the aim of the individual into general aims, crude instinct into moral inclination, natural independence into spiritual freedom, through the individual finding his good in the life of the whole and the whole in the frame of mind of the individual."[49]

By opposing Jewish emancipation, Bauer outraged a considerable slice of radical opinion, the ferocity of his publicly proclaimed antisemitism stirring a public scandal. He was condemned by Riesser and Marx along with many other critics, Jewish and non-Jewish, including a notable ally of Hess (and rival of Marx) promoting "True Socialism," their fellow (non-Jewish) Westphalian Karl Grün (1817–1887).[50] Unlike Bauer, Grün envisaged a "modernity" that did not necessitate the total abolition of theology and religion, only of religious authority. To Grün and Hess, the kind of separation of church and state prevailing in the United States would suffice since it separates the state from religion, imposing a "rule of law" according (or supposed to accord) equality to all non-Christians, Jews included. In his 1844 reply to Bauer, Grün argued, like Hess and Riesser, that equality before the law not only must accord equality of status between the religions but diminish gaps between the confessions, promoting reconciliation and unity. It was wrong to insist, like Bauer, Marx and most Young Hegelians, that the Jews had separated themselves from society; rather, it was Christian society that had degraded, marginalized and stigmatized the Jews.[51] "True Socialists," following Hess and Grün, were soon also to reject Marx's post-1844 doctrine of "class warfare," contending "that it blinded the workers," as Isaiah Berlin expressed it, "to those rights and ideals for the sake of which they fought."[52] Here, "True Socialism" was distinctly less distant from Radical Enlightenment than Marxism. Repudiated by the radicals, Bauer, after 1844, diverged more and more from his former pupils and followers. During the 1850s, he abandoned his mid-career phase as a radical enlightener and reverted fully back to his original right-wing stance, only now laced with anti-religious theorizing, his ever more virulent antisemitism henceforth assuming a markedly racist character. The late Bauer coupled materialism and atheism with furious rejection of Hess's racial equality: the "Jew," he insisted, "is a white negro, [even if] with a larger brain than the black."[53]

Unlike Marx and Bauer, Hess gradually came to see his own Spinozism and anti-Christianity as essentially "Jewish."[54] Nevertheless, during 1841–43 while they talked and worked together in Cologne, it was hard to discern much difference in vehemence between Hess's ethical *Antijudaismus* combined with support for Jewish rights and that of Marx. Although not published until 1844, it was while collaborating and conversing with Hess that Marx wrote his later notorious essay "Zur Judenfrage" equating world Jewry not with "capitalism," of which, as yet, "Marx before Marxism" had no conception, but with "egoism" (implying other men were less egoistic or less apt than Jews to embody the principle of "egoism") and with a purely commercial money economy, a money ethic now vilified and demonized equally by Hess and Marx. Jewry for them was the ultimate embodiment of the world's profit-driven economy and zeal for gain. Hess's essay "Über das Geldwesen" [On the Nature of Money] (1845) shows a striking parallelism with Marx's essay, especially in portraying Judaism and the Jews not just in highly derogatory fashion but as the ultimate embodiment of commerce and the money-driven economy.[55]

Hess later shifted to a very different perspective on the Jews; Marx never retracted or mitigated his unremitting *Antijudaismus*.[56] Keeping to it, he established what became a Marxist orientation and legacy that would have grave, far-reaching consequences for Jewry later in the nineteenth and early twentieth centuries. Marx's stance, envisaging the Jews as basically a financial and commercial elite and, consequently, a reactionary group, provided the Marxist movement generally with a license to ignore or downgrade the Jewish question, putting additional pressure on Jewish socialists to discard Jewishness altogether rather than identify, in the way Hourwitz, Auerbach and Riesser did, and Hess would later, with the aspirations, needs and anxieties of the Jewish people. Those like Hess and, later, the Yiddish-speaking *Bundists* of eastern Europe, opposing Marxism's outright dismissal of the call for Jewish cultural and national autonomy met not just with incomprehension and lack of sympathy but later came to be invariably and increasingly treated "contemptuously," as one historian expressed it, by the core Marxist leadership in both pre- and post-revolutionary Russia.[57]

In Marx's eyes the Jewish poor, the Jewish proletariat, had no independent existence.[58] "Moses Hess," observed Nachman Syrkin (1868–1924), the first thinker to propose "collective settlements," *Kibbutzim*, for the Jews of Palestine, "is not the founder of Zionism [. . .] but he is the founder of Socialist Judaism, the reviver of the Jewish revolutionary cultural idea, whose consequence is also political. Syrkin, the indefatigable activist and writer who first undertook the "thankless task" (in the wake of Theodor Herzl's launching of the Zionist movement) of being a "socialist among Zionists, and a Zionist among socialists," is often seen by historians as the founder of socialist Zionism as a movement. But Syrkin himself, on account of Hess's last book, *Rome and Jerusalem* (1861–62), venerated Hess as the true founder of Zionist socialism since Hess there combines socialism with presenting Jewish claims to be recognized as a distinct people and culture without lessening his insistence that "the present age [. . .] began with Spinoza and reached its world-historical existence in the great French Revolution."[59] Given that, by 1860, Hess felt Jewish regeneration required blending universal social justice and secular morality rooted in Spinozism with the specifics of cultural identity, it is indeed plausible to view Hess as the founder of "Socialist Zionism," the wing of socialism Syrkin promoted and which, he contended, removes and replaces "traditional Judaism" better and more constructively than either Reform Judaism or assimilation. During 1898–1901, Syrkin headed a student Zionist society in Zurich called the "Moses Hess Society," or *Hessiana*, a socialist movement following Hess in basing socialism on ethical universalism and humanism rather than Marxist class-warfare and the latter's predicated "dictatorship of the proletariat."[60]

Betraying few signs of his pending plunge from Radical Enlightenment into an inexorable materialist dialectic, *Zur Kritik* marks the close of Marx's "Spinozist" phase. By 1843, Marx had begun claiming great revolutions require more than just *Philosophismus*, even if this is still what chiefly counts. They need also a "passive element, a material basis." "The emancipation of Germany is the emancipation of man. The head of this emancipation is philosophy, its heart the proletariat. Philosophy cannot be actualized without the *Aufhebung* [abolition] of the proletariat; the proletariat cannot be abolished without the actualization of philosophy."[61] Still, every radical enlightener could readily accept that "theory will be realized in a people only insofar as it is the realization of their needs." Marx's notion that "it is not enough that thought strives to actualize itself, actuality must itself strive toward thought," amounts to only a faint foreshadowing of his subsequent vision of an inexorable process, a dialectic of shifts in property, economic relations and control of resources fueling escalating class warfare, that no radical enlightener could accept. Even if now at the starting point of his eventual break with Radical Enlightenment, in 1843, Marx was still broadly a radical enlightener.

MARX CONVERTS TO "MARXISM" (1844–1845)

Marx transferred to Paris, in October 1843. On leaving Cologne, he still adhered to an atheism, materialism and naturalism akin to those of Hourwitz, Frey, Börne, Heine and Hess. But before long, adjusting to the new milieu, discovering mass poverty and human degradation, and engaging for the first time with the reality of the "proletariat," reading Proudhon and other French socialists, and frequently meeting Engels,[62] he began identifying economic exploitation organized by class interest as the real driving force of history and basic cause of universal misery and false consciousness. These were shackles, physical and mental, to be cast off, he soon agreed with Engels, only by revolutionary processes driven by social forces, rooted in and shaped by economic developments. At this time commenced the subsequent lifelong collaboration between Marx and Engels which began at the venerable Café de la Regence, founded in 1718 on the Place du Palais Royale, once frequented by Diderot and later by the young Bonaparte. The aim of the coming revolution switched, in Marx's mind, from securing universal rights and equality based on democracy to capturing and totally transforming the economic system. No longer the chief motor, "philosophy," even if still useful for understanding the human condition, was now relegated to superstructure and pronounced irrelevant to advancing the revolutionary process and changing society for the benefit of all. With class war working toward the proletariat's seizure of power now the chief motor of universal liberation, the Enlightenment's role in elevating humanity found itself banished to the margins.

Neither Hess nor Heine contributed much to this most decisive shift in Marx's stance, which stemmed primarily from regular encounters with Engels and with French socialist leaders. Marx's lurch toward economics and labor issues, abandoning his earlier Spinozistic conception of democracy, moreover, went hand in hand with a growing dogmatism and intolerance of opponents like Bauer and Ruge, and soon also Hess, all who rejected his new posture. Veering into wholly fresh waters, Marx brusquely broke with former friends and allies wherever these proved reluctant to align with his ambitious new project.[63] His quarrel with Ruge, who considered his former ally dogmatic, irritable and hot-tempered, was paralleled to a degree by his simultaneous rupture, in 1844–45, with Hess and also Auerbach, who remained firmly convinced that only the more enlightened and better-educated element in society could be history's vehicle for elevating society to a higher level. In his literary endeavors, notably the *Schwarzwälder Dorfgeschichten* (1843), Auerbach expressed intense sympathy for village life and people reduced to poverty but, unlike the post-1844 Marx and Hess, still rejected socialism, remaining the fervent democrat whose ideological and political commitment had earlier cost him three months in prison, at Hohenasperg (1837). Hess chided and Heine derided, their famously gentle, withdrawn former friend eschewing communism and socialism, for dwelling in a fairy-tale world of Spinozism and sympathy for the poor, for refusing to join in their socialist *Erlösung der Menschheit* [redemption of mankind].[64]

Marx and Hess converged briefly in stressing redemption must apply to society as a whole and transform the collective will. Henceforward, they agreed also in rejecting the profit-based economy and embracing communism. Both believed the Enlightenment had failed and that communism offered a better prospect of transforming the human condition fundamentally, rendering mankind happier not with ideas and secular moral objectives but by abolishing money and private property, and resolving class conflict. For Marx and Hess communism was no longer a mere socialist theory but the indispensable doctrine sanctioned by factual reality that all worthwhile opponents of the *status quo* should support. Nevertheless, a wide gap quickly opened between them. For Hess, human suffering and alienation were universal facts, more the outcome of selfishness and human failings than of changing economic systems in any direct sense, so that he never felt drawn to rigorous economic analysis. To him, the notion of class warfare being inherent in economic development was a repugnant doctrine, while creating a better society via communism remained in essence an ethical project. Marx quickly tired of Hess's moralistic approach and idealism, seeing alienation and revolutionary potential as basic features of the proletariat he henceforth defined as a purely economic and social category.

Marx first met Heine, whose poetry he had long admired, some few weeks after arriving in Paris, probably in December 1843, apparently through Ruge, who arrived in Paris shortly after Marx. Heine is first recorded mentioning Marx when writing to Ruge in January 1844. Though certainly an interesting episode (sometimes blown up out of all proportion), the Heine-Marx encounter lasted barely a year, and in Marx's intellectual development can hardly be said to rival the Bauer-Marx or Hess-Marx relationship in importance, or possess the significance of Marx's early immersion in Spinoza. Still, Heine and Marx met frequently during that brief time and their interaction—and Engels's public comments and pronouncements about it—proved amicable to a degree unusual in both men's lives.[65] For as a rule, neither the sick and increasingly cantankerous Heine, nor the famously acerbic Marx, as Hess, Bauer and Ruge were all ruefully aware, was particularly cordial. On departing France, in February 1845, Marx assured Heine that leaving him was what he regretted most.[66]

The year 1844 was a notably fruitful one in Heine's literary career. Among his publications that year, his epic satirical masterpiece, *Deutschland. Ein Wintermärchen* [Germany, A Winter's Tale], was immediately banned by the

German states for its critical, irreverent tone and cutting remarks about German attitudes. Comprehensively radical rather than socialist in character, it reveals corrupt organized religion allied to malign royal government exercising a combined theologico-political tyranny over society and the life of the mind. Among its central themes is Heine's notion that it was chiefly medieval Christianity, basically a blend of "Dummheit und Bosheit" [stupidity and malignity], that engendered the antisemitism and hatred of Jews and Jewishness that in his day so profoundly marred German society.[67] Typical too was his notion that Jesus was an anti-Establishment rebel who "wanted to redeem the world" but was tricked by the Pharisee establishment, whose sole concern was to outlaw criticism of their presiding lawmaking function and fusion of church and state.[68]

No discernible change resulted from their conferring in either Heine's or Marx's ideological stance. Shared rejectionism of the existing order and radical temperament afforded some scope for a common revolutionary outlook, as did Heine's detestation of censorship and aristocracy, and his condemning autocratic government as rooted in ignorance and theological repression of the individual. Both were alive to the misery of the working poor and injustice of their plight. The Revolt of the Silesian Weavers, about which Heine wrote one of his most moving, socially engaged poems, "Die schlesischen Weber," occurred in 1844, the same year as their encounter.[69] Heine also expressed a strong premonition of the pent-up force of proletarian frustration, notably in his *Lutetia*, a collection of newspaper reports from the period 1840–43 for the *Augsburger Allgemeine Zeitung*, resentment that had "Kommunismus" as its "secret name." Yet, the new movement's relentless antagonism to the existing "bürgerliche Ordnung" [bourgeois order], and Marx's prediction of future class war made him uneasy. "How will it end? No-one knows but gods and goddesses acquainted with the future."[70] Privately, hints of discord seeped out with Marx depicting Heine as eloquent and discerning, certainly, but also timid, corrupt, a charmingly unreliable liar. While Marx made jibes about Heine behind his back, Heine felt a growing antipathy to the "clenched fists," as he caricatured the Communists, with their unappealing, unworkable "idea of absolute equality [. . .] that broods in their barbarous heads."[71]

For Heine, desirable emancipation with constructive results follows from individual and collective revolt against oppression rooted in insight, understanding and awareness, not revolt against a rigorously exploitative economic system by a massive social bloc.[72] Where Marx and Engels were to proclaim, in 1848, in the *Communist Manifesto*, that the "communists everywhere support every revolutionary movement against the existing social and political order of things," Heine, like Spinoza, believed the wrong kind of revolution, ineptly led by the ignorant, that is to say most revolutions, are merely one long ruinous disaster involving immense bloodshed for no gain.[73] Though Marx too had savored Spinoza only a few years earlier, he now, most strikingly in his *The Holy Family*, written between September and November 1844, tellingly classified Spinoza among the "metaphysicians" along with Descartes and Leibniz misleading and deluding mankind, terminology indicating Marx had now in substantial respects discarded him and his philosophy.[74] It is true that Spinoza and Marx continued to share key components of their philosophy in common—their identification of body and mind as one, their determinism, their fusing of nature and history as a single all-embracing process. But the focus on individual autonomy, freedom of expression and democracy had evaporated.

Spinoza's conflation of matter and thought, contended Marx, was not a pure form of materialism since he refused to elevate matter over thought any more than thought over matter. Matter and thought, in Spinoza, remain equal in status, parallel aspects of one and the same thing. The "ultimate identity" of matter and thought, in Hegel, by contrast, diverges from Spinoza in being a form of idealism subordinating matter to thought via dialectical negation of the negation. Since for Hegel one dimension is subordinate to the other and complete convergence of the two into one arises from the culmination of a dialectical process of negation producing negation. What in Spinoza remains a static state of nature, in Hegel becomes a complex historical process. Young Hegelians, and henceforth Marx especially, retained this distinctive feature of Hegel's thought while reversing Hegel's order of priorities: thought now becomes a passive adjunct subordinate to matter. Hegel and Marx hence equally diverged, albeit in opposition directions, from Spinoza and Heine, as well as Hess, with respect to their conserving parallelism of mind and matter, the equality of idea and object, thought and being.[75]

Expelled from France just over a year after moving there, at the Prussian crown's insistence, Marx transferred to Brussels. By 1845, his rupture with Radical Enlightenment was complete. What Marx retained from Hegel and the Young Hegelians had steered his mature thought onto a quite different trajectory from Spinoza's anti-theological imminentism, producing an irreversible iron law of history pushing toward a fixed goal, an unalterable process in which material forces feed unrelenting class warfare, which then underpins all subsequent developments, including the evolution of thought structures. Reacting with increasing exasperation to Hess's secular communistic theology and Marx's new economic determinism alike, Ruge, at this point, finally realized that socialism represents a quite different revolutionary path from that to which he and his fellow democratic radicals were devoted. To reduce individual significance to one's economic status and circumstance seemed to him to betray basic humanity as well as philosophy and democratic republican tradition. Ruge now summoned the enlightened to fight with all possible vigor and rescue the "true" enlightened individual from the communists' "mystical, reactionary claws."[76]

The meaningful "whole," held Ruge, is not economic society but the democratic republic. The leadership of the *Kommunisten* consisted of theorists promoting a new kind of dogmatic "religious sect," a secular theology Ruge judged fundamentally confused: they were sectarians promising the poor an utterly impossible, mystical new *Evangelium* of economic beatitude ill-advisedly concocted into an intolerant, uncompromising deviancy all too apt to wreck humanity's fight for democracy, freedom and enlightenment.[77] How right he was. Socialism of whatever variety Ruge, less accurately, henceforth viewed as a form of "mystification," a disastrously wrong turn for humanity bound to produce irresolvable disunity and strife between the rival oppositional blocs and movements.[78]

Europe's socialists, deluded and sidetracked according to the democratic radicals,[79] were weaving a new "theology" with the proletariat as redeemer, laced with old-style confessional wrangling to adorn it. Proudhon, Blanc, Blanqui, Fourier, Marx and the "artisan communists" were all soon at each others' throats; and along with this disastrous plethora of new "dogma" arose fresh forms of intolerance and dogmatism with excommunication of dissenters at formal meetings. This new style of inquisitorial procedure commenced with the condemnation and expulsion from Marx's movement of one of Germany's leading early communists, Wilhelm Weitling (1808–1871). In early adulthood a garment worker in Leipzig, Dresden and Vienna, Weitling had acquired his socialist leanings through reading and then activism in Parisian street battles during the late 1830s. His book, *Die Menschheit, wie sie ist und wie sie sein sollte* [Humanity As It Is, and As It Should Be], of 1838, combines a passionate plea for ending gross wealth inequality with a call to revolutionary action and renewal of the radical, democratic *Aufklärung*. All older notions about politics and society Weitling wanted jettisoned in favor of the brotherhood of all men, permanently erasing national and religious divisions. Capital should be reorganized into public funds vested in national banks, operated solely for the benefit of families and society. Partly inspired by Hess, and partly admiration of Babeuf and Buonarotti, Weitling was the first writer of the Western world to fuse a clear communist vision with calls for mass insurrection against the powers that be.[80] Tried and imprisoned in Zurich for sedition and blasphemy in 1845 (stating Jesus was a communist and Mary's illegitimate son), then deported from Switzerland, Weitling moved to Paris where, during 1846, he became prominent in socialist circles there.[81]

However, in March 1846, at a gathering of the Brussels *Kommunistisches Korrespondenzkomitee*, with Marx presiding, Weitling found himself formally arraigned and censored as part of a wider move to weed unwanted deviant strands from the communist movement—in particular, non-Marxist "artisan communism" and "philosophical communism."[82] Such dogmatic doctrinal manipulation, intolerance and power-seeking appalled Hess, but enabled Marx and Engels to consolidate their leadership of the budding communist movement in Europe. Even after Weitling permanently emigrated to New York, in late 1847, where his reputation among the German immigrants preceded him and where he at once began organizing workers' associations (as well as introducing improvements to sewing machines), becoming the effective founder of New World communism, the relentless feud between him and Marx continued unabated. By 1847, when he published his *Poverty of Philosophy* attacking Proudhon's approach, Marx had broken with, besides Weitling, Bauer, Grün, Ruge, Proudhon and partly with Heine and Hess. Unforgiving toward Weitling and Heine's friend Grün, and scornful of Hess, Marx developed a quite irrational hatred of Ruge, toward whom he now expressed a ferocious antagonism.[83]

In their *Communist Manifesto*, written in December 1847 and January 1848, during the early stages of the 1848 revolutions, Marx and Engels publicly denounced Hess's communism. They dismissed his and Grün's idealistic "True Socialism" and "philosophy of action" as philosophical nonsense derived from misused French sources, a tool of reactionary interests and a "robe of speculative cobwebs, embroidered with flowers of rhetoric."[84] By this point, with Marx having wholly eclipsed Weitling, Hess and Grün as a communist theoretician and leader, and with Hess starting to withdraw from his earlier activism, the rupture between Marx and Hess too became total.

In the *Communist Manifesto*, Marx and Engels announced that "communism is already acknowledged by all European Powers to be itself a Power."[85] Here they were correct and might have mentioned too, but did not, that theirs was a displacing power wresting the principal oppositional role from democratic republicanism and draining support from all alternative and rival socialist and communist movements. Marxist communism became a "power" under the personal control of Marx and Engels. Yet, it is hard to argue that Marx ever came close to matching Hess's passion for truth, freedom and justice, or radical enlighteners' insights into the nature of despotism and oppression. Among Marx's most characteristic innovations as a social theorist, he suggested, in a letter of 1852, was the idea that the class struggle he postulated "necessarily leads to the dictatorship of the proletariat," and that this "dictatorship" is the tool that will bring about the justice and happiness for all to be manifested in his eventual "classless society."[86] In its conflictual agenda, authoritarianism and displacement of any process of enlightening, it was a concept entirely remote from Heine and Hess and quintessentially remote from Radical Enlightenment. Ruge rightly believed it could only lead to a "police state" and "slavery."

The confessional wrangling blighted the principle of toleration and free criticism in Marxist circles, largely negating Marx's own earlier teaching on press freedom and liberty of expression. Hess, lending socialism an essentially ethical motivation, remained truer to Spinoza in some respects, whereas Marx, by 1845, explicitly distanced himself from Spinoza, straying further and further from the radical camp by basing Marxism on an unalterable ideological and economic logic,[87] one of the main factors prompting Hess's break with Marx's movement.[88] For Hess, it is not economic determinism that will rescue the poor and lift them to a new level of happiness but a general change of attitude, an ethical conversion submerging mankind's egoism, leading to social and political transformation. Where Marx substituted for Radical Enlightenment his doctrine of dialectical materialism and class warfare, Hess increasingly substituted his mystical this-worldly ethical messianism. Since, in Spinoza, not historical determinism but ethical truths proclaimed by the wise and by the republic, pursuit of virtue based on reason, are the exclusive route to human amelioration and maximizing human autonomy, and define the best society, true democratic republics by their nature must always remain provisional and precarious. For the late Hess, there can never be any final conclusion to the historical process in the manner predicted by Hegel, Marx, Engels and, earlier, also Hess himself.

"What is the best condition of whatever form of state," Spinoza summed up, "we can know easily from the goal of life in society which is nothing other than peace and security of life."[89] "The best state is one where men pass their lives harmoniously," that is, enjoy a life based on autonomy within nature's laws, "not one defined merely by circulation of the blood, and other things common to all animals, but based mostly on reason, the true virtue and life of the mind."[90] Marx, increasingly remote from such a perspective, ended up pushing determinism and materialism to the point that individual understanding of the world, individual agency and moral responsibility were all disastrously curtailed, a divergence from radical ideas originally prefigured perhaps in his early relative unresponsiveness to Spinoza's "justice" and "charity." If Spinoza and Marx were as one in affirming that miracles, revelation, divine providence and religious authority do not exist, and never have, Marx totally ignored, despite its sporadic presence in his extracts, Spinoza's insight that "true religion" and piety do exist. This was a lesson Hess never forgot. The essential difference between "religion" and "superstition," asserts Spinoza in a letter to Oldenburg (among the fragments Marx himself had annotated when a doctoral student), noting also that Christianity is not superior to other religions, is "haec ignorantiam, illa autem sapientiam pro fundamento habeat"—that the latter [superstition] has ignorance, the former [religion] wisdom for its basis.[91]

Spinoza, Hegel, Marx, Heine and Hess all sought worldly redemption, the higher state, the optimal condition of man, and the mechanism that transforms the picture from wretchedness to blessedness. Spinoza, Hess and Marx all championed "compatibilism," contending that our being determined by the force of nature does not mean lack of freedom to align with necessary truths, to choose between "religion" and "impiety," wisdom and ignorance, the common good and purely selfish options.[92] But in Spinoza's account, although he lived a century and a half before Marx, there is arguably less mystification and metaphysics regarding how all this occurs than in either Hess's utopia or Marx's projected culminating triumph of the proletariat. Doubtless, it was for this reason, above all, that efforts to reform Marxist theory in France in the 1960s and 1970s, in the wake of the "Prague Spring," and to an extent ever since, and in Latin America since the 1980s, have focused on the call, associated in particular with Louis Althusser (1918–1990), to use Spinoza's philosophy as the means to fill the gaps Marx's analysis leaves, to supplement Marx's account of the relationship between human motivation and desire and ideology, the prime and necessary correcting tool—to strip away what remained of teleological fixity, dogmatism and Hegelian metaphysics.[93] Paradoxically, as Frédéric Lordon noted, "although Marx comes after Spinoza, it is Spinoza who can now help us fill the gaps in Marx."[94]

Conclusion

Jewish Revolutionaries, 1650–1850

If 1848–49 was the "revolution of the intellectuals," the next few decades were an age of intellectual "disillusionment." The dismal failure of the 1848–49 revolutions, following those of 1830, only strengthened the belief of European governments that revolutionary opposition sufficiently organized and focused to overthrow absolute monarchy, force governments into conceding constitutions, and cut back aristocracy and ecclesiastical authority, arises from direct convergence of popular discontent with revolutionary ideas. Where there was no intellectual vanguard diffusing revolutionary concepts and strategies, or the latter is thoroughly suppressed, existing regimes had little or no reason to fear serious upset.

Conservative regimes, being mainly concerned with curbing revolutionary capability and potential, thus felt more or less safe in ignoring social injustice and destitution, as practically all did, as long as they were sufficiently armed against the "revolutionists," meaning the conspirators and the organized opposition's vanguard. They felt secure provided distress and discontent remained blind and had nothing to guide them, as long as opposition-minded intellectual cliques leading the revolutionary thrust remained firmly gagged. Social forces as such seemed to have little immanent relevance or consequence for those determined to keep power and privilege come what may, provided the nurturing and propagation of democratic republican—and, from the 1830s and 1840s, socialist—ideas were stifled and quashed as far as possible. Consequently, post-1848 monarchies more than ever focused their reactionary effort on purging universities, reading societies, secret organizations, the professorate, targeting the student body rather than attempting to remedy the real, or more precisely the underlying, causes of the disaffection—social injustice and increasing poverty.

After the final defeats of the revolutionary movements, in 1849, book, newspaper and journal censorship, preventing illicit gatherings, and policing universities, built up to new levels of intensity, squeezing the likes of Marx, Ruge, Bauer, Wirth, Mazzini, Ledru-Rollin, Lamartine, Michelet and many others, and stymying nearly all serious intellectual debate and philosophy in publicly funded institutions, organizations, mainstream publishing and churches, banishing subversive thought and systematic dissent, along with the great mass of "Forty-Eighters" cherishing revolutionary ideals, abroad, across the Atlantic or, once again, as in Spinoza's day and most of the eighteenth century, to the hidden margins and intellectual underground.[1]

But a crucially important difference developed between Radical Enlightenment and post-1848 anti-establishment philosophical defiance, especially in central and eastern Europe. The latter was no less estranged from respectability, government and churches than the underground Spinozism or machinations of the Diderot-d'Holbach circle of the Enlightenment era, just as atheistic in Nietzsche's day, and as scornful of academic orthodoxies, religious propriety, and commonplace thinking. But whereas anti-establishment radical philosophizing in Spinoza's time furtively vested its hopes in the future of society and political institutions, steering in a democratic republican direction, seeking to advance by diffusing radical ideas and eroding "superstition," innovative thought and culture in the nineteenth century's second half, except among socialists and Marxists, gave up all social and political ambition, predominantly leaning toward an altogether darker, more detached and pessimistic outlook. For decades the greatest intellectual and literary heroes of the age, following Schopenhauer and culminating in Nietzsche, Dostoyevsky, Lamartine and Baudelaire, even the lonely radical of Victorian England, John Stuart Mill, to a degree, abandoned hope of seeing anything much emerge in the short and medium term from either revolutionary politics, or gradualism. They persevered in developing their ideas, writing books, essays and poems in tense, often gloomy isolation, frequently living in poverty or dependence on others, or like Ruge in quiet and quaint retirement (in his case in Brighton), and, as with Ruge, Bauer, Hess, Lamartine, Michelet, Comte and Baudelaire, wholly or partly discarding their pre-1848 activism and immanent political perspectives.[2] The post-revolutionary era was an age of "art for art's sake" and strikingly remote philosophers. Post-1848 universal demoralization penetrated so deep that Flaubert could write one of his greatest novels, *Sentimental Education*, on precisely that topic.

This raised the further question of whether a genuine revolutionary republicanism opening the door to Jewish equality and meaningful integration into society and politics, encouraging participation in general intellectual and cultural life, was feasible at all in the near future; and, if still a practical proposition, could *Haskalah* revolt against the *shtetl* mentality, and political participation successfully blend with conserving Jewish identity as something distinct, meaningful and attainable?[3] The question became still more urgent amidst the stirrings of nationalism. Already by the 1820s and 1830s, Poland's democratic republicans favoring emancipation had begun debating whether emancipated Jews, and eventually all Poland's Jews, in order to become "Poles" must exchange Yiddish for Polish, quash their separate Jewishness and discard un-Polish pursuits like their post-1800 *Haskalah* enthusiasm for German studies (by no means confined just to Posen and Galicia).[4] Was Riesser, "among the most cultured of our German Jews," misguided or inspired, in demanding equality of rights while still cultivating Jewishness and Jewish culture, seeking cultural interaction and full participation in German political life, cultivating modern German rather than Yiddish, while simultaneously aiming to conserve core elements of Jewish tradition and forms of benevolence—exemplified nowhere more plainly than in the public addresses of the good-hearted Riesser himself?[5] In 1848, there was no easy answer; nor would there be over the next century.[6]

Democratic radicals of the 1830s and 1840s constituting the bulk of the European Left that was not socialist or Marxist (including the young Marx until 1844), as a rule did not doubt (Bauer was the great exception) that Jews needed, and should unconditionally be accorded, equal rights and access to general schooling and universities, along with a drastic curtailing of religious authority on both sides of the religious divide between—a curbing of rabbis and bishops equally. But beyond that they disagreed, especially the Jews among them, over whether their future was one of total assimilation into the wider society, or rather, as Maimon, Hourwitz, Nassy, Hartog Lémon, Auerbach, Riesser and (eventually) Hess called for, emancipation combined with and encouraging a separate Jewish identity and cultural existence.[7]

Here it is relevant to ask whether the earlier revolutionary tradition among the Jews themselves, down to 1848, displayed any coherent unifying character, and, if so, where exactly it was intended to lead. What kind of Jewish modernity had this tradition forged and did it envisage? Study of

Jewish revolutionaries participating in the French revolutions (1789–99, 1830, 1848–49), maintains Zosa Szajkowski, proves only that there was no typical Jewish pattern of revolution: Jews simply belonged to all factions and moved in all directions. But there is room to disagree with this hypothesis. It seems, rather, even where personal ambition or local tactics caused revolutionary Jews to align with the Montagne during the Terror, or attempt to, circumstances and conditioning over centuries brought out a deeply felt repugnance for the tyrannical, dogmatic, intolerant, bullying xenophobic tendency saturating *Robespierrisme* and Montagnard rhetoric and populist attitudes. This, in turn, further exacerbated Montagnard hostility to Jewish revolutionaries as overeducated, invidious cosmopolitan outsiders, as independent-minded critics disdaining the commonplace.

Jewish rejectionism of the existing *status quo* was rooted in what has sometimes been termed an "anarchic" tendency tinged with messianic longing.[8] But this "messianic" component was arguably mainly a yearning for the "ghetto walls" of "majoritarian sway" to come down, for provision of a freer, more autonomous existence for all, tending toward democratic republicanism. This meant the tradition of revolutionary Jews inherently clashed with the Counter-Enlightenment anti-intellectualism, Rousseauism and populist philistinism of *Robespierrisme* in some fundamental fashion. Where revolutionary Jews during the years 1792–94 preferred not to align with Hourwitz, Furtado and Nassy, and combat Montagnard populism, eschewing Brissotin circles during and after the brief civil war of the summer of 1793, like the Freys and Pereyra, they still chose uncompromisingly anti-Rousseauist, anti-*Robespierriste*, in effect quasi-Brissotin and *Dantoniste* positions and attitudes, as clearly emerges from Frey's *Philosophie sociale* attacking Rousseau, urging separation of state and religion and demanding freedom of expression and to criticize together with drastic curtailing of religious authority.

"La démocratie representative" is rejected by Rousseau but, according to Frey, the ex-Frankist Montagnard, remains the only legitimate structure of regime, the only form based on reason, the sole category where "the general will is continually manifested representatively by the most capable and fitting element, the one form robust, healthy and durable."[9] It appears, then, that there did, after all, exist a typical Jewish revolutionary posture that has thus far not been sufficiently profiled, a style integral to Radical Enlightenment closely linked to the fight for Jewish emancipation and, likewise, general emancipation, pushing for Enlightenment based on universal and equal rights, and representative democracy. Even the one great exception here, Ludwig Börne, is perhaps only an exception superficially, insofar, arguably, as he misread his hero "Robespierre." The main tendency, in any case, diverged sharply from Counter-Enlightenment reaction of whatever type whether *Robespierrisme,* religious orthodoxy, the Christian religious Right, "Holy Alliance" aristocratism, Panslavism or ultra-nationalism, while diverging too from the conservative, aristocratic Enlightenment of Montesquieu, Hume, Gibbon, Adam Smith and Voltaire, which made no effort, rather the contrary, to elevate the Jews' general image and wholly failed to push, or even hint at the need, for cancellation of Jewish disabilities and integration into society. If the Jewish revolutionary tradition was avowedly anti-Christian and anti-rabbinic, it was a revolutionary style equally adamant throughout on the overarching validity of equality of rights, justice for all, freedom of expression and curtailment of all forms of religious authority and religious policing.

If there existed a chain of revolutionary Jews from Spinoza to Marx convinced "justice, liberty and equality could be sovereigns of the world," and that they themselves were specially entrusted by circumstances with bringing about this redemption of all through the reign of truth,[10] it was a tradition perhaps partly deriving from the legacy of their religion, but equally, and arguably still more, from the two thousand years of oppression and degradation to which Jews had been subjected, and nowhere more so than in the stifling ghetto of papal Rome and the oppressive narrowness of the *shtetl* mentality. In 1789, no-one more vigorously expressed this Jewish revolutionary tradition than the minor French Jewish revolutionary whom the journalist Gorsas dubbed "the celebrated Hourwitz, author of an excellent work crowned by the Academy of Metz, reader in oriental languages at the Royal Library."[11] Hourwitz exhorted full equality of civil and political rights for Jews, together with political participation and military service in the national army of whatever nation they belonged to, without Jewry having to surrender its separate cultural and religious identity, and particular fields of language and historical study. An eager republican and egalitarian, he styled himself a French citizen but equally, and at the same time, a "Polish Jew."

Mendelssohn, the gentle revolutionary, found himself obliged by the requirements of caution, discretion and tactics to fuse strands of moderate and radical Enlightenment, sometimes descending into blatant self-contradiction in consequence.[12] Since his project involved launching a specifically Jewish

Enlightenment that would accompany Jewish emancipation, he needed to proceed without altogether alienating religious authority, his goal being impossible, he rightly grasped, if he wholly antagonized the Jewish orthodox who were up in arms against his reforms as it was. From his standpoint, a complete rupture made no sense and could only be counter-productive. As chief spokesman of the Jewish Enlightenment, he could not break with the rabbis, and hence could not wholeheartedly embrace Spinoza. Reason, he publicly maintained, confirms the reality of a benign Creator who knowingly governs the universe and immortality of the soul. Still, Mendelssohn was the first Jewish writer assiduously to work at rescuing Spinoza's image and message, helping re-install him in the history of mainstream modern philosophy. Spinoza's pathbreaking separation of philosophy from theology he emphatically endorsed, as he did much of his radical political thought, detaching the state from religion, and from monarchy and aristocracy, eager to see the Jewish community freed from all repressive censorship and coercive ecclesiastical oversight.

Mendelssohn was the epoch-making figure who established the model as to how, through independent study, assiduous self-development and self-education, individual Jews could escape the cramping limitations of tradition and religious observance and enter the world of Enlightenment and higher intellectual debate. His fame as a thinker and success in elevating himself to German intellectual life's upper echelons inevitably inspired many to follow the path of autodidactic self-formation, through reading, discussion and pursuit of intellectual excellence, striving to attain both self-liberation and gateways to European high culture and intellectual life.[13] In the longer run, though, it is hardly surprising that amidst the horrified bafflement and helpless passivity with which German Jewry watched the post-1880 titanic rise of organized mass antisemitism in central and western Europe as well as the United States and Russia, and, later still, the unparalleled horror of Nazism, many scholars of the post–World War II era construed Mendelssohn and the likes of Riesser and Auerbach as having led German Jewry onto a wrong track, being ultimately false guides leading their co-religionists to ruinous loss of identity, assimilation and destruction. Yet, in retrospect, this too seems simplistic. Jewish revolutionary tradition was a more complex, richer phenomenon than such judgments suggest.

Leo Strauss was by no means mistaken in pointing to the inherent weakness of Mendelssohn's "moderate Enlightenment" fixes, his approach's proneness to disintegrate under pressure, not wrong in maintaining Mendelssohn's "purified Spinozism" was just a convenient myth with no backbone.[14] Hannah Arendt scathingly attacked Mendelssohn's strategy, as the longing of an "obsequious bourgeois *Kulturmensch*" too addicted to German culture and acculturation, producing an unhealthy, self-denying German-Jewish thirst for *Bildung*. Arguably, though, neither formula is fully justified or gives a sufficiently balanced picture: Strauss was right that Mendelssohn's efforts to reconcile reason, emancipation and tradition were inherently fragile and apt to unravel, exposing its underlying Spinozism, but wrong to ignore the reality that it was precisely Mendelssohn's veiled radicalism that helped convert Spinoza into German Jewry's supreme icon of secularism and Jewish modernity. Arendt deplored the loss of Jewish awareness, identity and loyalty among German Jews bent on assimilation, but failed to note the positive features of Mendelssohn's veiled Spinozism for the achievement of a meaningful Jewish modernity. There was no other way Mendelssohn could have smuggled Radical Enlightenment elements into his German-Jewish concoction, his schema for *Haskalah*, and without such grounding there could be no concerted Jewish campaign for emancipation, equality, democracy and freedom of expression.

Enlightenment, insisted Condorcet shortly before his death at the hands of the viciously corrupt and tyrannical Montagnard factions that hijacked the Revolution and suspended the First Republic's constitution, of which he was the prime author, is the sole antidote to the ignorance, superstition, and credulity, and hence fanaticism, and populist intolerance that everywhere threatens the progress of humanity, the sole path to a higher level. Consequently, the representative democratic republic based on elections and representation he did so much to project can never be successfully established anywhere until superstition and ignorance are more effectively checked, countered and subdued.[15] If German Enlightenment created institutions and traditions too weak to stop Hitler and Nazism, then German and Jewish society's political redemption, and all human well-being, must await a future revived Enlightenment process that *is* strong enough to overcome modern multimedia ignorance-based populism, fascism and Counter-Enlightenment misdirected faith.

With the collapse of the 1848 Revolution and the French, German, Italian and Austro-Hungarian imperial and royal crackdown, in 1849–51, many democratic republican "Forty-Eighters" abandoned the revolutionary tradition, claiming the common people were simply not yet ready, that is, enlightened enough, to make their hopes and ideals feasible. Stamping out the last insurrectionary upsurge in Paris with the brutal suppression of the "Commune," in 1871, only confirmed the forlorn feelings prevalent since suppression of the French Second Republic, and of the anti-papal Roman republic, in 1849, that the revolutionary tradition in western Europe was finally dead.[16] The foremost philosophical loners of the nineteenth century, such as Schelling, Schopenhauer and Nietzsche, attacked Christianity arguably even more vehemently than had Spinoza long before. But, isolated and detached from society, they entirely dropped the attack on the political and social *status quo*, and all active involvement in countering the negative tendencies of the era, even though Nietzsche (mainly privately) was thoroughly contemptuous of the new ultra-nationalism, racism, imperialism and antisemitism. Those few who persevered in still fighting the princes, aristocracy and churches were, in a sense, back to square one, where Spinoza had found himself in the 1660s and 1670s. Little wonder, therefore, that Nietzsche, in his middle period, excitedly recognized himself and Spinoza as brothers-in-arms in their joint struggle against conventional notions and belief. But as regards actively subverting monarchy, aristocracy, churches and the social order, Nietzsche was anything but Spinoza's "brother-in-arms."

No veteran of 1848–49 subsequently stayed more engaged with social and political reality than Karl Marx, at any rate up to a point. From late 1847 down to early 1849 he remained highly optimistic at the seemingly real prospect of immediate revolutionary success and furiously active in various international organizations based in Cologne, Brussels, Paris and London. Marx proved vigorous and alert as a communist revolutionary planner, working closely with Engels and paying close attention to the intricacies of the revolutions on all sides, especially to developments in Paris, where he briefly returned with his family, in March 1848, two weeks after the start of the revolution there. Still, it can hardly be said that his grasp of the escalating conflict between the democratic republican radicals, on one side, and the socialists with their working-class supporters on the other, ran very deep. Rather, he showed little sympathy or understanding for the revolution's socioeconomic context, or for the profound predicament in which the republican leaders, Lamartine, Ledru-Rollin and the rest, found themselves. Nor did he accurately explore the reasons for the eventual triumph of Napoleon III and ensuing collapse of the Second French Republic.

In April 1848, once free of Prussian government restraints for the moment, Marx took up revolutionary battle stations in Cologne where there were many impoverished and unemployed workers and revolutionary support was substantial. Together with several colleagues, especially Engels, he restarted his *Rheinische Zeitung*, briefly turning it into Germany's foremost radical national newspaper. For the next thirteen months, until forced into exile from Germany for the second time, no-one was more active locally as an orator, reporter and revolutionary critic. But it is significant that during his revolutionary activity in Cologne, he referred hardly at all to communism and class warfare either at the gatherings he attended, or in his paper. To appeal to regional and wider German discontent as it then was, he realized, he had to concentrate on calling for "democracy" and universal male suffrage, on stressing the need for "sovereignty of the people," for a united German "republic," to replace the present regime of princely courts.[17]

Meanwhile, ignoring or treating with contempt all who disagreed with him, the dogmatic tendency increasingly obtrusive in Marx since 1844 showed little sign of receding. The "democratic" rhetoric he provisionally adopted in 1848–49 did not prevent Marx remaining throughout notably contemptuous of the Frankfurt Assembly (May 1848–May 1849), the elected national legislature sitting in the Frankfurt Paulskirche [St. Paul's Church] in which Riesser, elected vice president, was one of the most prominent orators. The Frankfurt Assembly, striving to reach broad concurrence and find a national constitutional, partly democratic solution to the political and social crisis which the revolutions had created right across Germany, drew no sympathy from Marx whatever. When it came to reporting the "June Days" in Paris, the "mini-civil war" between the republican radicals and the socialists that erupted when the "National Workshops" were inadvisably closed, and which did more than anything else to undermine the Second Republic, Marx's *Neue Rheinische Zeitung* saw all justification as being entirely on one side and was almost alone among national papers in Europe in unequivocally siding with the socialists. Indeed, he went so far as to call the "June Days," which wrecked the Republic's prospects completely, and deeply dismayed Germany's democratic republicans, the "destruction of all the delusions and illusions of the February revolution," an abjuring of the revolution of the democratic republicans and glorification of class-struggle bitterly condemned at the time by the democratic republicans.[18] A year later, refusing to support the Frankfurt Assembly in its final throes or the democratic armed risings in the Rhineland, with the 1848–49 revolutions facing defeat everywhere (except Switzerland), Marx fled Germany and soon the continent, taking refuge in London, in August 1849, but remained active in the "Communist League" and other organizations for still another year or so, until all hope of a revolutionary revival had expired.

From 1850 Marx notably withdrew from his former activism. He could no more see promising signs of immanent or medium-term revolutionary reawakening among the masses than the rest of the international exiled revolutionary fraternity. Living in Soho, a London district where many refugee "Forty-Eighters" congregated, he took personal refuge in the inexorable logic of his dialectic of class warfare, with the inevitable victory of the "proletariat" waiting in the wings and bound to stride triumphantly on stage one day, however long the wait. He withdrew from his 1847–50 bout of frenzied revolutionary activism into long years of solitary study, much of it sitting in the Reading Room of the British Museum, where he obtained his prized admission ticket in June 1850. Henceforth, he went even further than he had between 1844 and 1848 when he first began condemning the "bourgeois" delusions of the revolutionary democrats and republicans. After the defeat of 1848–49, he became still harsher and more dogmatic in rejecting the defeated democratic republican ideals of Ruge, Wirth and Riesser, of republicanism, representation and reforming the state through legislative means.

Those refusing to wholly abandon the dual fight on both fronts, against religious authority and the existing political order, like Heine, Hess and Marx, turned either to revolutionary socialism as their chief intellectual tool and schema, or else back to Spinoza, or, as in Hess's case, both. For his part, Ignać Einhorn, grandson of a rabbi of Vagújhely, in western Hungary, near the Slovak border, with his solid training in Hebrew and Jewish studies, a revolutionary activist equally committed to Jewish emancipation and Hungarian national renewal on a revolutionary basis, feeling as disillusioned as any by the failures of 1848, fled the following year to Leipzig, where he attended the university studying history, politics and philosophy. Einhorn took refuge in writing an academic thesis on Spinoza's political thought, a topic increasingly central to his post-1849 repulsed, defeated but still defiant revolutionary outlook. Publishing his *Spinozas Staatslehre*, at Dessau, in 1851, Einhorn underlined the absurdity of placing Spinoza's philosophy at the heart of modern thought as Mendelssohn, Lessing, Goethe, Herder, Fichte, Schelling, Hegel, Bauer and Feuerbach all did while entirely ignoring Spinoza's political and social ideas and their significance, or else dismissing them, as many erroneously did (and still do), as largely aligned with Hobbes.[19] The "grosse Bann" [great ban], as Einhorn called it, that seventeenth-century Sephardic Jewry imposed on Spinoza and his philosophy, subsequently broadened and maintained by the public's general view, was partially lifted by the late eighteenth and early nineteenth centuries, especially by Herder and German Idealism, but without ending the universally entrenched prejudice against Spinoza evident among religious leaders, most philosophers and intellectuals, and most of the political leaders heading the 1848 revolutions.

"Spinoza is still a troubling presence to some Jews," noted the Israeli philosopher Avishai Margalit, in April 2007. "So far as I know, not until recently was there a street in Israel named after him, in spite of the fact that David Ben-Gurion greatly admired him."[20] That is understandable, given Spinoza's hostility to all religious authority including the rabbis, his aversion to the Pharisaic temperament and tradition, his rejection of the idea of Jewish "election" by God as the "chosen people," and the dissolving effect of his thought on traditional belief and observance. In the mid-nineteenth century, society, churches, government and the academy, and not least Hegel, objected Einhorn, still conspired, just as Kant had earlier, to conceal from the general view something deeply relevant to everyone. In the seventeenth century, with every justification from their standpoint, theologians condemned Spinoza because he strove to topple theology and ecclesiastical sway, rejecting churchmen and religious authority more comprehensively than Hobbes or Locke, or any other thinker. But repudiating Spinoza and concerting efforts to marginalize his thought had senselessly persisted down to, and after, 1848–49 with far less justification than in the seventeenth and eighteenth centuries, an irrational ban tacitly acquiesced in by supposedly rational statesmen, academics and philosophers.

Even those philosophers most indebted to Spinoza's insights, like Hegel and Schelling, had shamelessly exploited the opportunity offered by ecclesiastical and popular condemnation, keeping him firmly under wraps philosophically and politically, in the manner of Kant abjectly hiding his revolutionary significance from public view while profiting from his philosophical greatness to further their own. Given the extent of their debt, Hegel, Schelling and Fichte had reprehensibly remained silent and been monstrously ungenerous in their publicly stated views and sentiments about Spinoza.[21] Moreover, while the true extent to which German Idealism revolved around *Spinozismus* remained concealed from the European public, from students and the academic sphere, Spinoza's political thought specifically, protested Einhorn, was being deliberately suppressed and buried by the academic establishment as part of the anti-democratic, pro-religion defensive strategy of all central and eastern Europe's princely courts and rulers.[22]

In 1851, prospects for a general appreciation of Spinoza's significance looked bleak to Ignaz Einhorn. In 1862, practically no-one agreed with Moses Hess when, now reconciled with his Jewish heritage after long estrangement, he emerged as an apologist for Jewish nationalism and resettlement in the Holy Land while still proclaiming Spinoza, as he had since the 1830s, as the "greatest thinker of all the centuries," and the most important for projecting the path of humanity's future.[23] If in the middle of the nineteenth century Spinoza was widely seen as nothing less, as Feuerbach dubbed him, in 1843, than "the Moses of modern freethinkers and materlialists," he was also still nothing more.[24] By the 1860s and 1870s, however, the situation was already changing significantly. Among a large segment of German Jewry, now becoming more secular and assimilated, and the growing radical *Haskalah* fringe in Poland, Lithuania and Russia, those forsaking orthodoxy while seeking a path midway between observance and assimilation, eagerly sought the ethical, political, literary and general reconstruction of a new kind of secular Jewish outlook and identity reconciling elements of tradition with modernity. It was at this point that Spinoza first began to emerge as the modern "Jewish" icon, hero and central figure.[25]

Regarding the Hebrew Bible as a cultural record and historical source rather than divine revelation, an object of secular study rather than the basis of religious authority, a whole wave of Jewish writers of the 1860s and 1870s generated a cultural nostalgia, a thirst for a lost Jewish world whose reconstruction through study, literature and revival of Hebrew could perhaps help shape the still unformed, largely unwritten and deeply uncertain secular Jewish identity of the future. It is useless, they and their twentieth-century heirs realized, to promote Jewish identity renewal within the confines of orthodoxy, Reform Judaism or the *shtetl* they had left behind, or to seek it within the surviving fragments of the contemporary Hasidic world, or the exotic, supposedly "authentic" pure "Jewishness" untouched by the travails of modernity, of eastern Jews, the Jewish traditions of the Orient—Yemenite or Bokharan. Not a few came to realize that an effective recipe combining progressive politics and benevolent reform with a tolerant secularism, blended with significant cultural elements of the Jewish past, was thinkable only via an anti-*shtetl*-minded Jewish secularism accurately identifying Jewish antecedents, uncovering authentic Jewish voices of revolutionary subversion preceding the radical *Haskalah* of the late eighteenth and early nineteenth centuries.

A truly authentic Jewish secular cultural tradition defined, renewed and revived had to lay special stress on study, rationalism and the quest for intellectual answers. It needed to be a tradition deeply preoccupied not just with one particular identity and cultural tradition but also with protecting minorities more broadly and securing equality of rights. Moderate *Haskalah* in Germany had undertaken such a salvaging function to an certain extent by sifting the Middle Ages and early modern era for everything in Jewish thought rationalistic, humanistic and of literary excellence that could be considered ethically "ennobling," focusing especially on the "Golden Age of Iberian Jewry," above all Maimonides and his followers. For the early modern era Joseph Delmedigo, Menasseh ben Israel and Orobio de Castro were the key heroes so imagined and elevated.[26] Radical *Haskalah* took up the challenge too but going dramatically further by detaching what could be regarded as ethically "ennobling" from religious values and concerns and, as part of this, following Heine and Hess, in not just resolutely re-incorporating Spinoza but placing him at the center of the story.

Given the prominence of revolutionary Jews in Europe during the age of the democratic revolutions (1775–1848), and in Poland-Lithuania in the rising of 1830 against the Czar, it was perhaps inevitable there would be more than minor ties and linkages, real and imagined, between the "Jewish revolutionaries" of the past and the new revolutionary movements welling up in late nineteenth-century eastern Europe. One obvious way forward for radical *Haskalah*, it emerged in Poland and Russia in the 1860s and 1870s, was to combine the notion that the Hasidim had conserved an authentic Jewish spiritual core with Jewish intellectual tradition while, here again, transcending the limits set by moderate *Haskalah*, as Solomon Maimon had done earlier when reconciling Hasidism with Spinozism via what he conceived as their common "pantheism." This was much the same path ventured down in the 1860s and 1870s by Hess and the "radical Haskalah" group around Abraham Krochmal in Poland.[27]

The first modern Russian Jewish revolutionaries, a new breed first emerging in the 1860s and early 1870s, in key instances followed just this progression from a Hasidic background to moderate *Haskalah,* and then radical secularism tinted by Jewish cultural identity before adding an admixture of revolutionary socialism too. Thus, the Hebrew poet Yehudah Leib Levin (1844–1925), from Minsk, who hailed from a Hasidic family, was drawn first, in the early 1860s, to Lubavitch Hasidism, then in the mid-1860s to *Haskalah*, only from the early 1870s, becoming a socialist revolutionary, but one, especially after the Kiev pogrom of 1872, much involved with questions of Jewish renewal and salvation. Aaron Lieberman (1845–1880) from a *shtetl* near Grodno, sometimes called the "father of Jewish socialism," studied in Petersburg and then, in the early 1870s, became a leader of a secret Jewish revolutionary socialist circle in Vilna. When this was broken up by the Czarist police, in June-July 1875, he escaped abroad, and continued propagating his socialist message, and brand of Marxism, but did so mainly in Hebrew and Yiddish, among other activities serving as editor in Vienna, until it was suppressed by the authorities, of the short-lived first Jewish and first Hebrew socialist periodical, *Ha-Emet* [The Truth] (1877–78).[28]

Just a few scattered individuals at first, in the 1860s, by the early 1870s a broad new social and cultural phenomenon was in the making. Russian Jewish revolutionary socialism linked to Marxism became an organized force led initially by two main cells of rabbinic seminary students, disillusioned with religion, based in Vilna and Mogilev. As early as 1872, a certain Arkadi Finkelstein was discovered clandestinely distributing anti-Czarist revolutionary literature among the students of the Vilna Rabbinical Seminary.[29] Vilna proved especially prolific in subversive students. The first "Vilna Circle," after being caught disseminating forbidden literature, was broken up by the police in 1875. But by then it had some thirty-eight members, several of whom, including Aaron Zundelevich (1852–1923), escaped abroad with Lieberman. Zundelevich, who had studied at the Vilna [Vilnius] Rabbinic Seminary until 1873, and helped turn Vilna into a major focus of revolutionary conspiracy, sought refuge in Königsberg, then Berlin, but soon returned to clandestine world of conspiracy in Russia where, in 1877, at Petersburg, he helped establish the first secret revolutionary press. Found involved in terrorist plots, he was imprisoned from 1880 to 1905.[30] Another Hebrew poet and *Haskalah* enthusiast fusing Jewish identity with a selective Marxism, closely associated with the Vilna Circle, was Isaac Kaminer (1834–1901), a graduate of Kiev University and a physician converted to socialism in Kiev in the 1860s, who later, after the early 1880s pogroms, strove to blend his *Haskalah*-tinted Marxist socialism with Zionism.[31]

Thus arose a widely diffused revolutionary secularizing underground, sworn to transform the social and political reality around them, soon encompassing a whole string of key centers of Jewish life in eastern Europe. By the late 1870s, there existed a remarkable network of Russian "circles," or local cells, of revolutionaries with a strikingly large proportion of Jewish participants, linking the Pale of Settlement centers—Vilna, Mogilev, Grodno, Minsk, Zhitomir and Odessa—not just with Petersburg, Moscow and Kiev but also (often via Vilna, Memel and Königsberg) with the exiled Russian revolutionary cells recently established in Berlin, Zurich, Paris and London's Whitechapel. In London appeared one of the most important general Russian socialist revolutionary papers of the era, *Vpered!* [Forward!] (1873–77), which was then smuggled back into Russia and disseminated by the clandestine cells. The burgeoning Jewish revolutionary network led by figures such as Lieberman, Kaminer, Finkelstein, Zundelevich, Lev Ginsburg, Lazar, Goldenberg and Natanson, included also noted revolutionary women such as Anna Epstein, Betsi Kaminskaia and Rozalia Idelson.[32]

Russian revolutionary cells in the 1870s and 1880s were generally divided between a whole array of ideological factions differing in their versions of socialism, and over strategy and tactics, some preferring a rural approach among the peasantry, others focusing on factory workers, some engaging in plotting assassination and terror, others refraining from terror tactics. All subscribed to a "secularism" rejecting all religious authority, all supernatural being and all divine governance of the world but in the case of the Jews among them a secularism able to incorporate significant cultural elements borrowed from religious tradition. Certainly, the Jewish revolutionaries found themselves just as split as their non-Jewish comrades into numerous different, sometimes warring factions—the Chaikovsky Circle, founded in the Petersburg medical academy in 1868–69, in which Natanson was a key member, consisted of Lavrists, Bakuninists, strict Marxists and more. Some, like Natanson and Zundelevich, did indeed avowedly reject their Jewish background and any notion of a separate Jewish collectivity and cultural tradition worth preserving. But it is equally evident that a large, crucial segment of this movement, with Levin, Kaminer and Lieberman as prime examples, all preaching versions of selective Marxism, strove to combine revolutionary socialism with conserving Jewish cultural identity and particularity.[33] Even Zundelevich developed a special interest in winning over Jewish workers. This latter concern became more marked later, in the 1890s, when the re-founded and now largely Marxist "Vilna Group" founded the General Jewish Workers' Association, or *Bund*, an organization vowing to transform the world and the Jews in it while retaining Jewishness as a meaningful separate cultural identity. This soon clashed with what became the dominant Marxist impulse in Russia, and internationally, aiming to change the world, equalizing all humanity without encouraging, or even allowing, cultural entities stressing their distinctiveness to emerge, discord developing, by 1920, in the new Soviet Union, into a brutal ideological conflict.[34]

Clearly, some Jewish centers of the Pale seemed more apt than others to nurture secularizing revolutionary tendencies blended with Jewish tradition and society. Vilna from the 1870s, despite its famous university, founded in 1579, being closed by the Czarist authorities due to its role in the 1830 Polish rising (and not re-opened until 1919), gained a renown as the "cradle of the Jewish socialist movement in eastern Europe" that lasted for decades,[35] colored by its rationalistic tradition of Jewish culture opposing the mysticism, messianism and emotionalism of Frankism and earlier Jewish messianic movements, and venerable record of anti-Hasidism entrenched still in its rabbinic seminary. During the nineteenth century, Lithuanian Jews (Litvaks) were indeed often looked on with distaste, bordering on hatred by many Polish and Ukrainian Jews for their scorning "Polish" Jewish "superstition" and mysticism and pretensions to greater *seychel*. *Seychel* was a Yiddish word general in Jewish eastern Europe but invested with special emphasis by Litvaks, designating hard-headed materialistic good sense, eagerness to avoid being wasteful or going down the wrong track, linked to, but distinct from wisdom acquired through study. It was a wisdom of the streets disdaining the "nonsense" spouted by the muddle-headed, eager to make the best of reality as it is. *Seychel* was a key feature of a folk rationalism shaping the distinctiveness of Litvakism that made its own contribution to Yiddish-speaking socialism.

By the 1870s, east European Jewry was caught up in a vast new drama of modernity versus tradition, secularism versus religious authority, participation in new youth groups and organizations at odds with the conservatism of the Jewish community councils. But even those repudiating all links with their Jewish path and uninterested in the quest for an authentic Jewish particularity, as revolutionary socialists arguably evinced typical Jewish traits. The impulse to self-improvement through intensive study of hallowed texts was ubiquitous, while sanctioning terror tactics, as Zundelevich did, was rare. Even Mark Andreyevich Natanson (1851–1919), a Lithuanian from near Kovno, as a medical student an organizer of the Chaikovsky Circle in Petersburg in the late 1860s, and in prison during 1869–71, later close to Russian conspirators plotting assassination, disapproved of planned terror and assassination as such. He also strongly disapproved of curbing the right to free expression and criticism, and eventually, after supporting the Bolshevik Revolution of 1917–19, broke with Lenin, in 1919, over the ban on other political parties and persecution of dissidents,[36] preferring to go into exile, in Switzerland, where he died the same year.

The uprooting of unprecedented numbers of young, often unmarried Jews, moving considerable distances within and also from the Pale of Settlement, not just for study in Petersburg or Moscow but from eastern to western Europe and, by the 1880s, emigrating *en masse* to the United States, South Africa and Australia, became a major factor in weakening ties with family, and religious observance, and, in the case of students converting to socialism, gravitating often also to sexual liberation and the idea of free love.[37] There was nothing untypical in Trotsky's parents, David and Aneta Bronstein, moving a great distance to a small outlying agricultural village, not far from Odessa, distant enough from their family and past to severely weaken old bonds. The Bronsteins became known for slackness of religious observance. The young Lev Davidovich Bronstein (Leon Trotsky; 1879–1940) felt even more remote from family, tradition and religion long before becoming an aspiring intellectual in Odessa, reading ardently and widely, which in turn prepared the way for his conversion to Marxism, in 1897.[38]

To those joining the quest for renewed authenticity of identity, it seemed most relevant, then, instead of eulogizing orthodox Hasidim or remote "Yemenites," to explore the gallery of great modern Jewish heretics—Uriel da Costa, Spinoza, Börne, Heine and Hess—who, despite being religious apostates, now seemed in some way to represent Jewish tradition and peoplehood in a secularized, wider, more modern but not yet fully defined sense. Spurred by rising antisemitism on all sides, fierce in the Ukraine, Lithuania, Poland and Russia as well as Hungary and all central Europe, and the brutal anti-intellectualism of Nazism, this widening European Jewish cultural quest eventually assumed a tone of deep alarm and urgency. For secular Jews, being Jewish suddenly meant finding oneself under intense pressure to redefine Jewishness as an intellectual and secular ethical tradition opposed to religious authority and all zealotry, but opposed also to Leninism, *Robespierrisme*, "Christian" Counter-Enlightenment, the Czarist nineteenth century, intolerant Polish and Magyar nationalism, Nazism and generally the sway of the bigoted and populist on every side. The fight was on to survive amidst a sea of hostility that among some strengthened resolve to find the inner resources to fight back. Yet, searching for a new ideal of Jewish identity, a viably modern

Jewish collective self-awareness and group identity, in reaction to nationalist antisemitism, Leninism, Stalinism and Nazism, became an agenda that, over the decades, itself tragically degenerated into a defensive, illiberal nationalism stiffened by messianic quasi-theological tendencies, eventually becoming deaf to Enlightenment reason and humanitarian values.[39]

Against the dangers without and the dangers within, no better remedy presented itself than enlightened reason. The menace of a narrow Jewish nationalism, no less than other kinds of bigotry, instigated a powerful dialectic contrary effect in pre-1933 Germany, a broad intensified reaffirmation of Enlightenment principles, culminating in Ernst Cassirer's *The Philosophy of the Enlightenment* (1932). Yet, "Enlightenment reason" on its own had obvious limits as far as retrieving, renewing and strengthening the kind of Jewish cultural awareness that can readily be combined and used to reinforce a modern-day Jewish secular democratic Left. A process of deep historical re-engagement is also needed. No-one has better brought out and underlined the "paradox of liberation" posed by modern secular revolutions than Michael Walzer. In his book *The Paradox of Liberation* (2015), Walzer powerfully delineates the tendency of many twentieth-century revolutions (giving India, Algeria and Israel as prime examples) to be self-defeating and unwittingly encourage conservative religious counterrevolution, as Left secular Zionism did by producing a revolutionary political and general culture too "thin," and too little rooted in the past, to inspire, morally uplift and sustain society's allegiance for any considerable span.[40]

In the changed, deeply fraught context of Weimar, no other Jewish figure could be found who could rival Spinoza as a Jewish and yet also general icon, except perhaps Heine, who, anyhow, with his cultural "Spinozism" was the exception proving the rule.[41] Ironic, paradoxical and improbable, the best rallying point and tool for unifying the many quarreling, divergent factions within Weimar Jewry—orthodoxy, Reform Judaism and secular Zionist and anti-Zionist—and the most useful to the many Jewish outcasts and refugees from the Russian Revolution huddling in Berlin, Königsberg, Bern and Zurich, in the 1920s and 1930s cursing all Marxism and communism, proved, yet again, to be the figure of Spinoza.[42] Not inconceivably, the same will prove to be true again in the future.

Spinoza's philosophy was "revolutionary" in at least three key respects—in assailing religious authority fundamentally, in decisively separating morality from theology, and in tying these two features closely to the new, late seventeenth-century originally principally Dutch democratic republican tendency (which strikingly continues to be *terra incognita* to practically all standard accounts of the history of modern political thought). But while this indubitably makes Spinoza a powerful revolutionary force in Western thought, author of a philosophy which continues even today to "open up horizons of liberation that can still be ours,"[43] does it make him also in some sense specifically a "Jewish revolutionary"?

There remains today a formidable argument, originating in Hermann Cohen and Leo Strauss, and recently best expressed by Daniel B. Schwartz in his *The First Modern Jew*, that the pervasive impact of Spinoza's revolt against the synagogue on Jewish enlighteners and other secularists in the nineteenth and twentieth centuries, not least Heine, Auerbach and Hess, was based on a potent myth: the real Spinoza possessed no sense of Jewish group identity that could be secularized. If he could plausibly be turned into a messianic figure promising secular redemption without Jewish allegiance of any sort, he offered no notion of any Jewish tradition beyond submission to religious law and observance. Hence, Spinoza, however much a source of modern Jewish secularist delusion, whatever his success in becoming "Rabbenu Baruch" [Our Rabbi Baruch] of the post-1850 radical *Haskalah*, provides no veritable path to a secular Jewish tradition or solution to the problem of modern Jewish ethical identity.[44]

This volume adopts a somewhat divergent position. The powerful attraction of Spinoza in the tradition of nineteenth-century Jewish secularism was indeed in part a constructed, if enduring, myth. But there *were* actually strands of Spinoza's mature outlook that do offer a ground plan for a secular democratic Jewishness rendering Spinoza the West's prototype of the enlightened "revolutionary Jew." There is the fact that Maimonides and medieval Jewish philosophy, especially its veiled subversive undercurrents, played a crucial role in the development of his philosophical approach while in his life's story studying the Hebrew Bible, and resorting to the best available scholarship in doing so, remained the orientating starting point for what he deemed a broader, more general understanding of the human reality. Thus, in his imagery, the Mosaic Hebrew republic was humanity's first recorded grand attempt to escape permanently from bondage, monarchy and all tyranny and fix the path for humanity's future efforts toward the democratic republic that forms the optimal context for human stability, co-operation and freedom.[45] Furthermore, his early life was decisively shaped by an exceptionally vibrant Jewish intellectual milieu in Amsterdam, at the time the center of the western Sephardic world. His background contributed too to his viewing church and Inquisition-based theologico-political tyranny, combining priestly doctrines with kingship as with Philip II's global empire, mankind's supreme tyranny of tyrannies. Further, there is no ignoring his viewing Christian martyrdom in scale and duration as basically a fake tradition in no way above Jewish martyrdom which, in his eyes, far outstripped it.

But above all, there is Spinoza's concept of a universal ethics of justice and charity as the creation not of any church or public institution but, rather, of a fiercely persecuted, hated and deeply vulnerable underground sect, an underground fraternity anchored exclusively in reason instead of faith and dogma, the idea that the best is achieved in the face of universal contempt and scorn. Spinoza's enlightened underground sect does not just spread *converso* skepticism about false "miracles" and "resurrections," but provides the key to what he envisages as a better human future, advancing a secular ethics edging surreptitiously forward, staunchly opposing oppression *and* the delusions of the majority. It hoped to work by eroding ignorance and blindness until eventually, partly guided and partly prodded, the great mass of the world's deceived credulous is ushered into the democratic republican revolution. Finally, there is Spinoza's idea that society, until it becomes sufficiently enlightened, cannot gain any realistic, meaningful notion of what its own best interest is, and must inevitably be systematically cheated by kings, aristocrats, churchmen and demagogues (or "false prophets") serving the privileged and the few, leaving society disfigured by wars that achieve nothing for most but cost them dear in lives and resources, just as remains the position in the world today. Right or wrong, such positions are perhaps best understood as genuine components of a Jewish secularist democratic (and secularized Marrano) identity.

Arguably, then, one can in some sense justifiably call Spinoza a "Jewish thinker" and "Jewish revolutionary," a thinker propagating ideas of great relevance to Jews everywhere about the relation of religion to politics and religion to community, about freedom of thought, war, religious laws, martyrdom, the survival of the Jewish people and, from the eighteenth century onwards, the significance of the Hebrew language. In educating themselves for life in the world of today, when asked: what is the relation of Judaism and Jewishness to "modernity," can even the cream of Jewish orthodoxy, asked Margalit, any longer avoid the specter of Spinoza?[46]

Spinoza's best-known remark about Jews occurs at the end of chapter 3 of the *Tractatus Theologico-Politicus* (1670), where he observes that the practice of circumcision "has so much importance as almost to persuade me that this thing alone will preserve their nation for ever, and in fact, were it not that the principles of their religion weaken their courage, I would believe unreservedly that at some time, given the opportunity, since all things are changeable, they might re-establish their state, and God will choose them again."[47] As Spinoza's wording suggests, this was a matter he had pondered for some time, prompted doubtless not only by the huge messianic frenzy stirring the Jewish world in 1665–67 in the shape of Sabbatai Zevi and his following but by his own personal copy of Menasseh ben Israel's messianic *Esperança de Israel* (1650), with its expressions of hope that the Jews would eventually return to the Holy Land, a text dedicated to, among other community elders, Spinoza's father.

Attention here tends to fix on the (probably somewhat sarcastic) prediction that, should they recover their courage, the Jews might one day restore their political independence, a significant claim (dear to the hearts of Zionists down to Ben-Gurion and beyond), as this might seem to explain the means by which the Jewish people can restore themselves to normality, ending the discrimination and persecution of old. But equally significant is Spinoza's markedly negative attitude toward the Jews' continued communal separateness and their resulting non-involvement in the political affairs of the lands where they dwell, wherever they possess no separate state of their own. For while strict separation in non-Jewish societies ensures survival as a religious community based, in Spinoza's view, on "superstition," such voluntary segregation also causes Jews unceasingly to "incur the hatred of all." Doubtless, Spinoza was contemptuous of the Jews' lack of courage, the unmanly attitude which, in his view, prevented their fighting tyranny and striving for republican liberty. But, despite that, he still regarded the Jews' precarious survival as a distinct people over so many centuries as a unique and striking phenomenon.

Einhorn followed up his *Zur Judenfrage in Ungarn* [On the Jewish Question in Hungary] of 1847, by raising precisely the question raised here: was Spinoza just an isolated phenomenon, a lonely heretic and abstract thinker whose toleration theories, democratic republicanism and unparalleled attack on Scriptural authority helped prepare the ground for the Enlightenment, and who, even if unjustly marginalized by philosophers and historians of "modernity" and the revolutionary age, was nevertheless still an isolated figure largely irrelevant, remote and unconnected with "modern" developments?

Or did Spinoza initiate a revolutionary tradition of opposition to existing structures of authority that mid-nineteenth-century philosophers, scholars, teachers and churchmen did their utmost to sweep under the carpet, while he, nevertheless, remains of overriding importance in the rise of the modern democratic revolutionary consciousness and, within it, a vigorous new kind of ethical-cultural and also political Jewish "modernity"?

NOTES

INTRODUCTION

1. Levin, *Jewish Socialist Movements*, 26–29; Stern, *Jewish Materialism*, 118–23.
2. Levin, *Jewish Socialist Movements*, 32, 377–96, 402–5; Stern, *Jewish Materialism*, 123–39; Wistrich, *Jews of Vienna*, 487–88.
3. Wistrich, *Jews of Vienna*, 26–28; Hertz, *How Jews Became Germans*, 75, 186; Stern, *Jewish Materialism*, 29, 59, 91, 114–15.
4. Feiner, *Origins*, 6–7, 154–58, 184, 194, 216–17; Sorkin, *Jewish Emancipation*, 5–6, 354.
5. Sorkin, *Jewish Emancipation*, 71, 79, 91, 101, 117, 355.
6. There is, though, a striking difference of emphasis: the index in Sorkin's book gives four page references to the Enlightenment; here, there is no page where Enlightenment is not at the center of the story.
7. Goldfarb, *Emancipation*, 201; Wistrich, *Jews of Vienna*, 27, 37, 150.
8. On the background, definition and scope of the term "Radical Enlightenment," see Israel, "'Radical Enlightenment': A Game-Changing Concept," 15–47; and Israel, *The Enlightenment That Failed*, 1–33.
9. Higby, *Religious Policy*, 147–74; Sorkin, *Jewish Emancipation*, 157–58; Israel, *The Enlightenment That Failed*, 795–801.
10. Kovács, *Liberal Professions*, 17–19; Carvalho and Koyama, "Jewish Emancipation and Schism," 27–29.
11. Goldfarb, *Emancipation*, 195–201, 234–35.
12. Higby, *Religious Policy*, 318–19; Harris, "Public Opinion and the Proposed Emancipation," 67, 72–79; Sorkin, *Jewish Emancipation*, 164–65, 180–82, 185–86.
13. Eisenbach, "Jewish Population in Warsaw," 108–9, 116–17; Drozdowski, "Jews of Warsaw," 85.
14. Hundert, *Jews in Poland-Lithuania*, 230–31; Stone, "Knowledge of Foreign Languages," 204; Opalski and Bartal, *Poles and Jews*, 59, 62, 124; Drozdowski, "Jews of Warsaw," 85; Dynner, *Yankel's Tavern*, 110.
15. Hundert, "Re(de)fining Modernity in Jewish History," 142–45; Hundert, *Jews in Poland-Lithuania*, 45; Drozdowski, "Jews of Warsaw," 86–80; Eisenbach, "Jewish Population in Warsaw," 95–98, 100.

16. Israel, *European Jewry*, 171–76; Löwy, *Redemption and Utopia*, 15, 190; Dweck, *Dissident Rabbi*, 140–51.
17. Frankel, *Crisis, Revolution*, 244–73, especially 255–56; Sutcliffe, *What Are Jews For?*, 49–50, 57.
18. Katz and Popkin, *Messianic Revolution*, 138; Schama, *Belonging*, 446–51; Kieniewicz, "Assimilated Jews," 172.
19. Frankel, *Crisis, Revolution*, 258, 268–69, 274, 277.
20. Levin, *Jewish Socialist Movements*, 6–7; Israel, *European Jewry*, 212–13; Wistrich, *Laboratory*, 246, 248–49.
21. Melamed, "Salomon Maimon and the Rise," 68; Melamed, "Spinozism, Acosmism," 76–79.
22. Feiner, *Origins*, 134; Mitchell, *Voltaire's Jews*, xxvii.
23. Israel, *The Enlightenment That Failed*, 178–82, 460–83.
24. Morawe, "Heinrich Heine und die Strategie," 549–50.
25. Toland, *Reasons for Naturalizing*, 15–18, 25; Lurbe, "John Toland and the Naturalization," 41–42, 46–47.
26. Toland, *Reasons for Naturalizing*, 15, 18, 20; Lurbe, "John Toland and the Naturalization," 37.
27. Toland, *Reasons for Naturalizing*, 25; Bernardini and Lucci, *The Jews, Instructions*, 73.
28. Israel, *European Jewry*, 156–63.
29. Toland, *Reasons for Naturalizing*, 14–16; Champion, "Toleration and Citizenship," 143; Stuurman, *Invention of Humanity*, 271.
30. Champion, "Toleration and Citizenship," 142; Sutcliffe, *Judaism and Enlightenment*, 198–99; Leask, "Undivulged Event," 63–66; Birnbaum, "Est-il des moyens?," 16.
31. Spinoza, *Theological-Political Treatise*, 56; Brykman, *Judéité de Spinoza*, 45–46, 86.
32. Toland, *Reasons for Naturalizing*, 10–11, 20; Bernardini and Lucci, *The Jews, Instructions*, 58–59, 65.
33. Hudson, *The English Deists*, 97; Bernardini and Lucci, *The Jews, Instructions*, 60–61.
34. Toland, *Reasons for Naturalizing*, 17–18; Manuel, *Broken Staff*, 187.
35. Brykman, *Judéité de Spinoza*, 59–70; Sutcliffe, *What Are Jews For?*, 81, 85.
36. Stone, "Knowledge of Foreign Languages," 200; Feiner, *Origins*, 125–26, 145, 154–58.
37. Drozdowski, "Jews of Warsaw," 88, 91; Harris, *Nachman Krochmal*, 9–14, 17.
38. Wistrich, *Jews of Vienna*, 135.
39. Harris, *Nachman Krochmal*, 17–18; Opalski and Bartal, *Poles and Jews*, 35–36.
40. Harris, *Nachman Krochmal*, 46–53
41. Schwartz, "Our Rabbi Baruch," 26–27, 45–46.

CHAPTER 1. THE SUBVERSIVE BACKGROUND OF A REVOLUTIONARY THINKER

1. Spinoza, *Letters*, 343; Nadler, *Spinoza: A Life*, 339; Lavaert, *Vreijheid, gelijkheid*, 214.
2. Spinoza, *Letters*, 340–44.

3. Menasseh ben Israel, *Hope of Israel*, 61; Servaas van Rooijen, *Inventaire.*
4. Domínguez, "Presencia de Antonio Pérez," 187; Menasseh ben Israel, *Hope of Israel*, 149; Brykman, *Judéité de Spinoza*, 21–22; Bodian, *Dying in the Law*, 250n38.
5. Menasseh ben Israel, *Hope of Israel*, 149; Den Boer, "Isaac Orobio de Castro," 81.
6. Menasseh ben Israel, *Hope of Israel*, 150.
7. Liebman, "Tomas Treviño de Sobremente," 64–67; Israel, *Race, Class and Politics*, 246.
8. Nadler, *Spinoza's Heresy*, 166.
9. Yovel, *Spinoza and Other Heretics*, 50.
10. Vaz Dias and Van der Tak, "Spinoza, Merchant and Autodidact," 136, 138.
11. Révah, *Des Marranes à Spinoza*, 169; Borges Coelho, "Orígenes de Bento de Espinosa," 125.
12. Borges Coelho, "Orígenes de Bento de Espinosa," 127.
13. Spinoza, *Theological-Political Treatise*, 55; this statement Spinoza seems to have largely borrowed from Antonio Pérez.
14. Spinoza, *Theological-Political Treatise*, 55.
15. Smith, *Spinoza, Liberalism and the Question*, 200–201; Smith, *Reading Leo Strauss*, 31–32.
16. Menasseh ben Israel, *Hope of Israel*, 156.
17. Kamen, *Philip of Spain*, 310.
18. Kamen, *Philip of Spain*, 170.
19. Kamen, *Philip of Spain*, 172–73; Valladares, *Conquista de Lisboa*, 33.
20. Parker, *Grand Strategy*, 166.
21. Spinoza, *Briefwisseling*, 410; Spinoza, *Letters*, 341.
22. Van de Kamp, *Emanuel van Portugal*, 44–45.
23. Israel, *Diasporas Within*, 81–82.
24. Révah, *Des Marranes à Spinoza*, 127–28.
25. Révah, *Des Marranes à Spinoza*, 50; Nahon, "Rapports," 43; Israel, *Diasporas Within*, 256–57.
26. Deed of Jan Fransz. Bruyningh, 16 December 1596, *SR* 1 (1967): 111–12.
27. Gómez-Centurión Jiménez, *Felipe II, la empresa*, 181.
28. Martin and Parker, *The Spanish Armada*, 94; Parker, *Grand Strategy*, 167; Valladares, *Conquista de Lisboa*, 30, 32, 41–42.
29. Valladares, *Conquista de Lisboa*, 58, 74.
30. Quoted in Ruspio, "La presenza portoghese," 78.
31. Ruspio, "La presenza portoghese," 79.
32. Parker, *Grand Strategy*, 190, 360n37.
33. Israel, "Maurits en de wording," 71.
34. Parker, *Grand Strategy*, 215.
35. Den Tex, *Oldenbarnevelt*, 2:16, 18.
36. Servaas van Rooijen, *Inventaire.*
37. Bodian, "Some Ideological Implications," 209; Bodian, "Portuguese Jews in Amsterdam," 314.

38. Deed of Jan Fransz. Bruyningh, Amsterdam, 16 December 1596, *SR* 1 (1967): 111–12.
39. GA Amsterdam, NA vol. 967, fo. 302, deed signed by Michael d'Espinoza, Amsterdam, 20 July 1651; see also Israel, "Philosophy, Commerce," 133–34.
40. Vaz Dias and Van der Tak, *Spinoza, mercator et autodidactus*, 17.
41. Israel, *Diasporas Within*, 278, 298, 311.
42. Vaz Dias and Van der Tak, *Spinoza, mercator et autodidactus*, 14–16.
43. See Spinoza, *Opera*, 2:5; see also Spinoza, *Collected Works*, 1:7; De Dijn, *Spinoza, The Way to Wisdom*, 181–89.
44. Brykman, *Judéité de Spinoza*, 46; Israel, "Philosophy, Commerce," 125–26.
45. Israel, "Philosophy, Commerce," 126.
46. Spinoza, *Opera*, 2:6; Spinoza, *Collected Works*, 1:8.
47. Tosel, *Spinoza, ou l'autre (in)finitude*, 149–51; Casarino, "Marx before Spinoza," 195; Lordon, *Willing Slaves of Capital*, 8.
48. Spinoza, *Opera*, 2:274; Spinoza, *Collected Works*, 1:593
49. Israel, "Philosophy, Commerce," 139–41.
50. Gebhardt, "Juan de Prado," 277–82; Israel, "Philosophy, Commerce," 128.
51. Jelles, "Praefatio," in Spinoza, *Opera Posthuma*, i.
52. Israel, "Philosophy, Commerce," 133–34.
53. Spinoza to Jelles, The Hague, 17 February 1671, in Spinoza, *The Letters*, 243–44; Lavaert, *Vrijheid, gelijkheid*, 192.
54. Levi de Barrios, *Triumpho del Govierno Popular*, 85; Kaplan, *From Christianity*, 265; further on this lost *Apologia*, see Curley, "Spinoza's Lost Defense," 9–32.
55. Spinoza, *Theological-Political Treatise*, 47, 200–201; Brykman, *Judéité de Spinoza*, 78, 84–85, 98–103.
56. Spinoza, *Theological-Political Treatise*, 201; Spinoza, *Opera*, 3:194–95; Michael Silverthorne and I here translated "salus" as safety; but on reflection this now seems mistaken here.
57. Brykman, *Judéité de Spinoza*, 80, 97; James, "Freedom, Slavery and the Passions," 229.
58. Spinoza, *Theological-Political Treatise*, 258–59; Spinoza, *Opera*, 3:247; Giancotti Boscherini, *Lexicon Spinozanum*, 1:114–15 and 2:974.
59. Spinoza, *Opera*, 3:229; Spinoza, *Theological-Political Treatise*, 238.
60. Spinoza, *Opera*, 3:329; Spinoza, *Collected Works*, 2:569; Giancotti Boscherini, *Lexicon Spinozanum*, 1:116.
61. Spinoza, *Opera*, 3:352; Spinoza, *Collected Works*, 2:594; Giancotti Boscherini, *Lexicon Spinozanum*, 1:116.
62. Melamed, "Charitable Interpretations," 271–72.
63. Vernière, *Spinoza et la pensée française*, 485; Jonathan Israel, introduction to B. de Spinoza, *Theological-Political Treatise*, viiixxxiv, here xxx; Lavaert, *Vrijheid, gelijkheid*, 237–38.
64. Spinoza, *Theological-Political Treatise*, 202.
65. Melamed, "Charitable Interpretations," 271.
66. Steenbakkers, "Spinoza, beyond the Legends," 23.

67. Spinoza, *Collected Works*, 2:593n10.
68. Further on this point, see Israel, "'Radical Enlightenment': A Game-Changing Concept," 15–47, 37–39.
69. Wertheim, *Salvation through Spinoza*, 6–7; Bourel, *Moses Mendelssohn*, 98.
70. Smith, *Spinoza, Liberalism and the Question*, xii; Goetschel, "The Hyphen in the Theological-Political," 6–7.
71. Levin, *Jewish Socialist Movements*, 377–78; Frankel, *Crisis, Revolution*, 119, 126, 164–65, 173.
72. Smith, *Spinoza, Liberalism and the Question*, 203–4; Nadler, *A Book Forged in Hell*, 167–69.

CHAPTER 2. SPINOZA AND THE ORIGINS OF THE MODERN REVOLUTIONARY CONSCIOUSNESS (1650–1677)

1. See Rosenthal, "The Siren Song of Revolution," 11–32; see also Feuer, *Spinoza and the Rise of Liberalism*, 38–42. As examples of writers viewing Spinoza as a revolutionary Rosenthal cites Antonio Negri, myself and also Willi Goetschel, who "highlights" what he calls the "revolutionary power of Spinoza's thought" which "radiates forward to Moses Hess and a line of progressive thinker who—knowingly or not—discover through Heine the critical potential of Spinozist thought"; to these names we should add the eminent French philosopher Étienne Balibar (see Cooper, "Statesmen versus Philosophers," 45).
2. See Sara Hutton's review of Ducheyne, ed., *Reassessing the Radical Enlightenment*, *EHR* 133 (October 2018).
3. Cohen, *Spinoza on State and Religion*, 1–3; for Cohen's favourable early view of Spinoza, see Beiser, *Hermann Cohen*, 44–46.
4. Spinoza, *Tractatus Politicus*, 126; Verbeek, "Spinoza on Aristocratic and Democratic Government," 145–60.
5. Israel, "Banning of Spinoza's Works," 8–9; Saar, *Immanenz der Macht*, 51.
6. Spinoza, *Tractatus Politicus*, 126.
7. Spinoza, *Tractatus Politicus*, 120, 127; Lavaert, *Vrijheid, gelijkheid*, 237–38.
8. Feuer, *Spinoza and the Rise of Liberalism*, 150–53; Saar, *Immanenz der Macht*, 53.
9. Such confusion is notable in Verbeek, "Spinoza on Aristocratic and Democratic Government," 151–57.
10. Spinoza, *Theological-Political Treatise*, 252–59; Israel, *The Enlightenment That Failed*, 71–72.
11. On this topic, see my *Diasporas within a Diaspora*.
12. Révah, *Spinoza et le Dr Juan de Prado*, 64.
13. Révah, *Spinoza et le Dr Juan de Prado*, 61–68; Kaplan, "Discipline, Dissent," 397; Muchnik, *Une Vie marrane*, 173–74, 317, 414–15.
14. Muchnik, "Orobio contra Prado," 34.
15. Nadler, *Spinoza: A Life*, 90–93, 136–37, 142–43.
16. Alston, *Education and the State*, 121–22; Stern, *Jewish Materialism*, 91.

17. Alston, *Education and the State*, 130–37.
18. Spinoza to Van Blijenbergh, 5 January 1665, in Spinoza, *Briefwisseling*, 163.
19. Bayle, *Écrits sur Spinoza*, 22; see also Cohen, *Spinoza on State and Religion*, 3; Curley, "Spinoza's Lost Defense," 9–32.
20. Spinoza, *Tractatus Politicus* (Wernham ed.), 261; Lavaert, *Vrijheid, gelijkheid*, 244–45.
21. I explain this point in detail in my forthcoming biography of Spinoza.
22. Yovel, *Spinoza and Other Heretics*, 34.
23. Quoted in Klever, "Spinoza and Van den Enden in Borch's Diary," 315.
24. Begley, "Support and Distrust" (forthcoming).
25. Spinoza, *Opera*, 4:308; Spinoza, *Briefwisseling*, 400.
26. Spinoza, *Tractatus Politicus* (Wernham ed.), 2:260–61.
27. Curley, "Kissinger, Spinoza and Genghis Khan," 315, 329.
28. Spinoza, *Theological-Political Treatise*, 235–37.
29. Spinoza, *Theological-Political Treatise*, 236.
30. Spinoza, *Theological-Political Treatise*, 213–14; Saar, *Immanenz der Macht*, 334–37; Cooper, "Reevaluating Spinoza's Legacy," 475–78.
31. Spinoza, *Theological-Political Treatise*, 232–35; Cooper, "Reevaluating Spinoza's Legacy," 479–81.
32. Domínguez, "Presencia de Antonio Pérez," 174–75.
33. Spinoza, *Tractatus Politicus*, 364–65; Domínguez, "Presencia de Antonio Pérez," 175; Gascón Pérez, *Aragón en la monarquía*, 2:42.
34. Offenberg, "Spinoza's Library," 320; Servaas van Rooijen, *Inventaire*, no. 17, p. 678; Blanco Echauri, "Espinosa y el pensamiento político,"179; Domínguez, "Presencia de Antonio Pérez," 165.
35. Gascón Pérez, *Aragón en la monarquía*, 1:28–29.
36. Spinoza, *Tractatus Politicus*, 334; the "Antonio Pérez" to whom Spinoza refers has sometimes been confused with the "other Antonio Perez," a legal scholar at the University of Louvain (Leuven), author of a work entitled *Ius publicum* (1657), even though this Pérez makes no mention of Aragon or its revolt (see R. H. M. Elwes's translation of the *TTP*, 334).
37. Domínguez, "Presencia de Antonio Pérez," 169; Blanco Mayor, "Quevedo y Spinoza," 195.
38. Elliott, *Revolt of the Catalans*, 19.
39. Kamen, *Philip of Spain*, 212–13.
40. Gómez-Centurión Jiménez, *Felipe II*, 179; Valladares, *Conquista de Lisboa*, 72–73.
41. Gascón Pérez, *Aragón en la monarquía*, 2:26–29.
42. Gascón Pérez, *Aragón en la monarquía*, 2:27; Kamen, *Philip of Spain*, 290–91.
43. Domínguez, "Presencia de Antonio Pérez," 175; Boyden, "Fortune Has Stripped You," 30, 33.
44. Spinoza, *Tractatus Politicus*, 346–47; Van de Kamp, *Emanuel van Portugal*, 86–87.
45. Pérez, *Relaciones y cartas*, 1:208; Domínguez, "Presencia de Antonio Pérez," 172.
46. Pérez, *Relaciones y cartas*, 1:168.
47. Cooper, "Statesmen versus Philosophers," 29.

48. Jean-Baptiste Stouppe, *De Gods-Dienst der Hollanders*. Amsterdam, 1673.
49. Stouppe, *Religion des Hollandois*, 65–66; Israel, *Dutch Republic*, 639–40, 921; Nadler, *Spinoza: A Life*, 315; Popkin, *Spinoza*, 109–12; Lavaert, *Vrijheid, gelijkheid*, 210–11.
50. Stouppe, *Religion des Hollandois*, 66; Klever, "Spinoza's Life and Works," 43–44; Krop, *Spinoza*, 149.
51. Spinoza, *Theological-Political Treatise*, 6.
52. Spinoza, *Theological-Political Treatise*, 6.
53. Bontekoe, *Brief aen Johan Frederik Swetzer*, 23. I am indebted to Annette Munt for drawing my attention to this rare tract in the Library at Wolfenbüttel.
54. Spandaw, *De Onbedekte Spinosist*, "Opdragt."
55. Jacob Brucker, *Historia critica philosophiae*, iv–2:697, citing Herman Alexander Röell, *Dissertatio de religione rationali*, 6th ed. (Utrecht, 1713), 166. I owe this reference to Winfried Schröder (see Schröder, "Spinozam tota armenta in Belgio sequi ducem," 167).
56. Goldfarb, *Emancipation*, 17.
57. See Israel, *The Enlightenment That Failed*, 66–74.

CHAPTER 3. OROBIO DE CASTRO AND THE ENLIGHTENMENT MYTH OF THE SEPHARDIC UNIVERSAL ICONOCLAST

1. Da Costa, *Examination*, 15; Swetschinski, *Reluctant Cosmopolitans*, 265–66.
2. Da Costa, *Examination*, 55, 271; Kaplan, "Discipline, Dissent," 395–96.
3. Da Costa, *Examination*, 415–19.
4. Wilke, "Clandestine Classics," 57–59; Muchnik, "Orobio contra Prado," 34–35.
5. Harvey, "Return of Maimonideism," 254; Kaplan, "Discipline, Dissent," 394–95.
6. Leydekker, *Historische en theologische redeneringe*," Voor-reden," 2; Kaplan, "Discipline, Dissent," 394–95; Israel, "Philosophy, Deism," 174–75; Israel, *The Enlightenment That Failed*, 85–96.
7. Leydekker, *Historische en theologische redeneringe*, "Voor-reden," 2.
8. Orobio de Castro, *Prevenciones divinas*, 49, 52–53.
9. Nahon, *Métropoles et périphéries séfarades*, 107; Muchnik, *Une Vie marrane*, 83–85.
10. Fuks-Mansfeld, *Sefardim in Amsterdam*, 133; Swetschinski, *Reluctant Cosmopolitans*, 248, 279–80.
11. Kaplan, *From Christianity to Judaism*, 113–14; Wallet and Zwiep, "Locals: Jews," 909.
12. Sophie to Karl Ludwig, Amsterdam, 8 August 1679, in Bodemann, ed., *Briefwechsel der Herzogin Sophie*, 369.
13. Israel, "Diplomatic Career of Jeronimo Nunes da Costa," 167–90; Israel, "Gregorio Leti (1631–1701) and the Dutch Sephardi Elite," 267–84.
14. Spinoza, *Letters*, 249–51.
15. Sophie to Karl Ludwig, 9 March 1679, in Bodemann, ed., *Briefwechsel der Herzogin Sophie*, 353.

16. Orobio de Castro, *Certamen philosophicum*, 389; Israel, *Radical Enlightenment*, 307; Krop, *Spinoza*, 195–96; Kors, *Naturalism and Unbelief*, 91.
17. Yovel, *Spinoza and Other Heretics*, 57–59; Muchnik, *Une Vie marrane*, 68–89.
18. Gebhardt, "Juan de Prado," 285–90; Kaplan, *From Christianity to Judaism*, 126; Muchnik, "Orobio contra Prado," 37–38; Curley, "Spinoza's Lost Defense," 12–13, 31.
19. Levi de Barrios, *Triumpho del Govierno*, section "La Corona de la ley," 2; Révah, *Des Marranes à Spinoza*, 224–25; Kaplan, *From Christianity to Judaism*, 128–33.
20. Kaplan, *From Christianity to Judaism*, 135; Swetschinski, *Reluctant Cosmopolitans*, 271–74.
21. Kaplan, *From Christianity to Judaism*, 142–43; Muchnik, *Une Vie marrane*, 321, 443–47.
22. Carvalho, "Orobio de Castro," 235–36; Révah, *Spinoza et le Juan de Prado*, 90; Méchoulan, *Hispanidad y Judaismo*, 64; Yovel, *Spinoza and Other Heretics*, 51–52; Berti, *Anticristianesimo e libertà*, 48–49; Maia Neto, "Struggle against Unbelief," 433.
23. Orobio de Castro, *Observancia de la Divina Ley*, 2–4.
24. Caballero, "La crítica de Orobio de Castro a Spinoza," 231.
25. Quoted in Israel, *Radical Enlightenment*, 465.
26. Krop, *Spinoza*, 194.
27. De Rossi, *Bibliotheca Judaica Antichristiana* (Parma, 1800), 82–83.
28. Fuks-Mansfeld, *Sefardim in Amsterdam*, 176.
29. *Bibliothèque Universelle et Historique* 7 (1687): 293.
30. Israel, *Radical Enlightenment*, 465.
31. Marshall, *John Locke*, 604; Nuovo, *John Locke*, 218–19; Reventlow, "The Religious Way of John Locke," 16–19.
32. *Bibliothèque Universelle et Historique* 7:293; Van Rooden and Weselius, "Early Enlightenment and Judaism," 148; Simonutti, *Arminianesimo e tolleranza*, 75, 82–83.
33. Van Rooden and Weselius, "Early Enlightenment and Judaism," 146–47; Silvera, "Quando Dio deciderà," 407, 415.
34. Van Limborch, *De Veritate religionis christianae*, 137; Bayle, *Commentaire philosophique*, 155–56; Krop, *Spinoza*, 194–95.
35. Van Limborch, *De Veritate religionis christianae*, 74–76; Silvera, "Quando Dio deciderà," 407, 426; Nuovo, *John Locke*, 219.
36. Orobio de Castro, *Observancia de la Divina Ley*, 42; Van Limborch, *Vriendelyke onderhandeling*, 148–53.
37. Van Limborch, *Vriendelyke onderhandeling*, 112–13; Kaplan, *From Christianity to Judaism*, 252; Reventlow, "The Religious Way of John Locke," 13–14, 18.
38. *Histoire des Ouvrages des Scavans*, December 1687, 453.
39. Israel, "Orobio de Castro," 232–33.
40. *Acta Eruditorum*, 1688, 220
41. Witsius, *Meletemata Leidensia*, 354–89.

42. *Bibliothèque Universelle et Historique* 7:303; Popkin, Image of the Jew," 30.
43. Basnage, *Histoire des Juifs*, 9:1047–56; Marx, "Présentation," 110–11; Popkin, "Image of the Jew," 31.
44. Leibniz, *Theodicy*, 350.
45. Popkin, "Image of the Jew," 30; Benítez, "Orobio de Castro et la littérature clandestine," 219; Israel, *Radical Enlightenment*, 466, 568.
46. *Bibliotheca Sarraziana distrahenda par Abr. De Hondt et H. Scheurleer, Bibliop. Ad diem 16 Sept. 1715*, 21; Mulsow, *Radikale Frühaufklärung*, 1:62; Sutcliffe, "Judaism and Jewish Arguments," 102.
47. Popkin, "Jacques Basnage's *Histoire des Juifs*," 154–56.
48. See, for instance, Fabricius, *Delectus argumentorum*, 614–15.
49. O'Higgins, *Anthony Collins*, 23–24; Sutcliffe, "From Apologetics to Polemics," 101–2.
50. Collins, *Discourse of the Grounds*, 82; Berti, *Anticristianesimo e libertà*, 24–25; Tarantino, *Scrittoio di Anthony Collins*, 112.
51. See Pierre des Maizeaux notes on Orobio's *Prevenciones divinas*, BL MS Add. 4254, fo. 10; and also the summary of this text and notes by Des Maizeaux in BL MS Add. 4257, fos. 74–81.
52. O'Higgins, *Anthony Collins*, 38, 207; Tarantino, *Scrittoio di Anthony Collins*, 106, 112.
53. Collins, *Discourse of the Grounds*, 82; Israel, "Orobio de Castro," 238–39.
54. Wilke, "Clandestine Classics," 62–64; Israel, *Radical Enlightenment*, 684–703.
55. Fuks and Fuks-Mansfeld, *Hebrew and Judaic Manuscripts*, 1:128–36 and plate 12 (which is wrongly dated 1771 instead of 1713) and 2:92–110.
56. Fuks and Fuks-Mansfeld, *Hebrew and Judaic Manuscripts*, 1:128.
57. Fuks and Fuks-Mansfeld, *Hebrew and Judaic Manuscripts*, 1:131; Israel, "Gregorio Leti (1631–1701) and the Dutch Sephardi Elite," 277–78.
58. Paris: Bibliothèque de l'Arsenal MS 2240/2241, "Rabbi Isaac ben Abraham of Lithuania 'Hisuk Emuna,' ou l'Appuis de la Foi," preface by D.D.L.P.; Israel, "Philosophy, Deism," 199.
59. Nieto, *Matteh Dan*, preface and fos. 1–2, 5; Kaplan, "Karaites" in Early Eighteenth-Century Amsterdam," 276; Israel, "Philosophy, Deism," 186–87.
60. Benítez, "Orobio," 151–54; Sutcliffe, "Judaism and Jewish Arguments," 102; Israel, *Radical Enlightenment*, 583–86, 690.
61. Wade, *Clandestine Organization and Diffusion*, 229–30; Naville, *Paul Thiry d'Holbach*, 165–66; Kaplan, *From Christianity to Judaism*, 453.
62. Orobio de Castro, *Israel Vengé*, "Avis de l'éditeur."
63. Vercruysse, *Bibliographie descriptive*, 1770, F1.
64. Vercruysse, *Bibliographie descriptive*, 1770, F1; 1823, E6; 1838, E2; 1839, E1; and 1845, D1.
65. BL MS 4284, fo. 162v, Saint-Hyacinthe to Des Maizeaux, Paris, 23 October 1737; Carayol, *Thémiseul de Saint Hyacinthe*, 143.
66. See Benítez, "Liste et localisation," 17–25; and the fuller list in Benítez, "Matériaux pour un inventaire des manuscrits philosophiques clandestins,"

501–31; see also McKenna, "Sur l'hérésie dans la littérature clandestine," 301–4; Schröder, *Ursprünge des Atheismus*, 525–26; Sutcliffe, "Judaism and Jewish Arguments," 101–2.

67. Benítez, "Orobio de Castro," 224.
68. Benítez, "Orobio de Castro," 151–54; Sutcliffe, "Judaism and Jewish Arguments," 103.
69. Caballero, "Orobio d Castro," 240–300; Kaplan, *From Christianity to Judaism*, 269–70, 439–40; Benítez, "Orobio de Castro," 220.
70. Schwartz, *First Modern Jew*, 17.
71. Sheridan, *Nicolas Lenglet Dufresnoy*, 46–48, 50, 58, 76–77; Israel, *Radical Enlightenment*, 102–3.
72. *Journal Littéraire* (La Haye) 19 (1732): 1485–86; Benítez, "Orobio de Castro," 220; Brogi, *Cerchio dell' universo*, 160n.
73. Basnage, *Histoire des Juifs*, 9:1043.
74. Orobio de Castro, *Certamen philosophicum*, 389; Krop, *Spinoza*, 116, 123.
75. Bayle, *Dictionnaire historique et critique*, 4:258; Krop, *Spinoza*, 189–98.
76. Van Bunge, *Johannes Bredenburg (1643-1691)*, 230n68.
77. Orobio de Castro, *Certamen philosophicum*, 389.
78. Orobio de Castro, *Certamen philosophicum*, 432–33; Silvera, "Quando Dio deciderà," 409.
79. Van Bunge, *Johannes Bredenburg*, 205; Israel, *Radical Enlightenment*, 351–52; Kors, *Naturalism and Unbelief*, 91–92; Krop, *Spinoza*, 196–97.
80. [Cuffeler], *Specimen artis rationcinandi*, 1:65–66; Orobio de Castro, *Certamen philosophicum*, 389.
81. [Veyssière de La Croze], *Entretiens sur divers sujets*, 14–15, 18.
82. [Veyssière de La Croze], *Entretiens sur divers sujets*, 13–15, 31, 35–36.
83. [Veyssière de La Croze], *Entretiens sur divers sujets*, 38; *Merkwaardig en zonderling mond-gesprek*, 16–17, 34; Israel, "Was There a Pre-1740 Sephardic Jewish Enlightenment?," 13–14.
84. [Veyssière de La Croze], *Entretiens sur divers sujets*, 41.
85. Mulsow, *Radikale Frühaufklärung*, 1: 69, 82, 103; Fuks-Mansfeld, *Sefardim in Amsterdam*, 177–78; Israel, "Was There a Pre-1740 Jewish Enlightenment?," 13.
86. Palladini, *Die Berliner Hugenotten*, 40–41, 409.
87. Mulsow, *Enlightenment Underground*, 42.
88. Mulsow, *Enlightenment Underground*, 34.
89. Schröder, *Ursprünge des Atheismus*, 40n41.
90. Mulsow, *Enlightenment Underground*, 31–32.
91. Mulsow, *Enlightenment Underground*, 36; Tarantino, *Scrittoio di Anthony Collins*, 103.
92. Mulsow, *Enlightenment Underground*, 36.
93. Mulsow, *Enlightenment Underground*, 42–43.
94. Wolf, *Bibliotheca Hebraea* 3 (1727): 552.
95. BL Add. MS 4283, fo. 24; O'Higgins, *Anthony Collins*, 225.
96. Mulsow, *Enlightenment Underground*, 53.

97. Kaplan, *From Christianity to Judaism*, 451–53, 466–67.
98. [Veyssière de La Croze], *Entretiens sur divers sujets*, 38; Israel, "Philosophy, Deism," 184–85.
99. Kaplan, *Alternative Path*, 229; Mulsow, *Enlightenment Underground*, 44.
100. Mulsow, *Radikale Frühaufklärung*, 1:62; Kaplan, *From Christianity to Judaism*, 466–67.
101. [Veyssière de La Croze], *Entretiens sur divers sujets*, 311–12.
102. Houtteville, *Religion chrétienne prouvée par les faits* (1740) i, xliv–lii ; Houtteville, *Religion chrétienne prouvée par les faits* (1765), 1:299–300; Israel, "Orobio de Castro," 244.
103. Houtteville, *Religion chrétienne prouvée par les faits* (1765), 1:304–6; Israel, "Orobio de Castro," 245.
104. Kaplan, *From Christianity to Judaism*, 453–54.
105. Manuel, *Broken Staff*, 193–201; Sutcliffe, "Can a Jew Be a Philosophe?," 32–39; Israel, "Was There a Pre-1740 Jewish Enlightenment?," 6.
106. Feiner, *Origins*, 88; Israel, "Was There a Pre-1740 Jewish Enlightenment?," 7–8; Israel, "Philosophy, Deism," 178–79.
107. Altmann, *Moses Mendelssohn*, 23; Israel, "Philosophy, Deism," 185–86.
108. Gaspar, *Marquis d'Argens*, 136.
109. Gottlieb, *Faith and Freedom*, 23.
110. On the disagreement with Harvey Chisick as to whether d'Holbach was a crypto-republican, see Israel, *The Enlightenment That Failed*, 179–214.
111. Orobio de Castro-d'Holbach, *Israel Vengé*, "Avis de l'éditeur."
112. Orobio de Castro-d'Holbach, *Israel Vengé*, "Préface," 1–11
113. Orobio de Castro-d'Holbach, *Israel Vengé*, 78–80; Sutcliffe, "From Apologetics to Polemics," 100–101.
114. Orobio de Castro-d'Holbach, *Israel Vengé*, 110–11; Hertzberg, *French Enlightenment and the Jews*, 43–45.
115. Orobio de Castro-d'Holbach, *Israel Vengé*, 99–100.
116. Orobio de Castro-d'Holbach, *Israel Vengé*, 153.
117. Orobio de Castro-d'Holbach, *Israel Vengé*, 157–61.

CHAPTER 4. THE DESTABILIZING REVERBERATIONS OF THE EARLY *HASKALAH*

1. Freudenthal, "New Light on the Physician Aaron Salomon Gumpertz," 69.
2. Mirabeau, *Essai sur Moses Mendelssohn*, 7; Feiner, *Moses Mendelssohn*, 28–29, 33.
3. Mirabeau, *Essai sur Moses Mendelssohn*, 14; Bourel, *Moses Mendelssohn*, 71; Nisbet, *Gotthold Ephraim Lessing*, 165–67.
4. Mendelssohn to Gumpertz, Berlin, late June 1754, in Mendelssohn, *Gesammelte Schriften*, 11:10–11; Sutcliffe, *What Are Jews For?*, 83–84.
5. Altmann, *Moses Mendelssohn*, 31–32; Israel, *Radical Enlightenment*, 658; Goldenbaum, "Mendelssohns schwierige Beziehung," 275; Sutcliffe, "Quarreling over Spinoza," 172–73.

6. Goldenbaum, "Mendelssohns schwierige Beziehung," 278–79; Bourel, *Moses Mendelssohn*, 98, 100–101; Schwartz, *First Modern Jew*, 36.
7. Mendelssohn, *Philosophical Writings*, 104; Laerke, *Leibniz lecteur*, 51.
8. Mendelssohn, *Philosophical Writings*, 104, 106–7; Israel, *Radical Enlightenment*, 658; Israel, *Democratic Enlightenment*, 307; Altmann, *Moses Mendelssohn*, 31–35; Forster, "Herder and Spinoza," 59–60.
9. Mendelssohn, *Philosophical Writings*, 107; Israel, *Radical Enlightenment*, 659.
10. Lessing, *Gesammelte Werke*, 3:142–43; Gottlieb, "Introduction," xiv; Nisbet, *Gotthold Ephraim Lessing*, 296.
11. Israel *Radical Enlightenment*, 658; Goetschel, *Spinoza's Modernity*, 191–95; Forster, "Herder and Spinoza," 59–60.
12. Lessing, *Werke*, 2:245; Stiening, "Zur Bedeutung," 205, 212–13.
13. Lessing, *Werke*, 2:245–46; Herder, *Gott*, 95; Pätzold, *Spinoza-Aufklärung*, 28–29; Bourel, *Moses Mendelssohn*, 102.
14. Lessing, *Werke*, 2:246–47; Lessing, *Philosophical and Theological Writings*, 33–34; Nisbet, *Gotthold Ephraim Lessing*, 207–8.
15. Mendelssohn to Lessing, 11 August and 3 September 1757, in Mendelssohn, *Gesammelte Schriften*, 11:149, 158.
16. Altmann, *Moses Mendelssohn*, 149, 151; Sutcliffe, *What Are Jews For?*, 88.
17. Sheppard, *Leo Strauss and the Politics*, 68; Forster, "Herder and Spinoza," 60, 63–65.
18. Hess, *Germans, Jews and the Claims*, 94–95.
19. Arkush, "Questionable Judaism of Moses Mendelssohn," 34; Hess, *Germans, Jews and the Claims*, 93.
20. Goetschel, *Spinoza's Modernity*, 194–95; Päzold, *Spinoza, Aufklärung*, 99–100.
21. Altmann, *Moses Mendelssohn*, 170–74; Markworth, *Unsterblichkeit*, 39–44.
22. Arkush, "Questionable Judaism of Moses Mendelssohn," 30.
23. Feiner, *Moses Mendelssohn*, 47; Nirenberg, *Anti-Judaism*, 397.
24. Laerke, *Leibniz lecteur*, 556, 646, 805n, 926n.
25. Lessing, *Werke*, 2:243; Stiening, "Zur Bedeutung," 206–7.
26. Israel, *Democratic Enlightenment*, 188, 633–34; Hess, *Germans, Jews and the Claims*, 35; Laursen and Mannies, "Diderot and Diez," 297.
27. Dohm, *Denkwürdigkeiten*, 4:381–82; Blanning, "Frederick the Great," 268–69.
28. *Archivo Miranda*, 1:388; Dohm, *Denkwürdigkeiten*, 4:482–83.
29. Feiner, *Moses Mendelssohn*, 69; Gasper, *Marquis d'Argens*, 247–49; Schama, *Belonging*, 296–97.
30. Dohm, *Denkwürdigkeiten*, 4:484–87; Kochan, *Jews, Idols and Messiahs*, 58–60.
31. Dohm, *Denkwürdigkeiten*, 4:264–65; Beales, *Joseph II. Against*, 203–7.
32. Heinrich, "Debatte um 'bürgerliche Verbesserung,'" 261–62; Altmann, *Moses Mendelssohn*, 452; Sorkin, *Jewish Emancipation*, 64–69.
33. Dohm, *Denkwürdigkeiten*, 2:265.
34. Feiner, *Moses Mendelssohn*, 135–36; Sutcliffe, *What Are Jews For?*, 93.

35. Birnbaum, "Est-il des moyens?," 37; Yovel, *Dark Riddle*, 32.
36. Hammacher and Piske, *Anhang*, 368; Israel, *Democratic Enlightenment*, 188, 433, 633, 701.
37. Heinrich, "Debatte um 'bürgerliche Verbesserung,'" 828, 877–78. Roudaut does not include Dohm among the radical enlighteners, but does include Diez (Roudaut, "Ambiguités et limites," 124–25).
38. Bernardini, *La questione ebraica*, 79.
39. Israel, *Democratic Enlightenment*, 20, 188, 701–2.
40. Diez, *Apologie*, 85, 88–89, 93. For more on Diez, see Roudaut, "Ambiguités," 124–25.
41. Chr. W. von Dohm, *Geschichte der Engländer und Franzosen im östlichen Indien* (Leipzig, 1776).
42. Diez, *Benedikt von Spinoza*, title page.
43. Wekhrlin, *Das graue Ungeheuer*, 8 (1786): 210.
44. Diez, *Apologie*, 86–90; Diez, *Benedikt von Spinoza*, 40–41; Wekhrlin, *Das graue Ungeheuer* 4 (1785): 302–9.
45. Diez, *Benedikt von Spinoza*, 41.
46. Wekhrlin, *Das graue Ungeheuer* 8 (1786): 8–9.
47. Sorkin, *Transformation*, 23–24; Israel, *Revolutionary Ideas*, 327.
48. Dohm, *Denkwürdigkeiten*, 4:484–88; Israel, *Democratic Enlightenment*, 275–77.
49. Dohm, *Denkwürdigkeiten*, 4:483; Sutcliffe, *What Are Jews For?*, 94–95.
50. Hess, *Germans, Jews, and the Claims*, 3.
51. Kochan, *Jews, Idols and Messiahs*, 70–71; Walzer, *Jewish Political Tradition*, 1:82, 86.
52. Arkush, "Questionable Judaism of Moses Mendelssohn," 35–36.
53. Mendessohn, *Writings*, 39; Schapkow, *Role Model and Countermodel*, 67; Gottlieb, *Faith and Freedom*, 34.
54. Hiegentlich, "Reflections," 208.
55. Pelluchon, *Leo Strauss*, 38–40; Gottlieb, *Faith and Freedom*, 6–7.
56. Abramsky, "Crisis of Authority," 18.
57. Altmann, *Moses Mendelssohn*, 489–90; Schapkow, *Role Model and Countermodel*, 67.
58. Mendelssohn, "Vorrede," iii; Hess, *Germans, Jews, and the Claims*, 94.
59. Mendelssohn, "Vorrede," iv; Bourel, *Moses Mendelssohn*, 308.
60. Mendelssohn, "Vorrede," v; Mendelssohn, *Jerusalem*, 155.
61. Walzer, *Jewish Political Tradition*, 1:82; Goetschel, "The Hyphen in the Theological-Political," 6–7.
62. Mirabeau, *Essai sur Moses Mendelssohn*, 22–23; Kochan, *Jews, Idols and Messiahs*, 70–72; Goldenbaum, "Mendelssohns schwierige Beziehung," 292–93; Goodman, *History of Judaism*, 457–58.
63. Gottlieb, *Faith and Freedom*, 58.
64. Mendelssohn, *Jerusalem*, 108; Graetz, "Jewish Enlightenment," 286–88, 292.
65. Mendelssohn, *Jerusalem*, 107–8; Bourel, *Moses Mendelssohn*, 318–19.

66. Mendelssohn to Herz Homberg, Berlin, 1 March 1784, in Mendelssohn, *Gesammelte Schriften*, 8:177.
67. Mendelssohn, *Jerusalem*, 126–28; Graetz, "Jewish Enlightenment," 292.
68. Mendelssohn, *Jerusalem*, 139–40.
69. Mendelssohn, "Vorrede," viii, x–xi.
70. Mendelssohn, *Jerusalem*, 145–46; Feiner, *Origins*, 165.
71. Mendelssohn, "Vorrede"; Bourel, *Moses Mendelssohn*, 312–14; Feiner, *Origins*, 166; Goodman, *History of Judaism*, 458.
72. Lessing, "Education," 218.
73. Mendelssohn to K. G. Lessing, Berlin, February 1781 in Mendelssohn, *Gesammelte Schriften*, 8:7.
74. Schilson, "Lessing and Theology," 174–75.
75. Altmann, *Moses Mendelssohn*, 569.
76. Lessing, *Gesammelte Werke*, 2:322, 334–35; Sutcliffe, *What Are Jews For?*, 64, 85.
77. Lessing, *Gesammelte Werke*, 2:474; Bohnert, "Enlightenment," 356–58
78. Bohnen, "Lessing und Dänemark," 306–8.
79. Bourel, *Moses Mendelssohn*, 396.
80. [Knoblauch], *Taschenbuch*; 19, 44; Knoblauch, *Ueber Feerei*, 11–12.
81. Knoblauch, *Taschenbuch*, 19.
82. Knoblauch, *Euclides Anti-Thaumaturgicus*, 13.
83. Lichtenberg, *Werke*, 174.
84. Knoblauch, *Taschenbuch*, 44; Knoblauch, *Euclides Anti-Thaumaturgicus*, 39, 41.
85. Knoblauch, *Taschenbuch*, 45, 101–3; Knoblauch, *Euclides Anti-Thaumaturgicus*, 11–12.
86. No Hebrew translation of *Phaedon* appeared until after Mendelssohn's death when that of Isaiah Beer-Bing (1759–1805), of Metz, was published in 1788 (Altmann, *Moses Mendelssohn*, 189–92; Zwiep, "Jewish Enlightenment Reconsidered," 301–2).
87. Feiner, *Moses Mendelssohn*, 78–79, 126–28; Schulte, *Jüdische Aufklärung*, 63–68.
88. Abramsky, "Crisis of Authority," 19–20; Hiegentlich, "Reflections," 207, 210; Feiner, "Seductive Science," 133.
89. Altmann, *Moses Mendelssohn*, 378–79; Kümper, "Worte der Wahrheit," 158–60.
90. Altmann, *Moses Mendelssohn*, 467–81; Kümper, "Worte der Wahrheit," 155–56.
91. Socher, *Radical Enlightenment of Solomon Maimon*, 23–25; Feiner, "On the Threshold," 45.
92. Abramsky, "Crisis of Authority," 21, 24; Feiner, *Moses Mendelssohn*, 164.
93. Kümper, "Worte der Wahrheit," 163–64.
94. Goetschel, *Spinoza's Modernity*, 137; Crouter, *Friedrich Schleiermacher*, 68–69; Socher, *Radical Enlightenment of Solomon Maimon*, 34.

95. Goetschel, *Spinoza's Modernity* 197; Bourel, *Moses Mendelssohn*, 209, 334; Hess, *Germans, Jews*, 114–16; Arkush, "Questionable Judaism of Moses Mendelssohn," 35–36.

CHAPTER 5. MAIMON'S REBELLION AND MENDELSSOHN'S DILEMMA (1770–1800)

1. Schelling, *Ages of the World*, 105; Pinkard, *Hegel*, 30.
2. Zammito, "Most Hidden Conditions," 335–36; Boehm, *Kant's Critique of Spinoza*, 203–10.
3. Altmann, *Moses Mendelssohn*, 639–40; Bayer, "Spinoza," 319.
4. Socher, *Radical Enlightenment of Solomon Maimon*, 23–24; Feiner, "Seductive Science," 129.
5. Maimon, *Lebensgeschichte*, 260; Socher, *Radical Enlightenment of Solomon Maimon*, 32.
6. Socher, *Radical Enlightenment of Solomon Maimon*, 24.
7. Maimon, *Lebensgeschichte*, 96–100.
8. Maimon, *Lebensgeschichte*, 107–8; Schama, *Belonging*, 455–56.
9. Goldberg, "Jewish Marriage," 14, 27; Socher, *Radical Enlightenment of Solomon Maimon*, 30, 67.
10. Maimon, *Lebensgeschichte*, 202–5; Hundert, *Jews in Poland-Lithuania*, 192–93; Goodman, *History of Judaism*, 414–15.
11. Maimon, *Lebensgeschichte*, 302; Socher, *Radical Enlightenment of Solomon Maimon*, 50, 55–61.
12. Maimon, *Lebensgeschichte*, 139.
13. Maimon, *Lebensgeschichte*, 209–10; Freudenthal, "Philosopher between Two Cultures," 12.
14. Maimon, *Lebensgeschichte*, 190; Löwy, *Redemption and Utopia*, 22; Davies, *God's Playground*, 247.
15. Maimon, *Lebensgeschichte*, 189–91; Katz and Popkin, *Messianic Revolution*, xv–xvi, 138.
16. Maimon, *Lebensgeschichte*, 162–68; Schwartz, "Causa materialis," 128–29.
17. Maimon, *Lebensgeschichte*, 168, 178, 193; Harvey, "Portrait of Spinoza as a Maimonidean," 161–63; Schapkow, *Role Model and Countermodel*, 60; Socher, *Radical Enlightenment of Solomon Maimon*, 32, 75–77, 82, 98–99, 197n34.
18. Maimon, *Lebensgeschichte*, 271; Stone, "Knowledge of Foreign Languages," 214; Socher, *Radical Enlightenment of Solomon Maimon*, 2, 23–24; Melamed, "Salomon Maimon and the Rise," 83–85.
19. Socher, *Radical Enlightenment of Solomon Maimon*, 30–32, 43; Kuehn, *Kant*, 214, 360.
20. Maimon, *Lebensgeschichte*, 152, 155–57, 172–73; Arkush, "Questionable Judaism of Moses Mendelssohn," 44; Melamed, "Salomon Maimon and the Rise," 68, 71, 73, 82–85.

21. Freudenthal, "Philosopher between Two Cultures," 2; Socher, *Radical Enlightenment of Solomon Maimon*, 33–34.
22. Socher, *Radical Enlightenment of Solomon Maimon*, 34.
23. Maimon, *Lebensgeschichte*, 40–41; Feiner, *Origins*, 172–73.
24. Schechter, "Rationalizing,"106; Trivellato, *Promise and Peril*, 158.
25. Rehberg, *Sämtliche Schriften*, 1:7–8; Beiser, *Enlightenment*, 306.
26. Rehberg, *Sämtliche Schriften*, 1:8; Bourel, *Moses Mendelssohn*, 391.
27. Lauermann and Schröder, "Textgrundlagen," 39–40.
28. Lichtenberg, *Schriften*, 4:649; Schüttler, *Mitglieder*, 48–50.
29. Ewald, "Vorrede," v–vi; Herder, *Gott*, 11n; Lauermann and Schröder, "Textgrundlagen," 39.
30. Ewald, "Vorrede," vii–viii; Schröpfer, *Schack Hermann Ewald*, 168–72, 182–85.
31. Nirenberg, *Anti-Judaism*, 397, 565.
32. Melamed, "Salomon Maimon and the Rise," 72.
33. Christ, "Johann Georg Hamann," 253; Beiser, "Enlightenment and Idealism," 26.
34. On this controversy, see Israel, *Democratic Enlightenment*, 315–25.
35. Janssens, "Problem," 180.
36. Arkush, "Solomon Maimon," 162–63; Melamed, "Salomon Maimon and the Rise," 83–84, 86–87.
37. Nisbet, *Gotthold Ephraim Lessing*, 632.
38. Altmann, *Moses Mendelssohn*, 652.
39. Whaley, *Religious Toleration*, 106–8; Nisbet, *Gotthold Ephraim Lessing*, 377–78, 554–59.
40. Mendelssohn, *Jerusalem*, 125–27.
41. Mendelssohn, *Jerusalem*, 165.
42. Mendelssohn, *Jerusalem*, 157, 167; Socher, *Radical Enlightenment of Solomon Maimon*, 34.
43. Pelluchon, *Leo Strauss and the Crisis*, 38–39.
44. Schmidt-Biggemann, *Theodizee*, 150; Goldenbaum, "Mendelssohns schwierige Beziehung," 304.
45. Strauss, "Einleitungen," xxxvi–ix; Altman, *Moses Mendelssohn*, 632–33.
46. Mendelssohn, *Morgenstunden*, 114–25; Schmidt-Biggemann, *Theodizee*, 154–55; Gottlieb, *Faith and Freedom*, 115–16.
47. Mendelssohn, *Morgenstunden*, 104; Israel, *Radical Enlightenment*, 649–50
48. Freudenthal, "Philosopher between Two Cultures," 10; Melamed, "Salomon Maimon and the Rise," 93–94; Socher, *Radical Enlightenment of Solomon Maimon*, 40.
49. Melamed, *Spinoza's Metaphysics*, 64, 68–69.
50. Mendelssohn, *Morgenstunden*, 107–9, 112; Israel, *Democratic Enlightenment*, 704.
51. Mendelssohn, *Morgenstunden*, 112; Bourel, *Moses Mendelssohn*, 430–32; Feiner, *Origins*, 92.
52. Rohls, "Herder's 'Gott,'" 280; Nisbet, *Gotthold Ephraim Lessing*, 639.
53. Maimon, *Essay*, 110; Heydenreich, *Natur und Gott*, 91–92.
54. Mendelssohn, *Morgenstunden*, 133.

55. Goldenbaum, "Mendelssohns schwierige Beziehung," 303.
56. Rohls, "Herder's 'Gott,'" 278.
57. Mendelssohn, *Morgenstunden*, 5; Reimarus, "Vorerrinerung," 3.
58. Mendelssohn, *An die Freunde Lessings*, 193.
59. Mendelssohn to Kant, 16 Octobrrt 1785, in Kant, *Briefwechsel*, 1:297–98; Altman, *Moses Mendelssohn*, 705.
60. Mendelssohn, *An die Freunde Lessings*, 187.
61. Mendelssohn, *An die Freunde Lessings*, 186–87.
62. Mendelssohn, *An die Freunde Lessings*, 188–89, 196–97.
63. Altmann, *Moses Mendelssohn*, 731; Gottlieb, *Faith and Freedom*, 48, 114.
64. Mendelssohn, *Morgenstunden*, 5; Reinhold, *Letters*, 24.
65. Altman, *Moses Mendelssohn*, 750–51.
66. Jakob to Kant, Halle, in Kant, *Briefwechsel*, 1:317–18.
67. Kant to Herz, 7 April 1786, in Kant, *Briefwechsel*, 1:323; Zammito, *Genesis*, 235–36; Beiser, *Hermann Cohen*, 272–74.
68. Kant to Jakob, 26 May 1786, in Kant, *Briefwechsel*, 1:329; Goldenbaum, "Kants Parteinahme," 176, 184.
69. Kant to Biester, 11 June 1786, in Kant, *Briefwechsel*, 1:330–31; Bolduc, *Kant et Spinoza*, 26–29, 56–65; Boehm, *Kant's Critique of Spinoza*, 202–3, 211–14, 220–22.
70. Kant, "What Does It Mean?," 7.
71. Kant, "What Does It Mean?," 4, 7, 11; Kuehn, *Kant*, 306.
72. Kant, "What Does It Mean?," 11; Neiman, *Unity of Reason*, 153.
73. Kant, "What Does It Mean?," 11–12.
74. Di Giovanni, "First Twenty Years," 426; Beiser, *Enlightenment*, 52.
75. Kant, "What Does It Mean?,"14; Zammito, *Genesis*, 240-41.
76. Reinhold, *Letters*, 28; Zammito, *Genesis*, 242.
77. Mendelssohn, *An die Freunde Lessings*, 189.
78. [Schulz], *Der entlarvte Moses Mendelssohn*, 5–6,17, 19; Janssens, "Problem," 180–81; Yovel, *Dark Riddle*, 13–14.
79. Kümper, "Worte der Wahrheit," 179–80.
80. Arkush, "Solomon Maimon," 158–59, 163; Socher, *Radical Enlightenment of Solomon Maimon*, 34
81. Maimon, *Lebensgeschichte*, 166.
82. Maimon, introduction to *Essay*, x–xi.
83. Buzaglo, *Solomon Maimon*, 1–2.
84. Quoted in Beiser, "Maimon and Fichte," 233.
85. Beiser, "Maimon and Fichte," 235–38; Freudenthal, "Maimon's Subversion," 148–49; Schwartz, "Causa materialis," 130–33.
86. Freudenthal, "Philosopher between Two Cultures,"11–12; Schwartz, "Causa materialis," 133–34, 138–39.
87. Strauss, "Testament of Spinoza," 216.
88. Curthoys, "Moses Mendelssohn," 65–66.
89. Pelluchon, *Leo Strauss and the Crisis*, 40–41; Israel, "Les 'Lumières radicales,'" 414–15.

90. Maimon, *Essay*, 2–3; Maimon, *Lebensgeschichte*, 302, 350.
91. Beiser, "Maimon and Fichte," 235–36, 238, 242; Freudenthal, "Maimon's Subversion," 144, 148; Yovel, *Dark Riddle*, 18–19; Socher, *Radical Enlightenment of Solomon Maimon*, 47; Melamed, "Salomon Maimon and the Rise," 74–75.

CHAPTER 6. DAVID NASSY'S NEW WORLD VISTAS (1770–1790)

1. Marcus, "Jews in the American Revolution," 117.
2. Marcus, "Jews in the American Revolution," 118–19.
3. Israel, "Philosophy, Deism," 174–84.
4. Cohen, *Jews in Another Environment*, 214.
5. Israel, "Was There a Pre-1740 Western Sephardic Enlightenment?," 4.
6. [Nassy], *Essai historique*, 1:157; Arbell, *Jewish Nation of the Caribbean*, 117.
7. [Nassy], *Essai historique*, 2:57; De Kom, *Wij slaven van Suriname*, 80; Israel, "David Nassy," 328.
8. Bijlsma, "David de Is. C. Nassy," 67; Seeligmann, "David Nassy," 26.
9. [Nassy], *Essai historique*, 1:182; Sint Nicolaas, *Shackles and Bonds*, 87, 91; Walet and Zwiep, "Locals: Jews," 906.
10. Bijlsma, "David de Isaac C.Nassy," 219–20.
11. Cohen, *Jews in Another Environment*, 63.
12. Arbell, *Jewish Nation of the Caribbean*, 226; Stipriaan, *Surinaams Contrast*, 297; for slave statistics, see Stipriaan, *Surinaams Contrast*, 28–29.
13. Van Lier, "Jewish Community in Surinam," 23; Stipriaan, *Surinaams Contrast*, 32–37, 297; Israel, *Diasporas Within*, 527–28.
14. Cohen, *Jews in Another Environment*, 74; Sint Nicolaas, *Shackles and Bonds*, 97–99.
15. Algemeen Rijksarchief, The Hague, archives of the Surinam Sephardic community (NPIG) vol. 1, Res. 1 June 1773 and Res. 20 July 1778.
16. Seeligmann, "David Nassy," 29; Israel, "Dutch Jews, David Nassy," 173; Wallet and Zwiep, "Locals: Jews," 919.
17. Goslinga, *Dutch in the Caribbean*, 309; Cohen, *Jews in Another Environment*, 16, 63–64; Fuks-Mansfeld, "Enlightenment and Emancipation," 172.
18. Cohen, *Jews in Another Environment*, 181–239; Israel, "Jewish Emancipation," 119.
19. Van Kempen, *Geschiedenis van de Surinaamse literatuur*, 1:3, 27, 191; and 2:34, 61.
20. Israel, *Democratic Enlightenment*, 495.
21. [Nassy], *Essai historique*, 2:34.
22. Cohen, *Jews in Another Environment*, 214.
23. Bijlsma, "David de Is. C. Nassy," 65, 68; Cohen, *Jews in Another Environment*, 113.
24. See Appendix A: "Catalogue of the Nassy Library," in Cohen, *Jews in Another Environment*, 203–4, 209, 214.
25. For this, see Israel, *The Enlightenment That Failed*, 227–36.
26. Winkle, "Johann Fredrich Struensee," 1–23.
27. [Nassy], *Essai historique*, 2:27–28.

28. Marcus, "Jews and the American Revolution," 107; Levine, *Seeking the Fabled City*, 21; Israel, *Expanding Blaze*, 196–97.
29. Sorkin, *Jewish Emancipation*, 230–32; Feiner, *Origins*, 166; Levine, *Seeking the Fabled City*, 39.
30. Marcus, "Jews and the American Revolution," 114–15, 213–14.
31. Demeunier, *L'Amérique indépendante*, 3:123–24; Sehat, *Myth*, 28, 54–55.
32. Ramsay, *History*, 2:535–37; Bromwich, *Intellectual Life of Edmund Burke*, 427–29; Sorkin, *Jewish Emancipation*, 74–75.
33. Bijlsma, "David de Is. C. Nassy," 69.
34. [Nassy], *Essai historique*, 2:76–77.
35. [Nassy], *Essai historique*, 2:60; Israel, "David Nassy," 331.
36. [Nassy], *Essai historique*, 2:78–79.
37. Van Vliet, *Elie Luzac (1721–1796). Boekverkoper van de Verlichting*, 232.
38. Goslinga, *Dutch in the Caribbean*, 361.
39. Cohen, *Jews in Another Environment*, 131–32.
40. Cohen, *Jews in Another Environment*, 133.
41. Schechter, "Rationalizing," 94–95, 103–5; Sutcliffe, "Voltaire in Context," 120–23.
42. Strum, "Isaac de Pinto's *Political Reflections*," 242–43.
43. De Pinto, *Réflexions critiques*, 23–37; Nijenhuis, *Een joodse philosophe*, 18, 26; Chisick, "Community and Exclusion in Rousseau and Voltaire," 84–85; Strum, "Isaac de Pinto's *Political Reflections*," 233.
44. [Nassy], *Essai historique*, 1:xxxvii; Schutte, *Nederlandsche Patriotten*, 57–59.
45. [Nassy], *Essai historique*, 1:180; Van Goor, *Nederlandse koloniën*, 166; Ben-Ur, *Cultural Heritage*, 179.
46. [Nassy], *Essai historique*, 2:182–83.
47. [Nassy], *Essai historique*, 2:175–76; Israel, "David Nassy," 332–34.
48. [Nassy], *Essai historique*, 2:179.
49. [Nassy], *Essai historique*, 2:180; on the place of Delisle in the Enlightenment, see Israel, *Democratic Enlightenment*, 675–83.
50. Bijlsma, "David de Is. C. Nassy," 65.
51. [Nassy], *Essai historique*, 1:181; Cohen, *Jews in Another Environment*, 99.
52. Israel, *Democratic Enlightenment*, 137–38, 667, 806–7.
53. [Nassy], *Essai historique*, 2:22–23; Cohen, *Jews in Another Environment*, 98.
54. [Nassy], *Essai historique*, 2:22; Arbell, *Jewish Nation of the Caribbean*, 116; Israel, "David Nassy," 325.
55. [Nassy], *Essai historique*, 1:ix; Israel, "Dutch Jews, David Nassy," 183–85.
56. [Nassy], *Essai historique*, 1:ix–x.
57. [Nassy], *Essai historique*, 1:xxi; Seeligmann, "David Nassy," 27.
58. Nassy, "Preface" to the *Essai*, xi, xxii–xxiv; Rauschenbach, "The Empire Writes Back," 159–60; Rauschenbach, "Patriots at the Periphery," 585.
59. [Nassy], *Essai historique*, 1:xxv; De Pinto, *Réflexions critiques*, 10–13, 23; Cohen, *Jews in Another Environment*, 113–14; Faur, "David Nassy," 97.
60. Israel, "Jewish Emancipation," 119–21.

CHAPTER 7. ZALKIND HOURWITZ (1751–1812) AND THE "GREAT REVOLUTION"

1. Hertzberg, *French Enlightenment and the Jews*, 7; Mitchell, *Voltaire's Jews*, 25–26.
2. Cérutti, *Bréviaire philosophique*, 10–11, 27.
3. Naigeon, *Adresse à l'Assemblée nationale sur la liberté des opinions, sur celle de la presse, etc.*, 100.
4. Arkush, "Montesquieu: A Precursor of Jewish Emancipation?," 55–58; Nirenberg, *Anti-Judaism*, 350–52.
5. Hertzberg, *French Enlightenment and the Jews*, 350–53, 366; Calmann, *Carrière of Carpentras*, 229–38, 249; Aston, *Religion and Revolution in France*, 72–80.
6. Sutcliffe, *Judaism and Enlightenment*, 251.
7. Roche, *France in the Enlightenment*, 364.
8. Wekhrlin, *Chronologen* 1 (1779): 76–87.
9. Sutcliffe, *Judaism and Enlightenment*, 249.
10. Gendzier, "Diderot and the Jews," 40–42, 53.
11. Mortier and Trousson, *Dictionnaire de Diderot*, 260; Girard, *Révolution française et le Juifs*, 62–63; Israel, *Democratic Enlightenment*, 69, 277, 436, 495, 620–21.
12. Mortier and Trousson, *Dictionnaire de Diderot*, 259–61.
13. [Cloots], *Lettre sur les Juifs*, 53–54, 72–73; Israel, *Democratic Enlightenment*, 495.
14. [Cloots], *Lettre sur les Juifs*, 45–46, 53–54.
15. [Cloots], *Lettre sur les Juifs*, 9.
16. [Cloots], *Lettre sur les Juifs*, 9, 66; Labbé, *Anarcharsis Cloots*, 64.
17. [Cloots], *Lettre sur les Juifs*, 70–72.
18. Loft, *Passion, Politics and Philosophie*, 225; Sutcliffe, *What Are Jews For?*, 64.
19. [Cloots], *Lettre sur les Juifs*, 75; Girard, *Révolution française et les Juifs*, 212–13.
20. Thompson, *Robespierre*, 431; Labbé, *Anacharsis Cloots*, 167–68, 235–36.
21. [Nassy], *Essai historique*, 1:xxxii; Cohen, *Jews in Another Environment*, 242.
22. Desprat, *Mirabeau*, 331, 334, 338–39; Birnbaum, "Est-il des Moyens?," 623–24.
23. Quoted in Loft, *Passion, Politics and Philosophie*, 232.
24. Loft, *Passion, Politics, and Philosophie*, 226–27.
25. Mirabeau, *Sur Moses Mendelssohn*, 4:16, 57, 61; Manuel, *Broken Staff*, 276.
26. [Cloots], *Lettre sur les Juifs*, 54; Mortier, *Anacharsis Cloots*, 68–69.
27. Girard, *Révolution française et les Juifs*, 62, 96.
28. Mirabeau, *Sur Moses Mendelssohn*, 19.
29. Mirabeau, *De la monarchie prussienne*, 5:55; Schechter, *Obstinate Hebrews*, 98–100; Karp, *Politics of Jewish Commerce*, 248.
30. Mirabeau, *Sur Moses Mendelssohn*, 73; Klaus, "Keeping Ahead," 173, 176.
31. Mirabeau, *De la monarchie prussienne*, 5:46, 55, 57.
32. Bourel, *Moses Mendelssohn*, 22, 35–36; Badinter, *Libres et égaux*, 79–80.
33. Jacques-André Naigeon, *Adresse à l'Assemblée nationale sur la liberté des opinions, sur celle de la presse, etc.*, 53.

34. Maréchal, *Dictionnaire des Athées*, 200.
35. Goldfarb, *Emancipation*, 6–7.
36. Hourwitz, *Apologie des Juifs*, preface, 14.
37. Malino, *A Jew in the French Revolution*, 10–11; Joskowicz, *Modernity of Others*, 77.
38. Malino, *A Jew in the French Revolution*, 12–13.
39. Hourwitz, *Apologie des Juifs*, 48–49, 56.
40. Hourwitz, *Apologie des Juifs*, 7.
41. Hourwitz, *Apologie des Juifs*, preface, 7 and 54–56; Schechter, *Obstinate Hebrews*, 127–28.
42. Hourwitz, *Apologie des Juifs*, 48–49, 56.
43. Hourwitz, *Apologie des Juifs*, 56; Malino, *A Jew in the French Revolution*, 47–48; Ruderman, *Jewish Enlightenment*, 106n46.
44. *La Chronique du Mois, ou les cahiers patriotiques* 1 (1792), section for March 26.
45. Schechter, *Obstinate Hebrews*, 128–29.
46. Birnbaum, "Est-il des moyens?," 49.
47. Loft, *Passion, Politics, and* Philosophie, 117; Lentz, *Roederer, 1734–1835*, 32–35.
48. Hertzberg, *French Enlightenment and the Jews*, 332–33.
49. Badinter, *Libres et égaux*, 73; Israel, *Revolutionary Ideas*, 27, 72–73.
50. Hourwitz, *Réponse à la question*, 87; Hourwitz, *Apologie des Juifs*, 1–2; Joskowicz, *Modernity of Others*, 78–79; Birnbaum, "Est-il des moyens?," 575; Klaus, "Keeping Ahead," 176.
51. Lentz, *Roederer*, 34–35; Goldfarb, *Emancipation*, 37.
52. Girard, *Révolution française et les Juifs*, 78; Badinter, *Libres et égaux*, 75–76; Malino, *A Jew in the French Revolution*, 27–28.
53. Lentz, *Roederer*, 35; Birnbaum, "Est-il des moyens?," 59, 573, 592–95.
54. Manuel, *Broken Staff*, 245; Birnbaum, "Est-il des Moyens?," 600–601.
55. Trigano, "French Revolution and the Jews," 186n2.
56. Hourwitz, *Réponse à la question*, 100.
57. Hourwitz, *Réponse à la question*, 100.
58. Girard, *Révolution française et les Juifs*, 76–77.
59. Goldfarb, *Emancipation*, 37–38; Lentz, *Roederer*, 33; Schechter, *Obstinate Hebrews*, 24–25.
60. Girard, *Révolution française et les Juifs*, 74–91; Mortier, *Anacharsis Cloots*, 67–69; Badinter, *Libres et égaux*, 72–74.
61. Thiéry, *Dissertation sur cette question: Est-il des moyens*, 29, 37–38.
62. Schechter, *Obstinate Hebrews*, 83–86; Trivellato, *Promise and Peril*, 147.
63. Thiéry, *Dissertation sur cette question: Est-il des moyens*, 79–82; Girard, *Révolution française et les Juifs*, 80–81, 84; Stuurman, *De Uitvinding van de mensheid*, 331.
64. Birnbaum, "Est-il des moyens?," 601
65. Goldstein Sepinwall, "Strategic Friendships," 200–201. Bernardini and Lucci downplay this contrast (see Bernardini and Lucci, *The Jews, Instructions*, 167–68).
66. Hourwitz, *Apologie des Juifs*, 7, 34; Trivellato, *Promise and Peril*, 147–48, 150.

67. Hourwitz, *Apologie des Juifs*, 29–30.
68. Hourwitz, *Apologie des Juifs*, 31–32; Malino, *A Jew in the French Revolution*, 54; Bloemgarten, *Hartog de Hartog Lémon*, 432, 437.
69. Malino, *A Jew in the French Revolution*, 75, 77.
70. Hourwitz, *Apologie des Juifs*, 39.
71. Seeligmann, "David Nassy," 36–37.
72. Hourwitz, *Apologie des Juifs*, 64–65; Trivellato, *Promise and Peril*, 150.
73. Hourwitz, *Réponse à la question*, 103; Feiner, *Origins*, 185.
74. Hourwitz, *Apologie des Juifs*, 42–43.
75. Hourwitz, *Apologie des Juifs*, 46–47; Hourwitz, *Origine des langues*, 65–67.
76. Badinter, *Libres et égaux*, 45.
77. Hourwitz, *Apologie des Juifs*, 37–38.
78. Feiner, *Origins*, 185; Goldstein Sepinwall, "Strategic Friendships," 191.
79. Hourwitz, *Réponse à la question*, 100.
80. Hourwitz, *Apologie des Juifs*, 39.
81. Girard, *Révolution française et les Juifs*, 80; Schechter, *Obstinate Hebrews*, 130.
82. BL Fr/ 170/6 H. Grégoire, "Motion en faveur des Juifs" (Paris, September 1789), iv.
83. BL Fr 170/6 Grégoire, "Motion en faveur des Juifs," 6–7, 12; Trivellato, *Promise and Peril*, 148–49, 153.
84. BL Fr 170/6 Grégoire, "Motion en faveur des Juifs," 15.
85. Goldstein Sepinwall, "Strategic Friendships,"191; Hermon-Belot, *L'Abbé Grégoire*, 152.
86. Cottebrune, *Mythe et réalité du "Jacobinisme allemande,"* 131.
87. BL Fr 170/6 Grégoire, "Motion en faveur des Juifs," xi; Furet and Richet, *Révolution française*, 94, 109.
88. Gorsas, *Courrier de Paris* 6, no. 117 (21 November 1789).
89. Badinter, *Libres et égaux*, 121, 140; Elyada, "Presse parisienne de droite et la question juive," 223.
90. Malino, *A Jew in the French Revolution*, 79, 121–23.
91. Gorsas, *Courrier de Versailles* 2, no. 52 (28 August 1789): 502–13.
92. Gorsas, *Courrier de Versailles* 2, no. 52 (28 August 1789): 508.
93. Gorsas, *Courrier de Paris*, 24 December 1789, 15–16; Battenberg, "Französische Revolution," 266; Loft, *Passion, Politics*, 232; Elyada, "Rhétorique antijuive," 142–43.
94. See *H-France Forum* 9, no. 1 (Winter 2013), no. 5, section replying to Baker.
95. Badinter and Badinter, *Condorcet*, 289–90; Hertzberg, *French Enlightenment and the Jews*, 297; Badinter, *Libres et égaux*, 141–42, 152–53.
96. Gorsas, *Courrier de Paris*, 25 December 1789, 4; Godechot, *Counter-Revolution*, 73; Israel, *Revolutionary Ideas*, 77, 108.
97. Sorkin, "Count Stanislas," 27, 40–43.
98. Sorkin, "Count Stanislas," 34–35.
99. Girard, *Révolution française et les Juifs*, 105–6.
100. Israel, *Revolutionary Ideas*, 88–89, 136–39, 160–62, 189, 197, 250, 515.

101. BL FR 170/17: *Opinion de M. L'évêque de Nancy député de Lorraine sur l'admissibilité des Juifs à la plénitude de l'état civil* (Paris, 1790), 12–13; Loft, "Mirabeau and Brissot," 615; Trigano, "French Revolution and the Jews," 180.
102. Badinter, *Libres et égaux*,141.
103. Israel, *Revolutionary Ideas*, 78–85.
104. Gorsas, *Courrier de Paris*, 30 January and 2 February 1790; Goldfarb, *Emancipation*, 84; Eisenbach, *Emancipation*, 61.
105. Labrosse and Rétat, *Naissance du journal révolutionnaire*, 169–71.
106. Gorsas, *Le Courrier de Paris dans les 83 départemens* (later entitled just *Le Courrier des LXXXIII départemens*) (journal, 1790–91) 1, no. 86 (1 October 1789): 1,19, 22; Badinter, *Libres et égaux*, 109–10, 115; Hermon-Belot, "L'Abbé Grégoire," 155–56; Nahon, *Juifs et judaïsme*, 165.
107. Hourwitz, *Apologie des Juifs*, 80; Battenberg, "Französische Revolution," 254.
108. Badinter, *Libres et égaux*, 123–27; Battenberg, "Französische Revolution," 251–53.
109. Nirenberg, *Anti-Judaism*, 367; Stuurman, *Invention of Humanity*, 354.
110. Despat, *Mirabeau*, 594.
111. Fontana, *Venise et la Révolution*, 391–92; Israel, *Revolutionary Ideas*, 183.
112. 28 January 1780, *Archives Parlementaires* 11:364–65; Jaher, *The Jews*, 72.
113. Sorkin, "Count Stanislas," 36–37; Nahon, *Juifs et judaïsme*, 167; Stuurman, *Invention of Humanity*, 355–56.
114. Malino, *A Jew in the French Revolution*, 98–99; Schechter, *Obstinate Hebrews*, 19, 31.
115. Gorsas, *Courrier de Paris*, 2 February 1790, 393–94.
116. Gorsas, *Courrier de Paris*, 2 February 1790, 394.
117. Gorsas, *Courrier de Paris*, 24 April 1790, 295–96; Godechot, *Counter-Revolution*, 29.
118. *Chronique de Paris* 1791, no. 11 (12 January 1791): 45–46. Hourwitz's letter is dated 9 January; Malino, generally accurate, dates this letter wrongly to 8 January (Malino, *A Jew in the French Revolution*, 102–3).
119. Malino, *A Jew in the French Revolution*, 47, 108, 240.
120. *Chronique de Paris* 1791, no. 11 (12 January 1791) : 45–46,
121. *Chronique de Paris* 1791 (11 January 1791): 13, 51; Malino, *A Jew in the French Revolution*, 103.
122. Elyada, "Rhétorique antijuive," 143–46; Nirenberg, *Anti-Judaism*, 366–67.
123. Zalkind Hourwitz, "Moyens d'empêcher la révélation du mot d'ordre dans les patrouilles," in Gorsas, *Courrier de Paris*, 1 December 1789, 265.
124. Hourwitz, *Origine des langues*, 45, 74.
125. Hourwitz, *Origine des langues*, 102, 104; Malino, *A Jew in the French Revolution*, 104–6.
126. Manuel, *Broken Staff*, 245.
127. Graetz, "Jewish Enlightenment," 312, 314–16.
128. Goldfarb, *Emancipation*, 126; Davies, *God's Playground*, 269; Schama, *Belonging*, 465.

129. Eisenbach, *Emancipation*, 8–9, 76; Drozdowski, "Jews of Warsaw," 90–91; Hundert, *Jews in Poland-Lithuania*, 217, 220.
130. Drozdowski, "Jews of Warsaw," 91; Zienkowska, "Jews Have Killed a Traitor," 134, 137, 144.
131. Israel, *European Jewry*, 184–91, 250; Goodman, *History of Judaism*, 421–22.
132. Israel, *European Jewry*, 249–50; Davies, *God's Playground*, 230; Zienkowska, "Jews Have Killed a Traitor," 143–44.
133. Hundert, *Jews in Poland-Lithuania*, 218; Stone, "Knowledge of Foreign Languages," 216.
134. Eisenbach, *Emancipation*, 76–77; Duzinkiewicz, *Fateful Transformations*, 68, 81, 260.
135. Hundert, *Jews in Poland-Lithuania*, 219; Goldberg, "Jewish Marriage," 15–16.
136. Eisenbach, *Emancipation*, 87–89; Birnbaum, "Est-il des moyens?," 581.
137. Mirabeau, *De la monarchie prussienne*, 5:46, 55–58.
138. Bourel, "Judéophobie savante," 130; Schapkow, *Role Model and Countermodel*, 82nn81, 82; Feiner, *Origins*, 181–82.
139. *Berlinische Monatsschrift*, ed. J. E. Biester and F. Gedike, 15 (January–June 1790): 370.
140. Hourwitz, *Apologie des Juifs*, preface, 10.
141. Hourwitz, *Apologie des Juifs*, 57; Hourwitz, *Origine des langues*, 44–48.
142. Hourwitz, *Apologie des Juifs*, 30–31.
143. Hourwitz, *Apologie des Juifs*, 31; Malino, *A Jew in the French Revolution*, 50–51; Koskowicz, *Modernity of Others*, 79–80.
144. Heinrich, "Debatte um 'bürgerliche Verbesserung,'" 2:820–24.
145. Sorkin, *Religious Enlightenment*, 126, 190; Israel, *Revolution of the Mind*, 120–21.
146. BL Fr 170/6 Grégoire, "Motion en faveur des Juifs," 21.
147. Sorkin, *Transformation of German Jewry*, 28; Altmann, *Moses Mendelssohn*, 40–44, 465–67; Bourel, "Judéophobie savante," 130–31, 137–38; Hess, *Germans, Jews and the Claims*, 39, 51–69.
148. Hourwitz, *Apologie des Juifs*, 57–58; Altmann, *Moses Mendelssohn*, 40–44, 467; Bourel,"Judéophobie savante," 130, 135.
149. Hourwitz, *Apologie des Juifs*, 13; Trigano, "French Revolution and the Jews," 180; Mitchell, *Voltaire's Jews*, 83.
150. Goldfarb, *Emancipation*, 83.

CHAPTER 8. JEWISH REVOLUTIONARIES AND THE TERROR (1793–1794)

1. Schechter, *Obstinate Hebrews*, 252.
2. Badinter, *Libres et égaux*, 173.
3. *Chronique de Paris* 1791, no. 42 (11 February 1791): 167; Malino, *A Jew in the French Revolution*, 110–11.
4. *Chronique de Paris* 1791, no. 42 (11 February 1791): 167.

5. Löwy, *Redemption and Utopia*, 42, 190; Israel, *Revolutionary Ideas*, 420–573; Israel, *The Enlightenment That Failed*, 457–96.
6. Frey, *Philosophie sociale*, 21.
7. Feiner, *Origins*, 65, 76; Maciejko, *Mixed Multitude*, 12.
8. Maciejko, *Mixed Multitude*, 15–17; Sutcliffe, *What Are Jews For?*, 104–5.
9. Feiner, *Origins*, 78–80; Löwy, *Redemption and Utopia*, 66–67; Maciejko, *Mixed Multitude*, 21–28, 31.
10. Eisenbach, *Emancipation*, 39; Hertz, *How Jews Became Germans*, 29–30.
11. Opalski and Bartal, *Poles and Jews*, 120–21; Eisenbach, "Jewish Population in Warsaw," 103; Sutcliffe, *What Are Jews For?*, 105.
12. Goodman, *History of Judaism*, 410–11.
13. Löwy, *Redemption and Utopia*, 42, 214n28; Davies, *God's Playground*, 247.
14. Ruderman, *Early Modern Jewry*, 144–45, 168–72; Löwy, *Redemption and Utopia*, 42, 66–67; Eisenbach, "Jewish Population in Warsaw," 103; Dynner, *Yankel's Tavern*, 70, 93, 202n104.
15. Scholem, *Du Frankisme au jacobinisme*, 12; Wöffle-Fischer, *Junius Frey*, 37–38, 83.
16. Greco, "Heresy, Apostasy," 445; Scholem, *Du Frankisme au jacobinisme*, 11–12.
17. Greco, "Heresy, Apostasy," 445–46.
18. Molitor, *Histoire*, 311, 324; Wöffle-Fischer, *Junius Frey*, 77; Israel, *Democratic Enlightenment*, 827.
19. Scholem, *Du Frankisme au jacobinisme*, 28–29, 40–43, 45; Maciejko, *Mixed Multitude*, 194–97, 224–26.
20. Molitor, *Histoire*, 311, 320–21; Wöffle-Fischer, *Junius Frey*, 76–78; Greco, "Heresy, Apostasy," 450.
21. Wöffle-Fischer, *Junius Frey*, 88–89; Kennedy, *Jacobin Clubs*, 48–49.
22. Kennedy, *Jacobin Clubs*, 188–99.
23. Kennedy, *Jacobin Clubs*, 49; Greco, "Heresy, Apostasy," 451.
24. Scholem, *Du Frankisme au Jacobinisme*, 69–70.
25. Bonald, *François Chabot*, 244, 248; Gross, *Fair Shares for All*, 135–36.
26. *Chronique de Paris* 1791, no. 201 (20 July 1791): 812; Israel, *Revolutionary Ideas*, 206.
27. Malino, *A Jew in the French Revolution*, 123.
28. Israel, *Revolutionary Ideas*, 304.
29. Malino, *A Jew in the French Revolution*, 123–24.
30. Nirenberg, *Anti-Judaism*, 375–76.
31. Nahon, *Juifs et judaïsme*, 161; Malino, "Furtado et les Juifs," 50; Joskowicz, *Modernity of Others*, 87.
32. Girard, *Révolution française et les Juifs*, 212–13.
33. Dumouriez, *Mémoires*, 2:42, 17–50; Thompson, *Robespierre*, 321; Szajkowski, *Jews and the French Revolutions*, 460; Israel, *Revolutionary Ideas*, 340, 421.
34. Wöffle-Fischer, *Junius Frey*, 33; Greco, "Heresy, Apostasy," 455n58.
35. Israel, *Revolutionary Ideas*, 313, 425.
36. Bonald, *François Chabot*, 248; Greco, "Heresy, Apostasy," 458–60.
37. Frey, *Aventures politiques*, 14–15.
38. Israel, *Revolutionary Ideas*, 458–66.

39. Frey, *Aventures politiques*, 17–18; Scholem, *Du Frankisme au jacobinisme*, 75–76.
40. Frey, *Aventures politiques*, 27–28; Israel, *Revolutionary Ideas*, 459–62.
41. Frey, *Aventures politiques*, 43, 57.
42. Szajkowski, *Jews and the French Revolutions*, 405–6, 461.
43. Israel, *Revolutionary Ideas*, 525–30.
44. Mathan, *Girondins*, 15, 270; Israel, *Revolutionary Ideas*, 508, 528–30.
45. Malino, "Furtado et le Juifs," 56; Nahon, *Juifs et judaïsme*, 173; Mathan, *Girondins*, 67.
46. Nahon, *Juifs et judaïsme*, 170–71; Slavin, *French Revolution in Miniature*, 19; Girard, *Révolution française et les Juifs*, 220–21.
47. Bonald, *François Chabot*, 272–86; Girard, *Révolution française et les Juifs*, 215–16.
48. Girard, *Révolution française et les Juifs*, 215; Greco, "Heresy, Apostasy," 441, 444–45.
49. Frey, *Philosophie sociale*, 39–41; Scholem, *Du Frankisme au jacobinisme*, 73; Wöffle-Fischer, *Junius Frey*, 98.
50. Frey, *Philosophie sociale*, 43–45; Gross, *Fair Shares for All*, 23, 26; Sonenscher, *Sans-Culottes*, 383.
51. Frey, *Philosophie sociale*, 2–4; Israel, *Enlightenment that Failed*, 290–315; 457–96.
52. Frey, *Philosophie sociale*, 3–4, 5, 95, 98–99, 114, 126–27; Wöffle-Fischer, *Junius Frey*, 98–99.
53. Frey, *Philosophie sociale*, 76.
54. Frey, *Philosophie sociale*, 11–13; Sonenscher, *Sans-Culottes*, 382.
55. Frey, *Philosophie sociale*, 111.
56. Frey, *Philosophie sociale*, 95–98; Greco, "Heresy, Apostasy, " 442.
57. Frey, *Philosophie sociale*, 70–71.
58. Frey, *Philosophie sociale*, 19; Israel, *Revolutionary Ideas*, 348–53; Israel, *Enlightenment That Failed*, 466–72.
59. Malino, "Furtado et les Juifs," 56, 59.
60. Frey, *Philosophie sociale*, 174–76; Greco, "Heresy, Apostasy," 458, 462.
61. Frey, *Philosophie sociale*, 178–81.
62. Frey, *Philosophie sociale*, 179–80.
63. Greco, "Heresy, Apostasy," 443; Sonenscher, *Sans-Culottes*, 383.
64. Frey, *Philosophie sociale*, 48–49; Greco, "Heresy, Apostasy," 462.
65. Cottebrune, *Mythe et realité*, 308.
66. Goldstein Sepinwall, "Strategic Friendships," 201.
67. Frey, *Aventures politiques*, 8, 27.
68. Hampson, *Life and Opinions*, 236; Malino, *A Jew in the French Revolution*, 137; Israel, *Revolutionary Ideas*, 487.
69. Thompson, *Robespierre*, 431; Israel, *Revolutionary Ideas*, 539.
70. Saint-Just, *Oeuvres complètes*, 682; Israel, *Revolutionary Ideas*, 546–51.
71. Hampson, *Life and Opinions*, 211, 216; Furet and Richet, *Révolution française*, 241.
72. Leuwers, *Robespierre*, 307; Martin, *Robespierre*, 235–37; Israel, *Revolutionary Ideas*, 534–41.

73. Malino, "Furtado et les Juifs," 50, 67; Martin, *Robespierre,* 231, 261.
74. Wöffle-Fischer, *Junius Frey*, 115–16; Girard, *Révolution française et les Juifs*, 200, 216; Jaume, *Discours jacobin*, 208–9.
75. Leuwers, *Robespierre,* 323–24; Martin, *Robespierre,* 231.
76. Wöffle-Fischer, *Junius Frey*, 131–32; Wahnich, *L'Impossible citoyen*, 202.
77. Girard, *Révolution française et les Juifs,* 212–13; Mathan, "Chef d'un groupe indulgent?," 119–20.
78. Hampson, *Life and Opinions*, 203; Jaume, *Discours jacobin*, 180, 214; Wahnich, *L'impossible citoyen*, 130.
79. Wahnich, *L'impossible citoyen*, 9–10, 208.
80. Szajkowski, *Jews and the French Revolutions*, 460; Israel, *Revolutionary Ideas*, 421, 539.
81. Desmoulins, *Vieux Cordelier*, 89, 115; Thompson, *Robespierre*, 436–39; Israel, *Revolutionary Ideas*, 539–40.
82. Jaume, *Discours jacobin,* 208–9; Israel, *Revolutionary Ideas*, 551.
83. Furet and Richet, *Révolution française*, 246; Israel, *Revolutionary Ideas*, 539–41, 555–56.
84. Wöffle-Fischer, *Junius Frey*, 127; Scholem, *Du Frankisme au jacobinisme*, 88–89.
85. Saint-Just, *Oeuvres complètes,* 746, 764–65; Malino, *A Jew in the French Revolution*, 138–40.
86. Malino, "Furtado et les Juifs," 52–54; Girard, *Révolution française et les Juifs,* 48–49; Sorkin, *Jewish Emancipation*, 125–26.

CHAPTER 9. REMAKING THE NEW WORLD (1790–1820)

1. Karp, *Politics of Jewish Commerce*, 97–98; Malino, "Furtado et les Juifs," 63.
2. Cohen, *Jews in Another Environment*, 174–77.
3. Arbell, *Jewish Nation*, 102–3.
4. [Nassy], *Essai historique*, 1:183–84 and 2:194–95; Cohen, *Jews in Another Environment*, 175.
5. Van Lier, "Jewish Community in Surinam," 24–25.
6. [Nassy], *Essai historique*, 2:63–64.
7. Davis, "Een joodse arts," 164.
8. Rush, *Letters of Benjamin Rush*, 2:660–61; Nassy, *Obervations,* 29, 36–37.
9. Nassy, *Obervations,* 10–13, 29–31, 34–37; Faur, "David Nassy," 87–89; Cohen, *Jews in Another Environment*, 38; Ben-Ur, "Cultural Heritage," 180n71; Davis, "Een joodse arts," 172n14.
10. Bloch, "Dr. David d'Isaac Nassy," 1228; Malino, "Furtado et les Juifs," 63.
11. Bloch, "Dr. David d'Isaac Nassy," 1228.
12. Israel, *Expanding Blaze*, 321–60.
13. Fatah-Black, "Patriot *coup d'état*," 130.
14. Emmanuel, *History of the Jews of the Netherlands Antilles*, 1:302.
15. Verheul, *Redevoering over de gelijkheid der menschen*, 7; Israel, "David Nassy," 325–26.

16. Van Kempen, *Geschiedenis van de Surinaamse literatuur*, 3:91–92; Israel, "David Nassy," 325.
17. Seeligmann, "David Nassy," 32–33.
18. Seeligmann, "David Nassy," 35–36.
19. Israel, *Revolutionary Ideas*, 626–94.
20. Fuks-Mansfeld, "Verlichting en emancipatie," 185; Cohen, *Jews in Another Environment*, 105.
21. Oostindie, "Slave Resistance, Colour Lines," 8–9, 15–16, 18; Jordaan, "Patriots, Privateers," 152.
22. Seeligmann, "David Nassy," 30–31.
23. [Nassy], *Lettre-politico-théologico-morale,* preface, xliii–xliv; Faur, "David Nassy," 92; Israel, "Dutch Jews, David Nassy," 175, 190.
24. Goslinga, *Dutch in the Caribbean,* 308–11; Van Goor, *De Nederlandse koloniën*, 386; Davis, "Een joodse arts," 172–73n17.
25. [Nassy], *Lettre-politico-théologico-morale* dedication, vi–vii; further on, Nassy lists those enlighteners who had defended the Jews as equals as Muratori, Dohm, Bernouilli, Mirabaud [Mirabeau], Cloots and the Abbé Grégoire.
26. Cloots, *Lettre sur les Juifs*, 45, 53–54.
27. [Nassy], *Essai historique*, 2:44; Israel, "Dutch Jews, David Nassy," 176–77.
28. De Kom, *Wij slaven van Suriname*, 36; Israel, "Dutch Jews, David Nassy," 180; Israel, *The Enlightenment That Failed*, 735, 746–47.
29. Fatah-Black, "Patriot *coup d'état*," 123–25; Jordaan, *Slavernij en vrijheid*, 197–201.
30. Arbell, *Jewish Nation of the Caribbean*, 292–93.
31. Emmanuel, *History of the Jews of the Netherlands Antilles*, 1:284–85; Loker, "Eighteenth-Century Plan," 135–37; Girard, *Toussaint Louverture*, 184; Jordaan, *Slavernij en vrijheid*, 187.
32. Jordaan, "Patriots, Privateers," 166, 158, 141–44, 149–50; Jordaan, *Slavernij en vrijheid,* 187, 209.
33. Girard, *Toussaint Louverture*, 184–85; Jordaan, "Patriots, Privateers," 150, 166.
34. Quoted in Loker, "Eighteenth-Century Plan," 137; Girard, *Toussaint Louverture*, 183–84.
35. Loker, "Eighteenth-Century Plan," 134, 137–38; Girard, "Black Talleyrand," 104–6.
36. Seeligmann, "David Nassy," 32; Wallet and Zwiep, "Locals: Jews," 919.
37. Algemeen Rijksarchief, The Hague, NPIG vol. 1, res. 22 August 1811; [Nassy], *Essai historique*, 2:39; Zwiep, "Naties worden burgers," 202.
38. Ben-Ur, "Cultural Heritage," 169–70; Cohen, *Jews in Another Environment*, 160–65.
39. [Nassy], *Essai historique*, 1:xxxvi–xxvii; Israel, "David Nassy," 343.
40. Davis, "Een joodse arts," 168–71.
41. Davis, "David Nassy's "Furlough," cue 29.
42. Bloch, "Dr. David d'Isaac Nassy," 1228; Israel, "David Nassy," 343.
43. Rush to Sharp, Philadelphia, undated, August 1791, in Rush, *Letters of Benjamin Rush*, 1:608.

44. Rush, *Letters of Benjamin Rush*, 2:654.
45. Israel, *Expanding Blaze*, 367–38, 374, 376–37, 407–9.
46. Davis, "David Nassy's "Furlough," cues 32 and 37.
47. Nassy, "Discours préliminaire" (10 December 1798), xlvi.
48. Davis, "David Nassy's "Furlough," cue 42.
49. [Nassy], *Essai historique*, 1:59–61; Israel, "David Nassy," 343–44.
50. Stipriaan, *Surinaams Contrast*, 289–91
51. Van Lier, "Jewish Community in Surinam," 23–24.
52. Davis, "Een joodse arts," 164.
53. On this general topic, see Israel, "Dutch Jews, David Nassy," 173–90.
54. Israel, *Revolutionary Ideas*, 57–60, 97; Israel, *Expanding Blaze*, 321–60; Israel, *The Enlightenment That Failed*, 255–89.
55. [Nassy], *Lettre-politico-théologico-morale*, 8.
56. Rauschenbach, "Patriots at the Periphery," 599, 601–2, 605.
57. Nassy, "A Letter of David Nassy" (1799), 186.
58. Nassy, "Discours préliminaire" (10 December 1798), xvi; Rauschenbach, "Patriots at the Periphery," 598.
59. Nassy, "Discours préliminaire" (10 December 1798), xxvi–xxviii.
60. Israel, *The Enlightenment That Failed*, 876–84.
61. Nassy, "Discours préliminaire" (10 December 1798), xiv, xxxiii–xxxiv.
62. Nassy, "Discours préliminaire" (10 December 1798), xiv.
63. Rauschenbach, "Patriots at the Periphery," 597–98.
64. Nassy, "Discours préliminaire" (10 December 1798), lix–lxi.
65. Israel, *The Enlightenment That Failed*, 860–62, 874–75, 877, 879–80, 894.
66. Cardot, *Curazao hispánico*, 424–25, 433; Oostindie, "Slave Resistance, Colour Lines," 12–14, 16.
67. Oostindie, "Slave Resistance, Colour Lines," 2.
68. Euwens, "Admiral Pedro Luis Brión," 460; Arbell, *Jewish Nation of the Caribbean*, 159.
69. Davis, "Een joodse arts," 166; Lynch, *Simón Bolívar*, 64.
70. Arbell, *Jewish Nation*, 159–60.
71. Cardot, *Curazao hispánico*, 457, 464; Emmanuel, *History of the Jews of the Netherlands Antilles*, 1:289, 298–99, 826; Arbell, *Jewish Nation*,160.
72. Emmanuel, *History of the Jews of the Netherlands Antilles*, 1:299; Arana, *Bolívar: American Liberator*, 175, 191; Van der Veen, *Groot-Nederland*, 66.
73. Euwens, "Admiral Pedro Luis Brión," 449–50, 457; Jordaan, "Patriots, Privateers," 148, 152, 166.
74. Arana, *Bolívar: American Liberator*, 178–79, 193, 198; Lynch, *Simón Bolívar*, 100, 134.
75. Euwens, "Admiral Pedro Luis Brión," 450; Arana, *Bolívar:American Liberator*, 201–2; Brown, "Impious Adventurers," 85.
76. Brown, "Impious Adventurers," 94–96.
77. Arbell, *Jewish Nation* 160, 302; Arana, *Bolívar: American Liberator*, 314, 455; Israel, *Expanding Blaze*, 455.

78. Brown, "Rebellion at Riohacha," 81, 86, 96–97; Brown, "Impious Adventurers," 227–28; Arana, *Bolívar:American Liberator,* 187–88; Van der Veen, *Groot- Nederland,* 42, 44, 64–66; Lynch, *Simón Bolívar,* 97.
79. Euwens, "Admiral Pedro Luis Brión," 456–57, 460–61.

CHAPTER 10. THE DISSIDENT JEWS OF *FELIX LIBERTATE* (1787–1800)

1. Davies, "Friendship in the Revolution," 72.
2. Heinrich, "Debatte um 'bürgerliche Verbesserung,'" 821.
3. Michman and Aptroot, *Storm in the Community,* 7, 13; Sorkin, *Transformation of German Jewry,* 43–44.
4. Michman and Aptroot, *Storm in the Community,* 7–8.
5. Hartog Lémon, *Aanspraak uitgesproken,* 4, 8; Michman, *Dutch Jewry,* 67–68, 71.
6. Israel, "Ideology," 88–89.
7. Goldstein Sepinwall, "Strategic Friendships," 193.
8. Michman, "Jewish Soldiers," 288–89; Wallet and Zwiep, "Locals: Jews,'" 917–18.
9. Quoted in Seeligmann, "David Nassy," 35; Zwiep, "Naties worden burgers," 215–16.
10. Michman, "Jewish Soldiers," 289.
11. Michman, *Dutch Jewry,* 6–7.
12. Caransa, *Vrijmetselarij en Jodendom,* 113; Israel, *Democratic Enlightenment,* 830.
13. De Vries, *Beschaven! Letterkundige genootschappen,* 165, 385; Zwiep, "Jewish Enlightenment Reconsidered," 307.
14. Hagen, "Zaal van staatsmannen," 127.
15. Altena, *Gerrit Paape,* 611.
16. Michman, "Emancipatie van de Joden," 79.
17. Hagen, "Zaal van staatsmannen," 125.
18. Bloemgarten, *Hartog de Hartog Lémon,* 39–40, 52; Rädecker, "Making Jews Dutch," 33, 37.
19. Van der Burg, *Nederland onder Franse invloed,* 37.
20. Michman, "Emancipatie van de de Joden," 80; Caransa, *Vrijmetselarij en jodendom,* 76.
21. Hagen, "Zaal van staatsmannen," 126.
22. Michman, *Dutch Jewry,* 2–3.
23. Michman, "Jewish Soldiers," 289; Sonnenberg-Stern, *Emancipation and Poverty,* 57–58, 61.
24. Wallet and Zwiep, "Locals: Jews," 902, 904; Rädecker, "Moses is tot [de] Raad," 26.
25. Fuks-Mansfeld, "Enlightenment and Emancipation," 171; Sorkin, *Jewish Enlightenment,* 31.
26. Prak, *Republikeinse veelheid,* 228.
27. Prak, *Republikeinse veelheid,* 229.
28. Fuks-Mansfeld, "Verlichting en emancipatie," 185; Cohen, *Jews in Another Environment,* 105.
29. [Nassy], *Lettre-politico-théologico-morale,* préface, xliii–xliv.

30. Fuks-Mansfeld, "Verlichting en emancipatie," 185; Cohen, *Jews in Another Environment*, 105; Michman, "Jewish Soldiers," 290–91; Caransa, *Vrijmetselarij en Jodendom*, 75–76.
31. Michman, "Emancipatie van de Joden," 80.
32. Seeligmann, "David Nassy," 32; Israel, "Dutch Jews, David Nassy," 175–76.
33. Michman, *Dutch Jewry*, 141n135.
34. Bloemgarten, *Hartog de Hartog Lémon*, 44–48; Michman and Aptroot, *Storm in the Community*, 5–6.
35. Bloemgarten, *Hartog de Hartog Lémon*, 41, 67; Rädecker, "Making Jews Dutch," 32, 171.
36. Bloemgarten, *Hartog de Hartog Lémon*, 37; Sonnenberg-Stern, *Emancipation and Poverty*, 58, 61.
37. Hartog Lémon, *Aanspraak gedaan*, 13–14; Hiegentlich, "Reflections," 210; Schama, *Patriots and Liberators*, 262.
38. Bloemgarten, *Hartog de Hartog Lémon*, 48–50; Rädecker, "Making Jews Dutch," 114–15.
39. Michman, *Dutch Jewry*, 57; Rädecker, "Making Jews Dutch," 120–21.
40. Berger, "Yiddish on the Borderline," 116–17; Feiner, *Origins*, 224.
41. Bloemgarten, *Hartog de Hartog Lémon*, 72–73; Michman and Aptroot, *Storm in the Community*, 8, 16, 22.
42. Hartog Lémon, *Aanspraak uitgesproken*, 1–2; Michman, *Dutch Jewry*, 59; Hiegentlich, "Reflections," 210–11.
43. Altena, *Gerrit Paape*, 457, 538, 754–55n111.
44. Hartog Lémon, *Aanspraak gedaan*, 3–4; Michman and Aptroot, *Storm in the Community*, 6–7.
45. Michman, "Emancipatie van de Joden," 78–79; Zwiep, "Naties worden burgers," 203.
46. Salvadori, *1799: Gli ebrei italiani*, 5–6; Goldfarb, *Emancipation*, 93–94; Sorkin, *Jewish Emancipation*, 102–6.
47. Salvadori, *1799: Gli ebrei italiani*, 6, 89–90, 100–103; Godechot, *Counter-Revolution*, 336–37; Grab, *Napoleon and the Transformation*, 157.
48. Israel, *Expanding Blaze*, 497–500; Godechot, *Counter-Revolution*, 337.
49. Michman, "Emancipatie van de Joden," 78.
50. Michman, "Emancipatie van de Joden," 78; Fuks-Mansfeld, "Enlightenment and Emancipation," 180; Joor, *Adelaar en het Lam*, 179–80.
51. Gompes and Ligtelijn, *Spiegel van Amsterdam*, 61; Rädecker, "Moses is tot [de] Raad," 26.
52. Michman, *Dutch Jewry*, 59n15; Rädecker, "Making Jews Dutch," 49; Salvadori, *1799: Gli ebrei italiani*, 6.
53. Bloemgarten, *Hartog de Hartog Lémon*, 39, 211.
54. Hartog Lémon, *Aanspraak uitgesproken*, 4–6; Bloemgarten, *Hartog de Hartog Lémon*, 27.
55. Hiegentlich, "Reflections," 215; Aptroot, "Yiddish, Dutch and German," 205, 208, 211.

56. Aptroot, "Yiddish, Dutch and German," 202–3; Berger, "Yiddish on the Borderline," 122.
57. Michman, *Dutch Jewry*, 68–71, 73–76; Aptroot, "Yiddish, Dutch and German," 203; Wallet and Zwiep, "Locals, Jews," 908–9.
58. *Diskurs gehalten tvishn yehudem*, 46–47; Zwiep, "Naties worden burgers," 206–8.
59. *Diskurs gehalten tvishn yehudem*, 42–43; Rädecker, "Making Jews Dutch," 101–4.
60. Hartog Lémon, *Aanspraak uitgesproken*, 8–11; Sonnenberg-Stern, *Emancipation and Poverty*, 117–18.
61. Michman, *Dutch Jewry*, 77–78; Aptroot, "Yiddish, Dutch and German," 207; Zwiep, "Naties worden Burgers," 205, 216; Rädecker, "Moses is tot [de] Raad," 23; Wallet and Zwiep, "Locals: Jews," 918.
62. Bloemgarten, *Hartog de Hartog Lémon*, 27–30.
63. Hartog Lémon, *Aanspraak gedaan*, 3–4, 13–14; Bloemgarten, *Hartog de Hartog Lémon*, 110.
64. Van der Burg, *Nederland onder Franse invloed*, 42; Prak, *Republikeinse veelheid*, 230.
65. Michman, *Dutch Jewry*, 79–80.
66. Hagen, "Zaal van staatsmannen," 134–35; Rädecker, "Making Jews Dutch," 36.
67. Altena, *Gerrit Paape*, 457; Bloemgarten, *Hartog de Hartog Lémon*, 143.
68. Michman, *Dutch Jewry*, 29.

CHAPTER 11. NAPOLEON AND THE JEWS (1796–1815)

1. Nipperdey, *Germany*, 1–11, 54–64; Whaley, *Germany*, 619–20; Battenberg, "Jews in Ecclesiastical Territories," 251–53; Kerautet, "Napoleon und Deutschland, " 25–29.
2. Nipperdey, *Germany*, 8–9, 57, 63; Severin-Barbout, "Gesellschaft im Umbruch," 144–48
3. Mintzker, *Defortification*, 145–72; Kerautret, "Napoleon und Deutschland," 31–36.
4. Whaley, *Germany*, 619–20; Battenburg, "Jews in Ecclesiastical Territories," 247, 251, 267 273–74.
5. Broers, *Europe under Napoleon*, 111.
6. Sperber, *Karl Marx*, 11–12; Stedman Jones, *Karl Marx*, 8, 18, 22–23.
7. Goldfarb, *Emancipation*, 209; Sperber, *Karl Marx*, 12; Avineri, *Karl Marx*, 5–7.
8. Jarrett, *Congress of Vienna*, 141; Hertz, *How Jews Became Germans*, 128.
9. Hobsbawm, *Age of Revolution*, 196–97; Sorkin, *Jewish Emancipation*, 111.
10. Ohles, *Germany's Rude Awakening*, 14–15.
11. Sorkin, *Transformation of German Jewry*, 29; Sorkin, *Jewish Emancipation*, 111.
12. Higby, *Religious Policy*, 309; Sorkin, *Transformation of German Jewry*, 27–28.
13. Higby, *Religious Policy*, 315–19; Grab, *Napoleon and the Transformation*, 105; Sorkin, *Transformation of German Jewry*, 29; Jersch-Wenzel, "Legal Status," 23–24.
14. Quoted in Einsenbach, *Emancipation*, 134.

15. Eisenbach, *Emancipation*, 133, 135.
16. Hartog Lémon, *Aanspraak uitgesproken*, 6, 8–9; Schechter, *Obstinate Hebrews*, 222–23.
17. Eisenbach, *Emancipation*, 132–34; Goldfarb, *Emancipation*, 96–102; Wallet, "Napoleon's Legacy," 293.
18. Grab, "Jewish Education," 272.
19. Michman, *Dutch Jewry*, 90–92; Bloemgarten, *Hartog de Hartog Lémon*, 196–97, 204–6.
20. Zwiep, "Jewish Enlightenment Reconsidered," 286–89, 293–94, 301–2.
21. Malino, "Furtado et les Juifs," 60–64.
22. Gallingani, *Napoleone e gli ebrei*, 51–52.
23. Gallingani, *Napoleone e gli ebrei*, 54.
24. Grab, "Jewish Education," 283; Wallet, "Napoleon's Legacy," 293.
25. Grab, "Jewish Education," 277–78.
26. Grab, "Jewish Education," 278.
27. Fuks-Mansfeld, "Enlightenment," 180; Rädecker, "Making Jews Dutch," 50.
28. Michman, *Dutch Jewry*, 39, 107–23, 139–42, 206; Bloemgarten, *Hartog de Hartog Lémon*, 207–10, 220; Zwiep, "Naties worden burgers," 209–10; Sonnenberg-Stern, *Emancipation and Poverty*, 62–63, 117–18.
29. Bloemgarten, *Hartog de Hartog Lémon*, 241–42; Wallet and Zwiep, "Locals: Jews," 920.
30. Joor, *Adelaar en het Lam*, 179–80; Bloemgarten, *Hartog de Hartog Lémon*, 425–27, 429; Gompes and Ligtelijn, *Spiegel van Amsterdam*, 58.
31. Hartog Lémon, *Aanspraak uitgesproken*, 4, 8; Bloemgarten, *Hartog de Hartog Lémon*, 210.
32. Michman, "De emancipatie," 80; Rädecker, "Making Jews Dutch," 169–70.
33. Fuks-Mansfeld, "Arduous Adaptation," 208; Wallet and Zwiep, "Locals: Jews," 920.
34. Wallet, "Napoleon's Legacy," 294; Westerburg, "Kirchenpolitik im Reformstaat," 194.
35. Grab, *Napoleon and the Transformation*, 101; Severin-Barboutie, "Gesellschaft im Umbruch," 149–51; Westerburg, "Kirchenpolitik im Reformstaat," 203–4.
36. Hertz, *How Jews Became Germans*, 134–35; Goldfarb, *Emancipation*, 124–26.
37. Westerburg, "Kirchenpolitik im Reformstaat," 204–5; Carvalho and Koyama, "Jewish Emancipation," 8–9.
38. Hartog Lémon, *Aanspraak uitgesproken*, 9–11; Lowenstein, "Two Silent Minorities," 12–13; Hess, *Germans, Jews*, 16–17.
39. Jersch-Wenzel, "Legal Status," 25–26; Stedman Jones, *Karl Marx*, 22.
40. Szulc, "A Gracious Act or Merely a Regulation?," 26–28.
41. Sorkin, *Transformation of German Jewry*, 34–35; Szulc, "A Gracious Act or Merely a Regulation?," 35–36.
42. Salvadori, *1799: Gli ebrei italiani*, 5–6; Schwartz, *Ghetto*, 49–52; Schechter, *Obstinate Hebrews*, 199–201; Grab, "Jewish Education," 273.
43. Kümper, "Worte der Wahrheit," 155–57, 160; Sorkin, *Religious Enlightenment*, 193.

44. Sorkin, *Religious Enlightenment*, 210–12; Goldfarb, *Emancipation*, 110; Elon, *Pity of It All*, 66–67; Hess, *German, Jews*, 179–83.
45. Altmann, *Moses Mendelssohn*, 478–83; Kümper, "Worte der Wahrheit," 165–67, 178–80; Feiner, "On the Threshold," 44–45; Lowenstein, "Two Silent Minorities," 9, 13, 17.
46. Sorkin, *Transformation of German Jewry*, 54–55; Graetz, "From Corporate Community," 76; Feiner, "On the Threshold," 44–45.
47. Sorkin, *Transformation of German Jewry*, 126, 128.
48. Bloemgarten, *Hartog de Hartog Lémon*, 205–6.
49. Grab, "Jewish Education," 279.
50. Graetz, "From Corporate Community," 78; Caransa, *Vrijmetselarij en Jodendom*, 75–76.
51. Joor, *Adelaar en het Lam*, 180–81.
52. Joor, *Adelaar en het Lam*, 140–41; Bloemgarten, *Hartog de Hartog Lémon*, 382–87.
53. Bloemgarten, *Hartog de Hartog Lémon*, 363, 369–70, 422; Caransa, *Vrijmetselari en jodendom*, 114.
54. Michman, *Dutch Jewry*, 43.
55. Michman, *Dutch Jewry*, 211, 216–24.
56. Bloemgarten, *Hartog de Hartog Lémon*, 400–407.
57. Michman, "De Emancipatie," 82.
58. Eisenbach, *Emancipation*, 137–43; Jarrett, *Congress of Vienna*, 202–3.
59. Aaslestad, *Place and Politics*, 249–50, 308, 282–83; Broers, *Europe under Napoleon*, 127–28, 142, 199.
60. Schwartz, *Ghetto*, 51, 64, 80, 87; Grab, "Jewish Education," 289.
61. Palmer, *Bernadotte*, 246.
62. Menkis, "In This Great, Happy and Enlightened Colony," 317–18; Sorkin, *Jewish Emancipation*, 231–32.
63. Arendt, *Rahel Varnhagen*, 147.

CHAPTER 12. HEINE, BÖRNE AND THE POST-NAPOLEONIC JEWISH REVOLUTIONARY TRADITION (1810–1840)

1. Ruge, "Self-Critique," 246; Heine, *Ludwig Börne: Eine Denkschrift*, 35; Hess, *Germans, Jews*, 193–203.
2. Mansel, *Paris between Empires*, 188; Bensusssan, *Moses Hess*, 12–13; Sorkin, *Jewish Emancipation*.
3. *British Envoys*, 2:148–49; Yovel, *Dark Riddle*, 91.
4. Herzig, "Process," 63–65; Graetz, "From Corporate Community," 77–78.
5. Quoted in Graetz, "From Corporate Community," 78.
6. Nickel, *Revolutionsgedanken*, 172.
7. Löwy, *Redemption and Utopia*, 190; Sutcliffe, "Ludwig Börne," 215, 228.
8. Morawe, "Heinrich Heine und die Strategie," 548, 560; Goetschel, *Heine and Critical Theory*, 195–96.

9. Quoted in Brod, *Heinrich Heine*, 36.
10. Sammons, *Heinrich Heine*, 56–57.
11. Yovel, *Dark Riddle*, 91–92.
12. Cohen, "Heinrich Heine und das Judenthum," 186; Goetschel, "Heine's Spinoza," 208; Morawe, "Heinrch Heine und die Strategie," 457–58.
13. Arendt, *Rahel Varnhagen*, 178–85; Goetschel, "Heine's Spinoza," 208–9; Schama, *Belonging*, 539–40.
14. Morawe, "Heinrich Heine und die Strategie," 546–47; Kouvelakis, *Philosophy and Revolution*, 76–77, 121.
15. Szulc, "A Gracious Act or Merely a Regulation," 28, 36; Levinger, *Enlightened Nationalism*, 121–22.
16. Heine, "Über Polen," 680–81; Sammons, *Heinrich Heine*, 87–89
17. Heine, "Über Polen," 682.
18. Schapkow, *"Die Freiheit zu philosophieren,"* 110–11; Goetschel, "Heine's Spinoza," 215; Skolnik, "Kaddish for Spinoza," 174.
19. Wertheim, *Salvation through Spinoza*, 48–50.
20. Sammons, *Heinrich Heine*, 101–2.
21. Heine, *Ludwig Börne: Eine Denkschrift*, 17–18; Ott, *Querelle de Heine*, 15.
22. Schapkow, *"Freiheit zu philosophieren,"* 103–11; Rippmann, *"Freiheit ist das Schönste,"* 177; Schwartz, *First Modern Jew*, 67–68; for the Heine quote, see Goetschel, *Heine and Critical Theory*, 193–94.
23. Hess, *Rome and Jerusalem*, 33; Schneider, *Fanny Lewald*, 17–18.
24. Eitan, "A Duel," 275–85; Goldfarb, *Emancipation*, 138–39, 143–45; Nipperdey, *Germany*, 218; Levinger, *Enlightened Nationalism*, 115.
25. Hertz, *How Jews Became Germans*, 161; Sutcliffe, "Ludwig Börne," 226–27; Kieniewicz, "Assimilated Jews," 173; Hess, *German, Jews*, 175, 189, 207.
26. *British Envoys*, 1:112; Herzig, "Process," 65–66; Hertz, *How Jews Became Germans*, 160–63.
27. *British Envoys*, 1:112; Jasper, *Keinem Vaterland*, 36–39.
28. *British Envoys*, 2:8; Hertz, *How Jews Became Germans*, 160–61, 173, 202.
29. Sutcliffe, "Ludwig Börne," 223; Elon, *Pity of It All*, 139.
30. Schneider, *Fanny Lewald*, 17–18, 27; Hess, *Rome and Jerusalem*, 25; Hertz, *How Jews Became Germans*, 175–77.
31. Hobsbawm, *Age of Revolution*, 231, 259; Israel, *The Enlightenment That Failed*, 850–51; Goetschel, *Heine and Critical Theory*, 205–6.
32. Finch, *French Literature*, 63.
33. Wistrich, *Revolutionary Jews*, 50–51.
34. Ruge, "Self-Critique," 245–47.
35. Ruge, "Self-Critique," 245–46; Salfi, *L'Italie au dix-neuvième siècle*, 14–15, 42–44; Aaslestad, *Place and Politics*, 282–92, 313–20.
36. Ruge, "Self-Critique," 246–47.
37. Heine, *On the History*, 132–33; Ruge, "Self-Critique," 259; Moran, *Toward the Century*, 187–88.
38. Wende, *Radikalismus im Vormärz*, 21, 28.

39. Goltschnigg and Steinecke, *Heine und die Nachwelt*, 172; Schwartz, *First Modern Jew*, 67; Goldfarb, *Emancipation*, 166.
40. Wende, *Radikalismus im Vormärz*, 27; Schapkow, *"Freiheit zu philosophieren,"* 111; Goldfarb, *Emancipation*, 165–67.
41. Vital, *Origins*, 28; Hobsbawm, *Age of Revolution*, 109; Nickel, *Revolutionsgedanken*, 83; Elon, *Pity of It All*, 133, 142–43; Sutcliffe, *What Are Jews For?*, 136.
42. Heine, *Ludwig Börne: Eine Denkschrift*, 32–33; Ott, *Querelle de Heine*, 12, 14, 17; Elon, *Pity of It All*, 131–32.
43. Bethencourt, *The Inquisition*, 421; Israel, *The Enlightenment That Failed*, 711–15.
44. Hobsbawm, *Age of Revolution*, 183; Petiteau, "La Restauration," 31–32; Duprat, "Le Sacre de Charles X," 69–70; Price, *Perilous Crown*, 52–55.
45. Börne, *Studien*, 21–22; Rippmann, *"Freiheit ist das Schönste,"* 179–80; Nickel, *Revolutionsgedanken*, 174.
46. Jasper, *Keinem Vaterland geboren*, 155–56; Bock, *Ludwig Börne*, 199–200; Elon, *Pity of It All*, 139.
47. Heine, *Ludwig Börne: Eine Denkschrift*, 56; Karl Marx, *The Revolutions*, ed. Fernbach, 180; Perraudin, *Literature, the Volk*, 33n6; Mansel, *Paris between Empires*, 276, 305, 385.
48. Aprile, "Des cantons suisses," 85–88; Wegert, *German Radicals*, 108–10, 112; Nipperdey, *Germany*, 324–27.
49. Börne, *Briefe aus Paris*, 1:160, 175–76; Ohles, *Germany's Rude Awakening*, 96–97; Maissen, *Geschichte der Schweiz*, 186–87.
50. Jasper, *Keinem Vaterland geboren*, 153; Israel, *The Enlightenment That Failed*, 528–32.
51. Arendt, *On Revolution*, 263; Israel, *The Enlightenment That Failed*, 779.
52. Ramm, *Germany*, 161–62; Wegert, *German Radicals*, 110–11; Nipperdey, *Germany*, 324.
53. Börne, *Briefe aus Paris*, 2:14–16; Ohles, *Germany's Rude Awakening*, 12, 25–27; Nipperdey, *Germany*, 324–25, 330.
54. Wegert, *German Radicals*, 116–17; Elon, *Pity of It All*, 139.
55. Sheehan, "The German States," 262–63; Israel, *Expanding Blaze*, 540–41.
56. Heine, *On the History*, 244; Heine, *Ludwig Börne: Eine Denkschrift*, 113.
57. Wende, *Radikalismus im Vormärz*, 13, 23–25.
58. Nipperdey, *Germany*, 326–27; Moran, *Toward the Century*, 266.
59. Nipperdey, *Germany*, 327; Wende, *Radikalismus im Vormärz*, 23.
60. Jasper, *Keinem Vaterland geboren*, 178–90; Rose, *German Question/Jewish Question*, 138–39; Sutcliffe, "Ludwig Börne," 229, 231.
61. Heuberger, *Ludwig Börne*, 20; Moran, *Toward the Century*, 268.
62. Görisch and Mayer, *Untersuchungsberichte*, 42, 276–77, 280–81, 358; Wende, *Radikalismus*, 41–44.
63. *Rede von Johann Georg August Wirth*, 1–3; Moran, *Toward the Century*, 262–63, 266–68.
64. *Rede von Johann Georg August Wirth*, 4.

65. Wegert, *German Radicals*, 153–56; Sperber, *Rhineland Radicals*, 112, 152, 175, 217–18.
66. Sperber, *Rhineland Radicals*, 112; Mansel, *Paris between Empires*, 352–53.
67. Wegert, *German Radicals*, 147–48; Wende, *Radikalismus im Vormärz*, 23–25.
68. Görisch and Mayer, *Untersuchungsberichte*, 11; Ohles, *Germany's Rude Awakening*, 37-41, 44.
69. Görisch and Meyer, *Untersuchungsberichte*, 42–43, 276–84.
70. Heine, *Ludwig Börne: Eine Denkschrift*, 54–55, 59; Elon, *Pity of It All*, 138, 140.
71. Heine, *Ludwig Börne: Eine Denkschrift*, 19, 36–37.
72. Heine, *Ludwig Börne: Eine Denkschrift*, 49–50, 208.
73. Heine, *On the History*, 134.
74. Jager, "After Atheism," 622; Roberts, *Shelley*, 30.
75. Hoagwood, *Skepticism and Ideology*, 174–76; Jager, "After Atheism," 613, 619–20; Roberts, *Shelley*, 83–85.
76. Hoagwood, *Skepticism and Ideology*, 144–45, 179–80; Foot, *Red Shelley*, 63.
77. Shelley, *Poetical Works*, 4:40–41; Hoagwood, *Skepticism and Ideology*, 179–80.
78. Sammons, *Heinrich Heine*, 176.
79. Börne, *Studien*, 94, 97.
80. Börne, *Studien*, 16; Heine, *Ludwig Börne: Eine Denkschrift*, 32.
81. Heine, *Ludwig Börne: Eine Denkschrift*, 60, Sammons, *Heinrich Heine*, 234–36.
82. Börne, "Ninth Letter" (Paris, 6 October 1830), in *Briefe aus Paris*, 1:83–86.
83. Ott, *Querelle de Heine*, 16, 22–23, 26, 29; Jasper, *Keinem Vaterland geboren*, 164–65, 176–77, 201–2.
84. Krohn, *"Streiter für Recht und Freiheit,"* 35.
85. Riesser, *Börne und die Juden*, 4.
86. Maissen, *Geschichte der Schweiz*, 216–17; Lewald, *Year of Revolutions*, 124–25.
87. Hess, *Rome and Jerusalem*, 40; Krohn, *"Streiter für Recht,"* 44; Goldfarb, *Emancipation*, 168–70; Elon, *Pity of It All*, 171.
88. Riesser, *Börne und die Juden*, 4, 12, 27; Rose, *German Question/Jewish Question*, 182–84.
89. Sorkin, *Transformation*, 144–46; Krohn, *"Streiter für Recht,"* 37–39; Goldfarb, *Emancipation*, 168–69.
90. Goltschnigg and Steinecke, *Heine und die Nachwelt*, 37; Rose, *German Question, Jewish Question*, 182–84; Sutcliffe, "Ludwig Börne," 225; Sorkin, *Jewish Emancipation*, 156–57, 166.
91. Butler, *Saint-Simonian Religion in Germany*, 147; Sutcliffe, *What Are Jews For?*, 145.
92. Heine, *On the History*, 115.
93. Heine, *On the History*, 116; Berlin, *Crooked Timber*, 257; Berlin, *Against the Current*, 424.
94. Berger, "Unzer Bruder Shpinoza," 254–56. After 1900, Cohen became notoriously hostile to Spinoza, coming to see him as a spur to nonreligious modern antisemitism, but the young Cohen was as much a Spinoza enthusiast as he later grew hostile (Beiser, *Hermann Cohen*, 5, 42–45, 276).

95. Heine, *Ludwig Börne: Eine Denkschrift*, 39–40, 109; Shavit, *Athens in Jerusalem*, 40–41.
96. Butler, *Saint-Simonian Religion in Germany*, 147–49; Goetschel, "Heine's Spinoza," 211–13; Rose, *German Question/ Jewish Question*, 159–60; Gottlieb, *Dream of Enlightenment*, 112.
97. Heine, *On the History*; Goetschel, "The Hyphen in the Theological-Political," 9–10.
98. Heine, *On the History*, 52, 110; Morawe, "Heinrich Heine und die Strategie," 558–60; Beiser, *Hermann Cohen*, 44.
99. Heine, *On the History*, 210–11; Mack, *German Idealism and the Jew*, 95; Shavit, *Athens in Jerusalem*, 40.
100. Brod, *Heinrich Heine*, 326–28; Mack, *Spinoza and the Specters*, 115–16; Mack, *German Idealism and the Jew*, 93–95; Goetschel, *Spinoza's Modernity*, 264.
101. Schapkow, *"Freiheit zu philosophieren,"* 104–5; Israel, "Lumières radicales," 415; Jasper, *Keinem Vaterland geboren*, 210.
102. Heine, *On the History*, 77; Goetschel, *Spinoza's Modernity*, 254–57.
103. Heine, *On the History*, 105.
104. Heine, *On the History*, 58; Heine, *Zur Geschichte*, 139; Goetschel, "Heine's Spinoza," 211, 215; Goetschel, *Heine and Critical Theory*, 222; Nirenberg, *Anti-Judaism*, 414–16.
105. Kouvelakis, *Philosophy and Revolution*, 106–7; Pinkard, *Hegel's Naturalism*, 189; Krop, *Spinoza*, 309; Yovel, *Dark Riddle*, 75, 206n15.
106. Morawe, "Heinrich Heine und die Strategie," 547–48.
107. Heine, *On the History*, 58.
108. Heine, *On the History*, 59, 71–75.
109. Heine, *On the History*, 68.
110. Heine, *Ludwig Börne: Eine Denkschrift*, 41.
111. Horch, "Friedrich Schiller, die Juden und das Judentum," 24, 33–34.
112. Wertheim, *Salvation through Spinoza*, 47; Stedman-Jones, *Karl Marx*, 70.
113. Goldfarb, *Emancipation*, 162; Hertz, *How Jews Became Germans*, 204.
114. Arendt, *Rahel Varnhagen*, 144.
115. Ruge, *Sämtliche Werke*, 3:45–46.
116. Ott, *Querelle de Heine*, 30–31, 36; Enzensberger, *Ludwig Börne*, 18–19, 31; Nickel, *Revolutionsgedanken*, 44–45.
117. Heine, *Ludwig Börne: Eine Denkschrift*, 92; Mansel, *Paris between Empires*, 323.
118. Perraudin, *Literature, the Volk*, 24, 29, 34n12; Enzensberger, *Ludwig Börne*, 18–19; Elon, *Pity of It All*, 137–38.
119. Lewald, *A Year of Revolutions*, 53–54; Kouvelakis, *Philosophy and the Revolution*, 118.
120. Nickel, *Revolutionsgedanken*, 79; Elon, *Pity of It All*, 139.
121. Heine, *Ludwig Börne: Eine Denkschrift*, 64–65, 72; Perraudin, *Literature, the Volk*, 19–22, 26, 29.
122. Heine, *Ludwig Börne: Eine Denkschrift*, 80.

123. Heine, *Ludwig Börne: Eine Denkschrift*, 518–19, 528–29; Perraudin, *Literature, the Volk*, 23–24.
124. Heine, *Ludwig Börne: Eine Denkschrift*, 85, 97; Kouvelakis, *Philosophy and the Revolution*, 115–16, 118.
125. Heine, *Ludwig Börne: Eine Denkschrift*, 59–60; Bock, *Ludwig Börne*, 194, 201, 222.
126. Börne, *Studien*, 78, 82, 85; Bock, *Ludwig Börne*, 341, 358–59.
127. Dresch, "Introduction et commentaire," 21, 33–34; Nickel, *Revolutionsgedanken*, 174.
128. Dresch, "Introduction et commentaire," 47; Jasper, *Keinem Vaterland geboren*, 204–6; Bock, *Ludwig Börne*, 193–94; Israel, *The Enlightenment That Failed*, 486–87.
129. Börne, *Studien*, 88; Jasper, *Keinem Vaterland geboren*, 208.
130. Börne, *Studien*, 97; Stedman Jones, *Karl Marx*, 139.
131. Börne, *Studien*, 89; Israel, *The Enlightenment That Failed*, 484–86.
132. Börne, *Studien*, 97–98, 105–6; Bock, *Ludwig Börne*, 221–22.
133. Börne, *Studien*, 82, 85, 88; Heine, *On the History*, 133.
134. Cohen, *Spinoza on State Religion*, 51, 81; Goldfarb, *Emancipation*, 167; Beiser, *Hermann Cohen*, 44–45.
135. Lewald, *Year of Revolutions*, 58–61; Morawe, "Heinrich Heine und die Strategie," 583; Israel, *Revolutionary Ideas*, 450–502.
136. Börne, *Sämtliche Schriften*, 3:813; Enzensberger, *Ludwig Börne*, 21–22, 34, 371; Sammons, *Heinrich Heine*, 236.
137. Heine, *Ludwig Börne: Eine Denkschrift*, 32.
138. Goltschnigg and Steinecke, *Heine und die Nachwelt*, 191; Kouvelakis, *Philosophy and Revolution*, 80; Rippmann, *"Freiheit ist das Schönste,"* 174; Mack, *German Idealism and the Jew*, 94–95.
139. For a fuller explanation of the tripartite internal ideological conflict within the French Revolution, a topic rarely well understood or explained, see Israel, *Revolutionary Ideas,* chapters 1, 14, 16, and 25.
140. Dresch, "Introduction et commentaire, " 24–25, 37, 57; Börne, *Studien*, 63–66, 93; Jasper, *Keinem Vaterland geboren*, 220–21.
141. Börne, *Studien*, 127; Jasper, *Keinem Vaterland geboren*, 214.
142. Dresch, "Introduction et commentaire," 38; Börne, *Studien*, 38, 58, 125, 138.
143. Rippmann, *"Freiheit ist das Schönste,"* 169; Jasper, *Keinem Vaterland geboren*, 209, 220.
144. Heine, *Ludwig Börne: Eine Denkschrift*, 94; Enzensberger, *Ludwig Börne*, 371; Rippmann, *"Freiheit ist das Schönste,"* 174, 177, 186.
145. Rippmann, *"Freiheit ist das Schönste,"* 174; Goldfarb, *Emancipation*, 229–30; Perraudin, *Literature, the Volk*, 19; Goetschel, *Heine and Critical Theory*, 75–77.
146. Ruge, *Briefwechsel*, 1:334–35.
147. Ruge, *Briefwechsel*, 1:331; Elon, *Pity of It All*, 139–42.
148. Ruge, *Sämtliche Werke*, 3:5, 12, 39, 46; Ruge, *Briefwechsel*, 1:334–35.
149. Ruge, *Briefwechsel*, 1:336; Elon, *Pity of It All*, 136–38.
150. Marcuse, "Heine and Marx," 115–16.

151. Ruge, *Briefwechsel*, 1:363–64.
152. Cohen, "Heinrich Heine und das Judenthum," 188; Bienenstock, "Hermann Cohens Heine," 192–94.
153. Goltschnigg and Steinecke, *Heine und die Nachwelt*, 38.
154. Bienenstock, "Hermann Cohens Heine," 192.
155. Morawe, "Heinrich Heine und die Strategie," 548–50; Sheppard, *Leo Strauss and the Politics*, 40–41, 49–50; Gottlieb, *Dream of Enlightenment*, 111–12.

CHAPTER 13. MOSES HESS (1812–1875) AND "THE NEW JERUSALEM"

1. Weiss, *Moses Hess*, 26–28; Bensussan, *Moses Hess*, 10; Goldfarb, *Emancipation*, 210.
2. Avineri, notes to Hess, *Holy History*, 40n6; Goetschel, "Heine's Spinoza," 214.
3. Haubtmann, *Proudhon*, 649–50, 656–57; Stedman Jones, *Karl Marx*, 166; Sutcliffe, *What Are Jews For?*, 101.
4. Hess, *Rome and Jerusalem*, 32–33; Vital, *Origins*, 13–14, 36; Wistrich, *Revolutionary Jews*, 47–48; Goldfarb, *Emancipation*, 190–91; Frankel, *Crisis, Revolution*, 24–25, 28–29.
5. Quoted in Vital, *Origins*, 211; see also Hess, *Rome and Jerusalem*, 34; and Frankel, *Crisis, Revolution*, 57.
6. Quoted in Silberner, *Moses Hess*, 49, 55–57.
7. Silberner, *Moses Hess*, 49; Weiss, *Moses Hess*, 43, 46–47; Stepelevich, *Young Hegelians*, 10, 13.
8. Schwartz, *First Modern Jew*, 121; Berlin, *Life and Opinions*, 7, 13.
9. Rose, *German Question/Jewish Question*, 306–8; Avineri, *Moses Hess*, 32.
10. Heller, *Moses Hess*, 12–13; Kouvelakis, *Philosophy and Revolution*, 127; Schwartz, *First Modern Jew*, 164.
11. Berlin, *Life and Opinions*, 6; Weiss, *Moses Hess*, 47–49; Sutcliffe, *What Are Jews For?*, 164.
12. Schapkow, *"Die Freiheit zu philosophieren,"* 107; Schwartz, *First Modern Jew*, 164.
13. Hess, *Holy History*, 45–46; Heller, *Moses Hess*, 13.
14. Hess, *Holy History*, 136–39; Avineri, *Moses Hess*, 208; Gottlieb, *Faith and Freedom*, 134–35.
15. Hess, *Holy History*, 40–41; Kouvelakis, *Philosophy and Revolution*, 126–28.
16. Lundgren, *Moses Hess on Religion*, 57.
17. Lundgren, *Moses Hess on Religion*, 61–64; Goldfarb, *Emancipation*, 220–21.
18. Lundgren, *Moses Hess on Religion*, 59–60; Goldfarb, *Emancipation*, 215; Avineri, *Karl Marx*, 38–40.
19. Hess, *Europäische Triarchie*, 27.
20. Hess, *Europäische Triarchie*, 10; Stedman Jones, *Karl Marx*, 207.
21. Brod, *Heinrich Heine*, 325; Stedman Jones, *Karl Marx*, 141–42.
22. Hess, *Europäische Triarchie*, 147–49; Rose, *German Question/Jewish Question*, 328, 330.

23. Hess, *Europäische Triarchie*, "Vorwort"; Lundgren, *Moses Hess on Religion*, 27; Bensussan, *Moses Hess*, 71, 73, 85.
24. Hess, *Europäische Triarchie*, 9–12; Avineri, *Karl Marx*, 65.
25. Na'aman, *Emanzipation und Messianismus*, 124–25; Stedman Jones, *Karl Marx*, 134, 142–43.
26. Na'aman, *Emanzipation und Messianismus*, 142.
27. Weiss, *Moses Hess*, 51; Israel, *The Enlightenment That Failed*, 324–30.
28. Hess, *Europäische Triarchie*, 61, 150–51; Heller, *Moses Hess*, 15; Berlin, *Life and Opinions*, 16; Bensussan, *Moses Hess*, 36–37; Kouvelakis, *Philosophy and Revolution*, 138–41.
29. Weiss, *Moses Hess*, 51.
30. Hess, *Holy History*, 105; Goldfarb, *Emancipation*, 218; Stedman Jones, *Karl Marx*, 142, 183.
31. Quoted in Avineri, *Moses Hess*, 188.
32. Hess, *Holy History of Mankind*, 39; Schama, *Belonging*, 573–74.
33. Ruge, *Zwei Jahre in Paris*, 1:64–65, 69, 75–76; Weiss, *Moses Hess*, 66; Haubtmann, *Proudhon*, 743.
34. Ruge, *Zwei Jahre in Paris*, 1:64; Hess, *Rome and Jerusalem*, 32.
35. Reinalter, "Arnold Ruge," 67; Wende, *Radikalismus im Vormärz*, 112–13, 128.
36. Reinalter, "Arnold Ruge," 66; Weiss, *Moses Hess*, 111.
37. Haubtmann, *Proudhon*, 649–50, 656–57, 658, 662–63; Vincent, *Pierre-Joseph Proudhon*, 117–18, 142.
38. Heine, *On the History*, 78–79; Stedman Jones, *Karl Marx*, 207.
39. Ruge, *Briefwechsel*, 1:278.
40. Hess, *Holy History*, 101.
41. Hess, *Holy History*, 71; Rose, *German Question/Jewish Question*, 18–19, 48–50.
42. Hess, *Holy History*, 79–80; Avineri, *Moses Hess*, 37; Goldfarb, *Emancipation*, 211.
43. Berlin, *Life and Opinions*, 11; Weiss, *Moses Hess*, 49.
44. Hess, *Holy History*, 82, 84; Lundgren, *Moses Hess on Religion*, 23.
45. Haubtmann, *Proudhon*, 447, 454, 620; Avineri, *Karl Marx*, 57; Stedman Jones, *Karl Marx*, 165–68, 224–25; Mansel, *Paris between Empires*, 391.
46. Wende, *Radikalismus im Vormärz*, 126–28.
47. Avineri, *Moses Hess*, 104–5.
48. Frey, *Philosophie sociale*, 210–11.
49. Wistrich, "Socialism and Judeophobia," 128–29.
50. Quoted in Haubtmann, *Proudhon*, 739, 743; Wistrich, "Socialism and Judeophobia," 120–21, 128.
51. Hobsbawm, *Age of Revolution*, 122–23, 127; Price, *Perilous Crown*, 293–94.
52. Haubtmann, *Proudhon*, 446–47; Hobsbawm, *Age of Revolution*, 122–23, 455, 461.
53. Reinalter, "Arnold Ruge," 66–67; Rosen, *Bruno Bauer and Karl Marx*, 212.
54. Rosen, *Bruno Bauer and Karl Marx*, 21–22, 235, 240.
55. Rosen, *Bruno Bauer and Karl Marx*, 224–26.
56. Hamerow, *Restoration, Revolution, Reaction*, 65–66.

57. Lamartine, *Histoire*, 1:16–17; Fortescue, *Alphonse de Lamartine*, 44, 64, 99.
58. Sammons, *Heinrich Heine*, 299, 301.
59. Berlin, *Against the Current*, 288, 458–89; Sperber, *Karl Marx*, 181–82; Stedman Jones, *Karl Marx*, 225–27.
60. Hess, *Holy History*, 63; Löwy, *Redemption and Utopia*, 190.
61. Hess, *Rome and Jerusalem*, 32.
62. Avineri, *Moses Hess*, 86; Goetschel, *Spinoza's Modernity*, 260, 276.
63. Hess, *Rome and Jerusalem*, 41.
64. Hess, *Rome and Jerusalem*, 30, 36, 67; Schwartz, *First Modern Jew*, 120–21.
65. Hess, *Rome and Jerusalem*, 72; Frankel, *Crisis, Revolution*, 173, 178.
66. Hess, *Rome and Jerusalem*, 40–41; Harvey, "Spinoza's Counterfactual Zionism," 239–41; Shavit, *Athens in Jerusalem*, 195–97, 396–97; Yovel, *Dark Riddle*, 215n.
67. Vital, *Origins*, 246–47; Berlin, *Against the Current*, 292–95, 425–26, 457–58.

CHAPTER 14. KARL MARX AND THE SOCIALIST REVOLUTION

1. Stedman Jones, *Karl Marx*, 29; Avineri, *Karl Marx*, 1, 9–10.
2. Fischer, *Socialist Response*, 64–65; Avineri, *Karl Marx*, 10–11.
3. Karl Marx to Heinrich Marx, 10 November 1837, in Marx, *Early Texts*, 2, 7–8; Goldfarb, *Emancipation*, 157–58; Avineri, *Karl Marx*, 16–17, 20.
4. Rotenstreich, "For and Against Emancipation," 11; Rosen, *Bruno Bauer and Karl Marx*, 194–95.
5. David McLellan, introduction to Marx, *Early Texts*, xiii.
6. Quoted in Rubel, "Marx à la recontre de Spinoza," 10; Avineri, *Karl Marx*, 21–22.
7. Marx, *Early Texts*, 13; Hull, "Marx's Anomalous Reading," 19, 28; Stedman Jones, *Karl Marx*, 79–83.
8. Rubel, "Marx à la recontre de Spinoza," 8; David McLellan, introduction to Marx, *Early Texts*, xiii.
9. Rubel, "Marx à la recontre de Spinoza," 8; Israel, *The Enlightenment That Failed*, 93–94.
10. Marx, "Cahier," 98–99; see Spinoza, *Letters*, 132.
11. Hulak, "Spinoza après Marx," 487; Tatián, *Spinoza, filosofía terrena*, 180–81; Bianchi, "Marx's Reading of Spinoza," 35; Fischbach, *Production des hommes*, 165.
12. Tosel, *Spinoza, ou l'autre (in)finitude*, 131; Casarino, "Marx before Spinoza," 180–81, 219.
13. Reproduced in *Cahiers Spinoza*, ed. A. Igoin, A. Lecrivain, Alexandre Matheron, Pierre-François Moreau, and M. Schneider, Paris, 1 (1977): 31–157; see also Rubel, "Marx à la recontre de Spinoza," 13–14; and Hulak, "Spinoza après Marx," 485–86.
14. Marx and Engels, *Exzerpte und Notizen*, 234; Spinoza, *Theological-Political Treatise*, 81; Spinoza, *Opera*, 3:81.
15. Marx and Engels, *Exzerpte und Notizen*, 247; Marx, "Cahier," 86–87.

16. Dobbs-Weinstein, *Spinoza's Critique of Religion*, 68; Bianchi, "Marx's Reading of Spinoza," 40–41; Fischbach, *Production des hommes*, 40–43, 166.
17. Tosel, "Pour une étude systématique," 129–30; Rubel, "Marx à la recontre de Spinoza," 12; Rosen, *Bruno Bauer and Karl Marx*, 109–10, 173–74.
18. Ruge, *Briefwechsel*, 1:239; Bianchi, "Marx's Reading of Spinoza," 47; Israel, *The Enlightenment That Failed*, 904–7.
19. Hess, *Briefwechsel*, 79–80. Hess to B. Auerbach, Köln, 2 Sept. 1841; Berlin, *Karl Marx*, 67; Marcuse, "Heine and Marx," 112.
20. Rose, *German Question, Jewish Question*, 226; Schwartz, *First Modern Jew*, 56–57.
21. Wistrich, *Jews of Vienna*, 172; Löwy, *Redemption and Utopia*, 36–37.
22. Na'aman, *Emanzipation und Messianismus*, 115–16; Kouvelakis, *Philosophy and Revolution*, 130; Evans, "Marx and the *Rheinische Zeitung*," 2–3.
23. Hess, *Briefwechsel*, 80; Silberner, "Moses Hess als Begründer," 24; Lundgren, *Moses Hess*, 28–30.
24. Silberner, "Moses Hess als Begründer," 19–20.
25. Karl Marx, *Early Texts*, 39, 42.
26. Karl Marx, *Early Texts*, 64–67; Tosel, "Pour une étude systématique," 130–31; Hull, "Marx's Anomalous Reading," 21–22.
27. Marx and Engels, *Exzerpte und Notizen*, 240–41; Marx, "Cahier," 60–61; Dobbs-Weinstein, "The Paradox," 200–202; Morfino, "Marx lettore di Spinoza, " cues 42, 51, 112–13.
28. Hull, "Marx's Anomalous Reading," 22.
29. Dobbs-Weinstein, *Spinoza's Critique of Religion*, 67; Tosel, *Spinoza, ou l'autre (in)finitude*, 133–34.
30. Quoted in Dobbs-Weinstein, *Spinoza's Critique of Religion*, 67; Kouvelakis, *Philosophy and Revolution*, 304; Morfino, "Marx lettore di Spinoza," cues 112, 113, and 114.
31. Marx to Ruge, undated, Cologne, May 1843, Marx Engels Internet Archive, Letters Archive, *Deutsch-Französische Jahrbücher* (1843).
32. Marx to Ruge, undated, March (1843), Marx Engels Internet Archive, Letters Archive, *Deutsch-Französische Jahrbücher* (1843); Rosen, *Bruno Bauer and Karl Marx*, 148–49, 224, 231–32.
33. Dobbs-Weinstein, *Spinoza's Critique of Religion*, 68; Igoin, "De l'ellipse de la théorie," 215–16; Matheron, "*Traité Theologico-Politique* vu par le jeune Marx," 160, 212.
34. Marx, *The Revolutions*, 12; Na'aman, *Emanzipation und Messianismus*, 115.
35. Marx, *Critique of Hegel's "Philosophy of Right,"* 138, 142; Rosen, *Bruno Bauer and Karl Marx*, 214.
36. Rose, *Jewish Philosophical Politics*, 155; Avineri, *Karl Marx*, 25–26.
37. Marx, *Critique of Hegel's "Philosophy of Right,"* 29.
38. Matheron, "*Traité Theologico-Politique* vu par le jeune Marx," 182–83.
39. Karl Marx, "Remarks on the Latest Prussian Instruction on the Censorship," in Marx, *Early Texts*, 29–30; Rubel, "Marx à la recontre de Spinoza," 15.

40. Rosen, *Bruno Bauer and Karl Marx*, 176.
41. Evans, "Marx and the *Rheinische Zeitung*," 2–3, 24–25.
42. Avineri, "Marx and Jewish Emancipation," 445–50; Levin, *Jewish Socialist Movements*, 104.
43. Marx to Ruge, Cologne, 13 March 1843, Marx Engels Internet Archive, Letters Archive, *Deutsch-Französische Jahrbücher* (1843); Marx, *Early Texts*, 60; Evans, "Marx and the *Rheinische Zeitung*," 9.
44. Wistrich, "Socialism and Judeophobia," 118; Nirenberg, *Anti-Judaism*, 433–34, 437; Rotenstreich, "For and Against Emancipation," 9, 13–14.
45. Rotenstreich, "For and Against Emancipation," 3–6; Rose, *German Question/Jewish Question*, 263–76.
46. Bauer, *Geschichte der Politik, Cultur und Aufklärung*, 1:233–37.
47. Wistrich, "Socialism and Judeophobia," 118–19.
48. Hull, "Marx's Anomalous Reading," 25; Rotenstreich, "For and Against Emancipation," 23–24.
49. Evans, "Marx and the *Rheinische Zeitung*," 6.
50. Rotenstreich, "For and Against Emancipation," 11.
51. Rotenstreich, "For and Against Emancipation," 21–22.
52. Berlin, *Karl Marx*, 137, 157n.
53. Rotenstreich, "For and Against Emancipation," 32–34; Rose, *German Question/Jewish Question*, 274–78.
54. Berlin, *Against the Current*, 297–301, 457; Rose, *Jewish Philosophical Politics*, 268–70.
55. Fischer, *Socialist Response*, 40–42.
56. Berlin, *Karl Marx*, 252.
57. Frankel, *Crisis, Revolution, and Russian Jews*, 158–68, 300 Stern, *Jewish Materialism*, 15, 115, 130.
58. Levin, *Jewish Socialist Movements*, 105–7.
59. Kochan, *Jews, Idols and Messiahs*, 182–83.
60. Fischer, *Socialist Response*, 42; Levin, *Jewish Socialist Movements*, 382, 385.
61. Marx, *Critique of Hegel's "Philosophy of Right,"* 142.
62. Mansel, *Paris between Empires*, 390.
63. Stedman Jones, *Karl Marx*, 123, 156–57, 159, 161.
64. Rose, *German Question, Jewish Question*, 234–35; Elon, *Pity of It All*, 167.
65. Mansel, *Paris between Empires*, 390; Stedman Jones, *Karl Marx*, 150, 154, 208–12.
66. Avineri, *Karl Marx*, 55–57; Sammons, *Heinrich Heine*, 261–65.
67. Heine, *Deutschland*, 43, 174; Elon, *Pity of It All*, 144–45.
68. Heine, *Deutschland*, 85, 178; Elon, *Pity of It All*, 142–43.
69. Marcuse, "Heine and Marx," 118; Stedman Jones, *Karl Marx*, 162–63; Goetschel, *Heine and Critical Theory*, 49–50.
70. Kouvelakis, *Philosophy and Revolution*, 83.
71. Quoted in Marcuse, "Heine and Marx," 120–21; Berlin, *Karl Marx*, 97–98; Elon, *Pity of It All*, 144.

72. Sammons, *Heinrich Heine*, 262–63; Marcuse, "Heine and Marx," 116.
73. Marx and Engels, *Communist Manifesto*, 65; Marcuse, "Heine and Marx," 124.
74. Moreau, "La réception du spinozisme aux XIXe et XXe siècles," 248; Bianchi, "Marx's Reading of Spinoza," 49, 55.
75. Tosel, *Spinoza, ou l'autre (in)finitude*, 129; Albiac, "Sujets determinés," 105.
76. Ruge, *Polemische Briefe*, 374, 377; Stedman Jones, *Karl Marx*, 155–56, 334.
77. Ruge, *Polemische Briefe*, 412; Israel, *The Enlightenment That Failed*, 917–18.
78. Ruge, *Polemische Briefe*, 390, 398, 412; Wende, *Radikalismus im Vormärz*, 127–28; Vaccaro, *Socialismo e umanesimo*, 274, 278–80.
79. Albiac, "Sujets determinés," 100–101.
80. Haubtmann, *Proudhon*, 444–45.
81. Haubtmann, *Proudhon*, 632, 637.
82. Weitling to Hess, Brussels, 31 March 1846, in Hess, *Briefwechsel*, 150–51.
83. Weiss, *Moses Hess*, 72–76; Marx, *The Revolutions*, 1:36, 65; Stedman Jones, *Karl Marx*, 156, 334, 343.
84. Marx and Engels, *Communist Manifesto*, 59; Heller, *Moses Hess*, 18, 21; Berlin, *Karl Marx*, 136–37.
85. Marx and Engels, *Communist Manifesto*, 33.
86. Marx to Weydemeyer, London, 5 March 1852, in Marx and Engels, *Selected Works*, 2:452.
87. Lundgren, *Moses Hess on Religion*, 2.
88. Tosel, "Pour un étude systématique," 132–33; Vaccaro, *Socialismo e umanesimo*, 281.
89. Spinoza, *Political Treatise*, in Curley, *Collected Works*, 2:529.
90. Spinoza, *Political Treatise*, in Curley, *Collected Works*, 2:530; Bove, "Bêtes ou automates," 157.
91. Marx, "Cahier," 124–25; Israel, *The Enlightenment That Failed*, 921.
92. Smith, *Spinoza's Book of Life*, 78–79; Albiac, "Sujets determinés," 105, 107; Bove, "Bêtes ou automates," 157.
93. Matheron, "Louis Althusser," 89–92; Albiac, "Spinoza/Marx," 11; Tatián, *Spinoza, filosofía terrena*,12, 181–83; also on this, see the article by Jason Read, "Of Labour and Human Bondage: Spinoza, Marx and the 'Willing Slaves' of Capitalism," in the *Los Angeles Review of Books*, 9 December 2014.
94. Lordon, *Willing Slaves of Capital*, x.

CONCLUSION. JEWISH REVOLUTIONARIES, 1650–1850

1. Hollingdale, "Hero as Outsider," 74; Burrow, *Crisis of Reason*, 24–29, 54–55.
2. Hollingdale, "Hero as Outsider," 74–77; Israel, *The Enlightenment That Failed*, 923–42.
3. Malino, *A Jew in the French Revolution*, 206–7; Girard, *Révolution français et les Juifs*, 75–76, 89, 104.
4. Opaski and Bartal, *Poles and Jews*, 30–33, 72–76; Wistrich, *Jews of Vienna*, 134–35.
5. Lewald, *Year of Revolutions*, 124–25, 140; Elon, *Pity of It All*, 175–77.

6. Hess, *Rome and Jerusalem*, 40; Davies, *God's Playground*, 60, 247.
7. Davies, *God's Playground*, 25, 46, 68–69, 76; Sorkin, "Emancipation and Assimilation," 32–33.
8. Löwy, *Redemption and Utopia*, 190; Sutcliffe, *What Are Jews For?*, 57, 85, 105.
9. Frey, *Philosophie sociale*, 234–35. Girard writes "bon disciple de Rousseau et de Voltaire," which is misleading (see Girard, *Révolution français et les Juifs*, 215).
10. Löwy, *Redemption and Utopia*, 190.
11. Gorsas, *Courrier de Paris*, 2 February 1790, 394; Badinter, *Libres et égaux*, 172–73.
12. Kochan, *Jews, Idols and Messiahs*, 70–72.
13. Curthoys, "Moses Mendelssohn," 65–66; Feiner, *Moses Mendelssohn*, 215.
14. Pelluchon, *Leo Strauss and the Crisis*, 40–41; Gottlieb, *Faith and Freedom*, 116–17.
15. Israel, *The Enlightenment That Failed*, 503–4, 545–46, 553–54, 585–86, 611–12; Israel, *Revolutionary Ideas*, 534–35.
16. Lewald, *Year of Revolutions*, 16; Mansel, *Paris between Empires*, 432.
17. Stedman-Jones, *Karl Marx*, 261–62, 264, 267, 292; Sperber, *Rhineland Radicals*, 273, 300–301.
18. Quoted in Stedman Jones, *Karl Marx*, 271; Sperber, *Rhineland Radicals*, 301–4, 352.
19. Einhorn, *Spinozas Staatslehre*, 7.
20. Margalit, "Lessons of Spinoza," 73.
21. Einhorn, *Spinozas Staatslehre*, 10; Bolduc, *Kant et Spinoza*, 26–28.
22. Einhorn, *Spinozas Staatslehre*, 9–10.
23. Hess, *Rome and Jerusalem*, 17; Wistrich, *Jews of Vienna*, 394.
24. Feuerbach, *Principles*, 24.
25. Brenner, *Renaissance*, 130; Wertheim, *Salvation through Spinoza*, 12.
26. Schapkow, *Role Model and Countermodel*, 56.
27. Hess, *Rome and Jerusalem*, 41–44; Schapkow, *Role Model and Countermodel*, 57; Schwartz, "Our Rabbi Baruch," 45–46.
28. Stern, *Jewish Materialism*, 5–6, 11, 16, 71, 117–18.
29. Bukhbinder, "History of the Jewish Labor Movement," 428, 430; Venclova, *Vilnius*, 144–45.
30. Glatzer, *Franz Rosenzweig*, 216–18; Levin, *Jewish Socialist Movements*, 30–31, 35, 41; Stern, *Jewish Materialism*, 120, 123.
31. Stern, *Jewish Materialism*, 11, 15–16, 117, 237n29; Sapir, "Jewish Socialists," 365–67.
32. Sapir, "Jewish Socialists," 365, 368, 372, 377; Stern, *Jewish Materialism*, 116, 118, 121, 236.
33. Sapir, "Jewish Socialists," 383–84; Stern, *Jewish Materialism*, 5–6, 16, 116–17, 124–26.
34. Goldman, *My Disillusionment in Russia*, 228–30, 240–41, 246.
35. Stern, *Jewish Materialism*, 22, 143.
36. Goldman, *My Disillusionment in Russia*, 202–6, 208–10.
37. Stern, *Jewish Materialism*, 121.
38. Wistrich, *Revolutionary Jews*, 190, 192, 199; Service, *Trotsky*, 17, 42–43.
39. Wertheim, *Salvation through Spinoza*, 12–13, 30–31.

40. Walzer, *The Paradox of Liberation*; Cooper, "Turn to Tradition," 78–79.
41. Brenner, *Renaissance,* 131–34; Goetschel, *Spinoza's Modernity,* 272–76.
42. Wertheim, *Salvation through Spinoza*, 13–14.
43. Fischbach, *Production des hommes*, 171.
44. Schwartz, *First Modern Jew,* 189–98; Schwartz, "Our Rabbi Baruch," 45–46; Smith, *Reading Leo Strauss*, 31–32, 75–76.
45. Israel, introduction to Spinoza, *Theological-Political Treatise,* xvi, xxiv–xxx; Dobbs-Weinstein, "The Paradox," 198–203; Cooper, "Reevaluating Spinoza's Legacy," 476–78.
46. Margalit, "Lessons of Spinoza," 73–74.
47. Spinoza, *Tractatus Theologico-Politicus*, 55; Smith, *Spinoza, Liberalism and the Question*, 203–5; Harvey, "Spinoza's Counterfactual Zionism," 239, 241–43; Cooper, "Reevaluating Spinoza's Legacy," 481.

BIBLIOGRAPHY

ABBREVIATIONS

AHRF	*Annales historiques de la Révolution française*
BL	British Library, London
BMGN	*Bijdragen en Mededelingen betreffende de Geschiedenis der Nederlanden*
BN	Paris Bibliothèque Nationale
DJH	*Dutch Jewish History.* Proceedings of the Symposium on the History of the Jews of the Netherlands (Hebrew University of Jerusalem–Tel Aviv University).
EHR	*English Historical Review*
GA Amsterdam	Gemeentearchief Amsterdam (Amsterdam municipal archives)
GSJ	Moses Mendelssohn, *Gesammelte Schriften Jubiläumausgabe.* 38 vols. Stuttgart–Bad Cannstatt, 1971–.
JHI	*Journal of the History of Ideas*
JHPh	*Journal of the History of Philosophy*
JSS	*Jewish Social Studies*
LBIY	*The Leo Baeck Institute Yearbook*
PAJHS	*Publications of the American Jewish Historical Society*
SDIJ	*Simon-Dubnow-Institut Jahrbuch* (Yearbook)
SR	*Studia Rosenthaliana*
TTP	Benedict de Spinoza, *Tractatus Theologico-Politicus* (1670)

PRIMARY SOURCES

d'Argens, Jean-Baptiste de Boyer, marquis. *The Jewish Spy: Being a Philosophical, Historical and Critical Correspondence, By Letters which Lately pass'd between certain Jews in Turkey, Italy, France etc.* 4 vols. Dublin, 1753.

———. *Lettres Chinoises ou Correspondance philosophique, historique et critique.* 5 vols. The Hague, 1739.

———. *Lettres Juives.* Edited by J. Marx. 3 vols. Paris, 2013.

Basnage, Jacques. *Histoire des Juifs, depuis Jésus-Christ jusqu'à present.* 9 vols. The Hague, 1716.

Bauer, Bruno. *Geschichte der Politik, Cultur und Aufklärung des achtzehnten Jahrhunderts*. 2 vols. Berlin, 1844.

Bayle, Pierre. *Commentaire philosophique sur les paroles de Jésus-Christ, "Contrains les d'entrer."* Edited by Jean-Michel Gros. Paris, 1992.

———. *Dictionnaire historique et critique*. 4 vols. Rotterdam, 1700.

———. *Écrits sur Spinoza*. Edited by Charles-Daubert and Pierre-François Moreau. Paris, 1983.

Berlinische Monatsschrift. Edited by J. E. Biester and F. Gedike. 28 vols. Berlin, 1783–96.

Bibliotheca Sarraziana distrahenda par Abr. De Hondt et H. Scheurleer, Bilio Ad diem 16 Sept. 1715. The Hague, 1715.

Bodemann, E., ed. *Briefwechsel der Herzogin Sophie von Hannover mit ihrem Bruder dem Kurfürsten Karl Ludwig von der Pfalz*. Leipzig, 1885.

Bontekoe, Cornelis. *Brief Aen Johan Frederik Swetzer, Gesegt Dr Helvetius, Geschreven en Uytgegeven: Tot een Korte Apologie voor den Grote Philosooph Renatus Descartes en sijne regtsinnige navolgers*. The Hague, 1680.

Börne, Ludwig. *Briefe aus Paris, 1830–31*. 2 vols. Hamburg, 1832.

———. *Studien über Geschichte und Menschen der französischen Revolution*. Edited by Joseph Dresch. Lyon, 1952.

British Envoys to Germany, 1816–1866. Edited by S. Freitag, P. Wende and M. Mösslang. Vol. 1: *1816–29*. Cambridge, 2000. Vol. 2: *1830–47*. Cambridge, 2002.

[Cérutti, Joseph-Antoine]. *Bréviaire philosophique, ou Histoire du Judaïsme, du Christianisme et du Déisme*. N.p. [Paris ?], 1791.

Chronique de Paris (revolutionary journal). Paris, 1789–93.

Cloots, Anacharsis. *Lettre sur les Juifs à un ecclésiastique de mes amis*. Berlin, 1783.

Collins, Anthony. *A Discourse of the Grounds and Reasons of the Christian Religion*. London, 1724.

[Cuffeler, Abraham Johannes]. *Specimen artis ratiocinandi naturalis & artificialis ad pantosophiae principia manuducens*. "Hamburg" [Amsterdam?], 1684.

Da Costa, Uriel. *Examination of Pharisaic Traditions*. Edited by H. P. Salomon and I. S. D. Sassoon. Leiden, 1993.

De Pinto, Isaac. *Réflexions critiques*. In *Lettres de Quelques Juifs Portugais et Allemands à M. de Voltaire*, 2nd ed., [edited by Abbé Guenée], 7–43. Paris, 1769.

Démeunier, Jean-Nicolas. *L'Amérique indépendante, ou, Les différentes constitutions des Treize Provinces qui se sont érigées en républiques, sous le nom d'États-Unis de l'Amérique*. 3 vols. Ghent, 1790.

Desmoulins, Camille. *Le Vieux Cordelier* (journal: 1793–84). Edited by P. Pachet. Paris, 2010.

Diez, Heinrich Friedrich. *Apologie der Duldung und Pressefreyheit*. N.p. [Dessau?], 1781.

———. *Benedikt von Spinoza nach Leben und Lehren*. Dessau, 1783.

Diskurs gehalten tvishn yehudem in shif fun Itert [Utrecht] *nakh Amsterdam*. Amsterdam, 1797. In *Storm in the Community: Yiddish Polemical Pamphlets of Amsterdam Jewry 1797–98*, edited and translated by Jozeph Michman and Marion Aptroot, 28–61. Cincinatti, OH, 2002.

Dohm, Christian Wilhelm von. *Denkwürdigkeiten meiner Zeit, oder Beiträge zur Geschichte vom letzten Viertel des achtzehnten und vom Anfang des neunzehnten Jahrhunderts (1778 bis 1806).* 4 vols. Lemgo-Hannover, 1814.

———. *Geschichte der Engländer und Franzosen im östlichen Indien.* Leipzig, 1776.

———. *Über die bürgerliche Verbesserung der Juden.* Berlin, 1781.

Dumouriez, Charles-François. *Mémoires écrits par lui-meme.* 2nd ed. Frankfurt-Leipzig, 1794.

Einhorn, Ignac. *Spinozas Staatslehre: Zum ersten Male dargestellt.* Dessau, 1851.

Ewald, Schack Hermann. "Vorrede." In *Zwei Abhandlungen*, by B. de Spinoza, i–viii. Leipzig, 1785.

Fabricius, Johann Albert. *Delectus argumentorum et syllabis scriptorum qui veritatem religionis Christianae adversus atheos, epicureos lucubrationibus suis asseruerunt.* Hamburg, 1725.

Fare, Anne-Louis-Henri de la. *Opinion de M. l'évêque de Nancy député de Lorraine sur l'admissibilité des Juifs à la plénitude de l'état civil.* Paris, 1790.

Feuerbach, Ludwig. *Principles of the Philosophy of the Future.* Indianapolis, IN, 1986.

Fontana, A., et al., eds. *Venise et la Révolution française: Les 470 dépêches des ambassadeurs de Venise au Doge, 1786–1795.* Paris, 1997.

Frey, Lucius Junius [alias Moses Dobruska]. *Les Aventures politiques du Père Nicaise, ou l'Anti-Fédéraliste.* Paris, 1793.

———. *Philosophie sociale, dédiée au peuple françois.* Paris, 1793.

Goldman, Emma. *My Disillusionment in Russia.* 1923. New York, 2003.

Gorsas, Antoine-Joseph. *Le Courrier de Paris dans les 83 départemens* (later titled *Le Courrier des LXXXIII départemens*) (journal, 1790–91).

Hartog Lémon, Hartog de. *Aanspraak gedaan in de Societeit Felix Libertate op den 18 Februarij.* Amsterdam, 1795.

———. *Aanspraak uitgesproken in de kerk der Nieuwe Joodsche Gemeente binnen Amsterdam, Ten gelegenheid der inwyding derzelve op den 23 Junij 1797.* Amsterdam, 1797.

Heine, Heinrich. *Deutschland, a Winter's Tale.* Edited by T. J. Reed. 2nd ed. London, 1997.

———. *Ludwig Börne: Eine Denkschrift.* Edited by H. Koopman. In *Heinrich Heine: Historisch-kritische Gesamtausgabe der Werke,* edited by M. Windfuhr, vol. 11. Hamburg, 1978.

———. *On the History of Religion and Philosophy in Germany.* Edited by T. Pinkard. Cambridge, 2007.

———. "Über Polen." In *Reisebilder mit zeitgenössischen Illustrationen*, by Heine, 673–711. Frankfurt, 1980.

———. *Zur Geschichte der Religion und Philosophie in Deutschland.* In *Sämtliche Werke*, by Heine, 12 vols., 15:294. Hamburg, 1861.

Herder, Johann Gottfried. *Gott, Einige Gespräche über Spinoza's System.* 1787. 2nd ed. Gotha, 1800.

Hess, Moses. *Briefwechsel.* Edited by E. Silberner. The Hague, 1959.

———. *Die europäische Triarchie.* Leipzig, 1841. Reprint, Amsterdam, 1971.

———. *The Holy History of Mankind and Other Writings*. Edited by Shlomo Avineri. Cambridge, 2004.

———. *Rome and Jerusalem*. Translated by M. J. Bloom. New York, 1958.

Heydenreich, Karl Heinrich. *Natur und Gott nach Spinoza*. Leipzig, 1789.

Hourwitz, Zalkind. *Apologie des Juifs*. Paris, 1789. (BL Fr 170/8).

———. *Origine des langues*. Paris, n.d. [1808].

———. *Réponse à la question: Est-il des moyens de rendre les Juifs plus utiles et plus heureux en France?* (1787). In Birnbaum, "Est-il des moyens?," 87–104.

Houtteville, Claude-François, Abbé. *La Religion chrétienne prouvée par les faits*. 2 vols. Paris, 1740.

Israel, Menasseh ben. *The Hope of Israel*. Edited by H. Méchoulan and G. Nahon. Oxford, 2004.

Kant, Immanuel. *Briefwechsel*. Edited by H. E. Fischer. 3 vols. Munich, 1912.

———. "What Does It Mean to Orientate Oneself in Thinking?" In *Religion within the Boundaries of Mere Reason*, by Kant, edited by A. Wood and G. di Giovanni, 3–14. Cambridge, 1998.

[Knoblauch, Karl von]. *Euclides Anti-Thaumaturgicus, oder demonstrativer Beweis von der Unmöglichkeit hyperphysischer Begebenheiten*. "Germanien" [Weissenfels?], 1791.

———. *Taschenbuch für Aufklärer und Nichtaufklärer auf das Jahr 1791*. Berlin, 1790.

———. *Ueber Feerey. Auch ein Beitrag zu den Theorien des Wunderbaren*. Berlin, 1791.

Leibniz, G. W. *Theodicy: Essays on the Goodness of God and Freedom of Man and the Origin of Evil*. 1710. Edited by A. Farrer. La Salle, IL, 1985.

Lessing, Ephraim Gotthold. "The Education of the Human Race" (1777). In *Philosophical and Theological Writings*, by Lessing, translated and edited by H. B. Nisbet, 217–40. Cambridge, 2005.

———. *Gesammelte Werke*. Edited by P. Rilla. 10 vols. Berlin, 1954–58.

———. *Werke in drei Bänden*. Edited by P. H. G. Göpfert. Munich, 1982

Leti, Gregorio. *Teatro Belgico, o vero ritratti historici, chronologici, politici, e geografici delle Sette Provincie Unite*. 2 vols. Amsterdam, 1690.

Levi de Barrios, Daniel [Miguel]. *Triumpho del Govierno Popular en la casa de Jacob*. Amsterdam, 1683.

Lewald, Hanna Ballin. *A Year of Revolutions: Fanny Lewald's Recollections of 1848*. Providence, RI, 1997.

Leydekker, Melchior. *Historische en theologische redeneringe over het onlangs uitgegeven boek van* [. . .] *Balthasar Bekker*. Utrecht, 1692.

Lichtenberg, Georg Christoph. *Schriften und Briefe*. Edited by W. Promies. 6 vols. Munich, 1968.

———. *Werke: Aphorismen-Briefe-Aufsätze-Essays*. Hamburg, 1967.

Maimon, Solomon. *Essay on Transcendental Philosophy*. London, 2010.

———. *Lebensgeschichte*. Edited by Jakob Fromer. Munich, 1911.

Malouet, Pierre-Victor. *Mémoires*. 2 vols. Paris, 1868.

Maréchal, Sylvain. *Dictionnaire des Athées*. Edited by Jean-Pierre Jackson. Paris, 2008.

Marx, Karl. "Cahier: Spinoza's *Tractatus Theologico-Politicus.*" *Cahiers Spinoza* 1 (1977): 31–157.

———. *Critique of Hegel's "Philosophy of Right."* Edited by Joseph O'Mally. Cambridge, 1970.

———. *Early Texts.* Edited by David McLellan. Oxford, 1971.

———. *The Revolutions of 1848: Political Writings.* Vol. 1. Edited by David Fernbach. Harmondsworth, 1973.

Marx, Karl, and Friedrich Engels. *Exzerpte und Notizen bis 1842.* Berlin, 1976.

———. *Die heilige Familie und Schriften von Marx von Anfang 1944 bis Anfang 1845.* In *Gesamtausgabe, Erste Abteilung,* by Marx/Engels, vol. 3. Berlin, 1932. Reprint, Moscow, 1970.

———. *The Holy Family, or Critique of Critical Critique.* Moscow, 1956.

———. *Manifesto of the Communist Party* (1848). In *Selected Works in Two Volumes,* by Marx and Engels, 5th impr., 2 vols., 1:13–65. Moscow, 1962.

Mendelssohn, Moses. *An die Freunde Lessings* (1786). In *GSJ*, vol. 3, part ii, 177–218.

———. *Gesammelte Schriften Jubiläumausgabe* (*GSJ*). 38 vols. Stuttgart–Bad Cannstatt, 1971–.

———. *Jerusalem oder über Macht und Judenthum* (1783). In *GSJ*, vol. 8, edited by A. Altmann, 99–204.

———. *Morgenstunden oder Vorlesungen über das Daseyn Gottes.* In *GSJ*, vol. 3, part ii, 1–175.

———. *Writings on Judaism, Christianity and the Bible.* Edited by Michah Gottlieb. Lebanon, NH, 2011.

Merkwaardig en zonderling mond-gesprek, tusschen een gereformeerd christen en een portugeesche jood mitsgaders de bekering dezer laatste. Amsterdam, 1757.

Michman, Jozeph, and Marion Aptroot, eds. *Storm in the Community: Yiddish Polemical Pamphlets of Amsterdam Jewry, 1797–1798.* Cincinnati, OH, 2002.

Mirabeau, Gabriel-Honoré, comte de. *Essai sur Moses Mendelssohn, sur la réforme politique des Juifs, et en particulier sur la révolution tentée en leur faveur en 1753 dans la Grande Bretagne.* "Londres" [Berlin?], 1787.

———. *De la monarchie prussienne sous Frédéric le Grand.* 6 vols. "Londres," 1788.

Molitor, Franz Joseph, *Histoire de l'ordre des Frères de Saint Jean l'Évangéliste d'Asie et d'Europe.* Milan, 1989.

Naigeon, Jacques-André. *Adresse à l'Assemblée nationale sur la liberté des opinions, sur celle de la presse, etc.* Paris, 1790.

[Nassy, David de Ishac Cohen]. "Discours préliminaire." In *Lettre politico-théologico-morale sur les Juifs,* by Nassy, 1–lx. Paramaribo, 1798.

———. *Essai historique sur la colonie de Surinam.* 2 vols. Paramaribo, 1788.

———. "A Letter of David Nassy, of Surinam." Edited by S. Oppenheim. *PAJHS* 23 (1915): 185–86.

———. *Lettre-politico-théologico-morale sur les Juifs.* Paramaribo, 1798.

———. *Observations sur la cause, la nature et le traitement de la maladie épédemique qui règne à Philadelphie.* Philadelphia, 1793.

Nieto, David. *De la Divina Providencia.* 1704. 2nd ed. London, 1716.

Orobio de Castro, Isaac. *Certamen philosophicum, propugnatae veritatis divinae ac naturalis.* Amsterdam, 1703.
———. *Israel Vengé, ou Exposition naturelle des prophètes hebraïques que les chrétiens appliquent à Jésus, leur prétendu Messie.* Edited by d'Holbach. "Londres," 1770.
———. *La Observancia de la Divina Ley de Mosseh.* Edited by Jacobo Israel Garzón. Barcelona, n.d.
———. *Prevenciones divinas contra la vana idolatría de las gentes.* Edited by M. Silvera. Florence, 2013.
Pérez, Antonio. *Relaciones y cartas.* 2 vols. Madrid, 1986.
Ramsay, David. *The History of the American Revolution.* Edited by I. H. Cohen. 2 vols. Indianoplis, IN, 1989.
Rehberg, August Wilhelm. *Sämtliche Schriften.* 4 vols. Hanover, 1828–29.
Reimarus, Johann Albrecht Heinrich. "Vorerinnerung von dem Daseyn Gottes und der menschlichen Seele." In *Abhandlungen von den vornehmsten Wahrheiten*, by Reimarus, 5th ed., 1–46. Hamburg, 1781.
Reinhold, Karl Reinhold. *Letters on the Kantian Philosophy.* Edited by Karl Ameriks. Cambridge, 2005.
Riesser, Gabriel. *Börne und die Juden.* Altenburg, 1832.
Ruge, Arnold. *Anekdota.* 2 vols. Zurich and Winterthur, 1843.
———. *Briefwechsel und Tagebuchblätter aus den Jahren 1825–1880.* Edited by P. Nerrlich. 2 vols. Berlin, 1886.
———. *Polemische Briefe.* Mannheim, 1847.
———. *Sämtliche Werke.* 2nd ed. 4 vols. Mannheim, 1847.
———. "A Self-Critique of Liberalism" (1843). In *The Young Hegelians. An Anthology*, edited by L. S. Stepelevich, 237–59. Atlantic Highlands, NJ, 1983.
———. *Zwei Jahre in Paris: Studien und Erinnerungen.* 2 vols. Leipzig, 1846.
Rush, Benjamin. *Letters of Benjamin Rush.* Edited by L. H. Butterfield. 2 vols. Princeton, NJ, 1951.
Saint-Just, Antoine-Louis de. *Oeuvres complètes.* Edited by A. Kupiec and M. Abensour. Paris, 2004.
Salfi, Francesco Severio. *L'Italie au dix-neuvième siècle.* Paris, 1821.
Schelling, F. W. J. *The Ages of the World.* Translated by P. Lawrence. Albany, NY, 2019.
[Schulz, Johann Heinrich]. *Der entlarvte Moses Mendelssohn.* Amsterdam, 1786.
Shelley, Percy Bysshe. *The Poetical Works.* Edited by H. Buxton Forman. 5 vols. London, 1892.
Spandaw, Willem. *De Onbedekte Spinosist in de persoon van Pontiaan van Hattem.* Goes, 1700.
Spinoza, Benedict de. *Briefwisseling.* Edited and translated by Fokke Akkerman et al. Amsterdam, 1992.
———. *The Collected Works.* Edited by Edwin Curley. 2 vols. Princeton, NJ, 1985–2016.
———. *The Letters.* Translated by S. Shirley. Indianapolis, IN, 1995.
———. *Opera.* Edited by Carl Gebhardt. 5 vols. Heidelberg, 1925. Reprint, 1987.
———. *Theological-Political Treatise.* 1670. Edited by J. I. Israel. Cambridge, 2007.

———. *Tractatus Politicus*. In *The Political Works*, by Spinoza, edited by A. G. Wernham. Oxford, 1958.

———. *Tractatus Politicus*. In Spinoza, *Collected Works*, edited by Curley, vol. 2.

Stouppe, J. B. *La Religion des Hollandois*. Cologne, 1673.

Thiéry, Claude Antoine. *Dissertation sur cette question: Est-il des moyens de rendre les Juifs plus heureux et plus utiles en France?* Paris, 1788.

Toland, John. *Reasons for Naturalizing the Jews in Great Britain and Ireland*. London, 1714.

Van Limborch, Philippus. *De Veritate religionis christianae Amica Collatio con erudito judaeo*. Gouda, 1687.

———. *Vriendelyke onderhandeling met een geleerden Jood over de waarheit van den christelycken godsdienst*. Amsterdam, 1723.

Verheul, Abraham, *Redevoering over de gelijkheid der menschen, beschouwd als dat algemeen beginsel, het welk den vrijen Nederlander tot gids behoort te strekken in het vestigen zijner politiecque en burgerlijke vrijheid*. Amsterdam, 1795.

[Veyssière de La Croze, Mathurin]. *Entretiens sur divers sujets d'histoire et de religion entre Mylord Bolingbroke, et Isaac d'Orobio, rabin des Juifs portugais à Amsterdam*. "Londres" [Amsterdam ?], 1770.

Wekhrlin, Wilhelm Ludwig. *Das graue Ungeheuer* (periodical, 31 vols., Nuremberg, 1784–87).

Wirth, Johann Georg August. *Rede von Johann Georg August Wirth auf dem Hambacher Fest 1832*. In *Das Nationalfest der Deutschen zu Hambach*, by Wirth, 31–41. Neustadt an der Haardt, 1832.

Witsius, Herman. *Meletemata Leidensia quibus continentur praelectiones de vita et rebus gestis Pauli Apostoli*. Leiden, 1703.

Wolf, Johann Christoph. *Bibliotheca Hebraea*. 4 vols. Hamburg, 1715–33.

SECONDARY SOURCES

Aaslestad, Katherine. *Place and Politics, Local Identity, Civic Culture and German Nationalism*. Leiden, 2005.

Abramsky, Chimen. "The Crisis of Authority within European Jewry in the Eighteenth Century." In *Studies in Jewish Religious and Intellectual History Presented to Alexander Altmann*, edited by S. Stein and R. Loewe, 13–28. Tuscaloosa, AL, 1979.

Albiac, Gabriel. "Sujets déterminés: Entre Althusser et Lacan, Spinoza." In *Lectures contemporainies de Spinoza*, edited by Cl. Cohen-Boulakia, M. Delbraccio, and Pierre-François Moreau, 95–107 Paris, 2012.

Alston, Patrick L. *Education and the State in Tsarist Russia*. Stanford, CA, 1969.

Altena, Peter. *Gerrit Paape (1752–1803), Levens en werken*. Nijmegen, 2012.

Altmann, Alexander. *Moses Mendelssohn: A Biographical Study*. London, 1973.

Aprile, Silvie. "Des cantons suisses aux États allemands." In *La Liberté guidant les peuples—Les révolutions de 1830 en Europe*, edited by Aprile, J. C. Caron, and E. Fureix. Toulouse, 2013.

Aptroot, Marion. "Yiddish, Dutch and German among Late 18th century Amsterdam Jewry." In Israel and Salverda, eds., *Dutch Jewry*, 201–11.
Arana, Marie. *Bolívar: American Liberator.* London, 2014.
Arbell, Mordechai. *The Jewish Nation of the Caribbean: The Spanish-Portuguese Jewish Settlements in the Caribbean and the Guianas.* Jerusalem, 2002.
Arendt, Hannah. *On Revolution.* New York, 1963.
———. *Rahel Varnhagen, the Life of a Jewess.* London, 1957.
Arkush, A. "Montesquieu: A Precursor of Jewish Emancipation?" In Zinguer and Bloom, eds., *L'Antisémitisme éclairé*, 45–59, 113.
———. "The Questionable Judaism of Moses Mendelssohn." *New German Critique* 77 (1999): 29–44.
———. "Solomon Maimon and His Jewish Philosophical Predecessors." In Brann and Sutcliffe eds., *Renewing the Past*, 14–66.
Aston, Nigel. *Religion and Revolution in France 1780–1804.* Basingstoke, 2000.
Avineri, Shlomo. *Karl Marx: Philosophy and Revolution.* New Haven, CT, 2019.
———. "Marx and Jewish Emancipation." *JHI* 25, no. 3 (1964): 445–50.
———. *Moses Hess: Prophet of Communism and Zionism.* New York, 1985.
Badinter, Elisabeth, and Robert Badinter. *Condorcet: Un intellectuel en politique.* Paris, 1988.
Badinter, Robert. *Libres et égaux: L'Emancipation des Juifs (1789–1791).* Paris, 1989.
Balibar, Étienne. *Spinoza et la politique.* 1984. 4th ed. Paris, 2019.
Barnikol, Ernst. *Das entdeckte Christentum im Vormärz: Bruno Bauers Kampf gegen Religion und Christentum.* Jena, 1927.
Bartoszewski, Wladyslaw, and A. Polonsky, eds. *The Jews in Warsaw.* Oxford, 1991.
Battenberg, J. F. "Die Französische Revolution und die Emanzipation der Juden im Elsass und Lothringen." In *Die Französische Revolution und die Oberrheinlande 1789–1798*, edited by Volker Rödl, *Oberheinische Studien* 9, 245–73. Ostfildern, 1991.
———. "Jews in Ecclesiastical Territories of the Holy Roman Empire." In *In and Out of the Ghetto: Jewish-Gentile Relations in Late Medieval and Early Modern Germany*, edited by R. Po-chia Hsia and H. Lehmann, 247–74. Cambridge, 1995.
Bayer, Oswald. "Spinoza im Gespräch zwischen Hamann und Jacobi." In *Spinoza im Deutschland des achtzehnten Jahrhunderts*, edited by Eva Schürmann, N. Waszek, and F. Weinreich, 319–25. Stuttgart, 2002.
Beiser, Frederick. *Enlightenment, Revolution and Romanticism. The Genesis of Modern German Political Thought (1790–1800).* Cambridge, MA, 1992.
———. "The Enlightenment and Idealism." In *The Cambridge Companion to German Idealism*, edited by K. Ameriks, 18–36. Cambridge, 2000.
———. *German Idealism: The Struggle against Subjectivism, 1781–1801.* Cambridge, MA, 2002.
———. *Hermann Cohen: An Intellectual Biography.* Oxford, 2018.
———. "Maimon and Fichte." In Freudenthal, ed., *Salomon Maimon*, 233–48.
Benítez, Miguel. *Le Foyer clandestin des Lumières: Nouvelles recherches sur les manuscrits clandestins.* 2 vols. Paris, 2013.

———. “Liste et localisation des traités clandestins.” In *Le Matérialisme du XVIIIe et la littérature clandestine*, edited by Olivier Bloch, 17–25. Paris, 1982.
———. “Matériaux pour un inventaire des manuscrits philosophiques clandestins des XVIIe et XVIIIe siècles.” *Rivista di Storia della filosofia* 3 (1988): 501–31.
———. “Orobio de Castro et la littérature clandestine.” In *Le Matérialisme du XVIIIe siècle et la littérature clandestine*, edited by Olivier Bloch, 219–26. Paris, 1982.
Bensussan, Gérard. *Moses Hess: La Philosophie, le socialisme* (1836–1845). Hildesheim, 2006.
Ben-Ur, Aviva. “The Cultural Heritage of Eurafrican Sephardi Jews in Suriname.” In *The Jews in the Caribbean*, edited by J. S. Gerber, 169–93. Oxford, 2014.
Berger, Shhlomo. “Unzer Bruder Shpinoza: Modern Yiddish Writers and the Amsterdam Freethinker.” *SR* 30 (1996): 254–56.
———. “Yidddish on the Borderline of Modernity: Language and Literature in Early Modern Ashkenazi Culture.” *SDIJ* 6 (2007): 113–22.
Berlin, Isaiah. *Against the Current. Essays in the History of Ideas.* Edited by Henry Hardy. 2nd ed. Princeton, NJ, 2013.
———. *The Crooked Timber of Humanity. Chapters in the History of Ideas.* Edited by Henry Hardy. 2nd ed. Princeton, NJ, 2013.
———. *Karl Marx.* Edited by Henry Hardy. 5th ed. Princeton, NJ, 2013.
———. *The Life and Opinions of Moses Hess.* Cambridge, 1959.
Bernardini, Paolo, and Diego Lucci. *The Jews, Instructions for Use: Four Eighteenth-Century Projects for the Emancipation of European Jews.* Boston, 2012.
Berti, Silvia. *Anticristianesimo e libertà: Studi sul primo Illuminismo.* Bologna, 2012.
Bethencourt, Francisco. *The Inquisition: A Global History, 1478–1834.* Cambridge, 2011.
Bianchi, Bernardo. “Marx’s Reading of Spinoza: On the Alleged Influence of Spinoza on Marx.” *Historical Materialism* 26 (2018): 35–58.
Bienenstock, Myriam. “Hermann Cohens Heine und der Kampf um Spinoza.” *Heine Jahrbuch* 2010, 192–200.
Bijlsma, R. “David de Is. C. Nassy, Author of the *Essai historique sur Surinam.*” In Cohen, ed., *The Jewish Nation in Surinam*, 65–73. Amsterdam, 1982.
Birnbaum, Pierre. “Est-il de moyens de rendre les Juifs plus utiles et plus heureux?” *Le Concours de l’Académie de Metz.* 1787. Paris, 2017.
Blanco Echauri, Jésus. “Espinosa y el pensamiento político del Barroco español.” In Domínguez, ed., *Spinoza y España*, 179–90.
Blanco Mayor, Carmelo. “Quevedo y Spinoza.” In Domínguez, ed., *Spinoza y España*, 191–99.
Bloch, H. “Dr. David d’Isaac Nassy.” *Journal of the American Medical Association* (10 February 1969): 1228.
Bloemgarten, Salvador. “De Amsterdamse Joden gedurende de eerste jaren van de Bataafse Republiek (1795–98).” *SR* 1 (1967): 66–96; and *SR* 2 (1968): 42–65.
———. *Hartog de Hartog Lémon: Joodse revolutionair in Franse Tijd.* Amsterdam, 2007.
Bock, Helmut. *Ludwig Börne: Vom Gettojuden zum Nationalschriftsteller.* Berlin, 1962.

Bodian, Miriam. *Dying in the Law of Moses: Crypto-Jewish Martyrdom in the Iberian World*. Bloomington, IN, 2000.

———. "The Portuguese Jews in Amsterdam and the Language of Liberty." *Journal of Levantine Studies* 6 (2016): 313–32.

———. "Some Ideological Implications of Marrano Involvement in the International Arena." In *Society and Community: Proceedings of the Second International Congress for Research of the Sephardi and Oriental Jewish Heritage*, edited by Abraham Haim, 207–17. Jerusalem, 1991.

Boehm, Omri. *Kant's Critique of Spinoza*. Oxford, 2014.

Bohnen, Klaus. "Lessing und Dänemark." In *Nation und Gelehrtenrepublik: Lessing im europäischen Zusammenhang* (Sonderband, Lessing Yearbook), edited by W. Barner and M. Reh, 305–14. Munich, 1984.

Bohnert, Christiane. "Enlightenment and Despotism: Two Worlds in Lessing's *Nathan the Wise*." In *Impure Reason: Dialectic of Enlightenment in Germany*, edited by W. Daniel Wilson and R. Holub, 344–63. Detroit, 1993.

Bolduc, Carl. *Kant et Spinoza: Rencontre paradoxale*. Paris, 2015.

Bonald, Louis-Gabriel Amboise, vicomte de. *François Chabot, Membre de la Convention (1756–1794)*. Paris, 1908.

Borges Coelho, Antonio. "Los Orígenes de Bento de Espinosa." In *Familia, Religión y negocio: El Sefardismo en las relaciones entre el mundo ibérico y los Países Bajos en la edad moderna*, edited by Jaime Contreras, Bernardo J. García, and Inacio Pulido. Madrid, 2002.

Bourel, Dominique. "La Judéophobie savante dans l'Allemagne des Lumières: Johann David Michaelis." In Zinguer and Bloom, eds., *L'Antisémitisme éclairé*, 125–38.

———. *Moses Mendelssohn: La naissance du judaïsme moderne*. Paris, 2004.

Bove, Laurent. "'Bêtes out automates': La Différence anthropologique dans la politique spinoziste." In *Lectures contemporaines de Spinoza*, edited by Moreau et al., 157–78.

Boyden, J. M. "Fortune Has Stripped You of Your Splendour: Favorites and Their Fates in Fifteenth- and Sixteenth-Century Spain." In *The World of the Favourite*, edited by J. H. Elliott and L. W. B. Brockliss, 26–37. New Haven, CT, 1999.

Brann, R., and Adam Sutcliffe, eds. *Renewing the Past, Reconfiguring Jewish Culture from al-Andalus to the* Haskalah. Philadelphia, 2004.

Brenner, Michael. *The Renaissance of Jewish Culture in Weimar Germany*. New Haven, CT, 1996.

Brod, Max. *Heinrich Heine: The Artist in Revolt*. London, 1956.

Broers, Michael. *Europe under Napoleon*. 1996. New ed., London, 2015.

Brogi, Stefano. *Il Cerchio dell' universo: Libertinismo, Spinozismo e filosofia della natura in Boulainvilliers*. Florence, 1993.

Bromwich, David. *The Intellectual Life of Edmund Burke*. Cambridge, MA, 2014.

Brown, Matthew. "Impious Adventurers: Mercenaries, Honour and Patriotism in the Wars of Independence in Gran Colombia." University of London, Ph.d. diss., 2004.

———. "Rebellion at Riohacha, 1820." *Jahrbuch für Geschichte Lateinamerikas* 42 (1964): 77–98.

Brykman, Geneviève. *La Judéité de Spinoza*. Paris, 1972.
Bukhbinder, Naum Abramovich. "A History of the Jewish Labour Movement in Russia." In *The Posen Library of Jewish Civilization* VIII, edited by T. M. Endelman et al., 427–30. New Haven, CT, 2020.
Burrow, J. W. *The Crisis of Reason: European Thought, 1848–1914*. New Haven, CT, 2000.
Butler, E. M. *The Saint-Simonian Religion in Germany: A Study of the Young German Movement*. Cambridge, 1926.
Buzaglo, Meir. *Solomon Maimon: Monism, Skepticism and Mathematics*. Pittsburgh, PA, 2002.
Caballero, P. "La Crítica de Orobio de Castro a Spinoza." In A. Domínguez, ed., *Spinoza y España*, 229–38.
Calmann, M. *The Carrière of Carpentras*. Oxford, 1984.
Caransa, Ab. *Vrijmetselarij en jodendom: De wereld een tempel*. Hilversum, 2001.
Carayol, E. *Thémiseul de Saint Hyacinthe*. Paris-Oxford, 1984.
Cardot, Carlos Felice. *Curazao hispánico: Antagonismo flamenco-español*. Caracas, 1982.
Carvalho, Jean-Paul, and M. Koyama. "Jewish Emancipation and Schism: Economic Development and Religious Change." *Journal of Comparative Economics* 44 (2016): 562–84.
Carvalho, Joaquim de. "Orobio de Castro e o espinosismo." *Memorias da Academia das Ciencias de Lisboa: Clase de Letras* 2 (1936): 183–252.
Casarino, Cesare. "Marx before Spinoza: Notes toward an Investigation." In *Spinoza Now*, edited by D. Vardoulakis, 179–234. Minneapolis, 2011.
Champion, Justin. "Toleration and Citizenship in Enlightenment England: John Toland and the Naturalization of the Jews, 1714–1753." In *Toleration in Enlightenment Europe*, edited by Ole Grell and Roy Porter, 133–56. Cambridge, 2000.
Chisick, Harvey. "Community and Exclusion in Rousseau and Voltaire: The Case of the Jews." In Zinguer and Bloom, eds., *L'Antisémitisme éclairé*, 77–104.
Christ, Kurt. "Johann Georg Hamann (1730–1788): Eine Portraitskizze." In *Johann Georg Hamann, 1788. Quellen und Forschungen*, edited by R. Knoll, 233–76. Bonn, 1988.
Cohen, Hermann. "Heinrich Heine und das Judenthum." In *Heine und die Nachwelt*, 184–88. Berlin, 2006.
———. *Spinoza on State and Religion, Judaism and Christianity*. Translated by R. S. Shine. Jerusalem, 2014.
Cohen, Robert, ed. *The Jewish Nation in Surinam: Historical Essays*. Amsterdam, 1982.
———. *Jews in Another Environment: Surinam in the Second Half of the Eighteenth Century*. Leiden, 1991.
Cooper, Julie. "Reevaluating Spinoza's Legacy for Jewish Political Thought." *Journal of Politics* 79 (2017): 473–84.
———. "Statesmen versus Philosophers: Experience and Method in Spinoza's *Political Treatise*." In Melamed and Sharp, eds., *Spinoza's Political Treatise*, 29–46.

———. "The Turn to Tradition in the Study of Jewish Politics." *Annual Review of Political Science* 19 (2016): 67–87.

Cottebrune, Anne. *Mythe et réalité du "Jacobinisme allemande": Des "Amis de la Révolution" face à l'épreuve de la réalité révolutionnaire.* Lille, 2001.

Crouter, Richard. *Friedrich Schleiermacher: Between Enlightenment and Romanticism.* Cambridge, 2005.

Crouter, Richard, and J. Klassen, eds. *A Debate on Jewish Emancipation and Christian Theology in Old Berlin.* Indianapolis, IN, 2004.

Curley, Edwin. "Kissinger, Spinoza and Genghis Khan." In *The Cambridge Companion to Spinoza*, edited by Don Garrett. Cambridge, 1996,

———. "Spinoza's Lost Defense." In Melamed, ed., *The Young Spinoza*, 9–51.

Curthoys, Ned. "Moses Mendelssohn and the Character of Virtue." In *Representing Humanity in the Age of Enlightenment*, edited by Alexander Cook, 65–78. London, 2013.

Dagron, Tristan. *Toland et Leibniz. L'Invention du néo-Spinozisme.* Paris, 2009.

Davies, Helen M. "Friendship in the Revolution: A Sephardic Correspondence." *French History and Civilization: Papers for the George Rudé Seminar* 4 (2011): 65–80.

Davis, Natalie Zemon. "David Nassy's "Furlough" and the Slave Mattheus." In *New Essays in American Jewish History*, edited by P. S. Nadell et al., 79–93. Cincinatti, OH, 2010.

———. "Een joodse arts in het achttiende-eeuwse Suriname." In *Joden in de Cariben*, edited by Julie-Marthe Cohen, 158–73. Zutphen, 2015.

Davies, Norman. *God's Playground: A History of Poland.* Vol. 2: *1795 to the Present.* Oxford, 1981.

De Dijn, Herman. *Spinoza: The Way to Wisdom.* West Lafayette, IN, 1996.

De Kom, Anton. *Wij slaven van Suriname.* 1934. Reprint, Amsterdam, 1999.

Den Boer, Harm. "Isaac Orobio de Castro as a Writer." In Wilke, ed., *Isaac Orobio*, 72–92.

Den Tex, Jan. *Oldenbarnevelt.* 5 vols. Haarlem, 1960–72.

De Vries. Marleen de. *Beschaven! Letterkundige genootschappen in Nederland, 1750–1800.* Nijmegen, 2001.

Desprat, Jean-Paul. *Mirabeau: L'excès et le retrait.* Paris, 2008.

Divendal, Joost. "Mozes Cohen Belinfante, Jew to the Depth of His Soul." *SR* 31 (1997): 94–138.

Dobbs-Weinstein, Idit. "The Paradox of a Perfect Democracy: From Spinoza's *Theological-Political Treatise* to Marx's Critique of Ideology. In *Between Hegel and Spinoza: A Volume of Critical Essays*, edited by H. Sharp and J. E. Smith, 189–208. London, 2012.

———. *Spinoza's Critique of Religion and Its Heirs, Marx, Benjamin, Adorno.* Cambridge, 2015.

Domínguez, Atilano. "Presencia de Antonio Pérez en Spinoza." In Domínguez, ed., *Spinoza y España*, 165–78.

———., ed. *Spinoza y España: Actas del congreso internacional sobre "Relaciones entre Spinoza y España."* Murcia, 1994.

Dresch, Joseph. "Introduction et commentaire." In Ludwig Börne, *Studien*, 1–52.

Drozdowski, Marian. "The Jews of Warsaw under King Stanislaw August." In Bartoszewaki and Polonsky, eds., *The Jews in Warsaw*, 84–94.

Duprat, Annie. "Le Sacre de Charles X: Justifications et critiques." In *Repenser la Restauration, actes du colloque de Saint-Quentin-en-Yvelines de septembre 2003*, edited by Jean-Yves Mollier et al., 69–84. Paris, 2005.

Duzinkiewicz, Janusz. *Fateful Transformations: The Four Years' Parliament and the Constitution of May 3, 1791*. New York, 1993.

Dweck, Yaacob. *Dissident Rabbi: The Life of Jacob Sasportas*. Princeton, NJ, 2019.

Dynner, Glenn. *Yankel's Tavern: Jews, Liquor, and Life in the Kingdom of Poland*. Oxford, 2014.

Eckstein, Walter. "Rousseau and Spinoza: Their Political Theories and Their Conceptions of Ethical Freedom." *JHI* 5 (1944): 259–91.

Eisenbach, Artur. *The Emancipation of the Jews of Poland*. Oxford, 1991.

———. "The Jewish Population in Warsaw at the End of the Eighteenth Century." In Bartoszewaki and Polonsky, eds., *The Jews in Warsaw*, 95–126.

Eitan, Ruthie. "A Duel of Victorious Violence?" In Zinguer and Bloom, eds., *L'Antisémitisme éclairé*, 275–85.

Elliott, J. H. *The Revolt of the Catalans (1598–1640)*. Cambridge, 1963.

Elon, Amos. *The Pity of It All: A Portrait of Jews in Germany 1743–1933*. London, 2002.

Elyada, Ouzi. "La Presse parisienne de droite et la question juive sous la Révolution française." In *Les Juifs en France au XVIIIe siècle*, edited by B. Blumenkrantz, 223–38. Paris, 1994.

———. "La rhétorique antijuive dans la presse contre-révolutionnaire 1789–1792." In Zinguer and Bloom, eds., *L'Antisémitisme éclairé*, 141–50.

Emmanuel, I. S., and Emmanuel, S. A. *History of the Jews of the Netherlands Antilles*. 2 vols. Cinncinatti, OH, 1970.

Enzensberger, Hans Magnus. *Ludwig Börne und Heinrich Heine: Ein deutsches Zerwürfnis*. Frankfurt, 1997.

Euwens, P. A. "Admiral Pedro Luis Brión." *Nieuwe-West-Indische Gids* 3 (1922): 449–65.

Evans, Michael. "Marx and the *Rheinische Zeitung*." *Manchester Papers in Politics* 5 (1995): 1–26.

Fatah-Black, Karwan. "The Patriot *coup d'état* in Curaçao, 1796." In Klooster and Oostindie, eds., *Curaçao in the Age of Revolutions*, 123–40.

Faur, José. "David Nassy: On Prejudice and Related Matters." In *Neveh Ya'akov: Jubilee Volume Presented to Dr. Jaap Meijer*, edited by L. Dasberg and Jonathan Cohen, 87–116. Assen, 1982.

Feiner, Shmuel. *Moses Mendelssohn: Sage of Modernity*. New Haven, CT, 2010.

———. "On the Threshold of the "New World"—*Haskalah* and Secularization in the Eighteenth Century." *SDIJ* 6 (2007): 33–45.

———. *The Origins of Jewish Secularization in Eighteenth-Century Europe.* Philadelphia, 2011.

———. "Seductive Science and the Emergence of the Secular Jewish Intellectual." *Science in Context* 15 (2002): 121–35.

Feuer, Lewis S. *Spinoza and the Rise of Liberalism.* 1958. Reprint, Westport, CT, 1983.

Finch, Alison. *French Literature: A Cultural History.* Cambridge, MA, 2010.

Fischbach, Franck, *La Production des hommes: Marx avec Spinoza.* 2005. 2nd ed. 2018.

Fischer, Lars. *The Socialist Response to Antisemitism in Imperial Germany.* Cambridge, 2007.

Foot, Paul. *Red Shelley.* 1984. New ed., London, 2004.

Forster, Michael N. "Herder and Spinoza." In Förster and Melamed, eds., *Spinoza and German Idealism*, 5–84.

Förster, E., and Yitzchak Melamed, eds. *Spinoza and German Idealism.* Cambridge, 2012.

Fortescue, William. *Alphonse de Lamartine: A Political Biography.* London, 1983.

Francesconi, Federica. "From Ghetto to Emancipation: The Role of Moise Formiggini." *Jewish History* (2010): 331–54.

Frankel, Jonathan. *Crisis, Revolution, and Russian Jews.* Cambridge, 2009.

Freudenthal, Gad. "New Light on the Physician Aaron Salomon Gumpertz: Medicine, Science and Early *Haskalah* in Berlin." *Zutot: Perspectives on Jewish Culture* 3 (2003): 66–77.

Freudenthal, Gideon. "Maimon's Subversion of Kant's *Critique of Pure Reason.*" In Freudenthal, ed., *Salomon Maimon*, 144–75.

———. "A Philosopher between Two Cultures." In Freudenthal, ed., *Salomon Maimon*, 1–17.

———., ed. *Salomon Maimon: Rational Dogmatist, Empirical Skeptic: Critical Reassessments.* Dordrecht, 2003.

Fuks, L., and R. G. Fuks-Mansfeld. *Hebrew and Judaic Manuscripts in Amsterdam Public Collections.* 2 vols. Leiden, 1973–75.

Fuks-Mansfeld, R. G. "Enlightenment and Emancipation from c. 1750 to 1814." In *History of the Jews in the Netherlands*, edited by J. C. H. Blom, R. G. Fuks-Mansfeld, and I. Schöffer, 164–91. Oxford, 2002.

———. *De Sefardim in Amsterdam tot 1795.* Hilversum, 1989.

———. "Verlichting en emancipatie omstreeks, 1750–1814." In *Geschiedenis van de Joden in Nederland*, edited by J. C. H. Blom et al., 177–203. Amsterdam, 1995.

Furet, François, and D. Richet. *La Révolution française.* Paris, 1963.

Gallingani, Daniela. *Napoleone e gli ebrei: Atti dell Assemblea degli Israeliti di Parigi e dei verbali del Gran Sinderio (1806–1807).* Paris, 1991.

Garber, Dan. "Superheroes in the History of Philosophy: Spinoza, Super-Rationalist." *Journal of the History of Philosophy* 53, no. 3 (2015): 507–22.

García-Alonso, Marta, ed. *Les Lumières radicales et le politique: Études critiques sur les travaux de Jonathan Israel.* Paris, 2017.

Garrett, Don. "A Reply on Spinoza's Behalf." In Forster and Melamed, eds., *Spinoza and German Idealism*, 248–64.

Gascón Pérez, Jesús. *Aragón en la monarquía de Felipe II*. 2 vols. Zaragoza, 2007.
Gasper, Julia, *The Marquis d'Argens: A Philosophical Life*. Lanham, MD, 2014.
Gebhardt, Carl. "Juan de Prado." *Chronicum Spinozanum* 3 (1923): 269–91.
Gendzier, S. J. "Diderot and the Jews." *Diderot Studies* 16 (1973): 35–54, edited by O. Fellows and D. Guiragossian.
Giancotti Boscherini, Emilia. *Lexicon Spinozanum*. 2 vols. The Hague, 1971.
Girard, Patrick. *La Révolution française et les Juifs*. Paris, 1989.
Girard, Philippe. "Black Talleyrand: Toussaint Louverture's Diplomacy, 1798–1802." *William and Mary Quarterly*, 3rd ser., 66 (2009): 87–124.
———. *Toussaint Louverture: A Revolutionary Life*. New York, 2016.
Glatzer, Nahum. *Franz Rosenzweig*. New York, 1953.
Godechot, Jacques. *The Counter-Revolution: Doctrine and Action, 1789–1804*. London, 1972.
Goetschel, W. *Heine and Critical Theory*. London, 2019.
———. "Heine's Spinoza." *Idealistic Studies* 33 (2003): 207–21.
———. "The Hyphen in the Theological-Political: Spinoza to Mendelssohn, Heine and Derrida." *Religions* 10 (2019): 1–13.
———. *Spinoza's Modernity: Mendelssohn, Lessing and Heine*. Madison, WI, 2004.
Goldberg, Cad Alan. *Modernity and the Jews in Modern Social Thought*. Chicago, 2017.
Goldberg, Jacob. "Jewish Marriage in Eighteenth-Century Poland." In *Jews in Early Modern Poland*, edited by Gershon Hundert, *Polin: Studies in Polish Jewry* 10, 3–39. London, 1997.
Goldenbaum, Ursula. "Kants Parteinahme für Mendelssohn im Spinoza-Streit 1786." In *Kant und die Berliner Aufklärung: Akten des IX Kant-Kongresses*, edited by Rolf-Peter Horstmann et al., 5:176–85. Berlin, 2001.
———. "Mendelssohns schwierige Beziehung zu Spinoza." In *Spinoza im Deutschland des achtzehnten Jahrhunderts*, edited by E. Schurmann, N. Waszek, and F. Weinreich, 265–317. Stuttgart–Bad Cannstatt, 2002.
Goldfarb, Michael. *Emancipation: How Liberating Europe's Jews from the Ghetto Led to Revolution and Renaissance*. Melbourne, 2009.
Goldstein Sepinwall, Alyssa. "Strategic Friendships: Jewish Intellectuals, the Abbé Grégoire and the French Revolution." In Brann and Sutcliffe, eds., *Renewing the Past*, 189–212.
Goltschnigg, D., and H. Steinecke, eds. *Heine und die Nachwelt: Geschichte seiner Wirkung in den deutschsprachigen Ländern* 1 (1856–1906). Berlin, 2006.
Gómez-Centurión Jiménez, Carlos. *Felipe II, la empresa de Inglaterra y el comercio septentrional (1566–1609)*. Madrid, 1988.
Gompers, Loes, and M. Ligtelijn. *Spiegel van Amsterdam: Geschiedenis van Felix Meritis*. Amsterdam, 2007.
Goodman, Martin. *A History of Judaism*. 2017. New ed., London, 2019.
Görisch, Reinhard, and Thomas Michael Mayer. *Untersuchungsberichte zur republikanischen Bewegung in Hessen 1831–1834*. Frankfurt, 1982.
Goslinga, Cornelis. *The Dutch in the Caribbean and the Guyanas, 1680–1791*. Assen, 1985.

Gottlieb, Anthony. *The Dream of Enlightenment: The Rise of Modern Philosophy.* New York, 2016.
Gottlieb, Michah. *Faith and Freedom: Moses Mendelssohn's Theological-Political Thought.* Oxford, 2011.
———. Introduction to Mendelssohn, *Writings*, xi–xxvii.
Grab, Alexander. "Jewish Education in Napoleonic Italy—The Case of the Ginnasio in Reggio Emilia." *SDIJ* 6 (2007): 269–89.
———. *Napoleon and the Transformation of Europe*. Basingstoke, 2003.
Graetz, Michael. "From Corporate Community to Ethnic-Religious Minority, 1750–1830." *LBIYB* 37 (1992): 71–82.
———. "The Jewish Enlightenment." In *German-Jewish History in Modern Times*, edited by M. A. Meyer, 262–374. New York, 1996.
Greco, Silvana. "Heresy, Apostasy, and the Beginnings of Social Philosophy." *Materia giudaica* 20/21 (2015/16): 439–64.
Gross, Jean-Pierre. *Fair Shares for All: Jacobin Egalitarianism in Practice.* Cambridge, 1997.
Hagen, Edwina. "Een zaal van staatsmannen, niet van godgeleerden: Godsdienstige sentimenten in de Nationale Vergadering." In *Het Bataafse experimen: Politiek en cultuur rond 1800*, edited by Frans Grijzenhout, Nick van Sas, and W.Velema, 125–53. Nijmegen, 2013.
Hamerow, Theodore. *Restoration, Revolution, Reaction: Economics and Politics in Germany, 1815–1871.* 1958. New ed., Princeton, NJ, 1966.
Hampson, Norman, *The Life and Opinions of Maximilien Robespierre.* London, 1974.
———. *Saint-Just.* Oxford, 1991.
Harris, James F. "Public Opinion and the Proposed Emancipation of the Jews in Bavaria in 1849–1850." *LBIYB* 35 (1989): 67–80.
Harris, Jay. *Nachman Krochmal: Guiding the Perplexed of the Modern Age.* New York, 1991.
Harvey, Warren Zev. "A Portrait of Spinoza as a Maimonidean." *JHPh* 19 (1981): 151–72.
———. "The Return of Maimonideism." *Jewish Social Studies* 42 (1980): 249–68.
———. "Spinoza's Counterfactual Zionism." *Iyyun: The Jerusalem Philosophical Quarterly* 62 (July 2013): 235–44.
Haubtmann, Pierre. *Pierre-Joseph Proudhon: Sa Vie et sa pensée (1809–1849).* Paris, 1982.
Hausdorff, D. *Jizkor: Platenatlas van drie en een halve eeuw geschiedenis van de joodse gemeente te Rotterdam.* Baarn, 1978.
Heinrich, Gerda. "Die Debatte um "bürgerliche Verbesserung" der Juden 1781–1786." In *Apell an das Publikum: Die öffentliche Debatte in der deutschen Aufklärung 1687–1796*, edited by Ursula Goldenbaum, 2 vols., 2:813–95. Berlin, 2004.
Heller, Joseph E. *Moses Hess.* London, 1950.
Hermann, Jacqueline. "An Undesired King: Some Notes on the Political Trajectory of D. Antonio, Prior of Crato." *Revista Brasileira de Historia* 30 (2010): 139–64.
Hermon-Belot, R. *L'Abbé Grégoire: La Politique et la vérité.* Paris, 2000.
Hertz, Deborah. *How Jews Became Germans: The History of Conversion and Assimilation in Berlin.* New Haven, CT, 2007.

Hertzberg, Arthur. *The French Enlightenment and the Jews: The Origins of Modern Anti-Semitism.* New York, 1968.
Herzig, Arno. "The Process of Emancipation from the Congress of Vienna to the Revolution of 1848–1849." *LBIYB* 37 (1992): 61–69.
Hess, Jonathan. *Germans, Jews and the Claims of Modernity.* New Haven, CT, 2002.
Heuberger, Georg. *Ludwig Börne: a Frankfurt Jew Who Fought for Freedom.* Frankfurt, 1996.
Hiegentlich, F. P. "Reflections on the Relationship between the Dutch *Haskalah* and the German *Haskalah.*" In *DJH*, edited by Michman, 1 (1984): 207–18.
Higby, Chester Penn. *The Religious Policy of the Bavarian Government during the Napoleonic Period.* 1918. Reprint, New York, 1967.
Hoagwood, T. A. *Skepticism and Ideology. Shelley's Political Prose and Its Philosophical Context from Bacon to Marx.* Iowa City, IA, 1988.
Hobsbawm, Eric. *The Age of Revolution, 1789–1848.* 1962. New ed., New York, 1996.
Holland, Eva E. "The World of Moses Mendelssohn." *LBIYB* 36 (1991): 27–43.
Hollingdale, R. J. "The Hero as Outsider." *The Cambridge Companion to Nietzsche*, edited by B. Magnus and K. M. Higgins, 71–89. Cambridge, 1996.
Horch, Hans Otto. "Friedrich Schiller, die Juden und das Judentum." *Aschkenaz-Zeitschrift für Geschichte und Kultur der Juden* 16 (2006): 17–36.
Hudson, Wayne. *The English Deists.* London, 2009.
Hulak, Florence, "Spinoza après Marx, ou le problème de l'ontologie marxienne." *Revue de Métaphysique et de Morale* 56 (2007): 483–98.
Hull, Gordon. "Marx's Anomalous Reading of Spinoza." *Interpretation* 28 (2000): 18–31.
Hundert, Gershon. *Jews in Poland-Lithuania in the Eighteenth Century: A Genealogy of Modernity.* Berkeley and Los Angeles, 2004.
———. "Re(de)fining Modernity in Jewish History." In *Rethinking European Jewish History*, edited by J. Cohen and M. Rosman, 133–45. Oxford, 2009.
Igoin, Albert. "De l'ellipse de la théorie politique de Spinoza chez le jeune Marx." *Cahiers Spinoza* 1 (1977): 213–28.
Israel, Jonathan. "The Banning of Spinoza's Works in the Dutch Republic." In *Disguised and Overt Spinozism around 1700*, edited by Wiep van Bunge and Wim Klever, 3–14. Leiden, 1996.
———. "El comercio de los judíos sefardíes de Amsterdam con los conversos de Madrid a través del suoeste francés." In *Familia, religión y negocio: El Sefardismo en las relaciones entre el mundo ibérico y los Países Bajos en la Edad Moderna*, edited by Jaime Contreras et al., 373–90. Antwerp, 2002.
———. "David Nassy and the Political Emancipation of Dutch and Dutch Caribbean Jewry (1785–1797)." In *Paths to Modernity: A Tribute to Yosef Kaplan*, edited by A. Bar-Levav et al., 321–47. Jerusalem, 2018.
———. *Democratic Enlightenment: Philosophy, Revolution and Human Rights, 1750–1790.* Oxford, 2012.
———. *Diasporas within a Diaspora: Jews, Crypto-Jews and the World Maritime Empires (1540–1740).* Leiden, 2002.

———. "The Diplomatic Career of Jeronimo Nunes da Costa: An Episode in Dutch-Portuguese Relations of the Seventeenth Century." *BMGN* 98 (1983): 167–90.

———. "Dutch Golden Age Politics and the Rise of the Radical Enlightenment." In *The Dutch Legacy: Radical Thinkers in the 17th Century and the Enlightenment*, edited by S. Lavaert and W. Schröder, 35–60. Leiden, 2017.

———. "The Dutch Jewish Enlightenment in Surinam, 1770–1800." In *The Religious Cultures of Dutch Jewry*, edited by Yosef Kaplan and Dan Michman, 183–202. Leiden, 2017.

———. "Dutch Jews, David Nassy, and the "General Revolution" in the Caribbean (1770–1800)." *SR* 44 (2012): 173–90.

———. *Dutch Primacy in World Trade, 1585–1740*. Oxford, 1989.

———. *The Dutch Republic: Its Rise, Greatness, and Fall, 1477–1806*. Oxford, 1995.

———. *The Enlightenment That Failed: Ideas, Revolution, and Democratic Defeat, 1748–1830*. Oxford, 2019.

———. *European Jewry in the Age of Mercantilism, 1550–1750*. Oxford, 1985.

———. *The Expanding Blaze: How the American Revolution Ignited the World, 1775–1848*. Princeton, NJ, 2017.

———. "Gregorio Leti (1631–1701) and the Dutch Sephardi Elite at the Close of the Seventeenth Century." In *Jewish History: Essays in Honour of Chimen Abramsky*, edited by A. Rappport-Albert and S. J. Zipperstein, 267–84. London, 1988.

———. "Ideology and Social Change: Jewish Emancipation in European Revolutionary Consciousness (1780–1800)." In *The Jew as Legitimation: Jewish-Gentile Relations beyond Antisemitism and Philosemitism*, edited by David Wertheim, 83–101. London, 2017.

———. "Jewish Emancipation in the Western World (1780–1860): What Kind of Enlightenment Made it Possible?" *Proceedings of the Israel Academy of Sciences and Humanities* 9, no. 6 (2018): 109–29.

———. "Les 'Lumières radicales' comme théorie générale de la modernité démocratique séculière, et ses critiques." In *Les Lumières radicales et le politique: Études critiques sur les travaux de Jonathan Israel*, edited by Marta García-Alonso, 387–436. Paris, 2017.

———. "Maurits en de wording van de buitenlandse politiek." In *Maurits, Prins van Oranje*, edited by Kees Zandvliet, 65–75. Zwolle, 2000.

———. "Philosophy, Commerce, and the Synagogue: Spinoza's Expulsion from the Portuguese Jewish Community in 1656." In Israel and Salverda, eds., *Dutch Jewry*, 125–40. Leiden, 2002.

———. "Philosophy, Deism, and the Early Jewish Enlightenment (1655–1740)." In *The Dutch Intersection: The Jews and the Netherlands in Modern History*, edited by Yosef Kaplan, 173–201. Leiden, 2008.

———. *Race, Class and Politics in Colonial Mexico, 1610–1670*. Oxford, 1975.

———. "'Radical Enlightenment': A Game-Changing Concept." In *Reassessing the Radical Enlightenment*, edited by Steffen Ducheyne, 15–47. Abingdon, 2017.

———. *Revolutionary Ideas: An Intellectual History of the French Revolution from "The Rights of Man" to Robespierre*. Princeton, NJ, 2014.

———. "Was There a Pre-1740 Sephardic Jewish Enlightenment?" *Arquivos do Centro Cultural Calouste Gulbenkian* 48 (2004) 3–20.

Israel, Jonathan, and Reinier Salverda, eds. *Dutch Jewry: Its History and Secular Culture (1500–2000).* Leiden, 2002.

Jacob, Margaret. *The Secular Enlightenment.* Princeton, NJ, 2019.

Jager, Colin. "Shelley after Atheism." *Studies in Romanticism* 49 (2010): 611–13.

Jaher, Frédéric. *The Jews and the Nation: Revolution, Emancipation, State Formation and the Liberal Paradigm in America and France.* Princeton, NJ, 2002.

James, Susan. "Freedom, Slavery and the Passions." In *The Cambridge Companion to Spinoza's Ethics*, edited by O. Koistinen, 223–41. Cambridge, 2009.

Janssens, David. "The Problem of the Enlightenment: Strauss, Jacobi, and the Pantheism Controversy." In *Reorientation: Leo Strauss in the 1930s*, edited by M. D. Yaffe and R. S. Ruderman, 171–90. Basingstoke, 2014.

Jarrett, Mark. *The Congress of Vienna and Its Legacy.* London, 2014.

Jasper, Willi. *Keinem Vaterland geboren: Ludwig Börne, Eine Biographie.* Hamburg, 1989.

Jaume, Lucien. *Le Discours Jacobin et la démocratie.* Paris, 1989.

Jersch-Wenzel, Stefi. "Legal Status and Emancipation." In *German-Jewish History in Modern Times*, edited by Michael Meyer, vol. 2: *1780–1871*, 5–50. New York, 1996.

Joor, Johan. *De Adelaar en het Lam: Onrust, opruiing en onwilligheid in Nederland ten tijde van het Koninkrijk Holland en de Inlijving bij het Franse keizerrijk (1806–1813).* Amsterdam, 2000.

Jordaan, Han. "Patriots, Privateers and international Politics." In *Curaçao in the Age of Revolutions, 1795–1800*, edited by Wim Klooster and Gert Oostindie, 141–69. Leiden, 2011.

———. *Slavernij en vrijheid op Curaçao.* Zutphen, 2013.

Joskowicz, Ari. *The Modernity of Others: Jewish Anti-Catholicism in Germany and France.* Stanford, CA, 2014.

Kamen, Henry. *Philip of Spain.* New Haven, CT, 1997.

Kaplan, Yosef. *An Alternative Path to Modernity: The Sephardi Diaspora in Western Europe.* Leiden, 2000.

———. "Discipline, Dissent, and Communal Authority in the Western Sephardic Diaspora." In *The Cambridge History of Judaism*, edited by J. Karp and A. Sutcliffe, vol. 7: *1500–1815*, 15–29. Cambridge, 2018.

———. *From Christianity to Judaism: The Story of Isaac Orobio de Castro.* Oxford, 1989.

———. "The Intellectual Ferment in the Spanish-Portuguese Community of Seventeenth-Century Amsterdam." In *Moreshet Sepharad: The Sephardic Legacy*, edited by Haim Beinart, vol. 2, 600–621. Jerusalem, 1992.

———. "Joden in de Republiek tot omstreeks 1750—religieus, cultureel en sociaal leven." In *Geschiedenis van de Joden in Nederland*, edited by J. C. H. Blom et al., 129–73, 413–19, 452–60. Amsterdam, 1995.

———. "Karaites" in Early Eighteenth-Century Amsterdam." In *Sceptics, Millenarians and Jews*, edited by D. S. Katz and Jonathan Israel, 196–236. Leiden, 1990.

———. "More Than Thirty Years after Its Publication." In Wilke, ed., *Isaac Orobio*, 15–29.
———. "Political Concepts in the World of the Portuguese Jews of Amsterdam during the Seventeenth Century." In *Menasseh ben Israel and His World*, edited by Kaplan, H. Méchoulan, and R. H. Popkin, 45–62. Leiden, 1989.
Karp, Jonathan. *The Politics of Jewish Commerce: Economic Thought and Emancipation in Europe, 1638–1848*. Cambridge, 2008.
Katz, David S., and R. H. Popkin. *Messianic Revolution: Radical Religious Politics to the End of the Second Millennium*. 1999. New ed., London, 2000.
Kennedy, M. L. *The Jacobin Clubs in the French Revolution: The Middle Years*. Princeton, NJ, 1988.
Kerautret, Michel. "Napoleon und Deutschland." In *Napoleon und das Königreich Westphalen*, edited by Andreas Hewig et al., 19–37. Marburg, 2008.
Kessler, Mario. *Moses Hess and Ferdinand Lassalle: Pioneers of Social Emancipation*. Berlin, 2013.
Kieniewicz, Stefan. "Assimilated Jews in Nineteenth-Century Warsaw." In Bartoszewski and Polonsky, eds., *Jews in Warsaw*, 171–80.
Klaus, Carrie. "Keeping Ahead of the English? A Defense of the Jews by Cornelie Wouters, Baroness de Vasse (1790)." In *Virtue, Liberty and Toleration: Political Ideas of European Women, 1400–1800*, edited by Jacqueline Broad and Karen Green, 171–88. Dordrecht, 2007.
Klever, Wim. "Spinoza and Van den Enden in Borch's Diary in 1661 and 1662." *Studia Spinozana* 5 (1989): 311–25.
———. "Spinoza's Life and Works." In *The Cambridge Companion to Spinoza*, edited by Don Garrett, 13–59. Cambridge, 1996.
Klooster, Wim, and Gert Oostindie, eds. *Curaçao in the Age of Revolutions, 1795–1800*. Leiden, 2011.
Kochan, Lionel. *Jews, Idols and Messiahs: The Challenge of History*. Oxford, 1990.
Koltun-Fromm, K. *Moses Hess and Modern Jewish Identity*. Bloomington, IN, 2001.
Kors, Alan Charles. *Naturalism and Unbelief in France, 1650–1720*. Cambridge, 2016.
Kouvelakis, Stathis. *Philosophy and Revolution from Kant to Marx*. London, 2003.
Kovács, Mária. *Liberal Professions and Illiberal Politics: Hungary from the Habsburgs to the Holocaust*. Washington, DC, 1994.
Krohn, Helga. *"Dem Streiter für Recht und Freiheit": Gabriel Riesser zum 200. Geburtstag*. Frankfurt, 2006.
Krop, Henri. *Spinoza, een paradoxale icoon van Nederland*. Amsterdam, 2014.
Kuehn, Manfred. *Kant: A Biography*. Cambridge, 2001.
Kümper, Michael. "'Worte der Wahrheit und des Friedens' oder 'Worte des Friedens und der Wahrheit'? Die deutsche Übersetzung von Naphtali Hartwig Wesselys pädagogischem Pamphlet *Divrei shalom ve'emet* durch David Friedländer." In *Berliner Aufklärung: Kulturwissenschaftliche Studien*, 2 vols., edited by U. Goldenbaum and A. Košenina, 2:165–78. Hanover, 2001–3.
Labbé, François. *Anacharsis Cloots, le prussien francophile*. Paris, 1999.

Labrosse, Claude, and Pierre Rétat. *Naissance du journal révolutionnaire, 1789*. Lyon, 1989.
Laerke, Mogens. *Leibniz lecteur de Spinoza*. Paris, 2008.
Lauermann, M., and M. B. Schröder. "Textgrundlagen der deutschen Spinoza-Rezeption im 18. Jahrhundert." In *Spinoza im Deutschland des achtzehnten Jahrhunderts*, edited by E. Schürmann, N. Waszek, and F. Weinreich, 39–85. Stuttgart, 2002.
Laursen, J. Christian, and Whitney Mannies. "Diderot and Diez: Complicating the Radical Enlightenment." In García-Alonso, ed., *Lumières radicales et le politique*, 281–302.
Lavaert, Sonja. *Vrijheid, gelijkheid, veelheid: Het moderne demokratie-denken van Machiavelli tot Spinoza en zijn kring*. Brussels, 2020.
Leask, Ian, "The Undivulged Event in Toland's *Christianity Not Mysterious*." In *Atheism and Deism Revalued: Heterodox Religious Identities in Britain, 1650–1800*, edited by Wayne Hudson, D. Lucci, and J. R. Wigelsworth, 63–80. Farnham, 2014.
Lentz, Thierry. *Roederer*. Metz, 1989.
Leuwers, Hervé. *Robespierre*. Paris, 2014.
Levin, Nora. *Jewish Socialist Movements, 1871–1917: While Messiah Tarried*. London, 1978.
Levine, Allan. *Seeking the Fabled City: The Canadian Jewish Experience*. Toronto, 2018.
Levinger, Matthew. *Enlightened Nationalism. The Transformation of Prussian Political Culture, 1806–1848*. Oxford, 2000.
Liberles, Robert. "Dohm's Treatise on the Jews: A Defense of the Enlightenment." *LBIYB* 33 (1988): 29–42.
Liebman, S. B. "Tomas Treviño de Sobremente: A Jewish Mexican Martyr." *Jewish Social Studies* 42 (1980): 63–74.
Loft, Leonore. "Mirabeau and Brissot Review Christian Wilhelm Von Dohm and the Jewish Question." *History of European Ideas* 13 (1991): 605–22.
———. *Passion, Politics and* Philosophie: *Rediscovering J. P. Brissot*. Westport, CT, 2002.
Loker, Zvi. "An Eighteenth-Century Plan to Invade Jamaica: Isaac Yeshurun Sasportas—French Patriot or Jewish Radical Idealist?" *TJSHE* 28 (1981/82): 132–44.
Lordon, Frédéric. *Willing Slaves of Capital: Spinoza and Marx on Desire*. Translated by G. Ash. London, 2014.
Lowenstein, Steven. "Two Silent Minorities: Orthodox Jews and Poor Jews in Berlin 1770–1823." *LBIY* 36 (1991): 3–25.
Löwy, Michael. *Redemption and Utopia: Jewish Libertarian Thought in Central Europe*. 1988. English translation by Hope Heaney, new ed., London, 2017.
Lundgren, Svante. *Moses Hess on Religion, Judaism and the Bible*. Åbo, 1992.
Lurbe, Pierre. "John Toland and the Naturalization of the Jews." *Eighteenth-Century Ireland* 14 (1999): 37–49.
Luttrell, B. *Mirabeau*. Hemel Hempstead, 1990.
Lynch, John. *Simón Bolívar*. New Haven, CT, 2006.

Maciejko, Pawel. *The Mixed Multitude: Jacob Frank and the Frankist Movement, 1755-1816*. Philadelphia, 2011.
Mack, Michael. *German Idealism and the Jew*. Chicago, 2003.
———. *Spinoza and the Specters of Modernity*. New York, 2010.
Maia Neto, José R. "The Struggle against Unbelief in the Portuguese Jewish Community of Amsterdam after Spinoza's Excommunication." In *Heterodoxy, Spinozism and Free Thought in the Early Eighteenth Century*, edited by S. Berti, F. Charles-Daubert, and R. H. Popkin, 425–37. Dordrecht, 1996.
Maissen, Thomas. *Geschichte der Schweiz*. Baden im Aargau, 2010.
Malino, Frances. "Furtado et les Juifs portugais." *AHRF* 235 (1979): 49–66.
———. *A Jew in the French Revolution: The Life of Zalkind Hourwitz*. Oxford, 1996.
Mandel, Arthur. *Le Messie militant ou La Fuite du Ghetto: Histoire de Jacob Frank et du mouvement frankiste*. Milan, 1989.
Mansel, Philip. *Paris between Empires, 1814-1852: Monarchy and Revolution*. 2001. New ed., London, 2003.
Manuel, Frank E. *The Broken Staff: Judaism through Christian Eyes*. Cambridge, MA, 1992.
Marcus, Jacob R. "Jews and the American Revolution." *American Jewish Archives* 27 (1975): 103–257.
Marcuse, Ludwig. "Heine and Marx: A History and a Legend." *Germanic Review* 30 (1955): 110–24.
Margalit, Avishai. "The Lessons of Spinoza." *New York Review of Books*, 12 April 2007, 73.
Marshall, John. *John Locke, Toleration and Early Enlightenment Culture*. Cambridge, 2006.
Martin, C., and Geoffrey Parker. *The Spanish Armada*. Harmondsworth, 1988.
Martin, Jean-Clément. *Robespierre: La fabrication d'un monstre*. Paris, 2016.
Marx, Alexander. *Studies in Jewish History and Booklore*. New York, 1944.
Marx, Jacques. "Présentation" to d'Argens's *Lettres Juives*, 3 vols., 1:11–153. Paris, 2013.
Mathan, Anne de. "Le Chef d'un groupe indulgent?" In *Danton: Le Mythe et l'histoire*, edited by M. Biard and H. Leuwers, 113–26. Paris, 2016.
———. *Girondins jusqu'au tombeau: Une révolte bordelaise dans la Révolution*. Bordeaux, 2004.
Matheron, Alexandre. *Individu et communauté chez Spinoza*. Paris, 1988.
———. "*Traité Theologico-Politique* vu par le jeune Marx." *Cahiers Spinoza* 1 (1977): 159–212.
Matheron, François. "Louis Althusser et le "groupe Spinoza." In *Lectures contemporaines de Spinoza*, edited by Pierre-François Moreau et al., 77–93. Paris, 2012.
Mathorez, Jules. "Notes sur l'histoire de la colonie portugaise de Nantes." *Bulletin hispanique* 15, no. 3 (1913): 316–39.
McKenna, Antony. "Sur l'hérésie dans la littérature clandestine." *Dix-Huitième Siècle* 22 (1990): 301–13.
Méchoulan, Henry. *Hispanidad y Judaísmo en tiempos de Espinoza*. Salamanca, 1987.

Melamed, Yitzchak. "Charitable Interpretations and the Political Domestication of Spinoza, or, Benedict in the Land of the Secular Imagination." In *Philosophy and Its History: Aims and Methods in the Study of Early Modern Philosophy*, edited by Mogens Laerke, Justin Smith, and Eric Schliesser, 258–77. Oxford, 2013.

———. "Salomon Maimon and the Rise of Spinozism in German Idealism." *JHPh* 42 (2004): 67–96.

———. *Spinoza's Metaphysics: Substance and Thought*. Oxford, 2013.

———. "Spinozism, Acosmism, and Hasidism: A Closed Circle." In *Der Begriff des Judentums in der klassischen deutschen Philosophie*, edited by A. Kravitz and J. Noller, 75–85. Tübingen, 2018.

———., ed. *The Young Spinoza: A Metaphysician in the Making*. Oxford, 2015.

Melamed, Yitzchak, and H. Sharp, eds. *Spinoza's "Political Treatise": A Critical Guide*. Cambridge, 2018.

Menkis, Richard. "In This Great, Happy and Enlightened Colony: Abraham de Sola on Jews, Judaism and Emancipation in Victorian Montreal." In Zinguer and Bloom, eds., *L'Antisémitisme éclairé*, 313–31.

Michman, Jozeph. *Dutch Jewry during the Emancipation Period, 1787–1815*. Amsterdam, 1995.

———. "De emancipatie van de Joden in Nederland." *BMGN* 96 (1981): 78–82.

———. "Jewish Soldiers in the Batavian Republic and under French Rule." In *DJH*, edited by Michman, 3 (1993): 285–308.

Mignini, Filippo. "Nuovi contribute per la datazione e l'interpetazione del *Tractatus de Intellectus Emendatione*." In *Spinoza nel 3500 anniversario della nascità*, edited by E. Giancotti, 515–25. Naples, 1985.

Mintzker, Yair. *The Defortification of the German City, 1689–1866*. Cambridge, 2012.

Mitchell, Harvey. *Voltaire's Jews and Modern Jewish Identity: Rethinking the Enlightenment*. Abingdon, 2008.

Moran, Daniel. *Toward the Century of Words: Johann Cotta and the Politics of the Public Realm in Germany, 1795–1832*. Berkeley, CA, 1990.

Morawe, Bodo. "Heinrich Heine und die Strategie der radikalen Aufklärung: Toland's *Pantheisticon*, Mesliers *Mémoire*, Holbach's *System der Natur*." *Deutsche Vierteljahrschrift für Literaturwissenschaft und Geistesgeschichte* 81 (2007): 546–83.

Moreau, Pierre-François. "La réception du spinozisme aux XIXe et XXe siècles." In *Lectures de Spinoza*, edited by Pierre-François Moreau and Charles Raymond, 243–53. Paris, 2006.

Mortier, Roland. *Anacharsis Cloots ou l'utopie foudroyée*. N.p., 1995.

Mortier, Roland, and Raymond Trousson, eds. *Dictionnaire de Diderot*. Paris, 1999.

Muchnik, Natalia. "Orobio contra Prado: A Trans-European Controversy." In Wilke, ed., *Isaac Orobio*, 31–56.

———. *Une Vie marrane: Les pérégrinations de Juan de Prado dans l'Europe du XVIIe siècle*. Paris, 2005.

Mulsow, Martin. *Enlightenment Underground: Radical Germany, 1680–1720*. Charlottesville, VA, 2015.

———. *Radikale Frühaufklärung in Deutschland 1680–1720*. 2 vols. Göttingen, 2018.
Na'aman, Shlomo. *Emanzipation und Messianismus: Leben und Werk des Moses Hess*. Frankfurt, 1982.
Nadler, Steven. *A Book Forged in Hell: Spinoza's Scandalous Treatise and the Birth of the Secular Age*. Princeton, NJ, 2011.
———. *Spinoza: A Life*. Cambridge, 1999.
———. "Spinoza on the Divinity of Scripture." In *Spinoza Research: To Be Continued*, 35–47. Uitgeverij Spinozahuis, 2016.
———. *Spinoza's Heresy: Immortality and the Jewish Mind*. Oxford, 2001.
Nahon, Gérard. *Juifs et judaïsme à Bordeaux*. Bordeaux, 2003.
———. *Métropoles et périphéries séfarades d'occident*. Paris, 1993.
———. "Les rapports des communautés judéo-portugaises de France avec celle d'Amsterdam du XVIIe au XVIIIe siècle." *SR* 10 (1976): 37–84 and 151–88.
Naville, Pierre. *Paul Thiry d'Holbach et la philosophie scientifique au XVIIe siècle*. 3rd ed. Paris, 1943.
Negri, Antonio. *Spinoza for Our Time*. 2003. English translation, New York, 2013.
Neiman, Susan. *The Unity of Reason: Rereading Kant*. New York, 1994.
Nickel, Jutta. *Revolutionsgedanken: Zur Lektüre der Geschichte in Heinrich Heines "Ludwig Börne. Eine Denkschrift."* Bielfeld, 2007.
Niekerk, Carl, ed. *The Radical Enlightenment in Germany: A Cultural Perspective*. Leiden, 2018.
Nijenhuis, I. J. A. *Een joodse philosophe: Isaac de Pinto (1717–1787)*. Amsterdam, 1992.
Nipperdey, Thomas. *Germany from Napoleon to Bismarck, 1800–1866*. Princeton, NJ, 1996.
Nirenberg, David. *Anti-Judaism: The Western Tradition*. New York, 2013.
Nisbet, H. B. *Gotthold Ephraim Lessing: His Life, Works, and Thought*. Oxford, 2013.
Nuovo, Victor. *John Locke: The Philosopher as Christian Virtuoso*. Oxford, 2017.
Offenberg, A. K. "Spinoza's Library: The Story of a Reconstruction." *Quaerendo* 3 (1973): 309–21.
O'Higgins, J. *Anthony Collins: The Man and His Works*. The Hague, 1970.
Ohles, Frederik. *Germany's Rude Awakening: Censorship in the Land of the Brothers Grimm*. Kent, OH, 1992.
Oostindie, Gert. "Slave Resistance, Colour Lines, and the Impact of the French and Haitian Revolutions in Curaçao." In Klooster and Oostindie, eds., *Curaçao in the Age of Revolutions*, 1–22.
Opalski, Magdalena, and Israel Bartal. *Poles and Jews: A Failed Brotherhood*. Hanover, NH, 1992.
Ott, Barthélemy. *La Querelle de Heine et de Börne: Contribution à l'étude des idées politiques et sociales en Allemagne de 1830 à 1840*. Lyon, 1935.
Pagden, Anthony. *The Enlightenment and Why It Still Matters*. Oxford, 2013.
Palladini, F. *Die Berliner Hugenotten und der Fall Barbeyrac: Orthdoxe und 'Sozinianer' im Refuge (1685–1720)*. Leiden, 2011.
Palmer, Alan. *Bernadotte: Napoleon's Marshal, Sweden's King*. London, 1990.
Parker, Geoffrey. *The Grand Strategy of Philip II*. New Haven, CT, 1998.

Pätzhold, D. *Spinoza, Aufklärung, Idealismus: Die Substanz der Moderne*. 1995. 2nd ed. Assen, 2002.
Pelluchon, Corine. *Leo Strauss and the Crisis of Rationalism: Another Reason, Another Enlightenment*. Albany, NY, 2014.
Perraudin, Michael. *Literature, the "Volk," and the Revolution in mid-19th Century Germany*. New York, 2001.
Petiteau, Nathalie. "La Restauration face aux vétérans de l'Empire." In *Repenser la Restauration, actes du colloque de Saint-Quentin-en-Yvelines de septembre 2003*, edited by Jean-Yves Mollier et al., 31–43. Paris, 2005.
Pinkard, Terry. *Hegel: A Biography*. Cambridge, 2000.
———. *Hegel's Naturalism: Mind, Nature, and the Final Ends of Life*. Oxford, 2012.
Popkin, Richard H. "Les Caraïtes et l'émancipation des Juifs." *Dix-Huitième Siècle* 13 (1981): 137–47.
———. "Image of the Jew in Clandestine Literature circa 1700." In *Filosofia e religione nella letteratura clandestina*, edited by Guido Canziani, 13–34. Milan, 1994.
———. "Jacques Basnage's *Histoire des Juifs* and the Bibliotheca Sarraziana." *SR* 21 (1987): 154–62.
———. *Spinoza*. Oxford, 2004.
———. "Spinoza's Earliest Philosophical Years (1655–61)." *Studia Spinozana* 4 (1988): 37–55.
Prak, Maarten. *Republikeinse veelheid, democratisch enkelvoud: Sociale verandering in het Revolutietijdvak 's-Hertogenbosch, 1770–1820*. Nijmegen, 1999.
Price, Munro. *The Perilous Crown: France between Revolutions 1814–1848*. London, 2007.
Rädecker, Tsila. "Making Jews Dutch: Secular Discourse and Jewish Responses, 1796–1848." Ph.D. diss., University of Groningen, 10 September 2015.
———. "'Moses is tot [de] Raad verheven': De integratie van Amsterdamse, Rotterdamse en Haagse Joden in de 19de eeuw." *Holland* (2016): 23–26.
Ramm, Agatha. *Germany 1789-1919. A Political History*. London, 1967.
Rauschenbach, Sina. "The Empire Writes Back: David Nassy and Jewish Creole Historiography in Colonial Suriname." In *The Sephardic Atlantic. Colonial Histories and Postcolonial Perrspectives*, edited by Rauschenbach and Jonathan Schorch, 159–82. London, 2018.
———. "Patriots at the Periphery: David Nassy, the French Revolution, and the Emancipation of the Dutch Jews." In *Religious Changes and Cultural Transformations in the Early Modern Western Sephardic Communities*, edited by Yosef Kaplan, 581–610. Leiden, 2019.
Ravven, Heidi. "Spinoza's Rupture with Tradition—His Hints of a Jewish Modernity." In *Jewish Themes in Spinoza's Philosophy*, edited by Ravven and L. E. Goodman, 187–223. Albany, NY, 2002.
Reinalter, Helmut. "Arnold Ruge, der Vormärz und die Revolution 1848/9." In *Die Junghegelianer: Aufkärung, Literatur, Religionskritik und politisches Denken*, edited by Reinalter, 139–59. Frankfurt, 2019.
Reuveni, Gideon. "Emancipation through Consumption: Moses Mendelssohn and the Idea of Marketplace Citizenship." *LBIYB* 59 (2014): 7–22.

Révah, I. S. "Aux origines de la rupture spinozienne." *Revue des Études Juives* 99 (1961): 359–431.
———. *Des Marranes à Spinoza*. Paris, 1995.
———. *Spinoza et le Juan de Prado*. Paris, 1959.
Reventlow, Henning Graf. "The Religious Way of John Locke from the *Essay* to the *Paraphrase* (1690–1704)." In *Locke and Biblical Hermeneutics: Conscience and Scripture*, edited by L. Simonutti, 11–20. Cham, Switzerland, 2019.
Riedel, Manfred. *Between Tradition and Revolution: The Hegelian Transformation of Political Philosophy*. Cambridge, 1984.
Rippmann, Inge. *"Freiheit ist das Schönste und Höchste in Leben und Kunst": Ludwig Börne zwischen Literatur und Politik*. Bielefeld, 2004.
Roberts, Hugh. *Shelley and the Chaos of History: A New Politics of Poetry*. University Park, PA, 1997.
Roche, Daniel. *France in the Enlightenment*. Cambridge, MA, 1998.
Rohls, Jan. "Herder's 'Gott.'" In *Johann Gottfried Herder: Aspekte seines Lebenswerks*, edited by M. Kessler and V. Lepin, 271–91. Berlin, 2005.
Rose, Paul Lawrence. *German Question/Jewish Question: Revolutionary Antisemitism from Kant to Wagner*. Princeton, NJ, 1990.
Rose, Sven-Erik. *Jewish Philosophical Politics in Germany, 1789-1848*. Lebanon, NH, 2014.
Rosen, Zvi. *Bruno Bauer and Karl Marx: The Influence of Bauer on Marx's Thought*. The Hague, 1977.
Rosenthal, Michael. "The Siren Song of Revolution." *Crossmark Graduate Faculty Philosophy Journal* 34 (2013): 11–32.
———. "What Is Real about 'Ideal Constitutions'? Spinoza on Political Explanation." In Melamed and Sharp, eds., *Spinoza's "Political Treatise,"* 12–28.
———. "Why Spinoza Chose the Hebrews: The Exemplary Function of Prophecy in the *Theological-Political Treatise*." In *Jewish Themes in Spinoza's Philosophy*, edited by H. M. Ravven and L. E. Goodman, 225–60. Albany, NY, 2002.
Rotenstreich, Nathan. "For and Against Emancipation: The Bruno Bauer Controversy." *LBIYB* 4 (1959): 3–36.
Roudaut, M. "Ambiguités et limites de la tolérance radicale de l'*Aufklärung*: Autour du débat sur 'l'amélioration civile des Juifs.'" In *Lumières radicales, radicalisme des Lumières*, edited by Jean Mondot and C. Larrère (*Lumières* no. 13), 117–34. Rouen, 2009.
Rubel, Maximilien. "Marx à la rencontre de Spinoza." *Cahiers Spinoza* 1 (1977): 7–28.
Ruderman, David. *Early Modern Jewry: A New Cultural History*. Princeton, NJ, 2010.
———. *Jewish Enlightenment in an English Key: Anglo-Jewry's Construction of Modern Jewish Thought*. Princeton, NJ, 2000.
Ruspio, Federica. "La Presenza portoghese a Venezia (fine del XVI—metà del XVII secolo)." Ph.D. diss., Università di Ca' Foscari di Venezia, 2006.
Saar, Martin. *Die Immanenz der Macht: Politische Theorie nach Spinoza*. Berlin, 2013.
Salvadori, Roberto. *1799: Gli Ebrei italiani nella bufera antigiacobino*. Florence, 1999.
Sammons, J. L. *Heinrich Heine: A Modern Biography*. Princeton, NJ, 1979.

Sapir, Boris. "Jewish Socialists around *Vpered*." *Intellectual Review for Social History* 10 (1965): 365–84.
Sarna, Jonathan. "The Impact of the American Revolution on American Jews." *Modern Judaism* 1 (1981): 149–60.
Schama, Simon. *Belonging: The Story of the Jews, 1492–1900*. London, 2017.
———. *Patriots and Liberators. Revolution in the Netherlands, 1780–1813*. London, 1977.
Schapkow, Carsten. *"Die Freiheit zu philosophieren": Jüdische Identität in der Moderne im Spiegel der Rezeption Baruch de Spinozas in der deutschsprachigen Literatur*. Bielefeld, 2001.
———. *Role Model and Countermodel: The Golden Age of Iberian Jewry and German Jewish Culture during the Era of Emancipation*. Lanham, MD, 2016.
Schechter, Ronald. *Obstinate Hebrews: Representations of Jews in France, 1715–1815*. Berkeley and Los Angeles, 2003.
———. "Rationalizing the Enlightenment: Postmodernism and Theories of Anti-Semitism." In *Postmodernism and the Enlightenment*, edited by Daniel Gordon, 93–116. London, 2001.
Schilson, Arno. "Lessing and Theology." In *A Companion to the Works of Ephraim Gotthold Lessing*, edited by B. Fischer and Th. C. Fox, 157–83. Rochester, NY, 2005.
Schmidt-Biggemann, W. *Theodizee und Tatsachen: Das philosophische Profil der deutschen Aufklärung*. Frankfurt, 1988.
Schneider, Gabriele. *Fanny Lewald*. Hamburg, 1996.
Scholem, Gershom. *Du frankisme au jacobinisme: La vie de Moses Dobruška alias Franz Thomas von Schönfeld alias Junius Frey*. Paris, 1981.
Schröder, Winfried. "Spinozam tota armenta in Belgio sequi ducem: The Reception of the Early Dutch Spinozists in Germany." In *Disguised and Overt Spinozism around 1700*, edited by W. van Bunge and W. Klever, 157–70. Leiden, 1996.
———. *Ursprünge des Atheismus*. Stuttgart, 1998.
Schröpfer, Horst. *Schack Hermann Ewald (1745–1822): Ein Kantianer in der thüringischen Residenzstadt Gotha*. Cologne, 2015.
Schulte, Christoph. *Die Jüdische Aufklärung*. Munich, 2002.
Schutte, G. J. *De Nederlandse Patriotten en de koloniën: Een onderzoek naar hun denkbeelden en optreden, 1770–1800*. Groningen, 1974.
Schüttler, Hermann. *Die Mitglieder des Illuminatenordens 1776–1787/93*. Munich, 1991.
Schwartz, Daniel B. *The First Modern Jew: Spinoza and the History of an Image*. Princeton, NJ, 2012.
———. *Ghetto: The History of a Word*. Cambridge, MA, 2019.
———. "'Our Rabbi Baruch': Spinoza and Radical Jewish Enlightenment." In *Secularism in Question: Jews and Judaism in Modern Times*, edited by Ari Joskowicz and Ethan Katz, 25–46. Philadelphia, 2015.
Schwartz, Stuart B. *All Can Be Saved: Religious Toleration in the Iberian Atlantic World*. New Haven, CT, 2008.
Schwartz, Yosef. "Causa Materialis: Solomon Maimon, Moses ben Maimon, and the Possibility of Philosophical Transmission." In *Salomon Maimon: Rational*

Dogmatist, Empirical Sceptic, edited by Gideon Freudenthal, 125–43. Dordrecht, 2003.

Seeligmann, Sigmund. "David Nassy of Surinam and His *Lettre Politico-Theologico-Morale sur Le Juifs*." *PAJHS* 22 (1914): 25–38.

Sehat, David. *The Myth of American Religious Freedom*. New York, 2011.

Servaas van Rooijen, A. J. *Inventaire des livres formant la bibliothèque de Bénédict Spinoza*. The Hague-Paris, 1888.

Service, Robert. *Trotsky: A Biography*. London, 2009.

Severin-Barbouti, Bettina. "Gesellschaft im Umbruch: Wirtschafts- und Sozialreformen im Königreich Westphalen." In *Napoleon und das Königreich Westphalen*, edited by A. Hedwig et al., 141–65. Marburg, 2008.

Shantz, Douglas H. "Religion and Spinoza: Jonathan Israel's Interpretation of the Enlightenment." In *Religious Minorities and Cultural Diversity in the Dutch Republic*, edited by August den Hollander, A. Noord, M. van Veen, and A. Voolstra, 208–21. Leiden, 2014.

Shavit, Yaacov. *Athens in Jerusalem: Classical Antiquity and Hellenism in the Making of the Modern Secular Jew*. London, 1997.

Sheehan, James. "The German States and the European Revolution." In *Revolution and the Meanings of Freedom in the Nineteenth Century*, edited by Isser Woloch, 246–79. Stanford, CA., 1996.

Sheppard, Eugene. *Leo Strauss and the Politics of Exile: The Making of a Political Philosopher*. Waltham, MA, 2006.

Sheridan, G. *Nicolas Lenglet Dufresnoy and the Literary Underworld of the* Ancien Régime. Oxford, 1989.

Silberner, Edmund. *Moses Hess: Geschichte seines Lebens*. Leiden, 1966.

———. "Moses Hess als Begründer und Redakteur der *Rheinischen Zeitung*." *Archiv für Sozialgeschichte* 4 (1964): 5–44.

Silvera, Miriam. "Quando Dio deciderà di redimere Israele: Vera e falsa redenzione nel pensiero di Isaac Orobio di Castro." *Sefarad* 77 (2017): 405–27.

Simonutti, Luisa. *Arminianesimo e tolleranza nel Seicento olandese*. Florence, 1984.

Sint Nicolaas, Eveline. *Shackles and Bonds: Suriname and the Netherlands since 1600*. Amsterdam, 2018.

Skolnik, Jonathan. "Heine and Haggadah: History, Narration, and Tradition in the Age of *Wissenschaft des Judentums*." In Brann and Sutcliffe, eds., *Renewing the Past*, 213–25.

———. "Kaddish for Spinoza: Memory and Modernity in Celan and Heine." *New German Critique* 77 (1999): 169–86.

Slavin, M. *The French Revolution in Miniature: Section Droits-de-l'Homme, 1789–1795*. Princeton, NJ, 1984.

Smith, Steven B. *Reading Leo Strauss: Politics, Philosophy, Judaism*. Chicago, 2006.

———. *Spinoza, Liberalism and the Question of Jewish Identity*. New Haven, CT, 1997.

Socher, Abraham P. *The Radical Enlightenment of Solomon Maimon*. Stanford, CA, 2006.

Sonenscher, M. *Sans-Culottes: An Eighteenth-Century Emblem in the French Revolution*. Princeton, NJ, 2008.

Sonnenberg-Stern, Karina. *Emancipation and Poverty: The Ashkenazi Jews of Amsterdam, 1796–1850*. Basingstoke, 2000.

Sorkin, David. "The Count Stanislas de Clermont-Tonnerre's 'To the Jews as a Nation . . .' the Career of a Quotation." Leo Baeck Institute Lecture. Jerusalem, 2012.

———. "Emancipation and Assimilation—Two Concepts and Their Application to German-Jewish History." *LBIY* 35 (1990): 17–33.

———. *Jewish Emancipation: A History across Five Centuries*. Princeton, NJ, 2019.

———. *The Religious Enlightenment: Protestants, Jews, and Catholics from London to Vienna*. Princeton, NJ, 2008.

———. *The Transformation of German Jewry 1780–1840*. New York, 1987.

Sperber, Jonathan. *Karl Marx: A Nineteenth-Century Life*. New York, 2013.

———. *Rhineland Radicals: The Democratic Movement and the Revolution of 1848–1849*. Princeton, NJ, 1991.

Stedman Jones, Gareth. *Karl Marx: Greatness and Illusion*. London, 2016.

Steenbakkers, Piet. "Spinoza, beyond the Legends." In *Spinoza Research: To Be Continued*. Uitgeverij Spinozahuis, 2016.

Stepelevich, L. S. *The Young Hegelians: An Anthology*. 1983. New ed., London, 1999.

Stern, Eliyahu. *Jewish Materialism: The Intellectual Revolution of the 1870s*. New Haven, CT, 2018.

Stiening, G. "Zur Bedeutung von Lessings Spinoza-Rezeption." In *Spinoza im Deutschland des achtzehnten Jahrhunderts*, edited by E. Schürmann, N. Waszek, and F. Weinreich, 193–220. Stuttgart, 2002.

Stipriaan, Alex van. *Surinaams Contrast: Roofbouw en Overleven in een Caraibische Plantagekolonie 1750–1863*. Leiden, 1993.

Stone, Daniel. "Knowledge of Foreign Languages among Eighteenth-Century Polish Jews." In *Jews in Early Modern Poland*, edited by Gershon D. Hundert, 200–218. London, 1997.

Strauss, Leo. "Einleitungen." In *GSJ*, vol. 3, pt. 2: xi–cx. Stuttgart, 1971.

———. "The Testament of Spinoza" (1932). In *Leo Strauss, Early Writings (1921–32)*, edited by Michael Zank. Albany, NY, 2002.

Strum, Daniel. "Isaac de Pinto's *Political Reflections* and the Beginning of the Jewish Political Economy." In *Paths to Modernity: A Tribute to Yosef Kaplan*, edited by Avriel Bar-Levav, C. B. Stuczynski, and Michael Heyd, 233–48. Jerusalem, 2018.

Stuurman, Siep. *The Invention of Humanity: Equality and Cultural Difference in World History*. Cambridge, MA, 2017.

———. *De Uitvinding van de mensheid: Korte wereldgeschiedenis van het denken over gelijkheid en cultuurverschil*. Amsterdam, 2009.

Sullam, Simon Levis. "Prescribing Toleration at the Paris Sanhedrin (1806–1807)." In *Toleration within Judaism*, edited by Martin Goodman et al., 111–29. Oxford, 2013.

Sutcliffe, Adam. "From Apologetics to Polemics: Isaac Orobio's Defenses of Judaism and Their Uses in the French Enlightenment." In Wilke, ed., *Isaac Orobio*, 93–104.

———. "Can a Jew Be a Philosophe? Isaac de Pinto, Voltaire, and Jewish Participation in the European Enlightenment." *JSS*, new ser., 6 (2000): 31–51.
———. *Judaism and Enlightenment*. Cambridge, 2003.
———. "Judaism and Jewish Arguments in the Clandestine Radical Enlightenment." In *Scepticisme, clandestinité et libre pensée*, edited by Gianni Paganini, M. Benítez, and J. Dybikowski, 97–113. Paris, 2002.
———. "Ludwig Börne, Jewish Messianism and the Politics of Money." *LBIYB* 57 (2012): 213–37.
———. "Quarreling over Spinoza: Moses Mendelssohn and the Fashioning of Jewish Philosophical Heroism." In Brann and Sutcliffe, eds., *Renewing the Past, Reconfiguring Jewish Culture*, 167–88.
———. "Voltaire in Context: The Emergence of Antijudaic Rhetoric in the French Early Enlightenment." In Zinguer and Bloom, eds., *L'Antisémitisme éclairé*, 115–24.
———. *What Are Jews For? History, Peoplehood and Purpose*. Princeton, NJ, 2020.
Swetschinski, Daniel M. *Reluctant Cosmopolitans: The Portuguese Jews of Seventeenth-Century Amsterdam*. London, 2000.
Szajkowski, Zosa. *Jews and the French Revolutions of 1789, 1830 and 1848*. New York, 1970.
Szulc, Michal. "A Gracious Act or Merely a Regulation of Economic Activity." *LBIYB* (2014): 23–36.
Tanguay, Daniel. *Leo Strauss: An Intellectual Biography*. New Haven, CT, 2003.
Tarantino, Giovanni. *Lo Scrittoio di Anthony Collins (1676–1729): I Libri e i tempi di un libero pensatore*. Milan, 2007.
Tatián, Diego. *Spinoza filosofía terrena*. Buenos Aires, 2014.
Thompson, J. M. *Robespierre*. 1935. New ed., Oxford, 1988.
Tosel, André. "Pour une étude systématique du rapport de Marx à Spinoza: Remarques et hypothèses." In *Spinoza au XIX siècle*, edited by A. Tosel, Pierre-François Moreau, and J. Salem. Paris, 2007.
———. *Spinoza, ou l'autre (in)finitude*. Paris, 2008.
Trigano, Shmuel. "The French Revolution and the Jews." *Modern Judaism* 10 (1990): 171–90.
Trivellato, Francesca. *The Promise and Peril of Credit: What a Forgotten Legend about Jews and Finance Tells Us about the Making of European Commercial Society*. Princeton, NJ, 2019.
Vaccaro, G. Battista. *Socialismo e umanesimo nel pensiero di Moses Hess (1837–1847)*. Naples, 1981.
Valladares, Rafael. *La Conquista de Lisboa: Violencia militar y comunicadad política en Portugal, 1578–1583*. Madrid, 2008.
Van Bunge, L. (Wiep). *Johannes Bredenburg (1643–1691): Een Rotterdamse Collegiant in de ban van Spinoza*. Rotterdam, 1990.
Van de Kamp, J. L. J. *Emanuel van Portugal en Emilia van Nassau*. Assen, 1980.
Van der Burg, Martijn. *Nederland onder Franse invloed: Culturele overdracht en staatsvorming in de napoleontische tijd 1799–1813*. Amsterdam, 2009.

Van der Tak, W. G. "Spinoza's Payments to the Portuguese-Israelitic Community, and the Language in Which He Was Raised." *SR* 16 (1982): 190–95.
Van der Veen, Sytze. *Groot-Nederland en Groot Colombia, 1815–1830.* Hilversum, 2015.
Van Goor, J. *De Nederlandse koloniën: Geschiedenis van de Nederlandse expansie, 1600–1975.* 1994. 2nd ed., 1997.
Van Kempen, Michiel. *Een geschiedenis van de Surinaamse literatuur.* 5 vols. Paramaribo, 2002.
Van Lier, R. A. J. "The Jewish Community in Surinam: A Historical Survey." In Cohen, ed., *The Jewish Nation in Surinam*, 19–23.
Van Rooden, Peter, and J. W. Weselius. "The Early Enlightenment and Judaism: The 'Civil Dispute' between Philippus van Limborch and Isaac Orobio de Castro (1687)." *SR* 21 (1987): 140–53.
Van Vliet, R., *Elie Luzac (1721–1796): Boekverkoper van de Verlichting.* Nijmegen, 2005.
Vaz Dias, A. M., and W. G. van der Tak, eds. *Spinoza, mercator et autodidactus: Oorkonden en andere authentieke documenten betreffende des wijsgeers jeugd en diens betrekkingen.* The Hague, 1932.
———. "Spinoza, Merchant and Autodidact." *SR* 16 (1982): 105–71.
Venclova, Tomas. *Vilnius: A Personal History.* Riverdale-on-Hudson, NY, 2009.
Verbeek, Theo. "Spinoza on Aristocratic and Democratic Government." In Melamed and Sharp, eds., *Spinoza's "Political Treatise,"* 145–60.
Vercruysse, Jérôme. *Bibliographie descriptive des écrits du Baron d'Holbach.* Section 1770. Paris, 1971.
Vernière, Paul. *Spinoza et la pensée française avant la Révolution.* 1954. 2nd ed. Paris, 1982.
Vincent, Steven. *Pierre-Joseph Proudhon and the Rise of French Republican Socialism.* New York, 1984.
Vital, David. *The Origins of Zionism.* Oxford, 1975.
Vlessing, Odette. "The Jewish Policy of King William I." In *DJH*, edited by Michman, 2 (1989): 177–90.
Wade, Ira. *The Clandestine Organization and Diffusion of Philosophic Ideas in France from 1700 to 1750.* New York, 1967.
Wahnich, Sophie. *L'impossible citoyen: L'Étranger dans le discours de la Révolution française.* Paris, 1997.
Wallet, Bart. "Napoleon's Legacy—National Government and Jewish Community in Western Europe." *SDIJ* 6 (2007): 291–309.
Wallet, Bart, and Zwiep, Irene. "Locals: Jews in the Early Modern Dutch Republic." In *The Cambridge History of Judaism*, edited by Jonathan Karp and Adam Sutcliffe, vol. 7: *The Early Modern World, 1500–1815*, 894–922. Cambridge, 2018.
Walther, Manfred. "Was/Is Spinoza a 'Jewish Philosopher'? Spinoza in the Struggle for a Modern Jewish Cultural Identity in Germany: A Meta-Reflection." *Studia Spinozana* 13 (1997): 207–37.
Walzer, Michael, *The Jewish Political Tradition.* Vol. 1. New Haven, CT, 2000.
———. *The Paradox of Liberation: Secular Revolutions and Religious Counterrevolution.* New Haven, CT, 2015.

Wegert, Karl H. *German Radicals Confront the Common People. Revolutionary Politics and Popular Politics, 1789–1849*. Mainz, 1992.
Weiss, Volker. *Moses Hess: Rheinischer Jude, Revolutionär, früher Zionist*. Cologne, 2015.
Wende, Peter. *Radikalismus im Vormärz: Untersuchungen zur politischen Theorie der frühen deutschen Demokratie*. Wiesbaden, 1975.
Wertheim, David J. *Salvation through Spinoza: A Study of Jewish Culture in Weimar Germany*. Leiden, 2011.
Westerburg, Jörg. "Die Kirchenpolitik im Reformstaat Königreich Westphalen." In *Napoleon und das Königreich Westphalen*, edited by A. Hedwig et al., 191–209. Marburg, 2008.
Whaley, Joachim. *Germany and the Holy Roman Empire*. Vol. 2: *1648–1806*. Oxford, 2012.
———. *Religious Toleration and Social Change in Hamburg, 1529–1819*. Cambridge, 1985.
Wilke, Carsten. "Clandestine Classics: Isaac Orobio and the Polemical Genre among the Dutch Sephardim." In Wilke, ed., *Isaac Orobio*, 57–76.
———., ed. *Isaac Orobio: The Jewish Argument with Dogma and Doubt*. Berlin, 2018.
Williams, David Lay. "Spinoza and the General Will." In *The General Will: The Evolution of a Concept*, edited by James Farr and David Lay Williams, 115–46. Cambridge, 2015.
Winkle, Stefan. "Johann Friedrich Struensee und das Judentum." *Jahrbuch des Instituts für Deutsche Geschichte* (Tel Aviv) 15 (1986): 9–10.
Wistrich, Robert S. *The Jews of Vienna in the Age of Franz Joseph*. 1989. New ed., London, 2006.
———. *Laboratory for World Destruction: Germans and Jews in central Europe*. Lincoln, NE, 2007.
———. *Revolutionary Jews from Marx to Trotsky*. London, 1976.
———. "Socialism and Judeophobia-Antisemitism in Europe before 1914." *LBIYB* 37 (1992): 11–45.
Wöffle-Fischer, Suzanne. *Junius Frey (1753–1794): Jude, Aristokrat und Revolutionär*. Frankfurt, 1997.
Yardeni, Myriam. *Anti-Jewish Mentalities in Early Modern Europe*. Lanham, MD, 1990.
Yovel, Y. *Dark Riddle: Hegel, Nietzsche and the Jews*. Oxford, 1998.
———. *Spinoza and Other Heretics*. Princeton, NJ, 1989.
Zammito, John H. *The Genesis of Kant's "Critique of Judgment."* Chicago, 1992.
———. "'The Most Hidden Conditions of Men of First Rank'—The Pantheist Current in Eighteenth-Century Germany 'Uncovered' by the Spinoza Controversy." *Eighteenth-Century Thought* (2003): 335–68.
Zienkowska, Krystyna. "'The Jews Have Killed a Traitor': The Socio-Political Background of a Riot in Warsaw in 1790." In Bartoszewski and Polonsky, eds., *The Jews in Warsaw*, 127–50.

Zinguer, Ilana, and S. Bloom, eds. *L'Antisémitisme éclairé: Inclusion et exclusion depuis l'époque des Lumières jusqu'à l'affaire Dreyfus*. Leiden, 2003.

Zwiep, I. E. "Jewish Enlightenment Reconsidered: The Dutch Eighteenth Century." In *Sepharad in Ashkenaz: Medieval Knowledge and Enlightened Jewish Discourse*, edited by A. Fontaine, A. Schatz, and I. Zwiep, 279–311. Amsterdam, 2007.

———. "De Naties worden burgers: Joods leven in de Lage Landen in de schaduw van de Verlichting (1750–1814)." In *Geschiedenis van de Joden in Nederland*, edited by H. Bom, D. Wertheim, H. Berg and B. Wallett, 197–274. Amsterdam, 2017.

INDEX

THE SAMUEL & ALTHEA STROUM LECTURES IN JEWISH STUDIES

Revolutionary Jews from Spinoza to Marx: The Fight for a Secular World of Universal and Equal Rights, Jonathan I. Israel

School Photos in Liquid Time: Reframing Difference, Marianne Hirsch and Leo Spitzer

What We Talk about When We Talk about Hebrew (and What It Means to Americans), edited by Naomi B. Sokoloff and Nancy E. Berg

The Jewish Bible: A Material History, David Stern

A Best-Selling Hebrew Book of the Modern Era: The Book of the Covenant of Pinḥas Hurwitz and Its Remarkable Legacy, David B. Ruderman

Agnon's Moonstruck Lovers: The Song of Songs in Israeli Culture, Ilana Pardes

Writing in Tongues: Yiddish Translation in the Twentieth Century, Anita Norich

Make Yourself a Teacher: Rabbinic Tales of Mentors and Disciples, Susan Handelman

The Jewish Life Cycle: Rites of Passage from Biblical to Modern Times, Ivan Marcus

Autobiographical Jews: Essays in Jewish Self-Fashioning, Michael Stanislawski

Studying the Jewish Future, Calvin Goldscheider

Popular Culture and the Shaping of Holocaust Memory in America, Alan Mintz

Imagining Russian Jewry: Memory, History, Identity, Steven J. Zipperstein

Judaism and Hellenism in Antiquity: Conflict or Confluence? Lee I. Levine

Portrait of American Jews: The Last Half of the 20th Century, Samuel C. Heilman

Gender and Assimilation in Modern Jewish History: The Roles and Representation of Women, Paula E. Hyman

The Kiss of God: Spiritual and Mystical Death in Judaism, Michael Fishbane

I. L. Peretz and the Making of Modern Jewish Culture, Ruth R. Wisse

Jewish Identity in the Modern World, Michael A. Meyer

Recent Archaeological Discoveries and Biblical Research, William G. Dever

The Invention of Hebrew Prose: Modern Fiction and the Language of Realism, Robert Alter

Jewish Mysticism and Jewish Ethics, Joseph Dan

Zakhor: Jewish History and Jewish Memory, Yosef Hayim Yerushalmi

The Holocaust in Historical Perspective, Yehuda Bauer

The Yiddish Art Song, performed by Leon Lishner, basso, and Lazar Weiner, piano (stereophonic record album)